McKlein

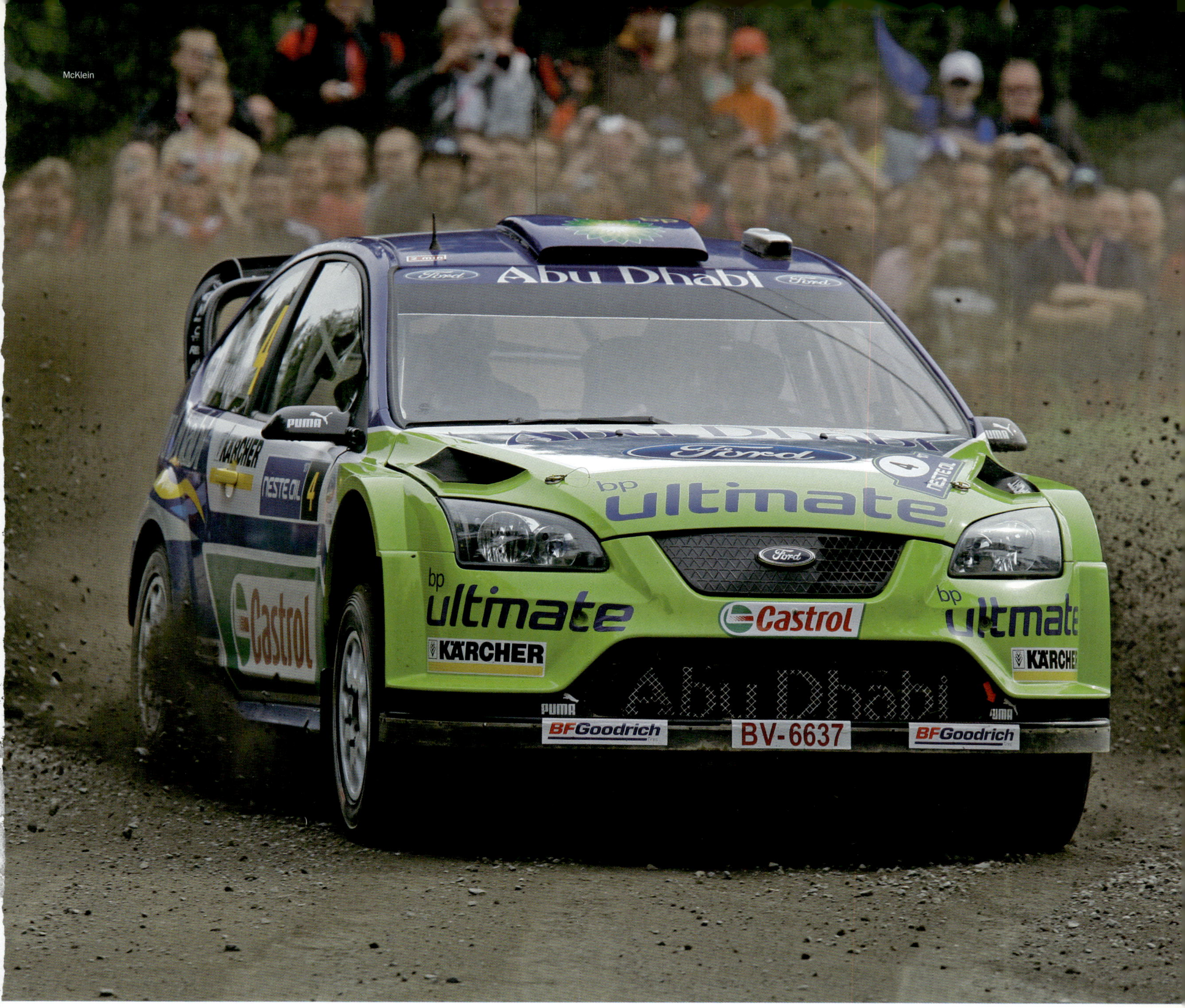


# RALLYCOURSE™

THE WORLD'S LEADING RALLY ANNUAL 2007

CMG PUBLISHING

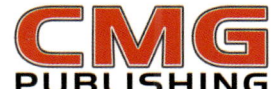

# CONTENTS

## RALLYCOURSE 2007-2008

is published by:
Crash Media Group Ltd
Number One
The Innovation Centre
Silverstone Circuit
Silverstone
Northants NN12 8GX
Telephone: +44 (0)870 3505044
Fax: +44 (0)870 3505088
Email: info@crash.net
Website: www.crashmediagroup.com

Printed in Italy by
ALSABA industrie grafiche,
Z.I. Belvedere S. Antonio
53034 Colle Val d'Elsa (SI)
Telephone: +39 (0)577 905311
Website: www.alsaba.it

© Crash Media Group Limited 2007
No part of this publication may be reproduced, stored in a retrieval system or transmitted, in any form or by any means, electronic, mechanical, photocopying, recording or otherwise, without prior permission in writing from Crash Media Group Ltd.

ISBN: 978-1905334-23-0

## DISTRIBUTORS

Gardners Books
1 Whittle Drive, Eastbourne,
East Sussex BN23 6QH
Telephone: +44 (0)1323 521555
E-mail: sales@gardners.com

Menoshire Ltd
Unit 13
21 Wadsworth Road
Perivale
Middlesex UB6 7LQ
Telephone: +44 (0)20 8566 7344
Fax: +44 (0)20 8991 2439

NORTH AMERICA
Motorbooks International
PO Box 1
729 Prospect Avenue
Osceola
Wisconsin 54020, USA
Telephone: 1 715 294 3345
Fax: 1 715 294 4448

| | |
|---|---|
| FOREWORD by the 2007 World Champion Sébastien Loeb | 05 |
| EDITOR'S INTRODUCTION | 06 |
| REVIEW OF THE YEAR by David Evans | 12 |
| THE TOP TEN DRIVERS OF 2007 by David Evans | 18 |
| WORLD CHAMPION by David Evans | 30 |
| COLIN McRAE by David Evans | 36 |
| SUZUKI by David Evans | 48 |
| RALLY IRELAND by David Evans | 52 |
| FRANÇOIS DUVAL by Anthony Peacock | 54 |
| TECHNICAL REVIEW by Rob Wilkins | 56 |
| OBITUARY TONY FALL by Mike Broad | 60 |
| GUY FRÉQUELIN by Anthony Peacock | 62 |
| WORLD CHAMPIONSHIP RALLIES by David Evans | 66 |
| WORLD RALLY CHAMPIONSHIP RESULTS by Paul Haines | 168 |
| CAR SPECIFICATIONS | 170 |
| INTERCONTINENTAL RALLY CHAMPIONSHIP by David Evans | 174 |
| PRODUCTION CAR WORLD RALLY CHAMPIONSHIP by Richard Rodgers | 178 |
| JUNIOR RALLY CHAMPIONSHIP by Anthony Peacock | 182 |
| REGIONAL CHAMPIONSHIPS by Richard Rodgers | 184 |
| BRITISH RALLY CHAMPIONSHIP by Gillian Bell | 188 |
| BRITISH NATIONAL REVIEW By Andrew Haill | 190 |

**editor**
DAVID EVANS

**publisher**
BRYN WILLIAMS

**art editor**
ROSANNE DAVIS

**sub-editor**
GILLIAN BELL

**results and statistics**
PAUL HAINES

**advertising sales**
SIMON MOORE

**chief photographers**
THE McKLEINS

**office manager**
WENDY SALISBURY

**illustrations**
ADRIAN DEAN
f1artwork@blueyonder.co.uk

### ACKNOWLEDGMENTS

Once again, the mainstay of the photographic genius in Rallycourse comes from the eyes and lenses of McKlein (Reinhard Klein, Bob McCaffrey, Colin McMaster, Tony Welan and Ross Hyde). Adding to the pictorial brilliance have been Gavin Lodge, Mark Griffin, Race&motion, Photo4, Crash.net, Gérard Rancinan, Gold & Goose, Gary Parravani and Brian Young - LINEAR Photographs.

The editor also has to thank the following people for making the whole Rallycourse process as trouble-free as possible: Gillian Bell, Anthony Peacock, Richard Rodgers, Andrew Haill, Mike Broad and Rob Wilkins. Finally, a big, big thanks to my wife Sandra (who makes her writing debut in Rallycourse this year) and daughter Georgia for all their love, support and tolerance through another hectic second half of the season. None of this would be possible without you.

www.rallycourse.com

# SÉBASTIEN LOEB
# C4MIDABLE

Congratulations Sébastien Loeb on your 4th consecutive Drivers' World Rally Championship win and well done to the entire Citroën Total WRT.^
You too can experience the car with the rally pedigree, in this Special Edition Citroën C4 by LOEB from £12,795.*
Call 0800 262 262 or visit www.citroen.co.uk/loeb

Official Government Fuel Consumption Figures (litres per 100km/mpg) and CO2 Emissions (g/km). Lowest: C4 by LOEB 1.6HDi 16V (110hp): Urban 6.1/46.3, Extra Urban 4.0/70.6, Combined 4.8/58.8 and 128 CO2. Highest: C4 by LOEB 1.6i 16V (110hp): Urban 9.5/29.7, Extra Urban 5.7/49.6, Combined 7.1/39.8 and 169 CO2.

*Manufacturer's 'on the road' recommended retail price for C4 by LOEB 1.6i 16V 110hp. Price, correct at time of going to press, includes VAT, delivery to dealer incl. number plates and VAT, Government First Registration Fee and 12 months' graduated vehicle excise duty. Black paint optional at extra cost. C4 by LOEB Special Edition models subject to availability, from participating dealers, and are excluded from all Manufacturer C4 offers. ^Subject to official FIA confirmation. CITROËN prefers TOTAL

# Foreword

By Sébastien Loeb
Rallycourse 2007

Hello from Geneva!
I have to say, there were times this year when it didn't look like I would be writing this foreword for Rallycourse...

But, the important thing is that my co-driver Daniel Elena and I never lost sight of the fact that we were always in with a good chance of winning the World Rally Championship. We never got to the stage where we were relying on other people to retire. Okay, when we came back from New Zealand, I knew that we had to win the next five rallies - but that was possible, so I told myself to try my hardest to do that.

And then in Ireland, Marcus gave us a little bit of a gift. But at the start, it looked difficult for us as we had a broken damper before the first stage and couldn't push from the start. I believe Marcus wanted to take profit of the situation, but...

In Wales, the drive was a little bit boring, but that was the way it had to be. And now we are champions again. Four times champions is incredible. This is just the best way possible for me to say a big thank you to somebody who helped me through my whole career. Citroen's team principal Guy Frequelin retires at the end of this season. Guy has been with me through my whole WRC career - and I owe him a lot. I hope the four titles and 36 wins we have managed together repays some of the faith he showed in me!

As well as Daniel, I have to thank the whole of Citroen Sport for this year. After a season away from the sport, we came back with a fantastic car in the C4 WRC.

Before I finish, we shouldn't forget that we lost another great man this year. And I'm sorry for your British fans, that, again, it was one of your best drivers. Colin McRae was my friend and I am really sorry for the loss of him, his son Johnny and his two family friends.

Nobody can replace Colin, so let's just keep our memories of him alive.

# From the editor

THIS year's World Rally Championship produced some of the best sport ever seen in the series' history. Following the tragic events of one Saturday in September, however, it was also tinged with enormous sadness. In the fullness of time, Sébastien Loeb's achievement in winning a fourth straight world title will doubtless fade as more follow; this season will be marked by the loss of Britain's first world champion and the WRC's first super-hero, Colin McRae.

As much as the sport mourns, thoughts have to be spared and hearts sent out to those closer to that tragic helicopter accident of early autumn. Colin, his son Johnny and family friends Graeme Duncan and Ben Porcelli were all lost on a day, which began like any other but ended with such stunningly sad news.

Given Colin's pre-eminence in the sport, every aspect of his spectacular and glittering career at the wheel of a rally car was scrutinised, which is why we have decided to let the pictures tell the story of Colin McRae.

In the midst of Britain's first Rally GB without the man McRae, there was more sad news - that of the loss of Tony Fall. Former British champion co-driver Mike Broad recounts his memories of one of the sport's great characters.

Through the dark days, which followed McRae's accident, the battle that raged for this year's world title between Loeb and Marcus Grönholm gave the WRC a much-needed focus. The gathering of drivers in Catalunya to pay their respects and the display of Colin's cars in Cardiff ensured the Scot was, quite rightly, never far from our thoughts. But at the same time - and as one considered what Colin would have wanted - there was a title to be won.

The history books will reflect Loeb's success on half of this year's rally, with the upshot of that fine points haul leaving him only needing fifth or better on the final round. Reflection on 2007 a few years down the line will conjure a very different picture from the reality; this was an absolute dogfight between the top two. And nowhere was the intensity of that battle better displayed than in New Zealand, where just three tenths of a second separated the pair at the end of the Hamilton-based event.

In the end, though, with the title in the palm of his hand, Grönholm dropped it. Having gone to Ireland four points adrift in the title chase, it looked as though this was going to be the one that got away from Loeb. Ford collected a second manufacturers' title in as many years in the Emerald Isle, but the wall that Grönholm clouted in the Lough Gill stage ended his hopes of a third world title in the twilight of his career.

But has Grönholm really gone? Who knows? There's still a strong inkling that he'll be back for more in 2008. He may drive in Sweden, or he may throw his lot in with one or more of the latest teenage sensations who are arriving by the bucketful in the WRC.

But Loeb is the champion, and what a champion he is. He's already the best of the best, but now he stands on the verge of becoming even better. He has won more WRC events than anybody else, but he could now become the first man to win five titles - and in fact the first to achieve five in a row. Through all of this success, Loeb - now a father - remains an utterly engaging and - his word - "concentrated" interviewee.

If there was nothing new at the top of the results column this year, there was certainly a new manufacturer in the service park. Or at least in a different part of the service park. There were question marks over the debut of Suzuki's SX4 WRC as late as August this year, before the car arrived on the scene in Corsica. As a precursor to its first full year in the sport in 2008, the globe's newest World Rally Car also tackled Rally GB. Despite finishing both events there were, ahem, issues to be dealt with. There's no doubt this has been an interesting season for those involved with the Japanese-French alliance. Read more about it on page 48.

If it's a technical insight you're after, Crash's Rob Wilkins takes a look at what's got the engineering types involved this year, while Anthony Peacock provides his usual refreshing approach to the diverse subject matters of François Duval and this year's Junior Rally Championship - a fascinating read on both parts.

Motorsport News' rallies editor Richard Rodgers does a similar job on the Production World Rally Championship, while also looking closely at what went on elsewhere in the world in his round up of all the FIA Regional Championships. Motor Sport's Gillian Bell provides her usual precision in a fascinating look at this year's British Rally Championship, while Andrew Haill considers the challenges facing the national arena following the 2007 season.

As usual, close attention is paid to the world champion, as we look at how Sébastien Loeb's laid-back approach has paid dividends again. It's not just Loeb at Citroën, though. His team principal and mentor Guy Fréquelin retired at the end of this season. Rallycourse looks back over the relationship the pair have built together.

Between the words on these pages, you'll find some of the best pictures taken anywhere this season. Again, we have to thank the McKleins for their undimmed enthusiasm and quality results in relaying what's seen on the stages. And providing the perfect foil for them were Gavin Lodge, Mark Griffin, Race&motion, Photo4, Crash.net, Gérard Rancinan, Gold & Goose, Gary Parravani and Brian Young - LINEAR Photographs.

With the help, energy, interest and desire of all these contributors, Rallycourse once again provides the perfect reflection on a sad and yet sensational year in the sport.

David Evans
Teddington

Main: Colin McRae at the wheel of his Subaru in the year he became Britain's first World Rally Champion. The rallying superstar is sadly missed
Race&motion

Inset: Loeb and Grönholm kept us all entertained with their titanic title battle
Photo4/Crash.net

Right: He masterminded Loeb's record-breaking rally career at Citroën, but team principal Guy Fréquelin is now heading into retirement

Far right: The WRC's newest car, the Suzuki SX4, made its debut in Corsica and was then showcased in Britain (pictured)

Bottom right: Hirvonen and the Ford boys celebrated the team's second consecutive manufacturers' championship win

Below: And it's goodbye from them: Grönholm and co-driver Timo Rautiainen have waved goodbye to the WRC, for now?

All photographs by McKlein

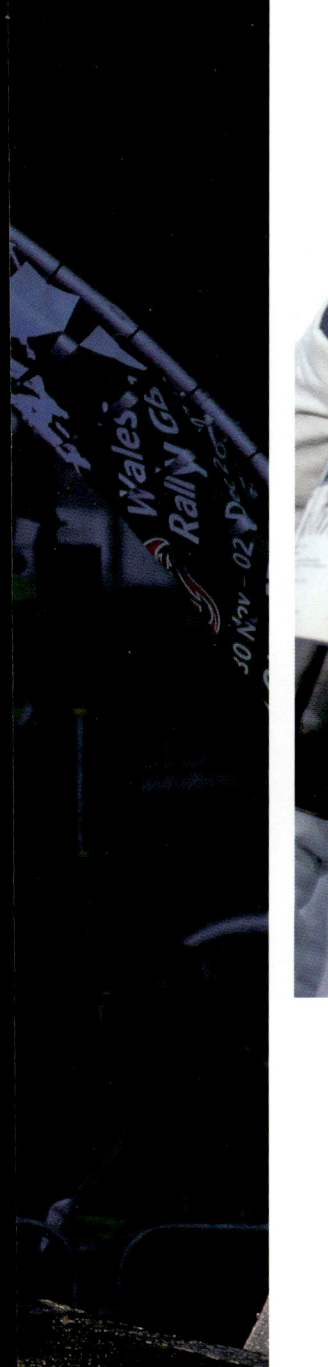

Team Abu Dhabi
2007 FIA Middle East Rally Championship

BP-Ford World Rally Team
2007 FIA World Rally Champion
WRC Official Destination Partner

Welcome to Abu Dhabi, where luxury and style are infused with traditional values of hospitality and respect. Where sunny weather, tranquil beaches, lush oases, vibrant city life and a mixture of culture and traditions come together to create a destination like no other. Explore the emirate's old souqs, sip a fragrant Arabic coffee, ride the dunes on an exhilarating desert safari or dive into a world of dazzling marine life.

**THERE'S SOMETHING FOR EVERYONE IN ABU DHABI.**

www.visitabudhabi.ae

ABU DHABI TOURISM AUTHORITY

# Lost opportunities and lost friends

A season where Marcus Grönholm came so close to winning his final
World Rally Championship was overshadowed by the death of Colin McRae
By David Evans

Main: Grönholm came achingly close to winning his third WRC title in his final year in the sport - but by Rally GB his hopes were fading

Inset: The WRC was rocked by the death of McRae in a helicopter crash near his Lanark home in September

All photographs by McKlein

Above: The Citroën team celebrates Loeb and Elena's latest championship success in Wales. The Frenchman has now equalled Tommi Mäkinen's record of four title wins in a row
McKlein

AS the years roll by in Marcus Grönholm's retirement, he will sit back in wonder at this, his final season in the World Rally Championship. But it's likely he won't be pondering the 30 rallies he won or the two drivers' titles he collected with Peugeot. It'll be the one that got away which will be the last to leave the Grönholm psyche. This year is going to be one that bugs the man they call "Bosse" for some time.

Ahead of Rally Ireland, Grönholm was four points up in the title chase and looking good. Three days around west coast lanes battered by the late autumn Atlantic squalls were never going to be an easy challenge, but Grönholm and his chief rival Sébastien Loeb had both crashed on the previous round in Japan, so surely they had learned their lesson? Surely there would be no more accidents…

There was. Leading the rally, Grönholm was desperate to press home his advantage when he fell foul of a right-hander close to the end of the Lough Gill test. For the second rally in succession, the Finn had failed to complete the fourth stage. This time, however, Loeb didn't follow him into retirement. This time the Frenchman stayed in the middle of the road to collect his eighth win of the season. Having been behind Grönholm in the points for six months, the advantage was now definitely with the Citroën driver. He took it and collected a fourth title in Wales a fortnight later.

There's a danger that what's been written so far underplays Loeb's role in this year's WRC, and that would be a big mistake. Eight wins are not the work of a moment and Loeb was on exceptional form this season. But the fact remains that this was a championship lost by Grönholm, rather than won by Loeb.

Ahead of the season, Grönholm and Ford had been quietly confident. After years of Citroën dominance with the exceptional Xsara WRC it was time for the new car, the C4 WRC. As with every new car, there were question marks over its reliability. For Ford, however, there were no such concerns.

There was also a question mark over Loeb's return to the sport. Monte Carlo in January was his first event in four months after breaking his arm the previous September. In the end, when it came to the rally, neither his car nor his arm let down the defending champion and he started his 2007 campaign with 10 points. There was trouble, however, for the sister C4 of Dani Sordo, which would become something of a theme through the year. If ever there was grief with one of the Citroëns, it was invariably the Spaniard who suffered.

At year's end Loeb admitted the pressure of running a new car had gotten to him. Clearly, after making more mistakes in one season than he had in the previous three championship-winning years, something was playing on his mind.

His first error was in Norway, where Loeb went off the road twice to miss out on scoring any points and drop from second to third in the drivers' standings. The next mistake was the one he would spend the rest of the year battling to make amends for: his crash in Sardinia which left Grönholm to take 10 points and the championship lead. From there the Finn didn't lose his grip on the top of the table until the penultimate round in Ireland.

Grönholm collected five wins along the way which, when combined with three victories from the ever-improving Mikko Hirvonen, helped to ensure that Ford would take a second consecutive manufacturers' award from 2007.

There wasn't just one young Finn who came to the fore this season, either. Hirvonen's fabulous run to score points on all but one event - and that amazing effort in Norway, where *nobody* could hold a candle to him - has been enough to garner him the lead role in Ford's WRC effort next season. A driver five years younger than him, Jari-Matti Latvala, is likely to be his teammate. Latvala has also had an exciting season. He will never forget this year, partly for getting to grips with asphalt and scoring his first career podium in Ireland, partly for leading in Japan, but mostly for being a Finn and leading in Finland - although he would probably like to forget the shunt which followed on stage three of the Jyväskylä-based event.

Hand-in-hand with Latvala's success has gone the development of the Stobart team. The Cumbrian firm moved into world rallying to help out Matthew Wilson and, in the process, has become a WRC brand in its own right. That it came within an ace of beating triple manufacturer world champion Subaru to third place in 2007 shows the effort put in by Latvala, Henning Solberg and Wilson.

Behind one of the most fascinating seasons on the stages, there was a political element that was never far from the surface. The new year was welcomed on the back of a World Motor Sport Council meeting last December which provided details of Vision 2012 - a document that was to become deeply debated in the following months.

Vision 2012 was, essentially, FIA president Max Mosley's thoughts on the way the WRC should be progressing. As the

## REVIEW OF THE YEAR

year wore on, there was more and more talk, but the issue was becoming increasingly cloudy. There appeared a desire for an early resolution to the question of regulations for World Rally Cars, but what was the answer?

As usual there were agendas aplenty on this subject, but it was a Super 2000-based formula, reportedly favoured by Mosley, which emerged as the favourite towards the end of the season. Getting the current teams to agree to such a move will be an enormous task. There has been major investment made by Ford, Citroën, Subaru and now Suzuki in the current formula and major technical changes will not be welcomed by those players. Whether that change is coming is still up in the air, as is the precise date for it. The teams remain adamant that the current World Rally Car formula is set until the end of 2012, but the FIA is equally adamant that the end of the road for the WR Car as we know it could come as soon as December 2009.

The foundations for this rumpus were well and truly set this season. In 2008 the battle between the sport's two biggest stakeholders - the teams and the FIA - will move up a gear as the future is defined.

One thing this year proved beyond all doubt is that the FIA retains the ability to make bold decisions. July's world council meeting delivered one such example: from 2009 onwards, the WRC will be reduced from 16 to 12 rallies. At the time this decision appeared to be the complete reverse of what people had been expecting. With five or six events chomping at the bit to be included in the calendar, reducing the number by four was unexpected to say the least. But there was a rider - those 12 rallies would only run every other year. Gone was the 16-round WRC; we now had to think in terms of a 24-rally series run over two years.

The organisers of new events such as Norway and Ireland are delighted with this news. Both of those rallies were well run, as was Portugal, which returned to the WRC this year, but it was doubtful all three would be accommodated within the confines of 16 rounds. Now, there's space for everybody and more, with Indonesia, China and Russia among those on the sidelines eyeing up the 2010 calendar.

The undiluted joy of Norway and co. was not shared by the traditional events, the ones that have been in the sport for the long run: Rally GB and Monte Carlo, for example. It wasn't long before there was talk of WRC classics such as Corsica doing deals with the Intercontinental Rally Challenge (IRC) in order to run a high-profile event every year.

Just running a rally, of whatever profile, is currently uppermost in the minds of Rally Australia's organisers. The event, now based on the Gold Coast, was expected to run in 2008 - that was until an announcement that it was still not ready. The Brisbane event should be good to go in '09.

Cyprus is another event with a question mark hanging over it following a disastrous rally this time. An argument between two Cypriot organising bodies boiled over and ended with stages being blocked, reducing the event to something of a farce. Despite that, the pressures of filling 24 slots in two years means Cyprus is on the menu for 2009, pending the good behaviour of the locals next year.

The season began with a much-modified Monte Carlo Rally (for the start, read car park in Valence rather than harbour side, Monaco), which clearly set something of a precedent as the season wore on. Night stages, as well as the Ardeche roads, returned for the traditional season opener, and by the end of the year Rally GB's route also sported a brace of tests run in the dark.

For next season, however, there could be more and more rallies moving away from the traditional cloverleaf set-up across three days. Despite considerable investment in the service park infrastructure, the use of remote service areas means a big shift away from central service towards more radical routes using stages much further away from rally headquarters. This is also a chance for organisers to be more innovative with their choice of stages, with the added benefit of avoiding the double use of tests.

WRC Commission president Morrie Chandler has

encouraged this sea change in event planning policy. Chandler is keen for rallies to avoid the predictability associated with the current timetable. Unfortunately, the teams - the ones who have shelled out all their cash on fancy hospitality centres in service - are far from happy that the cars are likely to be scarcely seen in service next season.

Beyond the calendar and technical regulations of the sport, there was one more tough decision that the FIA had to make in March. It was another announcement that drew surprise, as Pirelli was given the nod to supply the WRC's first-ever control tyre in 2008. Given BFGoodrich's monopoly on the supply of tyres this season - and the fact that Pirelli had failed to win an event in 2006 - BFG had been the odds-on favourite for the three-year deal on offer from the FIA. But a well-planned package from Pirelli had swung it in the Italian company's favour.

Just as the dust was beginning to settle on that news, Michelin - BFG's parent company - took things to the next level and began legal proceedings against the FIA. The case is ongoing, but such is Michelin and BFG's faith in its argument that it has continued to develop a control tyre - one that might never see the light of day.

If the FIA's Pirelli decision didn't go down well in some quarters of the service park, news of a longer-term commercial agreement was very well received. This deal, which is still being worked on, came on the back of the sale of International Sportsworld Communicators, the WRC's commercial rights holder, to All3Media. With mounting speculation of a financial crisis for ISC, things were looking increasingly bleak for the championship, but the announcement of an upbeat and enthusiastic media firm taking charge of ISC was the perfect tonic. North One Television, the WRC's TV production firm - owned by All3Media - will run ISC. North One is still finding its feet in the new world into which it has bravely stepped, but things are looking positive for the sport as there will be more investment to bankroll improved television and multi-media coverage.

The minutiae of the ISC deal was off the radar of most rally fans, the headline for them was about one man: David Richards. Having done all he could to lift the sport out of the obscurity which had blighted its commercial development for years, Richards was more than happy to hand it over to the new owner.

Above: We said goodbye to BFGoodrich in Wales. Pirelli has been named as the sole WRC tyre supplier for 2008, although Michelin is challenging the decision

Above middle: The legend that is Gronholm had plenty of support on his final event in GB. They do say imitation is the greatest form of flattery...

Top: Norway was one of two new events on the calendar, along with Ireland, and both were considered a success. Portugal also made its WRC return

All photographs by McKlein

# REVIEW OF THE YEAR

That, allied to the loss of Prodrive's Formula 1 project for next season, left DR with time on his hands. And as the results for the past two years had shown, that time would be best spent within the confines of the Subaru World Rally Team.

If the Banbury-based team had thought 2006 was bad, it was nothing compared with this year. Peter Solberg's tantrums of 2006 turned to tears in '07. It wouldn't be fair to label the Norwegian's year as an emotional rollercoaster, as that would imply the occasional high. The highs simply didn't come this year and a better analogy would be a free-fall parachute jump. The low point was undoubtedly Finland where, between the tears, Solberg labelled his Impress WRC2007 - among other things - as undriveable.

At that time there were stories doing the rounds about Solberg's forecasted departure from Subaru, despite his being tied to the team for a further two years. When, however, it became clear that neither Citroën nor Ford would be making space for the Norwegian, he wisely got his head down and focused on making the best of a bad lot.

This coincided with Richards declaring his intention to return full-time to the team, with a promise to "bang heads together" and eliminate "personal agendas".

It's doubtful that Richards ever truly left Subaru, but his return was not the only personnel change of the year. Going in the opposite direction was technical chief Steve Farrell, who was replaced - at least for the balance of the season - by Graeme Moore, one of the favoured engineers from the team's heyday. And any talk of engineering brains from Subaru's heyday would not be complete without the name of David Lapworth. He was also back on board, although he didn't make an appearance until November's Rally Ireland. The results from the last two events of the year may not have reflected the return of the two Davids, but there was certainly a different feel around the team.

What rally fans really want to know, however, is when Subaru will start winning again? Solberg's gifted win - under the worst possible circumstances - at Rally GB 2005 aside, you have to go all the way back to Mexico in March that year to find the team's last success. The S12 Impreza, revealed in 2006, was sufficiently bad that the team had to work on a new homologation - the S12B - in an effort to right some of the wrongs. That there will now be an 'S12C' (not that the car will be known as this internally) readied for Monte Carlo 2008 speaks volumes about the failings of the current car. The all-new Impreza, which was expected to start testing in April this year, had still not turned a wheel in December, and August '08 has become the new January in terms of a launch date. Despite the necessity to crack on with the new car, Subaru steadfastly refuses to give up on the saloon Impreza. Given that SWRT is stuck with it for the first six months of next year, the team's continued development of the current car is understandable, but there are those in the know who would prefer a policy of 100 per cent commitment to the new machine. As one team member pointed out, the current car has been off the pace for so long, what does another six months matter in the long run? Such sentiments are understandable, given the team's desire to turn the corner and start winning again.

For the first time since 2005 there will be two Japanese manufacturers involved in the WRC in '08. The other will be Suzuki, which ran its SX4 WRC in Corsica and Wales this year. There was continued speculation about the state of Suzuki's WRC programme for most of the season, and there was precious little information emanating from Hamamatsu. When the news did start to filter through, it became clear why there had been so little of it: not much had happened. The development programme for the SX4 was not as advanced as had been hoped. That was, according to sources, only partly down to funding issues - it was also partly due to continued indecision from the powers-that-be about the precise nature of the regulations for a World Rally Car beyond 2009.

There was plenty of sympathy for Suzuki. It had made the commitment to build a World Rally Car, but even before the car was finished, there were growing questions over how long its use would be permitted at the highest level.

Suzuki, however, is in. Mitsubishi, for now at least, is out.

One of the best-known WRC team bases - Mitsubishi Ralliart's Rugby factory, from where Andrew Cowan and Tommi Mäkinen had masterminded four consecutive drivers' titles - was effectively shut down this year. There are continued rumours of a new Mitsubishi team coming out of France, with a potential new WRC in 2010, but there is plenty of time for policy decisions and reversals between now and then.

One of the longest-standing commercial sponsors involved in the WRC also departed this season. OMV has backed Manfred Stohl for the last 15 years and even longer with his father Rudi before him. But this season was the last for the Austrian oil firm.

Having ended 2006 on a high with second on Rally GB and fourth in the championship in a Peugeot 307 WRC, much was expected of Stohl's return to Citroën Xsara WRC power for this year. In the end, Stohl's second full WRC campaign went off the rails. He was unhappy with the car for the first half of the season, and he then crashed comprehensively in Spain, Japan and Ireland. Stohl arrived at the finish of Rally GB with mixed feelings. There was relief that his difficult season was at a close, but sadness at the end of what has been one of the WRC's most enduring partnerships.

All the wheeling, dealing and political shenanigans that had run and run through the year were forgotten for all the wrong reasons one Saturday in September. Colin McRae had been killed. His helicopter had crashed in Scotland. Just as that news was beginning to filter through, worse followed - he hadn't been alone: his five-year-old son Johnny and two family friends, 37-year-old Graeme Duncan and six-year-old Ben Porcelli, had been with them. All perished.

McRae had been back in the news following an announcement that he was to join the Green Power Racing BMW team for Dakar in 2008. It beggared belief that it was time to prepare an obituary for Britain's other world champion, less than two years after the death of Richard Burns.

McRae's enthusiasm for his return to the sport had been infectious. He had competed on the Transiberico in a private Nissan in June where the result had been sacrificed by a clutch problem, but the pace had been there for all to see. A month later and the Scot was installed in the X3 and taking the fight to Mitsubishi and Volkswagen on Baja Espana. On top of all the Dakar talk, there were also rumours of a WRC return in 2008. The potential for seeing more of the 1995 champion generated a buzz about the sport.

Then it was gone and so was he - and in the most tragic of circumstances. Colin not being around anymore still doesn't make sense. Seeing his father Jim drive the 1995 Impreza across the start ramp on Rally GB in November was surreal in the extreme. The loss of the world's biggest, fastest and most spectacular rally driver certainly provided perspective on the other 'problems' which had hit the WRC through 2007.

*Below:* The ever-improving Latvala scored his maiden WRC podium finish in Ireland with third place. Afterwards he was tipped for a move to the works team

*Below middle:* Jimmy McRae drove son Colin's 1995 championship-winning Subaru as part of a tribute to the rally hero on Rally GB

*Bottom:* Suzuki made its long-awaited graduation to the WRC field with the SX4 in Corsica. Nicolas Bernardi had a troubled drive to 31st

All photographs by McKlein

*Opposite top:* Hirvonen will replace Grönholm as Ford's number one driver in 2008 after a great year which included three wins and points on every round but one

*Opposite bottom:* Petter Solberg had another trying year with the Subaru team, which reached a low point when he withdrew from Rally Finland, describing his car as "undriveable"

All photographs by McKlein

# The top 10 drivers of 2007

They weren't perfect all the time, but even so these are the standout guys who did the business in this year's WRC.
By David Evans

# SÉBASTIEN LOEB

## 1

AFTER a mountain bike shunt-enforced holiday of four months, Loeb didn't know what to expect from his broken left shoulder or the all-new C4 WRC beneath him when he arrived at the start of this year's Monte Carlo. He needn't have worried – it was business as usual on both counts. Neither the arm nor the car let him down. It did take a while for him to get the feeling with the C4 – and privately at least, he'd probably still say he doesn't have the same feeling he had with the factory Xsara – but it started to really come on song in Mexico. The León event was the setting for the car's first gravel win and 10-pointers in Portugal and Argentina followed in quick succession. Just when he looked on course for another incredible run of victories, he fell off the road in Sardinia. From that point of the season until the penultimate round in Ireland, he was playing catch-up to Grönholm. For a while in Japan it appeared to be going Loeb's way: Grönholm was out, and he was coasting. Then a mistake came from the right hand side of the C4, something that has never happened before – co-driver Daniel Elena called a note wrong and they joined Grönholm off the road. Normal service was resumed in Ireland, where Loeb made the best of his exceptional ability to find grip where others wouldn't dream of looking. After Grönholm's retirement, the Frenchman was never troubled on his way to 10 points. In Wales a fortnight later, he did what he had to do to clinch a fourth straight drivers' title. A slightly messier season than usual, but the result was the same: champion of the world.

| Round | Monte Carlo | Sweden | Norway | Mexico | Portugal | Argentina | Italy | Greece | Finland | Germany | New Zealand | Spain | Corsica | Japan | Ireland | Great Britain |
|---|---|---|---|---|---|---|---|---|---|---|---|---|---|---|---|---|
| Sébastien Loeb | 1 | 2 | 14 | 1 | 1 | 1 | R | 2 | 3 | 1 | 2 | 1 | 1 | R | 1 | 3 |

Key: R - retired, E - excluded

| Round | Monte Carlo | Sweden | Norway | Mexico | Portugal | Argentina | Italy | Greece | Finland | Germany | New Zealand | Spain | Corsica | Japan | Ireland | Great Britain |
|---|---|---|---|---|---|---|---|---|---|---|---|---|---|---|---|---|
| Marcus Grönholm | 3 | 1 | 2 | 2 | 4 | 2 | 1 | 1 | 1 | 4 | 1 | 3 | 2 | R | R | 2 |

Key: R - retired, E - excluded

# MARCUS GRÖNHOLM

## 2

OH bugger. This should have been the crowning glory on a fantastic career. Instead Grönholm froze at the most important moment of the year, like a rabbit in the headlights. When all he needed to do was bring the Focus RS WRC 07 home with some sensible points in the bag, he dropped it. Twice. Those are the negatives from this year (the biggest of which is a silver medal after 16 rallies). Now for the positives: New Zealand and Finland, two of the fastest rallies on the planet and two events where you need genitals the size of space hoppers. Grönholm won them both, and in some style. He fought off the prolonged challenge of team-mate Mikko Hirvonen in Finland – admitting along the way that his speed through Ouninpohja was bordering on the crazy – to become the first driver ever to win one WRC round seven times. But it was NZ that really caught the imagination of the rallying public. Grönholm and Loeb battled for three days around Hamilton. The lead changed four times between them and only once did anybody other than Loeb or Grönholm set fastest time on a stage (that was Atkinson on the superspecial). When Loeb nosed ahead on Saturday, it looked to be all over. The script usually played out with a French win. Not this time – Grönholm hit back and through awful weather on the Tasman coast he collected an astonishing victory that left the watching world agog. He had won by three tenths of a second and Loeb could barely believe it. The title had swung massively in favour of the Finn, yet still he managed to lose it.

McKlein

| Round | Monte Carlo | Sweden | Norway | Mexico | Portugal | Argentina | Italy | Greece | Finland | Germany | New Zealand | Spain | Corsica | Japan | Ireland | Great Britain |
|---|---|---|---|---|---|---|---|---|---|---|---|---|---|---|---|---|
| Jari-Matti Latvala | R | R | 5 | 7 | 8 | 4 | 9 | 12 | R | 8 | 5 | 7 | 4 | 25 | 3 | 10 |

Key: R - retired, E - excluded

# JARI-MATTI LATVALA

## 3

NEVER looked like a driver in his first full season in the sport. By mid-season Malcolm Wilson was talking in glowing terms of the latest Finn to drive one of his Fords. Then came Finland. Like his brethren who had passed down the hallowed tracks of Mökkiperä and the like before him, Latvala was lightening quick. Then he went off the road twice. Ouch. Wilson let him off with the first one, but was mightily miffed at the second shunt. Neither wrecked the Focus, but that Latvala didn't re-start made the point that there was a lesson to be learned. When he did the same in Japan (where he led and then binned it), there were question marks over how much had been learned… The one lesson Latvala undoubtedly learned was how to drive on asphalt. Last season it seemed all he had to do was look at a sealed surface and he was bouncing off the road. This time around he looked sure-footed and supremely confident as he waged an ultimately successful final-day war against a brace of Subarus in Corsica. And then came his crowing glory in Ireland. He was awesome on his way to third.

His ability to drive flat-chat under pressure on the dirt was also tested thoroughly, with New Zealand being a classic example. He traded seconds with Atkinson for the majority of Rally New Zealand. Yes, he lost out on the position, but he kept his car in one piece – something he would have struggled to do in the face of such a fierce fight 12 months earlier. He did plenty to merit all the talk of him being the man to step up and join Hirvonen in the BP Ford team for 2008.

McKlein

# MIKKO HIRVONEN

## 4

TWICE this year, Ford team principal Malcolm Wilson could have been forgiven for thinking the loss of Marcus Grönholm was nothing to worry about. One such occasion was in Norway, where such was Hirvonen's frantic pace from the outset that nobody else even got a look in. The younger of Ford's Finns went so fast that Sébastien Loeb kept on crashing trying to keep up. Hirvonen was immense on the second snow rally of the season. And then there was Finland. As Grönholm wound his Focus up and found the next level and another gear, Hirvonen kept on matching him. Hirvonen did flirt with disaster in a mammoth moment at the end of Ouninpohja, but even after that, he still looked up for more of the same. Still not quite a match for his team-mate (who has won the event seven times…) he was a good way clear of the rest of the field. So, what was the downside for Malcolm Wilson? It was an occasionally apathetic approach. When Hirvonen crashed in Corsica, he was perfectly miserable throughout Saturday and Sunday. Sure, everybody wants to win, but the wheel of his Focus hadn't ripped itself off and a weekend of driving a World Rally Car as fast as you dare remains an enormously attractive proposition to plenty of other drivers. That said this was another tough season for Hirvonen. He couldn't really challenge the two ahead enough to battle for the title *and* he was needed in third for the manufacturers' points. He did a good enough job, but could have shown more spark along the way – again in Ireland, where he admitted to being bored for the event's duration.

| Round | Monte Carlo | Sweden | Norway | Mexico | Portugal | Argentina | Italy | Greece | Finland | Germany | New Zealand | Spain | Corsica | Japan | Ireland | Great Britain |
|---|---|---|---|---|---|---|---|---|---|---|---|---|---|---|---|---|
| Mikko Hirvonen | 5 | 3 | 1 | 3 | 5 | 3 | 2 | 4 | 2 | 3 | 3 | 4 | 13 | 1 | 4 | 1 |

# DANI SORDO

## 5

GIVEN the machinery Sordo had at his disposal, he has to rank this as a disappointing season. Or does he? The trouble with Sordo is that he has slipped straight into the role of a WRC driver so easily, it's jolly easy to forget he's only contested one season in a World Rally Car prior to this one. After a year of learning the rallies in a Xsara WRC, there was a degree more pressure on the Spaniard's shoulders this year given his status as Citroën Sport number two. And, in turn, he did produce some sensible points-scoring drives – but the flashes of inspiration that made everybody stop and stare in 2006 seemed to have faded this time around. He was the threat everybody expected him to be at home, but he's struggled on the dirt and appeared unable to post the times without complete confidence in the car beneath him on the odd event. Trying to match up to one of the fastest drivers the world has ever seen is never going to be easy. But his team-mate Sébastien Loeb is an easy-going kind of fella who is more than happy to share his settings and offer advice to Sordo. So you do wonder if Sordo has made the best of having one of the most successful drivers around as a mentor. His season ended on a high with more podiums and a strong outing in Ireland, where he was clearly chomping at the bit to get out and have a crack – or should that be craic – at the man ahead. Unfortunately, the man ahead was Loeb – the only man in the world he wasn't permitted to overtake on the Emerald Isle.

| Round | Monte Carlo | Sweden | Norway | Mexico | Portugal | Argentina | Italy | Greece | Finland | Germany | New Zealand | Spain | Corsica | Japan | Ireland | Great Britain |
|---|---|---|---|---|---|---|---|---|---|---|---|---|---|---|---|---|
| Dani Sordo | 2 | 12 | 25 | 4 | 3 | 6 | 3 | 24 | R | R | 6 | 2 | 3 | 2 | 2 | 5 |

Key: R - retired, E - excluded

| Round | Monte Carlo | Sweden | Norway | Mexico | Portugal | Argentina | Italy | Greece | Finland | Germany | New Zealand | Spain | Corsica | Japan | Ireland | Great Britain |
|---|---|---|---|---|---|---|---|---|---|---|---|---|---|---|---|---|
| Petter Solberg | 6 | R | 4 | R | 2 | R | 5 | 3 | R | 6 | 7 | 6 | 5 | 16 | 5 | 4 |

Key: R - retired, E - excluded

# PETTER SOLBERG

**6**

SEEMED to take his eye off the ball this season. In fact, in Finland, his eye was never anywhere near the ball. Finland turned into big deal for Solberg, for all the wrong reasons. After a rotten pre-event test in the Impreza WRC2007, he arrived in Jyväskylä in then wrong frame of mind. That was carried through onto the stages, where the times were nowhere and the driver in tears. The car was parked up soon after on what was undoubtedly the former world champion's darkest day since joining Subaru. That all of this was played out to the backdrop of ever-increasing speculation that he would walk out of the team at the end of the season seemed more than just a co-incidence. By his own high standards, this was a shocker for Solberg. The car didn't work again, but what was – at times – more of a cause for concern was the fact that Petter appeared to have lost the heart to keep searching for the solution. Germany was a case in point. The Solberg look of exasperation is now so commonplace that the Solberg look of exultation formerly etched on his face when he met the same team personnel is hard to recall. The Solberg-Prodrive relationship has been tested severely this season, but the Solberg-Subaru relationship (ie the one with Japan) appears as strong as ever. His lack of podiums or the pace to threaten a podium has been hard enough to stomach this season. The best news came towards the end of the year, when David Richards and David Lapworth emerged in blue jackets again in Ireland. Suddenly, the trio of DR, Lappy and Hollywood was smiling again. The times in GB reflected the possible shoots of recovery…

McKlein

# CHRIS ATKINSON

**7**

THIS was a season of three parts for Atkinson. There was a purple patch in the middle where he was tremendous. At this time, while Petter Solberg found nothing but abject misery in Finland, Atkinson just got on with the job and fired the car through the trees at barely diminished speed. He never looked like winning a rally, but that was more down to the car than what he was doing in the driving seat. Prior to that, there were sticking points at the start of the year (his fine fourth in Monte aside). A narrow escape from what could have been the mother and father of all shunts in Portugal cost him the services of co-driver Glenn Macneall, who walked after that event. Rally New Zealand was a high point for Atkinson, backing up his fourth in Finland with a similar result on the North Island. At times in his rally-long battle with Latvala, you were just waiting for the news that Atko had gone off. That news never came. It looked as though the Queenslander had curbed his annoying habit of knocking corners off his Subaru. Then he signed his contract to stay with the team next season and everything appeared to go off the rails again. Yes, the speed was still there, but suddenly his car appeared magnetised to the side of the road again. There was a scary shunt in Japan and another off in Ireland. By that time, though, there was a school of thought that said: 'Why not chuck the car at the stages and set some times?' The Impreza WRC2007 wasn't a rally-winning package, so single-stage glory might have been nice. Atko appeared to deploy this policy; SWRT management didn't appear to appreciate it.

| Round | Monte Carlo | Sweden | Norway | Mexico | Portugal | Argentina | Italy | Greece | Finland | Germany | New Zealand | Spain | Corsica | Japan | Ireland | Great Britain |
|---|---|---|---|---|---|---|---|---|---|---|---|---|---|---|---|---|
| Chris Atkinson | 4 | 8 | 19 | 5 | R | 7 | 10 | 6 | 4 | 15 | 4 | 8 | 6 | R | 42 | 7 |

Key: R - retired, E - excluded

| Round | Monte Carlo | Sweden | Norway | Mexico | Portugal | Argentina | Italy | Greece | Finland | Germany | New Zealand | Spain | Corsica | Japan | Ireland | Great Britain |
|---|---|---|---|---|---|---|---|---|---|---|---|---|---|---|---|---|
| Henning Solberg | 14 | 4 | 3 | 9 | 11 | 5 | 4 | 5 | 5 | 13 | 9 | 10 | 9 | 3 | 16 | 14 |

# HENNING SOLBERG

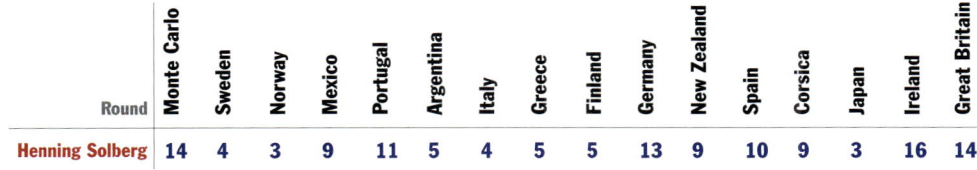

**W**OEFUL on the asphalt rallies, even if it was his first time. He seemed utterly perplexed by what was needed from the set-up of his car to make it go quickly in Corsica and Catalunya, which came as something of a shock given that he is usually a driver with a solid mechanical approach. The highlight for Solberg's first full year in the sport was undoubtedly Norway. He arrived at home on the back of a great rally in Sweden, where he had finished fourth just days earlier. In Norway, he seemed to find another gear again in the Focus, particularly through the final day. Fittingly, given the nation's blanket media coverage of the event, Norway was treated to the finest of family soap operas through the final day as Henning and brother Petter went head to head for fourth. It wasn't the win the locals had been hoping for, but it was a gripping scrap to the last. Beyond the snow rallies, this was a fairly ordinary season for the older Solberg who does have a surprising level of experience on many of the world rallies he tackled this year – and he certainly had a car that was still capable of winning WRC rounds. In Japan he made up for the lack of Loeb and Grönholm on the leaderboard to clinch another podium.

# JAN KOPECKY

THIS looks like being the popular Czech Republic driver's final World Rally Championship programme – and what a great way to go out. Sure, there has been the odd spillage here and there, but when you're driving a car that's three years out of date and trying to make up for the lack of technology beneath the bonnet by leaving your right foot on the loud pedal for longer, these things are going to happen. Kopecky belied the age of his Skoda Fabia and was never out of the top 10 in this year's championship, until the WRC crossed the Atlantic for Mexico. Flyaway rallies were never going to be part of his budget-driven programme, so he focused his attentions and efforts in Europe. The highlight of the year was fifth in Germany. By the time he got to Corsica – where he finished seventh – Kopecky looked like a man who had had enough. One mid-stage speed trap on leg two showed he was well down on an uphill section – despite unflinching commitment through the high-speed corners that led to the hill. The car was tired and it was beginning to tell. An Intercontinental Rally Challenge campaign for next season beckons, but that will be the WRC's loss. Had he been a couple of years older, he could have been the one to keep Skoda in the world championship. As it is, the pinnacle of the sport looks to have lost them both.

| Round | Monte Carlo | Sweden | Norway | Mexico | Portugal | Argentina | Italy | Greece | Finland | Germany | New Zealand | Spain | Corsica | Japan | Ireland | Great Britain |
|---|---|---|---|---|---|---|---|---|---|---|---|---|---|---|---|---|
| Jan Kopecky | 8 | 10 | 8 | X | 20 | X | R | 7 | R | 5 | X | R | 7 | X | X | 12 |

Key: R - retired, E - excluded

# PER-GUNNAR ANDERSSON

## 10

THE fight that ensued on the final round of this year's Junior Rally Championship should never have happened. If Andersson's right foot hadn't been so heavy on the public roads at home in Sweden, he would still have had his driving licence, would still have competed in Germany and probably had the title sorted out without the need for any last-gasp shenanigans in Corsica. Andersson has, once again, been the class of the Junior field. Having lifted this title for the first time in 2004, it's not unreasonable to think that he might have taken his fourth crown this season. In the end, it was his second. After two successful campaigns in what's supposed to be the WRC's feeder formula, you'd have thought somebody would have been ready to snap up the Swede and his undoubted speed. Seemingly not – not even his employer for the past four years, Suzuki. It seems Andersson doesn't have the budget for the second SX4 WRC, which is a massive shame. P-G is not only one of the quickest Swedes around, he's also a damned nice bloke who seems to have everything going for him to make it to the top.

| Round | Monte Carlo | Sweden | Norway | Mexico | Portugal | Argentina | Italy | Greece | Finland | Germany | New Zealand | Spain | Corsica | Japan | Ireland | Great Britain |
|---|---|---|---|---|---|---|---|---|---|---|---|---|---|---|---|---|
| **Per-Gunnar Andersson** | X | 32 | 18 (1) | X | 14 (1) | X | 14 (2) | X | X | X | X | 15 (1) | 20 (5) | X | X | X |

*\* Junior results in brackets*

# The king of cool

Sébastien Loeb's relaxed approach to his fourth straight WRC title win disguised the fact that this has been his toughest fight yet.
By David Evans

SUNDAY morning, Rally GB, just before 7am. As usual, Sébastien Loeb is lingering over his third espresso since he opened his eyes. Coffee in hand, he's casting an eye over three pictures that adorn the walls of the Citroën Sport hospitality area; there's one from each time he became world champion in the last three years. Lost in the moment temporarily, he doesn't hear co-driver Daniel Elena calling him back to their world. Elena sounds the horn on the C4 WRC and Loeb is back with it. In one motion, he necks the coffee, bins the cup, winks and throws a "See you later..." over his shoulder. He has a world championship waiting.

Four hours later and Loeb's back, to a hero's welcome for the fourth successive season. He's a champion again. Nobody has won more world titles than he has and only one person has ever claimed four on the trot before. He must be bouncing off the ceiling somewhere. Er, no. That's not Loeb's way.

"It's nice," he smiles. Not bothering with another question, I wait for him to fill the ensuing silence. Realising I want more than two words, he opens up: "This was the hardest championship for me. There is no doubt about that. Look at the mistakes I made - more than ever. The reason for that was that Marcus [Grönholm] had the perfect car. Normally, in the past, it has only been me who had the perfect car, but this time he had it as well. This made it hard for me; I had to be on my limit all the time. There was no time that I could slow down. But this is a great moment for the team and for me. Also it's a great moment for Guy [Fréquelin, retiring team principal], it's a nice way for him to leave and go into retirement."

The final round of the season, Rally Great Britain, was a breeze compared with what Loeb had been through previously. Look back 12 months, and he was barely able to sit in a car without being in a considerable amount of pain following his mountain bike accident in September 2006.

Four months away from a World Rally Car had given his shoulder injury good time to heal, but still it wasn't enough. Physios, consultants and specialists were saying that, given the operation the Frenchman had undergone, he shouldn't really have competed in Monte Carlo. Forget that.

Nothing, but nothing, was going to stop Loeb from stepping aboard the all-new Citroën C4 on the French firm's return to the world stage. Particularly as that return would come in Monte Carlo, one of Loeb's favoured events. Thinking back to the start of the season and Loeb admits he wasn't quite as laidback on the Thursday in Valence as he was come Sunday afternoon in Cardiff.

"I was really stressed before the start," he says. "I didn't know what to expect. I didn't know how the car would be compared with the competition. Okay, we had an idea from testing, but this is just testing, it's not competition. And then there was my arm: how would this be? And finally, we were competing at night. There was no snow and ice, but the weather was wet. It was so much not to know about. I was so relieved when we came out of the those stages in the lead."

Loeb's physio, Marc Germain, was on hand throughout to tend to the 33-year-old's every need. He says: "I've been looking after Seb for three years now and I know him inside out. One of his biggest strengths is the speed in which he recovers

**Main and inset:** Loeb admitted to being stressed at the start of the season as he returned from injury and got to grips with the new C4. But he won first time out in Monte Carlo, one of his favourite events

All photographs by Gérard Rancinan

*Above:* His wife Severine is usually with Loeb on events but missed much of this season prior to the birth of their first child, Valentine

*Above right:* Coffee in hand, Loeb reflects on his previous title successes in the Citroën Sport hospitality area at Rally GB, before going out and securing his fourth straight championship

*Top:* Retiring team boss Guy Fréquelin (second from left) has nurtured Loeb's WRC career and would love nothing better than to see the Frenchman and Elena go on to further success

*Opposite:* Loeb drove with his head on Rally GB, maintaining third position instead of going on a charge to be sure of his title win

All photographs by Gérard Rancinan unless specified

He certainly recovered from the injury and from any lingering doubts about his performance at the start of the year. The wins followed, four from six starts, before Loeb arrived in Sardinia. Midway through the final day of that event he had the rally in the palm of his hand. Then out of nowhere he cropped the C4. A three-point lead over Grönholm was converted in to a seven-point deficit to the Finn. Things got worse for Loeb when he was beaten by not just one Finn but two at the wheel of Ford Focuses in Finland. At the finish of his weekend in Jyväskylä, Loeb was contemplating at a 13-point difference to the championship leader.

But Loeb didn't let his head drop, he knew he had his asphalt bankers on the horizon. Sure enough, in the space of a fortnight, he'd slashed the gap to Grönholm to just four points with three rallies remaining.

Halfway through the second half of the season, New Zealand had given Loeb a wake-up call. Grönholm beat him in the tightest finish to a WRC round in history - just three tenths of a second separated them when they arrived at Hamilton for the final time.

"My approach to rallies is a little different to that of Marcus," says Loeb. "I take things slowly to begin with. Even from the shakedown, when I look at the times, he is usually faster than me. When I have my confidence with the car and with the road surface, then I begin to speed up."

This is usually on the second run at stages, starting on Friday afternoon. Looking back through the times for this year's championship, it was exceptionally rare for Loeb to be beaten by anybody on the afternoon of legs one and two.

Having done just that in New Zealand, he had duly moved ahead of Grönholm on the Saturday. From then on, there should have been a repeat of numerous past rallies: with the Ford disposed of, Loeb could just motor on to the win. Only this time, Grönholm made a major fight of it. The pair risked all in some of the worst conditions seen this year, as rain lashed the North Island coastline just outside Raglan. Loeb lost. Talking about it three months on, he still can't help but shake his head.

"It was incredible," he says. "Just incredible. Okay, I lost the rally, but still it was the highlight of the year for me. That is why I do this sport. That's why I'm here: for competition like that. It was the best rally."

Despite winning 36 world rallies and four titles - which, don't forget, could have been five had he managed to score one more point in 2003 - Loeb has stuck to the old adage about taking part and winning. But that's him. He's come from an average family and while he knows he's talented, he also knows he's on to a good thing.

Ask him what bothers him about his job and there's a double take, almost to confirm this is a serious question. He's thinking about it. In the middle of thinking about it, he throws in the good stuff.

"When I get back in the car and sit there, knowing I'm going to drive as fast as I can, then this is the best feeling," he says. "It is fantastic to be able to do what I do."

Above: Mechanical dramas were rare in the C4's maiden season well, on Loeb's car at least

Opposite top: He may have lost to Grönholm in New Zealand by just 0.3 seconds, but this was the rally that Loeb enjoyed the most this year, due to his great battle with the Finn

Opposite bottom: Loeb and Elena's partnership is an enduring one. The co-driver pace note mistake in Japan, his first in 10 years of them being together, was quickly forgotten by his driver

All photographs by Gérard Rancinan unless specified

Then comes this: "It's a little bit boring being at the airport all the time."

That's it, the only downside to being a four-time world champion. What about the ceaseless stream of questions from journalists across the globe?

Again, there's a slightly quizzical look. "I can't not answer them," he says. "It's the day they stop having questions for me that I will start worrying."

After four years of winning, there must be a secret to Loeb's success beyond a heavy right foot and a slightly lighter left one. What about some kind of ritual before each stage? Didier Auriol used to select fourth gear before the start of every stage.

"No," says Loeb. "I'm not interested in any of that. I think you should keep your head as clear as possible before the start of a rally. Forget everything and just focus on what you have in front of you. Doing things like this is fine, but what do you do when you get to the start of a stage and you don't have the time to put the car in gear? What happens then? Your head will be finished, because you haven't done what you always do. It's best to do nothing. Just drive."

It's a simple theory, but it's clearly the best. In fact, there's nothing complicated about Loeb. He's in tip-top physical condition, but when other drivers are out for a run in the morning, you can guarantee Loeb will still be fast asleep.

Germain is the man tasked with raising Loeb from his slumber each morning, and experience tells him to leave him as long as possible.

"Sébastien gets up at the last minute but hits the ground running," says Germain. "What he has done in the past has stood him in good stead for this."

It's true that the bus to take the drivers from the team hotel to the service park will be waiting for Loeb 99 per cent of the time. And 90 per cent of the time, when he does finally step aboard the bus, he's still got a cup of coffee in his hand.

Beyond the physical attributes, gymnastics has also taught Loeb plenty when its come to dealing with pressure. That's one of his biggest strengths - the pressure simply doesn't seem to get to him like it does other drivers. When was the last time you saw the laidback Loeb flustered? Exactly. Flustered is not an adjective usually found in the same sentence as the words Sébastien or Loeb.

"When I was very young, the pressure was very hard for me to succeed in gym," says Loeb. "When you have learned to cope with that, then what happens to me now is okay - I am older and I can deal with this much easier. I learned about pressure at a young age."

He is also learning more about the pressures of family life right now. The Monday after Rally Ireland, his first child arrived in the shape of Valentine Loeb. While his wife Severine stayed at home for most of Rally GB to look after the newborn, Loeb's father-in-law Richard Meny was close at hand in Wales with plenty of reassuring words.

"Sébastien is the son I never had," he says. "I am so proud of him. Usually, the whole family comes on the rallies, but this time is an exception. My wife has stayed back at home with Severine and the baby. Sébastien calls my daughter after every stage and she is following the event closely on the Internet."

Severine arrived in time for the finish of Rally GB. An emotional moment followed as the two celebrated another major achievement in their lives.

Motorsport-wise Citroën Sport team principal Guy Fréquelin has, to date, celebrated every one of Loeb's major milestones. Not any more. Fréquelin retires at the end of this season. It's fitting that the man known as Le Grizzli has the last word here.

"It will be strange on January 2," says Fréquelin, "when my alarm goes off and I don't know what to do. But I will only consider my mission complete when I see Citroën and the drivers continuing to win after my departure. I have known Sébastien and Daniel for a long time and they have made me and everybody Citroën Sport very proud. This will not stop."

# SÉBASTIEN LOEB

## A MAN WORTH TAKING NOTE OF

In rallying, it's all too easy to forget the fella sitting alongside the driver when things are going well. Down the years, co-drivers have talked of the solitude they can feel in their job. When everything goes right and the wins are coming, it's down to the driver. But one wrong call or one late note that causes an accident and the one without the wheel is squarely to blame.

That's precisely what happened to Daniel Elena and Sébastien Loeb in Japan this year. After 10 years of not making any mistakes, Elena got it wrong and - for some inexplicable reason - what he read and what he told his driver bore no resemblance.

Loeb set up the car for the corner as he had been told and nanoseconds later the pair were off the road. Sébastien remembers the immediate aftermath: "I just couldn't understand it," he says. "It didn't make sense. How had this happened? How were we off the road? Then Daniel told me he had made a mistake. Now I understood. Okay, this can happen."

The pair have competed on 98 rallies together now. It's fair to say they have a good idea of what makes each other tick. Elena says it's only when they get in the rally car and get away from service and the multitude of engineers and team personnel that they really get to relax.

"It's then that Sébastien and I get to breathe more easily," says Elena.

There was never any question of retribution for Elena's Japanese mistake. The pair have been through tougher times than that, particularly when they were starting out and certain parties within Citroën Sport were calling for a change in the partnership. Elena takes solace from those memories now.

He says: "I can't help but smile when I think of how long Seb and I have been together, despite the fact that very few people had confidence in me at the beginning. They wanted someone with more experience. With Seb's help, I had to fight to keep my job. There was little chance of me making progress if nobody was willing to give me a break."

The French-Monegasque pairing have stood - and sat - shoulder to shoulder through four world titles since. And there's no sign of this enduring partnership coming to an end any time soon.

# Colin McRae MBE
# 1968-2007

"He was a great friend. The whole world of motorsport will miss him"
David Coulthard

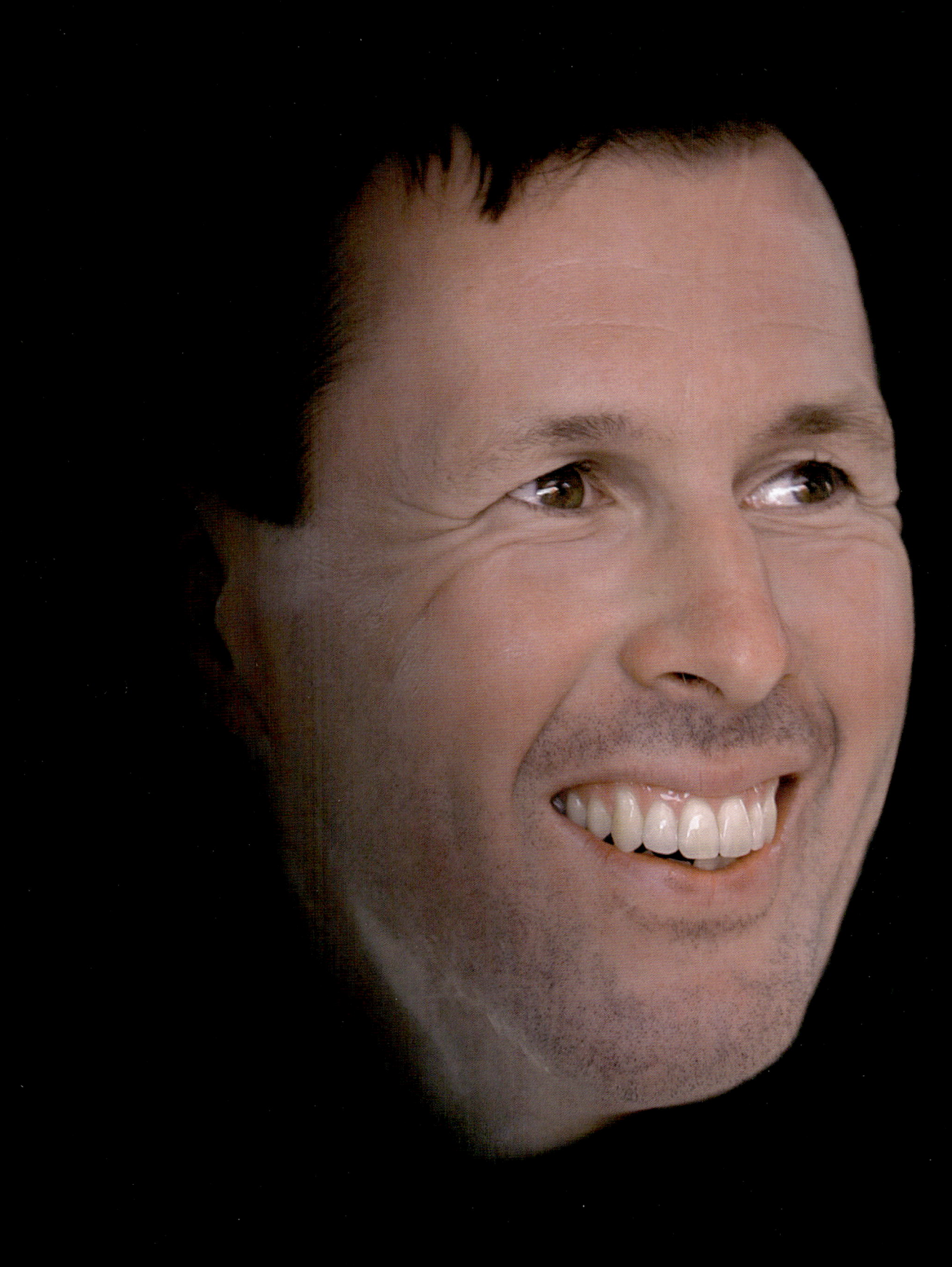

Colin was a global figure. We always knew what he did went much further than our local community in Scotland, but the memorial service to remember him, Johnny, Graeme and Ben in September really showed us that. I think deep down we knew how many people were really big fans of his, but seeing all those people in the High Street in Lanark was still quite amazing.

Competing at the Race of Champions at Wembley in Colin's place was really emotional for me. Doing all the interviews brought a lot of the feelings back and everything felt quite raw again. It really wasn't an easy thing to do, but it was special to drive one of Colin's Impreza 555s around the track - and to see how much it meant to the people out there.

The family has been overwhelmed by the messages of condolence and Colin would have been touched to think of the support his friends have given to the family.

Alister McRae,
December 2007

"Nothing was going to stop us being world champions in 1995" Derek Ringer

Left: McRae became an instant hit with the Finnish fans (and trees) by rolling his Legacy nine times on his way to eighth overall in 1992

Far left: Aged 21, McRae drove a factory Ford on the RAC. He showed blinding speed before rolling in Dyfi and then crashing into the Sierra of team-mate Franco Cunico in Kielder

Above left: The first of many... McRae and co-driver Derek Ringer celebrate WRC win number one in New Zealand, 1993

Above: After winning the British title in 1991, Prodrive sent McRae and his Rothmans Legacy to do a similar job at the Bettega Memorial Rallysprint

All photographs by McKlein unless specified

"He was my hero" Valentino Rossi | "We had incredible fights: one of us would win, the other would crash" Tommi Makinen

"Colin taught me so much about driving. He was one of my best friends" Petter Solberg

There was support for McRae everywhere. In his title-winning year, he only managed fifth in Corsica in a down-on-power Impreza, but he would go on to win the WRC's asphalt classic twice, amply demonstrating that his abilities stretched way beyond fast gravel rallies
Race&motion

"He was the people's champion" Malcolm Wilson   |   "Colin was a champion. End of story. Colin, forever" Carlos Sainz

"In 1995 I asked for his autograph. I still have it. He was such a character" Heikki Kovalainen

Above: The best of Britain! McRae and Richard Burns were great mates and rivals. It's unbelievable that they're both gone

Left: Colin came close to winning Australia 2005 on only his second outing in a works Skoda. He lost the result when the team failed to change a gearbox in the allotted time

Far left: The first and possibly sweetest win with Ford. New car or not, McRae was king of Kenya in 1999

Top left: Whether the car suited his style of driving or not, McRae was still spectacular to watch in the Citroën

Top right: Dakar was one of McRae's rally passions. He desperately wanted to win the rally raid and was on his way in 2005 when a big accident in the desert put paid to his chances. He was scheduled to return with BMW in January 2008

All photographs by McKlein

"Colin just drove faster than anybody else" David Lapworth

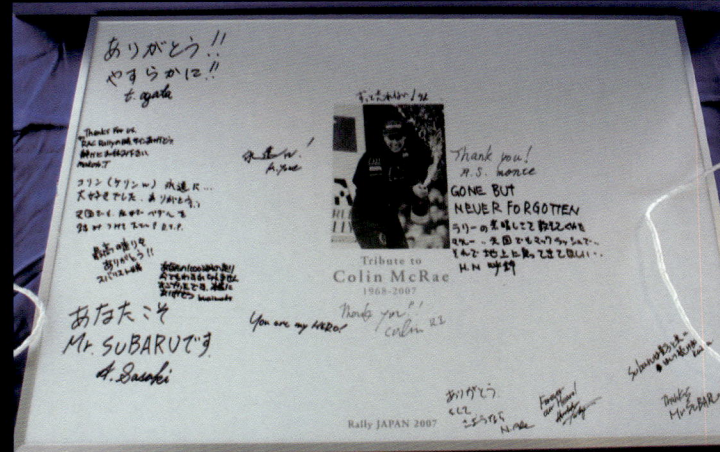

Clockwise from left: At the first WRC event after McRae's death, the drivers gathered in Spain to pay tribute to the former champion

Valentino Rossi and McRae shared a mutual respect and the loss of his friend hit the MotoGP ace hard

Alister and Stuart McRae drove Colin's 1995 Catalunya car at December's Race of Champions

More then 20,000 fans turned out for McRae's memorial service in his hometown of Lanark

Two of McRae's favourite cars were also in attendance at the service of celebration for Colin and Johnny on September 30

One of many Japanese tributes prepared for the McRae family

A lone piper played Flower of Scotland prior to the start of the memorial service

All photographs by McKlein unless specified

The situation was surreal beyond belief. Wembley Stadium on a chilly Sunday evening in December and a young fan, draped in a Saltire, was looking up at the big screen at the far end of the stadium with tears running down his face. This was nothing to do with football. The tears were for Colin McRae, and the event was London's first Race of Champions.

As I write it is three months and one day since McRae's helicopter crashed near his home in Lanark, Scotland, killing the 1995 world champion, his five-year-old son Johnny and family friends Graeme Duncan, 37, and Ben Porcelli, six. The passing of time has done nothing to dull the pain or make sense of a family's nightmare and British rallying's darkest hour. Colin McRae has gone. Unbelievable.

McRae was the first and the best of the Group A supermen. The nickname 'Supermac' said it all. If it could be done in a car, Colin would do it - regularly and more often than anybody else. That stunning ability to drive a car into a corner at a completely different angle, looking thoroughly out of shape on the way in yet gathered and composed on the way out, was what Colin was all about. In rallying, McRae would deliver his very own brand of shock and awe at almost every turn.

That was what made him great, and also what turned a family name formerly synonymous with his father Jimmy's five British titles into one of the biggest brands in the World Rally Championship. Colin McRae was worshipped across the globe - as the people who had travelled from around it to stand in honour of McRae at September's memorial service would testify.

But his was a story which started from humble beginnings: a tale of Talbot Sunbeams, Vauxhall Novas and not as much help from dad as people might think.

Unfortunately I missed out on the Sunbeam action, but I was captivated the first time I saw the name McRae on the side of the Nova. It was on the Welsh Rally in 1987 when, following a flotilla of midfield mediocrity, came the sight of the diminutive Vauxhall bouncing from the ditch on the inside of the road - the apex of the corner sufficiently chopped as to be well beneath the car - to the ditch on the outside. The topography of the manoeuvre slowed the car's velocity only momentarily; the breathless screaming of the 1300cc engine provided the aural evidence of McRae's planted right boot. There were seconds to be won everywhere and Colin was always in the hunt.

There was an aura about McRae in the early days. It was an aura that would evolve and morph itself into a variety of character traits in the years to come, but in the early days, it was based around invincibility and pure and simple enjoyment. A couple of months after I'd watched agog as the Nova danced between the trees in Wales came Colin's finest hour in the 1988 British Championship: ninth overall on his home international, the Scottish. Now that was a result to build on.

While British motorsport got excited about this result, McRae kept his feet firmly on the ground and sought to broaden his horizon of competition. That meant switching to cars like the venerable Nissan 240 RS and a variety of Ford Sierra Cosworths. If the cars differed, the results were becoming increasingly familiar: almost always a win, sometimes a crash, rarely anything else. The British and National class titles were solid achievements, but becoming the youngest ever Scottish Champion in 1988 highlighted his ability to outshine his peers in equal machinery.

In 1989, Ford provided a Group N Sierra for McRae junior to take on Pentti Airikkala's Mitsubishi Galant in the British series. It was a battle that was weighted ridiculously in favour of the Finn. Not only did he have vast experience of the stages, his car had a full compliment of driven wheels. McRae did his utmost to defy the laws of mechanical grip and provided more than the odd bent panel along the way.

These were tough times for McRae. The Audi Sport Rally in 1989 showed his immense potential as, armed with a Group A Sierra, he beat the sister car of his father. But then, on the bigger stage of the RAC a month later, he comprehensively binned the Ford, not helping his father's negotiations for 1990.

started and ended on a huge high - his first British win on the Cartel Rally and sixth on the RAC - but in the middle there was more bent metal. Now, more than ever, somebody had to take a punt on McRae and his wicked pace. That man was David Richards.

McRae joined Prodrive's fledgling Subaru programme and rewarded the team with back-to-back titles. With home glory secured, Richards and McRae looked to take on the world. Three years later, and that crown was in the bag too.

The 1995 title should have been the tip of the iceberg, but his knack of winning deserted McRae in his year as champion. He was stymied at every turn and came close to losing his seat as Richards' patience wore thin. You had to feel for Colin that season. He was doing his darndest, driving the door handles off the car, but while everything had flowed in his direction in '95, he was pushing water uphill 12 months on.

It didn't last. He was fiercely dominant in 1997, when only the dogged determination of Tommi Mäkinen and occasional frailty of the Impreza WRC combined to keep McRae off the top.

At the end of the following season, the unthinkable happened: McRae left Subaru. Lured by the challenge of helping to develop Ford's new Focus WRC and more than a fistful of dollars, the WRC's highest-paid driver moved to pastures new for 1999.

There can be little doubt that McRae was one of the fastest drivers ever to earn a living in the sport, but one aspect of rallying that the Scot was never given enough credit for was his ability to drive sensibly as well as speedily. It was just this trait that earned him and Ford a historic win on the Safari, with the Focus just a few months old. He then went on and won the next event, the Rally of Portugal, to prove the he and the Focus could live with anything else in the WRC in terms of pure pace.

A string of mechanical glitches kept McRae off the finishers' list for nine rallies from Argentina 1999 to Monte Carlo the following season. There was more disappointment in 2000, but by '01, Ford and M-Sport had ridden the Focus of glitches and successive wins in Argentina, Cyprus and Greece put McRae on pole for that illusive second title. That was until he binned the Ford in one of the highest speed and most spectacular accidents ever seen in the history of the series in Corsica.

Few would have believed that when McRae won the Safari in 2002 - making him the then-most successful driver in the history of the sport - it would be his last WRC victory. Ford failed to secure the finance to keep him the following year, when he moved to Citroën for a season in the Xsara WRC, which he found a troublesome beast. At the end of 2003, however, he was out of a drive. Astonishingly, there was no seat for the planet's most recognisable rally driver.

At the time, McRae appeared quite relaxed about the situation. Okay, he said, it wasn't on his terms, but after more than 10 years on the road he was ready for a break. A break to Colin meant two things: Le Mans and Dakar. He finished both and cherished the experiences. There were also brief forays back into the WRC with Skoda and Kronos Citroën, but it appeared that his time in the world championship was up.

Latterly, there had been talk of a return for 2008. Whether that would have happened or not didn't matter after the horrific crash in September. Suddenly, it wasn't just the WRC that needed McRae - now the world needed him. That he had gone just didn't compute. Motorsport, not just rallying, still feels the loss of one of its quickest, most-admired and idolised characters. And it always will.

However much pain and heartache the rally world feels, it can't come close to what Alison, Hollie, Margaret, Jim, Alister and Stuart have been through. All we can do is thank them for sharing Colin with us. As time passes and the legendary McRae stories are handed down from generation to generation, they will appear more fable than fact. But every one of them is true.

Those who saw Colin on the stages can count themselves lucky, those who knew him luckier still - and those who shared a bar bill with him, the luckiest of all.

# RESULTS

| 1985 | | |
|---|---|---|
| Kames Stages | Talbot Avenger | 14th |
| Galloway Hills Rally | Talbot Avenger | DNF |

| 1986 | | |
|---|---|---|
| Snowman Rally | Talbot Sunbeam | 27th |
| Valentine Rally | Talbot Sunbeam | 15th |
| Granite City Rally | Talbot Sunbeam | 54th |
| Autofit Rally | Talbot Sunbeam | 9th |
| Scottish Rally | Talbot Sunbeam | DNF |
| Border Rally | Talbot Sunbeam | 103rd |
| Lindisfarne Rally | Talbot Sunbeam | DNF |
| Kingdom Rally | Talbot Sunbeam | 18th |

| 1987 | | |
|---|---|---|
| Swedish Rally | Vauxhall Nova | 36th |
| Valentine Rally | Vauxhall Nova | 16th |
| Granite City Rally | Vauxhall Nova | DNF |
| Scottish Rally | Vauxhall Nova | DNF |
| Manx Rally | Vauxhall Nova | 1 class |
| Hackle Rally | Vauxhall Nova | 11th |
| RAC Rally | Vauxhall Nova | DNF |
| Trossachs Rally | Ford Sierra Cosworth | DNF |

| 1988 | | |
|---|---|---|
| Snowman Rally | Vauxhall Nova | 8th |
| Cartel Rally | Vauxhall Nova | 8th |
| Circuit of Ireland | Vauxhall Nova | DNF |
| Granite City Rally | Vauxhall Nova | 28th |
| Welsh Rally | Vauxhall Nova | 14th |
| Autofit Rally | Nissan 240RS | 2nd |
| Scottish Rally | Vauxhall Nova | 9th |
| Ypres Rally | Vauxhall Nova | DNF |
| Jim Clark Rally | Peugeot-Nissan 205 | 2nd |
| Tweedies Stages | Nissan 240RS | 1st |
| Manx National Rally | Peugeot 309 | DNF |
| Ulster Rally | Vauxhall Nova | 12th |
| Border Rally | Ford Sierra Cosworth | 1st |
| Kingdom Stages | Ford Sierra Cosworth | 2nd |
| Manx Rally | Vauxhall Nova | 14th |
| Quip Stages | Peugeot 309 | 29th |
| Hackle Rally | Ford Sierra Cosworth | 1st |
| Audi Sport Rally | Ford Sierra Cosworth | DNF |
| Trossachs Rally | Ford Sierra Cosworth | 2nd |
| RAC Rally | Peugeot 205 | DNF |

| 1989 | | |
|---|---|---|
| Swedish Rally | Ford Sierra XR 4x4 | 15th |
| Cartel Rally | Ford Sierra Cosworth | DNF |
| Skip Brown Rally | Ford Sierra Cosworth | DNF |
| Circuit of Ireland | Ford Sierra Cosworth | 12th |
| Granite City Rally | Ford Sierra Cosworth | DNF |
| Welsh Rally | Ford Sierra Cosworth | DNF |
| Manx National Rally | Ford Sierra Cosworth | 4th |
| Scottish Rally | Ford Sierra Cosworth | 6th |
| Kayel Graphics Rally | Ford Sierra Cosworth | DNF |
| Rally New Zealand | Ford Sierra Cosworth | 5th |
| Ulster Rally | Ford Sierra Cosworth | DNF |
| Cumbria National Rally | Ford Sierra Cosworth | 1st |
| Manx Rally | Ford Sierra Cosworth | DNF |
| Trackrod National Rally | Ford Sierra Cosworth | 1st |
| Audi Sport Rally | Ford Sierra Cosworth | 3rd |
| RAC Rally | Ford Sierra Cosworth | DNF |

| 1990 | | |
|---|---|---|
| Cartel Rally | Ford Sierra Cosworth | 1st |
| Circuit of Ireland | Ford Sierra Cosworth | 3rd |
| Welsh Rally | Ford Sierra Cosworth | DNF |
| Scottish Rally | Ford Sierra Cosworth | 2nd |
| Ypres Rally | Ford Sierra Cosworth | 4th |
| Ulster Rally | Ford Sierra Cosworth | 8th |
| Manx Rally | Ford Sierra Cosworth | 3rd |
| Hackle Rally | Ford Escort RS2000 | 1st |
| Audi Sport Rally | Ford Sierra Cosworth 4x4 | 2nd |
| RAC Rally | Ford Sierra Cosworth 4x4 | 6th |

| 1991 | | |
|---|---|---|
| Talkland Rally | Subaru Legacy RS | 1st |
| Circuit of Ireland | Subaru Legacy RS | 1st |
| Welsh Rally | Subaru Legacy RS | DNF |
| Scottish Rally | Subaru Legacy RS | 1st |
| Ulster Rally | Subaru Legacy RS | DNF |
| Manx Rally | Subaru Legacy RS | 1st |
| Audi Sport | Subaru Legacy RS | 3rd |
| RAC Rally | Subaru Legacy RS | DNF |

| 1992 | | |
|---|---|---|
| Swedish Rally | Subaru Legacy RS | 2nd |
| Vauxhall Sport Rally | Subaru Legacy RS | 1st |
| Pirelli Rally | Subaru Legacy RS | 1st |
| Acropolis Rally | Subaru Legacy RS | 4th |
| Scottish Rally | Subaru Legacy RS | 1st |
| Rally New Zealand | Subaru Legacy RS | DNF |
| Ulster Rally | Subaru Legacy RS | 1st |
| 1000 Lakes Rally | Subaru Legacy RS | 8th |
| Manx Rally | Subaru Legacy RS | 1st |
| Elonex Rally | Subaru Legacy RS | 1st |
| RAC Rally | Subaru Legacy RS | 6th |

| 1993 | | |
|---|---|---|
| Swedish Rally | Subaru Legacy RS | 3rd |
| Portugal Rally | Subaru Legacy RS | 7th |
| Safari Rally | Subaru Vivio | DNF |
| Tour de Corse | Subaru Legacy RS | 5th |
| Acropolis Rally | Subaru Legacy RS | DNF |
| Rally New Zealand | Subaru Legacy RS | 1st |
| Malaysia Rally | Subaru Legacy RS | 1st |
| Rally Australia | Subaru Legacy RS | 6th |
| Hong Kong-Peking Rally | Subaru Legacy RS | 2nd |
| RAC Rally | Subaru Impreza 555 | DNF |

| 1994 | | |
|---|---|---|
| Monte Carlo Rally | Subaru Impreza 555 | 10th |
| Portugal Rally | Subaru Impreza 555 | DNF |
| Tour de Corse | Subaru Impreza 555 | DNF |
| Acropolis Rally | Subaru Impreza 555 | DNF |
| Argentina Rally | Subaru Impreza 555 | DNF |
| Rally New Zealand | Subaru Impreza 555 | 1st |
| Rally Australia | Subaru Impreza 555 | 1st |
| Sanremo Rally | Subaru Impreza 555 | 5th |
| RAC Rally | Subaru Impreza 555 | 1st |

| 1995 | | |
|---|---|---|
| Monte Carlo Rally | Subaru Impreza 555 | DNF |
| Swedish Rally | Subaru Impreza 555 | DNF |
| Portugal Rally | Subaru Impreza 555 | 3rd |
| Tour de Corse | Subaru Impreza 555 | 5th |
| Malaysia Rally | Subaru Impreza 555 | DNF |
| Indonesia Rally | Subaru Impreza 555 | 1st |
| Rally New Zealand | Subaru Impreza 555 | 1st |
| Rally Australia | Subaru Impreza 555 | 2nd |
| Rally Catalunya | Subaru Impreza 555 | 1st |
| RAC Rally | Subaru Impreza 555 | 1st |

| 1996 | | |
|---|---|---|
| Swedish Rally | Subaru Impreza 555 | 4th |
| Thailand Rally | Subaru Impreza 555 | 1st |
| Safari Rally | Subaru Impreza 555 | 4th |
| Indonesia Rally | Subaru Impreza 555 | DNF |
| Acropolis Rally | Subaru Impreza 555 | 1st |
| Argentina Rally | Subaru Impreza 555 | DNF |
| 1000 Lakes Rally | Subaru Impreza 555 | DNF |
| Rally Australia | Subaru Impreza 555 | 4th |
| Rally Sanremo | Subaru Impreza 555 | 1st |
| Rally Catalunya | Subaru Impreza 555 | 1st |

| 1997 | | |
|---|---|---|
| Monte Carlo Rally | Subaru Impreza WRC97 | DNF |
| Swedish Rally | Subaru Impreza WRC97 | 4th |
| Safari Rally | Subaru Impreza WRC97 | 1st |
| Portugal Rally | Subaru Impreza WRC97 | DNF |
| Catalunya Rally | Subaru Impreza WRC97 | 4th |
| Tour de Corse | Subaru Impreza WRC97 | 1st |
| Argentina Rally | Subaru Impreza WRC97 | 2nd |
| Acropolis Rally | Subaru Impreza WRC97 | DNF |
| China Rally | Subaru Impreza WRC97 | 1st |
| Rally New Zealand | Subaru Impreza WRC97 | DNF |
| Finland Rally | Subaru Impreza WRC97 | DNF |
| Indonesia Rally | Subaru Impreza WRC97 | DNF |
| Sanremo Rally | Subaru Impreza WRC97 | 1st |
| Rally Australia | Subaru Impreza WRC97 | 1st |

*The perfect final shot for Colin. Here's Mr McRae doing what he did best, utterly sideways with the taps wide open. There'll never be another like him*
McKlein

| | | |
|---|---|---|
| **1998** | | |
| Monte Carlo Rally | Subaru Impreza WRC98 | 3rd |
| Swedish Rally | Subaru Impreza WRC98 | DNF |
| Safari Rally | Subaru Impreza WRC98 | DNF |
| Portugal Rally | Subaru Impreza WRC98 | 1st |
| Catalunya Rally | Subaru Impreza WRC98 | WDN |
| Tour de Corse | Subaru Impreza WRC98 | 1st |
| Argentina Rally | Subaru Impreza WRC98 | 5th |
| Acropolis Rally | Subaru Impreza WRC98 | 1st |
| Rally New Zealand | Subaru Impreza WRC98 | 5th |
| Finland Rally | Subaru Impreza WRC98 | DNF |
| Sanremo Rally | Subaru Impreza WRC98 | 3rd |
| Rally Australia | Subaru Impreza WRC98 | 4th |
| RAC Rally | Subaru Impreza WRC98 | DNF |
| **1999** | | |
| Monte Carlo Rally | Ford Focus WRC | EXC |
| Swedish Rally | Ford Focus WRC | DNF |
| Safari Rally | Ford Focus WRC | 1st |
| Portugal Rally | Ford Focus WRC | 1st |
| Catalunya Rally | Ford Focus WRC | WDN |
| Tour de Corse | Ford Focus WRC | 4th |
| Argentina Rally | Ford Focus WRC | DNF |
| Acropolis Rally | Ford Focus WRC | DNF |
| Rally New Zealand | Ford Focus WRC | DNF |
| Finland Rally | Ford Focus WRC | DNF |
| China Rally | Ford Focus WRC | DNF |
| Sanremo Rally | Ford Focus WRC | DNF |
| Rally Australia | Ford Focus WRC | DNF |
| RAC Rally | Ford Focus WRC | DNF |
| **2000** | | |
| Monte Carlo Rally | Ford Focus WRC | DNF |
| Swedish Rally | Ford Focus WRC | 3rd |
| Safari Rally | Ford Focus WRC | DNF |
| Portugal Rally | Ford Focus WRC | DNF |
| Catalunya Rally | Ford Focus WRC | 1st |
| Argentina Rally | Ford Focus WRC | DNF |
| Acropolis Rally | Ford Focus WRC | 1st |
| Rally New Zealand | Ford Focus WRC | 2nd |
| Finland Rally | Ford Focus WRC | 2nd |
| Cyprus Rally | Ford Focus WRC | 2nd |
| Tour de Corse | Ford Focus WRC | DNF |
| Sanremo Rally | Ford Focus WRC | 6th |
| Rally Australia | Ford Focus WRC | DNF |
| RAC Rally | Ford Focus WRC | DNF |
| **2001** | | |
| Monte Carlo Rally | Ford Focus WRC | DNF |
| Swedish Rally | Ford Focus WRC | 9th |
| Portugal Rally | Ford Focus WRC | DNF |
| Catalunya Rally | Ford Focus WRC | DNF |
| Argentina Rally | Ford Focus WRC | 1st |
| Cyprus Rally | Ford Focus WRC | 1st |
| Acropolis Rally | Ford Focus WRC | 1st |
| Safari Rally | Ford Focus WRC | DNF |
| Finland Rally | Ford Focus WRC | 3rd |
| Rally New Zealand | Ford Focus WRC | 2nd |
| Sanremo Rally | Ford Focus WRC | 8th |
| Tour de Corse | Ford Focus WRC | 11th |
| Rally Australia | Ford Focus WRC | 5th |
| Rally GB | Ford Focus WRC | DNF |
| **2002** | | |
| Monte Carlo Rally | Ford Focus WRC | 4th |
| Swedish Rally | Ford Focus WRC | 6th |
| Tour de Corse | Ford Focus WRC | DNF |
| Catalunya Rally | Ford Focus WRC | 6th |
| Cyprus Rally | Ford Focus WRC | 6th |
| Argentina Rally | Ford Focus WRC | 3rd |
| Acropolis Rally | Ford Focus WRC | 1st |
| Safari Rally | Ford Focus WRC | 1st |
| Finland Rally | Ford Focus WRC | DNF |
| Rally Deutschland | Ford Focus WRC | 4th |
| Sanremo Rally | Ford Focus WRC | 8th |
| Rally New Zealand | Ford Focus WRC | DNF |
| Rally Australia | Ford Focus WRC | DNF |
| Rally GB | Ford Focus WRC | 5th |
| **2003** | | |
| Monte Carlo Rally | Citroën Xsara WRC | 2nd |
| Swedish Rally | Citroën Xsara WRC | 5th |
| Rally Turkey | Citroën Xsara WRC | 4th |
| Rally New Zealand | Citroën Xsara WRC | DNF |
| Argentina Rally | Citroën Xsara WRC | DNF |
| Acropolis Rally | Citroën Xsara WRC | 8th |
| Cyprus Rally | Citroën Xsara WRC | 4th |
| Rally Deutschland | Citroën Xsara WRC | 4th |
| Finland Rally | Citroën Xsara WRC | DNF |
| Rally Australia | Citroën Xsara WRC | 4th |
| Sanremo Rally | Citroën Xsara WRC | 6th |
| Tour de Corse | Citroën Xsara WRC | 5th |
| Catalunya Rally | Citroën Xsara WRC | 9th |
| Rally GB | Citroën Xsara WRC | 4th |
| **2004** | | |
| Dakar | Nissan Pickup | 20th |
| Le Mans 24 Hours | Ferrari 550 | 9th |
| **2005** | | |
| Dakar | Nissan Pickup | DNF |
| Rally GB | Skoda Fabia WRC | 7th |
| Rally Australia | Skoda Fabia WRC | DNF |
| **2006** | | |
| Rally Turkey | Citroën Xsara WRC | DNF |
| **2007** | | |
| Rali Transiberico | Nissan Pickup | 30th |
| Baja Espana | BMW X3 | 3rd |

DNF - did not finish
WDN - withdrawn
EXC - excluded

# Power to the people carrier

Suzuki faces a tall order in 2008 - to turn the SX4 from small people carrier into serious WRC contender on a limited budget and in a multi-national team environment. By David Evans

THERE have always been a number of reasonably eccentric competition vehicles over the years, as part of the rich tapestry of motorsport. Volvo once entered the British Touring Car Championship using an 850 estate, while a few years ago Renault decided that it would be fun to drop a Formula 1 engine into an Espace. Now it's Suzuki's turn to go rallying in a people carrier.

Admittedly the SX4 is a very small people carrier (if this archaic term is still alive: modern marketing speak probably makes it a Crossover Transport Lifestyle Solution). But it's still squatter and higher than most vehicles, which hardly makes it an ideal choice as the basis of a World Rally Car - on paper at least.

Nonetheless, Suzuki has a colourful history of making rally cars out of shopping trolleys. In the late 1990s there was the Baleno estate Formula 2 car, and even the Junior World Rally Championship-winning Ignis was hardly a beauty. "If we don't win any rallies with it," commented one team member at the time, "at least we can use it to deliver pizzas."

As it turned out they did win rallies with it - several of them in fact. Not bad for a vehicle that appeared to have all the aerodynamic properties of a house brick. Underneath its fairly ugly skin, the Ignis had simple and consequently reliable engineering, which enabled P-G Andersson to claim the 2004 Junior title. The same basic philosophy was carried through to the Super 1600 Swift (which won the Junior championship this year) and now the SX4 World Rally Car.

True, the SX4 WRC didn't shatter any speed records on its two solitary outings this year, in Corsica and Great Britain. But neither did the Ignis when it first came out. Japanese businessmen are by nature cautious (until it's time for drinks after work). In this case, Suzuki's evolutionary and low-key approach could well pay dividends.

**Main:** The new Suzuki SX4 was welcomed onto the world stage in Corsica, where it survived the twists and turns of the asphalt classic
Race&motion

**Above right:** Suzuki Sport boss 'Monster' Tajima has a tough task in overseeing the SX4's continued development on a limited budget, but he's thinking podiums in 2008
McKlein

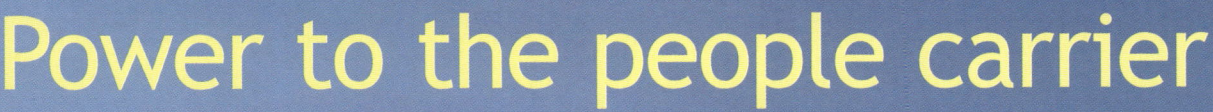

Suzuki said that it wasn't looking at the SX4 WRC's stage times this year, which is just as well as they were always outside the top 10. On asphalt in Corsica, they were not far off the top 10 though, whereas on the gravel of Great Britain it was markedly slower. In fairness, the SX4 was tuned for longevity rather than speed, and Sebastian Lindholm (in the car for GB) may well have struggled to set top-10 times in a factory Ford or Citroën. Nothing against Lindholm, who is a talented test driver, perfect gentleman and a deserving seven-time Finnish champion. There's no escaping the fact though that he is 46 years old and last competed on Rally GB in 1998.

Nicolas Bernardi, who drove in Corsica, was a better bet for a result - but even he had only driven there twice, in 2001 and '05, with just an eighth-place finish to his name. Suzuki's charismatic boss Nobuhiro 'Monster' Tajima has always been at pains to point out that the 2007 campaign was about gaining experience with test drivers, before it all gets more serious in '08.

Nonetheless, his prediction of podiums at the end of the coming year seems a touch optimistic to say the least - particularly given that Suzuki is operating on a budget that is much smaller than most. This has inevitably led to frustrations among the technical staff. Whereas at M-Sport, for example, a part can almost be thought of in the morning and on the car the same afternoon, there is a complicated chain of command at Suzuki, which means that everything decided in the Paris factory has to be approved by Japan. This can be a long and laborious process. As befits a man with such large hands, 'Monster' Tajima keeps an iron fist on both proceedings and the purse strings.

So far, he says that testing probably went slightly better than expected. "If we had done these tests and rallies and nothing had broken, then I would have been quite worried," commented Tajima. "However, we did not have too many problems either. So it is positive."

Evidence of this comes from the fact that the SX4 WRC finished both rallies it entered in 2007, albeit with a little help from the SupeRally system. More encouragingly, the things that did break were comparatively minor. The first thing to go wrong didn't even exist: Bernardi switched off the SX4 WRC during the afternoon of leg one in Corsica as he believed that the water temperature had risen too high. In actual fact, it was a relatively harmless differential temperature warning that had caused the alert. Then there was a broken fuel injector on day two, before Bernardi ended up 31st at the finish after losing time on the final day following a hydraulic gearshift problem. That evening there was champagne in the Suzuki service area: the atmosphere was upbeat.

In Wales, Lindholm effectively missed all of the first day after a stone cut a brake pipe on the opening stage. Following that setback, he got through the rest of the stages to finish 27th. These aren't show-stopping results, but fundamentally the car is reliable. With a clean run, and drivers a bit closer to the sharp end of the field, it would have been entirely possible to finish within the top 10 on both rallies: a creditable enough result for the first two events of any new car's career. Let alone a people carrier.

Technical director Michel Nandan has always maintained that one of the biggest problems with the SX4 as a World Rally Car was the fact that it is so tall, making the aerodynamics of it challenging. The rest of the car's dimensions, according to Lindholm, are spot on. "It actually reminds me a lot of the old Peugeot 206," says the Finn, referring to the car that both he and his cousin Marcus Grönholm have used to very good effect over the years. "Because the wheelbase is short it reacts to changes in direction quite quickly, and also the engine is powerful, which is another characteristic of the 206." The influence of Nandan (who designed both cars) is probably the biggest factor behind the similarity, but the Frenchman staunchly maintains that he had no intention just to pen a 206 WRC replica.

"You have to play to the strengths of the base product you've got, but you need to know how to look for those strengths," he says. Although the SX4's height was initially a problem, it at least meant that there was sufficient room to have good suspension travel: a major issue with many more compact cars (including the 206). The SX4 WRC has better potential than the Peugeot 307 WRC already, which was not one of Nandan's finest hours. Nonetheless, even the unloved 307 still won rallies and national championships. So it's all possible for the little SX4 WRC, which from some angles actually looks endearing. It's just a question of putting the correct resources behind it.

One of the key factors, of course, will be its drivers. Toni Gardemeister has been confirmed for the lead driver role and in terms of speed and personality there could be no better choice. If things go well on the engineering side, the 32-year-old will put the car into the points on more than one occasion. He's also just as good on asphalt as on gravel: an important consideration at this stage of the development as Suzuki desperately needs an all-rounder to give consistent feedback (as opposed to Lindholm and Bernardi, who are very much specialists in their fields).

The only concern might be Gardemeister's occasional tendency to settle into a rut if the car is not competitive, as he did sometimes during his three years with Skoda. Remarkably for a driver of his talents, Toni is cheap as well: a major consideration for a team that uses a large tent rather than a bespoke hospitality unit. The team's 'motorhome' is 10 years old, but this means nothing: the all-conquering Mitsubishi team relied on a couple of ageing vans and a tent throughout its heyday, and up until this year Ferrari lagged considerably behind in the motorhome arms race that characterises Formula 1. Tajima's philosophy is refreshingly pragmatic, with far greater attention paid to realities than appearances. Rather than shell out money for a test driver at the very start of the Suzuki programme, he preferred to conduct the initial testing himself. His approach is best described as 'hands on'.

Driver number two in 2008 is P-G Andersson, the only man to have won the Junior championship twice. The second Suzuki drive was a carrot that Tajima enjoyed dangling under the nose of several of his young drivers, but ultimately it would have been hard to justify not giving it to the most successful product of Suzuki's Junior programme.

### THERE ONCE WAS AN UGLY DUCKING...

At the start of 2002 the Junior World Rally Championship was just one year old, having been spectacularly claimed by the phenomenon that is Sébastien Loeb in its first season. Big things were expected of the series, and so an official championship launch was staged before the 2002 Monte Carlo Rally.

The concrete and glass Grimaldi Forum, Monaco's premier conference centre, played host to the presentation. The all-conquering Citroën Saxo lined up for the photoshoot along with some intriguing new arrivals such as the short-lived MG ZR S1600 (driven by Gwyndaf Evans). One newcomer, however, was late. When the Suzuki truck finally turned up, apologetically disgorging its contents of three angular Ignises, the onlookers struggled to contain their mirth. One seasoned journalist described Suzuki's squat yellow charger as the "ugliest rally car since the BX4TC".

With an underwhelming driver line-up of Kazuhiko Niwa, Juha Kangas and Nikolaus Schelle, the team's prospects were hardly stellar - and so it proved during the first rally. Just over two years later, P-G Andersson won the Junior championship in the new five-door Ignis: a car even uglier than its predecessor.

The moral of this particular story is that even though the SX4 WRC isn't going to win any rallies or beauty competitions at this stage in its career, it might just spring an almighty surprise if history decides to repeat itself.

Of course, the challenges at World Rally Car level are much greater than those faced by a Super 1600 team. But Suzuki's fundamental ability to turn round what appeared to be a hopeless - and for some people downright laughable - situation is what counts. Those who mocked at the bug-like yellow cars in the swanky surroundings of Monte Carlo nearly six years ago have had the smiles wiped off their faces since.

Right: The SX4 could end up having the shortest lifespan of any World Rally Car, should the regulations take on a Super 2000 twist in 2010

Far right: Tech boss Nandan, who also designed the Peugeot 206, says the SX4's height posed aerodynamic problems at first but has also allowed for good suspension travel

Below right: Lindholm gave the car its asphalt debut in Wales. He says the SX4 reminds him of the super-successful 206, with similarly responsive steering and good engine power

Below: Bernardi had the honour of giving the SX4 its rally debut in Corsica. He finished 31st after a few technical problems, but set times not far outside the top 10

All photographs by McKlein

## PLANNING FOR THE FUTURE

Whatever happens in the future, there is one record that the SX4 WRC seems virtually assured of. With the new World Rally Car format (whatever it may be) possibly being introduced as early as 2010, the SX4 WRC could be the world's shortest-lived World Rally Car.

To what extent it lives on after that time depends largely on the format the new rules take, but Suzuki has already begun work on a Super 2000 car based on the SX4. If - as FIA president Max Mosley has hinted - the new era of World Rally Car is based on S2000, possibly with a turbo as well, then Suzuki could end up with a head start.

Uncertainty over the future regulations (and hence the lifespan of the new SX4 WRC) nearly killed the project before it even saw the light of day. "I had to persuade the Suzuki board to continue, even though I could not tell them what the rules would be in the future," said Tajima. "I can see why it was difficult for them to understand. Nothing was guaranteed."

In order to cover all the bases, Suzuki is working on the development of a new SX4 S2000 challenger in parallel to that of the WRC car. Tajima is also quick to spot a business opportunity, with the potential of selling the car both to competitors doing the Intercontinental Rally Challenge and national championships. "We are spreading the word that Suzuki is not just all about bikes," he says. "Our cars are also sporty and fun."

The company's advertising slogan is "way of life". With Suzuki offering rally cars at more or less every level - thanks to the introduction of the Group N Swift as well - this could well become true.

## SUZUKI

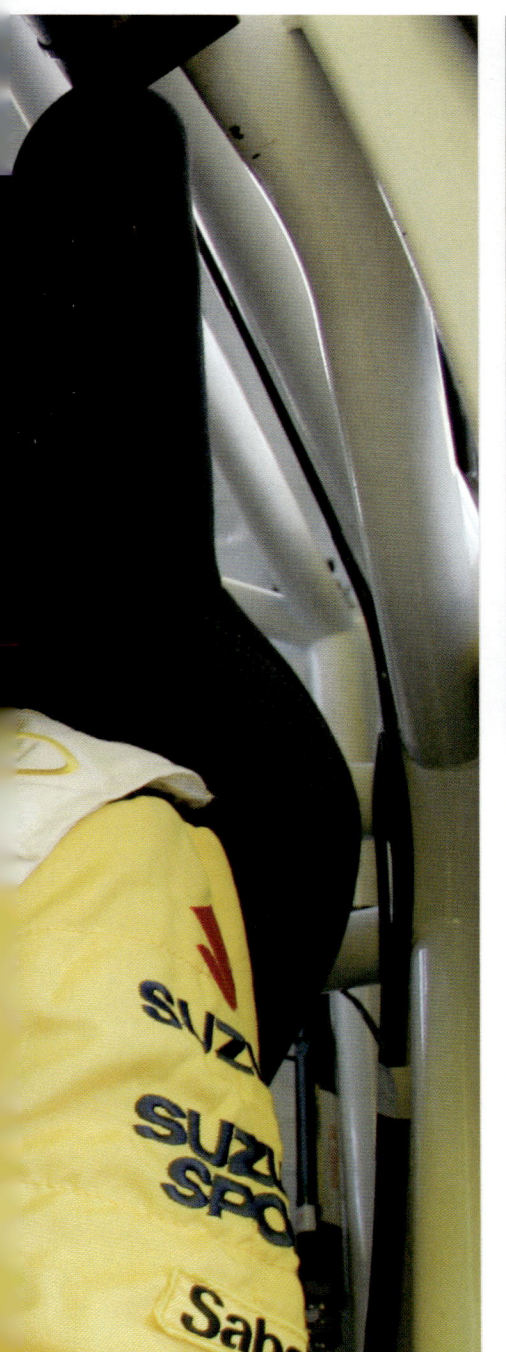

go through him (and the inevitable delays that this brings). Critics may call it a culture of fear, but this is standard Japanese business practice and also one that didn't do some of the world's greatest leaders - such as Napoleon - any harm when it came to empire-building.

Tajima also has to walk a delicate tightrope between his newly-formed Suzuki World Rally Team and the parent company, Suzuki Motor Corporation. Even Ford's rally team, which has swept up the manufacturers' championship for the past two seasons, has been constantly threatened with review and possible closure over the years. For anybody in Tajima's situation (Malcolm Wilson, Richard Taylor, Olivier Quesnel) it's a nightmare. At least Tajima has the advantage of coming from the same culture and knowing Suzuki Motor Corporation inside out, which will be an invaluable asset when it comes to maintaining good relations.

He's not yet sure where he will be based most of the time, but the likelihood is that Tajima will spend some time at the rally workshop in Paris but much of it in Japan as well. It would be hard for him to be based permanently in Europe because he has other business interests. As even David Richards found out though, it can be hard to focus on too many things at once. And Tajima hasn't even called time on his own competitive career yet on some of the world's legendary hillclimbs - such as Pikes Peak - in his Suzuki Vitara.

These cautionary tales are not intended to paint a pessimistic picture, but merely to underline the difficulties

The flip side is that Andersson has next to no four-wheel drive experience, barring a couple of outings in a Group N car. When he came into the Junior championship in 2004, he only had a couple of previous outings in a Super 1600 car to his name - and he still managed to blitz his opposition. The lean and hungry Andersson could be just what is needed to keep Gardemeister honest.

But the team's success (or not) in the future will mainly depend on how three very different cultures - Scandinavian, Japanese and French - work together. Satisfying team objectives while pleasing Japanese paymasters is a big ask, as many of the European team members in Subaru and Mitsubishi have attested over the years. Add to that a newly-appointed Scandinavian element (who all tend to stick together in their own little Mafia) and there's an interesting cocktail for potential trouble and private agendas. With the axis of power split between Paris and Japan, some of the free thinkers may see it as an opportunity to pursue their personal self-interests above those of the team.

He doesn't mention this explicitly, but Tajima is well aware of the danger: hence his rigid insistence that everything must

that any new team faces coming into the mind-numbingly competitive arena of the World Rally Championship - particularly with a limited budget and a Japanese management structure. The most important thing is to be aware of those problems and spend that budget wisely, exactly as Andrew Cowan did during Mitsubishi's winning era. It's not impossible, just very difficult. Suzuki's basic strengths are a decent enough car, some talented individuals and a corporate insistence on quality. Now these strengths have to be put to work - which is the hard bit.

Of course there are still a lot of people and facilities to be put in place and we haven't seen the full potential yet. Tajima is the undisputed team principal but he needs a day-to-day lieutenant to manage the team as well. Getting the right person in as team manager - and also beefing up the engineering department to take some pressure off Nandan - will be key to success next year.

Not much gets past Tajima. As he once jokingly pointed out, gesturing at his head, "I have 64K of memory. Standard equipment on Tajima." He's going to need all of it in the seasons to come.

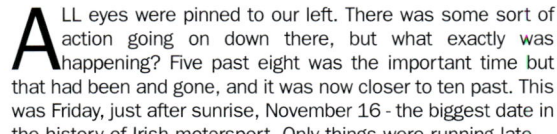

**Above:** The Princess Royal took up the task of waving off the crews at the Stormont Parliament buildings, which hosted the opening superspecial stage

**Top:** Rallying has huge popularity in Ireland - fans lined the stages to get a glimpse of their heroes in action

**Right top:** Ireland has dreamed of hosting a WRC round and its debut on the world stage was considered a success by all

**Right bottom:** Norway ran as another new event this year after the Swedish Rally, allowing the teams to tackle two snow events in a row

All photographs by McKlein unless specified

ALL eyes were pinned to our left. There was some sort of action going on down there, but what exactly was happening? Five past eight was the important time but that had been and gone, and it was now closer to ten past. This was Friday, just after sunrise, November 16 - the biggest date in the history of Irish motorsport. Only things were running late.

Then the lights flicked on and the noise started. A mile away from the field where we had gathered, Marcus Grönholm was on stage, Irish style.

The anticipation was incredible. People flattened themselves against the stone walls that lined the route in order to get an inch or two closer to the great man. When Sébastien Loeb's C4 arrived two minutes later, jaws dropped. The faces were a picture. It was *that* man, in *their* backyard. There would probably have been less excitement if Han Solo had landed the Millennium Falcon in the field next door and Chewbacca had asked if anybody wanted to join the Rebel Alliance.

In case you're wondering, the reason for the delayed start was a timing glitch at the beginning of the stage. Apparently the marshals didn't know how to work the clocks. At the time, knowing looks passed from hack to hack. We'd all covered rallies in Ireland in years gone by, and we'd all had the odd 'where's the time control gone?' moment. The big question was, was this the thin end of the wedge?

No. The handful of seconds lost at the start of the Geevagh test didn't even register.

Rally Ireland was an exceptional event; it was as if it had been in the World Rally Championship calendar for years.

Nobody was taking anything for granted, though. Anybody who has spectated in Ireland has marvelled at the thousands of fans clinging to the rocks at Moll's Gap, or just how many people can be crammed into a farm entrance in Wexford or the Macroom service area in Cork. So when the news came that the best rally drivers on the planet were coming to the north-west of Ireland, the rest of the nation began to make plans to decamp around Sligo and Enniskillen. There was concern for the organisers with regards to hosting a round of the WRC from a technical perspective. If the know-how doesn't exist locally, it can easily be imported in the shape of a Fred Gallagher or Simo Lampinen-type figure to act as clerk of the course and a similarly experienced team to install the necessary infrastructure. What nobody can control is the number of people across the country that might wake up in the morning and say, 'Hmm, let's go to Rally Ireland'.

The event's popularity was potentially going to be its undoing. This was what the likes of event promoter Ronan Morgan were genuinely concerned about. Failing to control spectators, as we have seen in Monte Carlo, Sanremo and in years gone by Catalunya, can do a great deal of harm. With everything else in place, the last thing Morgan and his men wanted was the nation's fever to get in the way.

What seemed to make matters worse ahead of the event was that there would be no charge for getting into the stages. You could just park up at the side of the main road and then hike - admittedly, usually a fair distance - into a field at the side of the stage. As Rally GB can testify, increasing the entry fee is a great way of limiting the numbers: it's simple supply and demand. Ireland wasn't up for that, though. This was the nation's moment and the organisers wanted the nation to share it.

Route co-ordinator Gordon Noble had spent months planning for just this scenario and much of the route was actually constructed around which access roads and fields would be available as viewing points on which day. One prime example is the Ballinamallard stage that ran on day two.

"Obviously we wanted to include the stage," said Noble, "but it was quite out of character with the rest of the day's stages. The intention was to run that stage with its plentiful supply of great places to watch, with really easy access, to soak up as many of the spectators as possible. It worked all around. We kept the people in the areas we wanted them in, they had a great day and we didn't have any problems with excessive numbers."

In the end, as the spectator figures rose up and past the 150,000 mark, Noble didn't have the slightest concern. Everything was in place - nothing was going to spoil this party.

As a sporting exercise, Rally Ireland ticked all the boxes. Colin McRae had talked for years about his hopes of seeing a WRC round in Ireland - and the Isle of Man, come to think of it - but, while the rest of us thought this something of a pipedream,

# Ireland paradise

The coming together of Ireland and the World Rally Championship surpassed all expectations. Well, once it got going anyway.

By David Evans

Morgan was quietly confident.

"Max [Mosley, FIA president] made me a promise," said Morgan. "He said that when the time was right and it was applicable, we would bring the WRC to Ireland. That's just what's happened now. And while I might be a bit biased, these are among the best roads in the world."

And who were we to argue? There was near-universal agreement from the drivers. Marcus Grönholm probably thinks otherwise, but that was the nature of this rally. It was always going to catch out the unwary or those who didn't treat it with the utmost respect. Grönholm pushed too hard in Lough Gill and paid the price.

Beyond the sport, it was impossible to ignore the political importance of this event. Having grown up with the troubles of the 1970s, the mention of Belfast and Stormont conjured up a mental image that had little to do with rally cars. Laughable didn't come into the prospect of Ian Paisley and Martin McGuinness being in the same room - let alone talking about rally cars - before the Northern Irish Assembly was reformed. Yet, on the eve of the rally, there were two of the biggest men in Irish politics, putting their polar extreme views to one side for the common good of the Irish and world rallying. This was a whole new kind of fever. And then, to top it all, the Princess Royal turned up and waved the crews away.

Ari Vatanen is a man who knows a bit about rallying and politics as a former world champion turned Member of the European Parliament. He put the thing in context, saying: "When I came here in the British championship on the Ulster Rally, we would see a normal city in Belfast with normal people. Then an army patrol would come around the corner with the last man walking backwards and training his rifle on where the snipers might be. It took your breath away, but it was normal life. Now look at it - it's a wonderful place. This is an incredible event. You know, what we have in these rally cars are the fastest doves of peace in the world! This shows that, no matter how difficult things can be in politics, sport can find a way forward. And in this case it's found a way forward flat-out!"

Rally Ireland was a success in all corners. Finally, the WRC had arrived in the lanes that had been cut through this land with just one purpose in mind…

## A BREATH OF FRESH AIR FOR THE WRC

In terms of competing FIA Candidate rallies, Ireland had a great deal to live up to after the success of the two events that had gone before it.

Rally Norway was the first to run this season, coming a week after Sweden. Prior to the start, there had been the odd concern about a lack of snow in the Hamar region, but nobody need have worried. It snowed and snowed hard, ensuring Norway was the perfect host for a winter round of the championship. The only thing that let down the nation was the absence of the name Solberg at the top of the timesheets. Otherwise, from an organisational and sporting perspective, this rally was fantastic.

Organisationally, Portugal was hit hard on the eve of the start, when Armindo Araújo's Mitsubishi Lancer WR 05 went off and injured five spectators at shakedown. The organisers were fined £25,000 by the FIA for not taping off the spectator areas correctly. An accident involving rally fans is the last thing anybody wants, but for a nation whose sport was blighted by Joachim Santos's 1986 crash - in which six people died - this was the worst start possible.

By the ceremonial start and superspecial in Faro Stadium later that day, the news had come through that the fans were all fine. Now the show could get on the road. And what an amazing show it was - watching so many Group B cars in so little time was pure heaven. When three days of fierce competition followed without incident - save for Ford's rear windows being too light and some incredibly wet weather - then Portugal looked to have safeguarded its return to the championship.

The other two official Candidate Rallies were set for 2008, but only Jordan is going ahead, after South Africa ran out of cash and had to withdraw its entry. Given the new structure of the WRC calendar - 24 rallies in two years - it's a good thing there are so many spaces to fill. These new rallies are coming in and raising the bar for the existing events. It's amazing to see the enthusiasm and desire of those new rallies - the very antithesis of the apathy and indolence that has overtaken some of the traditional events.

# The lone warrior

A complicated character by nature, François Duval has found himself fighting his own corner in the WRC, but that's the way he prefers it. By Anthony Peacock

FRANÇOIS Duval is not so much at a career crossroads as at a career Spaghetti Junction. For those unfamiliar with it, the Gravelly Hill interchange in Birmingham (nicknamed 'Spaghetti Junction' by a sub-editor of the Birmingham Evening Mail) can potentially take you to 18 different places, none of which you would ever want to be in. Get it right and your prize is a passport out of Birmingham.

François Duval is trying to escape from his metaphorical Birmingham, having recently taken a couple of wrong turns into a few insalubrious suburbs of the action.

The young Belgian has a colourful and well-documented past: he shot to fame under the tutelage of Ford through the British Rally Championship and Junior World Rally Championship in 2001 and '02, before being unexpectedly promoted to a full factory drive alongside Markko Märtin in a revamped Ford team that put the emphasis on youth. It was a massive gamble on the part of team principal Malcolm Wilson, and despite (or maybe because of) the fact that his two young drivers got on about as well as Fernando Alonso and Lewis Hamilton it sort of worked. Duval achieved his first podium in only his fourth drive in a World Rally Car and demonstrated the sort of speed that marked him out as a future champion.

But nobody has ever argued about his talent. Malcolm Wilson maintains to this day that Duval was one of the most naturally gifted drivers ever to sit in a Focus WRC, and in 2004 the Belgian - who was still only 23 at the start of the year, with fewer than 35 world rallies under his belt - went on to score five podiums. Wilson did not hesitate to offer him a four-year contract.

Which was where the trouble started. In the middle of 2004 the mighty Carlos Sainz announced his retirement, which would leave a seat free at Citroën. To cut a long story short, Duval took it. To all the world it seemed that the Belgian had turned his back on four years at Ford in favour of just one year at Citroën, as in November 2004 the PSA Group announced that Peugeot and Citroën would be pulling out of world rallying. Only one other factor, leaving aside the opportunity to beat Sébastien Loeb in the same car, could have motivated him: money.

Speaking frankly about the whole episode for the first time, nearly three years later, Duval maintains that this was all revisionist history.

"At the time I signed the contract with Citroën, it was for a two-year deal," he says unblinkingly. "The decision for Citroën and Peugeot to pull out was made after I had signed. So it's not true to say that I signed just for one year." His piercing, blue-eyed gaze remains steady. "At the time, there was not a lot I could say. But if I had known then that it would be for one year only…"

He doesn't need to complete the sentence. Suddenly his quixotic behaviour at the time begins to make some sort of sense: he must have been even more stunned than the rest of us when he found out that Citroën was quitting, and he could hardly turn round to Malcolm Wilson and say that he had changed his mind now that his signature was safely on a contract at Velizy.

At least there was the money though: reputed to be double the sum that Ford was offering. Duval allows himself the ghost of a smile. "Well, actually, that didn't really make any difference," he says.

Taken at face value, this could mean that it was not money that motivated him to drive for Citroën - merely the prospect of beating Loeb. Or could he be referring to his suspension from the team for two events in 2005? Rumour has it that one of the conditions of his return was a greatly reduced financial settlement for the rest of the season.

He's not saying, but his friends maintain that Duval really did believe he could beat Loeb and that it was just the car making the difference. He was probably remembering the 2001 Junior World Championship, where Loeb's Saxo walked all over his Puma. Duval's very first rally in the Xsara, where he kept pace with his new team-mate before smacking a telegraph pole, probably reinforced that impression. As for Loeb, he still says that Duval was one of the people who pushed him hardest on asphalt - particularly in Germany.

It's a strange situation for the Belgian. Everybody is willing to be very complimentary about him (apart from Citroën boss Guy Fréquelin, who admitted that signing Duval was "a mistake") but no teams are exactly tripping over themselves to have him back.

Of course there are some vague possibilities at Ford, which may or may not be over by the time this goes to press. Duval says that despite everything, he's maintained good relations with Malcolm Wilson. "We've spoken and I do not think there are any hard feelings," he says. "Of course I'd like to drive for Ford next year if there is a chance and that's one of the things we are working on."

At the time though, there were indeed some hard feelings: Duval didn't see out the 2004 season with Ford as Malcolm Wilson replaced him with Mark Higgins for Rally GB. Nonetheless, even in the heat of the moment, Wilson maintained a grudging respect.

"He's a brave boy, I'll give him that," said Wilson at the end of 2004. "If he thinks he can go and beat Sébastien [Loeb], good luck to him…"

The problem is more his personality, which can be most accurately described as enigmatic, although one person at Ford has called it "a nightmare" and another person at Citroën has called it "stupid". Duval is admittedly not the easiest person to get on with, which explains why he is currently on his fourth co-driver. But he is entirely lacking in hypocrisy - a refreshingly rare character trait at this level - and you are never going to please everyone. François doesn't even try: what you see is what you get.

It's important to see everybody in his or her correct context. Duval was born in the heart of rural Belgium near the town of Chimay (which is best known for its community of trappist monks that brew indecently strong beer). As a child he lived a semi-monastic lifestyle in which his father was the dominant figure; he still describes his father as his best friend now.

François left school as early as he could to work in his father's garage: one of the biggest Toyota specialists in the region. The garage fascinated him so much that he was not particularly interested in going out much as a teenager - he preferred fiddling with the cars and driving them. He's still in the garage every day now. "That's my job," he puts it simply. "When I'm not at a rally, that's where you'll find me." The garage buys and sells used Toyotas, scouring the classified ads for good prospects. Duval will often go to view a car and pick it up, even if it is a smelly old Carina with a past life as a minicab.

"I like working there: it's good fun," he says. Those who label him arrogant have got it totally wrong: he is entirely devoid of pretension. But he does sometimes have problems conducting human relationships: his first co-driver, Jean-Marc Fortin, was fired by text message. Having been thrust into an unexpectedly public and political environment at such a young age, is that entirely surprising?

In any case, a few hard knocks have smoothed the rough edges off Duval. As well as the Citroën saga there was the debacle with Skoda last year, which netted only one half-decent result: sixth in Catalunya. He drove it again - briefly - on the Acropolis Rally this year, before wisely deciding to call it a day. The Skoda campaign got off to a bad start when energy drink firm Kizz Me (which also briefly appeared on last year's Kronos-run Citroën Xsaras) promised a pile of money, but did not deliver. After that, Duval had to rely on a meagre budget from Skoda Belgium.

"That wasn't really the way to go rallying: I felt let down by that experience," says François. Of course it was still fun because it was driving a car but we didn't really stand a chance. That's life."

To keep his hand in, Duval raced a Porsche in Belgium as well as doing a few Belgian championship events. This was what he was reduced to, after five years as a factory driver, but not once did he let his head drop. He still believed in himself and still enjoyed what he was doing. The sixteenth century English poet John Donne famously wrote that "no man is an island" - but he had never met François Duval.

Then a number of circumstances reported elsewhere came together. Kronos Citroën needed another driver following the enforced departure of Daniel Carlsson due to budgetary problems. The Citroën factory team needed a 'spoiler' to stop Marcus Grönholm scoring too many points at the top of the WRC. It turned out that the Belgian motorsport federation (RACB) had a bit of cash going begging too. It was the opportunity that Duval had been waiting for and he ended up with two drives in a properly prepared Xsara WRC, for Germany and Catalunya.

At the end of leg one in Germany he was leading Sébastien Loeb, which was probably of greater satisfaction than his eventual second place overall. In Spain he finished fifth. The point had been proven - but François is not desperate to hammer it home. His complacency may at times be infuriatingly hard for people to understand but that's fundamentally because he is happy with what he's got. He is an island.

"Of course I want a factory drive next year and I'm working hard to get it, but it's not going to destroy my life if I don't," he says. "I know that I'm good enough at the top level; I'll still drive cars and I'll still like it. What sort of cars and where is the thing I don't know yet."

One of the possibilities for next year is Suzuki, and he has been linked to a Peugeot drive with Kronos on the Intercontinental Rally Challenge as well. Duval hasn't given up on the WRC yet - even if it sometimes seems that it has given up on him.

Opposite: Duval drove a Kronos-run Xsara in Germany and led Loeb at the end of leg one. He finished second, helping Citroën to limit the success of Grönholm and Ford

Opposite inset: Nicky Grist presents Duval with the Star Driver Award at Monte Carlo 2004. He finished on the podium five times with the team that year

Above: The Belgian was hailed by Ford boss Malcolm Wilson as being one of the most naturally gifted drivers he'd seen before his WRC debut

Middle: Duval flew for Ford in Australia '04, but he didn't see out the year with the team after agreeing a deal with Citroën and was replaced by Mark Higgins for Rally GB

Top: The move to Citroën in 2005 turned out to be a disappointment. The team pulled out of the WRC at the end of the year and François was dropped for a time mid-season

All photographs by McKlein

Main: The '07 Focus was launched in Finland and scored a one-two on its debut. Ford went on to secure its second manufacturers' title in a row

Right: Ford technical director Christian Loriaux believes his car is the quickest on the stages and the most reliable

All photographs by McKlein

### THE ENVIRONMENTAL IMPACT

Rallying, like all forms of motorsport, is responding to environmental concerns. A number of rally cars are already competing at different levels that are more energy efficient, and subsequently more green than the norm.

In Sweden and Catalunya this year, for example, several bio-ethanol cars took part and the Fiesta Sporting Trophy will include bio-fuelled cars only from 2008. In addition Stohl Racing, the team owned by WRC driver Manfred Stohl, is competing in and actually winning rounds of the Austrian Rally Championship with a Mitsubishi Lancer that is converted to run on bio-gas.

Energy Efficient Motorsport (EEMS) is supporting Oaktek, which is running a Honda Insight hybrid in the Formula 1000 rally series in the UK. "Those kinds of cars are really the first generation of energy efficient rally cars that we are seeing," says Marc de Jong, who works as a consultant for EEMS in the UK.

"It is the responsibility of everybody to ensure the sport acts - it is with the legislator, the organiser and the participant. I think it is a big social issue that all of us have to find a solution for. Frankly speaking, if we don't find a solution people are going to see motorsport as part of the problem."

Suzuki's technical manager Michel Nandan agrees that action must be taken: "If things can be done in motorsport and especially in rallying we have to do it. The FIA understands this and bio-fuels will be introduced quite soon."

TECHNICAL REVIEW

# Small advances in technology

How do you gain an advantage against your WRC rivals when the rules are restricted and costs are cut? Ford has led the way, with Citroën snapping at its heels. By Rob Wilkins

"NOWADAYS, none of them are good years technology-wise. There is an economy of crisis," says BP Ford World Rally Team technical director Christian Loriaux. "It is hard for all the manufacturers - and the motorsport budgets are smaller. In view of that, the organising body the FIA is trying to reduce costs. We are limiting the technology more and more every day, and it is quite restricted because of cost implications."

That is the climate in which all the manufacturers currently compete in the WRC. Reliability is crucial, as always, but with the regulations now demanding parts that last longer and longer, this is the latest challenge. The trend started in 2006 when engines were paired and other limitations were brought in restricting the number of times you could change the suspension, the gearboxes and so on. In '07 engines had to do three rally distances - not one or two, not 350 kilometres (the average distance for an event) but 1050 kilometres.

The top two teams, the BP Ford World Rally Team and the Citroën Total World Rally Team, have made it look easy - or relatively so. The Focus WRC has been pretty much bullet-proof and the C4 WRC hasn't been too far off either.

Ford began the 2007 season with the Focus RS WRC 06 and it wasn't until halfway through the year that the new car was introduced. The Focus RS WRC 07 was very much an evolution. "There weren't tons of changes, because the '06 car was already so evolved and competitive. It was difficult to make it much better," explains Loriaux, the man who heads up the M-Sport team of 20-25 designers and engineers responsible for the design, development and running of the car. "But we refined a fair bit in terms of aerodynamics with a new rear wing. We had a new front bumper too because with the original one we had very little time for testing and it was too low. The front of the front bumper dragged on the ground all the time.

"There was also constant development on the engine and a lot of weight-saving on that and on all the other components on the car. There was probably a weight-saving of 20 kilos and more on the car, which helped us to lower the centre of gravity and improve the weight distribution."

All those refinements, while minor in isolation, made a real cumulative difference to the whole package. "There is a lot of fine-tuning now because to find 25 kilos in a car, which is already optimised, you need to find something like 250 parts where you can save 100 grams. It's not a matter of changing one part and saving 20 or 25 kilos," says Loriaux. "It's a pretty laborious job and sometimes you think, 'Are we pushing it a bit too far?' But it's needed if you want to succeed and keep on winning."

And win the car did. First time out in Finland Marcus Grönholm and Mikko Hirvonen finished one-two to give the '07 Focus the perfect debut. Indeed Marcus and Mikko blitzed the opposition on their home round, winning 20 of the 23 stages in total and finishing comfortably ahead of Citroën's Sébastien Loeb.

"Usually we do back-to-backs tests when we do a new car, but this time, because the changes were not so massive, we didn't do that," says Loriaux. "We knew the car's behaviour was better because we could see the handling was superior in certain places. But we couldn't really tell how much better and faster it would be, and we were a bit surprised by how much we were in front of the opposition when we started competing with it in Finland. But that was good to see and we weren't about to complain!

"I'd like to think it's the fastest car out there and I think we have pretty much proven that," he adds. "The car has proven it is fast on everything because we have won on snow, on rough gravel and nearly on asphalt too. So far it has been the most reliable car as well. It seems the team has done a good job and hopefully we will get the rewards."

Loriaux believes the car doesn't have any particular

shortcomings: "Okay, to start with the Focus is quite a big car compared to the C4. As such we have more drag and a higher centre of gravity because the car is higher. On paper, then, we have got a small disadvantage, but we seem to be able to cope with it."

Ford's hard work with the new car paid off when the M-Sport team wrapped up its second consecutive manufacturers' championship on the penultimate round in Ireland.

Citroën has been on the back foot a bit this year, but that is not to say the C4 WRC, which was brought in to replace the Xsara, has not been good. Indeed like the Focus RS WRC 07 it shone immediately and Loeb and Dani Sordo finished one-two on the season-opening Rallye Monte Carlo.

The C4 had a long gestation period and was originally intended to make its WRC debut in 2006. When Citroën opted for a 'semi-sabbatical' year, however, that was pushed back to '07. Despite being in development so long the car's birth wasn't problem-free and rule changes forced it to be altered from a fully-active machine, which it was originally intended to be, into a car with mechanical front and rear differentials.

Citroën technical director Xavier Mestelan-Pinon says this change wasn't too difficult to make, especially as the team had already done it with the C4's predecessor. "It was exactly the same job that we did on the Xsara and because we used the same gearbox and rear axle [with the C4] it was very easy for us to switch between both technologies," he explains. "When we changed the differentials the only problem was to find the right set-up."

As for what the C4's main strengths are, Mestelan-Pinon is guarded: "Ask the drivers," he says. "It is very difficult to answer that question. You need a lot of things to make a good car - good engine, good balance, good gearbox, good shock absorbers, good traction, good reliability and so on."

Pressed on how it compares to its rivals, he is similarly elusive: "The best thing is to look at the results. This year all the manufacturers are very close. We have maybe made more mistakes this year than the other manufacturers. We have had too many problems, but we are working on it for the future."

Early on Loeb struggled with the C4 and didn't feel 100 per cent comfortable in the car. Sordo echoed his concerns, but both have since found the C4's sweet spot, thanks to some minor changes and a lot of testing. "Sébastien drove many, many kilometres and after it was easier for him," says

## TECHNICAL REVIEW

Right: Loeb was tasked with guiding the new C4 during its maiden season but had been more comfortable in the Xsara

Opposite top: Nicolas Bernardi gave the all-new Suzuki SX4 its WRC debut in Corsica. He obeyed orders to reach the finish despite retiring from the first two legs

Opposite bottom: Brice Tirabassi drove a Peugeot 207 Super 2000 car in Corsica and served notice of the car's pace by beating several World Rally Cars. S2000 rules are likely to be adopted in the future by the WRC

Below: The C4 did have some teething problems and Sordo failed to finish on two successive rallies due to engine-related problems

All photographs by McKlein

Mestelan-Pinon. "Of course we changed a little bit the position of Sébastien in the car and now his seat is higher. I think the most important thing, however, is that Sébastien did many tests before Monte Carlo so that he could learn the new car and the revisions."

All in all the C4 has delivered: "The car is fast but the reliability is maybe not enough at the moment. But we have good performance if we compare it to the other manufacturers."

While Ford and Citroën have taken the laurels this season the other manufacturer team, the Prodrive-run Subaru World Rally Team, has continued to struggle. The Banbury-based outfit hasn't won a rally now since 2005 and when the '07-spec Impreza, which featured a number of 'small evolutions', was wheeled out for Rally Mexico, round four in the championship, it made little difference.

Even before the year began David Lapworth, who returned to the SWRT fold in May as a consultant, admitted things were not looking especially promising. "We have known for a while that this was going to be a tough period, because of the life cycle of the car," he said at the end of '06. "Ford has got a new car and so has Citroën. Subaru's turn is really 2008. There is a nice step, an interim car for '07, which will help. I don't think it will be a great year, but 2008 should be."

Petter Solberg's co-driver Phil Mills agrees that the team has a lot to do to catch up: "It seems that Ford and Citroen have got the upper hand on us. Their cars are a totally different concept to our car, which is quite an old concept now and is starting to show its age a little bit in comparison."

It's not all doom and gloom though and Mills is positive about the future, even if it doesn't look like the Impreza WRC2008 will be ready for the 76th Rallye Monte Carlo - the event that traditionally heralds the start of the season. "It will turn around. We have got a new car - that is a new concept car, like the other two cars I just mentioned," he says. "All sorts of modifications are coming along and we're looking forward to the future very much."

Another team looking to the future is Suzuki. The Japanese manufacturer will graduate from the Junior championship in 2008 with the all-new SX4 WRC. Suzuki will be out to build on its successes with the Ignis S1600 and the Swift S1600, which included two Junior driver titles in 2004 and '07, but it will now face a far tougher challenge at the senior level.

Much of 2007 has been devoted to testing with the SX4 and the car finally made its debut on the Tour de Corse - albeit somewhat later than first planned, after an outing in Finland was abandoned.

Michel Nandan, formerly with Peugeot and Toyota, is the man at the helm as technical manager. He doesn't underestimate the challenge, but he is confident Suzuki will get there. "Performance-wise the car is still behind. There is still a lot of work to do, but this is quite normal for a new car and a new team" he says. "But from the base of the car and knowing what can be done in the future, it is a good start. We have to work quite hard though in order to 'grow up' and be competitive like our main rivals. This will not happen in a few rallies, but the plan is within one or two years to reach this level.

"The car has some advantages because of its size," adds Nandan. "It is quite a small car with good dimensions, and even if some dimensions like the height aren't so good for a competition car, it doesn't have a big effect in rallying. In general the base is good and the car is a good compromise to be a WRC machine. The disadvantages are, as I mentioned, that the car is quite high. But this is in general a tendency for all the cars now, the new evolutions. This is a bit of a disadvantage in terms of aerodynamics, but on rallies this is less important than in circuit racing."

Nandan faces a different challenge to when he was with Peugeot and working on the 307 WRC. "With Suzuki the team will be a bit smaller and the investment, so far, is just at the beginning," he explains. "The team and the SX4 WRC need to improve. But it is still a good challenge because we have to build the team. We are starting from zero, everything has to be done. Suzuki is a very, very new competitor in this business."

The size of the team isn't the only difference, as the regulations have of course also moved on. "There are quite a lot of things now that are not allowed anymore," says Nandan. "The cars are much more basic. While it is true you can still invest a lot of money there has been a big reduction, especially in parts that can be used. Compared to a few years ago there are a lot of limitations on these parts - like the engine.

"We are limited in the number of body shells we can use during the year and also in the parts we can change during an event - like the turbo charger, the gearbox and the suspension. It is going in the direction of reliability. These limitations are reducing a lot of the costs, which is good for motorsport. Cost is the biggest problem for the manufacturer."

Nandan says that an advantage with the SX4 WRC is that it can be adapted to Super 2000 regulations relatively easily. "When the car was designed we were thinking about this possibility," he says. "It's true that it can be made into a S2000 car quite quickly. It's not a very big job - at least in terms of design. Of course in terms of parts it will be different. For example, the body shell is quite specific for a WRC car. But the main layout can be the same and quite a lot of parts can actually be used for S2000."

Such flexibility may prove handy in the years to come, as S2000 cars may form the basis for the top level in the WRC. The World Motor Sport Council confirmed as much in June, when it announced: "From 2012 it was agreed in principle that World Rally Cars will be four-wheel drive and turbo-charged, based on mass-produced Group N and S2000-specification cars."

BP Ford WRT team boss Malcolm Wilson thinks this won't make too much of a difference. "In real terms the regulations are not going to change much from where we are now," he said in the summer. "It is still going to be four-wheel drive and turbo-charged engines. So it's going to be a similar situation to where we are now and I don't think it's the change people were envisaging."

### SUPER 2000: A TURN-OFF?

The FIA has yet to decide on the future direction for the World Rally Championship, and while it may be based around Super 2000, the details are currently sketchy.

But BP Ford technical director Christian Loriaux has real concerns about the proposals and isn't convinced that S2000 is the way to go.

"I think S2000 cars will be pretty slow and boring to watch," he says. "In a way I can see that they could reduce the costs a bit. But the cost of the car is not a big factor in the overall cost of the championship. I'm worried that they will be less spectacular and will put people off following rallying rather than attracting them.

"There is a need for a change, but I'm not convinced that S2000 is the way to go. We should keep the car with the minimum of power and do a re-set with new regulations to make the cars cheaper, but still we need to make sure we keep them spectacular."

His counterpart at Citroën Xavier Mestelan-Pinon is also unconvinced by S2000. "It should be an interesting car for the customers, he says. "Currently it is a cheaper car, but if all the teams work on this car for the WRC, then the price will increase. I don't know if it is the right route for the future. The technical rules seem good, but is it a good thing to have the same car for the customers and the official team? I don't know."

Suzuki's Michel Nandan believes that S2000 is a good base for a competition car. "It would probably be more accessible for different manufacturers, but it is a completely different car in terms of performance," he says. "Maybe the top category should be a compromise between the WRC and the S2000. I think the FIA will decide quite soon what will be the future but for now, or at least for the next three years, the regulations are for WRCs."

# OBITUARY

Former co-driver and close friend Mike Broad recalls his memories of Tony Fall, who died on December 1, this year.

## TONY FALL 1940-2007

I first met Tony Fall somewhere in South America in 1970. I was 21 and a junior official on the World Cup Rally. I didn't have anything to do when I got to the finish in Mexico, so Tony found me a job and took me under his wing. We'd been friends ever since. Friends and fellow competitors, that is. I competed with him on numerous occasions and whenever we did, there was always a story to tell. Actually, there was always a story to tell whether we were competing or not. He was a real character.

I guess we really began to work closely when he started the Dealer Opel Team. I bumped into him, quite by chance, at Silverstone. He told me what he was doing and told me his former co-driver Mike Wood had retired. Did I fancy coming to work with him in the car? I certainly did.

Our first event was the Welsh in 1974 and we finished fourth overall in the Kadett. At the time, Tony was trying to retire from driving, but he didn't seem able to actually stop - there was always another car that needed testing. It was a good thing he didn't retire before the Scottish of that year. We were running the same Kadett, but this time we had quite a few problems. Curiously, those problems all seemed to come on the road sections, which dropped us miles back down the order.

"Don't look at the times," I remember Tony saying, his tone underlining the fact that he didn't expect much from this event. That said, you can imagine our - and everybody's - surprise to find that we were leading at the first halt at Ayr, even though we were less than a minute away from going OTL. We were leading Vatanen, Clark, all the boys. Tony got really excited and drove us into a mountain the next day.

As well as that, he put me in charge of promoting the DOT programme through forum evenings and things like that. Around RAC time, as you can imagine, this was really busy - but it was so much fun.

One of Tony's best attributes was his light-hearted approach to taking things seriously. This was tested to the extreme on the 1982 RAC Rally. Everybody remembers this one, but to be on the inside when it was going on (I was co-driving Russell Brookes in a Chevette) was incredible. Walter Röhrl was one of Tony's drivers in 1982. By the time the RAC came around, Walter was world champion. He didn't need to start the event and made it quite clear he didn't want to. He was leaving DOT for Lancia the following year, so he didn't see the point. Tony was having none of it. After Walter had missed some pre-event functions, Tony told him to make sure he was at the next one - or he wouldn't be taking the start.

At the time, I don't think Walter or anybody thought Tony would go through with it. But Tony could be a blunt Yorkshireman and a damned strong character when he wanted. When Walter didn't turn up, Tony told him to go home and the car was pulled. Well, we couldn't believe it. An hour or so after it had happened and Walter was on the train back to London. You'd never have thought anything like that had even gone on - Tony was back to his best, on top form again.

Walter's 1982 world title at the wheel of the Ascona 400 was significant in that it was the last time a two-wheel-drive car won the championship. After that, the Audis and the four-wheel-drive revolution took over. Unfortunately Opel's answer - like that of Lancia - was lightweight, powerful, but rear-wheel drive. The Manta 400 was a wonderful machine, but no match for the Quattros. Tony was well aware of this situation but his actions, I believe, demonstrated his business acumen and forward-thinking approach. Conscious of the fact that the Audis were taking over the world, Tony saw a big gap in domestic markets, so he made sure the preferred markets like Britain, Sweden, Holland, Belgium, Spain and Italy had plenty of 400s so they could keep on winning the national championships.

While keeping the Opel flag flying with Henri Toivonen in a Manta, Tony was working hard behind the scenes to get the Astra 4S project up and running. He managed it and was only beaten by the rule change that came at the end of 1986.

When Tony returned to Britain in the early 1990s, he took charge of the Safety Devices rollcage firm. This was right up his street. He turned the company around and made a big success out of it. It took him back to his cars and his people. He loved the fact that if you wanted a cage for a 260Z, you had to come to him - he was the one with the jigs. It was great to see him really enjoying himself again.

All photographs by McKlein

There was a great moment at Stoneleigh Park earlier this year. Tony was sitting at a table and signing autographs. There wasn't much time for him to pause and look up between signatures. Little did he know, Yvonne Mehta had slipped a Tour Brittania entry form into a programme and asked for his autograph. Before he knew it - and to Yvonne's delight - he'd been tricked into a Tour entry. The pair of them had a ball.

Yvonne and her late husband Shekhar had been great friends with Tony, and had shared a love of Africa and rallying in that part of the world. People have pointed out recently that if Tony had to go, going on an event like the Safari in Africa would be just about the perfect way for him to leave this world.

It doesn't make it any easier on those he leaves behind - particularly his wife Pat and the rest of his family - but at least we know he'd have gone with a smile on his face.

Mike Broad

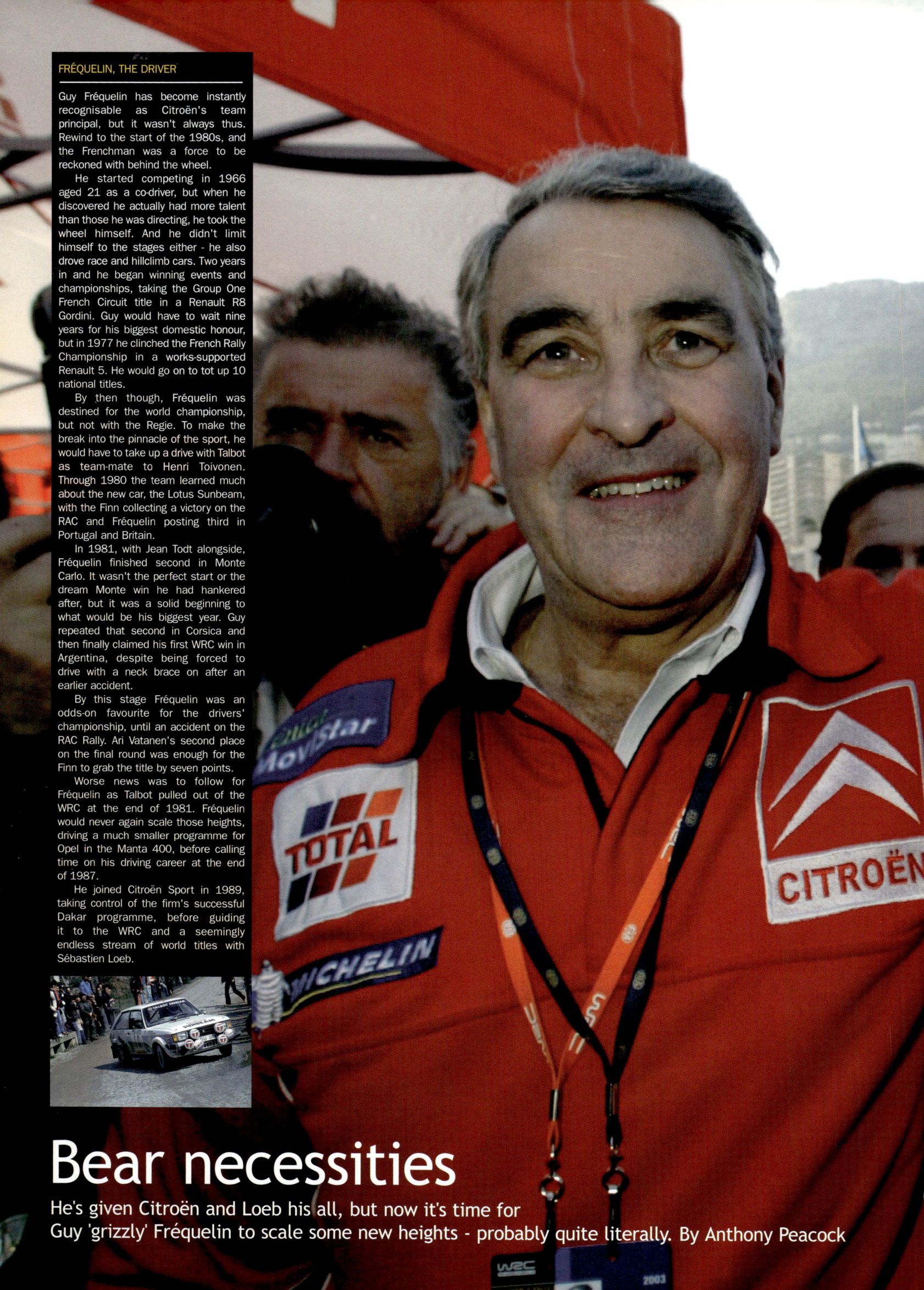

### FRÉQUELIN, THE DRIVER

Guy Fréquelin has become instantly recognisable as Citroën's team principal, but it wasn't always thus. Rewind to the start of the 1980s, and the Frenchman was a force to be reckoned with behind the wheel.

He started competing in 1966 aged 21 as a co-driver, but when he discovered he actually had more talent than those he was directing, he took the wheel himself. And he didn't limit himself to the stages either - he also drove race and hillclimb cars. Two years in and he began winning events and championships, taking the Group One French Circuit title in a Renault R8 Gordini. Guy would have to wait nine years for his biggest domestic honour, but in 1977 he clinched the French Rally Championship in a works-supported Renault 5. He would go on to tot up 10 national titles.

By then though, Fréquelin was destined for the world championship, but not with the Regie. To make the break into the pinnacle of the sport, he would have to take up a drive with Talbot as team-mate to Henri Toivonen. Through 1980 the team learned much about the new car, the Lotus Sunbeam, with the Finn collecting a victory on the RAC and Fréquelin posting third in Portugal and Britain.

In 1981, with Jean Todt alongside, Fréquelin finished second in Monte Carlo. It wasn't the perfect start or the dream Monte win he had hankered after, but it was a solid beginning to what would be his biggest year. Guy repeated that second in Corsica and then finally claimed his first WRC win in Argentina, despite being forced to drive with a neck brace on after an earlier accident.

By this stage Fréquelin was an odds-on favourite for the drivers' championship, until an accident on the RAC Rally. Ari Vatanen's second place on the final round was enough for the Finn to grab the title by seven points.

Worse news was to follow for Fréquelin as Talbot pulled out of the WRC at the end of 1981. Fréquelin would never again scale those heights, driving a much smaller programme for Opel in the Manta 400, before calling time on his driving career at the end of 1987.

He joined Citroën Sport in 1989, taking control of the firm's successful Dakar programme, before guiding it to the WRC and a seemingly endless stream of world titles with Sébastien Loeb.

# Bear necessities

He's given Citroën and Loeb his all, but now it's time for Guy 'grizzly' Fréquelin to scale some new heights - probably quite literally. By Anthony Peacock

Main: Guy Fréquelin has been credited with turning Sébastien Loeb from a shy novice into a four-time world champion

Inset: Fréquelin, seen here in Portugal in 1980, was a rapid driver and came close to capturing the world crown the following year

All photographs by McKlein

### THE SEB AND GUY STORY...

**1998**
Loeb contests the Citroën Saxo Kit Car Cup and wins all the rounds. He first appears on Fréquelin's radar aged 24.

**1999**
Loeb repeats his 1998 success.

**2000**
Gains support from Citroën Sport for the French Gravel Championship, which he wins in a Saxo kit car. He is then offered a Xsara kit car for the Rallye du Var at the end of the year. He wins the event and Fréquelin notes at the time: "A star has been born."

**2001**
Loeb stars in the Super 1600 World Rally Championship (now known as the Junior Rally Championship), winning five rallies from five starts to take the title in a factory-backed Saxo kit car. In addition to that, he wins his first outright French title in a Xsara kit car. He also makes his first major hit in the WRC proper, harrying Gilles Panizzi through a wet Sanremo to finish second on his debut in the Xsara WRC.

**2002**
Unsurprisingly, Fréquelin signs up Loeb for a part-programme in the Xsara WRC. Loeb wins in Monte Carlo but is relegated to second place after a stewards' meeting, due to a tyre infringement. That first official win follows later in the season in Germany - an event where he remains unbeaten to this day.

**2003**
Loeb is signed for a full WRC programme alongside Colin McRae and Carlos Sainz. He soon outshines the pair of them with his first win in Monte, then misses out on the world championship by just one point.

**2004**
World champion. Not only does he lift his first title, but he and Fréquelin also celebrate Loeb winning as many rallies (six) as anybody else has ever managed in a single season.

**2005**
This time Loeb beats the record, winning 10 rounds of the championship. He also breaks another record - that of the longest winning streak in the sport when he remains unbeaten for six rallies midway through the year. Another championship season.

**2006**
Loeb declines the offer of a Ford contract. Despite Fréquelin and the official Citroën team not taking part in the WRC, Loeb drives a Citroën for private team Kronos and remains loyal to the Xsara, albeit in a different colour. Fréquelin remains active in the background. Along the way, in Japan, Loeb becomes the most successful driver in the history of the sport by winning his 27th WRC event. Another title soon follows, despite Loeb missing the last four rounds due to a shoulder injury.

**2007**
Back to the official Citroën Sport team and Loeb and Fréquelin prove the partnership is as strong as ever by taking the C4 to a debut win on the Monte Carlo Rally. A fourth title follows before Fréquelin's retirement.

---

GUY Fréquelin has been called a number of things in his time, but this is probably the first occasion that even he has seen his full title in print: ursos arctos horribilis.

As the Latin name for the grizzly bear suggests, it is a savage beast that has even been known to prey upon other bears when especially hungry. Luckily, Fréquelin's nickname of 'grizzly' stems not from any cannibalistic tendencies but from his burly physique.

It was actually one of his biggest rivals, Bernard Darniche, who thought of the nickname. Darniche was so impressed by Fréquelin's determined drive on the 1977 Rallye de la Chataigne, with a Renault Alpine A310 in appalling weather conditions, that he christened Fréquelin "the grizzly bear from the countryside". Somehow the nickname stuck.

'Grizzly' has a sharp tongue and an iron will, which is how both he and Citroën Sport have managed to survive for the last 17 years. But having postponed his departure twice already, at the age of nearly 63 Fréquelin has new mountains to climb.

Quite literally: last year he paraglided from Mount Acotango, which is on the border between Bolivia and Chile, and now he wants to go back for more. He's talking about Kilimanjaro, even some of the Himalayas that are more than 8000 metres high. This is not going to be a conventional retirement.

"My job was almost impossible to put down, but rallying functions at an amazing pace now," he points out. "There are so many different things that I have to be on top of, so many things to focus on, and of course I have dedicated myself 100 per cent to all of them all of the time. I can't imagine working in any other way. So it's normal that you get tired of the constant travel, the 13-hour days, the snatched holidays. There are other things I want to do with my life."

Such as more hang-gliding: another one on his eclectic list of hobbies, along with wine tasting and hill walking. None of this is surprising though, as everything he does is pushed to the extreme. He is an unapologetic disciplinarian, the last of the patriarchal breed of team bosses.

Sébastien Loeb certainly looks upon him as a father figure. "Yes of course, he is like a father for me," says the Frenchman. "Guy, without a doubt, has been one of the most important and influential figures in my life."

This comes as no surprise, but what is more revealing is the fact that Loeb sees a softer side to the grizzly exterior. "With Guy, everything is quite relaxed," he says unexpectedly. "He's not a dictator: we choose the car set-up and the tyres we want. Most of the time, he just lets us do as we feel. There's no stress or pressure."

That wasn't always the case. When Loeb was driving the Formula 2 Xsara in the 2001 French Championship, he was threatened with the sack if he went too quickly on the superspecial stages (as Fréquelin believed he posed a big risk for little gain). Two years later, Loeb was made to sacrifice his own drivers' title ambitions on Rally Great Britain in order to guarantee the manufacturers' championship for Citroën.

At the time he was disappointed, but now he says that: "It's normal. You have to think of the team."

Loeb has built up the same sort of rapport with Citroën and Fréquelin as Michael Schumacher enjoyed at Ferrari with Jean Todt: one of Fréquelin's former co-drivers and the reason why he came to be at the helm of Citroën Sport.

It wasn't actually Fréquelin's intention to retire from driving in 1989. The year before he had won the French Championship again in a Peugeot 205 T16, and he started the '89 season in Peugeot's Dakar 205 T16 (with which he finished fourth). "Quite suddenly, I was proposed as Guy Verrier's successor at the head of Citroën's competitions department through Jean Todt," remembers Fréquelin. "I was surprised. Then I thought to myself: 'You're 44 years old. These are chances that don't come up very often.' I finished the Dakar on January 16. On January 22 I met Citroën's two managing directors. I started my new job on February 1."

He remained there right up to December 2007, building an impressive record of achievement along the way. One of his first moves back into rallying was to take Citroën to Dakar, with the ZX Rally Raid car in the mid-1990s, but it was only a matter of time before he would look for a way into the World Rally Championship.

With PSA Group stablemates Peugeot already comfortably installed, it looked like any four-wheel drive Xsara would be limited to seeing action only in the French Championship - which was the decision that the PSA board understandably reached. Somehow, Fréquelin managed to persuade them to change their minds and allow the Xsara WRC to compete in the world championship against Peugeot.

Not only that, but he did it again after it was announced that both Peugeot and Citroën would be pulling out of rallying at the end of 2005. Just over a year later, Citroën was back with an all-new car for the start of the 2007 season.

It would be easy to conclude that Fréquelin has a stash of secret photographs depicting every single board member bound and gagged in leather with a lady of ill repute. But while

Fréquelin undoubtedly knows where all the bodies are buried in an extremely political environment - another benefit of experience - the simple truth is that he is extremely persuasive. "Negotiating with Guy has never been easy!" says Loeb. "He knows how to get his own way."

As a youngster, Fréquelin had no choice. He grew up in the Haute Marne area of France: an agricultural backwater to the north east of the country that is roughly equivalent to Norfolk. "It's a tough place where you have to work hard if you want to get out," says Fréquelin - and most people did. But while his elder brother went away to technical college, and Guy himself passed the right exams to follow in his footsteps, their parents explained that there was only money to send one of the children to college. For Guy, it was back to the farm - where he was eventually expected to take over from his father. That would have happened, had Guy not found a job at a driving school in the evenings that allowed him to take part in club rallies at weekends.

Aged 22 he married Chantal - whom he had known since he was 16 - and moved out of the farm into a rented council house on the outskirts of Langres, not far from where he grew up. The couple lived off Chantal's meagre wages from the French post office, while Guy was finally able to devote himself to driving full-time: a plan he had formulated years earlier.

A few good results in showroom-specification Renaults meant that he was invited to take over a Renault dealership and make some proper money for the first time in his life. But he didn't touch any of it: his wages were all re-invested in rallying.

The turning point was in 1976, when Fréquelin rented a Porsche 911 for the Monte Carlo Rally with a budget of 45,000 francs (the equivalent of about £4100 now). He found himself leading, in front of all the established stars like Sandro Munari, before eventually finishing seventh overall and first in class. Gerard Larrousse, who was competitions director for Renault at the time, offered him a factory drive in an Alpine, and shortly afterwards the legend of the 'grizzly' was born.

The point of this potted biography - which Loeb is well familiar with - is this: Fréquelin has had to work tremendously hard and make huge sacrifices for everything he achieved. Consequently, he has a pathological horror of anybody not pulling their weight or taking things for granted. If you understand that, as Loeb soon did, then you will get on just fine with him. Show the wrong attitude, as François Duval did, and you won't even last a season.

Loeb, strangely, says that he cannot recall the first time he

met Guy Fréquelin. "Of course I was always aware of him, but I can't remember the exact occasion. Maybe because it just feels like he's been around all the time."

In the time they've worked together, they have formed a remarkable bond. It will be interesting to see if Loeb is at all destabilised in the post-Fréquelin era, but the chances are that the Frenchman would keep cranking out the wins even with Paris Hilton as his team boss. The handling of Dani Sordo - whom Fréquelin kept on a tight leash - will be a bigger challenge for Fréquelin's successor Olivier Quesnel.

"One of the things I will be most proud of in my retirement is the way that we brought Sébastien up to the level where he is now," says Fréquelin. "That beats any satisfaction I had as a driver. And actually Sébastien has allowed me to continue my career as a driver in a way: when I see him go past on the stages I always think that there's a little bit of me behind the wheel as well. Working with Seb has been a pleasure from start to finish. But nobody is irreplaceable. Life carries on, and it's time to let somebody else have some fun."

Loeb too is surprisingly unsentimental about Fréquelin's departure. Too much emotion has no place in a quasi-Presbyterian work ethic. "Guy has been a fantastic person to lead the team, but I am sure that Olivier will do a very good job too. There is a very good structure in place now."

True enough, but the service area will still be missing something next year. Although Loeb might not miss a rib-crunching bear hug every time he wins.

**Above:** Sébastien Loeb's victory in Mexico in March 2007 marked the first on gravel for the all-new Citroën C4

**Left:** Fréquelin's organisational prowess is synonymous with Citroën's success in world rallying

**Bottom left:** Fréquelin isn't one for hanging around in service parks and regular travels to stages to feedback information to his engineers

**Top left:** Loeb's win in Sardinia in 2004 was one of six he claimed during his first title-winning season

All photographs by McKlein

## WORLD RALLY CHAMPIONSHIP
# 2007

| | |
|---|---|
| MONTE CARLO RALLY | 68 |
| UDDEHOLM SWEDISH RALLY | 74 |
| RALLY NORWAY | 80 |
| RALLY MEXICO | 86 |
| RALLY DE PORTUGAL | 94 |
| RALLY ARGENTINA | 100 |
| RALLY D'ITALIA | 106 |
| ACROPOLIS RALLY | 112 |
| RALLY FINLAND | 118 |
| RALLYE DEUTSCHLAND | 124 |
| RALLY NEW ZEALAND | 130 |
| RALLYE DE ESPANA | 138 |
| RALLYE DE FRANCE | 144 |
| RALLY JAPAN | 150 |
| RALLY IRELAND | 156 |
| WALES RALLY GB | 162 |

## The FIA World Rally Championship Round 1
# Monte Carlo Rally

THE blues were red again. Sébastien Loeb's hair was longer and floppier. Monaco was nowhere to be seen and neither, for that matter, was the snow. Other than that, it was normal service on the Monte Carlo Rally. That man Loeb, driving a Citroën C4 WRC, won. Naturellement.

Guy Fréquelin was still overseeing things at Citroën as it made its return to the upper echelons of global rallying. Strangely, the man known as 'The Bear' has a most un-bear-like attitude ahead of rallies. You would expect a bear's confidence to flow freely. Let's face it; in the animal world there aren't many rivals that the bear can't have. Yet Fréquelin is the antithesis of all that. He's naturally pessimistic. He and Loeb had clearly worried themselves silly about this. It was Fréquelin's first time out since Citroën's WRC departure in November 2005, while Loeb returned to the stages following a four-month absence brought about by a broken arm sustained when he fell off his mountain bike the previous September.

"I don't know so much," said Loeb on the eve of the event. "The arm has been okay in testing, but what about the long stage? I don't know. And the car? It's been good in testing, but what about the rally? I don't know."

Predictably, all Fréquelin could talk about was pace and ability - but it was the pace and ability of the Ford and Marcus Grönholm that concerned him. In the end, and equally predictably, the Frenchmen needn't have worried. They romped home.

A last-gasp tweak to Loeb's C4 at pre-event shakedown made a good car great (or should that be great car perfect?) for the reigning world champion. Happy with its handling, he set out into damp Ardeche on Thursday night to blitz the brace of stages the Automobile Club de Monaco had organised. Returning to service, Loeb was smiling.

"I really didn't know what to expect," said the man now sitting on a 23-second lead.

One thing he probably didn't expect was the ferocity of the challenge coming from his team-mate Dani Sordo. The Spaniard, in his first ever factory WRC drive, was on startling form through St Pierreville the next morning. He beat Loeb by a whopping 16.2 seconds. Loeb was visibly shaken. He couldn't and wouldn't let this happen. These were his roads and his mountains. They weren't big enough for two fast Citroëns. Loeb hit back and put Sordo firmly in his place.

Citroën also put Ford firmly in its place, determined to show that Grönholm's success here 12 months ago had been a blip rather than a shift in Monte Carlo Rally performance. Grönholm's Ford was comfortably the third fastest car throughout the event, but the Finn admitted there was little - if anything - he could do about the pair ahead of him.

Grönholm's Ford team-mate Mikko Hirvonen and Subaru's Chris Atkinson were engaged in a fabulous fight for fourth. After the stresses and strains of the mountain roads, the pair arrived in Monaco with just over a second separating them. Atkinson was inch-perfect and fastest, while Hirvonen made a couple of mistakes and ended up fifth.

Grönholm was unable to repeat his 2006 victory on a snow-free Monte
McKlein

Sordo
CITROËN
TOTAL
738 DYN 78
BFGoodrich

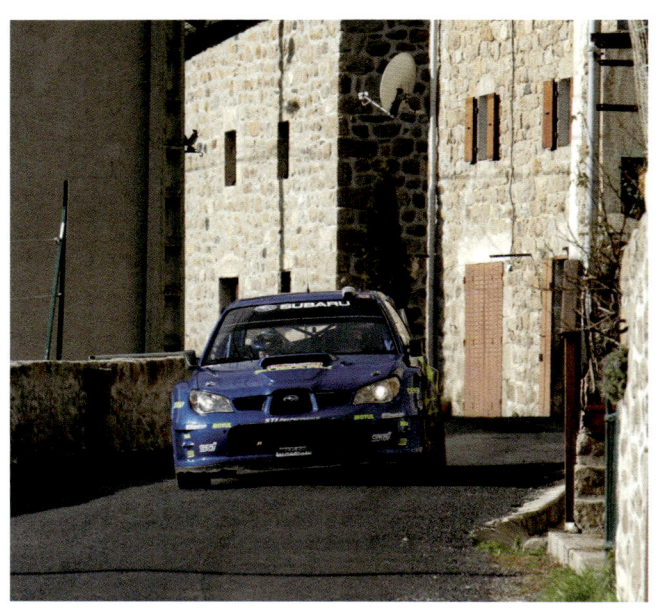

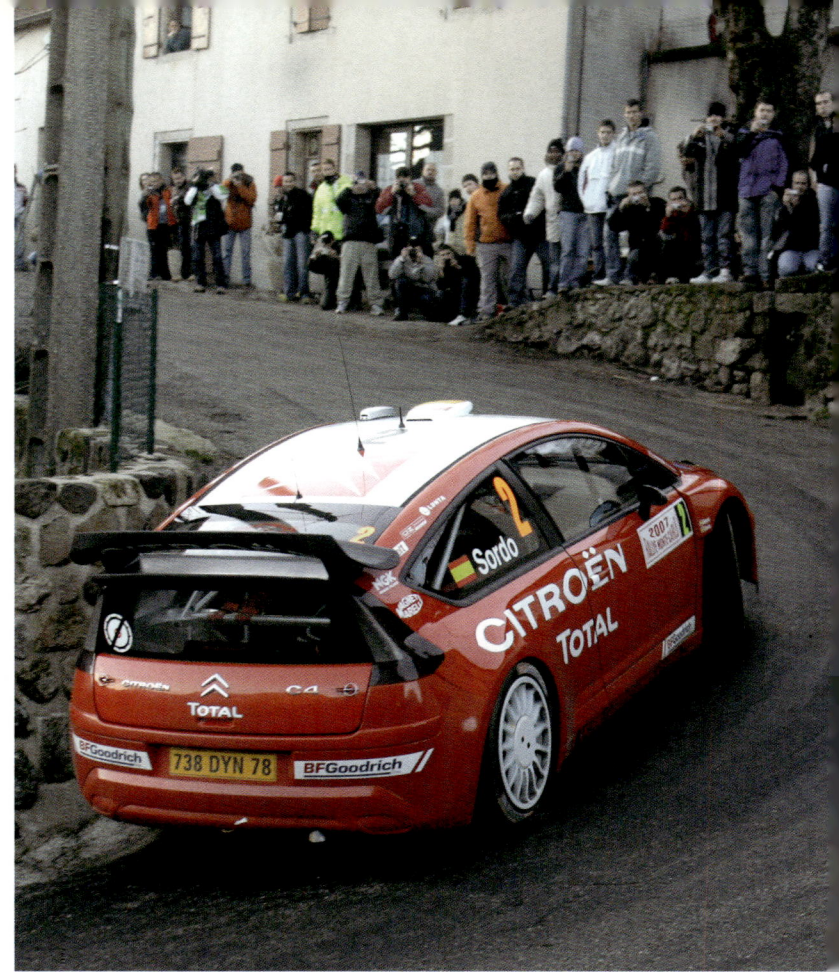

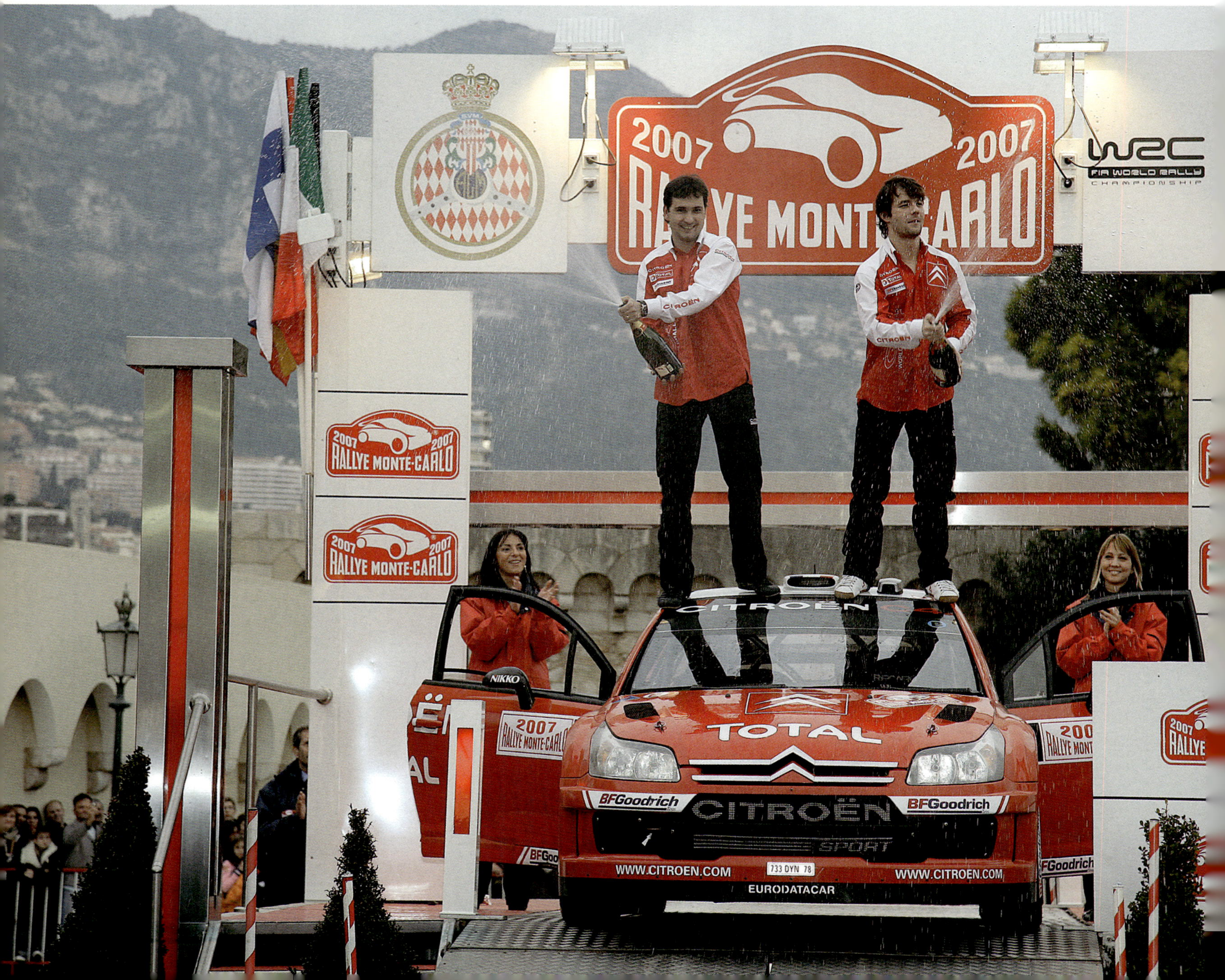
2007
2007
RALLYE MONTE-CARLO
FIA WORLD RALLY CHAMPIONSHIP
TOTAL
CITROËN
BFGoodrich
WWW.CITROEN.COM
733 DYN 78
EURODATACAR

MONTE CARLO RALLY

Bottom Left: After months on the sidelines, waiting for his broken arm to heal, Loeb returned with a debut win in the C4

Far Left: A subdued Solberg collected sixth on his first event on BFGoodrich rubber

Centre: Sordo was on sublime form, worrying Loeb briefly before taking second

Left: Atkinson clinched fourth after a fabulous battle around the Monaco Grand Prix track...

Below: ... and it was Hirvonen who lost out in that tussle on the final stage

All photographs by McKlein unless specified

The Monte has always been a happy hunting ground for French amateur drivers. This year it was Jean-Marie Cuoq guiding his 307 into ninth.
McKlein

## The FIA World Rally Championship Round 1
# Monte Carlo Results
### January 18-21 2007

### FINISH LINES...

Subaru really hadn't expected much from this event. The new car was not due until Mexico in March, so the first three rallies were about points and possible podiums, as well as damage limitation and reading between the lines. Atkinson accomplished the team's objectives with fourth place, but Petter Solberg was strangely subdued. He admitted he was finding it tough to get to grips with the BF Goodrich tyres he was using for the first time. Any plans he might have had about pushing further up the leaderboard were ended by a monster moment on SS10, when the Impreza WRC2006 understeered off the road in top gear... Toni Gardemeister confirmed there was still plenty of life left in the Mitsubishi Lancer WR 05 with some solid times and seventh overall on his debut in the car. Skoda man Jan Kopecky took the final point, while local hero Jean-Marie Cuoq made his WRC debut in the top 10 with ninth in a Peugeot 307 WRC... There was much to talk about in this year's World Rally Championship opener. Still troubled by criticism following last year's chaotic route, the organisers came up with a completely new idea for this season. The Monte Carlo Rally was based in Valence, miles and miles from Monaco and the Alpes Maritimes. The rally did visit the principality, but it only paid lip service with a Sunday morning superspecial. Also new, or at least returning, were night stages. Opinion on the changes was divided. WRC commercial guru David Richards likened the service park to a car boot sale, but the stages themselves were fabulous - except for the fact that every kilometre was bone-dry... Following the organisers' decision to move the event to Valence, there were fewer competitors on this rally - and no round of either the Production or Junior series, due to there being no room in a smaller than usual service park.

### RUNNING ORDER

| | | | |
|---|---|---|---|
| 1 | Sébastien Loeb/ Daniel Elena | Citroën C4 WRC | Gr A |
| 3 | Marcus Grönholm/ Timo Rautiainen | Ford Focus RS WRC 06 | Gr A |
| 4 | Mikko Hirvonen/ Jarmo Lehtinen | Ford Focus RS WRC 06 | Gr A |
| 5 | Manfred Stohl/ Ilka Minor | Citroën Xsara WRC | Gr A |
| 2 | Daniel Sordo/ Marc Martí | Citroën C4 WRC | Gr A |
| 7 | Petter Solberg/ Phil Mills | Subaru Impreza WRC 2006 | Gr A |
| 27 | Xavier Pons/ Xavier Amigo | Mitsubishi Lancer WRC05 | Gr A |
| 10 | Henning Solberg/ Cato Menkerud | Ford Focus RS WRC 06 | Gr A |
| 26 | Toni Gardemeister/ Jakke Honkanen | Mitsubishi Lancer WRC05 | Gr A |
| 8 | Chris Atkinson/ Glenn Macneall | Subaru Impreza WRC 2006 | Gr A |
| 9 | Jari-Matti Latvala/ Miikka Anttila | Ford Focus RS WRC 06 | Gr A |
| 18 | Jan Kopecky/ Filip Schovanek | Skoda Fabia WRC | Gr A |
| 19 | Gareth MacHale/ Paul Nagle | Ford Focus RS WRC 04 | Gr A |
| 16 | Matthew Wilson/ Michael Orr | Ford Focus RS WRC 06 | Gr A |
| 20 | Eamonn Boland/ Francis Regan | Ford Focus RS WRC 04 | Gr A |
| 21 | Jean-Marie Cuoq/ David Marty | Peugeot 307 WRC | Gr A |
| 61 | Philippe Roux/ Eric Jordan | Peugeot 307 WRC | Gr A |
| 62 | Frédéric Romeyer/ Marie-Ange Lachand | Peugeot 206 WRC | Gr A |
| 74 | Andreas Aigner/ Klaus Wicha | Mitsubishi Lancer Evo 9 | Gr N |
| 75 | Olivier Burri/ Fabrice Gordan | Subaru Impreza WRX Sti | Gr N |

### SPECIAL STAGE TIMES

**SS1 St Jean en Royans - Col de Lachau (28.52km)**
1 S.Loeb/D.Elena (Citroën C4 WRC) 13m58.7s; 2 D.Sordo/M.Martí (Citroën C4 WRC) 14m07.2s; 3 M.Grönholm/T.Rautiainen (Ford Focus RS WRC 06) 14m13.5s; 4 P.Solberg/P.Mills (Subaru Impreza WRC 2006) 14m22.7s; 5 M.Hirvonen/J.Lehtinen (Ford Focus RS WRC 06) 14m26.1s; 6 J.Kopecky/F.Schovanek (Skoda Fabia WRC) 14m29.5s

**SS2 La Cime du Mas - Col de Gaudissart (17.88km)**
1 Loeb/Elena (Citroën) 9m31.2s; 2 Grönholm/Rautiainen (Ford) 9m45.5s; 3 Sordo/Martí (Citroën) 9m46.6s; 4 C.Atkinson/G.Macneall (Subaru Impreza WRC2006) 9m55.2s; 5 Hirvonen/Lehtinen (Ford) 9m55.5s; 6 M.Stohl/I.Minor (Citroën Xsara WRC) 9m59.6s

**SS3 St Pierreville - Antraiques 1 (46.02km)**
1 Sordo/Martí (Citroën) 29m43.4s; 2 Loeb/Elena (Citroën) 29m59.6s; 3 Grönholm/Rautiainen (Ford) 30m01.1s; 4 Atkinson/Macneall (Subaru) 30m03.5s; 5 T.Gardemeister/J.Honkanen (Mitsubishi Lancer WRC05) 30m10.1s; 6 Stohl/Minor (Citroën) 30m14.7s

**SS4 Burzet - Lachamp Raphael 1 (16.48km)**
1 Loeb/Elena (Citroën) 9m39.3s; 2 Sordo/Martí (Citroën) 9m39.4s; 3 Grönholm/Rautiainen (Ford) 9m43.0s; 4 Solberg/Mills (Subaru) 9m50.4s; 5 J.M.Latvala/M.Anttila (Ford Focus RS WRC 06) 9m51.6s; 6 Hirvonen/Lehtinen (Ford) 9m52.0s

**SS5 St Martial - Le Chambon - Beleac 1 (12.81km)**
1 Sordo/Martí (Citroën) 8m00.7s; 2 Loeb/Elena (Citroën) 8m01.9s; 3 Grönholm/Rautiainen (Ford) 8m03.8s; 4 Solberg/Mills (Subaru) 8m05.9s; 5 Hirvonen/Lehtinen (Ford) 8m06.9s; 6= Stohl/Minor (Citroën), Gardemeister/Honkanen (Mitsubishi) 8m08.9s

**SS6 St Pierreville - Antraiques 2 (46.02km)**
1 Loeb/Elena (Citroën) 28m29.7s; 2 Sordo/Martí (Citroën) 28m46.8s; 3 Grönholm/Rautiainen (Ford) 28m54.1s; 4 Hirvonen/Lehtinen (Ford) 28m59.7s; 5 Atkinson/Macneall (Subaru) 29m00.8s; 6 Solberg/Mills (Subaru) 29m10.3s

**SS7 Burzet - Lachamp Raphael 2 (16.48km)**
1 Sordo/Martí (Citroën) 9m43.2s; 2 Loeb/Elena (Citroën) 9m44.3s; 3 Grönholm/Rautiainen (Ford) 9m49.3s; 4 Atkinson/Macneall (Subaru) 9m50.3s; 5 Solberg/Mills (Subaru) 9m51.8s; 6 Gardemeister/Honkanen (Mitsubishi) 9m54.4s

**SS8 St Martial - Le Chambon - Beleac 2 (12.81km)**
1 Loeb/Elena (Citroën) 8m16.4s; 2 Sordo/Martí (Citroën) 8m19.0s; 3 J-M.Cuoq/D.Marty (Peugeot 307 WRC) 8m26.1s; 4 Grönholm/Rautiainen (Ford) 8m26.5s; 5 Gardemeister/Honkanen (Mitsubishi) 8m27.3s; 6 Solberg/Mills (Subaru) 8m30.8s

**SS9 Labatie d'Andaure - Lalouvesc 1 (19.67km)**
1 Loeb/Elena (Citroën) 10m47.2s; 2 Sordo/Martí (Citroën) 10m48.3s; 3 Grönholm/Rautiainen (Ford) 10m57.3s; 4 Solberg/Mills (Subaru) 11m01.1s; 5 Hirvonen/Lehtinen (Ford) 11m02.1s; 6 Cuoq/Marty (Peugeot) 11m03.8s

**SS10 St Bonnet le Froid 1 (25.93km)**
1 Atkinson/Macneall (Subaru) 12m42.7s; 2 Grönholm/Rautiainen (Ford) 12m46.3s; 3 Latvala/Anttila (Ford) 12m49.9s; 4 Sordo/Martí (Citroën) 12m50.0s; 5= Solberg/Mills (Subaru), Cuoq/Marty (Peugeot) 12m50.4s

**SS11 Lamastre - St Barthelemy Grozen 1 (18.76km)**
1 Hirvonen/Lehtinen (Ford) 11m46.9s; 2 Loeb/Elena (Citroën) 11m48.1s; 3 Grönholm/Rautiainen (Ford) 11m52.7s; 4 Kopecky/Schovanek (Skoda) 11m54.9s; 5 Latvala/Anttila (Ford) 11m55.0s; 6 Gardemeister/Honkanen (Mitsubishi) 11m55.7s

**SS12 Labatie d'Andaure - Lalouvesc 2 (19.67km)**
1 Hirvonen/Lehtinen (Ford) 10m45.1s; 2 Solberg/Mills (Subaru) 10m45.9s; 3 Grönholm/Rautiainen (Ford) 10m50.0s; 4= Loeb/Elena (Citroën), Kopecky/Schovanek (Skoda) 10m53.0s; 6 Sordo/Martí (Citroën) 10m53.3s

**SS13 St Bonnet le Froid 2 (25.93km)**
1 Atkinson/Macneall (Subaru) 12m32.4s; 2 Sordo/Martí (Citroën) 12m34.5s; 3 Latvala/Anttila (Ford) 12m37.8s; 4

# MONTE CARLO RALLY

Solberg/Mills (Subaru) 12m38.7s; 5 Hirvonen/Lehtinen (Ford) 12m40.0s; 6 Loeb/Elena (Citroën) 12m41.2s

**SS14 Lamastre - St Barthelemy Grozen 2 (18.76km)**
1 Hirvonen/Lehtinen (Ford) 11m30.5s; 2 Atkinson/Macneall (Subaru) 11m38.5s; 3 Solberg/Mills (Subaru) 11m42.8s; 4 Loeb/Elena (Citroën) 11m47.7s; 5 Gardemeister/Honkanen (Mitsubishi) 11m49.2s; 6 Grönholm/Rautiainen (Ford) 11m49.9s

**SS15 Monaco (2.80km)**
1 Atkinson/Macneall (Subaru) 1m49.9s; 2 Grönholm/Rautiainen (Ford) 1m50.4s; 3 Hirvonen/Lehtinen (Ford) 1m50.9s; 4 Gardemeister/Honkanen (Mitsubishi) 1m51.0s; 5 Loeb/Elena (Citroën) 1m51.2s; 6 Stohl/Minor (Citroën) 1m52.8s

Cars who retired and subsequently restarted and were classified under SupeRally regs:
27 Pons/Amigo  Mitsubishi Lancer WRC05
  Transmission  SS3  Gr A

## MAJOR RETIREMENTS
9 Latvala/Anttila  Ford Focus RS WRC 06
  Accident  SS14  Gr A
74 Aigner/Wicha  Mitsubishi Lancer Evo 9
  Mechanical  SS9  Gr N

## FIA CLASS WINNERS
A8 Over 2000cc  Loeb/Elena
  Citroën C4 WRC
A7 1600-2000cc  Monnet/Monnet
  Peugeot 206 RC
A6 1400-1600cc  Prokop/Tomanek
  Citroën C2
N4 Over 2000cc  Burri/Gordan
  Subaru Impreza WRX Sti

## RALLY LEADERS
Overall: SS1-15 Loeb

## SPECIAL STAGE ANALYSIS

|  | 1st | 2nd | 3rd | 4th | 5th | 6th |
|---|---|---|---|---|---|---|
| Loeb (Citroën) | 6 | 4 | - | 2 | 1 | 1 |
| Sordo (Citroën) | 3 | 6 | 1 | 1 | - | 1 |
| Atkinson (Subaru) | 3 | 1 | - | 3 | 1 | - |
| Hirvonen (Ford) | 3 | - | 1 | 1 | 5 | 1 |
| Grönholm (Ford) | - | 3 | 9 | 1 | - | 1 |
| P.Solberg (Subaru) | - | 1 | 1 | 5 | 2 | 2 |
| Latvala (Ford) | - | - | 2 | - | 2 | - |
| Cuoq (Peugeot) | - | - | 1 | - | 1 | 1 |
| Kopecky (Skoda) | - | - | - | 2 | - | 1 |
| Gardemeister (Mitsubishi) | - | - | - | 1 | 3 | 3 |
| Stohl (Citroën) | - | - | - | - | - | 4 |

## WORLD CHAMPIONSHIP POINTS
**Drivers**
1 Loeb 10; 2 Sordo 8; 3 Grönholm 6; 4 Atkinson 5; 5 Hirvonen 4; 6 P.Solberg 3; 7 Gardemeister 2; 8 Kopecky 1
**Manufacturers**
1 Citroën Total WRT 18; 2 BP-Ford WRT 10; 3 Subaru WRT 8; 4 OMV-Kronos Citroën WRT 2; 5 Stobart M-Sport Ford RT 1

## ROUTE DETAILS
Total route of 1185.02km of which 328.54km were competitive on 15 stages
**Leg 1** Thursday 18 January, 2 special stages totalling 46.40km
**Leg 2** Friday 19 January, 6 special stages totalling 150.62km
**Leg 3** Saturday 20-Sunday 21 January, 7 special stages totalling 131.52km

## RESULTS
1 Sébastien Loeb/ Citroën C4 WRC
  Daniel Elena  3h10m27.4s  Gr A
2 Daniel Sordo/ Citroën C4 WRC
  Marc Martí  3h11m05.6s  Gr A
3 Marcus Grönholm/ Ford Focus RS WRC 06
  Timo Rautiainen  3h11m50.2s  Gr A
4 Chris Atkinson/ Subaru Impreza WRC 2006
  Glenn Macneall  3h12m55.5s  Gr A
5 Mikko Hirvonen/ Ford Focus RS WRC 06
  Jarmo Lehtinen  3h12m55.7s  Gr A
6 Petter Solberg/ Subaru Impreza WRC 2006
  Phil Mills  3h13m39.4s  Gr A
7 Toni Gardemeister/ Mitsubishi Lancer WRC05
  Jakke Honkanen  3h14m05.5s  Gr A
8 Jan Kopecky/ Skoda Fabia WRC
  Filip Schovanek  3h15m06.8s  Gr A
9 Jean-Marie Cuoq/ Peugeot 307 WRC
  David Marty  3h16m27.1s  Gr A
10 Manfred Stohl/ Citroën Xsara WRC
  Ilka Minor  3h17m04.7s  Gr A

47 starters, 39 finishers

## RECENT WINNERS
1964 Paddy Hopkirk/Henry Liddon  Mini Cooper S
1965 Timo Mäkinen/Paul Easter  Mini Cooper S
1966 Pauli Toivonen/Ensio Mikander  Citroen DS21
1967 Rauno Aaltonen/Henry Liddon  Mini Cooper S
1968 Vic Elford/David Stone  Porsche 911T
1969 Björn Waldegård/Lars Helmer  Porsche 911S
1970 Björn Waldegård/Lars Helmer  Porsche 911T
1971 Ove Andersson/David Stone  Alpine Renault A110
1972 Sandro Munari/Mauro Mannucci  Lancia Fulvia
1973 Jean-Claude Andruet/'Biche'  Alpine Renault A110
1975 Sandro Munari/Mauro Mannucci  Lancia Stratos
1976 Sandro Munari/Silvio Maiga  Lancia Stratos
1977 Sandro Munari/Silvio Maiga  Lancia Stratos
1978 Jean-Pierre Nicolas/Vincent Laverne  Porsche 911 Carrera
1979 Bernard Darniche/Alan Mahé  Lancia Stratos
1980 Walter Röhrl/Christian Geistdörfer  Fiat 131 Abarth
1981 Jean Ragnotti/Jean-Marc Andrié  Renault 5 Turbo
1982 Walter Röhrl/Christian Geistdorfer  Opel Ascona 400
1983 Walter Röhrl/Christian Geistdorfer  Lancia Rally 037
1984 Walter Röhrl/Christian Geistdorfer  Audi Quattro A2
1985 Ari Vatanen/Terry Harryman  Peugeot 205 Turbo 16
1986 Henri Toivonen/Sergio Cresto  Lancia Delta S4
1987 Miki Biasion/Tiziano Siviero  Lancia Delta HF 4x4
1988 Bruno Saby/Jean-François Fauchille  Lancia Delta HF 4x4
1989 Miki Biasion/Tiziano Siviero  Lancia Delta Integrale
1990 Didier Auriol/Bernard Occelli  Lancia Delta Integrale 16v
1991 Carlos Sainz/Luis Moya  Toyota Celica GT4
1992 Didier Auriol/Bernard Occelli  Lancia Delta HF Integrale
1993 Didier Auriol/Bernard Occelli  Toyota Celica Turbo 4wd
1994 François Delecour/Daniel Grataloup  Ford Escort RS Cosworth
1995 Carlos Sainz/Luis Moya  Subaru Impreza 555
1996 Patrick Bernardini/Bernard Occelli  Ford Escort RS Cosworth
1997 Piero Liatti/Fabrizia Pons  Subaru Impreza WRC97
1998 Carlos Sainz/Luis Moya  Toyota Corolla WRC
1999 Tommi Mäkinen/Risto Mannisenmäki  Mitsubishi Lancer E6
2000 Tommi Mäkinen/Risto Mannisenmäki  Mitsubishi Lancer E6
2001 Tommi Mäkinen/Risto Mannisenmäki  Mitsubishi Lancer Evo
2002 Tommi Mäkinen/Kaj Lindström  Subaru Impreza WRC2001
2003 Sébastien Loeb/Daniel Elena  Citroën Xsara WRC
2004 Sébastien Loeb/Daniel Elena  Citroën Xsara WRC
2005 Sébastien Loeb/Daniel Elena  Citroën Xsara WRC
2006 Marcus Grönholm/Timo Rautiainen  Ford Focus RS WRC 06

| Stage Numbers | 1 | 2 | 3 | 4 | 5 | 6 | 7 | 8 | 9 | 10 | 11 | 12 | 13 | 14 | 15 |
|---|---|---|---|---|---|---|---|---|---|---|---|---|---|---|---|
| Loeb | 1 | 1 | 1 | 1 | 1 | 1 | 1 | 1 | 1 | 1 | 1 | 1 | 1 | 1 | 1 |
| Sordo | 2 | 2 | 2 | 2 | 2 | 2 | 2 | 2 | 2 | 2 | 2 | 2 | 2 | 2 | 2 |
| Grönholm | 3 | 3 | 3 | 3 | 3 | 3 | 3 | 3 | 3 | 3 | 3 | 3 | 3 | 3 | 3 |
| Atkinson | 9 | 6 | 4 | 4 | 4 | 4 | 4 | 4 | 4 | 4 | 4 | 5 | 5 | 4 | 4 |
| Hirvonen | 5 | 4 | 7 | 7 | 5 | 5 | 5 | 5 | 5 | 5 | 5 | 4 | 4 | 5 | 5 |
| P.Solberg | 4 | 5 | 9 | 9 | 8 | 7 | 7 | 7 | 6 | 6 | 6 | 6 | 6 | 6 | 6 |
| Gardemeister | 8 | 8 | 5 | 6 | 6 | 6 | 6 | 6 | 7 | 7 | 7 | 7 | 7 | 7 | 7 |
| Kopecky | 6 | 9 | 8 | 8 | 9 | 9 | 8 | 8 | 8 | 8 | 8 | 8 | 8 | 8 | 8 |
| Cuoq | 11 | 10 | 10 | 10 | 10 | 11 | 11 | 10 | 10 | 10 | 10 | 10 | 10 | 9 | 9 |
| Stohl | 7 | 7 | 6 | 5 | 8 | 9 | 9 | 11 | 11 | 11 | 11 | 11 | 11 | 10 | 10 |
| MacHale | 14 | 14 | 12 | 12 | 12 | 12 | 12 | 12 | 12 | 12 | 12 | 12 | 12 | 11 | 11 |
| Wilson | 15 | 15 | 14 | 13 | 13 | 13 | 13 | 13 | 14 | 13 | 13 | 13 | 13 | 12 | 12 |
| H.Solberg | 16 | 16 | 16 | 15 | 15 | 15 | 15 | 15 | 15 | 15 | 15 | 15 | 15 | 14 | 14 |
| Pons | 10 | 11 | 32 | 28 | 32 | 31 | 33 | 33 | 32 | 30 | 28 | 27 | 26 | 26 | 25 |
| Latvala | 12 | 12 | 11 | 11 | 11 | 10 | 10 | 9 | 9 | 9 | 9 | 9 | 9 | 9 | R |

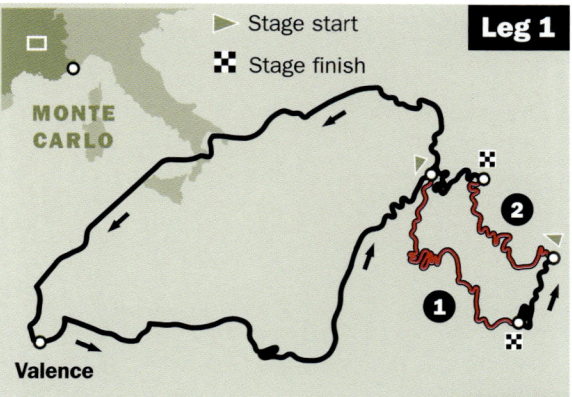

Leg 1

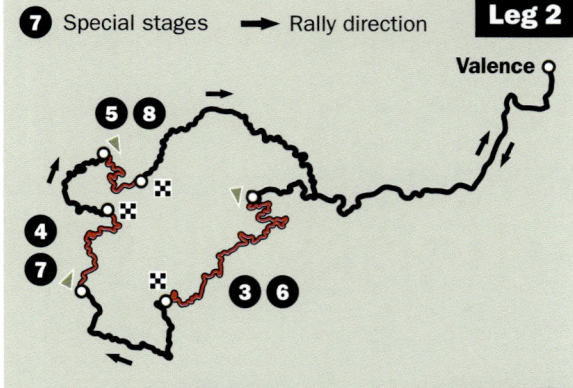

Leg 2

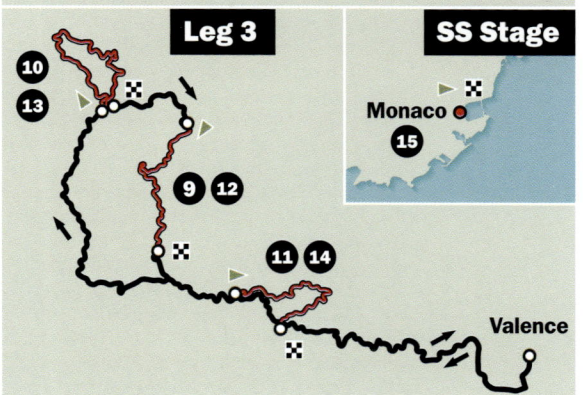

Leg 3 / SS Stage

## The FIA World Rally Championship Round 2
# Swedish Rally

**Above:** Loeb lost out in the tyre-choice gamble on the final morning. The Citroen driver settled for second in Sweden

**Opposite Top:** Carlsson impressed on his debut in a Citroen Xsara WRC, taking fourth on his home event

**Far Right:** The WRC is truly a multi-national sport...

**Right:** Solberg led early on, but then binned his Impreza trying to keep up with the machinery ahead

All photographs by McKlein

To the outsider at lunchtime on leg one of this year's Swedish Rally, it must have looked as though Subaru had spent the previous season sandbagging. Maybe the Impreza WRC 2006 really wasn't that bad. Following Chris Atkinson's belting Monte drive to fourth, Petter Solberg was now leading a world championship round. A day later and Solberg the hero became Solberg the villain. Trying desperately to cling to the coattails of Marcus Grönholm and Sébastien Loeb, who had subsequently passed his Subaru, the Norwegian slid off and ditched the car. Fourteen minutes passed before the Impreza could be manhandled back onto the road. Privately, the team was furious that this had happened. Everybody - Solberg included - knew full well that pushing wasn't on the agenda. The Impreza didn't have the pace of its rivals and Solberg, according to the team's strategy, should have known this, throttled back and taken the potential six points on offer. The best laid plans and all that. Instead, Solberg's car was withdrawn to save it for the following week's encounter in the 2003 world champion's backyard.

Out front, Grönholm had everything under control. He loves these lanes and knows them exceptionally well. The only potential hiccup for Ford came, just like last season, on the final morning. When the Fords of Jari-Matti Latvala and Matthew Wilson showed a loss of oil pressure, they were instructed to switch them off immediately. It turned out the extreme cold around the Hagfors service park (very extreme, like minus 23 degrees) had frozen a breather pipe on the car, leaving the motor gasping. Grönholm and team-mate Mikko Hirvonen, who had been third in the sister Focus, were instructed to pull over and slice open the pipe in question. This automotive tracheotomy ensured the Finns were able to pull back some of the ground lost to Citroen on the opening round. As had been the case so many times on the Swedish Rally, Loeb was faced with a conundrum. On the same tyre as Grönholm, he was not able to make any significant impact on the 11-second deficit he'd faced on Saturday morning. So, he gambled. He went for a long stud tyre on Saturday afternoon. But his number didn't come up. There wasn't enough snow for the seven-millimetre protrusion. The stud hit the gravel beneath the ice and began to overheat in the tyre. The battle was lost. Second would suffice. Hirvonen wasn't best pleased with third, feeling he'd missed the chance to make an impact at the top of the table.

On only his second outing in a Ford Focus, Henning Solberg was delighted with fourth, seeing it as the perfect preparation for the maiden WRC qualifier in his home nation of Norway, which began just five days after the Swedish Rally ended. Further impressive performances came from Daniel Carlsson on his debut in a Citroen Xsara WRC and Toni Gardemeister, who could have been looking at a podium finish had it not been for a driveshaft problem aboard the Mitsubishi on Saturday.

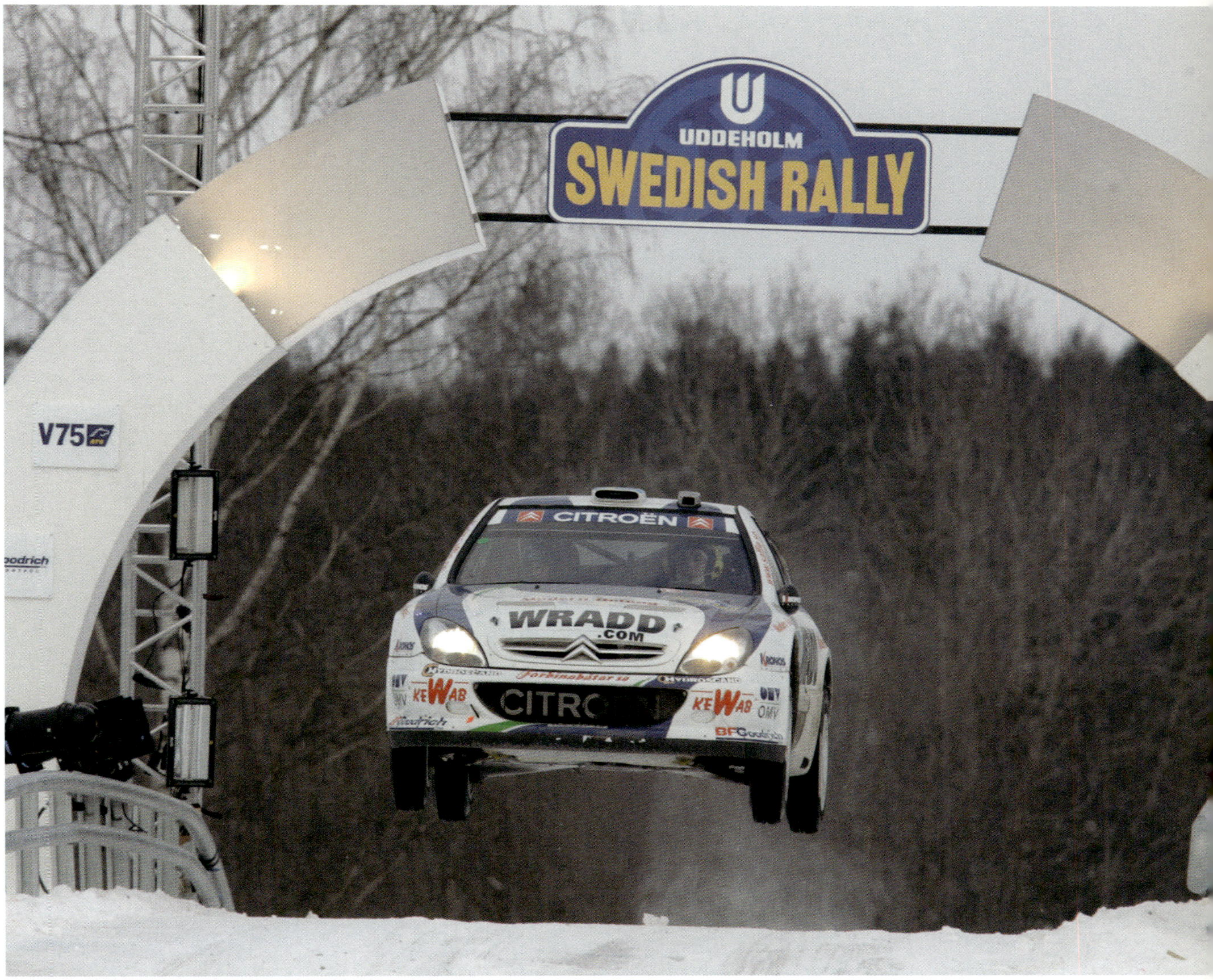
UDDEHOLM
SWEDISH RALLY
V75
CITROËN
WRADD .COM

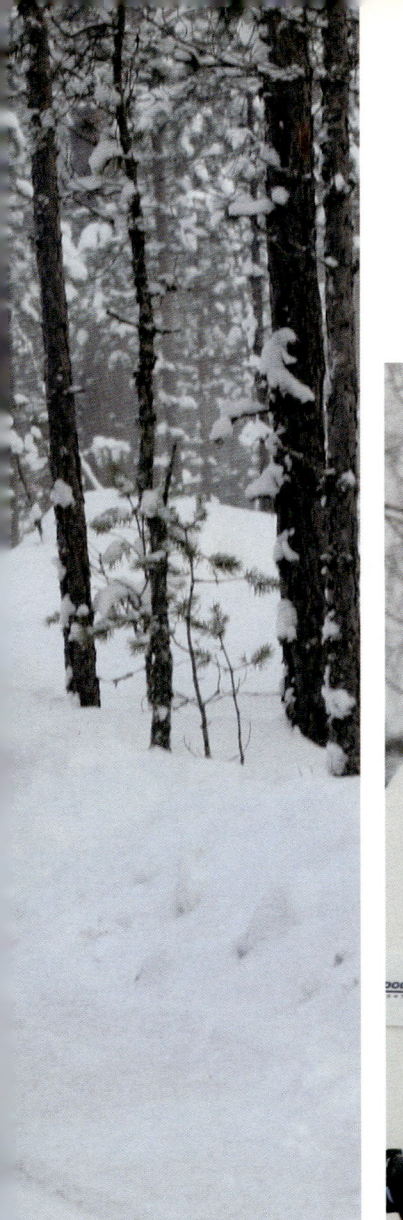

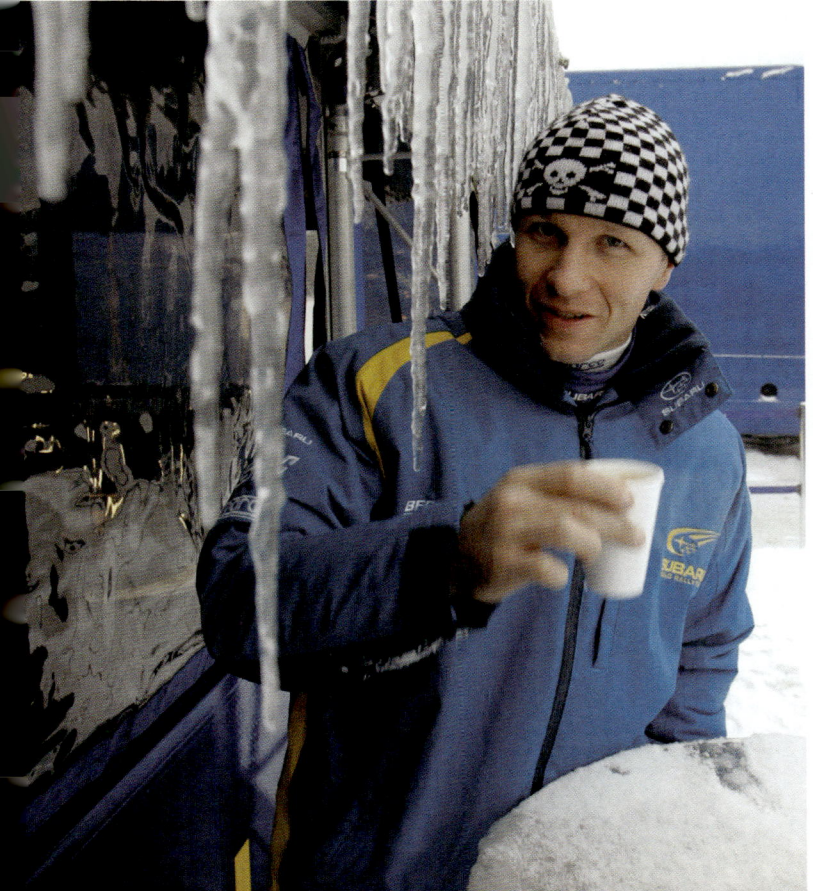

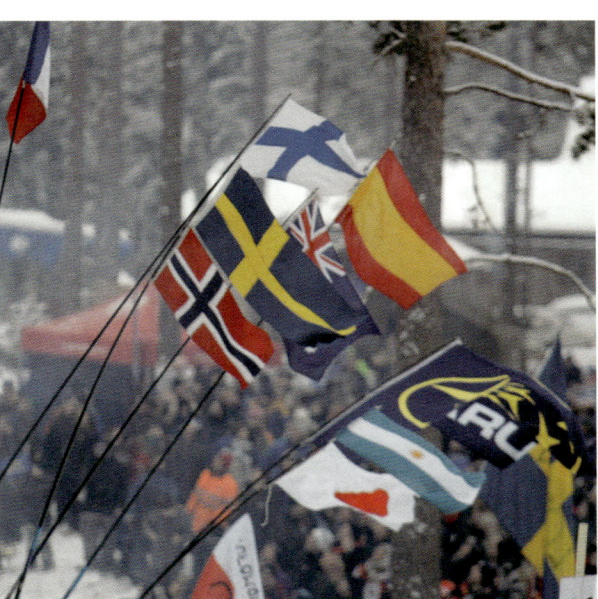

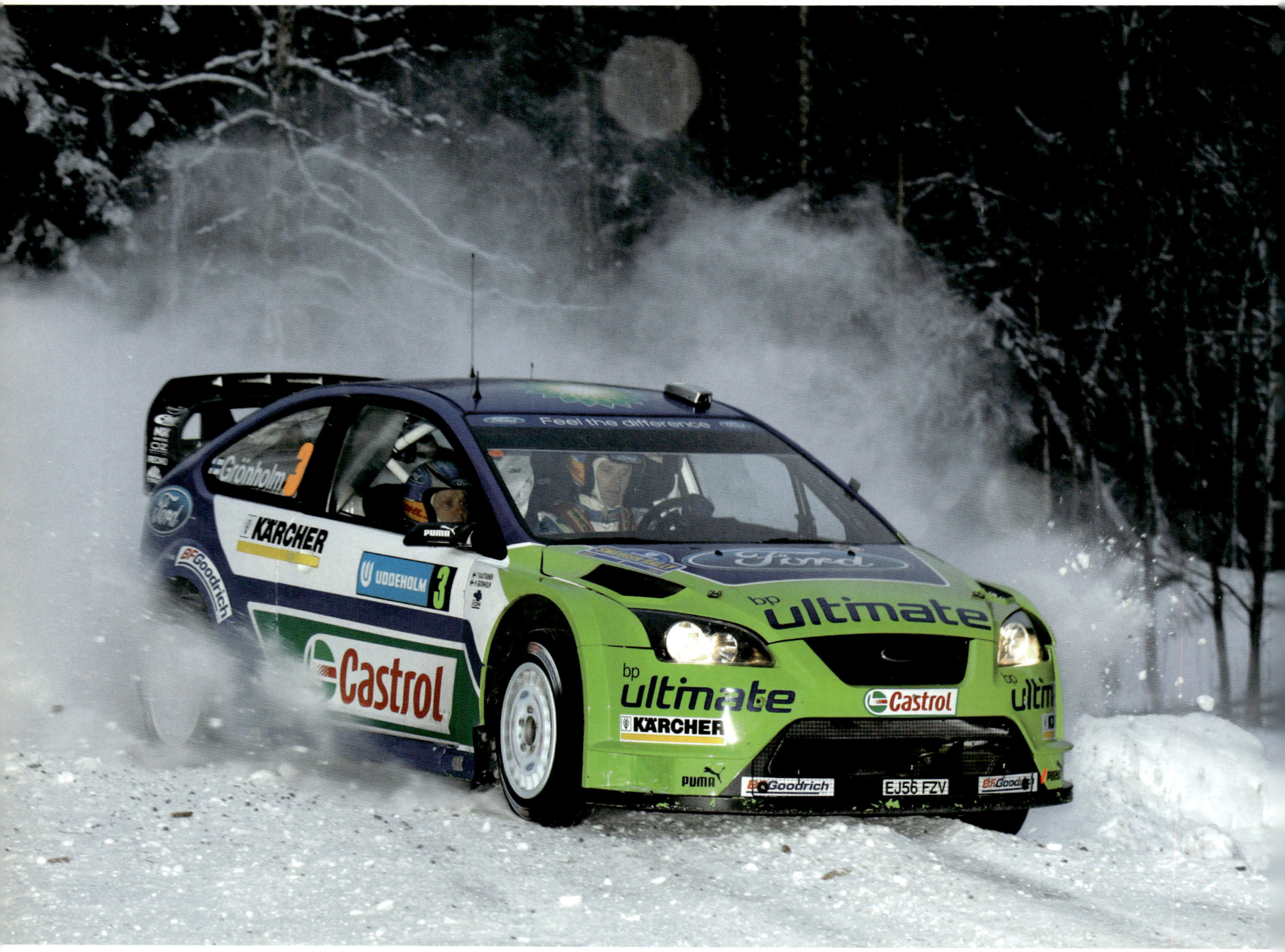
Feel the difference
Grönholm 3
KÄRCHER
UDDEHOLM 3
Castrol
bp
ultimate
PUMA
BFGoodrich
EJ56 FZV

EnPro
smartpanel
expert
EXIDE
BFGoodrich
EU55 CNX

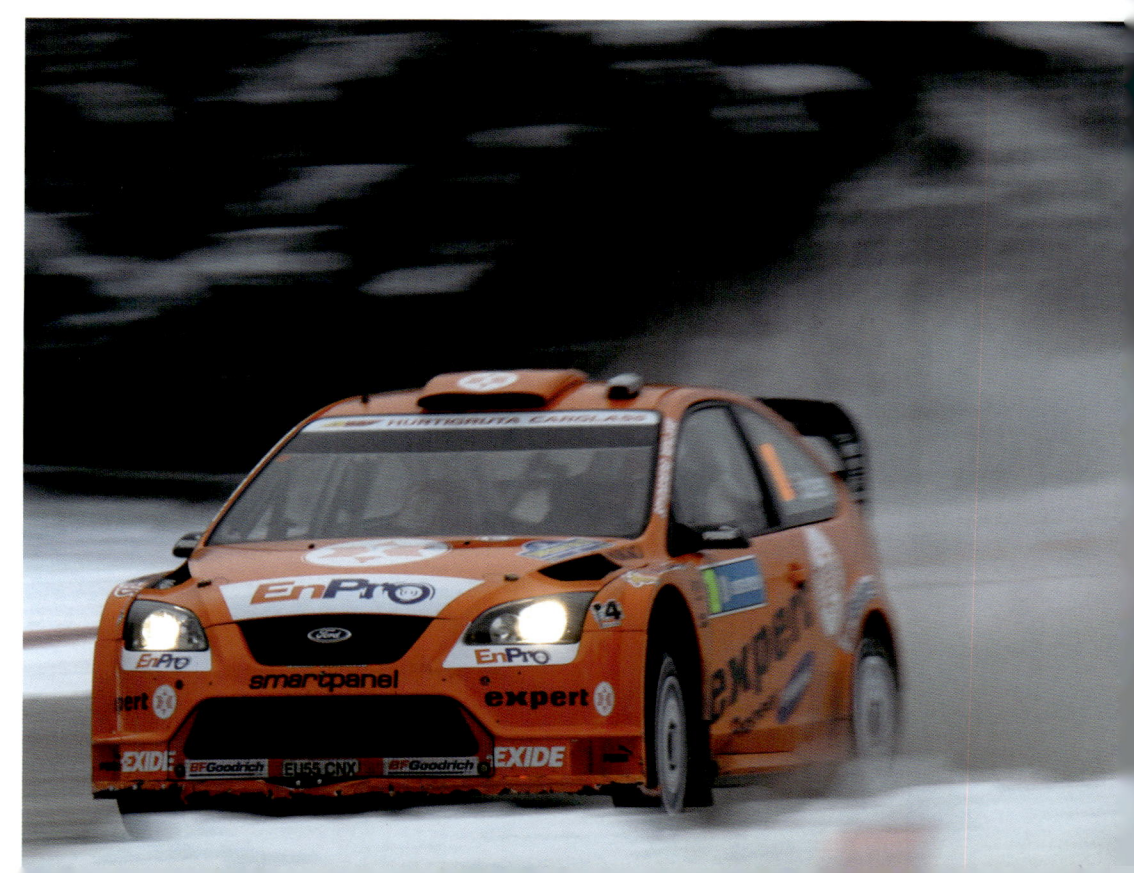

Photo4/Crash.net

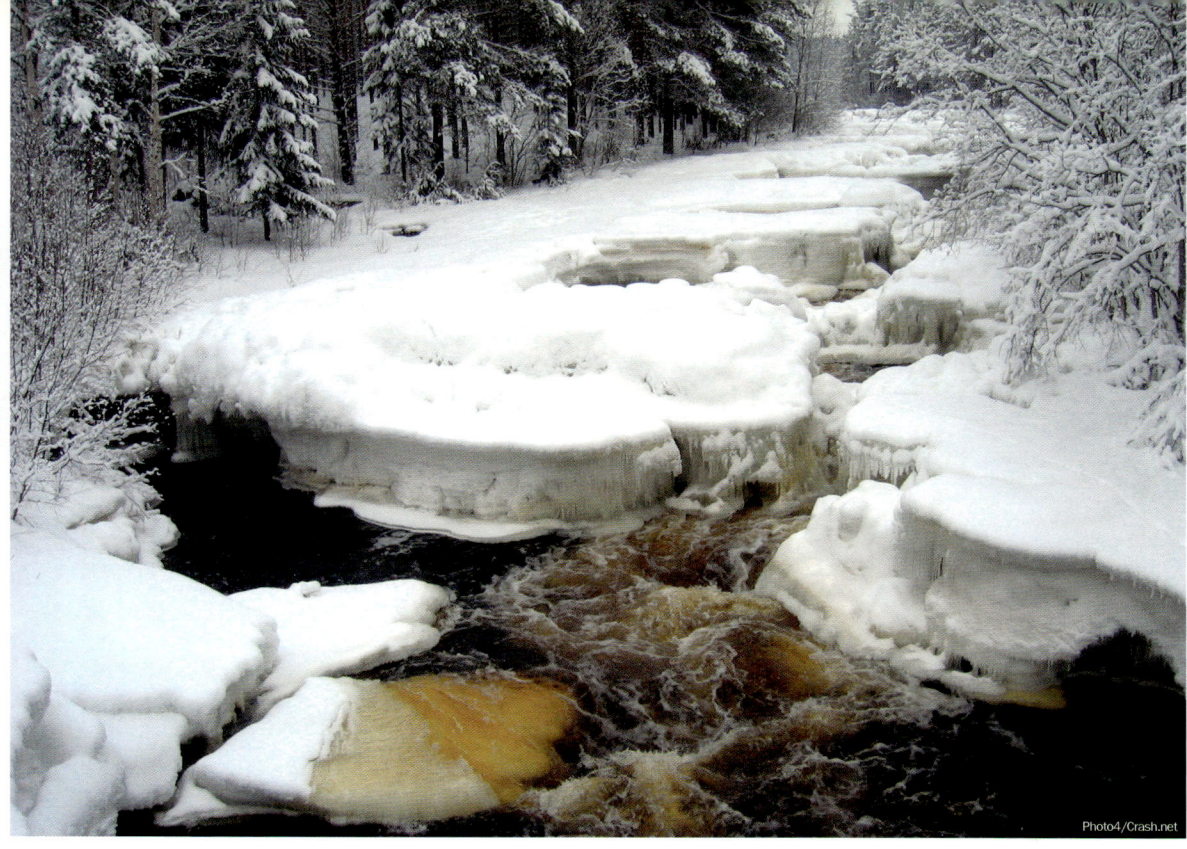

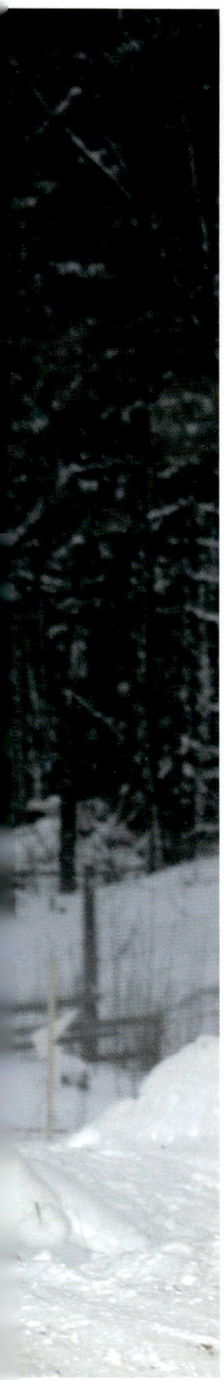

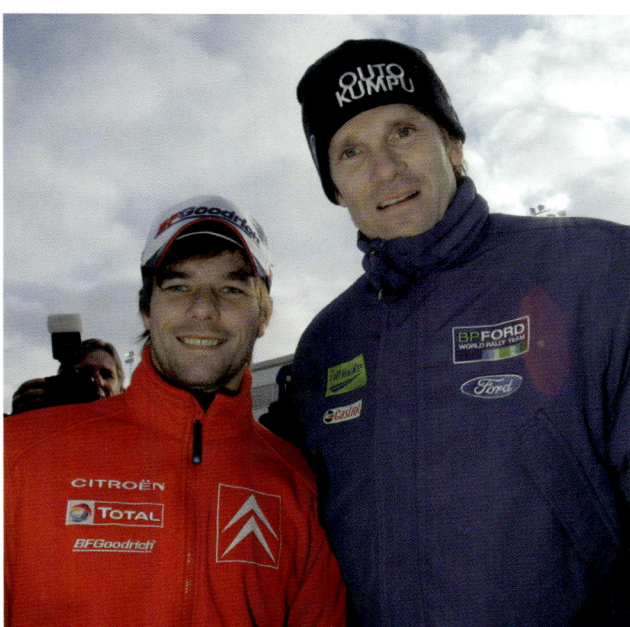

Far Left: Grönholm survived a final-morning mechanical scare to take his first win of the season in the Ford

Above: There was no shortage of snow on this year's Swedish...

Left: Nobody could touch Loeb and Grönholm on this first of two snow rally encounters this season.

Bottom Right: Going off the road and smashing the suspension on his Impreza cost Atkinson four points and kept the team busy

Bottom Left: If this was an event to forget for his brother, Henning Solberg upheld family honour in fourth

All photographs by McKlein unless specified

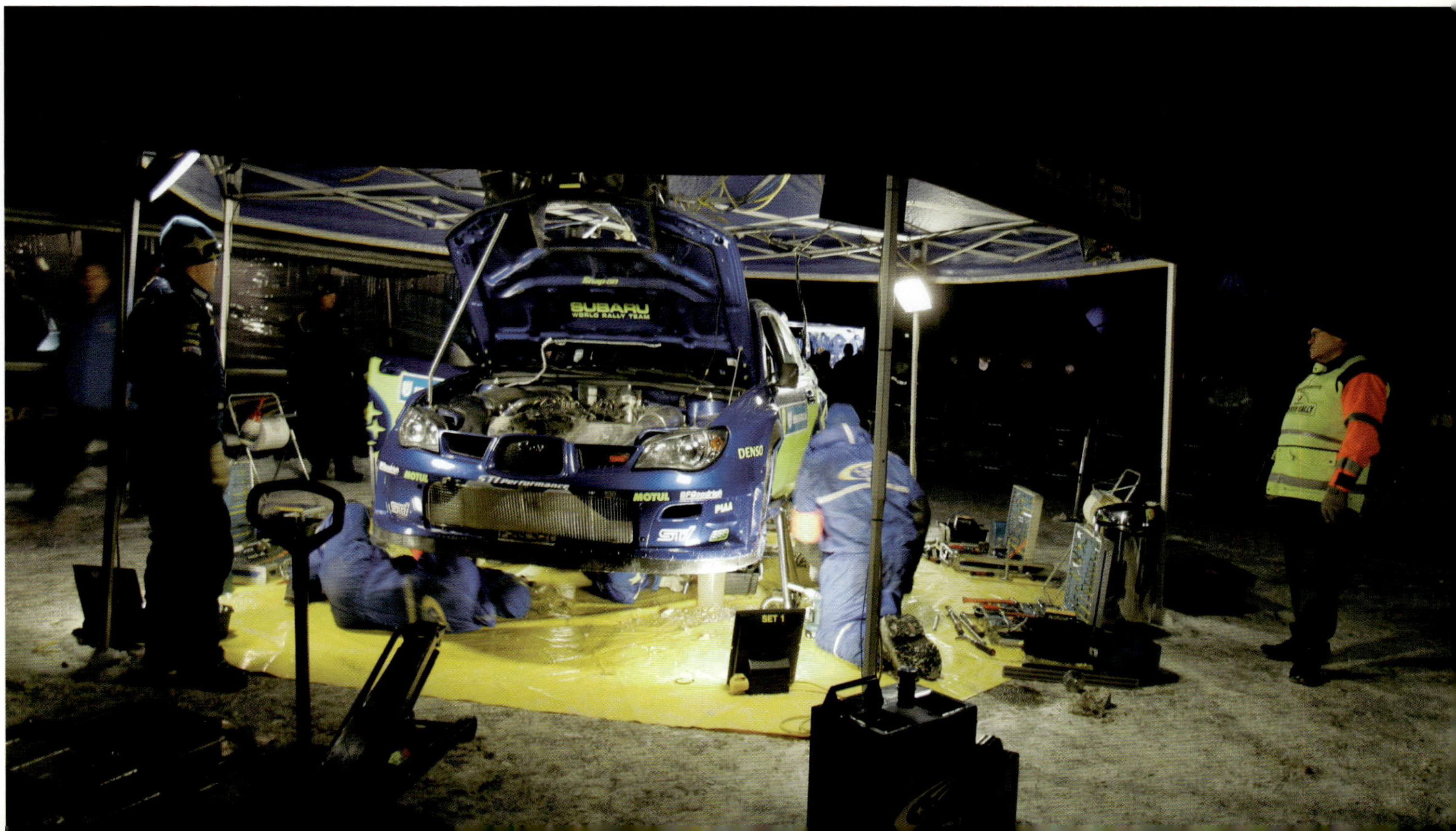

*Svedlund made the most of the post-event exclusion of Hanninen's Mitsubishi, winning Group N in his Impreza*
McKlein

# The FIA World Rally Championship Round 2
# Swedish Rally Results
### February 8-11 2007

### FINISH LINES...

With Solberg in a ditch, all Subaru eyes were on Chris Atkinson. He'd been running fifth for most of the event and looked a safe bet to hold on to those hard-earned four points. That was until he too dropped his Impreza into a ditch. With two stages to run, his car was left limping with broken left-rear suspension and transmission. Fifth turned into eighth... Toni Gardemeister did sterling work to set some cracking times in the 2005 Mitsubishi. He slipped back to sixth, however, when driveshaft problems struck in SS14. Manfred Stohl was seventh, leaving the final point for Atkinson... This event was also the opening round of this year's Production Car WRC and Mitsubishi man Juho Hänninen continued to impress. He won on the road, but was excluded for fuel pump irregularities. That left the door open for Oscar Svedlund (Subaru) to collect his maiden win in the category. Anton Alén led early on, but lost time with a puncture in SS12. He recovered to take second in his Subaru... There were high hopes for the WRC debut of Peugeot's 207 Super 2000, with the car being driven by Swedish privateer Jimmy Joge. Unfortunately for all concerned, the Peugeot only lasted for half of the first serious stage before the transmission cried enough... Argentinian driver Juan Pablo Raies contested the event as part of the Munchi's Ford World Rally Team. Given that this was his snow rally debut, the South American never looked like breaking any records for speed. He did, however, break the speed limit an unprecedented 29 times during the pre-event recce. It wasn't that which got him excluded though - it was not wearing a glove, which he'd lost while changing a wheel before the start of the final stage.

### RUNNING ORDER

| | | |
|---|---|---|
| 1 | Sébastien Loeb/<br>Daniel Elena | Citroën C4 WRC<br>Gr A |
| 2 | Daniel Sordo/<br>Marc Martí | Citroën C4 WRC<br>Gr A |
| 3 | Marcus Grönholm/<br>Timo Rautiainen | Ford Focus RS WRC 06<br>Gr A |
| 8 | Chris Atkinson/<br>Glenn Macneall | Subaru Impreza WRC 2006<br>Gr A |
| 4 | Mikko Hirvonen/<br>Jarmo Lehtinen | Ford Focus RS WRC 06<br>Gr A |
| 7 | Petter Solberg/<br>Phil Mills | Subaru Impreza WRC 2006<br>Gr A |
| 18 | Toni Gardemeister/<br>Jakke Honkanen | Mitsubishi Lancer WRC05<br>Gr A |
| 19 | Jan Kopecky/<br>Filip Schovanek | Skoda Fabia WRC<br>Gr A |
| 5 | Manfred Stohl/<br>Ilka Minor | Citroën Xsara WRC<br>Gr A |
| 10 | Henning Solberg/<br>Cato Menkerud | Ford Focus RS WRC 06<br>Gr A |
| 16 | Matthew Wilson/<br>Michael Orr | Ford Focus RS WRC 06<br>Gr A |
| 17 | Xavier Pons/<br>Xavier Amigo | Mitsubishi Lancer WRC05<br>Gr A |
| 9 | Jari-Matti Latvala/<br>Miikka Anttila | Ford Focus RS WRC 06<br>Gr A |
| 6 | Daniel Carlsson/<br>Denis Giraudet | Citroën Xsara WRC<br>Gr A |
| 21 | Mads Östberg/<br>Ole Unnerud | Subaru Impreza WRC 2005<br>Gr A |
| 25 | Gianluigi Galli/<br>Giovanni Bernacchini | Citroën Xsara WRC<br>Gr A |
| 23 | Patrik Flodin/<br>Maria Andersson | Subaru Impreza WRC 2005<br>Gr A |
| 20 | Thomas Schie/<br>Göran Bergsten | Ford Focus RS WRC 04<br>Gr A |
| 22 | Mats Jonsson/<br>Johnny Johansson | Ford Focus RS WRC 01<br>Gr A |
| 11 | Luis Perez-Companc/<br>José María Volta | Ford Focus RS WRC 06<br>Gr A |
| 12 | Juan Pablo Raies/<br>Jorge Perez-Companc | Ford Focus RS WRC 06<br>Gr A |

### SPECIAL STAGE TIMES

**SS1 Karststad Superspecial 1 (1.89km)**

1 T.Gardemeister/J.Honkanen (Mitsubishi Lancer WRC05) 1m31.9s; 2 M.Grönholm/T.Rautiainen (Ford Focus RS WRC 06) 1m32.4s; 3 P.Solberg/P.Mills (Subaru Impreza WRC 2006) 1m32.5s; 4 M.Hirvonen/J.Lehtinen (Ford Focus RS WRC 06) 1m33.3s; 5 J.M.Latvala/M.Anttila (Ford Focus RS WRC 06) 1m34.1s; 6 P.Flodin/M.Andersson (Subaru Impreza WRC 2005) 1m34.5s; PC A.Alén/T.Alanne (Subaru Impreza WRX Sti) 1m39.2s

**SS2 Likenas 1 (21.78km)**

1 Solberg/Mills (Subaru) 12m40.6s; 2 G.Galli/G.Bernacchini (Citroën Xsara WRC) 12m46.5s; 3 S.Loeb/D.Elena (Citroën C4 WRC) 12m46.6s; 4 Gardemeister/Honkanen (Mitsubishi) 12m46.8s; 5 D.Carlsson/D.Giraudet (Citroën Xsara WRC) 12m47.0s; 6 H.Solberg/C.Menkerud (Ford Focus RS WRC 06) 12m49.6s; PC K.Sohlberg/R.Pietiläinen (Subaru Impreza WRX Sti) 13m29.0s

**SS3 Hara 1 (11.31km)**

1 Galli/Bernacchini (Citroën) 6m22.6s; 2 Solberg/Menkerud (Ford) 6m24.1s; 3 Grönholm/Rautiainen (Ford) 6m24.8s; 4 Loeb/Elena (Citroën) 6m24.9s; 5 Solberg/Mills (Subaru) 6m26.9s; 6 Hirvonen/Lehtinen (Ford) 6m27.9s; PC O.Svedlund/B.Nilsson (Subaru Impreza WRX Sti) 6m45.5s

**SS4 Torntorp 1 (19.20km)**

1 Loeb/Elena (Citroën) 9m56.8s; 2 Grönholm/Rautiainen (Ford) 9m58.0s; 3 Gardemeister/Honkanen (Mitsubishi) 9m59.3s; 4 Solberg/Menkerud (Ford) 10m01.9s; 5 Solberg/Mills (Subaru) 10m02.2s; 6 Hirvonen/Lehtinen (Ford) 10m02.5s; PC J.Hänninen/M.Markkula (Mitsubishi Lancer Evo 9) 10m41.7s

**SS5 Likenas 2 (21.78km)**

1 Grönholm/Rautiainen (Ford) 12m21.5s; 2 Solberg/Mills (Subaru) 12m26.7s; 3 Hirvonen/Lehtinen (Ford) 12m27.9s; 4 Solberg/Menkerud (Ford) 12m29.1s; 5 Gardemeister/Honkanen (Mitsubishi) 12m29.6s; 6 C.Atkinson/G.Macneall (Subaru Impreza WRC 2006) 12m32.6s; PC Sohlberg/Pietiläinen (Subaru) 13m21.9s

**SS6 Hara 2 (11.31km)**

1 Grönholm/Rautiainen (Ford) 6m10.1s; 2 Hirvonen/Lehtinen (Ford) 6m12.3s; 3 Loeb/Elena (Citroën) 6m12.5s; 4 Latvala/Anttila (Ford) 6m13.9s; 5 Solberg/Menkerud (Ford) 6m14.7s; 6 Atkinson/Macneall (Subaru) 6m15.2s; PC Hänninen/Markkula (Mitsubishi), A.Aigner/K.Wicha (Mitsubishi Lancer Evo 9) 6m37.7s

**SS7 Vargasen 1 (24.62km)**

1 Loeb/Elena (Citroën) 13m57.7s; 2 Grönholm/Rautiainen (Ford) 14m03.5s; 3 Carlsson/Giraudet (Citroën) 14m08.9s; 4 Solberg/Menkerud (Ford) 14m09.3s 5 Hirvonen/Lehtinen (Ford) 14m10.0s; 6 Solberg/Mills (Subaru) 14m16.3s; PC Hänninen/Markkula (Mitsubishi), M.Prokop/J.Tomanek (Mitsubishi Lancer Evo 9) 14m44.2s

**SS8 Hagfors Sprint 1 (1.87km)**

1 Grönholm/Rautiainen (Ford) 2m00.0s; 2 Loeb/Elena (Citroën) 2m00.3s; 3 Solberg/Mills (Subaru) 2m01.5s; 4 Carlsson/Giraudet (Citroën) 2m01.6s; 5 D.Sordo/M.Martí (Citroën C4 WRC) 2m01.9s; 6 Hirvonen/Lehtinen (Ford) 2m02.1s; PC Hänninen/Markkula (Mitsubishi) 2m05.7s

**SS9 Lesjofors (10.48km)**

1 Loeb/Elena (Citroën) 5m45.1s; 2 Grönholm/Rautiainen (Ford) 5m46.3s; 3 Solberg/Mills (Subaru) 5m49.6s; 4 Hirvonen/Lehtinen (Ford) 5m53.5s; 5 Solberg/Menkerud (Ford) 5m54.5s; 6 Atkinson/Macneall (Subaru) 5m55.7s; PC Sohlberg/Pietiläinen (Subaru) 6m14.3s

**SS10 Liljendal (34.54km)**

1 Grönholm/Rautiainen (Peugeot) 17m50.3s; 2 Loeb/Elena (Citroën) 17m50.9s; 3 Gardemeister/Honkanen (Mitsubishi) 17m58.4s; 4 Hirvonen/Lehtinen (Ford) 17m59.3s; 5 Solberg/Menkerud (Ford) 18m01.1s; 6 Atkinson/Macneall (Subaru) 18m11.4s; PC Alén/Alanne (Subaru) 19m11.9s

**SS11 Torntorp 2 (19.20km)**

1 Grönholm/Rautiainen (Ford) 9m35.0s; 2 Gardemeister/Honkanen (Mitsubishi) 9m42.6s; 3 Hirvonen/Lehtinen (Ford) 9m43.4s; 4 Loeb/Elena (Citroën) 9m44.6s; 5 Solberg/Menkerud (Ford) 9m49.1s; 6

# UDDEHOLM SWEDISH RALLY

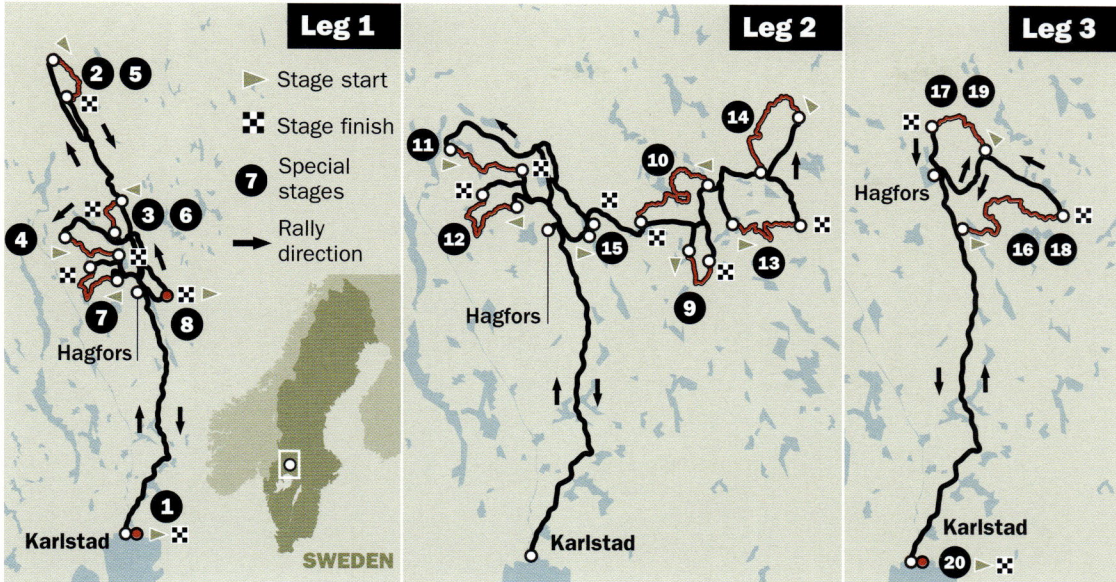

| | | | |
|---|---|---|---|
| 2 | Sébastien Loeb/ | Citroën C4 WRC | |
| | Daniel Elena | 3h09m34.5s | Gr A |
| 3 | Mikko Hirvonen/ | Ford Focus RS WRC 06 | |
| | Jarmo Lehtinen | 3h10m22.2s | Gr A |
| 4 | Henning Solberg/ | Ford Focus RS WRC 06 | |
| | Cato Menkerud | 3h10m50.5s | Gr A |
| 5 | Daniel Carlsson / | Citroën Xsara WRC | |
| | Denis Giraudet | 3h12m18.5s | Gr A |
| 6 | Toni Gardemeister/ | Mitsubishi Lancer WRC05 | |
| | Jakke Honkanen | 3h12m34.9s | Gr A |
| 7 | Manfred Stohl/ | Citroën Xsara WRC | |
| | Ilka Minor | 3h13m53.2s | Gr A |
| 8 | Chris Atkinson/ | Subaru Impreza WRC 2006 | |
| | Glenn Macneall | 3h14m55.4s | Gr A |
| 9 | Mads Östberg/ | Subaru Impreza WRC 2005 | |
| | Ole Unnerud | 3h16m27.7s | Gr A |
| 10 | Jan Kopecky/ | Skoda Fabia WRC | |
| | Filip Schovanek | 3h16m33.2s | Gr A |
| 58 starters, 43 finishers | | | |

### RECENT WINNERS

| | | |
|---|---|---|
| 1965 | Tom Trana/Gunnar Thermenius | Volvo 544 |
| 1966 | Ake Andersson/Sven-Olof Svedberg | Saab 96 |
| 1967 | Bengt Soderström/Gunnar Palm | Ford Lotus Cortina |
| 1968 | Björn Waldegård/Lars Helmer | Porsche 911T |
| 1969 | Björn Waldegård/Lars Helmer | Porsche 911S |
| 1970 | Björn Waldegård/Lars Helmer | Porsche 911S |
| 1971 | Stig Blomqvist/Arne Hertz | Saab 96 V4 |
| 1972 | Stig Blomqvist/Arne Hertz | Saab 96 V4 |
| 1973 | Stig Blomqvist/Arne Hertz | Saab 96 V4 |
| 1975 | Björn Waldegård/Hans Thorszelius | Lancia Stratos |
| 1976 | Per Eklund/Björn Cederberg | Saab 96 V4 |
| 1977 | Stig Blomqvist/Hans Sylvan | Saab 99 EMS |
| 1978 | Björn Waldegård/Hans Thorszelius | Ford Escort RS |
| 1979 | Stig Blomqvist/Björn Cederberg | Saab 99 Turbo |
| 1980 | Anders Kullang/Bruno Berglund | Opel Ascona 400 |
| 1981 | Hannu Mikkola/Arne Hertz | Audi Quattro |
| 1982 | Stig Blomqvist/Björn Cederberg | Audi Quattro A1 |
| 1983 | Hannu Mikkola/Arne Hertz | Audi Quattro A1 |
| 1984 | Stig Blomqvist/Björn Cederberg | Audi Quattro A2 |
| 1985 | Ari Vatanen/Terry Harryman | Peugeot 205 Turbo 16 |
| 1986 | Juha Kankkunen/Juha Piironen | Peugeot 205 Turbo 16 E2 |
| 1987 | Timo Salonen/Seppo Harjanne | Mazda 323 Turbo |
| 1988 | Markku Alén/Ilkka Kivimäki | Lancia Delta HF 4x4 |
| 1989 | Ingvar Carlsson/Per Carlsson | Mazda 323 Turbo |
| 1990 | Event cancelled | |
| 1991 | Kenneth Eriksson/Staffan Parmander | Mitsubishi Galant VR-4 |
| 1992 | Mats Jonsson/Lars Bäckman | Toyota Celica GT4 |
| 1993 | Mats Jonsson/Lars Bäckman | Toyota Celica Turbo 4wd |
| 1994 | Thomas Rådström/Lars Bäckman | Toyota Celica Turbo 4wd |
| 1995 | Kenneth Eriksson/Staffan Parmander | Mitsubishi Lancer RS-E2 |
| 1996 | Tommi Mäkinen/Seppo Harjanne | Mitsubishi Lancer RS-E3 |
| 1997 | Kenneth Eriksson/Staffan Parmander | Subaru Impreza WRC97 |
| 1998 | Tommi Mäkinen/Risto Mannisenmäki | Mitsubishi Lancer E4 |
| 1999 | Tommi Mäkinen/Risto Mannisenmäki | Mitsubishi Lancer E6 |
| 2000 | Marcus Grönholm/Timo Rautiainen | Peugeot 206 WRC |
| 2001 | Harri Rovanperä/Risto Pietiläinen | Peugeot 206 WRC |
| 2002 | Marcus Grönholm/Timo Rautiainen | Peugeot 206 WRC |
| 2003 | Marcus Grönholm/Timo Rautiainen | Peugeot 206 WRC |
| 2004 | Sébastien Loeb/Daniel Elena | Citroën Xsara WRC |
| 2005 | Petter Solberg/Phil Mills | Subaru Impreza WRC 2004 |
| 2006 | Marcus Grönholm/Timo Rautiainen | Ford Focus RS WRC 06 |

---

Solberg/Mills (Subaru) 9m49.8s; PC Hänninen/Markkula (Mitsubishi) 10m29.2s

**SS12 Vargasen 2 (24.62km)**
1 Grönholm/Rautiainen (Ford) 13m17.9s; 2 Hirvonen/Lehtinen (Ford) 13m24.7s; 3 Loeb/Elena (Citroën) 13m25.4s; 4 Solberg/Menkerud (Ford) 13m29.8s; 5 Carlsson/Giraudet (Citroën) 13m33.0s; 6 Gardemeister/Honkanen (Mitsubishi) 13m34.2s; PC Hänninen/Markkula (Mitsubishi) 14m24.8s

**SS13 Fredriksberg (24.75km)**
1 Grönholm/Rautiainen (Ford) 13m54.4s; 2 Solberg/Menkerud (Ford) 13m57.4s; 3 Hirvonen/Lehtinen (Ford) 13m57.9s; 4 Loeb/Elena (Citroën) 14m01.3s; 5= Gardemeister/Honkanen (Mitsubishi), M.Jonsson/J.Johansson (Ford Focus RS WRC 01) 14m04.2s; PC Alén/Alanne (Subaru) 15m02.1s

**SS14 Lejen (26.46km)**
1 Grönholm/Rautiainen (Ford) 14m41.8s; 2 Loeb/Elena (Citroën) 14m44.9s; 3 Hirvonen/Lehtinen (Ford) 14m50.6s; 4 Atkinson/Macneall (Subaru) 14m58.5s; 5 Latvala/Anttila (Ford) 15m00.8s; 6 J.Kopecky/F.Schovanek (Skoda Fabia WRC) 15m04.3s; PC Alén/Alanne (Subaru), Hänninen/Markkula (Mitsubishi) 15m47.1s

**SS15 Hagfors Sprint 2 (1.87km)**
1 M.Östberg/O.Unnerud (Subaru Impreza WRC 2005) 1m59.3s; 2 Latvala/Anttila (Ford) 2m00.7s; 3 T.Schie/G.Bergsten (Ford Focus RS WRC 04) 2m00.8s; 4 Kopecky/Schovanek (Skoda) 2m01.1s; 5 Hirvonen/Lehtinen (Ford) 2m01.3s; 6 Gardemeister/Honkanen (Mitsubishi) 2m01.9s; PC Hänninen/Markkula (Mitsubishi) 2m06.2s

**SS16 Backa 1 (30.95km)**
1 Atkinson/Macneall (Subaru) 16m31.6s; 2 Grönholm/Rautiainen (Ford) 16m32.9s; 3 Loeb/Elena (Citroën) 16m35.0s; 4 Hirvonen/Lehtinen (Ford) 16m36.5s; 5 Gardemeister/Honkanen (Mitsubishi) 16m38.5s; 6 Carlsson/Giraudet (Citroën) 16m42.3s; PC Hänninen/Markkula (Mitsubishi) 17m45.2s

**SS17 Malta 1 (11.25km)**
1 Solberg/Menkerud (Ford) 5m42.2s; 2 Grönholm/Rautiainen (Ford) 5m43.4s; 3 Loeb/Elena (Citroën) 5m44.9s; 4 Galli/Bernacchini (Citroën) 5m46.0s; 5 Atkinson/Macneall (Subaru) 5m46.7s; 6 Carlsson/Giraudet (Citroën) 5m47.6s; PC Alén/Alanne (Subaru), M.Baldacci/G.Agnese (Mitsubishi Lancer Evo 9) 6m14.7s

**SS18 Backa 2 (30.95km)**
1 Grönholm/Rautiainen (Ford) 16m30.0s; 2 Loeb/Elena (Citroën) 16m35.8s; 3 Gardemeister/Honkanen (Mitsubishi) 16m38.4s; 4 Solberg/Menkerud (Ford) 16m40.0s; 5 Hirvonen/Lehtinen (Ford) 16m40.1s; 6 Carlsson/Giraudet (Citroën) 16m44.5s; PC Hänninen/Markkula (Mitsubishi) 17m39.6s

**SS19 Malta 2 (11.25km)**
1 Grönholm/Rautiainen (Ford) 5m44.1s; 2 Loeb/Elena (Citroën) 5m46.1s; 3 Solberg/Menkerud (Ford) 5m47.8s; 4 Hirvonen/Lehtinen (Ford) 5m48.4s; 5 Gardemeister/Honkanen (Mitsubishi) 5m49.7s; 6 Sordo/Marti (Citroën) 5m52.0s; PC Hänninen/Markkula (Mitsubishi) 6m05.9s

**SS20 Karlstad Superspecial 2 (1.89km)**
1 Grönholm/Rautiainen (Ford) 1m40.7s; 2 Gardemeister/Honkanen (Mitsubishi) 1m42.2s; 3 Flodin/Andersson (Subaru) 1m42.3s; 4 Carlsson/Giraudet (Citroën) 1m43.2s; 5 L.Perez-Companc/J-M.Volta (Ford Focus RS WRC 06) 1m43.8s; 6 JP.Raies/J.Perez-Companc (Ford Focus RS WRC 06) 1m44.1s; PC Hänninen/Markkula (Mitsubishi) 1m44.3s

*Cars who retired and subsequently restarted and were classified under SupeRally regs:*
22 Jonsson/Johansson Ford Focus RS WRC 01
Steering SS11 Gr A

### MAJOR RETIREMENTS

| 7 | Solberg/Mills | Subaru Impreza WRC 2006 | | |
|---|---|---|---|---|
| | Withdrawn | SS12 | | Gr A |
| 16 | Wilson/Orr | Ford Focus RS WRC 06 | | |
| | Engine | SS16 | | Gr A |
| 17 | Pons/Amigo | Mitsubishi Lancer WRC05 | | |
| | Accident | SS5 | | Gr A |
| 9 | Latvala/Anttila | Ford Focus RS WRC 06 | | |
| | Engine | SS16 | | Gr A |
| 12 | Raies/Perez-Companc | Ford Focus RS WRC 06 | | |
| | Excluded | SS20 | | Gr A |

### FIA CLASS WINNERS

| A8 | Over 2000cc | Grönholm/Rautiainen Ford Focus RS WRC06 |
|---|---|---|
| A6 | 1600-2000cc | Strand/Ellison Citroën C2 |
| N4 | Over 2000cc | Svedlund/Nilsson Subaru Impreza WRX Sti |
| N3 | 1600-2000cc | Eriksson/Svensson Ford Fiesta ST |
| N2 | 1400-1600cc | Hytönen/Larsson Suzuki Ignis Sport |

### RALLY LEADERS
Overall: SS1 Gardemeister; SS2-4 P.Solberg; SS5-20 Grönholm
PC: SS1 Alén; SS2-13 Sohlberg; SS14-20 Hänninen

### SPECIAL STAGE ANALYSIS

| | 1st | 2nd | 3rd | 4th | 5th | 6th |
|---|---|---|---|---|---|---|
| Grönholm (Ford) | 11 | 6 | 1 | - | - | - |
| Loeb (Citroën) | 3 | 5 | 5 | 3 | - | - |
| Gardemeister (Mitsubishi) | 1 | 2 | 3 | 1 | 4 | 2 |
| H.Solberg (Ford) | 1 | 2 | 1 | 5 | 4 | 1 |
| P.Solberg (Subaru) | 1 | 1 | 3 | - | 2 | 2 |
| Galli (Citroën) | 1 | 1 | - | 1 | - | - |
| Atkinson (Subaru) | 1 | - | 1 | 1 | 1 | 4 |

---

Östberg (Subaru) 1 - - - -
Hirvonen (Ford) - 2 4 5 3 3
Latvala (Ford) - 1 - 1 2 -
Carlsson (Citroën) - - 1 2 2 3
Flodin (Subaru) - - 1 - - 1
Schie (Ford) - - 1 - - -
Kopecky (Skoda) - - - 1 - 1
Sordo (Citroën) - - - - 1 1
Jonsson (Ford) - - - - 1 -
Perez-Companc (Ford) - - - - 1 -
Raies (Ford) - - - - - 1

### WORLD CHAMPIONSHIP POINTS
**Drivers**
1 Loeb 18; 2 Grönholm 16; 3 Hirvonen 10; 4 Sordo 8; 5 Atkinson 6; 6= H.Solberg, Gardemeister 5; 8 Carlsson 4; 9 P.Solberg; 10 Stohl 2 etc

**Manufacturers**
1 Citroën Total WRT 27; 2 BP-Ford WRT 26; 3 Subaru WRT 10; 4 OMV-Kronos Citroën WRT 9; 5 Stobart M-Sport Ford RT 6

**Production Cup**
1 Svedlund 10; 2 Alén 8; 3 Sohlberg 6; 4 Aroujo 5; 5 Nutahara 4; 6 Arai 3; 7 Al Attiyah 2; 8 Frisiero 1

### ROUTE DETAILS
Total route of 1389.16km of which 341.20km were competitive on 20 stages
**Leg 1** Thursday 8-Friday 9 February, 8 Special Stages totalling 114.07km
**Leg 2** Saturday 10 February, 7 Special Stages totalling 142.63km
**Leg 3** Sunday 11 February, 5 Special Stages totalling 84.50km

### RESULTS
1 Marcus Grönholm/ Ford Focus RS WRC 06
  Timo Rautiainen 3h08m40.7s Gr A

| Position | Stage Numbers | 1 | 2 | 3 | 4 | 5 | 6 | 7 | 8 | 9 | 10 | 11 | 12 | 13 | 14 | 15 | 16 | 17 | 18 | 19 | 20 |
|---|---|---|---|---|---|---|---|---|---|---|---|---|---|---|---|---|---|---|---|---|---|
| | Grönholm | 2 | 4 | 4 | 2 | 1 | 2 | 1 | 1 | 1 | 1 | 1 | 1 | 1 | 1 | 1 | 1 | 1 | 1 | 1 | 1 |
| | Loeb | 20 | 9 | 6 | 4 | 5 | 3 | 2 | 2 | 2 | 2 | 2 | 2 | 2 | 2 | 2 | 2 | 2 | 2 | 2 | 2 |
| | Hirvonen | 4 | 10 | 10 | 8 | 6 | 6 | 5 | 5 | 5 | 4 | 3 | 3 | 3 | 3 | 3 | 3 | 3 | 3 | 3 | 3 |
| | H.Solberg | 10 | 5 | 5 | 6 | 4 | 4 | 4 | 4 | 4 | 3 | 4 | 4 | 4 | 4 | 4 | 4 | 4 | 4 | 4 | 4 |
| | Carlsson | 19 | 8 | 9 | 7 | 7 | 8 | 7 | 7 | 7 | 6 | 6 | 6 | 6 | 5 | 5 | 6 | 6 | 5 | 5 | 5 |
| | Gardemeister | 1 | 2 | 3 | 3 | 3 | 5 | 6 | 6 | 6 | 5 | 5 | 5 | 5 | 8 | 7 | 7 | 7 | 7 | 6 | 6 |
| | Stohl | 7 | 5 | 7 | 9 | 9 | 9 | 8 | 9 | 8 | 8 | 7 | 7 | 8 | 7 | 8 | 8 | 7 | 7 | 7 | 7 |
| | Atkinson | 13 | 11 | 11 | 11 | 10 | 10 | 9 | 9 | 9 | 7 | 8 | 8 | 7 | 6 | 6 | 5 | 5 | 6 | 8 | 8 |
| | Östberg | 11 | 15 | 15 | 14 | 12 | 12 | 11 | 11 | 11 | 10 | 10 | 10 | 11 | 10 | 9 | 9 | 9 | 9 | 9 | 9 |
| | Kopecky | 16 | 14 | 14 | 13 | 13 | 13 | 13 | 13 | 12 | 11 | 11 | 11 | 10 | 11 | 10 | 10 | 10 | 10 | 10 | 10 |
| | Flodin | 6 | 12 | 12 | 12 | 11 | 11 | 12 | 12 | 13 | 12 | 12 | 12 | 12 | 12 | 11 | 11 | 11 | 11 | 11 | 11 |
| | Sordo | 7 | 46 | 42 | 36 | 25 | 25 | 23 | 23 | 21 | 17 | 15 | 14 | 15 | 15 | 16 | 13 | 14 | 13 | 12 | 12 |
| | Galli | 9 | 3 | 2 | 5 | 8 | 20 | 24 | 18 | 16 | 14 | 14 | 14 | 14 | 17 | 14 | 13 | 12 | 13 | 13 | 13 |
| | Perez-Companc | 15 | 13 | 13 | 16 | 16 | 17 | 24 | 17 | 17 | 16 | 17 | 16 | 17 | 16 | 15 | 15 | 15 | 15 | 15 | 15 |
| | Raies | 58 | 54 | 51 | 49 | 47 | 44 | 42 | 40 | 40 | 38 | 36 | 37 | 34 | 33 | 33 | 28 | 28 | 25 | 25 | Ex |
| | Latvala | 5 | 7 | 8 | 10 | 8 | 7 | 10 | 10 | 10 | 9 | 9 | 9 | 9 | 9 | 9 | R | | | | |
| | Wilson | 17 | 17 | 18 | 17 | 15 | 15 | 16 | 16 | 16 | 14 | 14 | 16 | 16 | 17 | 14 | R | | | | |
| | P.Solberg | 3 | 1 | 1 | 1 | 2 | 2 | 3 | 3 | 3 | 34 | 33 | 31 | R | | | | | | | |
| | Pons | 30 | 56 | 56 | 53 | R | | | | | | | | | | | | | | | |

*Above:* Hirvonen was on inspired form to win the first ever WRC round in Norway

*Above right:* A week after Grönholm had dominated in Sweden, he was unable to match his team-mate across the border

*Right:* Henning Solberg gave home fans plenty to cheer, beating his brother Petter to the final podium spot

**All photographs by McKlein unless specified**

## The FIA World Rally Championship Round 3
# Rally Norway

IN the days between the Swedish and Norway rallies, Ford man Mikko Hirvonen talked of his frustration at a missed opportunity. It wasn't like the 26-year-old had been leading Sweden and then gone off. Nor had he been robbed by any kind of mechanical trouble. No, Hirvonen's malcontent lay solely with himself. In Norway, he would put that right. He was determined.

Hirvonen's co-driver Jarmo Lehtinen admitted he was bracing himself in the run-up to the event. "It's flat out for this one," he said. "I'm just going to read the notes and hold on!"

And that's just how it played out. Hirvonen caned the Focus from the second the lights turned green on stage one. This was a new event for everybody. Here and now, experience counted for absolutely nothing. Hirvonen was on sublime form. For three days, in astonishingly tricky conditions, he played with two of the finest drivers ever to grace the world championship; two drivers with 55 world rally wins and five drivers' titles between them: Sébastien Loeb and Marcus Grönholm. Try as they might, the winners of rounds one and two couldn't get close to Hirvonen, who had won one round of the championship. Loeb, in fact, twice binned his Citroën C4 WRC trying to catch the flying Ford. That's right. The unthinkable happened to the triple champion as he wedged the WRC's latest rally weapon in a snow bank on successive stages, spending eight minutes digging it out each time. Every time one of the other two went fastest, Hirvonen didn't panic. He merely picked his moment, wound the Focus up and pulled himself a couple of seconds clear again. It was inspirational stuff; a champion's drive if ever there was one.

Sunday night in Hamar was a joyous place for Ford, Hirvonen and the WRC. Some serious celebrating was done. Hirvonen had come of age in the finest fashion. Ford team principal Malcolm Wilson was smiling almost as much as his winner. As well he might - Grönholm and Henning Solberg backed up Hirvonen to ensure Ford of its first one-two-three in the world championship since the 1979 Rally New Zealand.

As Grönholm had tackled the Galway Rally in Ireland the week before Sweden, this event was his third on the bounce - and he admitted he was tired and ready for a break. On top of that, he felt his notes weren't entirely trustworthy. He hastened to add that these weren't excuses. All credit, in his words, to Mikko. His younger countryman had done the job. The Solbergs had been engaged in their own battle on the final day. Henning won through, despite panic setting in after he stalled the Ford at the start of the final stage, handing 10 seconds of a 17-second advantage to Petter. In the end it didn't matter. There was a Solberg on the podium, and that the driver was in orange not blue wasn't about to stop the nation's rally fans celebrating. The Subaru Solberg was fourth, following strict orders to bring the car home in one piece after failing to finish the previous round in Sweden.

RALLY NORWAY

Bottom left: Predictably, fourth-placed Solberg failed to deliver what would have been a dream home win for the former champ

Opposite left: Galli showed he'd lost none of his speed, sixth in a private Xsara

Left: Latvala set a fastest time on his way to fifth for the Stobart team

Below: Uncharacteristically, Loeb went off the road twice trying to catch the Fords

Bottom: Heavy snow falls made the correct stud length vital for the WRC's inaugural Norwegian trip

All photographs by McKlein

Andersson was untouchable among the Junior ranks, taking his first win of the season
McKlein

## The FIA World Rally Championship Round 3
# Rally Norway Results
### February 16-18 2007

### FINISH LINES...

Rally Norway was the first of the FIA Candidate rallies to run this season - and, privately, it received a favourable report from those watching from the world of officialdom. The event ran without any major problems and the roads - particularly The Mountain stage - received unanimous applause from the drivers... Suzuki driver Per-Gunnar Andersson began his fourth season with the Japanese team with a repeat of the round one win he scored in last year's Junior championship. The Swede's masterly control of his Swift in the snow was only momentarily lost, when he suffered a 360-degree spin in stage six. Once the win was safely in the bag, the former Junior champion grinned at the memory of the incident. "We knocked it down a couple of gears and carried on! It was quite exciting." That, however, was as exciting as it got. When his team-mate Urmo Aava, new to the factory team for this year, clipped a tree stump just under a mile into stage six he damaged the suspension and transmission and was forced to continue under SupeRally - although he did recover to clinch a class podium by the end. In the meantime, Andersson was left with a yawning gap between himself and second-placed driver Patrik Sandell, who ended the event seven minutes behind... This was the first event for the Renault Clio R3. Sandell admitted he had been changing the car's set-up throughout the rally and, despite the gap between himself and Andersson, he was happy with the two-litre machine.

### RUNNING ORDER

| | | |
|---|---|---|
| 1 | Sébastien Loeb/ | Citroën C4 WRC |
| | Daniel Elena | Gr A |
| 3 | Marcus Grönholm/ | Ford Focus RS WRC 06 |
| | Timo Rautiainen | Gr A |
| 4 | Mikko Hirvonen/ | Ford Focus RS WRC 06 |
| | Jarmo Lehtinen | Gr A |
| 2 | Daniel Sordo/ | Citroën C4 WRC |
| | Marc Martí | Gr A |
| 8 | Chris Atkinson/ | Subaru Impreza WRC 2006 |
| | Glenn Macneall | Gr A |
| 10 | Henning Solberg/ | Ford Focus RS WRC 06 |
| | Cato Menkerud | Gr A |
| 21 | Toni Gardemeister/ | Mitsubishi Lancer WRC05 |
| | Jakke Honkanen | Gr A |
| 6 | Daniel Carlsson/ | Citroën Xsara WRC |
| | Denis Giraudet | Gr A |
| 7 | Petter Solberg/ | Subaru Impreza WRC 2006 |
| | Phil Mills | Gr A |
| 5 | Manfred Stohl/ | Citroën Xsara WRC |
| | Ilka Minor | Gr A |
| 20 | Jan Kopecky/ | Skoda Fabia WRC |
| | Filip Schovanek | Gr A |
| 9 | Jari-Matti Latvala/ | Ford Focus RS WRC 06 |
| | Miikka Anttila | Gr A |
| 19 | Gianluigi Galli/ | Citroën Xsara WRC |
| | Giovanni Bernacchini | Gr A |
| 23 | Mads Østberg/ | Subaru Impreza WRC 2005 |
| | Ole Unnerud | Gr A |
| 18 | Thomas Schie/ | Ford Focus RS WRC 04 |
| | Göran Bergsten | Gr A |
| 25 | Juha Hänninen/ | Mitsubishi Lancer WRC05 |
| | Mikko Markkula | |
| 22 | Xavier Pons/ | Mitsubishi Lancer WRC05 |
| | Xavier Amigo | Gr A |
| 16 | Matthew Wilson/ | Ford Focus RS WRC 06 |
| | Michael Orr | Gr A |
| 24 | Anders Grøndal/ | Subaru Impreza WRC 2005 |
| | Trond Inge Ostbye | Gr A |
| 17 | Andreas Mikkelsen/ | Ford Focus RS WRC 04 |
| | Ola Floene | Gr A |
| 26 | Rune Dalsjø/ | Subaru Impreza WRC 2005 |
| | Jens Olav Løvhøiden | Gr A |
| 27 | Tord Linnerud/ | Peugeot 206 WRC |
| | Ragnar Engen | Gr A |
| 28 | Guy Wilks/ | Ford Focus RS WRC 04 |
| | Phil Pugh | Gr A |

### SPECIAL STAGE TIMES

**SS1 Loten 1 (30.03km)**
1 M.Hirvonen/J.Lehtinen (Ford Focus RS WRC 06) 16m14.1s; 2 M.Grönholm/T.Rautiainen (Ford Focus RS WRC 06) 16m25.3s; 3 J-M.Latvala/M.Anttila (Ford Focus RS WRC 06) 16m25.7s; 4 S.Loeb/D.Elena (Citroën C4 WRC) 16m31.1s; 5 T.Gardemeister/J.Honkanen (Mitsubishi Lancer WRC05) 16m31.9s; 6 P.Solberg/P.Mills (Subaru Impreza WRC 2006) 16m33.0s; JWC P-G.Andersson/J.Andersson (Suzuki Swift) 17m47.9s

**SS2 Haslemoen (11.92km)**
1 Loeb/Elena (Citroën) 8m08.4s; 2 Grönholm/Rautiainen (Ford) 8m10.3s; 3 Hirvonen/Lehtinen (Ford) 8m13.0s; 4 H.Solberg/C.Menkerud (Ford Focus RS WRC 06) 8m14.7s; 5 Gardemeister/Honkanen (Mitsubishi) 8m17.9s; 6 Solberg/Mills (Subaru) 8m18.5s; JWC Andersson/Andersson (Suzuki) 9m08.4s

**SS3 Loten 2 (30.03km)**
1 Hirvonen/Lehtinen (Ford) 16m09.9s; 2 Grönholm/Rautiainen (Ford) 16m10.6s; 3 G.Galli/G.Bernacchini (Citroën Xsara WRC) 16m20.0s; 4 Solberg/Menkerud (Ford) 16m21.6s; 5 Loeb/Elena (Citroën) 16m25.5s; 6 Latvala/Anttila (Ford) 16m27.8s; JWC U.Aava/K.Sikk (Suzuki Swift) 17m48.2s

**SS4 Grue (14.36km)**
1 Loeb/Elena (Citroën) 7m31.8s; 2 Galli/Bernacchini (Citroën) 7m32.7s; 3 Hirvonen/Lehtinen (Ford) 7m33.1s; 4 Solberg/Mills (Subaru) 7m33.4s; 5 Grönholm/Rautiainen (Ford) 7m34.9s; 6 Gardemeister/Honkanen (Mitsubishi) 7m36.6s; JWC Andersson/Andersson (Suzuki) 8m00.3s

**SS5 Opaker (14.64km)**
1 Latvala/Anttila (Ford) 7m59.8s; 2= Grönholm/Rautiainen (Ford), Loeb/Elena (Citroën) 8m03.8s; 4 Hirvonen/Lehtinen (Ford) 8m04.0s; 5 Galli/Bernacchini (Citroën) 8m07.9s; 6 M.Stohl/I.Minor (Citroën Xsara WRC) 8m08.9s; JWC Andersson/Andersson (Suzuki) 8m51.4s

**SS6 Kongsvinger (14.06km)**
1 Loeb/Elena (Citroën) 9m44.5s; 2 Hirvonen/Lehtinen (Ford) 9m47.7s; 3 Grönholm/Rautiainen (Ford) 9m50.2s; 4 Solberg/Mills (Subaru) 9m51.7s; 5 Latvala/Anttila (Ford) 9m53.2s; 6 J.Hänninen/M.Markkula (Mitsubishi Lancer WRC05) 9m59.5s; JWC Andersson/Andersson (Suzuki) 11m06.8s

**SS7 Finnskogen (21.29km)**
1 Loeb/Elena (Citroën) 12m42.3s; 2 Latvala/Anttila (Ford) 12m43.1s; 3 Hirvonen/Lehtinen (Ford) 12m45.8s; 4 Solberg/Mills (Subaru) 12m46.0s; 5 Grönholm/Rautiainen (Ford) 12m47.6s; 6 Solberg/Menkerud (Ford) 12m49.3s JWC Andersson/Andersson (Suzuki), Aava/Sikk (Suzuki) 13m55.0s

**SS8 Kirkanaer (6.75km)**
1 Loeb/Elena (Citroën) 5m48.9s; 2 Hirvonen/Lehtinen (Ford) 5m51.4s; 3 Grönholm/Rautiainen (Ford) 5m51.8s; 4 Solberg/Mills (Subaru) 5m55.5s; 5 D.Sordo/M.Martí (Citroën C4 WRC) 5m56.2s; 6 Solberg/Menkerud (Ford) 5m58.0s; JWC P.Sandell/E.Axelsson (Renault Clio) 6m25.2s

**SS9 Eleverum 1 (44.27km)**
1 Hirvonen/Lehtinen (Ford) 24m40.3s; 2 Grönholm/Rautiainen (Ford) 24m45.4s; 3 Loeb/Elena (Citroën) 24m54.5s; 4 Solberg/Mills (Subaru) 25m35.6s; 5 Latvala/Anttila (Ford) 25m40.6s; 6 X.Pons/X.Amigo (Mitsubishi Lancer WRC05) 25m44.9s; JWC Aava/Sikk (Suzuki) 27m25.6s

**SS10 Terningmoen (12.71km)**
1 Loeb/Elena (Citroën) 7m59.1s; 2 Grönholm/Rautiainen (Peugeot) 8m02.7s; 3 Hirvonen/Lehtinen (Ford) 8m03.6s; 4 Gardemeister/Honkanen (Mitsubishi) 8m06.4s; 5 Solberg/Mills (Subaru) 8m12.2s; 6 J.Kopecky/F.Schovanek (Skoda Fabia WRC) 8m13.5s; JWC Aava/Sikk (Suzuki) 8m52.4s

**SS11 Mountain 1 (24.36km)**
1 Hirvonen/Lehtinen (Ford) 14m01.8s; 2 Grönholm/Rautiainen (Ford) 14m04.5s; 3 Loeb/Elena (Citroën) 14m16.4s; 4

# RALLY NORWAY

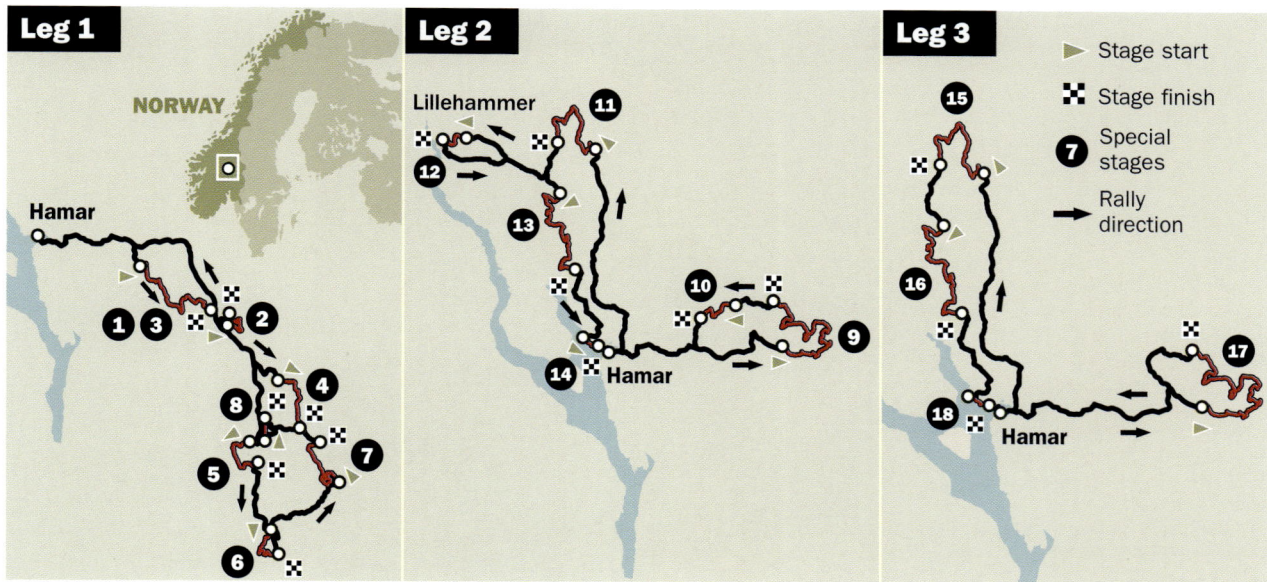

Gardemeister/Honkanen (Mitsubishi) 14m32.6s; 5 Solberg/Menkerud (Ford) 14m36.2s; 6 Kopecky/Schovanek (Skoda) 14m37.6s; JWC Andersson/Andersson (Suzuki) 15m41.1s

**SS12 Lillehammer (5.98km)**
1 Grönholm/Rautiainen (Ford) 4m33.9s; 2 Hirvonen/Lehtinen (Ford) 4m35.0s; 3 Solberg/Mills (Subaru) 4m38.2s; 4 Solberg/Menkerud (Ford) 4m40.4s; 5 Latvala/Anttila (Ford) 4m40.9s; 6 Gardemeister/Honkanen (Mitsubishi) 4m43.5s JWC Andersson/Andersson (Suzuki) 5m01.8s

**SS13 Ringsaker 1 (27.30km)**
1 Grönholm/Rautiainen (Ford) 16m29.7s; 2 Hirvonen/Lehtinen (Ford) 16m30.0s; 3 Solberg/Menkerud (Ford) 16m41.4s; 4 Solberg/Mills (Subaru) 16m45.0s; 5 Kopecky/Schovanek (Skoda) 16m47.8s; 6 Gardemeister/Honkanen (Mitsubishi) 16m48.9s; JWC Andersson/Andersson (Suzuki) 17m56.4s

**SS14 Hamar 1 (1.14km)**
1 Grönholm/Rautiainen (Ford) 1m13.8s; 2 Gardemeister/Honkanen (Mitsubishi) 1m15.3s; 3 Solberg/Mills (Subaru) 1m15.4s; 4 Hirvonen/Lehtinen (Ford) 1m15.5s; 5 Solberg/Menkerud (Ford) 1m16.0s; 6 Loeb/Elena (Citroën) 1m16.5s; JWC Sandell/Axelsson (Renault) 1m26.0s

**SS15 Mountain 2 (24.36km)**
1 Loeb/Elena (Citroën) 13m18.2s; 2 Solberg/Menkerud (Ford) 13m21.5s; 3 Hirvonen/Lehtinen (Ford) 13m27.8s; 4 Latvala/Anttila (Ford) 13m28.2s; 5 Grönholm/Rautiainen (Ford) 13m28.5s; 6 D.Carlsson/D.Giraudet (Citroën Xsara WRC) 13m35.1s; JWC Aava/Sikk (Suzuki) 14m45.2s

**SS16 Ringsaker 2 (27.30km)**
1 Solberg/Menkerud (Ford) 15m28.6s; 2 Grönholm/Rautiainen (Ford) 15m31.1s; 3 Hirvonen/Lehtinen (Ford) 15m32.7s; 4 Solberg/Mills (Subaru) 15m35.5s; 5 Latvala/Anttila (Ford) 15m36.6s; 6 C.Atkinson/G.Macneall (Subaru Impreza WRC 2006) 15m39.6s; JWC Aava/Sikk (Suzuki) 17m02.3s

**SS17 Hamar 2 (1.14km)**
1= Loeb/Elena (Citroën), Solberg/Mills (Subaru), Pons/Amigo (Mitsubishi) 1m11.8s; 4= Grönholm/Rautiainen (Ford), Hirvonen/Lehtinen (Ford) 1m12.1s; 6 Carlsson/Giraudet (Citroën) 1m12.2s; JWC Aava/Sikk (Suzuki) 1m20.9s

**SS18 Eleverum 2 (44.27km)**
1 Grönholm/Rautiainen (Ford) 24m10.3s; 2 Solberg/Menkerud (Ford) 24m15.3s; 3 Solberg/Mills (Subaru) 24m15.8s; 4 Hirvonen/Lehtinen (Ford) 24m19.2s; 5 Loeb/Elena (Citroën) 24m27.4s; 6 Latvala/Anttila (Ford) 24m28.2s; JWC Aava/Sikk (Suzuki) 26m19.3s

Cars who retired and subsequently restarted and were classified under SuperRally regs:

| | | | | |
|---|---|---|---|---|
| 2 | Sordo/Martí | Citroën C4 WRC | | |
| | Accident | SS9 | Gr A | |
| 23 | Östberg/Unnerud | Subaru Impreza WRC 2005 | | |
| | Steering | SS10 | Gr A | |
| 22 | Pons/Amigo | Mitsubishi Lancer WRC05 | | |
| | Accident | SS18 | Gr A | |
| 16 | Wilson/Orr | Ford Focus RS WRC 06 | | |
| | Accident | SS10 | Gr A | |

**MAJOR RETIREMENTS**

| | | | | |
|---|---|---|---|---|
| 21 | G'meister/Honkanen | Mitsubishi Lancer WRC05 | | |
| | Engine | SS14 | | |
| 18 | Schie/Bergsten | Ford Focus RS WRC 04 | | |
| | Gearbox | SS5 | Gr A | |
| 24 | Grøndal/Ostbye | Subaru Impreza WRC 2005 | | |
| | Gearbox | SS10 | Gr A | |
| 28 | Wilks/Pugh | Ford Focus RS WRC 04 | | |
| | Accident | SS9 | Gr A | |

**FIA CLASS WINNERS**
A8 Over 2000cc  Hirvonen/Lehtinen  Ford Focus RS WRC 06
A6 1600-2000cc  Andersson/Andersson  Suzuki Swift
N4 Over 2000 cc  Flodin/Andersson  Subaru Impreza WRX Sti
N3 1600-2000cc  Clark/Martin  Ford Fiesta ST

**RALLY LEADERS**
Overall: SS1-18 Hirvonen
JWC: SS1-18 Andersson

**SPECIAL STAGE ANALYSIS**

| | 1st | 2nd | 3rd | 4th | 5th | 6th |
|---|---|---|---|---|---|---|
| Loeb (Citroën) | 8 | 1 | 2 | 1 | 2 | 1 |
| Grönholm (Ford) | 4 | 8 | 2 | 1 | 3 | - |
| Hirvonen (Ford) | 4 | 4 | 6 | 4 | - | - |
| H.Solberg (Ford) | 1 | 2 | 1 | 6 | 3 | 2 |
| Latvala (Ford) | 1 | 1 | 1 | 1 | 4 | 2 |
| P.Solberg (Subaru) | 1 | - | 3 | 7 | 1 | 2 |
| Pons (Mitsubishi) | 1 | - | - | - | 1 | - |
| Galli (Citroën) | - | 1 | 1 | - | - | - |
| Gardemeister (Mitsubishi) | - | 1 | - | 2 | 2 | 3 |
| Kopecky (Skoda) | - | 1 | - | - | - | - |
| Sordo (Citroën) | - | - | - | - | 1 | - |
| Carlsson (Citroën) | - | - | - | - | - | 2 |
| Stohl (Citroën) | - | - | - | - | - | 1 |
| Atkinson (Subaru) | - | - | - | - | - | 1 |
| Hänninen (Mitsubishi) | - | - | - | - | - | 1 |

**WORLD CHAMPIONSHIP POINTS**
**Drivers**
1 Grönholm 24; 2 Hirvonen 20; 3 Loeb 18; 4 H.Solberg 11; 5= Sordo, P.Solberg 8; 7= Atkinson, Carlsson 6; 9 Gardemeister 5; 10 Latvala 4 etc
**Manufacturers**
1 BP-Ford WRT 44; 2 Citroën Total WRT 28; 3 Stobart M-Sport Ford RT 16; 4 Subaru WRT 15; 5 OMV-Kronos Citroën WRT 14
**Junior World Championship**
1 Andersson 10; 2 Sandell 8; 3 Aava 6; 4 Mölder 5; 5 Burkart 4; 6 Svenkerud 3; 7 Cortinovis 2; 8 Gallagher 1
**Production Cup**
1 Svedlund 10; 2 Alén 8; 3 Sohlberg 6; 4 Aroujo 5; 5 Nutahara 4; 6 Arai 3; 7 Al-Attiyah 2; 8 Frisiero 1

**ROUTE DETAILS**
Total route of 1127.62km of which 358.72km were competitive on 18 stages
Leg 1 Friday 16 February, 8 Special Stages totalling 142.51km
Leg 2 Saturday 17 February, 6 Special Stages totalling 117.42km
Leg 3 Sunday 18 February, 4 Special Stages totalling 98.79km

| Stage Numbers | 1 | 2 | 3 | 4 | 5 | 6 | 7 | 8 | 9 | 10 | 11 | 12 | 13 | 14 | 15 | 16 | 17 | 18 |
|---|---|---|---|---|---|---|---|---|---|---|---|---|---|---|---|---|---|---|
| Hirvonen | 1 | 1 | 1 | 1 | 1 | 1 | 1 | 1 | 1 | 1 | 1 | 1 | 1 | 1 | 1 | 1 | 1 | 1 |
| Grönholm | 2 | 2 | 2 | 2 | 2 | 2 | 2 | 2 | 2 | 2 | 2 | 2 | 2 | 2 | 2 | 2 | 2 | 2 |
| H.Solberg | 8 | 6 | 4 | 5 | 7 | 7 | 7 | 7 | 6 | 6 | 5 | 4 | 4 | 3 | 3 | 3 | 3 | 3 |
| P.Solberg | 6 | 7 | 7 | 7 | 5 | 4 | 4 | 4 | 4 | 4 | 3 | 3 | 3 | 4 | 4 | 4 | 4 | 4 |
| Latvala | 3 | 4 | 12 | 15 | 12 | 12 | 10 | 10 | 7 | 7 | 7 | 5 | 5 | 5 | 5 | 5 | 5 | 5 |
| Galli | 7 | 8 | 5 | 4 | 4 | 5 | 6 | 6 | 5 | 5 | 6 | 7 | 7 | 7 | 7 | 7 | 7 | 6 |
| Carlsson | 14 | 13 | 10 | 10 | 10 | 10 | 11 | 11 | 9 | 9 | 9 | 8 | 9 | 9 | 9 | 9 | 9 | 7 |
| Kopecky | 20 | 16 | 27 | 25 | 25 | 24 | 23 | 22 | 18 | 16 | 12 | 12 | 10 | 10 | 10 | 10 | 10 | 8 |
| Dalsjø | 21 | 22 | 20 | 19 | 19 | 19 | 19 | 19 | 15 | 13 | 15 | 11 | 11 | 11 | 11 | 11 | 11 | 9 |
| Mikkelsen | 15 | 14 | 13 | 12 | 15 | 15 | 15 | 15 | 14 | 12 | 14 | 14 | 13 | 13 | 13 | 13 | 13 | 10 |
| Stohl | 10 | 10 | 9 | 8 | 8 | 8 | 8 | 8 | 8 | 8 | 6 | 6 | 6 | 6 | 6 | 6 | 6 | 12 |
| Loeb | 4 | 3 | 3 | 3 | 3 | 3 | 3 | 3 | 3 | 3 | 11 | 18 | 18 | 17 | 16 | 16 | 16 | 14 |
| Pons | 19 | 17 | 18 | 18 | 18 | 18 | 17 | 17 | 12 | 11 | 10 | 9 | 8 | 8 | 8 | 8 | 8 | 16 |
| Hänninen | 11 | 18 | 16 | 13 | 13 | 12 | 12 | 10 | 10 | 10 | 10 | 16 | 15 | 15 | 18 | 17 | 17 | 17 |
| Atkinson | 9 | 9 | 9 | 9 | 9 | 9 | 9 | 29 | 28 | 26 | 25 | 23 | 23 | 21 | 20 | 20 | 19 |
| Sordo | 12 | 11 | 11 | 11 | 11 | 11 | 14 | 14 | 21 | 19 | 22 | 26 | 29 | 38 | 32 | 27 | 27 | 25 |
| Wilson | 16 | 15 | 14 | 17 | 17 | 16 | 16 | 13 | 22 | 20 | 24 | 26 | 36 | 30 | 28 | 28 | 26 |
| Östberg | 13 | 12 | 17 | 16 | 14 | 14 | 13 | 13 | 11 | 29 | 42 | 42 | 41 | 43 | 40 | 40 | 40 | 38 |
| Gardemeister | 5 | 5 | 6 | 6 | 6 | 6 | 5 | 5 | 39 | 35 | 29 | 28 | 25 | R |
| Wilks | 18 | 19 | 15 | 14 | 16 | 16 | 18 | 18 | R |

**RESULTS**
1 Mikko Hirvonen/ Jarmo Lehtinen  Ford Focus RS WRC 06  3h28m17.0s  Gr A
2 Marcus Grönholm/ Timo Rautiainen  Ford Focus RS WRC 06  3h28m26.5s  Gr A
3 Henning Solberg/ Cato Menkerud  Ford Focus RS WRC 06  3h32m01.6s  Gr A
4 Petter Solberg/ Phils Mills  Subaru Impreza WRC 2006  3h32m18.1s  Gr A
5 Jari-Matti Latvala/ Miikka Anttila  Ford Focus RS WRC 06  3h33m47.7s  Gr A
6 Gianluigi Galli/ Giovanni Bernacchini  Citroën Xsara WRC  3h35m22.2s  Gr A
7 Daniel Carlsson / Denis Giraudet  Citroën Xsara WRC  3h37m40.7s  Gr A
8 Jan Kopecky/ Filip Schovanek  Skoda Fabia WRC  3h40m06.9s  Gr A
9 Rune Dalsjø/ Jens Olav Løvhøiden  Subaru Impreza WRC 2005  3h41m48.8s  Gr A
10 Andreas Mikkelsen/ Ola Floene  Ford Focus RS WRC 04  3h42m45.7s  Gr A
74 starters, 64 finishers

**PREVIOUS WINNERS**
2006*Henning Solberg/Cato Menkerud  Peugeot 307 WRC
*Non-championship event

The FIA World Rally Championship Round 4

# Corona Rally Mexico

THE ends certainly justified the means, albeit briefly, as far as Subaru was concerned. The British-based team had never intended to build a new homologation of the Impreza WRC for this season. The 2006 car, it was hoped, would be good enough to see the team through until 2008, when the all-new hatchback version would be revealed. Last season's dire results forced a rethink. The fruits of that labour resulted in Petter Solberg leading for the first five stages in Mexico. After that, it was Sébastien Loeb all the way as the Frenchman demonstrated, with some force, that his Citroën C4 WRC wasn't about to be booted out of the limelight by a new blue car.

Fastest on the three stages that constituted the event's opening loop, Solberg's smile was justified when he returned to the service park in León. He announced that while there was still work to do on the car, he was happy - more than happy.

"I wasn't even trying this morning," he said. "I could have gone much harder. Even when I was told to cut the corner, I was still keeping the car on the road and going around all the rocks."

That's all very nice, but what about the main question? What about the trait that had become unflinchingly linked to the '06 Impreza? What about the understeer?

"It didn't," said Solberg, looking almost smug for the first time in ages. "Not even in the latter parts of the stages. This car has balance."

Two stages later, it also had no oil. Under braking for a corner early in Ortega 2 a stone flicked up into the wheel arch and hit the fan underneath the oil cooler. Part of one of the fan blades pierced the oil cooler and drained it of lubricant. The dry flat four battled on for eight miles before issuing a final warning via the dashboard. Solberg and the team heeded that warning and switched off the engine.

That left Loeb with a half-minute lead at the end of leg one. He wanted to double that before he started to think about feeling comfortable. But what of Citroën's nemesis on the previous two rounds? What of the Fords? Well, Marcus Grönholm was having one of his slowest starts to a WRC round in living memory and Mikko Hirvonen was embroiled in a four-way scrap for second.

By lunchtime on Saturday, Loeb was happy. The gap was a minute, now he could sit on it and watch the rest fight. He smiled as he saw his rival Grönholm's fastest time in SS11. "So, Marcus woke up," said the leader. He did so in some style, too. The Finn leapfrogged his way from fifth to second. From then on, Hirvonen, Dani Sordo and Chris Atkinson would be squabbling over third. Hirvonen was livid with himself, having spun in SS13. He would be playing catch up on the final morning. The Rally Norway winner did so perfectly. With dust hanging on the stages early on Sunday, Hirvonen extended himself and went quickest to put two Fords on the podium. Sordo, ears still ringing after a pre-event 'chat' with Citroën team principal Guy Fréquelin, took an impressive fourth, while Atkinson slipped to fifth with turbo trouble in the second Subaru.

Main: The Citroen demonstrated devastating pace and precision on its first time out on gravel roads
Race&motion

Inset: And it was Loeb who made the most of the C4, taking his second win of 2008
McKlein

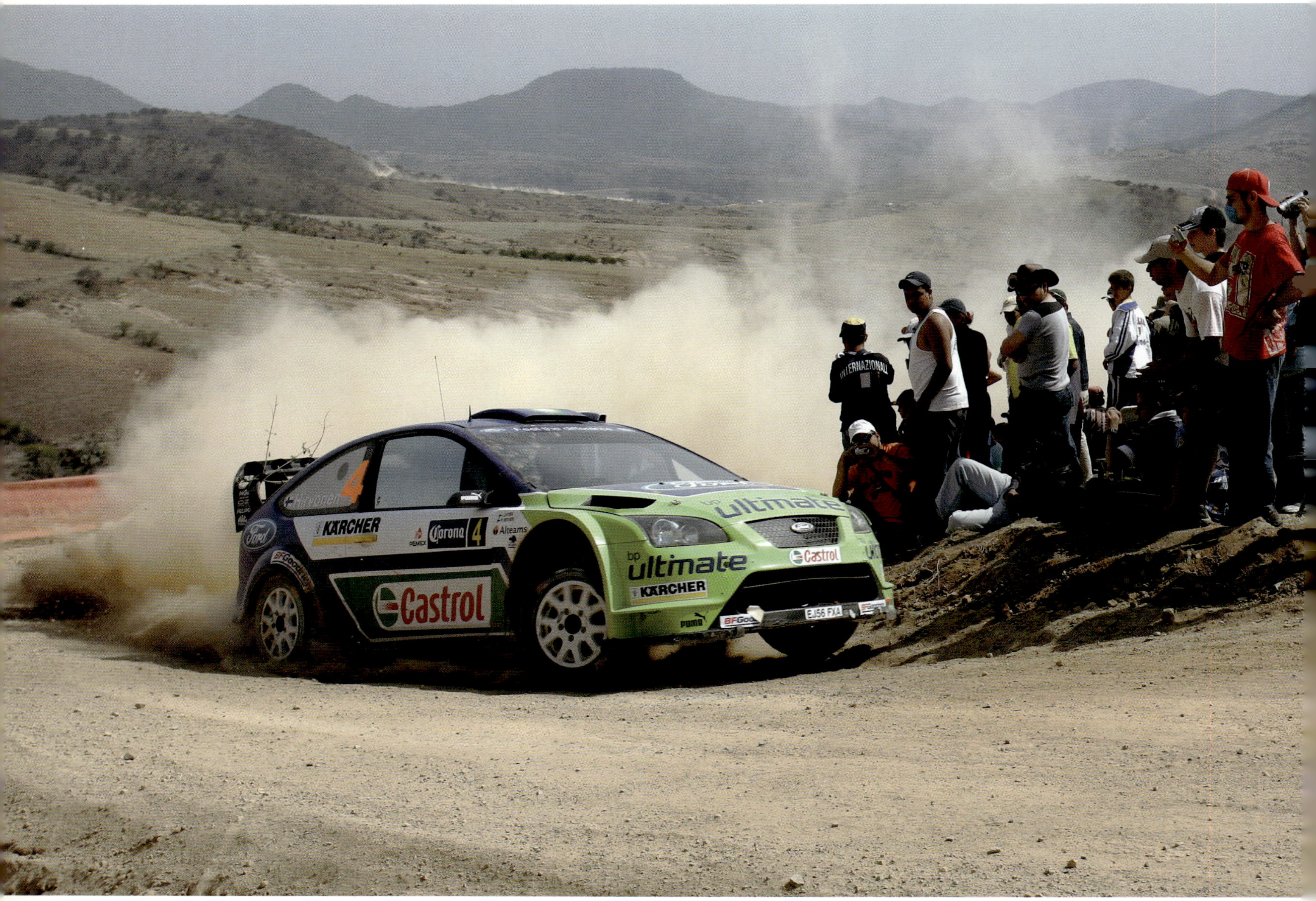
Castrol
ultimate
KÄRCHER
Corona
4
Castrol
EJ56 FXA

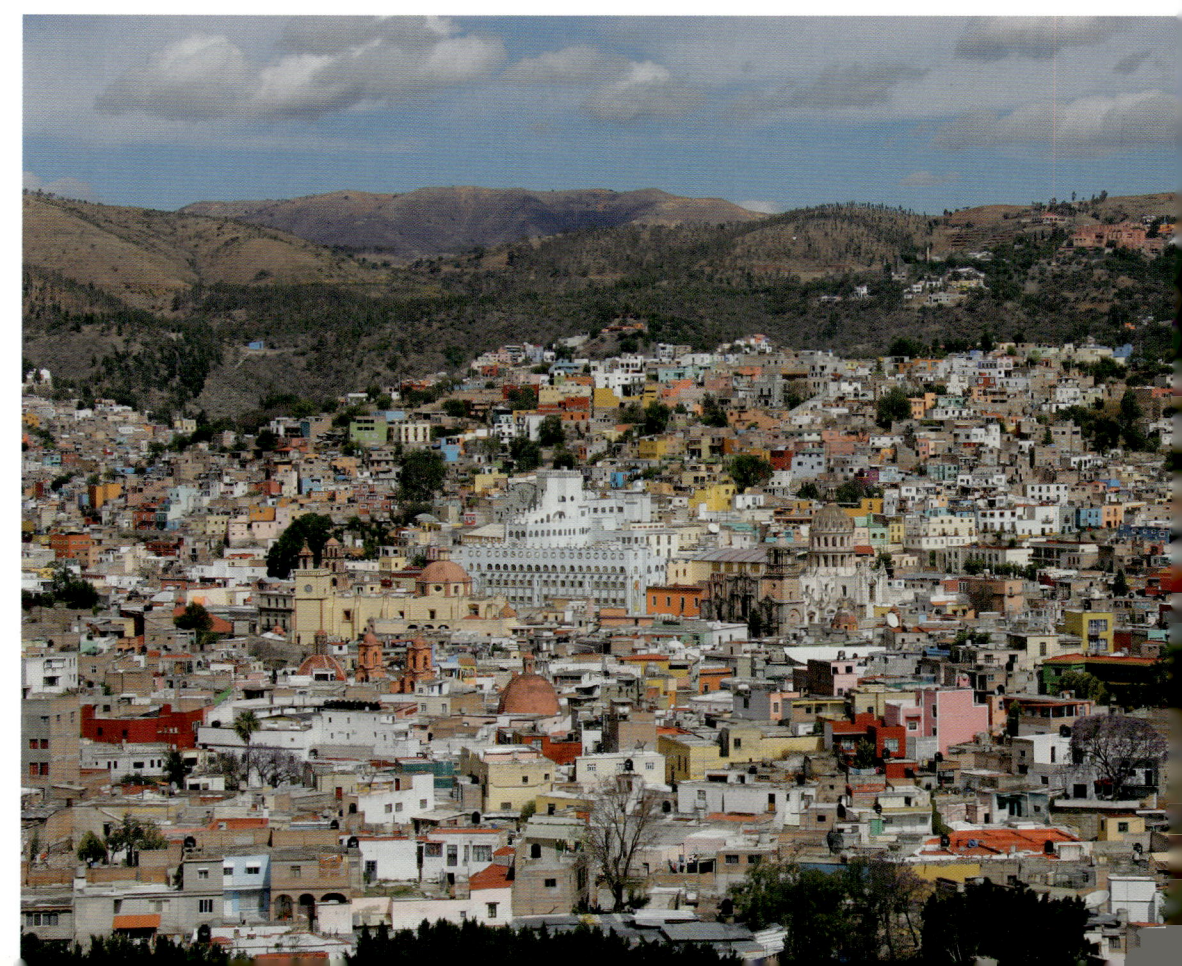

Opposite left: Grönholm made up for a slow start with second, but he was no match for Loeb in central America

Left: Sordo took a fine fourth on his gravel debut with the Citroen Sport team

Below: Former Subaru team-mates Solberg and Hirvonen share a joke

Bottom left: There's no shortage of colour at the ceremonial start in Guanajuato

All photographs by McKlein

PETTER
SOLBERG

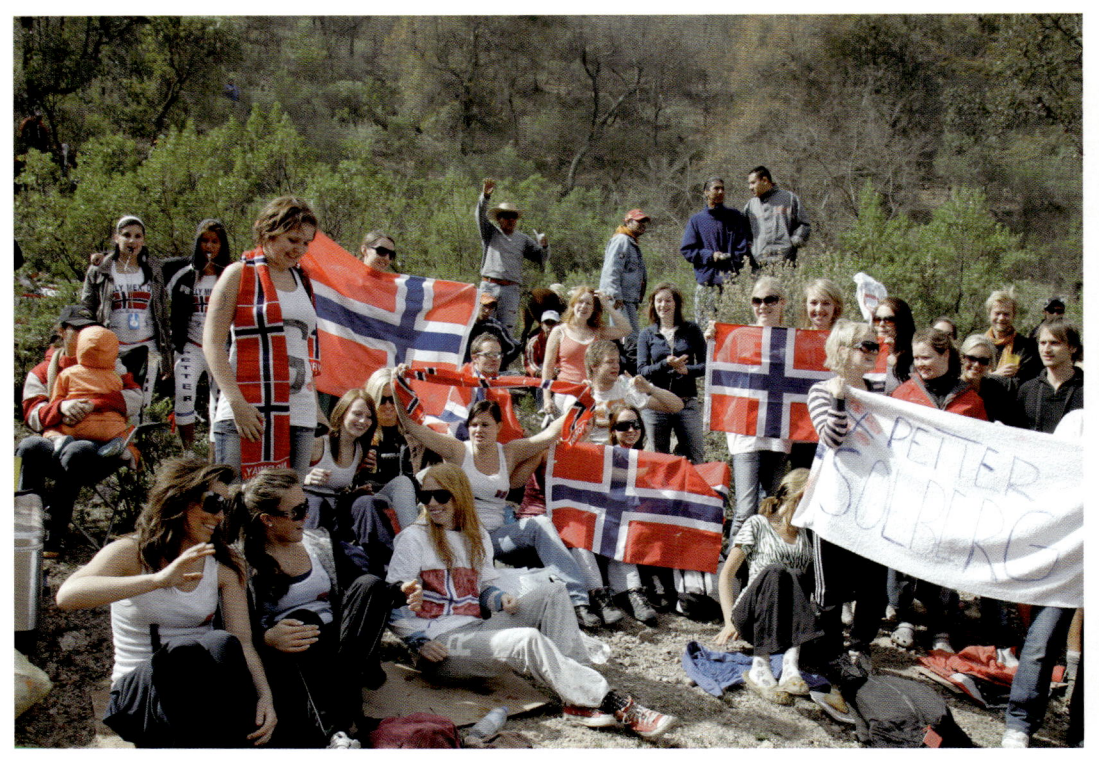

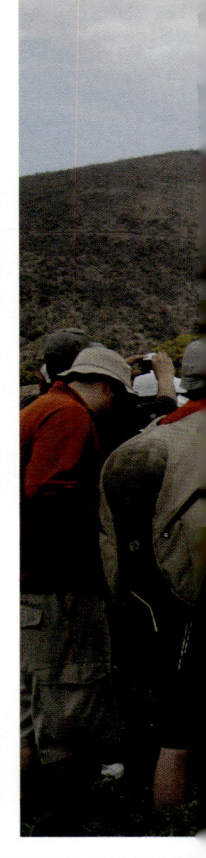

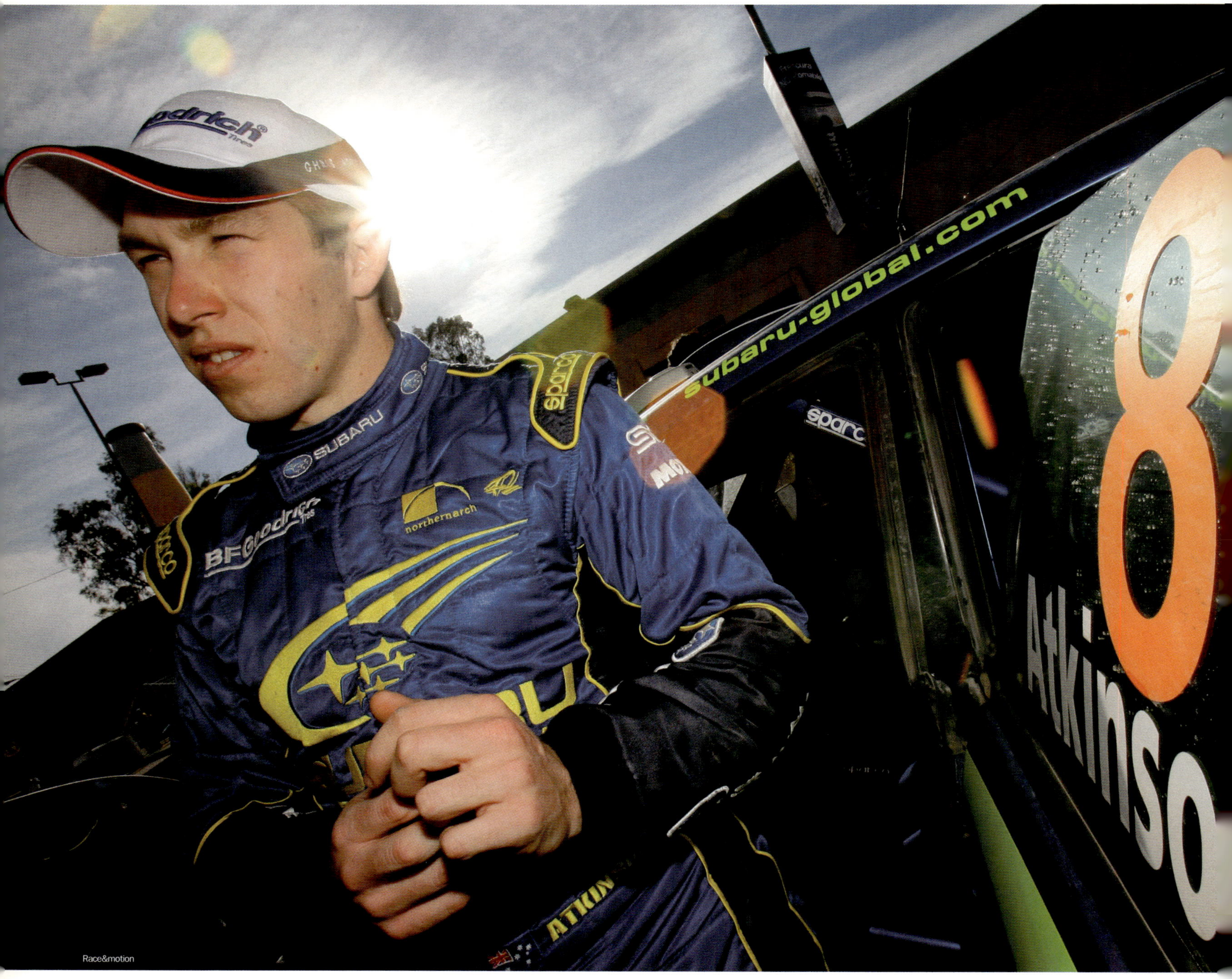
subaru-global.com
8
Atkinso
SUBARU
sparco
northernarch
ATKIN

CORONA RALLY MEXICO

Left: Turbo trouble cost Atkinson time and a possible third became fifth

Top left: Petter who? Solberg's female fan club was clearly visible in Mexico

Top right: Stohl was a subdued sixth in the Kronos/OMV Xsara

Above: Solberg led early on in the new Impreza, but was forced out after a stone damaged an oil pipe

All photographs by McKlein unless specified

Finally! After trying for three years, Higgins collected his first Production WRC win in Mexico
McKlein

## The FIA World Rally Championship Round 4
# Rally Mexico Results
### March 9-11 2007

### FINISH LINES...

The Stobart VK M-Sport team maintained its third position in the manufacturers' championship with seventh place for Jari-Matti Latvala. Matthew Wilson put the sister Focus RS WRC 06 in eighth overall, but with the Brit not registered for manufacturer points, a single point went to ninth-placed Henning Solberg - also a Stobart driver. The Norwegian entered Mexico on a high having clinched a podium at home. He came down to earth with a bump on SS1, however, when he rolled his Focus and spent the rest of the event trying to make up the time... For the second year in succession Rally Mexico was troubled by spectators who threw rocks at the cars, and placed rocks and other debris in the road. Rally winner Loeb put the problem into perfect perspective, saying: "Don't these people realise they're playing with our lives? It's not my fault if they don't want us to drive down this particular piece of road - I'm just doing my job"... After two years trying and coming close on numerous occasions, Britain's Mark Higgins finally took victory on a round of the Production Car WRC. The Mitsubishi Lancer driver led for all but one stage in a fabulously controlled drive. His chief rival early on had been Mirco Baldacci, but the San Marino man slipped back when he stopped to change a puncture on his Impreza. Fellow Subaru Group N runners Toshi Arai and Kristian Sohlberg were second and third respectively in the Production standings... Father and son duo Austin and Gareth MacHale wheeled out their 2004 and '06-spec Fords for this event, but neither finished. The older of the two, competing on gravel for the first time in two years, suffered suspension failure, while Gareth broke a track control arm on his car on leg two.

### RUNNING ORDER

| | | | |
|---|---|---|---|
| 3 | Marcus Grönholm/Timo Rautiainen | Ford Focus RS WRC 06 | Gr A |
| 4 | Mikko Hirvonen/Jarmo Lehtinen | Ford Focus RS WRC 06 | Gr A |
| 1 | Sébastien Loeb/Daniel Elena | Citroën C4 WRC | Gr A |
| 10 | Henning Solberg/Cato Menkerud | Ford Focus RS WRC 06 | Gr A |
| 2 | Daniel Sordo/Marc Martí | Citroën C4 WRC | Gr A |
| 7 | Petter Solberg/Phil Mills | Subaru Impreza WRC 2007 | Gr A |
| 8 | Chris Atkinson/Glenn Macneall | Subaru Impreza WRC 2007 | Gr A |
| 9 | Jari-Matti Latvala/Miikka Anttila | Ford Focus RS WRC 06 | Gr A |
| 5 | Manfred Stohl/Ilka Minor | Citroën Xsara WRC | Gr A |
| 17 | Gareth MacHale/Paul Nagle | Ford Focus RS WRC 06 | Gr A |
| 16 | Matthew Wilson/Michael Orr | Ford Focus RS WRC 06 | Gr A |
| 11 | Luis Pérez-Companc/José María Volta | Ford Focus RS WRC 06 | Gr A |
| 12 | Juan Pablo Raies/Jorge Pérez-Companc | Ford Focus RS WRC 06 | Gr A |
| 18 | Austin MacHale/Brian Murphy | Ford Focus RS WRC 03 | Gr A |
| 38 | Kristian Sohlberg/Risto Pietiläinen | Subaru Impreza WRX Sti | |
| 35 | Fumio Nutahara/Daniel Barritt | Mitsubishi Lancer Evo 9 | |
| 31 | Toshihiro Arai/Tony Sircombe | Subaru Impreza WRX Sti | Gr N |
| 39 | Nasser Al-Attiyah/Chris Patterson | Subaru Impreza WRX Sti | |
| 44 | Mauro Rongoni/Simone Scattolin | Mitsubishi Lancer Evo 9 | |
| 45 | Mirco Baldacci/Giovanni Agnese | Mitsubishi Lancer Evo 9 | Gr N |
| 41 | Leszek Kuzaj/Jarek Baran | Subaru Impreza WRX Sti | Gr N |

### SPECIAL STAGE TIMES

**SS1 Alfaro 1 (23.50km)**
1 P.Solberg/P.Mills (Subaru Impreza WRC 2007) 14m03.5s; 2 S.Loeb/D.Elena (Citroën C4 WRC) 14m06.4s; 3 C.Atkinson/G.Macneall (Subaru Impreza WRC 2007) 14m09.4s; 4 D.Sordo/M.Martí (Citroën C4 WRC) 14m11.0s; 5 M.Hirvonen/J.Lehtinen (Ford Focus RS WRC 06) 14m14.2s; 6 M.Grönholm/T.Rautiainen (Ford Focus RS WRC 06) 14m15.6s; PC M.Higgins/S.Martin (Mitsubishi Lancer Evo 9) 15m12.8s

**SS2 Ortega 1 (29.65km)**
1 Solberg/Mills (Subaru) 17m28.7s; 2 Atkinson/Macneall (Subaru) 17m31.1s; 3 Loeb/Elena (Citroën) 17m31.9s; 4 Sordo/Martí (Citroën) 17m38.6s; 5 Grönholm/Rautiainen (Ford) 17m39.0s; 6 M.Stohl/I.Minor (Citroën Xsara WRC) 17m40.3s; PC M.Baldacci/G.Agnese (Mitsubishi Lancer Evo 9) 18m52.3s

**SS3 El Cubilete 1 (17.87km)**
1 Solberg/Mills (Subaru) 9m45.6s; 2 Loeb/Elena (Citroën) 9m47.2s; 3 Sordo/Martí (Citroën) 9m49.7s; 4 Hirvonen/Lehtinen (Ford) 9m49.8s; 5 Grönholm/Rautiainen (Ford) 9m50.1s; 6 Stohl/Minor (Citroën) 9m51.8s; PC T.Arai/T.Sircombe (Subaru Impreza WRX Sti) 10m35.4s

**SS4 Alfaro 2 (23.50km)**
1 Loeb/Elena (Citroën) 13m47.0s; 2 Solberg/Mills (Subaru) 13m49.8s; 3 Sordo/Martí (Citroën) 13m50.5s; 4 Hirvonen/Lehtinen (Ford) 13m50.9s; 5 Atkinson/Macneall (Subaru) 13m54.0s; 6 Grönholm/Rautiainen (Ford) 13m56.0s; PC Higgins/Martin (Mitsubishi) 15m03.1s

**SS5 Ortega 2 (29.65km)**
1 Stohl/Minor (Citroën) 16m58.2s; 2 Loeb/Elena (Citroën) 16m58.3s; 3 Hirvonen/Lehtinen (Ford) 17m00.0s; 4 Atkinson/Macneall (Subaru) 17m00.4s; 5 Solberg/Mills (Subaru) 17m01.1s; 6 Grönholm/Rautiainen (Ford) 17m07.1s; PC Higgins/Martin (Mitsubishi) 18m28.8s

**SS6 El Cubilete 2 (17.87km)**
1 Loeb/Elena (Citroën) 9m37.5s; 2= Sordo/Martí (Citroën), Hirvonen/Lehtinen (Ford) 9m39.7s; 4 Stohl/Minor (Citroën) 9m43.5s; 5 Grönholm/Rautiainen (Ford) 9m43.9s; 6 Atkinson/Macneall (Subaru) 9m48.2s; PC Baldacci/Agnese (Mitsubishi) 10m22.5s

**SS7 Superspecial 1 (2.21km)**
1 Grönholm/Rautiainen (Ford) 1m42.6s; 2= Loeb/Elena (Citroën), Atkinson/Macneall (Subaru) 1m43.4s; 4 Sordo/Martí (Citroën) 1m43.9s; 5 Hirvonen/Lehtinen (Ford) 1m44.7s; 6 G.MacHale/P.Nagle (Ford Focus RS WRC 06) 1m45.6s; PC Higgins/Martin (Mitsubishi) 1m46.0s

**SS8 Superspecial 2 (2.21km)**
1 Atkinson/Macneall (Subaru) 1m42.0s; 2 Sordo/Martí (Citroën) 1m42.6s; 3 Loeb/Elena (Citroën) 1m42.7s; 4 Grönholm/Rautiainen (Ford) 1m43.2s; 5 Stohl/Minor (Citroën) 1m43.7s; 6 Hirvonen/Lehtinen (Ford) 1m44.1s; PC Arai/Sircombe (Subaru) 1m48.3s

**SS9 Ibarilla 1 (30.20km)**
1 Loeb/Elena (Citroën) 18m17.3s; 2 Hirvonen/Lehtinen (Ford) 18m24.8s; 3 Atkinson/Macneall (Subaru) 18m29.8s; 4 Grönholm/Rautiainen (Ford) 18m30.4s; 5 Sordo/Martí (Citroën) 18m36.8s; 6 Stohl/Minor (Citroën) 18m39.6s; PC K.Sohlberg/R.Pietiläinen (Subaru Impreza WRX Sti) 19m57.7s

**SS10 Duarte 1 (23.51km)**
1 Loeb/Elena (Citroën) 17m55.0s; 2 Grönholm/Rautiainen (Ford) 17m58.7s; 3 Sordo/Martí (Citroën) 18m02.6s; 4 Atkinson/Macneall (Subaru) 18m04.5s; 5 Hirvonen/Lehtinen (Ford) 18m05.6s; 6 Stohl/Minor (Citroën) 18m11.3s; PC Baldacci/Agnese (Mitsubishi) 19m08.2s

**SS11 Derramadero 1 (23.27km)**
1 Grönholm/Rautiainen (Ford) 14m01.6s; 2 Loeb/Elena (Citroën) 14m03.9s; 3 Sordo/Martí (Citroën) 14m11.7s; 4 Hirvonen/Lehtinen (Ford) 14m13.4s; 5 Atkinson/Macneall (Subaru) 14m16.3s; 6 Stohl/Minor (Citroën) 14m18.1s; PC Sohlberg/Pietiläinen (Subaru) 15m25.8s

**SS12 Ibarilla 2 (30.20km)**
1 Loeb/Elena (Citroën) 18m02.6s; 2 Grönholm/Rautiainen (Ford) 18m04.2s; 3 Hirvonen/Lehtinen (Ford) 18m06.0s; 4 Sordo/Martí (Citroën) 18m14.7s; 5 J-M.Latvala/M.Anttila (Ford Focus RS WRC 06) 18m21.7s; 6 Atkinson/Macneall (Subaru)

## CORONA RALLY MEXICO

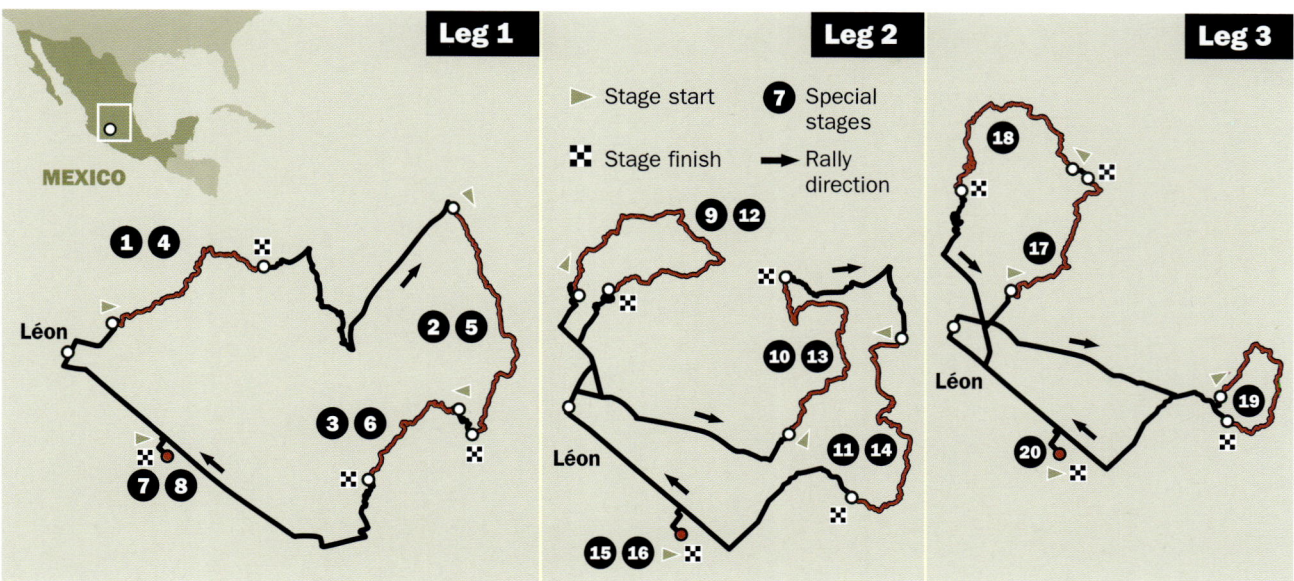

| Stage Numbers | 1 | 2 | 3 | 4 | 5 | 6 | 7 | 8 | 9 | 10 | 11 | 12 | 13 | 14 | 15 | 16 | 17 | 18 | 19 | 20 |
|---|---|---|---|---|---|---|---|---|---|---|---|---|---|---|---|---|---|---|---|---|
| Loeb | 2 | 2 | 2 | 2 | 2 | 1 | 1 | 1 | 1 | 1 | 1 | 1 | 1 | 1 | 1 | 1 | 1 | 1 | 1 | 1 |
| Grönholm | 6 | 5 | 5 | 6 | 7 | 6 | 5 | 5 | 5 | 42 | 2 | 2 | 2 | 2 | 2 | 2 | 2 | 2 | 2 | 2 |
| Hirvonen | 5 | 6 | 6 | 5 | 6 | 5 | 4 | 4 | 2 | 2 | 3 | 3 | 4 | 4 | 4 | 4 | 3 | 3 | 3 | 3 |
| Sordo | 4 | 4 | 4 | 4 | 5 | 4 | 3 | 3 | 4 | 5 | 4 | 4 | 3 | 3 | 3 | 3 | 4 | 4 | 4 | 4 |
| Atkinson | 3 | 3 | 3 | 3 | 3 | 2 | 2 | 2 | 3 | 4 | 5 | 5 | 5 | 5 | 5 | 5 | 5 | 5 | 5 | 5 |
| Stohl | 7 | 7 | 7 | 7 | 4 | 3 | 6 | 6 | 6 | 6 | 6 | 6 | 6 | 6 | 6 | 6 | 6 | 6 | 6 | 6 |
| Latvala | 8 | 8 | 8 | 8 | 9 | 7 | 7 | 7 | 7 | 7 | 7 | 7 | 7 | 7 | 7 | 7 | 7 | 7 | 7 | 7 |
| Wilson | 9 | 9 | 9 | 9 | 8 | 8 | 8 | 8 | 8 | 8 | 8 | 8 | 8 | 8 | 8 | 8 | 8 | 8 | 8 | 8 |
| H.Solberg | 32 | 28 | 25 | 23 | 21 | 20 | 19 | 19 | 15 | 13 | 12 | 10 | 9 | 9 | 9 | 9 | 9 | 9 | 9 | 9 |
| Higgins | 11 | 10 | 12 | 11 | 11 | 10 | 10 | 10 | 10 | 11 | 10 | 10 | 10 | 10 | 10 | 10 | 10 | 10 | 10 | 10 |
| Arai | 14 | 15 | 14 | 16 | 14 | 13 | 13 | 13 | 14 | 14 | 13 | 12 | 11 | 11 | 11 | 11 | 11 | 11 | 11 | |
| Raies | 18 | 21 | 20 | 18 | 16 | 15 | 15 | 15 | 16 | 16 | 15 | 14 | 14 | 13 | 13 | 13 | 14 | 13 | 13 | 12 |
| Baldacci | 12 | 11 | 13 | 13 | 12 | 11 | 11 | 11 | 11 | 10 | 11 | 13 | 12 | 13 | 14 | 15 | 15 | 15 | 14 | 14 |
| A.MacHale | 10 | 12 | 11 | 12 | 13 | 12 | 12 | 12 | 12 | 13 | 13 | 12 | 11 | 12 | 12 | 12 | 12 | 12 | 12 | R |
| G.MacHale | 26 | 14 | 10 | 10 | 10 | 9 | 9 | 9 | 9 | 9 | 9 | 9 | 9 | R | | | | | | |
| P.Solberg | 1 | 1 | 1 | 1 | 1 | R | | | | | | | | | | | | | | |

18m22.3s; PC Baldacci/Agnese (Mitsubishi) 19m51.7s

**SS13 Duarte 2 (23.51km)**
1 Grönholm/Rautiainen (Ford) 17m32.2s; 2 Loeb/Elena (Citroën) 17m34.6s; 3 Sordo/Martí (Citroën) 17m46.2s; 4 Atkinson/Macneall (Subaru) 17m46.5s; 5 Latvala/Anttila (Ford) 17m52.7s; 6 Stohl/Minor (Citroën) 17m55.5s; PC Higgins/Martin (Mitsubishi) 18m55.5s

**SS14 Derramadero 2 (23.27km)**
1 Loeb/Elena (Citroën) 13m49.4s; 2 Hirvonen/Lehtinen (Ford) 13m54.4s; 3 Grönholm/Rautiainen (Ford) 13m54.8s; 4 Sordo/Martí (Citroën) 13m55.5s; 5 H.Solberg/C.Menkerud (Ford Focus RS WRC 06) 14m03.3s; 6 Atkinson/Macneall (Subaru) 14m03.7s; PC Solhberg/Pietiläinen (Subaru) 15m07.6s

**SS15 Superspecial 3 (2.21km)**
1= Sordo/Martí (Citroën), Stohl/Minor (Citroën) 1m44.6s; 3 Grönholm/Rautiainen (Ford) 1m44.8s; 4 Loeb/Elena (Citroën) 1m45.3s; 5 Latvala/Anttila (Ford) 1m45.4s; 6 Atkinson/Macneall (Subaru) 1m45.9s; PC Arai/Sircombe (Subaru) 1m51.9s

**SS16 Superspecial 4 (2.21km)**
1 Grönholm/Rautiainen (Ford) 1m43.6s; 2 Sordo/Martí (Citroën) 1m43.7s; 3 Stohl/Minor (Citroën) 1m43.8s; 4 Loeb/Elena (Citroën) 1m44.5s; 5 Latvala/Anttila (Ford) 1m44.6s; 6= Atkinson/Macneall (Subaru), Hirvonen/Lehtinen (Ford) 1m45.1s; PC Arai/Sircombe (Subaru) 1m49.9s

**SS17 Leon (16.29km)**
1 Hirvonen/Lehtinen (Ford) 10m35.8s; 2 Loeb/Elena (Citroën) 10m39.7s; 3 Grönholm/Rautiainen (Ford) 10m40.8s; 4 Sordo/Martí (Citroën) 10m45.2s; 5 Latvala/Anttila (Ford) 10m47.1s; 6 Atkinson/Macneall (Subaru) 10m50.6s; PC Higgins/Martin (Mitsubishi) 11m33.8s

**SS18 Guanajuatito (23.34km)**
1 Grönholm/Rautiainen (Ford) 15m12.3s; 2 Loeb/Elena (Citroën) 15m13.8s; 3 Hirvonen/Lehtinen (Ford) 15m16.5s; 4 Sordo/Martí (Citroën) 15m20.6s; 5 Latvala/Anttila (Ford) 15m25.2s; 6 Atkinson/Macneall (Subaru) 15m31.9s; PC F.Nutahara/D.Barritt (Mitsubishi Lancer Evo 9) 16m42.1s

**SS19 Comanjilla (18.10km)**
1 Hirvonen/Lehtinen (Ford) 10m17.6s; 2 Sordo/Martí (Citroën) 10m22.8s; 3 Grönholm/Rautiainen (Ford) 10m24.6s; 4 Loeb/Elena (Citroën) 10m27.7s; 5 Latvala/Anttila (Ford) 10m28.4s; 6 Atkinson/Macneall (Subaru) 10m34.4s; PC Arai/Sircombe (Subaru) 11m26.3s

**SS20 Superspecial 5 (2.21km)**
1 Grönholm/Rautiainen (Ford) 3m23.6s; 2 Loeb/Elena (Citroën) 3m25.1s; 3= Atkinson/Macneall (Subaru), Stohl/Minor (Citroën) 3m25.8s; 5= Hirvonen/Lehtinen (Ford), Latvala/Anttila (Ford) 3m26.0s; PC Baldacci/Agnese (Mitsubishi) 3m29.4s

### MAJOR RETIREMENTS

| 7 | Solberg/Mills | Subaru Impreza WRC 2007 | | |
| | Engine | SS6 | Gr A | |
| 17 | G.MacHale/Nagle | Ford Focus RS WRC 06 | | |
| | Suspension | SS13 | Gr A | |
| 18 | A.MacHale/Murphy | Ford Focus RS WRC 03 | | |
| | Accident | SS18 | Gr A | |
| 39 | Al-Attiyah/Patterson | Subaru Impreza WRX Sti | | |
| | Suspension | SS2 | Gr N | |

### FIA CLASS WINNERS

| A8 Over 2000 cc | Loeb/Elena |
| | Citroën C4 WRC |
| A6 1400-1600cc | Guelfi/Lozano |
| | Peugeot 206 XS |
| N4 Over 2000 cc | Higgins/Martin |
| | Mitsubishi Lancer Evo 9 |

### RALLY LEADERS
Overall: SS1-5 P.Solberg; SS6-20 Loeb
PC: SS1-9 Higgins; SS10 Baldacci; SS11-20 Higgins

### SPECIAL STAGE ANALYSIS

| | 1st | 2nd | 3rd | 4th | 5th | 6th |
|---|---|---|---|---|---|---|
| Loeb (Citroën) | 6 | 9 | 2 | 3 | - | - |
| Grönholm (Ford) | 6 | 2 | 4 | 2 | 3 | 3 |
| P.Solberg (Subaru) | 3 | 1 | - | - | 1 | - |
| Hirvonen (Ford) | 2 | 3 | 3 | 3 | 4 | 2 |
| Stohl (Citroën) | 2 | - | 2 | 1 | 1 | 6 |
| Sordo (Citroën) | 1 | 4 | 5 | 7 | 1 | - |
| Atkinson (Subaru) | 1 | 2 | 3 | 3 | 2 | 8 |
| Latvala (Ford) | - | - | - | - | 8 | - |
| H.Solberg (Ford) | - | - | - | - | 1 | - |
| G.MacHale (Ford) | - | - | - | - | - | 1 |

### WORLD CHAMPIONSHIP POINTS
**Drivers**
1 Grönholm 32; 2 Loeb 28; 3 Hirvonen 26; 4 Sordo 13; 5 H.Solberg 11; 6 Atkinson 10; 7 P.Solberg 8; 8= Carlsson, Latvala 6; 10= Gardemeister, Stohl 5 etc

**Manufacturers**
1 BP-Ford WRT 58; 2 Citroën Total WRT 43; 3= Stobart M-Sport Ford RT, Subaru WRT 19; 5 OMV-Kronos Citroën WRT 17

**Junior World Championship**
1 Andersson 10; 2 Sandell 8; 3 Aava 6; 4 Mölder 5; 5 Burkart 4; 6 Svenkerud 3; 7 Cortinovis 2; 8 Gallagher 1

**Production Cup**
1 Sohlberg 12; 2 Arai 11; 3= Svedlund, Higgins 10; 5 Alén 8; 6 Nutahara 6; 7= Aroujo, Baldacci 5; 9 Pastrana 4; 10 Vojtech 3 etc

### ROUTE DETAILS
Total route of 849.55km of which 366.06km were competitive on 20 stages

**Leg 1** Friday 9 March, 8 Special Stages totalling 145.62km
**Leg 2** Saturday 10 March, 8 Special Stages totalling 158.38km
**Leg 3** Sunday 11 March, 4 Special Stages totalling 62.06km

### RESULTS

| 1 | Sébastien Loeb/ | Citroën C4 WRC | |
| | Daniel Elena | 3h48m13.3s | Gr A |
| 2 | Marcus Grönholm/ | Ford Focus RS WRC 06 | |
| | Timo Rautiainen | 3h49m09.1s | Gr A |
| 3 | Mikko Hirvonen/ | Ford Focus RS WRC 06 | |
| | Jarmo Lehtinen | 3h49m41.0s | Gr A |
| 4 | Daniel Sordo/ | Citroën C4 WRC | |
| | Marc Martí | 3h49m57.0s | Gr A |
| 5 | Chris Atkinson/ | Subaru Impreza WRC 2007 | |
| | Glenn Macneall | 3h50m37.4s | Gr A |
| 6 | Manfred Stohl/ | Citroën Xsara WRC | |
| | Ilka Minor | 3h51m58.8s | Gr A |
| 7 | Jari-Matti Latvala/ | Ford Focus RS WRC 06 | |
| | Miikka Anttila | 3h52m24.1s | Gr A |
| 8 | Matthew Wilson/ | Ford Focus RS WRC 06 | |
| | Michael Orr | 4h00m35.9s | Gr A |
| 9 | Henning Solberg/ | Ford Focus RS WRC 06 | |
| | Cato Menkerud | 4h02m29.0s | Gr A |
| 10 | Mark Higgins/ | Mitsubishi Lancer Evo 9 | |
| | Scott Martin | 4h08m44.5s | Gr N |

47 starters, 36 finishers

### RECENT WINNERS

| 1999* | Gabriel Marin/Javier Marin | Mitsubishi Lancer E6 |
| 2000* | Douglas Gore/Mark Nelson | Mitsubishi Lancer E6 |
| 2001* | Ramon Ferreyros/Raul Velit | Toyota Celica GT4 |
| 2002* | Harri Rovanperä/Risto Pietiläinen | Peugeot 206 WRC |
| 2003* | Marcos Ligato/Ruben Garcia | Mitsubishi Lancer E6 |
| 2004 | Markko Märtin/Michael Park | Ford Focus RS WRC03 |
| 2005 | Petter Solberg/Phil Mills | Subaru Impreza WRC2005 |
| 2006 | Sébastien Loeb/Daniel Elena | Citroën Xsara WRC |

*Non-championship event

# Rally Portugal
The FIA World Rally Championship Round 5

Opposite: **The almost local Sordo was the fans' favourite in third**

Left: **Petter Solberg bagged more data for the engineering team to check out with second for Subaru**

Below: **Post-event penalties for Grönholm would mean a bigger gap between Loeb and the Finn**

All photographs by McKlein

THERE was a degree of confusion all round. Sébastien Loeb had clearly taken the right tyre for the Silves stage. Surely the softer rubber beneath his Citroën would work far better than the tougher boots on Marcus Grönholm's Ford. But early in the 19-miler, Grönholm was faster. That changed soon after the mid-point, and it was almost as though Loeb had flicked a switch. In one sector he overturned Grönholm's advantage and romped home to another fastest time.

That one stage was a microcosm of this year's Rally Portugal. Loeb took his time, built his speed and then put his C4 in P1. Talking of that wet opening Saturday morning stage, the Frenchman said: "I wasn't sure about the grip. I knew the tyre was right, but I didn't know exactly how it would work on the surface. When I got the confidence, then I was happy to push, but not before.

"Look at the times from the shakedown stages," he added. "He [Grönholm] is always faster than me on the first run at the stage; it's always like this. I don't want to push myself or the car until I'm happy with both. Then I will. That's what I did here."

Grönholm's rally hadn't been the best, despite his lead early doors on Friday. He was plagued by some woeful tyre choices and a Saturday-evening investigation into the weight of his Focus by the FIA. The car was underweight, but the team's explanation placated the sport's governing body. Twenty hours later, the issue was raised again and this time Grönholm, along with the other six Focus RS WRC 06s, were kicked out. The rear windows in the cars were five millimetres too narrow. Second became fourth for Grönholm, promoting Subaru's Petter Solberg into the runner-up spot.

Grönholm's frustration at the loss of his early lead was mirrored throughout the Ford camp. Behind the scenes there was also increasing disquiet at the pace Loeb was showing. Three wins from five looked alarmingly familiar from the Frenchman.

As it was Loeb's second consecutive victory had narrowed the gap to Grönholm at the top of the table before the penalties were handed out. Now, and from a driver's perspective in the worst possible fashion, Loeb had the championship lead.

There was more good news for Citroën, as Dani Sordo collected an after-hours third position in his C4. The Spaniard's rise to be the fans' favourite had been as unsurprising as it was rapid. He delivered another consummate drive ahead of a rapturous close-to-home crowd.

If Portugal was all good for Citroën and pretty much all bad for Ford, it was half and half for Subaru. Solberg bagged more data on dirt, and his biggest points haul of the season in second. But his team-mate Chris Atkinson undid the good work of fourth in Mexico by crashing off the road on the Almodovar test, bouncing across a field in sixth gear. Soon after Atkinson's co-driver Glenn Macneall called time on their relationship. The two incidents, the team claimed, were not related. In reality, it was hard not to make the connection…

SUBARU
sparco
BFGoodrich
SUBARU
WORLD RALLY TEAM

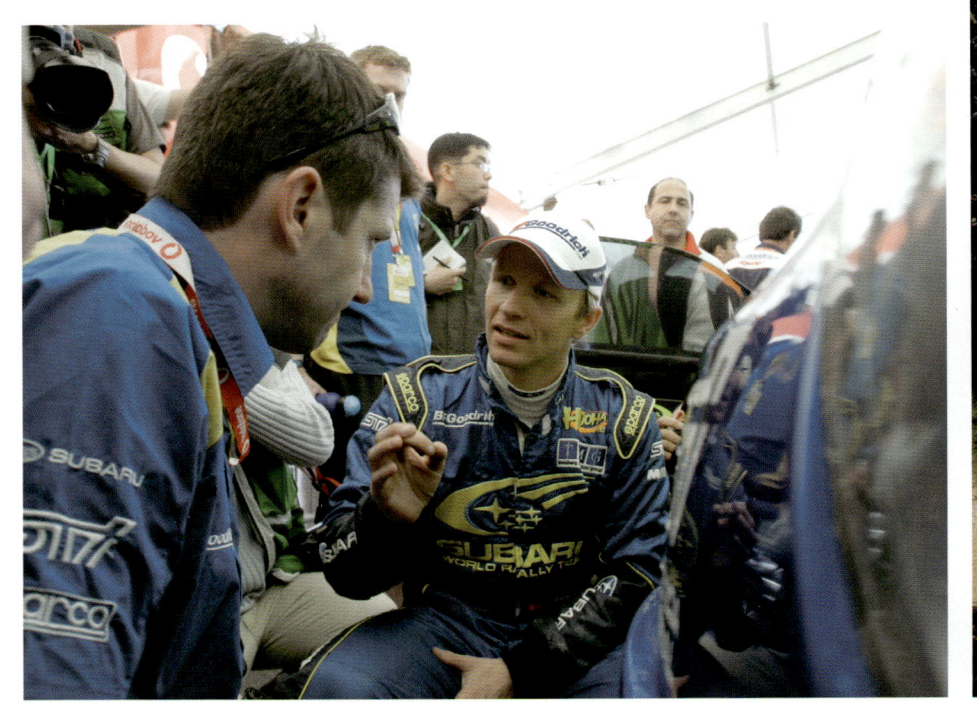

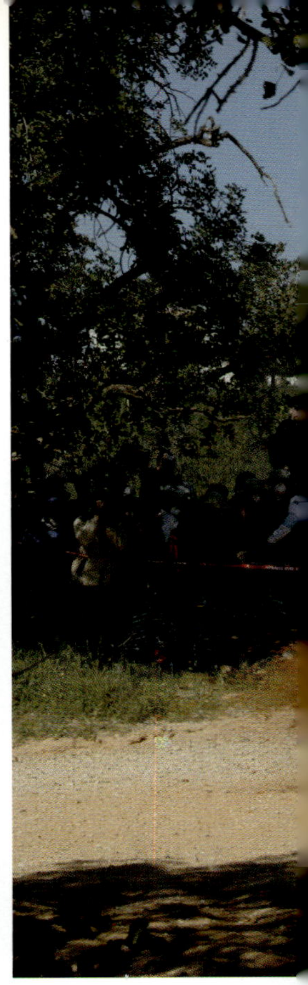

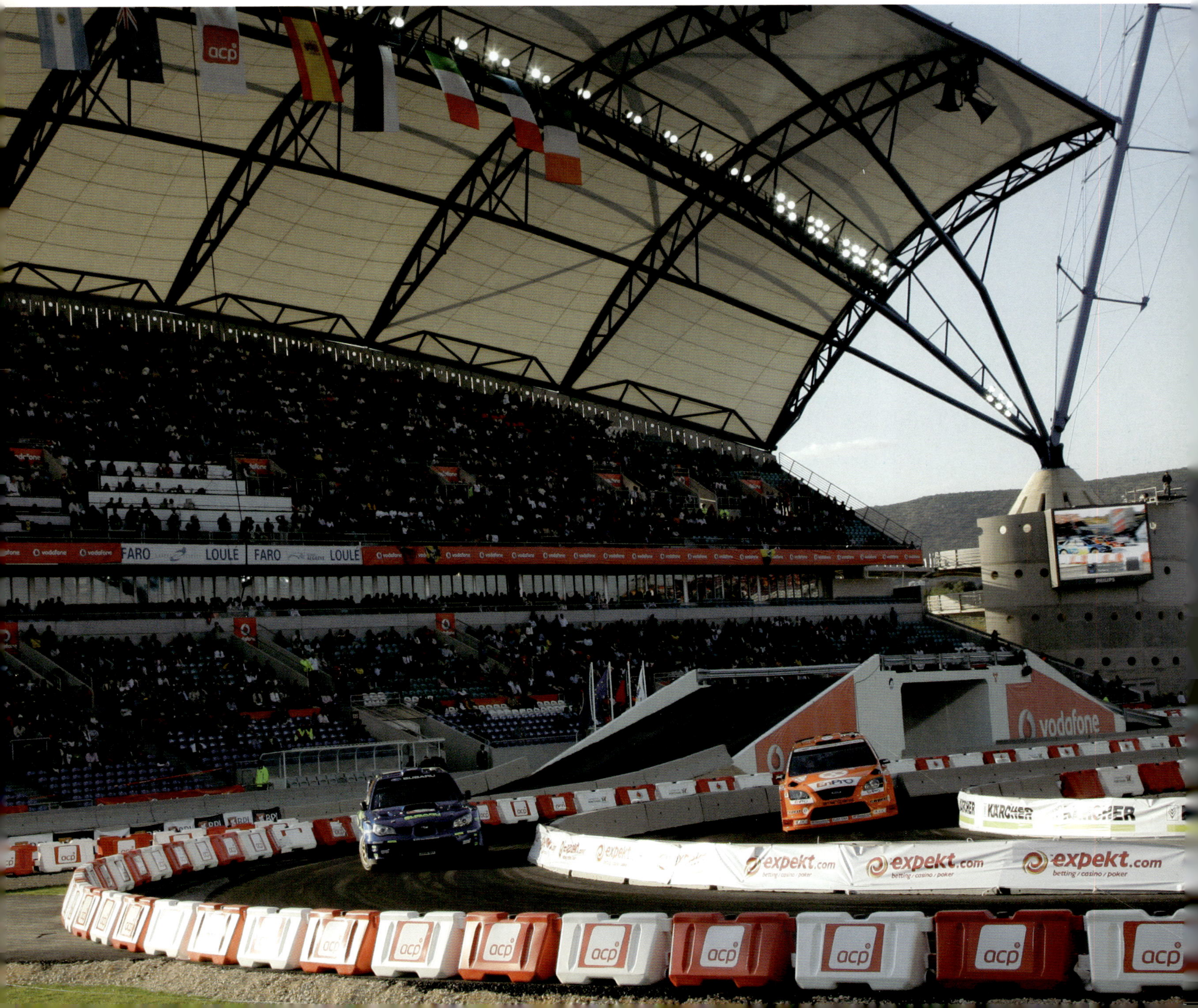
acp
FARO
LOULE
vodafone
expekt.com
betting / casino / poker
KÄRCHER

## RALLY PORTUGAL

**Opposite bottom:** Henning Solberg was among the Fords to lose out because his windows were too light. He seems to have the edge on his brother through this right-hander at the superspecial, though

**Opposite top:** Petter Solberg downloads his engineer Francois-Xavier Demaison

**Left:** Galli suffered a miserable event, unable to find any feeling in the Xsara

**Below:** Grönholm couldn't match Loeb's intuitive touch on tyre choice

All photographs by McKlein

*Another Junior round and another win for Suzuki man Andersson*
McKlein

# The FIA World Rally Championship Round 5
# Rally Portugal Results
### March 30-April 1 2007

## FINISH LINES...

Citroën privateers Daniel Carlsson and Gigi Galli moved up the order once Ford driver Jari-Matti Latvala's penalty was added to his time. The Xsara men were happy with the extra point, but Galli in particular was all at sea on this event. Shorn of ideas to make his PH Sport-run car faster, he elected to quicken local heart rates by standing atop of his moving Citroën to salute fans in the Algarve Stadium. Latvala was left with the final point in eighth place... This year's event was the first time the world championship had shown its face in Portugal since the washout that was 2001. This nation of passionate petrolheads demonstrated its fervour at the return of an old friend. Unfortunately, things didn't look good early on. For a rally that has suffered the highest number of spectator deaths - when Joaquim Santos crashed his RS200, killing three fans and injuring 30 in 1986 - the last thing it needed was crowd trouble. Those worst nightmares were realised at the earliest possible opportunity, when Armindo Araújo went off the road at the shakedown. His Mitsubishi collided with one photographer and four spectators standing in a 'no-go' area. One broken leg and a broken arm were the most serious injuries, but the event began under a cloud. The three days of competition ran without fault, but the FIA fined the organisers US$50,000 for the pre-event incident... Per-Gunnar Andersson demonstrated that the hare and tortoise theory still works on gravel rounds of the Junior series. Having suffered a puncture early on, the Suzuki-driving Swede throttled back instead of chasing his team-mate Urmo Aava hard. On the penultimate gravel test, Aava collected a puncture and P-G collected his second win in the series...

## RUNNING ORDER

| | | |
|---|---|---|
| 3 | Marcus Grönholm/<br>Timo Rautiainen | Ford Focus RS WRC 06<br>Gr A |
| 1 | Sébastien Loeb/<br>Daniel Elena | Citroën C4 WRC<br>Gr A |
| 4 | Mikko Hirvonen/<br>Jarmo Lehtinen | Ford Focus RS WRC 06<br>Gr A |
| 2 | Daniel Sordo/<br>Marc Martí | Citroën C4 WRC<br>Gr A |
| 10 | Henning Solberg/<br>Cato Menkerud | Ford Focus RS WRC 06<br>Gr A |
| 8 | Chris Atkinson/<br>Glenn Macneall | Subaru Impreza WRC 2007<br>Gr A |
| 7 | Petter Solberg/<br>Phil Mills | Subaru Impreza WRC 2007<br>Gr A |
| 6 | Daniel Carlsson/<br>Denis Giraudet | Citroën Xsara WRC<br>Gr A |
| 9 | Jari-Matti Latvala/<br>Miikka Anttila | Ford Focus RS WRC 06<br>Gr A |
| 5 | Manfred Stohl/<br>Ilka Minor | Citroën Xsara WRC<br>Gr A |
| 17 | Toni Gardemeister/<br>Jakke Honkanen | Mitsubishi Lancer WRC05<br>Gr A |
| 25 | Gianluigi Galli/<br>Giovanni Bernacchini | Citroën Xsara WRC<br>Gr A |
| 18 | Jan Kopecky/<br>Filip Schovanek | Skoda Fabia WRC<br>Gr A |
| 16 | Matthew Wilson/<br>Michael Orr | Ford Focus RS WRC 06<br>Gr A |
| 21 | Mads Østberg/<br>Ole Unnerud | Subaru Impreza WRC 2005<br>Gr A |
| 23 | Gareth MacHale/<br>Paul Nagle | Ford Focus RS WRC 06<br>Gr A |
| 22 | Armindo Araújo/<br>Miguel Ramalho | Mitsubishi Lancer WRC05<br>Gr A |
| 24 | Guy Wilks/<br>Phil Pugh | Ford Focus RS WRC 04<br>Gr A |
| 27 | Andreas Mikkelsen/<br>Ola Floene | Ford Focus RS WRC 04<br>Gr A |
| 45 | PG Andersson/<br>Jonas Andersson | Suzuki Swift<br>Gr A |

## SPECIAL STAGE TIMES

**SS1 Estadio Algarve 1 (2.20km)**

1 M.Grönholm/T.Rautiainen (Ford Focus RS WRC 06) 2m05.8s; 2 D.Sordo/M.Martí (Citroën C4 WRC) 2m08.1s; 3= S.Loeb/D.Elena (Citroën C4 WRC), P.Solberg/P.Mills (Subaru Impreza WRC 2007) 2m09.1s; 5 H.Solberg/C.Menkerud (Ford Focus RS WRC 06) 2m10.4s; 6 M.Hirvonen/J.Lehtinen (Ford Focus RS WRC 06) 2m10.7s; JWC A.Cortinovis/F.Zanella (Renault Clio R3) 2m17.6s

**SS2 Tavira 1 (19.92km)**

1 Hirvonen/Lehtinen (Ford) 14m07.5s; 2 Grönholm/Rautiainen (Ford) 14m09.5s; 3 Solberg/Mills (Subaru) 14m11.6s; 4 Loeb/Elena (Citroën) 14m12.6s; 5 Sordo/Martí (Citroën) 14m13.8s; 6= M.Stohl/I.Minor (Citroën Xsara WRC), D.Carlsson/D.Giraudet (Citroën Xsara WRC) 14m25.3s; JWC U.Aava/K.Sikk (Suzuki Swift) 15m55.8s

**SS3 Serra de Tavira 1 (24.37 km)**

1 Grönholm/Rautiainen (Ford) 16m30.1s; 2 Solberg/Mills (Subaru) 16m34.6s; 3 Loeb/Elena (Citroën) 16m36.5s; 4 Hirvonen/Lehtinen (Ford) 16m38.3s; 5 J-M.Latvala/M.Anttila (Ford Focus RS WRC 06) 16m39.9s; 6 Sordo/Martí (Citroën) 16m52.3s; JWC Aava/Sikk (Suzuki) 18m27.0s

**SS4 San Bras de Alportel 1 (16.70km)**

1 Loeb/Elena (Citroën) 11m24.3s; 2 Hirvonen/Lehtinen (Ford) 11m28.3s; 3 Latvala/Anttila (Ford) 11m32.9s; 4 Solberg/Mills (Subaru) 11m33.4s; 5 Grönholm/Rautiainen (Ford) 11m34.5s; 6 Sordo/Martí (Citroën) 11m39.5s; JWC Aava/Sikk (Suzuki) 12m41.8s

**SS5 Tavira 2 (19.92km)**

1 Grönholm/Rautiainen (Ford) 13m52.3s; 2 Solberg/Mills (Subaru) 13m52.8s; 3= Loeb/Elena (Citroën), Hirvonen/Lehtinen (Ford) 13m55.7s; 5 Sordo/Martí (Citroën) 14m03.1s; 6 Latvala/Anttila (Ford) 14m06.9s; JWC P-G.Andersson/J.Andersson (Suzuki Swift) 16m06.3s

**SS6 Serra de Tavira 2 (24.37km)**

1 Loeb/Elena (Citroën) 16m10.2s; 2 Grönholm/Rautiainen (Ford) 16m14.7s; 3 Latvala/Anttila (Ford) 16m19.5s; 4 Hirvonen/Lehtinen (Ford) 16m20.1s; 5 Solberg/Mills (Subaru) 16m23.6s; 6 Sordo/Martí (Citroën) 16m24.2s; JWC Aava/Sikk (Suzuki) 18m20.4s

**SS7 San Bras de Alportel 2 (16.70km)**

1 Loeb/Elena (Citroën) 11m10.6s; 2 Grönholm/Rautiainen (Ford) 11m15.2s; 3 Latvala/Anttila (Ford) 11m23.4s; 4 Hirvonen/Lehtinen (Ford) 11m23.7s; 5 Solberg/Mills (Subaru) 11m26.7s; 6 Sordo/Martí (Citroën) 11m28.9s; JWC Aava/Sikk (Suzuki) 12m34.2s

**SS8 Silves/Ourique 1 (30.69km)**

1 Loeb/Elena (Citroën) 21m36.5s; 2 Grönholm/Rautiainen (Ford) 21m38.5s; 3 Solberg/Mills (Subaru) 22m02.5s; 4 Hirvonen/Lehtinen (Ford) 22m05.4s; 5 Sordo/Martí (Citroën) 22m10.4s; 6 Latvala/Anttila (Ford) 22m28.6s; JWC Aava/Sikk (Suzuki) 24m21.0s

**SS9 Ourique 1 (24.87km)**

1 Loeb/Elena (Citroën) 14m59.9s; 2 Grönholm/Rautiainen (Ford) 15m05.7s; 3 Hirvonen/Lehtinen (Ford) 15m15.2s; 4 Solberg/Mills (Subaru) 15m15.8s; 5 Sordo/Martí (Citroën) 15m19.3s; 6 Latvala/Anttila (Ford) 15m33.5s; JWC Aava/Sikk (Suzuki) 16m54.0s

**SS10 Almodovar 1 (20.88km)**

1 Loeb/Elena (Citroën) 11m40.5s; 2 Grönholm/Rautiainen (Ford) 11m44.6s; 3 Hirvonen/Lehtinen (Ford) 11m52.0s; 4 Solberg/Mills (Subaru) 12m00.0s; 5 Sordo/Martí (Citroën) 12m02.0s; 6 Latvala/Anttila (Ford) 12m06.1s; JWC Aava/Sikk (Suzuki) 13m12.2s

**SS11 Silves/Ourique 2 (30.69km)**

1 Loeb/Elena (Citroën) 20m16.0s; 3 Grönholm/Rautiainen (Ford) 20m17.7s; 3 Hirvonen/Lehtinen (Ford) 20m26.5s; 4 Solberg/Mills (Subaru) 20m30.6s; 5 Latvala/Anttila (Ford) 20m42.9s; 6 G.Galli/G.Bernacchini (Citroën Xsara WRC) 20m55.1s; JWC Andersson/Andersson (Suzuki) 22m54.4s

**SS12 Ourique 2 (24.87km)**

1 Loeb/Elena (Citroën) 14m35.0s; 2 Solberg/Mills (Subaru) 14m45.1s; 3 Hirvonen/Lehtinen (Ford) 14m46.7s; 4 Grönholm/Rautiainen (Ford) 14m49.1s; 5 Sordo/Martí (Citroën) 14m59.9s; 6 Latvala/Anttila (Ford) 15m02.0s; JWC Andersson/Andersson (Suzuki) 16m18.8s

# RALLY PORTUGAL

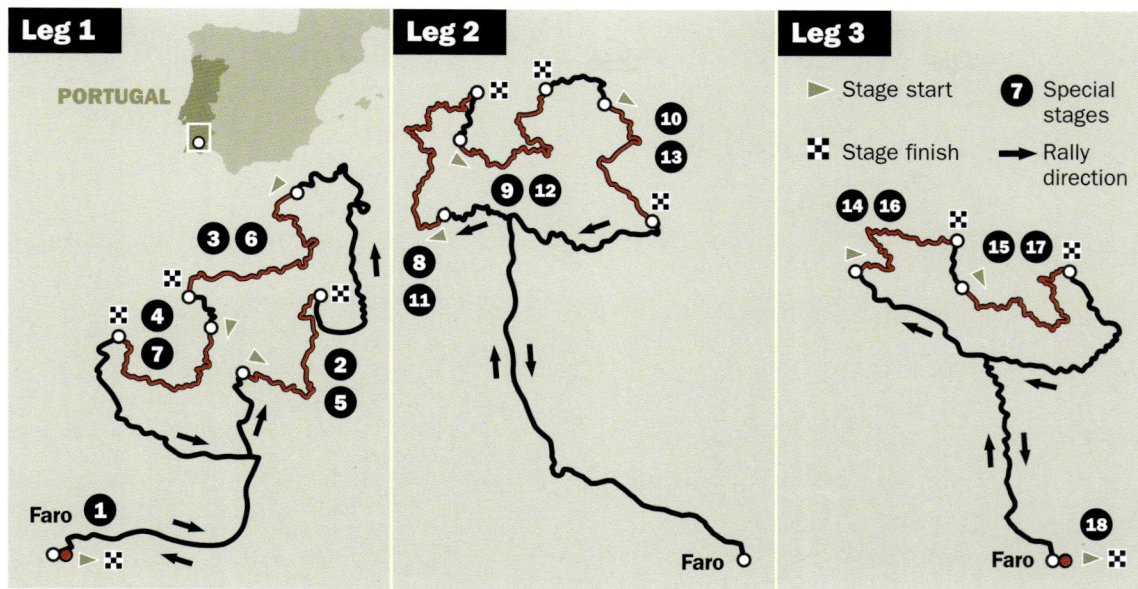

| Stage Numbers | 1 | 2 | 3 | 4 | 5 | 6 | 7 | 8 | 9 | 10 | 11 | 12 | 13 | 14 | 15 | 16 | 17 | 18 |
|---|---|---|---|---|---|---|---|---|---|---|---|---|---|---|---|---|---|---|
| Loeb | 3 | 4 | 4 | 2 | 2 | 2 | 1 | 1 | 1 | 1 | 1 | 1 | 1 | 1 | 1 | 1 | 1 | 1 |
| P.Solberg | 3 | 3 | 2 | 4 | 4 | 4 | 4 | 4 | 4 | 4 | 4 | 4 | 4 | 4 | 4 | 4 | 4 | 2 |
| Sordo | 2 | 5 | 5 | 5 | 5 | 5 | 5 | 5 | 5 | 5 | 5 | 5 | 5 | 5 | 5 | 5 | 5 | 3 |
| Grönholm | 1 | 1 | 1 | 1 | 1 | 1 | 2 | 2 | 2 | 2 | 2 | 2 | 2 | 2 | 2 | 2 | 2 | 4 |
| Hirvonen | 6 | 2 | 3 | 3 | 3 | 3 | 3 | 3 | 3 | 3 | 3 | 3 | 3 | 3 | 3 | 3 | 3 | 5 |
| Carlsson | 8 | 6 | 6 | 7 | 9 | 9 | 9 | 9 | 9 | 7 | 7 | 8 | 8 | 7 | 7 | 7 | 7 | 6 |
| Galli | 8 | 9 | 9 | 12 | 11 | 11 | 11 | 11 | 11 | 9 | 9 | 9 | 9 | 9 | 9 | 9 | 9 | 7 |
| Latvala | 44 | 18 | 11 | 9 | 7 | 6 | 6 | 6 | 6 | 6 | 6 | 6 | 6 | 6 | 6 | 6 | 6 | 8 |
| Stohl | 14 | 7 | 6 | 6 | 7 | 7 | 7 | 7 | 7 | 11 | 10 | 10 | 10 | 10 | 10 | 10 | 10 | 9 |
| Mikkelsen | 15 | 15 | 17 | 16 | 14 | 14 | 14 | 12 | 12 | 10 | 11 | 11 | 11 | 11 | 11 | 11 | 11 | 10 |
| H.Solberg | 5 | 13 | 12 | 11 | 10 | 10 | 10 | 10 | 8 | 8 | 7 | 7 | 7 | 8 | 8 | 8 | 9 | 11 |
| Wilson | 16 | 15 | 15 | 14 | 13 | 13 | 13 | 14 | 13 | 13 | 13 | 13 | 13 | 13 | 13 | 13 | 13 | 12 |
| MacHale | 13 | 17 | 16 | 15 | 15 | 15 | 15 | 15 | 15 | 14 | 14 | 14 | 14 | 14 | 14 | 14 | 13 | 13 |
| Kopecky | 18 | 53 | 63 | 65 | 59 | 56 | 57 | 49 | 43 | 39 | 35 | 31 | 26 | 25 | 23 | 23 | 22 | 20 |
| Araújo | 17 | 14 | 14 | 13 | 12 | 12 | 12 | 13 | 13 | 12 | 12 | 12 | 12 | 12 | 12 | 12 | 12 | R |
| Atkinson | 7 | 11 | 10 | 8 | 8 | 8 | 8 | 8 | 8 | R | | | | | | | | |
| G'meister | | | | 10 | 8 | 8 | 10 | R | | | | | | | | | | |
| Östberg | | | | 12 | 12 | 13 | R | | | | | | | | | | | |
| Wilks | | | 11 | 10 | R | | | | | | | | | | | | | |

**SS13 Almodovar 2 (20.88km)**
1 Loeb/Elena (Citroën) 11m38.6s; 2 Grönholm/Rautiainen (Ford) 11m48.3s; 3 Solberg/Mills (Subaru) 11m49.9s; 4 Hirvonen/Lehtinen (Ford) 11m52.7s; 5 Sordo/Martí (Citroën) 11m58.0s; 6 Latvala/Anttila (Ford) 12m01.4s; JWC Andersson/Andersson (Suzuki) 13m03.1s

**SS14 Loule/Almodovar 1 (17.60km)**
1 Hirvonen/Lehtinen (Ford) 11m18.0s; 2 Loeb/Elena (Citroën) 11m23.3s; 3 Grönholm/Rautiainen (Ford) 11m27.3s; 4 Solberg/Mills (Subaru) 11m31.5s; 5 Latvala/Anttila (Ford) 11m34.2s; 6 Carlsson/Giraudet (Citroën) 11m37.6s; JWC Andersson/Andersson (Suzuki) 12m37.0s

**SS15 Loule 1 (22.70km)**
1 Loeb/Elena (Citroën) 14m09.3s; 2 Grönholm/Rautiainen (Ford) 14m13.3s; 3 Hirvonen/Lehtinen (Ford) 14m15.4s; 4 Latvala/Anttila (Ford) 14m24.6s; 5 Solberg/Mills (Subaru) 14m26.5s; 6 Sordo/Martí (Citroën) 14m28.9s; JWC Andersson/Andersson (Suzuki) 15m34.5s

**SS16 Loule/Almodovar 2 (17.60km)**
1 Grönholm/Rautiainen (Ford) 11m11.1s; 2 Loeb/Elena (Citroën) 11m18.7s; 3 Hirvonen/Lehtinen (Ford) 11m19.0s; 4 Latvala/Anttila (Ford) 11m21.6s; 5 Solberg/Mills (Subaru) 11m23.7s; 6 Solberg/Menkerud (Ford) 11m25.5s; JWC Andersson/Andersson (Suzuki) 12m36.2s

**SS17 Loule 2 (22.70km)**
1 Grönholm/Rautiainen (Ford) 14m02.0s; 2 Loeb/Elena (Citroën) 14m09.5s; 3 Hirvonen/Lehtinen (Ford) 14m10.3s; 4 Latvala/Anttila (Ford) 14m17.7s; 5 Sordo/Martí (Citroën) 14m25.7s; 6 Solberg/Mills (Subaru) 14m27.4s; JWC Andersson/Andersson (Suzuki) 15m24.0s

**SS18 Estadio Algarve 2 (2.20km)**
1 Loeb/Elena (Citroën) 2m06.8s; 2 Sordo/Martí (Citroën) 2m10.0s; 3 G.MacHale/P.Nagle (Ford Focus RS WRC 06) 2m10.4s; 4 Grönholm/Rautiainen (Ford) 2m10.5s; 5 Carlsson/Giraudet (Citroën) 2m11.3s; 6 Galli/Bernacchini (Citroën) 2m12.0s; JWC Andersson/Andersson (Suzuki) 2m16.9s

Cars who retired and subsequently restarted and were classified under SuperRally regs:
18 Kopecky/S'vanek   Skoda Fabia WRC
   Brakes            SS2           Gr A

**MAJOR RETIREMENTS**
8  Atkinson/Macneall   Subaru Impreza WRC 2007
   Accident            SS10          Gr A
17 G'meister/Honkanen  Mitsubishi Lancer WRC05
   Excluded            SS4           Gr A
21 Östberg/Unnerud     Subaru Impreza WRC 2005
   Accident            SS4
22 Araújo/Ramalho      Mitsubishi Lancer WRC05
   Accident            SS17
24 Wilks/Pugh          Ford Focus RS WRC 04
   Accident            SS3

**FIA CLASS WINNERS**
A8  Over 2000 cc     Loeb/Elena
                     Citroën C4 WRC
A7  1600-2000cc      Rueda/Rozada
                     Renault Clio R3
A6  1400-1600cc      Andersson/Andersson
                     Suzuki Swift
N4  Over 2000 cc     Flodin/Andersson
                     Subaru Impreza WRX Sti

N3  1600-2000cc      Clark/Martin
                     Ford Fiesta ST
N2  1400-1600cc      Shean/Condessa
                     Citroën Saxo VTS

**RALLY LEADERS**
Overall: SS1-6 Grönholm; SS7-18 Loeb
JWC: SS1 Cortinovis; SS2-16 Aava; SS17-18 Andersson

**SPECIAL STAGE ANALYSIS**

|  | 1st | 2nd | 3rd | 4th | 5th | 6th |
|---|---|---|---|---|---|---|
| Loeb (Citroën) | 11 | 3 | 3 | 1 | - | - |
| Grönholm (Ford) | 5 | 9 | 1 | 2 | 1 | - |
| Hirvonen (Ford) | 2 | 1 | 8 | 5 | - | 1 |
| P.Solberg (Subaru) | - | 3 | 4 | 5 | 4 | 1 |
| Sordo (Citroën) | - | 2 | - | - | 8 | 5 |
| Latvala (Ford) | - | - | 3 | 3 | 3 | 6 |
| MacHale (Ford) | - | - | 1 | - | - | - |
| Carlsson (Citroën) | - | - | - | - | 1 | 2 |
| H.Solberg (Ford) | - | - | - | 1 | 1 | - |
| Galli (Citroën) | - | - | - | - | - | 2 |
| Stohl (Citroën) | - | - | - | - | - | 1 |

**WORLD CHAMPIONSHIP POINTS**
Drivers
1 Loeb 38; 2 Grönholm 37; 3 Hirvonen 30; 4 Sordo 19; 5 P.Solberg 16; 6 H.Solberg 11; 7 Atkinson 10; 8 Carlsson 9; 9 Latvala 7; 10= Gardemeister, Stohl, Galli 5 etc
Manufacturers
1 BP-Ford WRT 67; 2 Citroën Total WRT 59; 3 Subaru WRT 27; 4= Stobart M-Sport Ford RT, OMV-Kronos Citroën WRT 21
Junior World Championship
1 Andersson 20; 2 Aava 14; 3= Mölder 10; 4 Sandell 8; 5= Béres, Cortinovis 6; 7 Burkart 4; 8= Svenkerud, Rueda, Gallagher 3 etc
Production Cup
1 Sohlberg 12; 2 Arai 11; 3= Svedlund, Higgins 10; 5 Alén 8; 6 Nutahara 6; 7= Araújo, Baldacci 5; 9 Pastrana 4; 10 Vojtech 3; etc

**ROUTE DETAILS**
Total route of 1009.31km of which 357.10km were competitive on 18 stages
**Leg 1** Friday 30 March, 7 Special Stages totalling 122.79km
**Leg 2** Saturday 31 March, 6 Special Stages totalling 152.92km
**Leg 3** Sunday 1 April, 5 Special Stages totalling 81.39km

**RESULTS**
1  Sébastien Loeb/       Citroën C4 WRC
   Daniel Elena          3h53m33.1s        Gr A
2  Petter Solberg/       Subaru Impreza WRC 2007
   Phil Mills            3h56m47.0s
3  Daniel Sordo/         Citroën Xsara WRC
   Marc Martí            3h58m38.4s
4  Marcus Grönholm/      Ford Focus RS WRC 06
   Timo Rautiainen       3h59m10.2s        Gr A
5  Mikko Hirvonen/       Ford Focus RS WRC 06
   Jarmo Lehtinen        4h00m41.2s        Gr A
6  Daniel Carlsson/      Citroën Xsara WRC
   Denis Giraudet        4h01m46.3s        Gr A
7  Gianluigi Galli/      Citroën Xsara WRC
   Giovanni Bernacchini  4h03m12.7s        Gr A
8  Jari-Matti Latvala/   Ford Focus RS WRC 06
   Miikka Anttila        4h04m18.0s        Gr A
9  Manfred Stohl/        Citroën Xsara WRC
   Ilka Minor            4h06m19.1s        Gr A
10 Andreas Mikkelsen/    Ford Focus RS WRC 04
   Ola Floene            4h07m24.7s        Gr A
80 starters, 61 finishers

**RECENT WINNERS**
| 1970 | Simo Lampinen/John Davenport | Lancia Fulvia HF |
| 1971 | Jean-Pierre Nicolas/Jean Todt | Alpine Renault A110 |
| 1972 | Achim Warmbold/John Davenport | BMW 2002ti |
| 1973 | Jean-Luc Thérier/Jacques Jaubert | Alpine Renault A110 |
| 1974 | Rafaele Pinto/Arnaldo Bernacchini | Fiat 124 Abarth |
| 1975 | Markku Alen/Ilkka Kivimaki | Fiat 124 Abarth |
| 1976 | Sandro Munari/Silvio Maiga | Lancia Stratos |
| 1977 | Markku Alén/Ilkka Kivimaki | Fiat 131 Abarth |
| 1978 | Markku Alén/Ilkka Kivimaki | Fiat 131 Abarth |
| 1979 | Hannu Mikkola/Arne Hertz | Ford Escort RS |
| 1980 | Walter Röhrl/Christian Geistdörfer | Fiat 131 Abarth |
| 1981 | Markku Alén/Ilkka Kivimaki | Fiat 131 Abarth |
| 1982 | Michèle Mouton/Fabrizia Pons | Audi Quattro |
| 1983 | Hannu Mikkola/Arne Hertz | Audi Quattro A1 |
| 1984 | Hannu Mikkola/Arne Hertz | Audi Quattro A2 |
| 1985 | Timo Salonen/Seppo Harjanne | Peugeot 205 Turbo 16 |
| 1986 | Joaquim Moutinho/Edgar Fortes | Renault 5 Turbo |
| 1987 | Markku Alén/Ilkka Kivimaki | Lancia Delta HF 4x4 |
| 1988 | Miki Biasion/Carlo Cassina | Lancia Delta Integrale |
| 1989 | Miki Biasion/Tiziano Siviero | Lancia Delta Integrale |
| 1990 | Miki Biasion/Tiziano Siviero | Lancia Delta Integrale 16v |
| 1991 | Carlos Sainz/Luis Moya | Toyota Celica GT4 |
| 1992 | Juha Kankkunen/Juha Piironen | Lancia Delta HF Integrale |
| 1993 | François Delecour/Daniel Grataloup | Ford Escort RS Cosworth |
| 1994 | Juha Kankkunen/Nicky Grist | Toyota Celica Turbo 4wd |
| 1995 | Carlos Sainz/Luis Moya | Subaru Impreza 555 |
| 1996 | Rui Madeira/Nuno Silva | Toyota Celica GT-Four |
| 1997 | Tommi Mäkinen/Seppo Harjanne | Mitsubishi Lancer E4 |
| 1998 | Colin McRae/Nicky Grist | Subaru Impreza WRC98 |
| 1999 | Colin McRae/Nicky Grist | Ford Focus WRC |
| 2000 | Richard Burns/Robert Reid | Subaru Impreza WRC2000 |
| 2001 | Tommi Mäkinen/Risto Mannisenmäki | Mitsubishi Lancer Evo |
| 2002*| Didier Auriol/Thierry Barjou | Toyota Corolla WRC |
| 2003*| Armindo Araújo/Miguel Ramalho | Citroën Saxo Kit |
| 2004*| Armindo Araújo/Miguel Ramalho | Citroën Saxo Kit |
| 2005*| Daniel Carlsson/Mattias Andersson | Subaru Impreza WRX Sti (N) |
| 2006*| Armindo Araújo/Miguel Ramalho | Mitsubishi Lancer E8 (N) |

*Non-championship event

## The FIA World Rally Championship Round 6
# Rally Argentina

SURREAL didn't come close. Here lying on the floor, with seats, bags or whatever else appeared closest to a bed, were the millionaire drivers of the World Rally Championship. The time was approaching midnight in Buenos Aires and nobody knew when heads would be hitting pillows 450 miles west in Villa Carlos Paz. The Rally Argentina organisers' decision to run a superspecial stage in BA had backfired. And then some! In the end, Sébastien Loeb won the rally, but another superlative performance from the Frenchman was overshadowed by the events that preceded it. Farce and misfortune were the key players in this year's South American WRC round.

The problem was the fog. The stage in the River Plate stadium in Buenos Aires went off without any trouble, but when the weather closed in, there was little chance of the three WRC-chartered planes leaving the capital. Some people made it back in the early hours, but it was mid-morning on Friday when the rest returned. Mid-morning that was when they should have been thundering through the Translasierra Mountains. Leg one was scrapped because of the airborne delays, saving further egg on the organisers' faces - it turned out that the WRC cars hadn't made it back from the capital by road in time anyway. Largely the verdict was one of sympathy for the blind ambition shown by the organisers. The sport took a collective sharp intake of breath, however, when the rally's top brass said they intended to repeat the superspecial next season.

On the stages, it was all about Loeb again. Shorn of split times (he was running first on the road), the Frenchman said he was driving quite conservatively. It didn't show. Following the superspecials, five stages were run before he was beaten. But by then, he was comfortably up on Marcus Grönholm, and provided he could keep avoiding the stray dogs which seemed attracted to the front bumper of his speeding Citroen C4 WRC, he would be home and dry. Dry that was apart from the incredible downpour that hit Carlos Paz on the final morning, apparently to test the final reserves of the organisers' resolve. As mechanics were hauled from their beds to mop up the service park, Loeb nosed his way through the sodden and foggy Mina Clavero and Condor stages to clinch his third win on the trot and his fourth of the season.

Grönholm wasn't a million miles behind Loeb, but he might as well have been. The Ford driver didn't really look like winning - particularly when he went off on the first stage on Sunday morning. If the Finn was depressed, it was nothing compared with the dejection being experienced by Petter Solberg. His Subaru had been running comfortably third until stage 16 when Solberg clipped a rock, which flicked the Impreza onto two wheels. No problem there, but the landing damaged the radiator and caused a terminal engine problem. Whether we were calling Saturday leg one or leg two, it mattered little - the Norwegian was out.

Ford's Mikko Hirvonen was waiting in the wings, ready to collect yet another third place. Hirvonen had been unhappy at his inability to match the pace of those at the front, but he kept his car in one piece and bagged more valuable points. The final step of the podium is in danger of becoming Hirvonen's second home.

# RALLY ARGENTINA

**Below:** Despite struggling for pace in Argentina, Hirvonen collected another third place after Petter Solberg crashed out

**Opposite:** Running first on the road, Loeb took a conservative approach – but it didn't show as his lead grew

**Left:** Loeb found himself at the centre of attention in Argentina after scoring his third win on the trot

All photographs by McKlein

## RALLY ARGENTINA

*Below:* Henning Solberg battled through the fog to fifth place, helping the Stobart VK team back ahead of Subaru in the points

*Right:* Buenos Aires was the setting for the controversial superspecial, where drivers were stranded by bad weather

*Opposite top:* Solberg's Stobart VK team-mate Jari-Matti Latvala had a clean and impressive run to fourth

*Opposite bottom:* Sordo tackles the superspecial. He overcame hydraulic problems on board his Citroën to finish sixth

All photographs by McKlein

Federico Villagra put his local knowledge to full use to claim a second successive Group N win on home soil
McKlein

## The FIA World Rally Championship Round 6
# Rally Argentina Results
### May 3-6 2007

### FINISH LINES...

The Stobart VK team moved back past Subaru in the manufacturers' standings by finishing fourth and fifth, with Jari-Matti Latvala leading home the sister Ford Focus RS WRC 06 of Henning Solberg... Their joy wasn't shared in the third Stobart Ford of Matthew Wilson. His event ended on the first stage proper with an electrical fault on his Focus... Dani Sordo overcame hydraulic problems aboard his C4 to post sixth, with Chris Atkinson (Subaru) and Manfred Stohl (OMV Citroën) taking the final points... Local driver Federico Villagra made the most of his one-off entry in the Production Car World Rally Championship, seeing off a determined challenge from Toshi Arai to clinch his second successive Group N victory on his home round of the series. Just as he'd finished spraying champagne on the podium, he was asked if he'd like to replace Juan Pablo Raies in the Munchi's Ford World Rally Team, which must have left him tempted to pick up another bottle. For a man whose dream was to just find the cash for one WRC round in a World Rally Car, being asked if he'd like to drive a full-spec factory car for 10 rallies was not a difficult proposition... All the problems that beset this event were put into perspective when a rally fan was killed on the second day. The 49-year-old lady had been standing on the road section leading to SS14 when a local driver lost control of his car on right-hand bend and rolled into a group of spectators.

### RUNNING ORDER

| # | Driver/Co-driver | Car | Class |
|---|---|---|---|
| 1 | Sébastien Loeb/Daniel Elena | Citroën C4 WRC | Gr A |
| 3 | Marcus Grönholm/Timo Rautiainen | Ford Focus RS WRC 06 | Gr A |
| 4 | Mikko Hirvonen/Jarmo Lehtinen | Ford Focus RS WRC 06 | Gr A |
| 2 | Daniel Sordo/Marc Martí | Citroën C4 WRC | Gr A |
| 7 | Petter Solberg/Phil Mills | Subaru Impreza WRC 2007 | Gr A |
| 10 | Henning Solberg/Cato Menkerud | Ford Focus RS WRC 06 | Gr A |
| 8 | Chris Atkinson/Stéphane Prevot | Subaru Impreza WRC 2007 | Gr A |
| 9 | Jari-Matti Latvala/Miikka Anttila | Ford Focus RS WRC 06 | Gr A |
| 5 | Manfred Stohl/Ilka Minor | Citroën Xsara WRC | Gr A |
| 16 | Matthew Wilson/Michael Orr | Ford Focus RS WRC 06 | Gr A |
| 12 | Juan Pablo Raies/Jorge Perez-Compancr | Ford Focus RS WRC 06 | Gr A |
| 11 | Luis Perez-Companc/José María Volta | Ford Focus RS WRC 06 | Gr A |
| 38 | Kristian Sohlberg/Risto Pietiläinen | Subaru Impreza WRX Sti | Gr N |
| 31 | Toshihiro Arai/Tony Sircombe | Subaru Impreza WRX Sti | Gr N |
| 35 | Fumio Nutahara/Daniel Barritt | Mitsubishi Lancer Evo 9 | Gr N |
| 45 | Mirco Baldacci/Giovanni Agnese | Subaru Impreza WRX Sti | Gr N |
| 52 | Travis Pastrana/Bjorn Estrom | Subaru Impreza WRX Sti | Gr N |
| 49 | Stepan Vojtech/Michal Ernst | Mitsubishi Lancer Evo 9 | Gr N |
| 39 | Nasser Al-Attiyah/Chris Patterson | Subaru Impreza WRX Sti | Gr N |

### SPECIAL STAGE TIMES

**SS1 River Plate Stadium 1 (2.40km)**
1 M.Hirvonen/J.Lehtinen (Ford Focus RS WRC 06) 2m08.3s; 2 M.Grönholm/T.Rautiainen (Ford Focus RS WRC 06) 2m08.9s; 3 D.Sordo/M.Martí (Citroën C4 WRC) 2m09.1s; 4= S.Loeb/D.Elena (Citroën C4 WRC), P.Solberg/P.Mills (Subaru Impreza WRC 2007) 2m09.8s; 6 C.Atkinson/S.Prevot (Subaru Impreza WRC 2007) 2m11.0s; PC L.Kuzaj/J.Baran (Subaru Impreza WRX Sti) 2m15.2s

**SS2 Capilla del Monte 1 (22.95km)**
Cancelled due to delays in transporting drivers from Buenos Aires to Cordoba

**SS3 San Marcos 1 (19.23km)**
Cancelled due to delays in transporting drivers from Buenos Aires to Cordoba

**SS4 Villa Giardino 1 (15.50km)**
Cancelled due to delays in transporting drivers from Buenos Aires to Cordoba

**SS5 Valle Hermoso 1 (10.94km)**
Cancelled due to delays in transporting drivers from Buenos Aires to Cordoba

**SS6 Cosquin 1 (11.27km)**
Cancelled due to delays in transporting drivers from Buenos Aires to Cordoba

**SS7 Capilla del Monte 2 (22.95km)**
Cancelled due to delays in transporting drivers from Buenos Aires to Cordoba

**SS8 San Marcos 2 (19.23km)**
Cancelled due to delays in transporting drivers from Buenos Aires to Cordoba

**SS9 Estadio Cordoba 1 (2.40km)**
1 Hirvonen/Lehtinen (Ford) 2m31.7s; 2 J-M.Latvala/M.Anttila (Ford Focus RS WRC 06) 2m32.9s; 3 Loeb/Elena (Citroën) 2m33.1s; 4 Atkinson/Prevot (Subaru) 2m33.2s; 5 Sordo/Martí (Citroën) 2m33.3s; 6 Solberg/Mills (Subaru) 2m33.5s; PC M.Baldacci/G.Agnese (Subaru Impreza WRX Sti) 2m39.6s

**SS10 La Cumbre (18.70km)**
1 Loeb/Elena (Citroën) 15m35.1s; 2 Solberg/Mills (Subaru) 15m39.2s; 3 Grönholm/Rautiainen (Ford) 15m39.7s; 4 Hirvonen/Lehtinen (Ford) 15m46.7s; 5 Sordo/Martí (Citroën) 15m54.1s; 6 Latvala/Anttila (Ford) 15m58.3s; PC K.Sohlberg/R.Pietiläinen (Subaru Impreza WRX Sti) 16m49.6s

**SS11 Ascochinga (23.28km)**
1 Loeb/Elena (Citroën) 14m45.2s; 2 Grönholm/Rautiainen (Ford) 14m47.8; 3 Hirvonen/Lehtinen (Ford) 14m51.3s; 4 Solberg/Mills (Subaru) 14m54.1s; 5 Atkinson/Prevot (Subaru) 14m58.3s; 6 Sordo/Martí (Citroën) 14m59.7s; PC F.Villagra/D.Curletto (Mitsubishi Lancer Evo 9) 15m57.4s

**SS12 Villa Giardino 2 (15.50km)**
1 Loeb/Elena (Citroën) 11m02.6s; 2 Grönholm/Rautiainen (Ford) 11m03.2s; 3 Solberg/Mills (Subaru) 11m04.6s; 4 Hirvonen/Lehtinen (Ford) 11m12.2s; 5 Atkinson/Macneall (Subaru) 11m18.2s; 6 H.Solberg/C.Menkerud (Ford Focus RS WRC 06) 11m25.4s; PC M.Ligato/R.Garcia (Mitsubishi Lancer Evo 9) 12m13.1s

**SS13 Valle Hermoso 2 (10.94km)**
1 Loeb/Elena (Citroën) 7m11.3s; 2 Solberg/Mills (Subaru) 7m12.6s; 3 Grönholm/Rautiainen (Ford) 7m16.6s; 4 Hirvonen/Lehtinen (Ford) 7m19.4s; 5 Atkinson/Macneall (Subaru) 7m19.5s; 6 Sordo/Martí (Citroën) 7m21.6s; PC Villagra/Curletto (Mitsubishi) 7m46.4s

**SS14 Cosquin 2 (11.27km)**
1 Loeb/Elena (Citroën) 6m09.5s; 2 Grönholm/Rautiainen (Ford) 6m11.7s; 3 Solberg/Mills (Subaru) 6m18.0s; 4 Hirvonen/Lehtinen (Ford) 6m18.4s; 5 Latvala/Anttila (Ford) 6m19.0s; 6 Sordo/Martí (Citroën) 6m21.0s; PC Ligato/Garcia (Mitsubishi) 6m42.7s

**SS15 Santa Rosa 1 (21.40km)**
1 Grönholm/Rautiainen (Ford) 12m48.1s; 2 Loeb/Elena (Citroën) 12m50.7s 3 Solberg/Mills (Subaru) 13m00.0s; 4 Hirvonen/Lehtinen (Ford) 13m05.9s; 5 Solberg/Menkerud (Ford) 13m07.5s; 6 Latvala/Anttila (Ford) 13m08.4s; PC Ligato/Garcia (Mitsubishi) 14m15.1s

# RALLY ARGENTINA

**SS16 Las Bajadas (16.35km)**
1 Loeb/Elena (Citroën) 8m39.8s; 2 Grönholm/Rautiainen (Ford) 8m42.1s; 3 Solberg/Menkerud (Ford) 8m42.7s; 4 Solberg/Mills (Subaru) 8m45.4s; 5 Hirvonen/Lehtinen (Ford) 8m48.5s; 6 Sordo/Martí (Citroën) 8m49.1s; PC G.Pozzo/D.Stillo (Mitsubishi Lancer Evo 9) 9m33.7s

**SS17 Amboy (20.29km)**
1 Loeb/Elena (Citroën) 10m19.4s; 2 Grönholm/Rautiainen (Ford) 10m23.7s; 3 Hirvonen/Lehtinen (Ford) 10m28.3s; 4 Solberg/Menkerud (Ford) 10m33.3s; 5 Latvala/Anttila (Ford) 10m34.8s; 6 Sordo/Martí (Citroën) 10m36.1s; PC Pozzo/Stillo (Mitsubishi) 11m34.4s

**SS18 Santa Rosa 2 (21.40km)**
1 Grönholm/Rautiainen (Ford) 12m56.3s; 2 Loeb/Elena (Citroën) 12m56.5s; 3 Hirvonen/Lehtinen (Ford) 13m07.6s; 4 Solberg/Menkerud (Ford) 13m08.0s; 5 Latvala/Anttila (Ford) 13m09.2s; 6 Atkinson/Macneall (Subaru) 13m23.5s; PC Pozzo/Stillo (Mitsubishi) 14m18.3s

**SS19 Mina Clavero 1 (23.81km)**
1 Loeb/Elena (Citroën) 18m48.8s; 2 Grönholm/Rautiainen (Ford) 18m57.1s; 3 Atkinson/Macneall (Subaru) 19m10.6s; 4 Sordo/Martí (Citroën) 19m11.9s; 5 Latvala/Anttila (Ford) 19m12.4s; 6 Hirvonen/Lehtinen (Ford) 19m14.5s; PC Villagra/Curletto (Mitsubishi) 20m27.4s

**SS20 El Condor 1 (16.81km)**
1 Sordo/Martí (Citroën) 13m39.9s; 2 Loeb/Elena (Citroën) 13m49.4s; 3= Hirvonen/Lehtinen (Ford), Atkinson/Macneall (Subaru) 13m54.0s; 5 Solberg/Menkerud (Ford) 13m55.2s; 6 L.Perez-Companc/J-M.Volta (Ford Focus WRC 06) 13m55.3s; PC T.Arai/T.Sircombe (Subaru Impreza WRX Sti) 14m44.8s

**SS21 Mina Clavero 2 (23.81km)**
1 Loeb/Elena (Citroën) 18m51.2s; 2 Sordo/Martí (Citroën) 18m55.3s; 3 Grönholm/Rautiainen (Ford) 18m56.6s; 4 Hirvonen/Lehtinen (Ford) 19m10.3s; 5 Solberg/Menkerud (Ford) 19m13.9s; 6 Latvala/Anttila (Ford) 19m19.1s; PC Pozzo/Stillo (Mitsubishi) 20m25.2s

**SS22 El Condor 2 (16.81km)**
1 Sordo/Martí (Citroën) 13m46.8s; 2 Grönholm/Rautiainen (Ford) 13m47.9s; 3 Solberg/Menkerud (Ford) 13m53.4s; 4 Hirvonen/Lehtinen (Ford) 13m54.8s; 5 Loeb/Elena (Citroën) 13m56.0s; 6 Latvala/Anttila (Ford) 14m04.0s; PC Villagra/Curletto (Mitsubishi) 14m44.0s

**SS23 Estadio Cordoba 2 (2.40km)**
1 Loeb/Elena (Citroën) 2m25.4s; 2 Grönholm/Rautiainen (Ford) 2m26.7s; 3 Hirvonen/Lehtinen (Ford) 2m27.1s; 4 P.Flodin/M.Andersson (PC Subaru Impreza WRX Sti) 2m27.4s; 5 N.McShea/G.Noble (PC Subaru Impreza WRX Sti) 2m27.9s; 6 M.Wilson/N.Orr (Ford Focus RS WRC 06) 2m29.8s

Cars who retired and subsequently restarted and were classified under SuperRally regs:
16 Wilson/Orr — Ford Focus RS WRC 06 — Electrical — SS10 — Gr A
11 P-Companc/Volta — Ford Focus RS WRC 06 — Accident — SS10 — Gr A

## MAJOR RETIREMENTS
7 Solberg/Mills — Subaru Impreza WRC 2007 — Engine — SS17 — Gr A
18 Sohlberg/P'lainen — Subaru Impreza WRX Sti — Steering arm — SS12 — Gr N
45 Baldacci/Agnese — Subaru Impreza WRX Sti — Engine — SS22 — Gr N
35 Nutahara/Barritt — Mitsubishi Lancer Evo 9 — Out of fuel — SS21 — Gr N

39 Al-Attiyah/Patterson — Subaru Impreza WRX Sti — Lost wheel — SS18 — Gr N

## FIA CLASS WINNERS
A8 Over 2000cc — Loeb/Elena — Citroën C4 WRC
A6 1400-1600cc — Jauregui/Filippi — Peugeot 206
N4 Over 2000 cc — Villagra/Curletto — Mitsubishi Lancer Evo 9
N3 1600-2000cc — Machinea/Marongiu — Peugeot 206 RC
N2 1400-1600 cc — Bottazzini/De Luca — Honda Civic Vti

## RALLY LEADERS
Overall: SS1, SS9 Hirvonen; SS10-23 Loeb
PC: SS1 Kuzaj; SS9 M.Baldacci; SS10 Sohlberg; SS11-15 Villagra; SS16-17 Arai; SS18-23 Villagra
(SS2-8 cancelled)

## SPECIAL STAGE ANALYSIS

|  | 1st | 2nd | 3rd | 4th | 5th | 6th |
|---|---|---|---|---|---|---|
| Loeb (Citroën) | 10 | 3 | 1 | 1 | 1 | - |
| Grönholm (Ford) | 2 | 9 | 3 | - | - | - |
| Sordo (Citroën) | 2 | 1 | 1 | 1 | 2 | 5 |
| Hirvonen (Ford) | 2 | - | 5 | 7 | 1 | 1 |
| P.Solberg (Subaru) | - | 2 | 3 | 3 | - | 1 |
| Latvala (Ford) | - | 1 | - | - | 4 | 4 |
| H.Solberg (Ford) | - | - | 2 | 2 | 3 | 1 |
| Atkinson (Subaru) | - | - | - | 2 | 1 | 3 | 2 |
| Foldin (PC Subaru) | - | - | - | - | 1 | - |
| McShea (PC Subaru) | - | - | - | - | 1 | - |
| Wilson (Ford) | - | - | - | - | - | 1 |
| P-Companc (Ford) | - | - | - | - | - | 1 |

## WORLD CHAMPIONSHIP POINTS

**Drivers**
1 Loeb 48; 2 Grönholm 45; 3 Hirvonen 36; 4 Sordo 22; 5 P.Solberg 16; 6 H.Solberg 15; 7= Atkinson, Latvala 12; 9 Carlsson 9; 10 Stohl 6 etc

**Manufacturers**
1 BP-Ford WRT 81; 2 Citroën Total WRT 72; 3 Stobart M-Sport Ford RT 30; 4 Subaru WRT 29; 5 OMV-Kronos Citroën WRT 22

**Junior World Championship**
1 Andersson 20; 2 Aava 14; 3 Mölder 10; 4 Sandell 8; 5= Béres, Cortinovis 6; 7 Burkart 4; 8= Svenkerud, Rueda, Gallagher 3 etc

**Production Cup**
1 Arai 19; 2 Solberg 12; 3= Svedlund, Higgins, Villagra 10; 6 Alén 8; 7= Nutahara, Hänninen 6; 9= Araújo, Baldacci, Pozzo 5 etc

## ROUTE DETAILS
Total route of 1383.14km of which 247.60km were competitive on 16 stages (7 cancelled totalling 122.07km)
**Leg 1** Thursday 3 May - Friday 4 May, 2 Special Stages totalling 4.80km (7 cancelled totalling 122.07km)
**Leg 2** Saturday 5 April, 9 Special Stages totalling 159.16km
**Leg 3** Sunday 6 May, 5 Special Stages totalling 83.64km

## RESULTS
1 Sébastien Loeb/Daniel Elena — Citroën C4 WRC — 2h52m03.8s — Gr A
2 Marcus Grönholm/Timo Rautiainen — Ford Focus RS WRC 06 — 2h52m40.5s — Gr A
3 Mikko Hirvonen/Jarmo Lehtinen — Ford Focus RS WRC 06 — 2h54m19.0s — Gr A
4 Jari-Matti Latvala/Miikka Anttila — Ford Focus RS WRC 06 — 2h55m46.8s — Gr A
5 Henning Solberg/Cato Menkerud — Ford Focus RS WRC 06 — 2h56m13.9s — Gr A
6 Daniel Sordo/Marc Martí — Citroën C4 WRC — 2h56m27.4s — Gr A
7 Chris Atkinson/Stéphane Prevot — Subaru Impreza WRC 2007 — 2h56m47.2s — Gr A
8 Manfred Stohl/Ilka Minor — Citroën Xsara WRC — 2h57m24.0s — Gr A
9 Federico Villagra/Diego Curletto — Mitsubishi Lancer Evo 9 — 3h08m53.7s — Gr N
10 Toshihiro Arai/Tony Sircombe — Subaru Impreza WRX Sti — 3h09m03.0s — Gr N
70 starters, 41 finishers

## PREVIOUS WINNERS
1979* Jean Guichet/Jean Todt — Peugeot 504
1980 Walter Röhrl/Christian Geistdörfer — Fiat 131 Abarth
1981 Guy Fréquelin/Jean Todt — Talbot Sunbeam Lotus
1983 Hannu Mikkola/Arne Hertz — Audi Quattro A1
1984 Stig Blomqvist/Björn Cederberg — Audi Quattro A2
1985 Timo Salonen/Seppo Harjanne — Peugeot 205 Turbo 16
1986 Miki Biasion/Tiziano Siviero — Lancia Delta S4
1987 Miki Biasion/Tiziano Siviero — Lancia Delta HF 4x4
1988 Jorge Recalde/Jorge Del Buono — Lancia Delta Integrale
1989 Mikael Ericsson/Claes Billstam — Lancia Delta Integrale
1990 Miki Biasion/Tiziano Siviero — Lancia Delta Integrale 16v
1991 Carlos Sainz/Luis Moya — Toyota Celica GT4
1992 Didier Auriol/Bernard Occelli — Lancia Delta HF Integrale
1993 Juha Kankkunen/Nicky Grist — Toyota Celica Turbo 4wd
1994 Didier Auriol/Bernard Occelli — Toyota Celica Turbo 4wd
1995 Jorge Recalde/Märtin Christie — Lancia Delta HF Integrale
1996 Tommi Mäkinen/Seppo Harjanne — Mitsubishi Lancer E3
1997 Tommi Mäkinen/Seppo Harjanne — Mitsubishi Lancer E4
1998 Tommi Mäkinen/Risto Mannisenmäki — Mitsubishi Lancer E5
1999 Juha Kankkunen/Juha Repo — Subaru Impreza WRC99
2000 Richard Burns/Robert Reid — Subaru Impreza WRC2000
2001 Colin McRae/Nicky Grist — Ford Focus RS WRC
2002 Carlos Sainz/Luis Moya — Ford Focus RS WRC02
2003 Marcus Grönholm/Timo Rautiainen — Peugeot 206 WRC
2004 Carlos Sainz/Marc Martí — Citroën Xsara WRC
2005 Sébastien Loeb/Daniel Elena — Citroën Xsara WRC
2006 Sébastien Loeb/Daniel Elena — Citroën Xsara WRC
*Non-championship event

| Position | Stage Numbers | 1 | 9 | 10 | 11 | 12 | 13 | 14 | 15 | 16 | 17 | 18 | 19 | 20 | 21 | 22 | 23 |
|---|---|---|---|---|---|---|---|---|---|---|---|---|---|---|---|---|---|
| | Loeb | 4 | 3 | 1 | 1 | 1 | 1 | 1 | 1 | 1 | 1 | 1 | 1 | 1 | 1 | 1 | 1 |
| | Grönholm | 2 | 4 | 3 | 2 | 2 | 2 | 2 | 2 | 2 | 2 | 2 | 2 | 2 | 2 | 2 | 2 |
| | Hirvonen | 1 | 1 | 4 | 4 | 4 | 4 | 4 | 3 | 3 | 3 | 3 | 3 | 3 | 3 | 3 | 3 |
| | Latvala | 17 | 11 | 7 | 7 | 7 | 7 | 7 | 6 | 5 | 4 | 4 | 4 | 4 | 4 | 4 | 4 |
| | H.Solberg | 7 | 8 | 9 | 9 | 9 | 9 | 9 | 8 | 6 | 5 | 6 | 6 | 6 | 5 | 5 | 5 |
| | Sordo | 3 | 2 | 5 | 5 | 5 | 5 | 5 | 5 | 4 | 8 | 8 | 7 | 7 | 6 | 6 | 6 |
| | Atkinson | 6 | 6 | 6 | 6 | 6 | 5 | 6 | 6 | 7 | 6 | 5 | 5 | 6 | 7 | 7 | 7 |
| | Stohl | 9 | 7 | 8 | 8 | 8 | 8 | 8 | 9 | 8 | 7 | 7 | 8 | 8 | 8 | 8 | 8 |
| | Villagra | 22 | 16 | 11 | 10 | 10 | 10 | 10 | 10 | 11 | 11 | 10 | 9 | 9 | 9 | 9 | 9 |
| | Arai | 29 | 20 | 12 | 13 | 11 | 11 | 11 | 11 | 10 | 10 | 11 | 10 | 10 | 10 | 10 | 10 |
| | Raies | 16 | 12 | 14 | 15 | 14 | 14 | 15 | 15 | 14 | 13 | 12 | 12 | 12 | 12 | 12 | 12 |
| | P-Companc | 10 | 10 | 43 | 46 | 47 | 47 | 49 | 45 | 46 | 46 | 36 | 33 | 31 | 28 | 28 | |
| | Wilson | 8 | 9 | 42 | 45 | 46 | 46 | 48 | 44 | 45 | 45 | 37 | 34 | 32 | 30 | 30 | |
| | P.Solberg | 4 | 5 | 2 | 3 | 3 | 3 | 3 | 3 | R | | | | | | | |

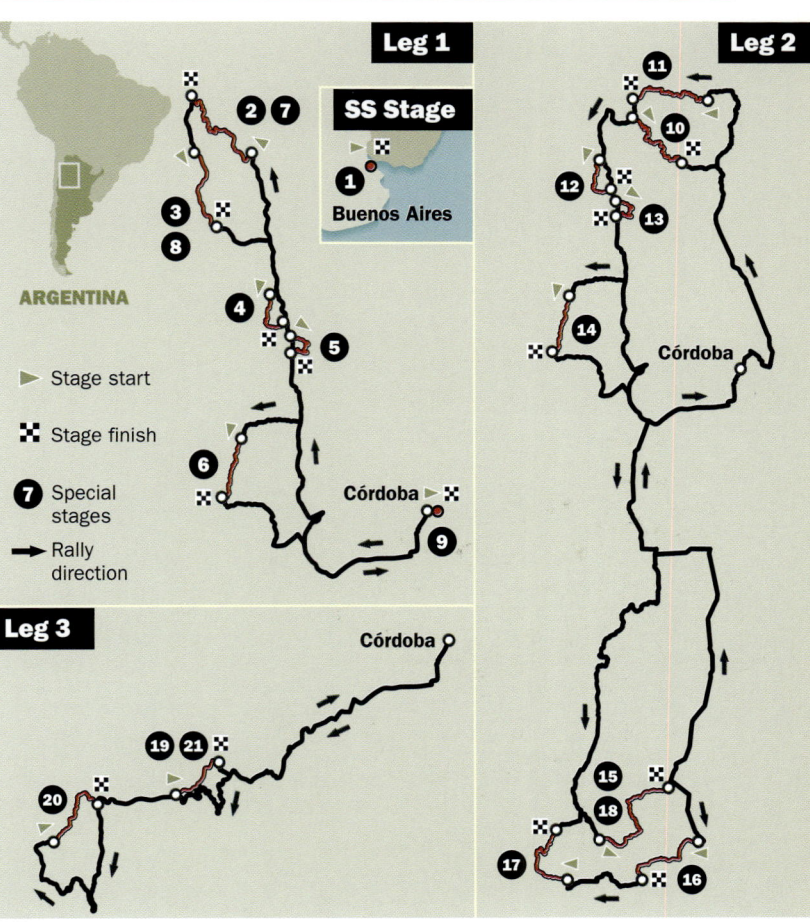

**Main:** Not only did Grönholm end Loeb's winning streak in Italy, he took a seven-point championship lead after the Frenchman crashed out

**Inset:** Marcus had thought the rally lost after he smashed a wheel against a rock in the Terranova stage, hence the less-than-sunny disposition

All photographs by McKlein

## The FIA World Rally Championship Round 7
# Rally d'Italia

MARCUS Gronholm looked up and saw the approaching pack of journalists. He turned on his heel and pretended to run in the opposite direction. "Please," he said, "no shit questions." The message was clear: 'Yes, Loeb's winning and yes this is the fourth rally on the trot I've been in this situation. Move on…'

A day later and Gronholm is happily fielding questions of every flavour. The reason being, the five-point deficit he was staring at on Sunday morning has been transformed into a seven-point lead, faster than you could say: "Watch your speed over that crest, Seb."

Unlike on previous rallies, where Sebastien Loeb had carved out some towering victories, it looked like this year's Rally d'Italia was going to be an event lost by Gronholm and Ford rather than won by the French. Loeb admitted he wasn't driving at his best. He didn't feel his usual confidence behind the wheel, he was having to force the pace and he wasn't happy. He – and the Citroën C4 WRC – just kept on pounding out the miles, though.

Until the Frenchman pounded his machine into a hedge after carrying too much speed through an easy right over crest not far after the start of San Giovanni. The C4 drifted into the undergrowth, bounced out, smacked a rock and mashed the front-left suspension. Game over. Loeb was off the road (in his car – rather than on his mountain bike) for the first time since Monte Carlo last year.

Gronholm had led on day one – once he'd elbowed countryman Jari-Matti Latvala out of the way – but was forced to give best to Loeb when his Focus RS WRC 06 smashed a wheel against a rock in Terranova. The impact damaged the hydraulic reservoir for the damper. Gronholm ended the test with flames around the offending wheel. The fire was simple enough to solve, it was just hydraulic fluid. The damage to his chances on this rally much more serious. Sure enough, as Gronholm limped through the following test, Loeb had romped past with the apparent invincibility of a man on his way to a fourth straight 2007 win. Loeb's task was made easier when a Gronholm's spare wheel fell out of the back of the car mid-way through Monte Lerno. As had been the case with his first problem, this had a knock-on effect: with a badly damaged right-rear tyre and the spare by the side of the road 30 miles away, the Ford man had to take his time through the 12 miles of Su Filigosu. Failure to make it back to service on four wheels and tyres would leave him in hot water with the stewards. As it was, not returning with the requisite five wheels aboard his Focus landed the team in front of them on Saturday evening. Luckily, common sense prevailed and no action was taken.

After a troublesome event, escaping the long arm of the law was reason enough to be cheerful for Gronholm. Mentally, this one had gone. Nothing, he reckoned, ever happened on a Sunday… Then it did and then Gronholm was smiling some more.

Gronholm's grin was more than matched by team principal Malcolm Wilson. The best Wilson could have hoped for from his men was a one-two. Mikko Hirvonen saw to it that the Cumbrian returned to Britain in the best possible fashion. Once again, Hirvonen turned in an inch-perfect drive. From his perspective, however, it just wasn't as fast enough. The decision to test a tyre-suspension package for the forthcoming Acropolis, which didn't work in Italy on the Saturday afternoon, was the only time Hirvonen wasn't smiling.

There was an incredible feeling by the end of this event that, had Loeb left Sardinia with another win, that would have been it. Now, though, it was game on.

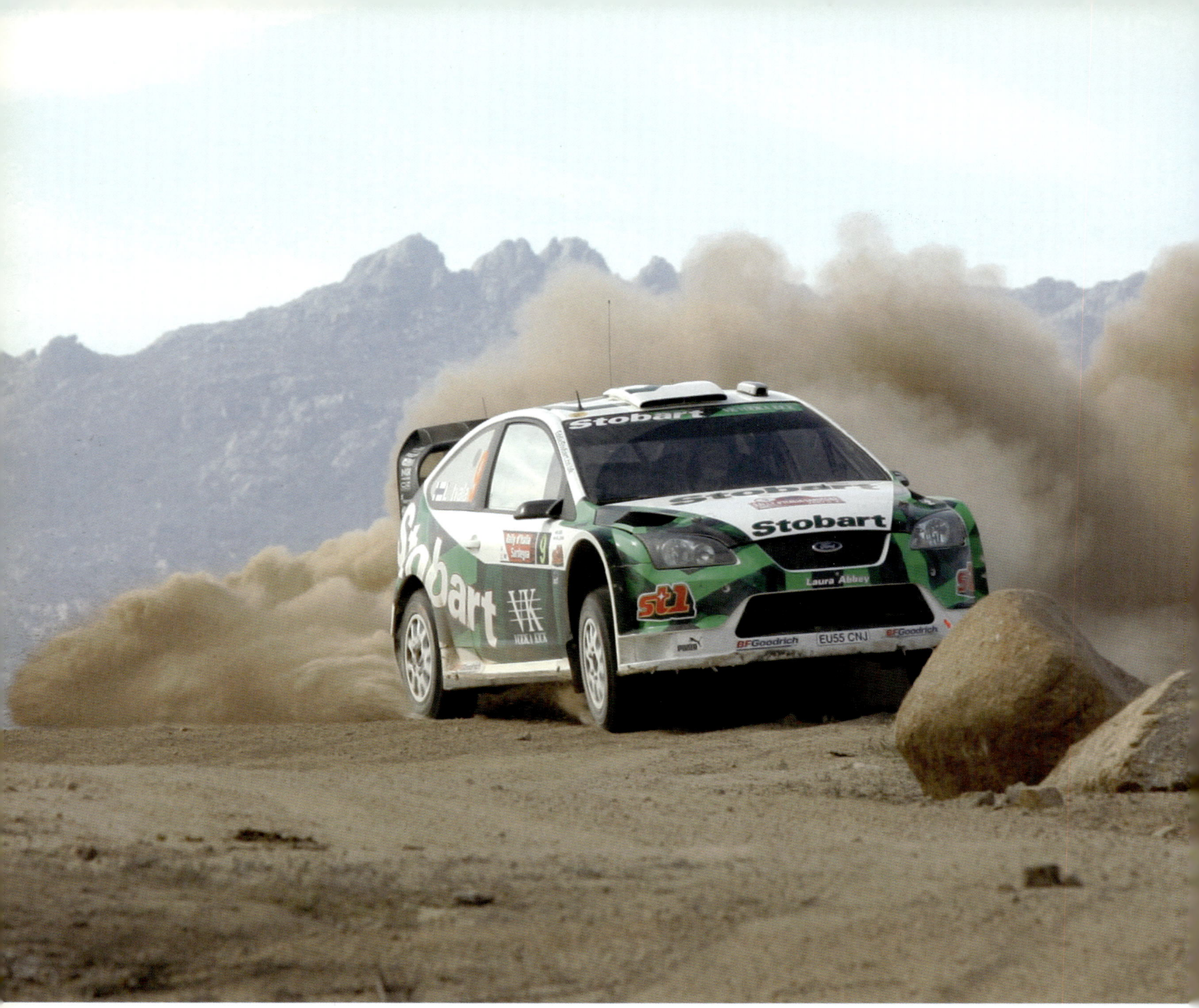
Stobart
Stobart
Stobart
Laura Abbey
st1
BFGoodrich
EU55 CNJ

CITROËN
TOTAL

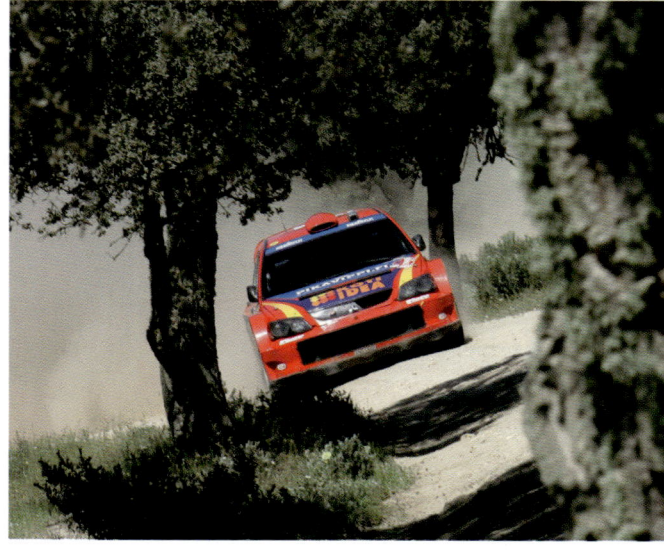

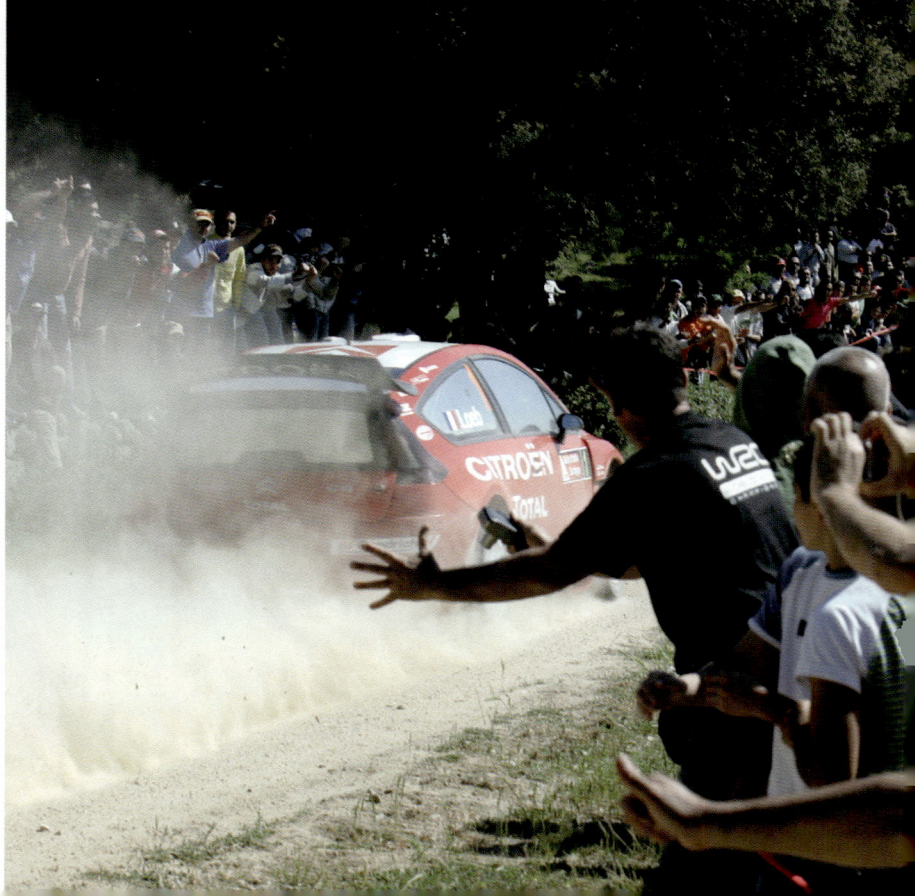

# RALLY D'ITALIA

**Above:** Henning Solberg had a tense final-day scrap with Sordo for third, narrowly missing out on the place

**Left:** Once again Sordo belied his lack of gravel experience to score valuable points for Citroën

**Middle Left:** He might have led, but Loeb wasn't happy with his performance in the C4 – and that was before he took a trip into the scenery

**Far left:** Mitsubishi man Gardemeister finished in the points in sixth, but was unhappy about his lack of pace

**Top left:** Latvala made a bright start, leading for the first three stages. Then Grönholm moved ahead in SS4 and the younger Finn retired with suspension damage on the next test

All photographs by McKlein

Aava got the better of Suzuki team-mate and chief JRC rival P-G Andersson to score a class win
McKlein

The FIA World Rally Championship Round 7
# Rally d'Italia Results

May 18-20 2007

## FINISH LINES...

Loeb's team-mate Dani Sordo salvaged something from Sardinia for Citroen, edging out Stobart driver Henning Solberg in a sensational final-day scrap for the final podium spot. Sordo continued to impress mightily, backing up his Argentinian form with another loose-surface performance way beyond his years... As much as Solberg would have wanted another podium, Stobart team boss Andrew Tinkler was over the moon with what his weekend in the sun had brought. When he woke on Friday morning, he couldn't have expected the kind of media attention lavished on the rally leader, but there it was: in black and white; stages one-to-three were headed by one of his cars, driven by Jari-Matti Latvala. Unfortunately for the Finn, he lost the lead in SS4 and then damaged his suspension on the next test, forcing him to retire from leg one. What a way to go out, though... Petter Solberg was a disgruntled fifth. His Subaru, like the one of tenth-placed team-mate Chris Atkinson, had returned to its bad old ways of delivering nothing but understeer once the stage was more than a handful of miles old... There was little more to cheer further down the leaderboard, as Toni Gardemeister (Lancer WR 05) and Manfred Stohl (Xsara WRC) were far from delighted at their lack of pace in sixth and seventh... Urmo Aava won the Junior Rally Championship element of the event. He and Suzuki team-mate Per-Gunnar Andersson both suffered their problems during the rally, but the issue was decided by day two puncture for the Swede.

## RUNNING ORDER

| | | |
|---|---|---|
| 1 | Sébastien Loeb/ Daniel Elena | Citroën C4 WRC Gr A |
| 3 | Marcus Grönholm/ Timo Rautiainen | Ford Focus RS WRC 06 Gr A |
| 4 | Mikko Hirvonen/ Jarmo Lehtinen | Ford Focus RS WRC 06 Gr A |
| 2 | Daniel Sordo/ Marc Martí | Citroën C4 WRC Gr A |
| 7 | Petter Solberg/ Phil Mills | Subaru Impreza WRC 2007 Gr A |
| 10 | Henning Solberg/ Cato Menkerud | Ford Focus RS WRC 06 Gr A |
| 8 | Chris Atkinson/ Stéphane Prevot | Subaru Impreza WRC 2007 Gr A |
| 9 | Jari-Matti Latvala/ Miikka Anttila | Ford Focus RS WRC 06 Gr A |
| 6 | Daniel Carlsson/ Denis Giraudet | Citroën Xsara WRC |
| 5 | Manfred Stohl/ Ilka Minor | Citroën Xsara WRC Gr A |
| 21 | Toni Gardemeister/ Jakke Honkanen | Mitsubishi Lancer WRC05 Gr A |
| 22 | Jan Kopecky/ Filip Schovanek | Skoda Fabia WRC Gr A |
| 16 | Matthew Wilson/ Michael Orr | Ford Focus RS WRC 06 Gr A |
| 23 | Mads Östberg/ Ole Unnerud | Subaru Impreza WRC 2005 Gr A |
| 24 | Gareth MacHale/ Paul Nagle | Ford Focus RS WRC 06 Gr A |
| 26 | Juha Hänninen/ Mikko Markkula | Mitsubishi Lancer WRC05 Gr A |
| 12 | Federico Villagra/ Jorge Perez-Companc | Ford Focus RS WRC 06 Gr A |
| 11 | Luis Perez-Companc/ José María Volta | Ford Focus RS WRC 06 Gr A |
| 45 | P-G Andersson/ Jonas Andersson | Suzuki Swift Gr A |
| 32 | Urmo Aava/ Kuldar Sikk | Suzuki Swift Gr A |

## SPECIAL STAGE TIMES

**SS1 Crastazza 1 (31.12km)**
1 J-M.Latvala/M.Anttila (Ford Focus RS WRC 06) 21m27.8s; 2 M.Grönholm/T.Rautiainen (Ford Focus RS WRC 06) 21m34.5s; 3 C.Atkinson/S.Prevot (Subaru Impreza WRC 2007) 21m34.8s; 4 P.Solberg/P.Mills (Subaru Impreza WRC 2007) 21m39.0s; 5 S.Loeb/D.Elena (Citroën C4 WRC) 21m40.2s; 6 M.Hirvonen/J.Lehtinen (Ford Focus RS WRC 06) 21m41.8s; JRC U.Aava/K.Sikk (Suzuki Swift) 23m42.3s

**SS2 Terranova 1 (21.20km)**
1 Loeb/Elena (Citroën) 15m14.9s; 2 Solberg/Mills (Subaru) 15m16.7s; 3 H.Solberg/C.Menkerud (Ford Focus RS WRC 06) 15m17.0s; 4 Grönholm/Rautiainen (Ford) 15m18.9s; 5 Latvala/Anttila (Ford) 15m21.7s; 6 Hirvonen/Lehtinen (Ford) 15m24.6s; JRC P-G.Andersson/J.Andersson (Suzuki Swift) 17m03.9s

**SS3 Monte Olia 1 (20.36km)**
1 Solberg/Menkerud (Ford) 14m52.9s; 2 Grönholm/Rautiainen (Ford) 14m53.9s; 3 Latvala/Anttila (Ford) 14m56.3s; 4 Solberg/Mills (Subaru) 14m56.9s; 5 Hirvonen/Lehtinen (Ford) 15m01.0s; 6 Loeb/Elena (Citroën) 15m01.1s; JRC Aava/Sikk (Suzuki) 16m28.6s

**SS4 Crastazza 2 (31.12km)**
1 Grönholm/Rautiainen (Ford) 20m51.9s; 2 Loeb/Elena (Citroën) 20m58.0s; 3 Latvala/Anttila (Ford) 20m58.7s; 4 Hirvonen/Lehtinen (Ford) 20m59.9s; 5 Solberg/Menkerud (Ford) 21m08.2s; 6 D.Sordo/M.Martí (Citroën C4 WRC) 21m14.4s; JRC Aava/Sikk (Suzuki) 23m41.9s

**SS5 Terranova 2 (21.20km)**
1 Loeb/Elena (Citroën) 14m44.9s; 2 Grönholm/Rautiainen (Ford) 14m57.2s; 3 Hirvonen/Lehtinen (Ford) 14m57.4s; 4 Sordo/Martí (Citroën) 14m59.5s; 5 Solberg/Menkerud (Ford) 15m01.2s; 6 Solberg/Menkerud (Ford) 15m11.9s; JRC Andersson/Andersson (Suzuki) 16m44.6s

**SS6 Monte Olia 2 (20.36km)**
1 Loeb/Elena (Citroën) 14m30.9s; 2 Hirvonen/Lehtinen (Ford) 14m34.4s; 3 Sordo/Martí (Citroën) 14m37.9s; 4 Solberg/Menkerud (Ford) 14m38.2s; 5 T.Gardemeister/J.Honkanen (Mitsubishi Lancer WRC05) 14m51.2s; 6 Grönholm/Rautiainen (Ford) 14m56.0s; JRC Andersson/Andersson (Suzuki) 16m05.2s

**SS7 Loelle 1 (22.56km)**
1 Loeb/Elena (Citroën) 13m40.6s; 2 Grönholm/Rautiainen (Ford) 13m42.9s; 3 Hirvonen/Lehtinen (Ford) 13m48.2s; 4 Sordo/Martí (Citroën) 13m56.1s; 5 Solberg/Mills (Subaru) 14m02.8s; 6 Solberg/Menkerud (Ford) 14m03.9s; JRC Andersson/Andersson (Suzuki) 15m16.0s

**SS8 Monte Lerno 1 (29.30km)**
1 Loeb/Elena (Citroën) 19m23.3s; 2 Grönholm/Rautiainen (Ford) 19m27.6s; 3 Hirvonen/Lehtinen (Ford) 19m34.5s; 4 Sordo/Martí (Citroën) 19m35.3s; 5 Solberg/Menkerud (Ford) 19m42.5s; 6 Solberg/Mills (Subaru) 19m46.5s; JRC Andersson/Andersson (Suzuki) 21m29.2s

**SS9 Su Filigosu 1 (19.47km)**
1 Loeb/Elena (Citroën) 12m36.3s; 2 Hirvonen/Lehtinen (Ford) 12m39.7s; 3 Sordo/Martí (Citroën) 12m45.0s; 4 Grönholm/Rautiainen (Ford) 12m48.8s; 5 Solberg/Menkerud (Ford) 12m52.7s; 6 Latvala/Anttila (Ford) 12m58.1s; JRC Andersson/Andersson (Suzuki) 13m57.8s

**SS10 Loelle 2 (22.56km)**
1 Grönholm/Rautiainen (Ford) 13m31.6s; 2 Loeb/Elena (Citroën) 13m33.2s; 3 Hirvonen/Lehtinen (Ford) 13m40.0s; 4 Solberg/Mills (Subaru) 13m40.1s; 5 Sordo/Martí (Citroën) 13m40.9s; 6 Solberg/Menkerud (Ford) 13m47.2s; JRC Aava/Sikk (Suzuki) 15m14.2s

**SS11 Monte Lerno 2 (29.30km)**
1 Loeb/Elena (Citroën) 18m58.7s; 2 Grönholm/Rautiainen (Ford) 18m59.5s; 3 Sordo/Martí (Citroën) 19m13.8s; 4 Solberg/Mills (Subaru) 19m14.2s; 5 Latvala/Anttila (Ford) 19m18.6s; 6 Solberg/Menkerud (Ford) 19m20.8s; JRC Aava/Sikk (Suzuki) 21m32.4s

**SS12 Su Filigosu 2 (19.47km)**
1 Grönholm/Rautiainen (Ford) 12m19.3s; 2 Loeb/Elena (Citroën) 12m23.5s; 3 Latvala/Anttila (Ford) 12m27.6s; 4 Sordo/Martí (Citroën) 12m28.6s; 5 Solberg/Mills (Subaru) 12m30.5s; 6 Hirvonen/Lehtinen (Ford) 12m33.4s; JRC Andersson/Andersson (Suzuki) 13m41.6s

# RALLY D'ITALIA

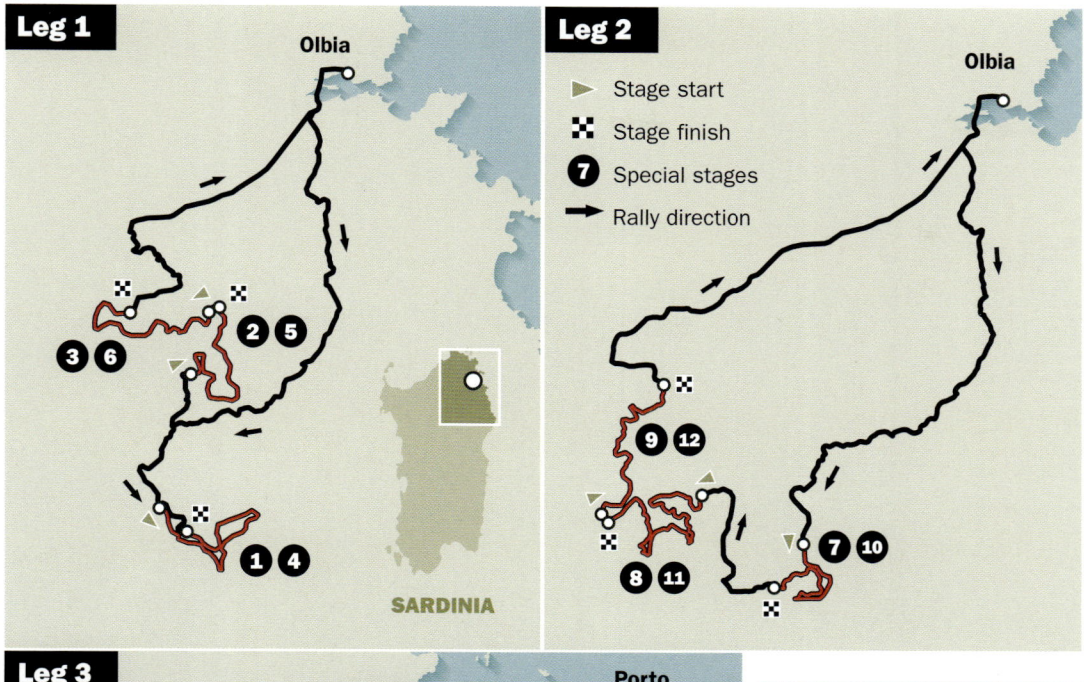

## ROUTE DETAILS
Total route of 1061.84km of which 342.86km were competitive on 18 stages
**Leg 1** Friday 18 May, 6 special stages totalling 145.40km
**Leg 2** Saturday 19 May, 6 special stages totalling 142.72km
**Leg 3** Sunday 20 May, 6 special stages totalling 54.74km

## RESULTS

| | | | | |
|---|---|---|---|---|
| 1 | Marcus Grönholm/ | Ford Focus RS WRC 06 | | |
| | Timo Rautiainen | 3h48m42.0s | Gr A | |
| 2 | Mikko Hirvonen/ | Ford Focus RS WRC 06 | | |
| | Jarmo Lehtinen | 3h49m11.2s | Gr A | |
| 3 | Daniel Sordo/ | Citroën C4 WRC | | |
| | Marc Martí | 3h50m03.8s | Gr A | |
| 4 | Henning Solberg/ | Ford Focus RS WRC 06 | | |
| | Cato Menkerud | 3h50m18.6s | Gr A | |
| 5 | Petter Solberg/ | Subaru Impreza WRC 2007 | | |
| | Phil Mills | 3h51m16.2s | Gr A | |
| 6 | Toni Gardemeister/ | Mitsubishi Lancer WRC05 | | |
| | Jakke Honkanen | 3h53m44.1s | Gr A | |
| 7 | Manfred Stohl/ | Citroën Xsara WRC | | |
| | Ilka Minor | 3h54m10.6s | Gr A | |
| 8 | Juna Hänninen/ | Mitsubishi Lancer WRC05 | | |
| | Mikko Markkula | 3h58m13.7s | Gr A | |
| 9 | Jari-Matti Latvala/ | Ford Focus RS WRC 06 | | |
| | Miikka Anttila | 4h00m09.7s | Gr A | |
| 10 | Chris Atkinson/ | Subaru Impreza WRC 2007 | | |

## Stage Numbers / Position

| | 1 | 2 | 3 | 4 | 5 | 6 | 7 | 8 | 9 | 10 | 11 | 12 | 13 | 14 | 15 | 16 | 17 | 18 |
|---|---|---|---|---|---|---|---|---|---|---|---|---|---|---|---|---|---|---|
| Grönholm | 2 | 2 | 2 | 1 | 1 | 2 | 2 | 2 | 2 | 2 | 2 | 2 | 1 | 1 | 1 | 1 | 1 | 1 |
| Hirvonen | 6 | 7 | 7 | 5 | 3 | 3 | 3 | 3 | 3 | 3 | 3 | 3 | 2 | 2 | 2 | 2 | 2 | 2 |
| Sordo | 10 | 10 | 9 | 8 | 6 | 5 | 5 | 5 | 5 | 5 | 5 | 4 | 3 | 3 | 3 | 3 | 3 | 3 |
| H.Solberg | 7 | 5 | 4 | 4 | 3 | 4 | 4 | 4 | 4 | 4 | 4 | 5 | 4 | 4 | 4 | 4 | 4 | 4 |
| P.Solberg | 4 | 4 | 3 | 6 | 5 | 6 | 6 | 6 | 6 | 6 | 6 | 6 | 5 | 5 | 5 | 5 | 5 | 5 |
| Gardemeister | 9 | 8 | 8 | 9 | 7 | 7 | 7 | 7 | 7 | 7 | 7 | 7 | 6 | 6 | 6 | 6 | 6 | 6 |
| Stohl | 8 | 9 | 10 | 10 | 8 | 8 | 8 | 8 | 8 | 8 | 8 | 8 | 7 | 7 | 7 | 7 | 7 | 7 |
| Hänninen | 11 | 11 | 11 | 11 | 9 | 12 | 11 | 10 | 10 | 9 | 9 | 9 | 8 | 8 | 8 | 8 | 8 | 8 |
| Latvala | 1 | 1 | 1 | 2 | 14 | 14 | 14 | 12 | 12 | 11 | 10 | 10 | 9 | 9 | 9 | 9 | 9 | 9 |
| Atkinson | 3 | 6 | 6 | 7 | 16 | 15 | 15 | 14 | 13 | 13 | 12 | 12 | 11 | 11 | 10 | 10 | 10 | 10 |
| Villagra | 16 | 17 | 16 | 16 | 15 | 13 | 12 | 11 | 11 | 12 | 11 | 11 | 10 | 10 | 11 | 11 | 11 | 11 |
| Wilson | 12 | 12 | 13 | 12 | 10 | 9 | 9 | 9 | 9 | 10 | 13 | 13 | 12 | 12 | 12 | 12 | 12 | 12 |
| Loeb | 5 | 3 | 5 | 3 | 2 | 1 | 1 | 1 | 1 | 1 | 1 | 1 | R | | | | | |
| Östberg | 13 | 13 | 12 | 13 | 12 | 11 | 13 | R | | | | | | | | | | |
| MacHale | 14 | 15 | 15 | 14 | 11 | 10 | 10 | R | | | | | | | | | | |
| P-Companc | 15 | 14 | 14 | 15 | 13 | 19 | 18 | R | | | | | | | | | | |

## SS13 S.Giovanni 1 (10.65km)
1 Hirvonen/Lehtinen (Ford) 7m21.9s; 2 Latvala/Anttila (Ford) 7m22.4s; 3 Solberg/Menkerud (Ford) 7m24.3s; 4 Sordo/Martí (Citroën) 7m25.0s; 5 M.Stohl/I.Minor (Citroën Xsara WRC) 7m29.3s; 6 Solberg/Mills (Subaru) 7m31.0s; JRC Aava/Sikk (Suzuki) 8m07.7s

## SS14 Monte Nuragone 1 (7.67km)
1 Solberg/Menkerud (Ford) 5m37.3s; 2 Solberg/Mills (Subaru) 5m41.9s; 3 Grönholm/Rautiainen (Ford) 5m42.0s; 4 Hirvonen/Lehtinen (Ford) 5m42.7s; 5 Sordo/Martí (Citroën) 5m43.0s; 6 Latvala/Anttila (Ford) 5m47.6s; JRC Andersson/Andersson (Suzuki) 6m22.9s

## SS15 Braniatogghlu 1 (9.30km)
1 Hirvonen/Lehtinen (Ford) 4m38.0s; 2 Sordo/Martí (Citroën) 4m40.2s; 3 Solberg/Menkerud (Ford) 4m41.5s; 4 Grönholm/Rautiainen (Ford) 4m41.8s; 5 Latvala/Anttila (Ford) 4m42.7s; 6 J.Hänninen/M.Markkula (Mitsubishi Lancer WRC05) 4m45.5s; JRC Andersson/Andersson (Suzuki) 12m02.9s

## SS16 S.Giovanni 2 (10.65km)
1 Sordo/Martí (Citroën) 7m06.4s; 2 Solberg/Menkerud (Ford) 7m08.2s; 3 Solberg/Mills (Subaru) 7m09.0s; 4 Hirvonen/Lehtinen (Ford) 7m09.5s; 5 Latvala/Anttila (Ford) 7m09.8s; 6 Grönholm/Rautiainen (Ford) 7m14.1s; JRC Andersson/Andersson (Suzuki) 7m47.2s

## SS17 Monte Nuragone 2 (7.67km)
1 Solberg/Menkerud (Ford) 5m29.4s; 2 Sordo/Martí (Citroën) 5m29.5s; 3 Grönholm/Rautiainen (Ford) 5m29.9s; 4 Latvala/Anttila (Ford) 5m31.2s; 5 Hirvonen/Lehtinen (Ford) 5m32.0s; 6 Gardemeister/Honkanen (Mitsubishi) 5m35.3s; JRC Andersson/Andersson (Suzuki) 6m11.6s

## SS18 Braniatogghlu 2 (9.30km)
1 Hirvonen/Lehtinen (Ford) 4m31.3s; 2 Sordo/Martí (Citroën) 4m31.7s; 3 Grönholm/Rautiainen (Ford) 4m32.3s; 4 Latvala/Anttila (Ford) 4m34.6s; 5 Hänninen/Markkula (Mitsubishi) 4m36.8s; 6 Solberg/Mills (Subaru) 4m38.3s; JRC Andersson/Andersson (Suzuki) 5m04.8s

Cars who retired and subsequently restarted and were classified under SuperRally regs:

| 9 | Latvala/Anttila | Ford Focus RS WRC 06 | | |
|---|---|---|---|---|
| | Suspension | SS5 | Gr A | |
| 8 | Atkinson/Prevot | Subaru Impreza WRC 2007 | | |
| | Suspension | SS5 | Gr A | |
| 22 | Kopecky/Schovanek | Skoda Fabia WRC | | |
| | Suspension | SS3 | Gr A | |
| 16 | Wilson/Orr | Ford Focus RS WRC 06 | | |
| | Suspension | SS10 | Gr A | |

## MAJOR RETIREMENTS

| 1 | Loeb/Elena | Citroën C4 WRC | | |
|---|---|---|---|---|
| | Accident | SS13 | Gr A | |
| 6 | Carlsson/Giraudet | Citroën Xsara WRC | | |
| | Withdrawn | SS1 | Gr A | |
| 22 | Kopecky/Schovanek | Skoda Fabia WRC | | |
| | Steering | SS10 | Gr A | |
| 11 | Perez-Companc/Volta | Ford Focus RS WRC 06 | | |
| | Mechanical | SS8 | Gr A | |
| 23 | Östberg/Unnerud | Subaru Impreza WRC 2005 | | |
| | Mechanical | SS7 | Gr A | |
| 24 | MacHale/Nagle | Ford Focus RS WRC 06 | | |
| | Accident | SS8 | Gr A | |

## FIA CLASS WINNERS

| A8 | Over 2000cc | Grönholm/Rautiainen Ford Focus RS WRC 06 |
|---|---|---|
| A7 | 1600-2000cc | Sandell/Axelsson Renault Clio R3 |
| A6 | 1400-1600cc | Aava/Sikk Suzuki Swift |
| N4 | Over 2000cc | Manfrinato/Pisano Subaru Impreza WRX Sti |
| N3 | 1600-2000cc | Clark/Martin Ford Fiesta ST |
| N2 | 1400-1600cc | Mela/Mela Citroën Saxo |

## RALLY LEADERS
Overall: SS1-3 Latvala; SS4-5 Grönholm; SS6-12 Loeb; SS13-18 Grönholm
JWC: SS1-7 Aava; SS8-9 Andersson; SS10-18 Aava

## SPECIAL STAGE ANALYSIS

| | 1st | 2nd | 3rd | 4th | 5th | 6th |
|---|---|---|---|---|---|---|
| Loeb (Citroën) | 7 | 3 | - | - | 1 | 1 |
| Grönholm (Ford) | 3 | 6 | 3 | 3 | - | 2 |
| Hirvonen (Ford) | 3 | 2 | 4 | 3 | 2 | 3 |
| H.Solberg (Ford) | 3 | 1 | 3 | 1 | 4 | 3 |
| Sordo (Citroën) | 1 | 3 | 3 | 5 | 2 | 1 |
| Latvala (Ford) | 1 | 1 | 3 | 2 | 4 | 2 |
| P.Solberg (Subaru) | - | 2 | 1 | 4 | 2 | 4 |
| Atkinson (Subaru) | - | - | 1 | - | - | - |
| Gardemeister (Mitsubishi) | - | - | - | - | 1 | 1 |
| Hänninen (Mitsubishi) | - | - | - | - | 1 | 1 |
| Stohl (Citroën) | - | - | - | - | 1 | - |

## WORLD CHAMPIONSHIP POINTS
**Drivers**
1 Grönholm 55; 2 Loeb 48; 3 Hirvonen 44; 4 Sordo 28; 5= P.Solberg, H.Solberg 20; 7= Atkinson, Latvala 12; 9 Carlsson 9; 10= Stohl, Gardemeister 8 etc

**Manufacturers**
1 BP-Ford WRT 99; 2 Citroën Total WRT 78; 3 Stobart M-Sport Ford RT 37; 4 Subaru WRT 34; 5 OMV-Kronos Citroën WRT 25

**Junior Rally Championship**
1 Andersson 28; 2 Aava 24; 3 Mölder 14; 4= Sandell, Béres, Burkart 9; 7= Cortinovis, Prokop 6; 9= Svenkerud, Rueda, Gallagher 3 etc

**Production Cup**
1 Arai 19; 2 Sohlberg 12; 3= Svedlund, Higgins, Villagra 10; 6 Alén 8; 7= Nutahara, Hänninen 6; 9= Aroujo, Baldacci, Pozzo 5 etc

| | | | | |
|---|---|---|---|---|
| | Stéphane Prevot | 4h05m01.4s | Gr A | |

82 starters, 67 finishers

## RECENT WINNERS

| 1970 | Jean-Luc Thérier/Marcel Callewaert | Alpine Renault A110 |
|---|---|---|
| 1971 | Ove Andersson/Arne Hertz | Alpine Renault A110 |
| 1972 | Amilcare Ballestrieri/Arnaldo Bernacchini | Lancia Fulvia |
| 1973 | Jean-Luc Thérier/Jacques Jaubert | Alpine Renault A110 |
| 1975 | Björn Waldegård/Hans Thorszelius | Lancia Stratos |
| 1976 | Björn Waldegård/Hans Thorszelius | Lancia Stratos |
| 1977 | Jean Claude Andruet/Christian Delferrier | Fiat 131 Abarth |
| 1978 | Markku Alén/Ilkka Kivimäki | Lancia Stratos |
| 1979 | Tony Fassina/Mauro Mannini | Lancia Stratos |
| 1980 | Walter Röhrl/Christian Geistdörfer | Fiat 131 Abarth |
| 1981 | Michèle Mouton/Fabrizia Pons | Audi Quattro |
| 1982 | Stig Blomqvist/Björn Cederberg | Audi Quattro A2 |
| 1983 | Markku Alén/Ilkka Kivimaki | Lancia Rallye 037 |
| 1984 | Ari Vatanen/Terry Harryman | Peugeot 205 Turbo 16 |
| 1985 | Walter Röhrl/Christian Geistdörfer | Audi Sport Quattro S1 |
| 1986 | Results Annulled | |
| 1987 | Miki Biasion/Tiziano Siviero | Lancia Delta HF 4x4 |
| 1988 | Miki Biasion/Tiziano Siviero | Lancia Delta Integrale |
| 1989 | Miki Biasion/Tiziano Siviero | Lancia Delta Integrale 16v |
| 1990 | Didier Auriol/Bernard Occelli | Lancia Delta Integrale 16v |
| 1991 | Didier Auriol/Bernard Occelli | Lancia Delta Integrale 16v |
| 1992 | Andrea Aghini/Sauro Farnocchia | Lancia Delta HF Integrale |
| 1993 | Franco Cunico/Steve Evangelisti | Ford Escort RS Cosworth |
| 1994 | Didier Auriol/Bernard Occelli | Toyota Celica Turbo 4wd |
| 1995 | Piero Liatti/Alex Alessandrini | Subaru Impreza 555 |
| 1996 | Colin McRae/Derek Ringer | Subaru Impreza 555 |
| 1997 | Colin McRae/Nicky Grist | Subaru Impreza WRC97 |
| 1998 | Tommi Mäkinen/Risto Mannisenmäki | Mitsubishi Lancer E5 |
| 1999 | Tommi Mäkinen/Risto Mannisenmäki | Mitsubishi Lancer E6 |
| 2000 | Gilles Panizzi/Hervé Panizzi | Peugeot 206 WRC |
| 2001 | Gilles Panizzi/Hervé Panizzi | Peugeot 206 WRC |
| 2002 | Gilles Panizzi/Hervé Panizzi | Peugeot 206 WRC |
| 2003 | Sébastien Loeb/Daniel Elena | Citroën Xsara WRC |
| 2004 | Petter Solberg/Phil Mills | Subaru Impreza WRC2004 |
| 2005 | Sébastien Loeb/Daniel Elena | Citroën Xsara WRC |
| 2006 | Sébastien Loeb/Daniel Elena | Citroën Xsara WRC |

**Right:** Loeb pointed to understeer and engine problems as reasons for being only fourth on leg one. He tried his hardest on soft tyres but only progressed to second

**Far right:** It had been a while since Petter Solberg had troubled the frontrunners – maybe that's why Loeb looks like he doesn't recognise him!

**Bottom right:** A determined Grönholm simply outpaced Loeb on this event, much to the Frenchman's chagrin

**Below:** Victory for Grönholm and co-driver Timo Rautiainen helped extend their lead to 10 points over Loeb in the title race

All photographs by McKlein unless specified

## The FIA World Rally Championship Round 8
# Acropolis Rally

SÉBASTIEN Loeb was carving his way into Marcus Grönholm's lead. After a troublesome opening leg in the Citroën C4 WRC, the Frenchman had dialled himself in and was now hounding the rally leader. With a couple of splits left to go in the tortuously long Agii Theodori test, Loeb was seven seconds up on the Ford. There was nothing between them. This was going to be a classic. Then, bang, both front tyres on the Citroën exploded and he dropped 25 seconds to Grönholm.

Way out west of the rally's Athens base was where Grönholm won this event. There was a natural tendency to feel sorry for Loeb. He had, after all, been quickest through the stage until that point. But this was no run-of-the-mill stage. This was the real deal; what the Acropolis is all about. Close to 50km and more than half an hour of flat-chat driving in the blazing sun, and all of the prizes were at the finish.

When Loeb arrived at the end of the stage, his front tyres were shredded and his legendary super-cool temperament tested. His challenge for the lead was over. Grönholm knew it, too. But Loeb wasn't going to say anything of the sort. What he would say, however, was that – in the absence of the uber-hard compound from BFGoodrich that he'd declined – he knew he had to pick his moment to push in the stage. Flat-out from the start would, he informed, only result in one thing. He didn't mention what it was – the flurry of activity around the red car parked close by said it all.

This was a masterly win from Grönholm, one he designed and built himself. Loeb pointed to understeer and being unhappy with his engine on leg one as reasons for him being in fourth (yes, fourth) place. He was also magnanimous enough to admit that Grönholm's pace had also been pretty special on Friday's roads north west of Athens. It was the latter problem that really hurt the Frenchman. Buoyed by the get out of jail card Loeb had handed him a fortnight earlier in Sardinia, when he binned the C4, the Ford man was going for double or quits in Greece. He was the one who held his nerve and it was Loeb's covers that went bust.

This time, however, it wasn't a two-horse race. The Subarus were in attendance. There had been plenty of pre-event talk about the return of David Lapworth and Graham Moore, and the departure of technical director Steve Farrell. Surely they couldn't have worked their magic in the handful of days they'd been back at the team before the start of round eight, could they? It certainly looked that way on Friday morning, when Chris Atkinson led and Petter Solberg was second. With or without the debatable advantage in road position, you'd still have got indecently long odds on a Subaru one-two at any stage of a WRC round on the form they've shown recently. But there they were.

They didn't last the pace. Atkinson dropped back with a puncture on the first run through Agii Theodori, and then struggled with the car's inconsistent handling. But Solberg continued to elbow his way into the Grönholm-Loeb show well into day two, only slowing when his Impreza's front-left damper gave up the ghost. Rather worryingly for Subaru, Atkinson's sister car suffered precisely the same fault, with the added bonus of a broken front-right driveshaft just to really test the Australian's patience. On the whole though, Subaru's improved pace was good news for the championship. Leg one had shown the increasing competitiveness of the series, with 10 seconds separating the top six cars. In the end though, there could only be one winner.

Photo 4/Crash.net

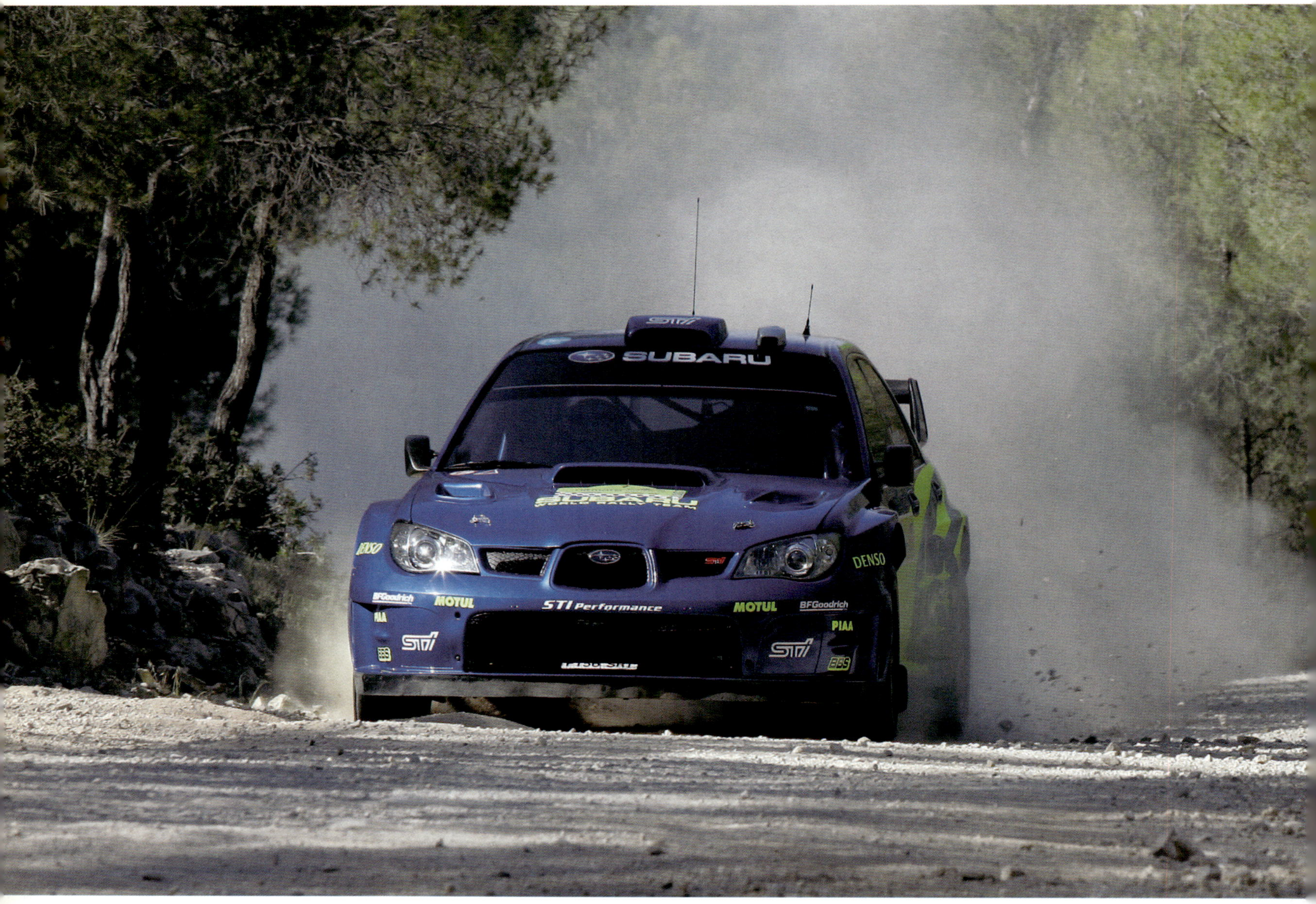
SUBARU
DENSO
MOTUL
STI Performance
BFGoodrich
PIAA

RECARO
Mobil

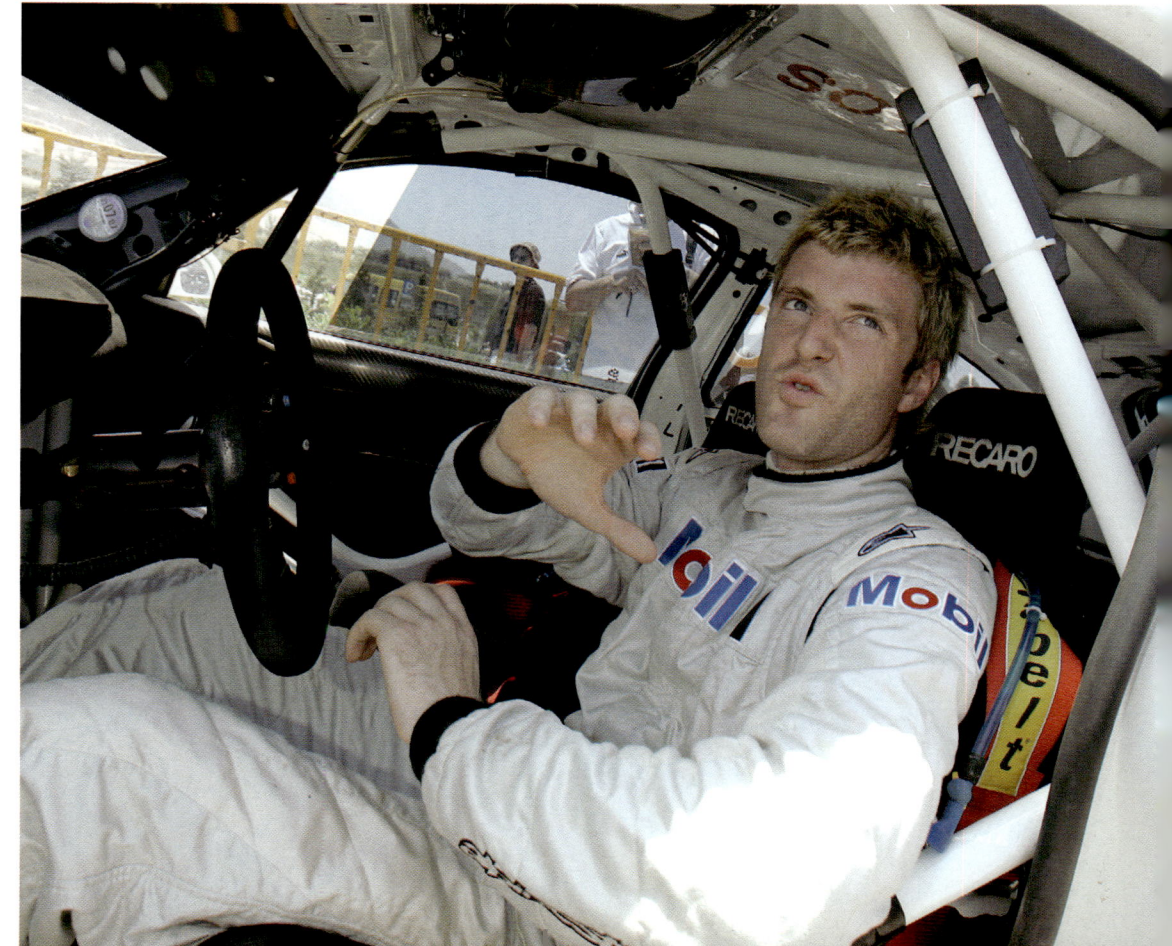

ACROPOLIS RALLY

Left: Atkinson was flying on leg one – he led a Subaru 1-2 before a costly puncture and inconsistent handling dropped him back to sixth at the finish

Below: Hirvonen survived a scary 100mph off-road moment to finish fourth, but the victory-hungry Finn had been hoping for much more

Opposite bottom: Guy Wilks gave British fans reason to cheer. He brought his '04-spec Focus home in ninth, ahead of fellow Brit Matthew Wilson

Opposite top: Petter Solberg had Grönholm and Loeb in his sights before a broken damper slowed his Impreza. Third was still a good result for the Norwegian

All photographs by McKlein

Toshi Arai opened up a healthy 14-point lead in the Production category with his first class win of the year
McKlein

## The FIA World Rally Championship Round 8
# Acropolis Rally Results
### June 1-3 2007

### FINISH LINES...

Mikko Hirvonen talked of his determination to go into the summer break on a high. He'd rolled over too easily in Sardinia. Not this time – he wanted another win. In the end, he was mightily lucky not to be rolling over literally, when he went off-road at close to 100mph on SS10. That near-shunt combined with punctures stuffed his chances of anything more than fourth place... Fellow Ford man Henning Solberg was fifth after a trouble-free and largely uninspired event for the Norwegian... Behind sixth-placed Chris Atkinson (whose event was anything but uninspired) was top privateer Jan Kopecky, who turned in a controlled drive – running with overheating rear brakes for much of the time – in his Skoda Fabia... OMV Citroën driver Manfred Stohl took the final point in a deeply disgruntled eighth place... There was better news for British rally fans in Greece, with Guy Wilks (Focus RS WRC 04) and Matthew Wilson (Focus RS WRC 06) rounding out the top 10... Toshi Arai scored his first Production Car win of the season and his first Group N win on the Acropolis Rally. The Japanese's success moved him 14 points clear of the chasing pack. If the main WRC field thought it had its fair share of punctures, it was nothing compared with the Production runners. Mark Higgins, Andreas Aigner and Juho Hanninen all led this event, but had their chances of winning ruined by deflations...

### RUNNING ORDER

| | | | |
|---|---|---|---|
| 3 | Marcus Grönholm/ | Ford Focus RS WRC 06 | |
| | Timo Rautiainen | Gr A | |
| 1 | Sébastien Loeb/ | Citroën C4 WRC | |
| | Daniel Elena | Gr A | |
| 4 | Mikko Hirvonen/ | Ford Focus RS WRC 06 | |
| | Jarmo Lehtinen | Gr A | |
| 2 | Daniel Sordo/ | Citroën C4 WRC | |
| | Marc Martí | Gr A | |
| 7 | Petter Solberg/ | Subaru Impreza WRC2007 | |
| | Phil Mills | Gr A | |
| 10 | Henning Solberg/ | Ford Focus RS WRC 06 | |
| | Cato Menkerud | Gr A | |
| 9 | Jari-Matti Latvala/ | Ford Focus RS WRC 06 | |
| | Miikka Anttila | Gr A | |
| 8 | Chris Atkinson/ | Subaru Impreza WRC2007 | |
| | Stéphane Prevot | Gr A | |
| 5 | Manfred Stohl/ | Citroën Xsara WRC | |
| | Ilka Minor | Gr A | |
| 19 | Jan Kopecky/ | Skoda Fabia WRC | |
| | Filip Schovanek | Gr A | |
| 16 | Matthew Wilson/ | Ford Focus RS WRC 06 | |
| | Michael Orr | Gr A | |
| 12 | Federico Villagra/ | Ford Focus RS WRC 06 | |
| | Jorge Pérez-Companc | Gr A | |
| 11 | Luis Pérez-Companc/ | Ford Focus RS WRC 06 | |
| | José Díaz | Gr A | |
| 17 | François Duval/ | Skoda Fabia WRC | |
| | Jean-François Elst | Gr A | |
| 18 | Guy Wilks/ | Ford Focus RS WRC 04 | |
| | Phil Pugh | Gr A | |
| 21 | Urmo Aava/ | Mitsubishi Lancer WRC05 | |
| | Kuldar Sikk | Gr A | |
| 15 | Aris Vovos/ | Subaru Impreza WRC2006 | |
| | El Em | Gr A | |
| 31 | Toshihiro Arai/ | Subaru Impreza WRX Sti | |
| | Tony Sircombe | Gr N | |
| 38 | Kristian Sohlberg/ | Subaru Impreza WRX Sti | |
| | Risto Pietiläinen | Gr N | |
| 34 | Mark Higgins/ | Mitsubishi Lancer Evo 9 | |
| | Scott Martin | Gr N | |

### SPECIAL STAGE TIMES

**SS1 Hippodrome 1 (3.20km)**
1 M.Hirvonen/J.Lehtinen (Ford Focus RS WRC 06) 2m50.8s; 2 M.Grönholm/T.Rautiainen (Ford Focus RS WRC 06) 2m51.0s; 3 S.Loeb/D.Elena (Citroën C4 WRC) 2m51.1s; 4 P.Solberg/P.Mills (Subaru Impreza WRC2007) 2m51.2s; 5 D.Sordo/M.Martí (Citroën C4 WRC) 2m51.3s; 6 H.Solberg/C.Menkerud (Ford Focus RS WRC 06) 2m52.6s; PC M.Higgins/S.Martin (Mitsubishi Lancer Evo 9), A.Araújo/M.Ramalho (Mitsubishi Lancer Evo 9) 3m00.1s

**SS2 Schimatari 1 (11.56km)**
1 Grönholm/Rautiainen (Ford) 10m17.6s; 2 Hirvonen/Lehtinen (Ford) 10m19.6s; 3 Solberg/Mills (Subaru) 10m22.2s; 4 J-M.Latvala/M.Anttila (Ford Focus RS WRC 06) 10m24.2s; 5 D.Sordo/M.Martí (Citroën C4 WRC) 10m24.6s; 6 C.Atkinson/S.Prevot (Subaru Impreza WRC2007) 10m26.9s; PC P.Flodin/M.Andersson (Subaru Impreza WRX Sti) 10m50.9s

**SS3 Thiva 1 (23.76km)**
1 Atkinson/Prevot (Subaru) 16m39.0s; 2 Solberg/Mills (Subaru) 16m46.9s; 3 Loeb/Elena (Citroën) 16m49.9s; 4 Grönholm/Rautiainen (Ford) 16m50.7s; 5 Sordo/Martí (Citroën) 16m51.0s; 6 Hirvonen/Lehtinen (Ford) 16m51.9s; PC A.Aigner/K.Wicha (Mitsubishi Lancer Evo 9) 17m42.7s

**SS4 Agia Sotira 1 (15.19km)**
1 Atkinson/Prevot (Subaru) 9m39.4s; 2 Hirvonen/Lehtinen (Ford) 9m41.8s; 3 Solberg/Mills (Subaru) 9m42.8s; 4 Sordo/Martí (Citroën) 9m44.0s; 5 Loeb/Elena (Citroën) 9m46.1s; 6 Solberg/Menkerud (Ford) 9m47.0s; PC T.Arai/T.Sircombe (Subaru Impreza WRX Sti) 10m37.2s

**SS5 Olympic Properties 1 (5.15km)**
1 Solberg/Mills (Subaru) 3m33.7s; 2 Atkinson/Prevot (Subaru) 3m34.5s; 3 Latvala/Anttila (Ford) 3m34.9s; 4 Loeb/Elena (Citroën) 3m35.0s; 5= Hirvonen/Lehtinen (Ford), Solberg/Menkerud (Ford) 3m37.1s; PC Aigner/Wicha (Mitsubishi) 3m43.4s

**SS6 Schimatari 2 (11.56km)**
1 Grönholm/Rautiainen (Ford) 10m10.1s; 2 Loeb/Elena (Citroën) 10m14.5s; 3 Hirvonen/Lehtinen (Ford) 10m16.4s; 4 Latvala/Anttila (Ford) 10m17.3s; 5 Solberg/Mills (Subaru) 10m18.1s; 6= Sordo/Martí (Citroën), Atkinson/Prevot (Subaru) 10m18.9s; PC Aigner/Wicha (Mitsubishi) 10m53.2s

**SS7 Thiva 2 (23.76km)**
1 Sordo/Martí (Citroën) 16m13.2s; 2 Grönholm/Rautiainen (Ford) 16m13.3s; 3 Loeb/Elena (Citroën) 16m14.0s; 4 Solberg/Mills (Subaru) 16m19.0s; 5 Hirvonen/Lehtinen (Ford) 16m22.8s; 6 Atkinson/Prevot (Subaru) 16m24.9s; PC J.Hänninen/M.Markkula (Mitsubishi Lancer Evo 9) 17m33.8s

**SS8 Agia Sotira 2 (15.19km)**
1 Loeb/Elena (Citroën) 9m25.6s; 2 Hirvonen/Lehtinen (Ford) 9m25.9s; 3 Sordo/Martí (Citroën) 9m26.4s; 4 Grönholm/Rautiainen (Ford) 9m26.7s; 5 Latvala/Anttila (Ford) 9m27.2s; 6 Atkinson/Prevot (Subaru) 9m28.3s; PC Hänninen/Markkula (Mitsubishi) 10m35.4s

**SS9 Imittos 1 (11.43km)**
Stage cancelled due to local protestors

**SS10 Agii Theodori 1 (48.88km)**
1 Grönholm/Rautiainen (Ford) 32m47.9s; 2 Loeb/Elena (Citroën) 32m58.6s; 3 Solberg/Mills (Subaru) 32m59.7s; 4 Sordo/Martí (Citroën) 33m24.5s; 5 Hirvonen/Lehtinen (Ford) 33m46.5s; 6 Solberg/Menkerud (Peugeot) 33m55.4s; PC Arai/Sircombe (Subaru), Hänninen/Markkula (Mitsubishi) 35m48.7s

**SS11 Loutraki 1 (9.18km)**
1 Loeb/Elena (Citroën) 7m21.1s; 2 Grönholm/Rautiainen (Ford) 7m21.9s; 3 Solberg/Mills (Subaru) 7m22.5s; 4 Sordo/Martí (Citroën) 7m27.3s; 5 Hirvonen/Lehtinen (Ford) 7m27.9s; 6 Atkinson/Prevot (Subaru) 7m28.1s; PC K.Sohlberg/R.Pietiläinen (Subaru Impreza WRX Sti) 7m54.1s

**SS12 Agia Triada 1 (10.80km)**
1 Solberg/Mills (Subaru) 7m24.5s; 2 Grönholm/Rautiainen (Ford) 7m29.2s; 3 Loeb/Elena (Citroën) 7m29.5s; 4 Atkinson/Prevot (Subaru) 7m32.0s; 5 Latvala/Anttila (Ford) 7m34.2s; 6 Hirvonen/Lehtinen (Ford) 7m35.1s; PC Higgins/Martin (Mitsubishi) 8m10.0s

**SS13 Olympic Properties 2 (5.15km)**
1 Solberg/Mills (Subaru) 3m23.4s; 2 Grönholm/Rautiainen (Ford) 3m23.6s; 3 Loeb/Elena (Citroën) 3m24.2s; 4 Latvala/Anttila (Ford) 3m26.5s; 5 Atkinson/Prevot (Subaru)

# ACROPOLIS RALLY

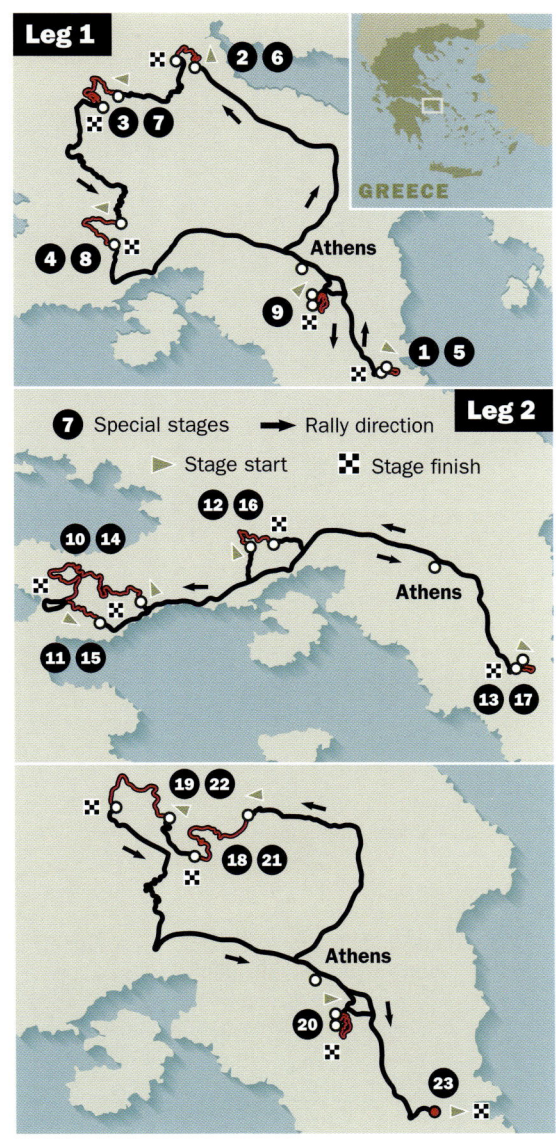

| Stage Numbers | 1 | 2 | 3 | 4 | 5 | 6 | 7 | 8 | 10 | 11 | 12 | 13 | 14 | 15 | 16 | 17 | 18 | 19 | 21 | 22 | 23 |
|---|---|---|---|---|---|---|---|---|---|---|---|---|---|---|---|---|---|---|---|---|---|
| Grönholm | 2 | 1 | 2 | 4 | 4 | 3 | 1 | 1 | 1 | 1 | 1 | 1 | 1 | 1 | 1 | 1 | 1 | 1 | 1 | 1 | 1 |
| Loeb | 3 | 7 | 6 | 6 | 6 | 5 | 4 | 4 | 3 | 2 | 3 | 3 | 3 | 3 | 2 | 2 | 2 | 2 | 2 | 2 | 2 |
| P.Solberg | 4 | 3 | 3 | 2 | 2 | 2 | 2 | 2 | 2 | 3 | 2 | 2 | 2 | 2 | 3 | 3 | 3 | 3 | 3 | 3 | 3 |
| Hirvonen | 1 | 2 | 4 | 3 | 4 | 6 | 5 | 5 | 5 | 4 | 4 | 4 | 4 | 4 | 4 | 4 | 4 | 4 | 4 | 4 | 4 |
| H.Solberg | 8 | 6 | 7 | 7 | 7 | 7 | 7 | 6 | 6 | 6 | 6 | 6 | 6 | 5 | 5 | 5 | 5 | 5 | 5 | 5 | 5 |
| Atkinson | 7 | 6 | 1 | 1 | 1 | 1 | 3 | 3 | 7 | 5 | 5 | 5 | 6 | 6 | 6 | 6 | 6 | 6 | 6 | 6 | 6 |
| Kopecky | 34 | 15 | 11 | 13 | 11 | 11 | 10 | 10 | 9 | 9 | 9 | 9 | 9 | 7 | 7 | 7 | 7 | 7 | 7 | 7 | 7 |
| Stohl | 10 | 9 | 9 | 9 | 9 | 9 | 9 | 9 | 8 | 8 | 7 | 8 | 8 | 8 | 8 | 8 | 8 | 8 | 8 | 8 | 8 |
| Wilks | 21 | 10 | 10 | 12 | 12 | 12 | 11 | 12 | 12 | 12 | 11 | 9 | 9 | 9 | 9 | 9 | 9 | 9 | 9 | 9 | 9 |
| Wilson | 10 | 13 | 17 | 17 | 16 | 14 | 13 | 13 | 13 | 12 | 10 | 10 | 10 | 10 | 10 | 10 | 10 | 10 | 10 | 10 | 10 |
| P.Companc | 13 | 11 | 13 | 10 | 10 | 10 | 12 | 11 | 11 | 11 | 11 | 11 | 11 | 11 | 11 | 11 | 11 | 11 | 11 | 11 | 11 |
| Latvala | 8 | 5 | 8 | 8 | 8 | 8 | 8 | 6 | 10 | 10 | 8 | 14 | 14 | 13 | 12 | 12 | 12 | 12 | 12 | 12 | 12 |
| Vovos | 23 | 17 | 16 | 14 | 13 | 16 | 16 | 15 | 14 | 14 | 13 | 11 | 11 | 12 | 12 | 12 | 13 | 13 | 13 | | |
| Sordo | 5 | 4 | 5 | 5 | 5 | 6 | 5 | 4 | 4 | 10 | 14 | 15 | 23 | 27 | 31 | 28 | 27 | 25 | 25 | 24 | |
| Villagra | 9 | 14 | 14 | 15 | 15 | 15 | 14 | 15 | 21 | 30 | 35 | 37 | 37 | 39 | 37 | 37 | 34 | 33 | 32 | | |
| Duval | 12 | 12 | 12 | 11 | R | | | | | | | | | | | | | | | | |

3m27.0s; 6 Solberg/Menkerud (Ford) 3m28.4s; PC Aigner/Wicha (Mitsubishi) 3m39.4s

### SS14 Agii Theodori 2 (48.88km)
1 Grönholm/Rautiainen (Ford) 32m33.0; 2 Solberg/Mills (Subaru) 32m52.9s; 3 Loeb/Elena (Citroën) 33m01.8s; 4 Solberg/Menkerud (Ford) 33m13.8s; 5 Atkinson/Prevot (Subaru) 33m14.9s; 6 Hirvonen/Lehtinen (Ford) 33m34.3s; PC Arai/Sircombe (Subaru) 35m32.0s

### SS15 Loutraki 2 (9.18km)
1 Loeb/Elena (Citroën) 7m14.7s; 2 Grönholm/Rautiainen (Ford) 7m17.6s; 3 Hirvonen/Lehtinen (Ford) 7m19.5s; 4 Solberg/Menkerud (Ford) 7m20.2s; 5 Solberg/Mills (Subaru) 7m23.8s; 6 Latvala/Anttila (Ford) 7m25.4s; PC Aigner/Wicha (Mitsubishi) 7m53.3s

### SS16 Agia Triada 2 (10.80km)
1 Loeb/Elena (Citroën) 7m17.2s; 2 Grönholm/Rautiainen (Ford) 7m19.6s; 3 Latvala/Anttila (Ford) 7m21.2s; 4 Hirvonen/Lehtinen (Ford) 7m21.3s; 5 Solberg/Menkerud (Ford) 7m22.9s; 6 M.Stohl/I.Minor (Citroën Xsara WRC) 7m29.4s; PC Hänninen/Markkula (Mitsubishi) 8m00.0s

### SS17 Hippodrome 2 (3.20km)
1 Loeb/Elena (Citroën) 2m52.8s; 2 Grönholm/Rautiainen (Ford) 2m53.5s; 3 Hirvonen/Lehtinen (Ford) 2m53.7s; 4 U.Aava/K.Sikk (Mitsubishi Lancer WRC05) 2m54.7s; 5 Latvala/Anttila (Ford) 2m54.8s; 6 Solberg/Menkerud (Ford) 2m54.9s; PC Higgins/Martin (Mitsubishi) 3m01.0s

### SS18 Avlonas 1 (20.00km)
1 Loeb/Elena (Citroën) 12m05.1s; 2 Grönholm/Rautiainen (Ford) 12m11.2s; 3 Hirvonen/Lehtinen (Ford) 12m17.1s; 4 Latvala/Anttila (Ford) 12m22.4s; 5 Solberg/Mills (Subaru) 12m23.4s; 6 Sordo/Martí (Citroën) 12m30.4s; PC M.Rauam/K.Kraag (Mitsubishi Lancer Evo 9) 13m23.7s

### SS19 Assopia 1 (17.87km)
1 Grönholm/Rautiainen (Ford) 10m58.6s; 2 Loeb/Elena (Citroën) 11m00.7s; 3 Hirvonen/Lehtinen (Ford) 11m06.5s; 4 Latvala/Anttila (Ford) 11m10.8s; 5 Solberg/Mills (Subaru) 11m15.5s; 6 Sordo/Martí (Citroën) 11m15.9s; PC Higgins/Martin (Mitsubishi) 12m00.5s

### SS20 Imittos 2 (11.43km)
Stage cancelled due to local protestors

### SS21 Avlonas 2 (20.00km)
1 Hirvonen/Lehtinen (Ford) 12m00.0s; 2 Latvala/Anttila (Ford) 12m00.4s; 3 Grönholm/Rautiainen (Ford) 12m01.0s; 4 Solberg/Mills (Subaru) 12m01.2s; 5 Loeb/Elena (Citroën) 12m03.5s; 6 Sordo/Martí (Citroën) 12m04.4s; PC M.Baldacci/G.Agnese (Subaru Impreza WRX Sti) 13m07.4s

### SS22 Assopia 2 (17.87km)
1 Latvala/Anttila (Ford) 10m47.8s; 2 Hirvonen/Lehtinen (Ford) 10m48.6s; 3 Loeb/Elena (Citroën) 10m49.5s; 4 Sordo/Martí (Citroën) 10m50.6s; 5 Solberg/Mills (Subaru) 10m50.8s; 6 Grönholm/Rautiainen (Ford) 10m52.8s; PC N.Al-Attiyah/C.Patterson (Subaru Impreza WRX Sti) 11m43.5s

### SS23 Hippodrome 3 (3.20km)
1 Sordo/Martí (Citroën) 2m55.4s; 2 Solberg/Mills (Subaru) 2m55.9s; 3 Grönholm/Rautiainen (Ford) 2m56.7s; 4 Loeb/Elena (Citroën) 2m56.8s; 5 F.Villagra/J.Pérez-Companc (Ford Focus RS WRC 06) 2m56.9s; 6 Hirvonen/Lehtinen (Ford) 2m57.3s; PC Higgins/Martin (Mitsubishi) 3m03.5s

Cars which retired and subsequently restarted and were classified under SuperRally regs:

| 2 | Sordo/Martí | Citroën C4 WRC | | |
| | Transmission | | SS12 | Gr A |
| 12 | Villagra/P-Companc | Ford Focus RS WRC 06 | | |
| | Clutch | | SS10 | Gr A |

### MAJOR RETIREMENTS
| 17 | Duval/Elst | Skoda Fabia WRC | | |
| | Engine | | SS5 | Gr A |

### FIA CLASS WINNERS
| A8 | Over 2000 cc | Grönholm/Rautiainen |
| | | Ford Focus RS WRC 06 |
| A7 | 1600-2000cc | 'Leonidas'/Kotsalis |
| | | Renault Clio R3 |
| A6 | 1400-1600 cc | Kaltsounis/Papageorgiou |
| | | Opel Corsa |
| A5 | Upto 1400cc | Makaronis/Vassiliadis |
| | | Toyota Yaris |
| N4 | Over 2000 cc | Arai/Sircombe |
| | | Subaru Impreza WRX Sti |

### RALLY LEADERS
Overall: SS1 Hirvonen; SS2 Grönholm; SS3-6 Atkinson; SS7-23 Grönholm
PC: SS1 Higgins, Araújo; SS2 Flodin; SS3 Aigner; SS4 Arai; SS5-7 Aigner; SS8-23 Arai
(SS9 and SS20 cancelled)

### SPECIAL STAGE ANALYSIS
| | 1st | 2nd | 3rd | 4th | 5th | 6th |
|---|---|---|---|---|---|---|
| Loeb (Citroën) | 6 | 3 | 7 | 2 | 2 | - |
| Grönholm (Ford) | 5 | 9 | 2 | 2 | - | 1 |
| P.Solberg (Subaru) | 3 | 3 | 4 | 3 | 5 | - |
| Hirvonen (Ford) | 2 | 4 | 5 | 1 | 4 | 4 |
| Atkinson (Subaru) | 2 | 1 | - | 1 | 2 | 5 |
| Sordo (Citroën) | 2 | - | 1 | 4 | 3 | 4 |
| Latvala (Ford) | 1 | 1 | 2 | 1 | 5 | 3 | 1 |
| H.Solberg (Ford) | - | - | - | 2 | 2 | 5 |
| Aava (Mitsubishi) | - | - | - | 1 | - | - |
| Villagra (Ford) | - | - | - | - | 1 | - |
| Stohl (Citroën) | - | - | - | - | - | 1 |

### WORLD CHAMPIONSHIP POINTS
**Drivers**
1 Grönholm 65; 2 Loeb 56; 3 Hirvonen 49; 4 Sordo 28; 5 P.Solberg 26; 6 H.Solberg 24; 7 Atkinson 15; 8 Latvala 12; 9= Carlsson, Stohl 9; 10 Gardemeister 8 etc

**Manufacturers**
1 BP-Ford WRT 114; 2 Citroën Total WRT 86; 3 Subaru WRT 43; 4 Stobart M-Sport Ford RT 41; 5 OMV-Kronos Citroën WRT 27; 6 Munchi's Ford RT 1

**Junior World Championship**
1 Andersson 28; 2 Aava 24; 3 Mölder 14; 4= Sandell, Béres, Burkart 9; 7= Cortinovis, Prokop 6; 9= Svenkerud, Rueda, Gallagher 3 etc

**Production Cup**
1 Arai 29; 2 Higgins 15; 3 Sohlberg 12; 4 M.Baldacci 11; 5= Svedlund, Villagra, Aigner 10; 8 Alén 8; 9 Pozzo 7; 10= Nutahara, Hänninen, Al-Attiyah 6 etc

### ROUTE DETAILS
Total route of 1572.33km of which 334.44km were competitive on 21 stages (2 cancelled totalling 22.86km)
**Leg 1** Thursday 31 May- Friday 1 June, 8 Special Stages totalling 109.42km
**Leg 2** Saturday 2 June, 8 Special Stages totalling 146.08km
**Leg 3** Sunday 3 June, 5 Special Stages totalling 41.07km

### RESULTS
| 1 | Marcus Grönholm/ | Ford Focus RS WRC 06 | |
| | Timo Rautiainen | 3h49m22.6s | |
| 2 | Sébastien Loeb/ | Citroën C4 WRC | |
| | Daniel Elena | 3h50m01.0s | |
| 3 | Petter Solberg/ | Subaru Impreza WRC2007 | |
| | Phil Mills | 3h50m56.7s | Gr A |
| 4 | Mikko Hirvonen/ | Ford Focus RS WRC 06 | |
| | Jarmo Lehtinen | 3h52m03.9s | Gr A |
| 5 | Henning Solberg/ | Ford Focus RS WRC 06 | |
| | Cato Menkerud | 3h54m15.3s | Gr A |
| 6 | Chris Atkinson/ | Subaru Impreza WRC2007 | |
| | Stéphane Prevot | 3h55m54.3s | Gr A |
| 7 | Jan Kopecky/ | Skoda Fabia WRC | |
| | Filip Schovanek | 3h57m38.4s | Gr A |
| 8 | Manfred Stohl/ | Citroën Xsara WRC | |
| | Ilka Minor | 3h58m18.8s | Gr A |
| 9 | Guy Wilks/ | Ford Focus RS WRC 04 | |
| | Phil Pugh | 3h59m15.8s | Gr A |
| 10 | Matthew Wilson/ | Ford Focus RS WRC 06 | |
| | Michael Orr | 4h00m02.2s | Gr A |

64 starters, 49 finishers

### RECENT WINNERS
| 1965 | Carl-Magnus Skogh/'Tandlakare' | Volvo 122S |
| 1966 | Bengt Söderstrom/Gunnar Palm | Ford Lotus Cortina |
| 1967 | Paddy Hopkirk/Ron Crellin | Mini Cooper S |
| 1968 | Roger Clark/Jim Porter | Ford Escort TC |
| 1969 | Pauli Toivonen/Matti Kolari | Porsche 911S |
| 1970 | Jean-Luc Thérier/Marcel Callewaert | Alpine Renault A110 |
| 1971 | Ove Andersson/Arne Hertz | Alpine Renault A110 |
| 1972 | Håkan Lindberg/Helmut Eisendle | Fiat 124 Spyder |
| 1973 | Jean-Luc Thérier/Christian Delferrier | Alpine Renault A110 |
| 1975 | Walter Röhrl/Jochen Berger | Opel Ascona |
| 1976 | Harry Kallström/Claes-Goran Andersson | Datsun 160J |
| 1977 | Björn Waldegård/Hans Thorszelius | Ford Escort RS |
| 1978 | Walter Röhrl/Christian Geistdörfer | Fiat 131 Abarth |
| 1979 | Björn Waldegård/Hans Thorszelius | Ford Escort RS |
| 1980 | Ari Vatanen/David Richards | Ford Escort RS |
| 1981 | Ari Vatanen/David Richards | Ford Escort RS |
| 1982 | Michèle Mouton/Fabrizia Pons | Audi Quattro |
| 1983 | Walter Röhrl/Christian Geistdörfer | Lancia Rally 037 |
| 1984 | Stig Blomqvist/Björn Cederberg | Audi Quattro A2 |
| 1985 | Timo Salonen/Seppo Harjanne | Peugeot 205 Turbo 16 |
| 1986 | Juha Kankkunen/Juha Piironen | Peugeot 205 Turbo 16 E2 |
| 1987 | Markku Alén/Ilkka Kivimäki | Lancia Delta HF 4x4 |
| 1988 | Miki Biasion/Tiziano Siviero | Lancia Delta Integrale |
| 1989 | Miki Biasion/Tiziano Siviero | Lancia Delta Integrale |
| 1990 | Carlos Sainz/Luis Moya | Toyota Celica GT4 |
| 1991 | Juha Kankkunen/Juha Piironen | Lancia Delta Integrale 16v |
| 1992 | Didier Auriol/Bernard Occelli | Lancia Delta HF Integrale |
| 1993 | Miki Biasion/Tiziano Siviero | Ford Escort RS Cosworth |
| 1994 | Carlos Sainz/Luis Moya | Subaru Impreza 555 |
| 1995 | Aris Vovos/Kostas Stefanis | Lancia Delta HF Integrale |
| 1996 | Colin McRae/Derek Ringer | Subaru Impreza 555 |
| 1997 | Carlos Sainz/Luis Moya | Ford Escort RS WRC |
| 1998 | Colin McRae/Nicky Grist | Subaru Impreza WRC98 |
| 1999 | Richard Burns/Robert Reid | Subaru Impreza WRC99 |
| 2000 | Colin McRae/Nicky Grist | Ford Focus RS WRC |
| 2001 | Colin McRae/Nicky Grist | Ford Focus RS WRC 01 |
| 2002 | Colin McRae/Nicky Grist | Ford Focus RS WRC 02 |
| 2003 | Markko Märtin/Michael Park | Ford Focus RS WRC 03 |
| 2004 | Petter Solberg/Phil Mills | Subaru Impreza WRC2004 |
| 2005 | Sébastien Loeb/Daniel Elena | Citroën Xsara WRC |
| 2006 | Marcus Grönholm/Timo Rautiainen | Ford Focus RS WRC 06 |

## The FIA World Rally Championship Round 9
# Rally Finland

THE Ford Focus RS WRC 07 lurched onto its right-hand side, cocking the left-front wheel high into the air. Mikko Hirvonen didn't flinch. His right foot was in danger of punching through the bulkhead; such was the force with which he was pushing the throttle. Such was the determination of the 27-year-old to win his home round of the championship. About 30 miles away, team principal Malcolm Wilson did flinch. He'd seen enough. Having watched Hirvonen howling through Ouninpohja in desperate pursuit of team leader and rally leader Marcus Grönholm, Wilson thought it was time to talk to his boys.

Twelve months ago, at the post-event press conference, Sébastien Loeb had spoken about wanting to beat Grönholm in Finland before the Finn retired. At the time Hirvonen chipped in that when Grönholm retired, the Frenchman would have him to deal with. This year, Hirvonen delivered on that promise. Engaged in a fascinating and utterly flat-out tussle, the Ford pair drew away from a chasing pack headed up by Loeb's Citroën`C4 WRC.

As the second day of the rally closed, however, Grönholm edged his way clear at the front. Hirvonen knew the fight was done for another year. His disappointment at not being able to find that final tenth of a second to win was negated by the way he had beaten Loeb. For Grönholm, there was enormous relief. He had expected this kind of effort from Hirvonen, but clearly he hadn't expected it to go on for so long or at such speed. In the end though, Grönholm got his record. Having seen Loeb smash record after record in recent WRC seasons, the Finn took the one that mattered most in his homeland. Prior to the start, Grönholm and Finnish rally uber-hero Markku Alen were level pegging on six wins apiece over the yumps. Not now. Grönholm became the first man ever to win a single WRC round seven times.

There was no denying the exhilaration Grönholm felt at winning, but almost immediately this opened up a new debate concerning his future. With the history books re-written and two – possibly three – titles in the bag, was this enough? Would he be back? Grönholm declined to comment, but the onlookers were adamant. His latest and arguably greatest win at home could have been the beginning of the end.

With Hirvonen second, Ford's – and Finland's – future in this neck of the woods looked assured, but what of Loeb? He had tried, pushed himself over his limit, scared himself and come back to the right side of his limit. Third and six points were far more attractive than no points and a headache.

That Loeb was almost two minutes ahead of fourth-placed Chris Atkinson came as little consolation to the C4 driver. That Atkinson was fourth came as a massive boost to the Subaru team. In an event that tested the Banbury outfit's PR skills to the limit, number one driver Petter Solberg pulled over on Saturday afternoon, declaring his Impreza WRC2007 simply undriveable. Atkinson battled on, suffering similar difficulties aboard his car, but still he equalled his best result of the season.

RALLY FINLAND

*Left:* Atkinson equalled his best result of the season in fourth despite problems with the Impreza. Team-mate Solberg had declared the car undriveable before switching it off

*Below:* Loeb clearly pushed hard in a bid to beat Grönholm in his backyard, but both the Finn and his compatriot Hirvonen were uncatchable

*Bottom right:* Marcus made history in Finland, going one better than fellow rally legend Markku Alén to win his home event a record seven times

*Bottom left:* Accidents in Finland tend to err on the large side, as Skoda Fabia driver Jan Kopecky found out on the Valkola test

All photographs by McKlein

**Opposite:** Hirvonen desperately wanted to win in Finland, to the point that team boss Malcolm Wilson had to rein him in, but at least he beat Loeb soundly

**Above left:** JRC driver Aava upgraded to a Mitsubishi Lancer WRC and finished seventh, to the delight of at least one of the Estonian's fans...

**Above top:** Rally fans packed service park at Jyväskylä and they weren't just there for the locals - witness this welcome for Citroën's stars

**Above:** Pons joined the Subaru ranks in Finland. He was sixth even after reversing into a tree on leg one

**Left:** Henning Solberg gave Ford further reason to cheer by taking his Stobart VK-backed Focus to fifth place

*All photographs by McKlein unless specified*

Reigning Junior champion Patrick Sandell capitalised on Suzuki's absence to score his sole class win of the year
McKlein

## The FIA World Rally Championship Round 9
# Rally Finland Results
### August 3-5 2007

### FINISH LINES...

This year's Rally Finland was the first WRC round in what is rapidly becoming known as the Abu Dhabi era. During the summer break, the Abu Dhabi Tourism Authority signed a deal to back the Ford team, and UAE driver Khalid Al Qassimi in particular. From the first stage onwards, however, it became clear from the ADTA branding at the side of the road that there was more to this programme than the Ford angle, with an all-round WRC deal on the cards... There was more Ford cheer in fifth place, as Henning Solberg bagged valuable points for the Stobart team. But his team-mate Jari-Matti Latvala was in Malcolm Wilson's bad books. Well, he was in Wilson's good books at first – as he led the event after the first stage proper – before he crashed in SS3 and then took a wheel off in SS7... Xevi Pons looked a touch bemused at the way his new Subaru handled on some of the stages, but in the main the Spaniard's first SWRT outing went well. That was apart from when he backed the car into a tree at quite high speed on Friday. Never mind, he still managed sixth... Urmo Aava's decision to hire a Mitsubishi WRC on the event closest to his Estonian home paid dividends with seventh, one place ahead of Subaru privateer Mads Ostberg, who collected his first ever WRC point in eighth... Reigning Junior champion Patrik Sandell (Renault) won his first round in 2007, picking up the pieces after early leader Martin Prokop crashed his C2.

### RUNNING ORDER

| | | |
|---|---|---|
| 3 | Marcus Grönholm/ | Ford Focus RS WRC 07 |
| | Timo Rautiainen | Gr A |
| 1 | Sébastien Loeb/ | Citroën C4 WRC |
| | Daniel Elena | Gr A |
| 4 | Mikko Hirvonen/ | Ford Focus RS WRC 07 |
| | Jarmo Lehtinen | Gr A |
| 2 | Daniel Sordo/ | Citroën C4 WRC |
| | Marc Martí | Gr A |
| 7 | Petter Solberg/ | Subaru Impreza WRC2007 |
| | Phil Mills | Gr A |
| 10 | Henning Solberg/ | Ford Focus RS WRC 06 |
| | Cato Menkerud | Gr A |
| 8 | Chris Atkinson/ | Subaru Impreza WRC2007 |
| | Stéphane Prevot | Gr A |
| 9 | Jari-Matti Latvala/ | Ford Focus RS WRC 06 |
| | Miikka Anttila | Gr A |
| 5 | Manfred Stohl/ | Citroën Xsara WRC |
| | Ilka Minor | Gr A |
| 14 | Jan Kopecky/ | Skoda Fabia WRC |
| | Filip Schovanek | Gr A |
| 16 | Matthew Wilson/ | Ford Focus RS WRC 06 |
| | Michael Orr | Gr A |
| 15 | Juha Hänninen/ | Mitsubishi Lancer WRC05 |
| | Mikko Markkula | Gr A |
| 11 | Luis Pérez-Companc/ | Ford Focus RS WRC 06 |
| | José María Volta | Gr A |
| 12 | Federico Villagra/ | Ford Focus RS WRC 06 |
| | Jorge Pérez-Companc | Gr A |
| 17 | Xavier Pons/ | Subaru Impreza WRC2007 |
| | Xavier Amigo | Gr A |
| 18 | Kristian Sohlberg/ | Mitsubishi Lancer WRC05 |
| | Risto Pietiläinen | Gr A |
| 19 | Mads Östberg/ | Subaru Impreza WRC2005 |
| | Ole Unnerud | Gr A |
| 20 | Urmo Aava/ | Mitsubishi Lancer WRC05 |
| | Kuldar Sikk | Gr A |
| 21 | Guy Wilks/ | Ford Focus RS WRC 04 |
| | Phil Pugh | Gr A |
| 22 | Jarmo Mikkonen/ | Peugeot 206 WRC |
| | Hannu Ervasto | Gr A |
| 23 | Andreas Mikkelsen/ | Ford Focus RS WRC 04 |
| | Ola Floene | Gr A |
| 25 | Khalid Al-Qassimi/ | Ford Focus RS WRC 06 |
| | Nicky Beech | Gr A |

### SPECIAL STAGE TIMES

**SS1 Killeri 1 (2.50km)**
1 C.Atkinson/S.Prevot (Subaru Impreza WRC2007) 1m20.6s; 2 M.Grönholm/T.Rautiainen (Ford Focus RS WRC 07) 1m20.8s; 3 S.Loeb/D.Elena (Citroën C4 WRC) 1m20.9s; 4 D.Sordo/M.Martí (Citroën C4 WRC) 1m21.2s; 5 P.Solberg/P.Mills (Subaru Impreza WRC2007) 1m21.3s; 6 J-M.Latvala/M.Anttila (Ford Focus RS WRC 06) 1m21.7s; JRC M.Prokop/J.Tomanek (Citroën C2) 1m30.0s

**SS2 Vellipohja 1 (17.20km)**
1 Latvala/Anttila (Ford) 8m18.7s; 2 M.Hirvonen/J.Lehtinen (Ford Focus RS WRC 07) 8m20.3s; 3= Grönholm/Rautiainen (Ford), Loeb/Elena (Citroën) 8m23.3s; 5 Atkinson/Prevot (Subaru) 8m23.6s; 6 M.Stohl/I.Minor (Citroën Xsara WRC) 8m26.0s; JRC Prokop/Tomanek (Citroën) 9m19.1s

**SS3 Mokkipera 1 (13.72km)**
1 Grönholm/Rautiainen (Ford) 6m47.5s; 2 Loeb/Elena (Citroën) 6m49.6s; 3 Hirvonen/Lehtinen (Ford) 6m50.3s; 4 Atkinson/Prevot (Subaru) 6m50.8s; 5 Sordo/Martí (Citroën) 6m55.5s; 6 H.Solberg/C.Menkerud (Ford Focus RS WRC 06) 6m56.0s; JRC Prokop/Tomanek (Citroën) 7m45.0s

**SS4 Palsankyla 1 (13.31km)**
1 Hirvonen/Lehtinen (Ford) 6m47.4s; 2 Grönholm/Rautiainen (Ford) 6m48.4s; 3 Latvala/Anttila (Ford) 6m49.0s; 4 Loeb/Elena (Citroën) 6m52.7s; 5 Solberg/Menkerud (Ford) 6m54.7s; 6 Atkinson/Prevot (Subaru) 6m55.3s; JRC Prokop/Tomanek (Citroën) 7m41.1s

**SS5 Vellipohja 2 (17.20km)**
1 Grönholm/Rautiainen (Ford) 8m10.1s; 2 Hirvonen/Lehtinen (Ford) 8m10.6s; 3 Loeb/Elena (Citroën) 8m11.5s; 4 Solberg/Mills (Subaru) 8m12.1s; 5 Atkinson/Prevot (Subaru) 8m14.1s; 6 Latvala/Anttila (Ford) 8m16.3s; JRC Prokop/Tomanek (Citroën) 9m14.0s

**SS6 Mokkipera 2 (13.72km)**
1= Grönholm/Rautiainen (Ford), Hirvonen/Lehtinen (Ford) 6m42.7s; 3 Solberg/Mills (Subaru) 6m43.4s; 4 Loeb/Elena (Citroën) 6m44.1s; 5= Atkinson/Prevot (Subaru), Latvala/Anttila (Ford) 6m45.6s; JRC Prokop/Tomanek (Citroën) 7m38.1s

**SS7 Palsankyla 2 (13.31km)**
1 Grönholm/Rautiainen (Ford) 6m36.1s; 2 Hirvonen/Lehtinen (Ford) 6m36.5s; 3 Solberg/Mills (Subaru) 6m38.3s; 4 Loeb/Elena (Citroën) 6m38.5s; 5 Atkinson/Prevot (Subaru) 6m41.4s; 6 Solberg/Menkerud (Ford) 6m42.9s; JRC P.Sandell/E.Axelsson (Renault Clio R3) 7m38.3s

**SS8 Urria (9.96km)**
1 Grönholm/Rautiainen (Ford) 4m36.6s; 2 Hirvonen/Lehtinen (Ford) 4m36.8s; 3 Loeb/Elena (Citroën) 4m37.8s; 4 Atkinson/Prevot (Subaru) 4m38.2s; 5 Solberg/Mills (Subaru) 4m40.0s; 6 Solberg/Menkerud (Ford) 4m41.9s; JRC Prokop/Tomanek (Citroën) 5m14.1s

**SS9 Lautapera (8.69km)**
1 Grönholm/Rautiainen (Ford) 3m56.7s; 2 Hirvonen/Lehtinen (Ford) 3m58.4s; 3 Loeb/Elena (Citroën) 3m59.3s; 4 J.Hänninen/M.Markkula (Mitsubishi Lancer WRC05) 4m02.8s; 5 Sordo/Martí (Citroën) 4m03.4s; 6 Solberg/Mills (Subaru) 4m04.3s; JRC Sandell/Axelsson (Renault) 4m32.2s

**SS10 Jukojarvi (22.25km)**
1 Grönholm/Rautiainen (Ford) 10m35.6s; 2 Hirvonen/Lehtinen (Ford) 10m36.7s; 3 Loeb/Elena (Citroën) 10m40.2s; 4 Atkinson/Prevot (Subaru) 10m44.6s; 5 Solberg/Mills (Subaru) 10m49.7s; 6 Stohl/Minor (Citroën) 10m55.4s; JRC J.Nikara/P.Nikara (Honda Civic Type-R) 12m10.0s

**SS11 Killeri 2 (2.50km)**
1 Grönholm/Rautiainen (Ford) 1m20.7s; 2 Loeb/Elena (Citroën) 1m20.8s; 3 Sordo/Martí (Citroën) 1m20.9s; 4 Atkinson/Prevot (Subaru) 1m21.0s; 5= Hirvonen/Lehtinen (Ford), Solberg/Mills (Subaru) 1m21.3s; JRC Sandell/Axelsson (Renault) 1m30.6s

**SS12 Kaipolanvuori (13.46km)**
1 Loeb/Elena (Citroën) 6m53.4s; 2 Grönholm/Rautiainen (Ford) 6m55.6s; 3 Hirvonen/Lehtinen (Ford) 6m56.0s; 4 Solberg/Mills (Subaru) 6m59.1s; 5 Atkinson/Prevot (Subaru)

RALLY FINLAND

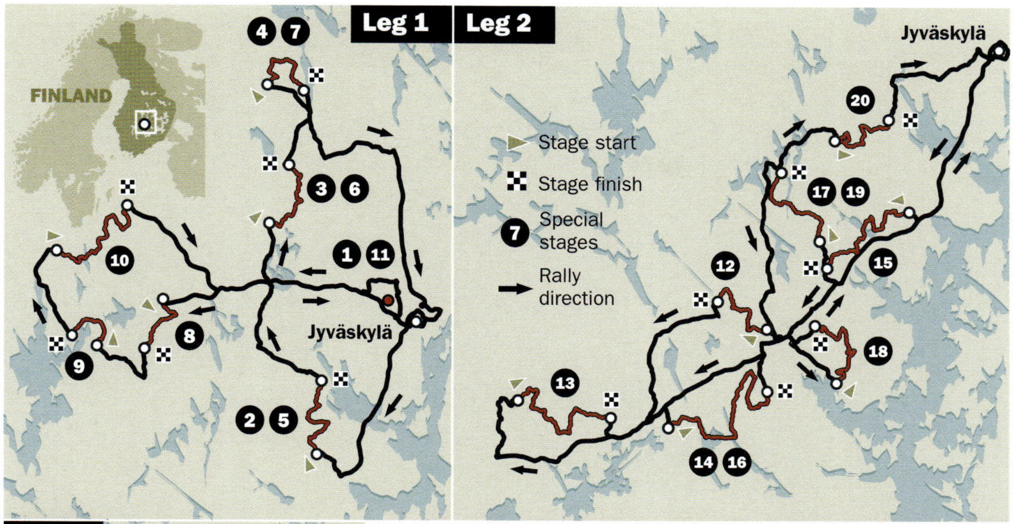


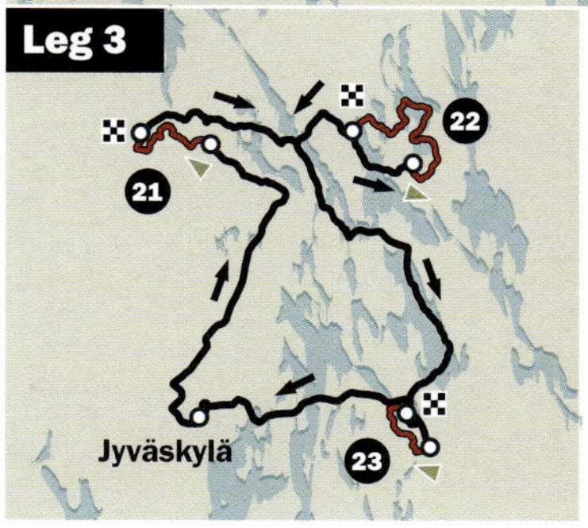


| Position / Stage Numbers | 1 | 2 | 3 | 4 | 5 | 6 | 7 | 8 | 9 | 10 | 11 | 12 | 13 | 14 | 15 | 16 | 17 | 18 | 19 | 20 | 21 | 22 | 23 |
|---|---|---|---|---|---|---|---|---|---|---|---|---|---|---|---|---|---|---|---|---|---|---|---|
| Grönholm | 2 | 3 | 1 | 2 | 1 | 1 | 1 | 1 | 1 | 1 | 1 | 1 | 1 | 1 | 1 | 1 | 1 | 1 | 1 | 1 | 1 | 1 | 1 |
| Hirvonen | 7 | 2 | 2 | 1 | 2 | 2 | 2 | 2 | 2 | 2 | 2 | 2 | 2 | 2 | 2 | 2 | 2 | 2 | 2 | 2 | 2 | 2 | 2 |
| Loeb | 3 | 4 | 3 | 3 | 3 | 3 | 3 | 3 | 3 | 3 | 3 | 3 | 3 | 3 | 3 | 3 | 3 | 3 | 3 | 3 | 3 | 3 | 3 |
| Atkinson | 1 | 4 | 4 | 4 | 4 | 4 | 4 | 4 | 4 | 4 | 4 | 4 | 4 | 4 | 4 | 4 | 4 | 4 | 4 | 4 | 4 | 4 | 4 |
| H.Solberg | 9 | 10 | 8 | 7 | 7 | 7 | 7 | 6 | 7 | 7 | 7 | 7 | 7 | 6 | 5 | 5 | 5 | 5 | 5 | 5 | 5 | 5 | 5 |
| Pons | 11 | 12 | 12 | 12 | 9 | 9 | 9 | 10 | 10 | 11 | 11 | 11 | 10 | 8 | 6 | 6 | 6 | 6 | 6 | 6 | 6 | 6 | 6 |
| Aava | 15 | 9 | 9 | 8 | 12 | 12 | 11 | 11 | 11 | 10 | 10 | 10 | 9 | 9 | 7 | 7 | 7 | 7 | 7 | 7 | 7 | 7 | 7 |
| Östberg | 16 | 14 | 13 | 13 | 13 | 13 | 13 | 14 | 16 | 16 | 16 | 15 | 13 | 11 | 10 | 9 | 9 | 8 | 8 | 8 | 8 | 8 | 8 |
| Wilks | 13 | 12 | 10 | 10 | 11 | 11 | 12 | 12 | 12 | 12 | 12 | 12 | 11 | 10 | 9 | 8 | 8 | 9 | 9 | 9 | 9 | 9 | 9 |
| Wilson | 20 | 17 | 16 | 16 | 16 | 15 | 15 | 15 | 14 | 14 | 14 | 13 | 12 | 12 | 12 | 10 | 10 | 11 | 11 | 11 | 10 | 10 | 10 |
| P-Companc | 18 | 16 | 15 | 14 | 14 | 14 | 14 | 13 | 13 | 13 | 13 | 14 | 14 | 13 | 11 | 11 | 12 | 13 | 13 | 13 | 12 | 12 | 11 |
| Mikkelsen | 19 | 18 | 17 | 15 | 15 | 16 | 16 | 16 | 15 | 15 | 15 | 16 | 15 | 14 | 13 | 12 | 13 | 12 | 12 | 12 | 11 | 11 | 12 |
| Villagra | 14 | 20 | 19 | 20 | 20 | 19 | 19 | 18 | 18 | 19 | 19 | 19 | 18 | 18 | 16 | 15 | 15 | 15 | 15 | 15 | 14 | 14 | 14 |
| Kopecky | 17 | 15 | 14 | 17 | 21 | 21 | 17 | 19 | 19 | 17 | 17 | 17 | 16 | 15 | 14 | 13 | 11 | 10 | 10 | 10 | R | | |
| P.Solberg | 5 | 7 | 6 | 6 | 5 | 5 | 5 | 5 | 5 | 5 | 5 | 5 | 5 | 7 | 8 | R | | | | | | | |
| Sordo | 4 | 8 | 7 | 5 | 6 | 6 | 6 | 7 | 6 | 6 | 6 | 6 | 6 | 5 | R | | | | | | | | |
| Hänninen | 10 | 11 | 11 | 11 | 10 | 10 | 10 | 9 | 9 | 9 | 9 | 9 | 8 | R | | | | | | | | | |
| Stohl | 8 | 6 | 5 | 9 | 8 | 8 | 8 | 8 | 8 | 8 | 8 | 8 | R | | | | | | | | | | |
| Latvala | 6 | 1 | 31 | 22 | 17 | 17 | R | | | | | | | | | | | | | | | | |
| Sohlberg | 12 | R | | | | | | | | | | | | | | | | | | | | | |

7m02.4s; 6 Sordo/Martí (Citroën) 7m04.1s; JRC Sandell/Axelsson (Renault) 7m56.2s

**SS13 Juupajoki (22.13km)**

1 Grönholm/Rautiainen (Ford) 11m19.3s; 2 Hirvonen/Lehtinen (Ford) 11m20.8s; 3 Loeb/Elena (Citroën) 11m24.2s; 4 Atkinson/Prevot (Subaru) 11m35.2s; 5 Sordo/Martí (Citroën) 11m37.0s; 6 Solberg/Mills (Subaru) 11m42.4s; JRC Prokop/Tomanek (Citroën) 12m50.8s

**SS14 Ouninpohja 1 (33.00km)**

1 Grönholm/Rautiainen (Ford) 15m35.3s; 2 Hirvonen/Lehtinen (Ford) 15m40.1s; 3 Atkinson/Prevot (Subaru) 15m40.8s; 4 Loeb/Elena (Citroën) 15m42.2s; 5 Sordo/Martí (Citroën) 15m57.1s; 6 Solberg/Menkerud (Ford) 16m05.9s; JRC C.Rautenbach/D.Senior (Citroën C2) 17m54.3s

**SS15 Leustu (21.27km)**

1 Grönholm/Rautiainen (Ford) 10m12.6s; 2 Hirvonen/Lehtinen (Ford) 10m15.0s; 3 Loeb/Elena (Citroën) 10m17.8s; 4 Solberg/Menkerud (Ford) 10m23.7s; 5 Atkinson/Prevot (Subaru) 10m27.5s; 6 M.Östberg/O.Unnerud (Subaru Impreza WRC2005) 10m41.1s; JRC Nikara/Nikara (Honda) 11m50.1s

**SS16 Ouninpohja 2 (33.00km)**

1 Grönholm/Rautiainen (Ford) 15m19.8s; 2 Hirvonen/Lehtinen (Ford) 15m22.8; 3 Loeb/Elena (Citroën) 15m24.6s; 4 Solberg/Menkerud (Ford) 15m32.8; 5 Atkinson/Prevot (Subaru) 15m34.8s; 6 X.Pons/X.Amigo (Subaru Impreza WRC2007 15m51.9s; JRC J.Mölder/K.Becker (Suzuki Swift) 17m46.4s

**SS17 Ehikki 1 (14.88km)**

1 Grönholm/Rautiainen (Ford) 6m52.2s; 2 Hirvonen/Lehtinen (Ford) 6m56.2s; 3 Loeb/Elena (Citroën) 6m56.5; 4 Solberg/Menkerud (Ford) 7m05.2s; 5 Atkinson/Prevot (Subaru) 7m07.1s; 6 J.Kopecky/F.Schovanek (Skoda Fabia WRC) 7m12.8s; JRC A.Bettega/S.Scattolin (Suzuki Ignis) 7m55.7s

**SS18 Himos (18.55km)**

1 Grönholm/Rautiainen (Ford) 10m09.8s; 2 Hirvonen/Lehtinen (Ford) 10m10.8s; 3 Solberg/Menkerud (Ford) 10m15.9s; 4 Loeb/Elena (Citroën) 10m18.5s; 5 Atkinson/Prevot (Subaru) 10m22.6s; 6 Kopecky/Schovanek (Skoda) 10m26.7s; JRC T.Suominen/J.Ottman (Suzuki Swift) 11m42.1s

**SS19 Ehikki 2 (14.88km)**

1 Hirvonen/Lehtinen (Ford) 6m47.4s; 2 Grönholm/Rautiainen (Ford) 6m48.0s; 3 Loeb/Elena (Citroën) 6m50.3s; 4 Solberg/Menkerud (Ford) 6m55.7s; 5 Atkinson/Prevot (Subaru) 7m00.1s; 6 Kopecky/Schovanek (Skoda) 7m03.5s; JRC Bettega/Scattolin (Suzuki) 7m49.5s

**SS20 Surkee (14.89km)**

1 Hirvonen/Lehtinen (Ford) 8m13.6s; 2 Grönholm/Rautiainen (Ford) 8m14.1s; 3 Loeb/Elena (Citroën) 8m19.5s; 4 Atkinson/Prevot (Subaru) 8m30.6s; 5 Solberg/Menkerud (Ford) 8m31.4s; 6 U.Aava/K.Sikk (Mitsubishi Lancer WRC05) 8m33.6s; JRC Suominen/Ottman (Suzuki) 9m21.1s

**SS21 Valkola (10.38km)**

1 Grönholm/Rautiainen (Ford) 5m35.9s; 2 Hirvonen/Lehtinen (Ford) 5m36.0s; 3 Loeb/Elena (Citroën) 5m38.2s; 4= Atkinson/Prevot (Subaru), M.Wilson/M.Orr (Ford Focus RS WRC 06) 5m42.9s; 6 Pons/Amigo (Subaru) 5m44.5s; JRC Nikara/Nikara (Honda) 6m20.0s

**SS22 Lankamaa (22.82km)**

1 Grönholm/Rautiainen (Ford) 11m07.2s; 2 Hirvonen/Lehtinen (Ford) 11m09.2; 3 Loeb/Elena (Citroën) 11m12.5s; 4 Atkinson/Prevot (Subaru) 11m17.4s; 5 Solberg/Menkerud (Ford) 11m24.7s; 6 Pons/Amigo (Subaru) 11m27.1s; JRC Nikara/Nikara (Honda) 12m32.7s

**SS23 Ruuhumaki (7.53 km)**

1 Grönholm/Rautiainen (Ford) 3m57.8s; 2 Hirvonen/Lehtinen (Ford) 3m59.5s; 3 Loeb/Elena (Citroën) 3m59.6s; 4 Pons/Amigo (Subaru) 4m01.1s; 5 Solberg/Menkerud (Ford) 4m01.5s; 6 G.Wilks/P.Pugh (Ford Focus RS WRC 04) 4m01.7s; JRC Rautenbach/Senior (Citroën) 4m30.0s

## MAJOR RETIREMENTS

| | | | |
|---|---|---|---|
| 2 | Sordo/Martí | Citroën C4 WRC | |
| | Mechanical | SS15 | Gr A |
| 7 | Solberg/Mills | Subaru Impreza WRC2007 | |
| | Handling | SS16 | Gr A |
| 9 | Latvala/Anttila | Ford Focus RS WRC 06 | |
| | Accident | SS7 | Gr A |
| 5 | Stohl/Minor | Citroën Xsara WRC | |
| | Accident | SS13 | Gr A |
| 14 | Kopecky/Sch'nek | Skoda Fabia WRC | |
| | Accident | SS21 | Gr A |
| 15 | Hänninen/Markkula | Mitsubishi Lancer WRC05 | |
| | Mechanical | SS14 | Gr A |
| 18 | Sohlberg/P'läinen | Mitsubishi Lancer WRC05 | |
| | Accident | SS2 | Gr A |

## FIA CLASS WINNERS

| | | |
|---|---|---|
| A8 | Over 2000 cc | Grönholm/Rautiainen |
| | | Ford Focus RS WRC 07 |
| A7 | 1600-2000cc | Sandell/Axelsson |
| | | Renault Clio R3 |
| A6 | 1400-1600 cc | Kosciuszko/Szczepaniak |
| | | Renault Clio |
| A5 | Upto 1400cc | Saari/Leppala |
| | | VW Polo GTi |
| N4 | Over 2000 cc | Flodin/Andersson |
| | | Subaru Impreza WRX Sti |
| N3 | 1600-2000cc | Koitia/Toomas |
| | | Honda Civic Type-R |

## RALLY LEADERS

Overall: SS1 Atkinson; SS2 Latvala; SS3 Grönholm; SS4 Hirvonen; SS5-23 Grönholm

JWC: SS1-13 Prokop; SS14-23 Sandell

## SPECIAL STAGE ANALYSIS

| | 1st | 2nd | 3rd | 4th | 5th | 6th |
|---|---|---|---|---|---|---|
| Grönholm (Ford) | 17 | 5 | 1 | - | - | - |
| Hirvonen (Ford) | 4 | 15 | 2 | - | 1 | - |
| Loeb (Citroën) | 1 | 2 | 15 | 5 | - | - |
| Atkinson (Subaru) | 1 | - | 1 | 8 | 10 | 1 |
| Latvala (Ford) | 1 | - | 1 | - | 1 | 2 |
| P.Solberg (Subaru) | - | - | 2 | 2 | 4 | 2 |
| H.Solberg (Ford) | - | - | 1 | 4 | 4 | 4 |
| Sordo (Citroën) | - | - | 1 | 1 | 4 | 1 |
| Pons (Subaru) | - | - | - | 1 | - | 3 |
| Hänninen (Mitsubishi) | - | - | - | 1 | - | - |
| Wilson (Ford) | - | - | - | 1 | - | - |
| Kopecky (Skoda) | - | - | - | - | - | 3 |
| Stohl (Citroën) | - | - | - | - | - | 2 |
| Aava (Mitsubishi) | - | - | - | - | - | 1 |
| Wilks (Ford) | - | - | - | - | - | 1 |

## WORLD CHAMPIONSHIP POINTS

**Drivers**

1 Grönholm 75; 2 Loeb 62; 3 Hirvonen 57; 4= Sordo, H.Solberg 28; 6 P.Solberg 26; 7 Atkinson 20; 8 Latvala 12; 9= Carlsson, Stohl 9; 10 Gardemeister 8 etc

**Manufacturers**

1 BP-Ford WRT 132; 2 Citroën Total WRT 92; 3 Subaru WRT 48; 4 Stobart M-Sport Ford RT 45; 5 OMV-Kronos Citroën WRT 27; 6 Munchi's Ford RT 6

**Junior World Championship**

1 Andersson 28; 2 Aava 24; 3 Sandell 19; 4 Mölder 14; 5= Béres, Burkart 9; 7 Pinomäki 8; 8= Cortinovis, Prokop, Kosciuszko 6 etc

**Production Cup**

1 Arai 29; 2 Higgins 15; 3 Sohlberg 12; 4 M.Baldacci 11; 5= Svedlund, Villagra, Aigner 10; 8 Alén 8; 9 Pozzo 7; 10= Nutahara, Hänninen, Al-Attiyah 6 etc

## ROUTE DETAILS

Total Route of 1375.15km of which 360.34km were competitive on 23 stages

**Leg 1** Thursday 2 August - Friday 3 August, 11 special stages totalling 133.49km

**Leg 2** Saturday 4 August, 9 special stages totalling 186.10km

**Leg 3** Sunday 5 August, 3 special stages totalling 40.75km

## RESULTS

| | | | |
|---|---|---|---|
| 1 | Marcus Grönholm/ | Ford Focus RS WRC 07 | |
| | Timo Rautiainen | 2h57m26.1s | Gr A |
| 2 | Mikko Hirvonen/ | Ford Focus RS WRC 07 | |
| | Jarmo Lehtinen | 2h57m50.3s | Gr A |
| 3 | Sébastien Loeb/ | Citroën C4 WRC | |
| | Daniel Elena | 2h58m36.0s | Gr A |
| 4 | Chris Atkinson | Subaru Impreza WRC2007 | |
| | Stéphane Prevot | 3h00m28.9s | Gr A |
| 5 | Henning Solberg/ | Ford Focus RS WRC 06 | |
| | Cato Menkerud | 3h01m55.5s | Gr A |
| 6 | Xavier Pons/ | Subaru Impreza WRC2007 | |
| | Xavier Amigo | 3h04m26.6s | Gr A |
| 7 | Urmo Aava/ | Mitsubishi Lancer WRC05 | |
| | Kuldar Sikk | 3h05m05.7s | Gr A |
| 8 | Mads Östberg/ | Subaru Impreza WRC2005 | |
| | Ole Unnerud | 3h06m58.0s | Gr A |
| 9 | Guy Wilks/ | Ford Focus RS WRC 04 | |
| | Phil Pugh | 3h07m05.5s | Gr A |
| 10 | Matthew Wilson/ | Ford Focus RS WRC 06 | |
| | Michael Orr | 3h08m39.5s | Gr A |

97 starters, 70 finishers

## PREVIOUS WINNERS

| | | |
|---|---|---|
| 1970 | Hannu Mikkola/Gunnar Palm | Ford Escort TC |
| 1971 | Stig Blomqvist/Arne Hertz | Saab 96 V4 |
| 1972 | Simo Lampinen/Klaus Sohlberg | Saab 96 V4 |
| 1973 | Timo Mäkinen/Henry Liddon | Ford Escort RS1600 |
| 1974 | Hannu Mikkola/John Davenport | Ford Escort RS1600 |
| 1975 | Hannu Mikkola/Atso Aho | Toyota Corolla |
| 1976 | Markku Alén/Ilkka Kivimäki | Fiat Abarth 131 |
| 1977 | Kyosti Hämaläinen/Martí Tiukkanen | Ford Escort RS |
| 1978 | Markku Alén/Ilkka Kivimäki | Fiat Abarth 131 |
| 1979 | Markku Alén/Ilkka Kivimäki | Fiat Abarth 131 |
| 1980 | Markku Alén/Ilkka Kivimäki | Fiat Abarth 131 |
| 1981 | Ari Vatanen/David Richards | Ford Escort RS |
| 1982 | Hannu Mikkola/Arne Hertz | Audi Quattro |
| 1983 | Hannu Mikkola/Arne Hertz | Audi Quattro A1 |
| 1984 | Ari Vatanen/Terry Harryman | Peugeot 205 Turbo 16 |
| 1985 | Timo Salonen/Seppo Harjanne | Peugeot 205 Turbo 16 E2 |
| 1986 | Timo Salonen/Seppo Harjanne | Peugeot 205 Turbo 16 E2 |
| 1987 | Markku Alén/Ilkka Kivimäki | Lancia Delta 4x4 |
| 1988 | Markku Alén/Ilkka Kivimäki | Lancia Delta Integrale |
| 1989 | Mikael Ericsson/Claes Billstam | Mitsubishi Galant VR-4 |
| 1990 | Carlos Sainz/Luis Moya | Toyota Celica GT4 |
| 1991 | Juha Kankkunen/Juha Piironen | Lancia Delta Integrale 16v |
| 1992 | Didier Auriol/Bernard Occelli | Lancia Delta HF Integrale |
| 1993 | Juha Kankkunen/Denis Giraudet | Toyota Celica Turbo 4wd |
| 1994 | Tommi Mäkinen/Seppo Harjanne | Ford Escort RS Cosworth |
| 1995 | Tommi Mäkinen/Seppo Harjanne | Mitsubishi Lancer RS-E3 |
| 1996 | Tommi Mäkinen/Seppo Harjanne | Mitsubishi Lancer RS-E3 |
| 1997 | Tommi Mäkinen/Seppo Harjanne | Mitsubishi Lancer E4 |
| 1998 | Tommi Mäkinen/Seppo Harjanne | Mitsubishi Lancer E5 |
| 1999 | Juha Kankkunen/Juha Repo | Subaru Impreza WRC99 |
| 2000 | Marcus Grönholm/Timo Rautiainen | Peugeot 206 WRC |
| 2001 | Marcus Grönholm/Timo Rautiainen | Peugeot 206 WRC |
| 2002 | Marcus Grönholm/Timo Rautiainen | Peugeot 206 WRC |
| 2003 | Markko Märtin/Michael Park | Ford Focus RS WRC03 |
| 2004 | Marcus Grönholm/Timo Rautiainen | Peugeot 307 WRC |
| 2005 | Marcus Grönholm/Timo Rautiainen | Peugeot 307 WRC |
| 2006 | Marcus Grönholm/Timo Rautiainen | Ford Focus RS WRC 06 |

Above: Duval inherited second place after Grönholm lost time rearranging the rear suspension on his Ford in the final stage

Above right: The rally's close proximity to the French and Belgian borders always guarantees a huge turnout of fans

Far right: Sordo suffered the second of two engines failures on consecutive events in Germany

Right: Loeb loves the German asphalt – he's won there six times on the trot now. Hirvonen was Ford's top man in third

All photographs by McKlein unless specified

# RALLYE DEUTSCHLAND

## The FIA World Rally Championship Round 10
# Rallye Deutschland

CITROËN team principal Guy Fréquelin was deeply concerned during leg one of Rally Deutschland. The World Rally Championship media had been filled with stories of how Ford had unlocked supersonic pace from its Focus RS WRC 07; Fréquelin's number one driver Sébastien Loeb hadn't won an event for three months; Dani Sordo's C4 WRC had suffered the same mysterious failure which had beset the car 14 days earlier in Finland; and now this. Now the C4's predecessor, the Xsara WRC, was beating Citroën's current World Rally Car. It was little wonder Fréquelin wasn't overly communicative at breakfast on leg two.

An hour or so later, and Fréquelin was looking a touch more comfortable. By lunch, he was smiling - albeit nervously. Ahead of the event, Fréquelin had accepted that the threat of François Duval in a Xsara WRC was a real one. While the telegraphed menace of the new Focus failed to materialise, the Belgian gave his former team a real scare on Friday.

For once, Loeb and Citroën made a duff tyre choice for the opening afternoon in the vineyards. Expecting rain, the C4s were fitted with soft BFGoodrich rubber. The rain never came, although it was of no real consequence for the number two car when Sordo ground to a halt.

Loeb was forced to forfeit his lead to Duval. Having not driven the Xsara since he left Citroën Sport after winning in Australia 2005, Duval was understandably playing down his potential. Then, he was leading. The obvious question pertained to how much benefit Duval was gaining from running a fully-active 2005-specification Xsara. Loeb reckoned there would be a degree of help in tight corners and under braking.

Duval took the comment on board and then pointed to the engine beneath Loeb's bonnet. "That thing has much more power," he said. "Watching it go off the line is incredible. We don't even have a launch system on this car."

That quarrel was quelled first thing on Saturday when Duval spun his Xsara on the second corner. Then he did it again three miles further into the St Wendeler test. His overnight advantage of just over a second was turned into a 15-second deficit to Loeb. A stage later and Duval was down to third as Marcus Grönholm stole second.

From that point onwards, Loeb extended his advantage and controlled the rally from the front, collecting a record-breaking sixth consecutive win in Germany. Behind him, Grönholm looked to have the measure of Duval - until a cow standing at the side of the final stage distracted the Finn. Mishearing the ensuing note, Grönholm slid wide and smashed the right-rear wheel of his Focus. Second became fourth in an instant.

Ford was still represented on the podium, however, by Mikko Hirvonen. The younger Finn had been in the thick of the fight until he whacked a straw bale on Saturday and then gambled on the wrong tyres on Sunday morning.

When Loeb returned to the Citroën service area on Sunday afternoon, Fréquelin was waiting for him as usual. The two celebrated together, but the champagne wasn't sprayed with its usual verve. Their reserve was a nod to the eight-point lead Grönholm retained in the title race and Citroën's inability to unearth the engine fault which was spoiling its chances of clinching a fourth manufacturers' crown in five years.

# RALLYE DEUTSCHLAND

*Above:* Latvala was under pressure to reach the finish after crashing out last time in Finland. He did just that and collected a point for eighth

*Above right:* Hirvonen tackles the super-special, which was run through the centre of host city Trier

*Far right:* Grönholm's series lead was slashed from 13 points to eight by Loeb following the Finn's final-stage blunder

*Middle right:* Subaru completed a gearbox and clutch change on Solberg's car in just 11 minutes before the final day – maybe that's why he looks so shocked. The Norwegian finished sixth

*Right:* Jan Kopecky scored his best result of the season in Germany, taking the Skoda Fabia to fifth place

All photographs by McKlein unless specified

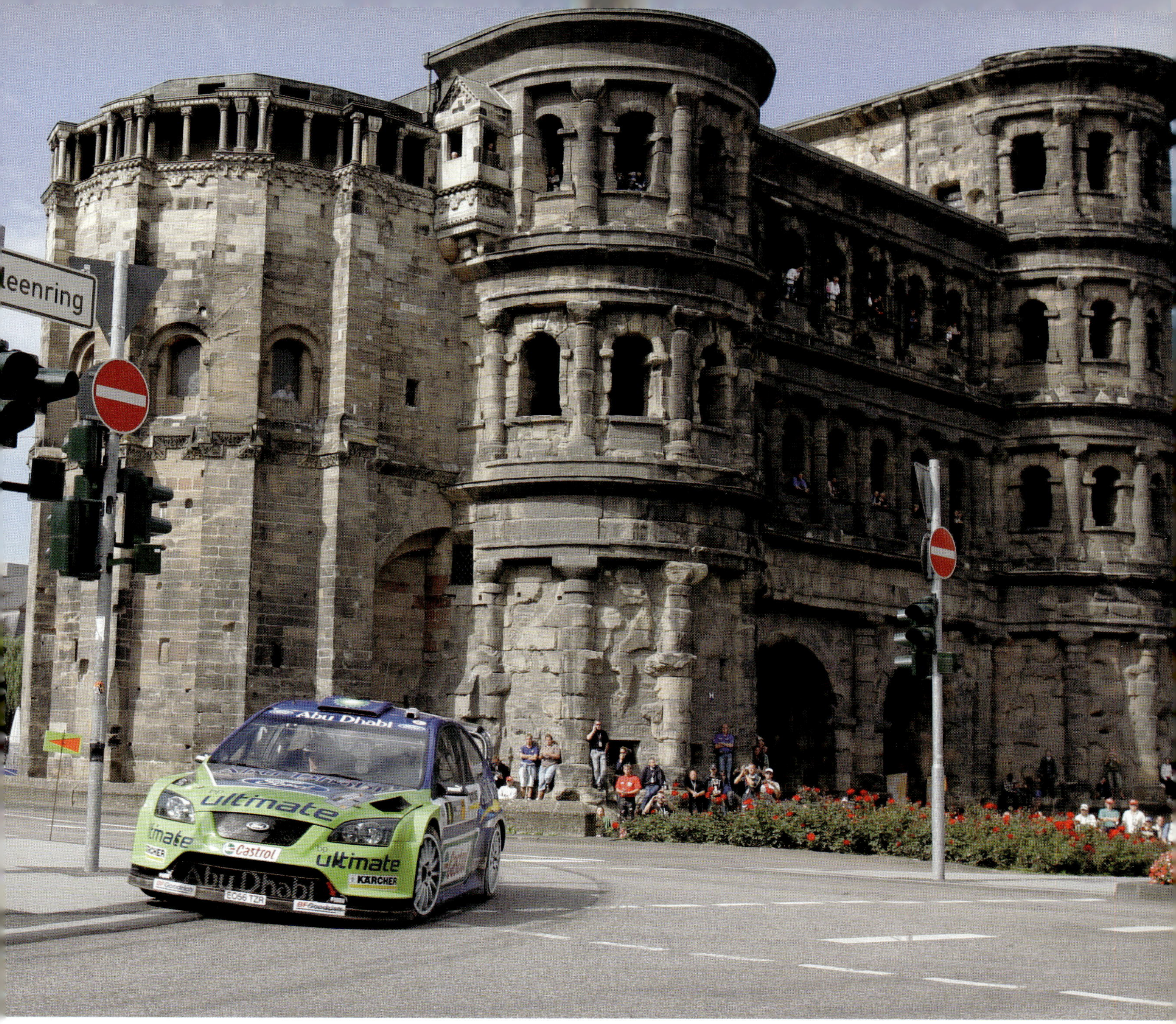
eenring
Abu Dhabi
ultimate
Castrol
KÄRCHER
EO56 TZR

WWW.ABUDHABITOURISM.AE
Grönholm
KÄRCHER
Abu Dhabi
Castrol
BFGoodrich
EU07 SSX

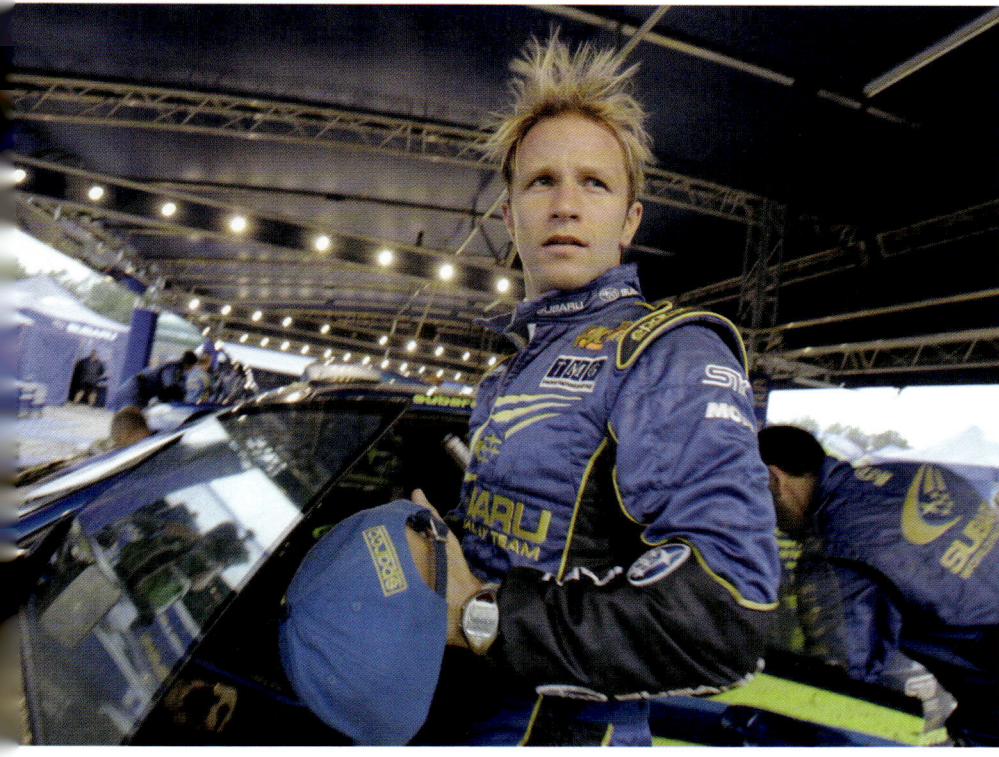

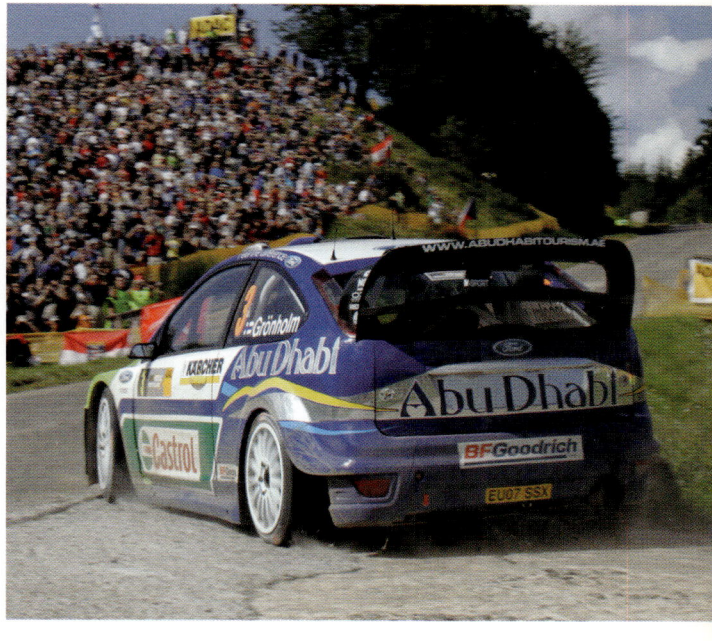

Citroën C2 driver Martin Prokop scored the first of two 2007 Junior wins in Germany. It made up for the previous round in Finland where he'd crashed out of the lead
McKlein

The FIA World Rally Championship Round 10     August 17-19 2007
# Rallye Deutschland Results

## FINISH LINES...

The fierce nature of the battle for podium positions was repeated all the way down top 10, with Skoda privateer Jan Kopecky emerging from a fascinating scrap with Toni Gardemeister's Citroën to clinch fifth. Gardemeister had begun the final day looking odds on to take the place, despite gearbox and handling difficulties through the rally, only to be let down by a penultimate stage puncture... Subaru's Petter Solberg also took full advantage of the Finn's trouble, edging him out of sixth on the final leaderboard. After a disastrous event last time out in Finland, Germany was more promising for the 2003 world champion. Apart from a sticky patch on Saturday, when the Impreza returned to its ill-handling worst, this was a solid event for the Norwegian. He never looked like threatening those ahead, but at least he got points on the board. The same could not be said for his team-mate Chris Atkinson. It was a rally of extremes for the Australian: he was either extremely quick or extremely far off the road. For the second rally in succession Atkinson was in the fight for fourth, but this time he missed out by crashing twice on Sunday morning... Jari-Matti Latvala arrived in Germany determined not to crash on asphalt for the fifth consecutive event. He fought with Xevi Pons early on, but when the Spaniard's engine let go, the way was clear for Latvala to collect the final point for Stobart... After coming close in Finland, Martin Prokop (Citroën C2) won the Junior Rally Championship comfortably from Urmo Aava's Suzuki.

## RUNNING ORDER

| | | | |
|---|---|---|---|
| 3 | Marcus Grönholm/ Timo Rautiainen | Ford Focus RS WRC 07 | Gr A |
| 1 | Sébastien Loeb/ Daniel Elena | Citroën C4 WRC | Gr A |
| 4 | Mikko Hirvonen/ Jarmo Lehtinen | Ford Focus RS WRC 07 | Gr A |
| 2 | Daniel Sordo/ Marc Martí | Citroën C4 WRC | Gr A |
| 10 | Henning Solberg/ Cato Menkerud | Ford Focus RS WRC 06 | Gr A |
| 7 | Petter Solberg/ Phil Mills | Subaru Impreza WRC2007 | Gr A |
| 8 | Chris Atkinson/ Stéphane Prevot | Subaru Impreza WRC2007 | Gr A |
| 9 | Jari-Matti Latvala/ Miikka Anttila | Ford Focus RS WRC 06 | Gr A |
| 5 | Manfred Stohl/ Ilka Minor | Citroën Xsara WRC | Gr A |
| 14 | Toni Gardemeister/ Jakke Honkanen | Citroën Xsara WRC | Gr A |
| 15 | Jan Kopecky/ Filip Schovanek | Skoda Fabia WRC | Gr A |
| 20 | Xavier Pons/ Xavier Amigo | Subaru Impreza WRC2007 | Gr A |
| 16 | Matthew Wilson/ Michael Orr | Ford Focus RS WRC 06 | Gr A |
| 17 | Guy Wilks/ Phil Pugh | Ford Focus RS WRC 04 | Gr A |
| 18 | Andreas Mikkelsen/ Ola Floene | Ford Focus RS WRC 04 | Gr A |
| 19 | Thomas Schie/ Göran Bergsten | Ford Focus RS WRC 04 | Gr A |
| 6 | François Duval/ Patrick Pivato | Citroën Xsara WRC | Gr A |
| 21 | Khalid Al-Qassimi/ Nicky Beech | Ford Focus RS WRC 06 | Gr A |
| 23 | Mark Van Eldik/ Michel Groenewoud | Subaru Impreza WRC2006 | Gr A |
| 24 | Erik Wevers/ Jalmar Van Weeren | Skoda Fabia WRC | Gr A |
| 25 | Peter Van Merksteijn/ Erwin Berkhof | Ford Focus RS WRC 06 | Gr A |

## SPECIAL STAGE TIMES

**SS1 Rutwertal/Fell 1 (19.79km)**
1 S.Loeb/D.Elena (Citroën C4 WRC) 11m04.2s; 2 F.Duval/P.Pivato (Citroën Xsara WRC) 11m07.2s; 3 D.Sordo/M.Martí (Citroën C4 WRC) 11m08.0s; 4 C.Atkinson/S.Prevot (Subaru Impreza WRC2007) 11m09.1s; 5 P.Solberg/P.Mills (Subaru Impreza WRC2007) 11m10.9s; 6 M.Hirvonen/J.Lehtinen (Ford Focus RS WRC 07) 11m12.6s; JRC M.Prokop/J.Tomanek (Citroën C2) 12m20.9s

**SS2 Grafschaft Veldenz 1 (23.40km)**
1 Loeb/Elena (Citroën) 13m12.4s; 2 M.Grönholm/T.Rautiainen (Ford Focus RS WRC 07) 13m13.3s; 3 Duval/Pivato (Citroën) 13m15.6s; 4 Sordo/Martí (Citroën) 13m16.2s; 5 Hirvonen/Lehtinen (Ford) 13m21.8s; 6 Solberg/Mills (Subaru) 13m22.5s; JRC Prokop/Tomanek (Citroën) 14m48.0s

**SS3 Schones Moselland 1 (21.46km)**
1 Duval/Pivato (Citroën) 12m22.9s; 2 Loeb/Elena (Citroën) 12m23.3s; 3 Sordo/Martí (Citroën) 12m24.2s; 4 Grönholm/Rautiainen (Ford) 12m26.2s; 5 Solberg/Mills (Subaru) 12m28.7s; 6 Hirvonen/Lehtinen (Ford) 12m31.3s; JRC Prokop/Tomanek (Citroën) 13m47.2s

**SS4 Rutwertal/Fell 2 (19.79km)**
1 Hirvonen/Lehtinen (Ford) 11m34.2s; 2 Duval/Pivato (Citroën) 11m34.7s; 3 Loeb/Elena (Ford) 11m37.5s; 4= Grönholm/Rautiainen (Ford), Atkinson/Prevot (Subaru) 11m39.6s; 6 X.Pons/X.Amigo (Subaru Impreza WRC2007) 11m41.6s; JRC Prokop/Tomanek (Citroën) 12m51.5s

**SS5 Grafschaft Veldenz 2 (23.40km)**
1 Duval/Pivato (Citroën) 13m30.6s; 2 Loeb/Elena (Citroën) 13m31.9s; 3 Hirvonen/Lehtinen (Ford) 13m32.0s; 4 Grönholm/Rautiainen (Ford) 13m32.7s; 5 Atkinson/Prevot (Subaru) 13m33.1s; 6 Sordo/Martí (Citroën) 13m33.4s; JRC Prokop/Tomanek (Citroën) 15m00.6s

**SS6 Schones Moselland 2 (21.46km)**
1 Atkinson/Prevot (Subaru) 12m18.5s; 2 Duval/Pivato (Citroën) 12m19.9s; 3 Hirvonen/Lehtinen (Ford) 12m21.7s; 4 Grönholm/Rautiainen (Ford) 12m22.1s; 5 Loeb/Elena (Citroën) 12m22.9s; 6 T.Gardemeister/J.Honkanen (Citroën Xsara WRC) 12m29.2s; JRC Prokop/Tomanek (Citroën) 13m40.3s

**SS7 St Wendeler Land 1 (16.37km)**
1 Hirvonen/Lehtinen (Ford) 8m52.6s; 2 Loeb/Elena (Citroën) 8m52.9s; 3 Gardemeister/Honkanen (Citroën) 8m56.5s; 4 J.Kopecky/F.Schovanek (Skoda Fabia WRC) 8m58.3s; 5 Grönholm/Rautiainen (Ford) 8m58.4s; 6 J-M.Latvala/M.Anttila (Ford Focus RS WRC 06) 9m00.5s; JRC U.Aava/K.Sikk (Suzuki Swift) 9m55.4s

**SS8 Bosenberg 1 (19.00km)**
1 Loeb/Elena (Citroën) 10m39.5s; 2 Grönholm/Rautiainen (Ford) 10m43.0s; 3 Hirvonen/Lehtinen (Ford) 10m43.3s; 4 Atkinson/Prevot (Subaru) 10m45.6s; 5 Duval/Pivato (Citroën) 10m49.8s; 6= Latvala/Anttila (Ford), Pons/Amigo (Subaru) 10m50.1s; JRC Aava/Sikk (Suzuki) 11m58.3s

**SS9 Erzweiler 1 (16.51km)**
1 Grönholm/Rautiainen (Ford) 9m55.9s; 2 Loeb/Elena (Citroën) 9m56.5s; 3 Atkinson/Prevot (Subaru) 9m59.7s; 4 Hirvonen/Lehtinen (Ford) 10m00.6s 5 Solberg/Mills (Subaru) 10m02.1s; 6 Duval/Pivato (Citroën) 10m02.7s; JRC Prokop/Tomanek (Citroën) 11m04.0s

**SS10 Panzerplatte 1 (30.54km)**
1 Loeb/Elena (Citroën) 17m57.4s; 2 Grönholm/Rautiainen (Ford) 17m59.6s; 3 Atkinson/Prevot (Subaru) 18m02.3s; 4 Duval/Pivato (Citroën) 18m07.4s; 5 Hirvonen/Lehtinen (Ford) 18m10.7s; 6 Solberg/Mills (Subaru) 18m14.4s; JRC Prokop/Tomanek (Citroën) 19m56.6s

**SS11 St Wendeler Land 2 (16.37km)**
1 Hirvonen/Lehtinen (Ford) 8m51.6s; 2 Duval/Pivato (Citroën) 8m51.9s; 3 Loeb/Elena (Citroën) 8m52.2s; 4 Grönholm/Rautiainen (Ford) 8m52.4s; 5 Gardemeister/Honkanen (Citroën) 8m52.5s; 6 Kopecky/Schovenak (Skoda) 8m53.2s; JRC A.Burkart/M.Kölback (Citroën C2) 9m51.1s

**SS12 Bosenberg 2 (19.00km)**
1 Atkinson/Prevot (Subaru) 10m27.4s; 2 Loeb/Elena (Citroën) 10m32.5s; 3 Duval/Pivato (Citroën) 10m35.2s; 4 Hirvonen/Lehtinen (Ford) 10m36.2s; 5 Grönholm/Rautiainen

# RALLYE DEUTSCHLAND

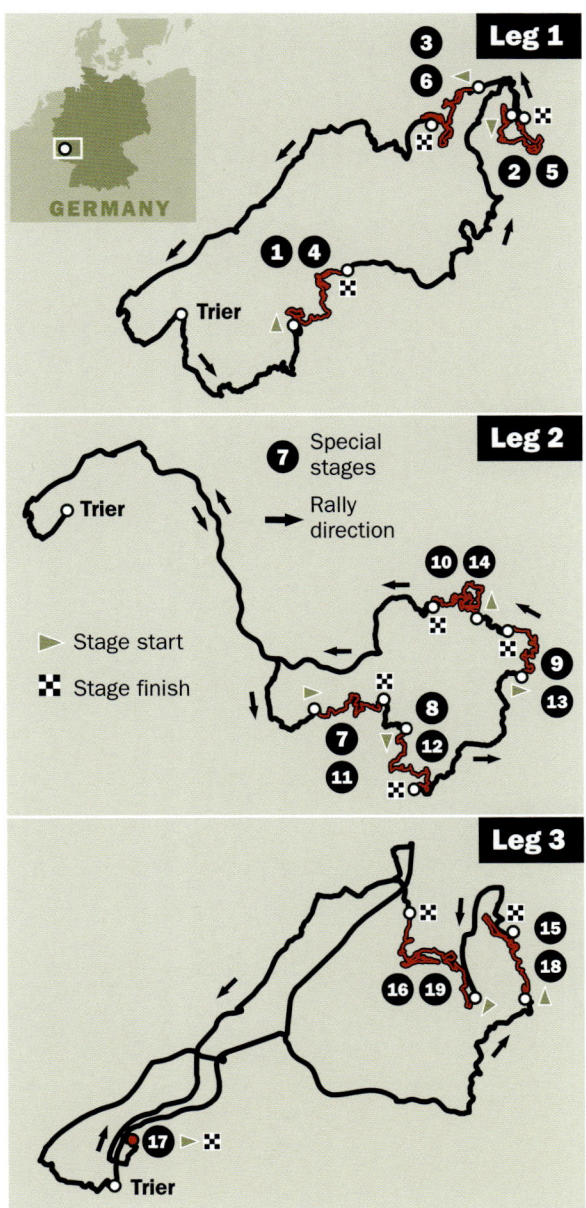

| Stage Numbers | 1 | 2 | 3 | 4 | 5 | 6 | 7 | 8 | 9 | 10 | 11 | 12 | 13 | 14 | 15 | 16 | 17 | 18 | 19 |
|---|---|---|---|---|---|---|---|---|---|---|---|---|---|---|---|---|---|---|---|
| Loeb | 1 | 1 | 1 | 1 | 1 | 2 | 1 | 1 | 1 | 1 | 1 | 1 | 1 | 1 | 1 | 1 | 1 | 1 | 1 |
| Duval | 2 | 2 | 2 | 2 | 2 | 1 | 2 | 4 | 4 | 3 | 3 | 3 | 4 | 3 | 3 | 3 | 3 | 3 | 2 |
| Hirvonen | 6 | 6 | 6 | 5 | 5 | 4 | 3 | 2 | 3 | 4 | 4 | 4 | 3 | 4 | 4 | 4 | 4 | 4 | 3 |
| Grönholm | 7 | 4 | 4 | 3 | 3 | 3 | 4 | 3 | 2 | 2 | 2 | 2 | 2 | 2 | 2 | 2 | 2 | 2 | 4 |
| Kopecky | 11 | 9 | 9 | 9 | 8 | 6 | 6 | 6 | 6 | 5 | 5 | 5 | 5 | 5 | 6 | 6 | 6 | 5 | 5 |
| P.Solberg | 5 | 5 | 5 | 6 | 7 | 9 | 9 | 9 | 8 | 6 | 8 | 8 | 7 | 7 | 7 | 7 | 7 | 6 | 6 |
| Gardemeister | 9 | 7 | 7 | 7 | 6 | 5 | 5 | 5 | 5 | 7 | 6 | 6 | 6 | 6 | 5 | 5 | 5 | 7 | 7 |
| Latvala | 12 | 10 | 10 | 10 | 10 | 8 | 7 | 7 | 7 | 9 | 9 | 9 | 9 | 9 | 8 | 8 | 8 | 8 | 8 |
| Wilson | 14 | 13 | 13 | 13 | 12 | 11 | 11 | 11 | 10 | 10 | 10 | 10 | 11 | 10 | 9 | 9 | 9 | 9 | 9 |
| Wilks | 100 | 97 | 90 | 84 | 64 | 49 | 39 | 29 | 24 | 20 | 17 | 17 | 13 | 12 | 12 | 12 | 12 | 10 | 10 |
| H.Solberg | 13 | 12 | 12 | 12 | 12 | 16 | 16 | 25 | 22 | 17 | 17 | 16 | 13 | 10 | 15 | 19 | 18 | 18 | 17 | 16 | 13 |
| Atkinson | | 4 | 90 | 51 | 33 | 21 | 15 | 13 | 12 | 13 | 12 | 11 | 11 | 10 | 9 | 10 | 10 | 12 | 15 |
| Pons | 8 | 8 | 8 | 8 | 9 | 7 | 9 | 9 | 9 | 8 | 8 | 8 | 8 | 10 | 1 | 1 | 13 | 18 | |
| Stohl | 10 | 11 | 11 | 11 | 11 | 10 | 10 | 10 | 11 | R | | | | | | | | | |
| Sordo | 3 | 3 | 3 | 4 | 4 | R | | | | | | | | | | | | | |

(Ford) 10m36.6s; 6= Kopecky/Schovanek (Skoda), Solberg/Mills (Subaru) 10m39.2s; JRC Aava/Sikk (Suzuki) 11m51.4s

### SS13 Erzweiler 2 (16.51km)
1 Loeb/Elena (Citroën) 9m45.5s; 2 Atkinson/Prevot (Subaru) 9m47.5s; 3 Gardemeister/Honkanen (Citroën) 9m48.6s; 4 Grönholm/Rautiainen (Ford) 9m49.6s; 5 Solberg/Mills (Subaru) 9m49.7s; 6 Hirvonen/Lehtinen (Ford) 9m50.0s; JRC Aava/Sikk (Suzuki) 10m55.3s

### SS14 Panzerplatte 2 (30.54km)
1 Atkinson/Prevot (Subaru) 17m49.8s; 2 Loeb/Elena (Citroën) 17m51.7s; 3 Duval/Pivato (Citroën) 17m52.0s; 4 Grönholm/Rautiainen (Ford) 17m54.4s; 5 Hirvonen/Lehtinen

(Ford) 17m57.7s; 6 Solberg/Mills (Subaru) 17m57.8s; JRC Prokop/Tomanek (Citroën) 19m46.3s

### SS15 Dhrontal 1 (11.14km)
1 Duval/Pivato (Citroën) 6m59.2s; 2 Atkinson/Prevot (Subaru) 7m01.3s; 3 Grönholm/Rautiainen (Ford) 7m01.8s; 4 Solberg/Mills (Subaru) 7m02.1s; 5 Gardemeister/Honkanen (Citroën) 7m03.2s; 6 Kopecky/Schovanek (Skoda) 7m06.5s; JRC C.Rautenbach/D.Senior (Citroën C2) 7m55.0s

### SS16 Moselwein 1 (18.70km)
1 Duval/Pivato (Citroën) 10m40.3s; 2 Grönholm/Rautiainen (Ford) 10m40.4s; 3 Loeb/Elena (Citroën) 10m43.2s; 4 Solberg/Mills (Subaru) 10m47.2s; 5 Gardemeister/Honkanen (Citroën) 10m48.0s; 6 Hirvonen/Lehtinen (Ford) 10m52.0s;

JRC Burkart/Kölback (Citroën) 12m05.5s

### SS17 Super Special Circus Maximus Trier (4.36km)
1 Duval/Pivato (Citroën) 3m11.4s; 2 Grönholm/Rautiainen (Ford) 3m11.9s; 3 Solberg/Mills (Subaru) 3m13.5s; 4 Loeb/Elena (Citroën) 3m13.8s; 5 Kopecky/Schovanek (Skoda) 3m14.1s; 6 Hirvonen/Lehtinen (Ford) 3m15.0s; JRC Prokop/Tomanek (Citroën) 3m34.2s

### SS18 Dhrontal 2 (11.14km)
1 Duval/Pivato (Citroën) 6m53.4s; 2 Grönholm/Rautiainen (Ford) 6m57.2s; 3 Loeb/Elena (Citroën) 7m01.0s; 4 Solberg/Mills (Subaru) 7m01.2s; 5 Kopecky/Schovanek (Skoda) 7m02.0s; 6 Latvala/Anttila (Ford) 7m04.8s; JRC Rautenbach/Senior (Citroën) 7m54.2s

### SS19 Moselwein 2 (18.70km)
1 Duval/Pivato (Citroën) 10m32.7s; 2 Solberg/Mills (Subaru) 10m40.7s; 3 Loeb/Elena (Citroën) 10m41.3s; 4 Gardemeister/Honkanen (Citroën) 10m46.2s; 5 Hirvonen/Lehtinen (Ford) 10m47.2s; 6 Latvala/Anttila (Ford) 10m47.6s; JRC Rautenbach/Senior (Citroën) 11m59.3s

Cars which retired and subsequently re-started and were classified under SuperRally regs:

| 10 | Solberg/Menkerud | Ford Focus RS WRC 06 | | |
| | Accident | SS5 | Gr A | |
| 10 | Solberg/Menkerud | Ford Focus RS WRC 06 | | |
| | Accident | SS13 | Gr A | |
| 8 | Atkinson/Prevot | Subaru Impreza WRC2007 | | |
| | Accident | SS16 | Gr A | |
| 20 | Pons/Amigo | Subaru Impreza WRC2007 | | |
| | Engine | SS15 | Gr A | |
| 18 | Mikkelsen/Floene | Ford Focus RS WRC 04 | | |
| | Accident | SS2 | Gr A | |
| 21 | Al-Qassimi/Beech | Ford Focus RS WRC 06 | | |
| | Engine | SS14 | Gr A | |
| 25 | V-Merksteijn/Berkhof | Ford Focus RS WRC 06 | | |
| | Mechanical | SS13 | Gr A | |

### MAJOR RETIREMENTS
| 4 | Sordo/Martí | Citroën C4 WRC |
| | Engine | SS6 | Gr A |
| 5 | Stohl/Minor | Citroën Xsara WRC |
| | Engine | SS10 | Gr A |
| 19 | Schie/Bergsten | Ford Focus RS WRC 04 |
| | Hydraulics | SS5 | Gr A |
| 24 | Wevers/Van Weeren | Skoda Fabia WRC |
| | Mechanical | SS1 | |

### FIA CLASS WINNERS
| A8 | Over 2000cc | Loeb/Elena |
| | | Citroën Xsara WRC |
| A7 | 1600-2000cc | Mohe/Walker |
| | | Renault Clio R3 |
| A6 | 1400-1600 cc | Prokop/Tomanek |
| | | Citroën C2 |
| A5 | Upto 1400cc | Hohlheimer/Kippe |
| | | Fiat Seicento Sporting |
| N4 | Over 2000 cc | Van Den Heuvel/Kolman |
| | | Mitsubishi Lancer Evo 9 |
| N3 | 1600-2000cc | Mysliwietz/Schumacher |
| | | Honda Civic Type-R |
| N2 | 1400-1600cc | Niegel/Kachel |
| | | Suzuki Swift Sport |
| N1 | Upto 1400cc | Ottosson/Ottosson |
| | | VW Polo GTi |

### RALLY LEADERS
Overall: SS1-5 Loeb; SS6 Duval; SS7-19 Loeb
JWC: SS1-19 Prokop

### SPECIAL STAGE ANALYSIS
| | 1st | 2nd | 3rd | 4th | 5th | 6th |
|---|---|---|---|---|---|---|
| Duval (Citroën) | 7 | 4 | 3 | 1 | 1 | 1 |
| Loeb (Citroën) | 5 | 6 | 5 | 1 | 1 | - |
| Atkinson (Subaru) | 3 | 2 | 2 | 3 | 1 | - |
| Hirvonen (Ford) | 3 | - | 3 | 2 | 4 | 5 |
| Grönholm (Ford) | 1 | 6 | 1 | 7 | 2 | - |
| P.Solberg (Subaru) | - | 1 | 1 | 3 | 4 | 4 |
| Gardemeister (Citroën) | - | - | 2 | 1 | 3 | 1 |
| Sordo (Citroën) | - | - | 2 | 1 | - | 1 |
| Kopecky (Skoda) | - | - | - | 1 | 2 | 3 |

| Latvala (Ford) | - | - | - | - | 4 |
| Pons (Subaru) | - | - | - | - | 2 |

### WORLD CHAMPIONSHIP POINTS
**Drivers**
1 Grönholm 80; 2 Loeb 72; 3 Hirvonen 63; 4 P.Solberg 29; 5= Sordo, H.Solberg 28; 7 Atkinson 20; 8 Latvala 13; 9 Gardemeister 10; 10= Carlsson, Stohl 9 etc

**Manufacturers**
1 BP-Ford WRT 143; 2 Citroën Total WRT 102; 3 Subaru WRT 53; 4 Stobart M-Sport Ford RT 50; 5 OMV-Kronos Citroën WRT 35; 6 Munchi's Ford RT 6

**Junior World Championship**
1 Aava 32; 2 Andersson 28; 3 Sandell 19; 4 Mölder 17; 5 Prokop 16; 6 Burkart 14; 7 Beres 13; 8 Rautenbach 11; 9 Pinomäki 8; 10= Cortinovis, Kosciuszko 6 etc

**Production Cup**
1 Arai 29; 2 Higgins 15; 3 Sohlberg 12; 4 M.Baldacci 11; 5= Svedlund, Villagra, Aigner 10; 8 Alén 8; 9 Pozzo 7; 10= Nutahara, Hänninen, Al-Attiyah 6 etc

### ROUTE DETAILS
Total Route of 1227.04km of which 356.27km were competitive on 19 stages
**Leg 1** Friday 17 August, 6 special stages totalling 128.60km
**Leg 2** Saturday 18 August, 8 special stages totalling 164.86km
**Leg 3** Sunday 19 August, 5 special stages totalling 62.81km

### RESULTS
| 1 | Sebastien Loeb/ | Citroën C4 WRC | |
| | Daniel Elena | 3h27m27.5s | Gr A |
| 2 | François Duval/ | Citroën Xsara WRC | |
| | Patrick Pivato | 3h27m47.8s | Gr A |
| 3 | Mikko Hirvonen/ | Ford Focus RS WRC 07 | |
| | Jarmo Lehtinen | 3h28m46.6s | Gr A |
| 4 | Marcus Grönholm/ | Ford Focus RS WRC 07 | |
| | Timo Rautiainen | 3h29m04.0s | Gr A |
| 5 | Jan Kopecky/ | Skoda Fabia WRC | |
| | Filip Schovanek | 3h30m34.6s | Gr A |
| 6 | Petter Solberg/ | Subaru Impreza WRC2007 | |
| | Phil Mills | 3h30m42.2s | Gr A |
| 7 | Toni Gardemeister/ | Citroën Xsara WRC | |
| | Jakke Honkanen | 3h31m05.0s | Gr A |
| 8 | Jari-Matti Latvala/ | Ford Focus RS WRC 06 | |
| | Miikka Anttila | 3h32m56.8s | Gr A |
| 9 | Matthew Wilson/ | Ford Focus RS WRC 06 | |
| | Michael Orr | 3h38m31.7s | Gr A |
| 10 | Guy Wilks/ | Ford Focus RS WRC 04 | |
| | Phil Pugh | 3h47m15.3s | Gr A |

102 starters, 88 finishers

### RECENT WINNERS
| 1982 | *Erwin Weber/Matthias Berg | Opel Ascona 400 |
| 1983 | *Walter Röhrl/Christian Geistdörfer | Lancia Rally 037 |
| 1984 | *Hannu Mikkola/Christian Geistdörfer | Audi Sport Quattro |
| 1985 | Kalle Grundel/Peter Diekmann | Peugeot 205T16 |
| 1986 | *Michèle Mouton/Terry Harryman | Peugeot 205T16 |
| 1987 | *Jochi Kleint/Manfred Hiemer | VW Golf GTI-16v |
| 1988 | *Robert Droogmans/Ronny Joosten | Ford Sierra RS Cosworth |
| 1989 | *Patrick Snijers/Dany Colebunders | Toyota Celica GT4 |
| 1990 | *Robert Droogmans/Ronny Joosten | Lancia Delta Integrale |
| 1991 | *Piero Liatti/Luciano Tedeschini | Lancia Delta Integrale 16V |
| 1992 | *Erwin Weber/Manfred Hiemer | Mitsubishi Galant VR-4 |
| 1993 | *Patrick Snijers/Dany Colebunders | Ford Escort RS Cosworth |
| 1994 | *Dieter Depping/Peter Thul | Ford Escort RS Cosworth |
| 1995 | *Enrico Bertone/Massimo Chiapponi | Toyota Celica Turbo 4WD |
| 1996 | *Dieter Depping/Fred Berssen | Ford Escort RS Cosworth |
| 1997 | *Dieter Depping/Dieter Hawranke | Ford Escort RS Cosworth |
| 1998 | *Matthias Kahle/Dieter Schneppenheim | Toyota Corolla WRC |
| 1999 | *Armin Kremer/Fred Berßen | Subaru Impreza WRC97 |
| 2000 | *Henrik Lundgaard/Jens Christian Anker | Toyota Corolla WRC |
| 2001 | *Philippe Bugalski/Jean-Paul Chiaroni | Citroën Xsara WRC |
| 2002 | Sébastien Loeb/Daniel Elena | Citroën Xsara WRC |
| 2003 | Sébastien Loeb/Daniel Elena | Citroën Xsara WRC |
| 2004 | Sébastien Loeb/Daniel Elena | Citroën Xsara WRC |
| 2005 | Sébastien Loeb/Daniel Elena | Citroën Xsara WRC |
| 2006 | Sébastien Loeb/Daniel Elena | Citroën Xsara WRC |

*Non-championship event

The FIA World Rally Championship Round 11
# Rally New Zealand

Grönholm came out on top in a sensational battle with Loeb in New Zealand, beating the Citroën driver by just 0.3 seconds
Race&motion

**Above: Ford ace Grönholm had refused to give up when Loeb edged ahead on leg two. He kept pushing even through the pain barrier when he aggravated an old shoulder injury**
McKlein

STANDING waiting for the cars to go into the final stage, Ford team principal Malcolm Wilson walked out to the back of the Mystery Creek main building. Running a stage around rally headquarters had been a way for the Rally New Zealand organisers to bring the sport to the people on a Sunday afternoon. It afforded Wilson and his opposite number at Citroën Guy Fréquelin a perfect view of the end of the most sensational rally in the history of the championship.

As the crews arrived back in Hamilton from the stunning west-coast stages, there was seven tenths of a second separating Marcus Grönholm's Focus and Sébastien Loeb's C4. The watching world, let alone the drivers themselves, could scarcely believe what was going on. The previous three days of flat-out driving across the middle of the North Island had, however, hinted at a finish of this nature.

Grönholm had stolen the early march with a monster charge through the first loop, mindful of the fact that Loeb had not seen these roads at competitive speeds courtesy of his broken shoulder 12 months ago. Having taken 7.2 seconds out of Loeb in the opener, he doubled that lead on the ensuing run through Waitomo Caves. The combination of a drying road and Loeb's exceptional ability to find more speed on the second run at stages netted the Frenchman 1.8 seconds through the afternoon.

The next morning posed a typically tricky tyre choice. It hadn't rained overnight, but the middle stage of the morning loop was muddy enough to warrant soft rubber: Grönholm went with it. Loeb went harder and reaped the benefit through the long Franklin test, taking 11.3 seconds out of the leader. The Finn's mood darkened further when Loeb passed him in Te Akau North in the afternoon. The event, if not the championship, was at a pivotal point. So many times before, Loeb had waltzed off over the horizon once he was ahead by a nose. Grönholm simply wasn't having it that morning.

As the cars were fettled for the final day, Wilson admitted there was something about his boys that morning. "They certainly seem up for it," he said.

Up for it they were. Capitalising on a Loeb error in the opener, Grönholm retook the lead, with Loeb hitting back in the next two. Grönholm's run through Whaanga Coast, the last of the loop before a remote tyre zone in Raglan, was spoiled when he aggravated an old shoulder injury early in the stage. Pushing through the pain barrier, he contained the time loss and took aim at Loeb for the second loop. Once again, Grönholm went for a softer tyre than his rival and this time it worked a treat – he was fastest on all three stages, including a masterful run through Whaanga Coast, which had everybody rooted to the split-sector timing screens in the service park.

So, back to Mystery Creek, and Grönholm was first. Promising co-driver Timo Rautiainen a sensible run, he was nevertheless confident of maintaining his slender gap to Loeb to the finish. Then disaster. They ran wide in two corners. The perfect run had turned messy. Grönholm ended the stage and jumped on the roof of his car to watch Loeb across the line. The time was beamed back. The Frenchman had only done him for four tenths. Quick as a flash, maths done, Marcus was dancing on the roof.

Loeb was gracious in defeat, but – along with the rest of the team – looked slightly bemused. How had he lost? This wasn't part of the script. With Grönholm's title lead back up to 10 points the Finn's shimmying was mirrored a hundred yards away where Wilson and the boys were boogying too.

RALLY NEW ZEALAND

Below: Loeb was working at a disadvantage having missed this event 12 months ago, but having followed Grönholm through leg one he led on the second day

Bottom right: The strain of his fight with Grönholm seemed to take its toll on Loeb – he probably felt even worse at the finish!

Bottom Left: Hirvonen's third place helped Ford to increase its manufacturers' lead over Citroën to a healthy 46 points

All photographs by McKlein

# RALLY NEW ZEALAND

Below: Rising star Jari-Matti Latvala battled with Subaru's Chris Atkinson for fourth place, missing out by just 4.6 seconds

Right: New Zealand flew the flag and brought out the girls for its WRC round – considered among the finest in the championship

Middle right: Fourth was a great result for Atkinson on the WRC round closest to his home on the Gold Coast

Far right: Ford team boss Malcolm Wilson had a perfect view of the last stage which finished at rally HQ – his joy at the result matched Grönholm's

Bottom right: Mechanical trouble on board his Citroën relegated Sordo to just seventh place and two points

All photographs by McKlein unless specified

Junior driver Urmo Aava was back out in a Mitsubishi Lancer WRC and, as in Finland, finished in the points again - this time in eighth place
McKlein

## The FIA World Rally Championship Round 11
August 31- Sept 2 2007
# Rally New Zealand Results

### FINISH LINES...

There was more to celebrate for Wilson with Mikko Hirvonen collecting third place to open up Ford's manufacturer championship lead to 46 points over Citroën. Hirvonen's hopes of challenging for the win were dashed when he took tyres that were too hard for the first loop and dropped half a minute to the men ahead... Australian Chris Atkinson did a fantastic job on the WRC round closest to his Queensland roots, beating Jari-Matti Latvala in a frantic final-day fight for fourth. Once again, Atkinson's impressive speed left team-mate Petter Solberg in the shade as the Norwegian struggled with the Subaru Impreza's handling. Solberg ended the rally one place behind Citroën's Dani Sordo in seventh... Urmo Aava collected a point for the private Mitsubishi team in eighth... The competition in the Production Car element of the field was almost as exciting as that for overall glory. Pre-event favourite Toshi Arai dropped three minutes stopping to change a day-one puncture. Britain's Niall McShea then lead for the majority of the rally, before succumbing to an astonishing charge back through the field from Arai. Like Grönholm and Loeb, this one went down to the wire, with 1.6 seconds separating the two Imprezas ahead of the final stage. Tying on time gave Arai the win and McShea nightmares about where he'd let it slip... There were more nightmares for Alister McRae. The Scotsman, returning to the world championship for the first time in almost a year, drove an NZ-sourced Mitsubishi perfectly for three days. Despite running unfamiliar tyres and having a new co-driver, the former British champion was on course for a perfect return and a comfortable Group N victory when he was forced to stop and change a puncture on the final significant stage. It should have been a belter of a win but turned into a forgettable ninth.

### RUNNING ORDER

| | | | |
|---|---|---|---|
| 3 | Marcus Grönholm/ Timo Rautiainen | Ford Focus RS WRC 07 | Gr A |
| 1 | Sébastien Loeb/ Daniel Elena | Citroën C4 WRC | Gr A |
| 4 | Mikko Hirvonen/ Jarmo Lehtinen | Ford Focus RS WRC 07 | Gr A |
| 7 | Petter Solberg/ Phil Mills | Subaru Impreza WRC2007 | Gr A |
| 2 | Daniel Sordo/ Marc Martí | Citroën C4 WRC | Gr A |
| 10 | Henning Solberg/ Cato Menkerud | Ford Focus RS WRC 06 | Gr A |
| 8 | Chris Atkinson/ Stéphane Prevot | Subaru Impreza WRC2007 | Gr A |
| 9 | Jari-Matti Latvala/ Miikka Anttila | Ford Focus RS WRC 06 | Gr A |
| 5 | Manfred Stohl/ Ilka Minor | Citroën Xsara WRC | Gr A |
| 14 | Xavier Pons/ Xavier Amigo | Subaru Impreza WRC2007 | Gr A |
| 15 | Urmo Aava/ Kuldar Sikk | Mitsubishi Lancer WRC05 | Gr A |
| 16 | Matthew Wilson/ Michael Orr | Ford Focus RS WRC 06 | Gr A |
| 12 | Federico Villagra/ Jorge Pérez-Companc | Ford Focus RS WRC 06 | Gr A |
| 11 | Luis Pérez-Companc/ José Maria Volta | Ford Focus RS WRC 06 | Gr A |
| 31 | Toshihiro Arai/ Tony Sircombe | Subaru Impreza WRX Sti | Gr N |
| 45 | Mirco Baldacci/ Giovanni Agnese | Subaru Impreza WRX Sti | Gr N |
| 54 | Gabriel Pozzo/ Daniel Stillo | Mitsubishi Lancer Evo 9 | Gr N |
| 36 | Juha Hänninen/ Mikko Markkula | Mitsubishi Lancer Evo 9 | Gr N |
| 35 | Fumio Nutahara/ Daniel Barritt | Mitsubishi Lancer Evo 9 | Gr N |
| 46 | Armindo Araújo/ Miguel Ramalho | Mitsubishi Lancer Evo 9 | Gr N |
| 53 | Niall McShea/ Gordon Noble | Subaru Impreza WRX Sti | Gr N |

### SPECIAL STAGE TIMES

**SS1 Pirongia West 1 (18.30km)**
1 M.Grönholm/T.Rautiainen (Ford Focus RS WRC 07) 13m40.5s; 2 S.Loeb/D.Elena (Citroën C4 WRC) 13m47.7s; 3 M.Hirvonen/J.Lehtinen (Ford Focus RS WRC 07) 13m54.1s; 4 C.Atkinson/S.Prevot (Subaru Impreza WRC2007) 13m56.5s; 5 J-M.Latvala/M.Anttila (Ford Focus RS WRC 06) 14m00.9s 6 D.Sordo/M.Martí (Citroën C4 WRC) 14m06.1s; PC T.Arai/T.Sircombe (Subaru Impreza WRX Sti) 14m46.4s

**SS2 Waitomo 1 (43.88km)**
1 Grönholm/Rautiainen (Ford) 28m47.8s; 2 Loeb/Elena (Citroën) 28m55.4s; 3 Hirvonen/Lehtinen (Ford) 29m07.8s; 4 Atkinson/Prevot (Subaru) 29m18.1s; 5 Latvala/Anttila (Ford) 29m20.4s; 6 Sordo/Martí (Citroën) 29m21.8s; PC J.Hänninen/M.Markkula (Mitsubishi Lancer Evo 9) 30m51.3s

**SS3 Pirongia West 2 (18.30km)**
1 Loeb/Elena (Citroën) 13m32.4s; 2 Grönholm/Rautiainen (Ford) 13m33.0s; 3 Hirvonen/Lehtinen (Ford) 13m35.9s; 4 P.Solberg/P.Mills (Subaru Impreza WRC2007) 13m47.4s; 5 Sordo/Martí (Citroën) 13m47.6s; 6 Latvala/Anttila (Ford) 13m47.8s; PC R.Mason/S.Randall (Subaru Impreza WRX Sti) 14m38.8s

**SS4 Waitomo 2 (43.88km)**
1 Loeb/Elena (Citroën) 28m20.4s; 2 Grönholm/Rautiainen (Ford) 28m21.1s; 3 Hirvonen/Lehtinen (Ford) 28m31.0s; 4 Sordo/Martí (Citroën) 28m38.2s; 5 Atkinson/Prevot (Subaru) 28m40.0s; 6 Latvala/Anttila (Ford) 28m40.4s; PC A.Araújo/M.Ramalho (Mitsubishi Lancer Evo 9) 30m30.4s

**SS5 Mystery Creek 1 (3.14km)**
1 Atkinson/Prevot (Subaru) 2m56.2s; 2 Loeb/Elena (Citroën) 2m57.2s; 3 Solberg/Mills (Subaru) 2m57.6s; 4 Grönholm/Rautiainen (Ford) 2m57.7s; 5= Latvala/Anttila (Ford), M.Wilson/M.Orr (Ford Focus RS WRC 06) 2m59.8s; PC N.McShea/G.Noble (Subaru Impreza WRX Sti) 3m05.5s

**SS6 Port Waikato (17.21km)**
1 Loeb/Elena (Citroën) 9m33.2s; 2 Grönholm/Rautiainen (Ford) 9m36.3s; 3 Hirvonen/Lehtinen (Ford) 9m36.7s; 4 Latvala/Anttila (Ford) 9m37.9s; 5 Solberg/Mills (Subaru) 9m44.3s; 6 Sordo/Martí (Citroën) 9m44.5s; PC M.Baldacci/G.Agnese (Subaru Impreza WRX Sti) 10m14.5s

**SS7 Possum (13.88km)**
1 Grönholm/Rautiainen (Ford) 10m38.2s; 2 Hirvonen/Lehtinen (Ford) 10m41.0s; 3 Latvala/Anttila (Ford) 10m41.6s; 4 Loeb/Elena (Citroën) 10m43.2s; 5 Atkinson/Prevot (Subaru) 10m44.7s; 6 Sordo/Martí (Citroën) 10m48.4s; PC Arai/Sircombe (Subaru) 11m10.3s

**SS8 Franklin (31.57km)**
1 Loeb/Elena (Citroën) 21m15.7s; 2 Grönholm/Rautiainen (Ford) 21m27.0s; 3 Hirvonen/Lehtinen (Ford) 21m29.1s; 4 Latvala/Anttila (Ford) 21m39.2s; 5 Atkinson/Prevot (Subaru) 21m39.7s; 6 Sordo/Martí (Citroën) 21m43.1s; PC Arai/Sircombe (Subaru) 22m40.0s

**SS9 Mystery Creek 2 (3.14km)**
1 Grönholm/Rautiainen (Ford) 2m54.7s; 2 Loeb/Elena (Citroën) 2m55.1s; 3 Atkinson/Prevot (Subaru) 2m55.3s; 4 Solberg/Mills (Subaru) 2m56.4s; 5 Hirvonen/Lehtinen (Ford) 2m57.2s; 6 Sordo/Martí (Citroën) 2m57.4s; PC G.Pozzo/D.Stillo (Mitsubishi Lancer Evo 9) 3m04.0s

**SS10 Te Akau South (31.92km)**
1 Loeb/Elena (Citroën) 18m25.0s; 2 Grönholm/Rautiainen (Ford) 18m25.3s; 3 Latvala/Anttila (Ford) 18m26.4s; 4 Hirvonen/Lehtinen (Ford) 18m29.3s; 5 Atkinson/Prevot (Subaru) 18m34.6s; 6= Solberg/Mills (Subaru), Sordo/Martí (Citroën) 18m40.5s; PC Mason/Randall (Subaru) 19m38.0s

**SS11 Te Akau North (32.36km)**
1 Loeb/Elena (Citroën) 16m59.8s; 2 Grönholm/Rautiainen (Ford) 17m05.2s; 3 Hirvonen/Lehtinen (Ford) 17m15.0s; 4 Latvala/Anttila (Ford) 17m15.4s; 5 Atkinson/Prevot (Subaru) 17m16.1s; 6 Sordo/Martí (Citroën) 17m27.0s; PC Hänninen/Markkula (Mitsubishi) 18m14.0s

**SS12 Maungatawhiri 1 (5.34km)**
1 Grönholm/Rautiainen (Ford) 2m41.3s; 2 Loeb/Elena (Citroën) 2m43.1s; 3 Solberg/Mills (Subaru) 2m44.4s; 4 Latvala/Anttila (Ford) 2m44.7s; 5 Atkinson/Prevot (Subaru) 2m45.6s; 6 Hirvonen/Lehtinen (Ford) 2m46.7s; PC Hänninen/Markkula (Mitsubishi) 2m57.1s

# RALLY NEW ZEALAND

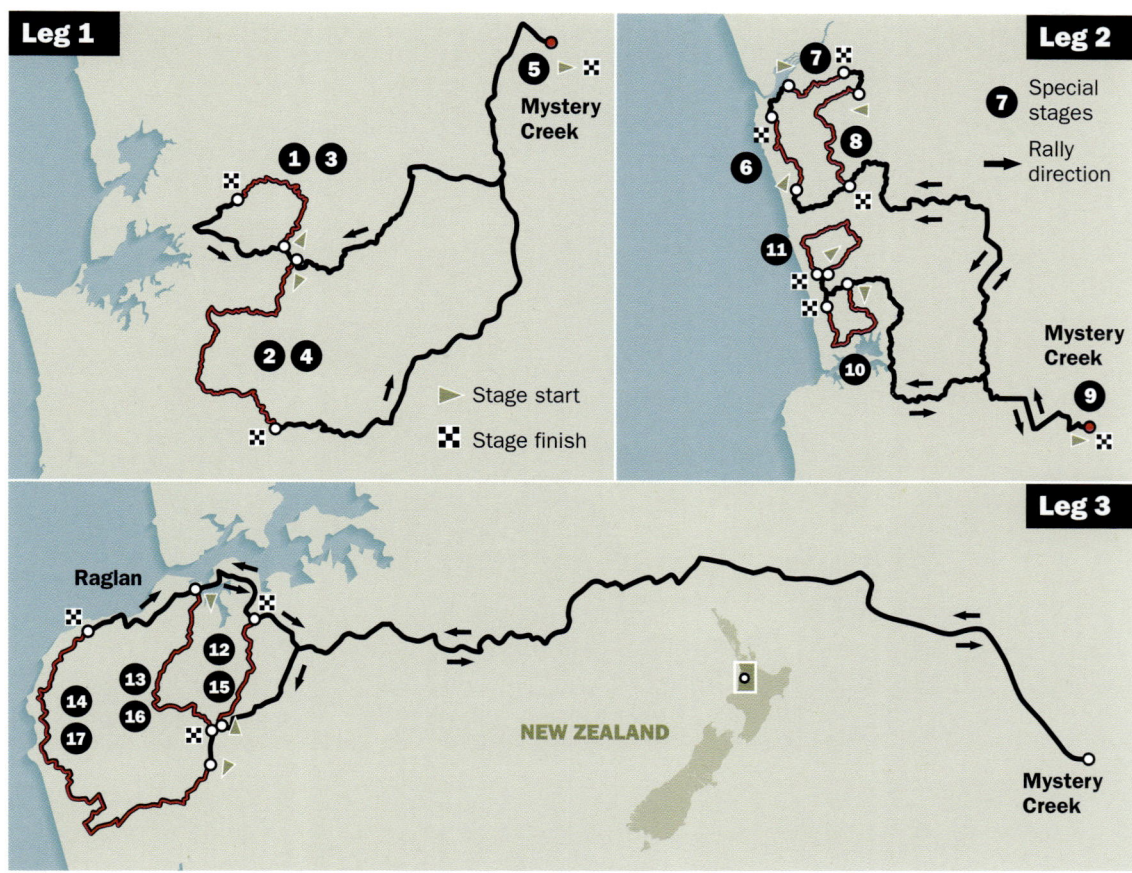

Pinomäki 8; 10= Cortinovis, Kosciuszko 6 etc
**Production Cup**
1 Arai 39; 2 Higgins 15; 3= Sohlberg, Pozzo 12; 5= M.Baldacci, McShea 11; 7= Svedlund, Villagra, Aigner, Nutahara 10 etc

### ROUTE DETAILS
Total route of 1255.98km of which 353.56km were competitive on 18 stages
**Leg 1** Friday 31 August, 5 special stages totalling 127.52km
**Leg 2** Saturday 1 September, 6 special stages totalling 130.10km
**Leg 3** Sunday 2 September, 7 special stages totalling 95.94km

### RESULTS
| | | | | |
|---|---|---|---|---|
| 1 | Marcus Grönholm/ | | Ford Focus RS WRC 07 | |
| | Timo Rautiainen | | 3h52m53.9s | Gr A |
| 2 | Sébastien Loeb/ | | Citroën C4 WRC | |
| | Daniel Elena | | 3h52m54.2s | Gr A |
| 3 | Mikko Hirvonen/ | | Ford Focus RS WRC 07 | |
| | Jarmo Lehtinen | | 3h54m36.7s | Gr A |
| 4 | Chris Atkinson/ | | Subaru Impreza WRC2007 | |
| | Stéphane Prevot | | 3h55m26.2s | Gr A |
| 5 | Jari-Matti Latvala/ | | Ford Focus RS WRC 06 | |
| | Miika Anttila | | 3h55m30.8s | Gr A |
| 6 | Daniel Sordo/ | | Citroën C4 WRC | |
| | Marc Martí | | 3h56m35.9s | Gr A |
| 7 | Petter Solberg/ | | Subaru Impreza WRC2007 | |
| | Phil Mills | | 3h56m48.6s | Gr A |
| 8 | Urmo Aava/ | | Mitsubishi Lancer WRC05 | |
| | Kuldar Sikk | | 4h02m10.2s | Gr A |
| 9 | Henning Solberg/ | | Ford Focus RS WRC 06 | |
| | Cato Menkerud | | 4h02m48.5s | Gr A |
| 10 | Matthew Wilson/ | | Ford Focus RS WRC 06 | |
| | Michael Orr | | 4h03m13.8s | Gr A |

68 starters, 59 finishers

### PREVIOUS WINNERS
| Year | Driver/Co-driver | Car |
|---|---|---|
| 1979 | Hannu Mikkola/Arne Hertz | Ford Escort RS1800 |
| 1980 | Timo Salonen/Seppo Harjanne | Datsun 160J |
| 1981* | Jim Donald/Kevin Lancaster | Ford Escort RS1800 |
| 1982 | Björn Waldegård/Hans Thorszelius | Toyota Celica GT |
| 1983 | Walter Röhrl/Christian Geistdörfer | Lancia Rally 037 |
| 1984 | Stig Blomqvist/Bjorn Cederberg | Audi Quattro A2 |
| 1985 | Timo Salonen/Seppo Harjanne | Peugeot 205 Turbo 16 |
| 1986 | Juha Kankkunen/Juha Piironen | Peugeot 205 Turbo 16 E2 |
| 1987 | Franz Wittmann/Jorg Pattermann | Lancia Delta HF 4x4 |
| 1988 | Sepp Haider/Ferdinand Hinterleitner | Opel Kadett GSi |
| 1989 | Ingvar Carlsson/Per Carlsson | Mazda 323 Turbo |
| 1990 | Carlos Sainz/Luis Moya | Toyota Celica GT4 |
| 1991 | Carlos Sainz/Luis Moya | Toyota Celica GT4 |
| 1992 | Carlos Sainz/Luis Moya | Toyota Celica Turbo 4WD |
| 1993 | Colin McRae/Derek Ringer | Subaru Legacy RS |
| 1994 | Colin McRae/Derek Ringer | Subaru Impreza 555 |
| 1995 | Colin McRae/Derek Ringer | Subaru Impreza 555 |
| 1996 | Richard Burns/Robert Reid | Mitsubishi Lancer E3 |
| 1997 | Kenneth Eriksson/Staffan Parmander | Subaru Impreza WRC97 |
| 1998 | Carlos Sainz/Luis Moya | Toyota Corolla WRC |
| 1999 | Tommi Mäkinen/Risto Mannisenmäki | Mitsubishi Lancer Evo |
| 2000 | Marcus Grönholm/Timo Rautiainen | Peugeot 206 WRC |
| 2001 | Richard Burns/Robert Reid | Subaru Impreza WRC2001 |
| 2002 | Marcus Grönholm/Timo Rautiainen | Peugeot 206 WRC |
| 2003 | Marcus Grönholm/Timo Rautiainen | Peugeot 206 WRC |
| 2004 | Petter Solberg/Phil Mills | Subaru Impreza WRC2004 |
| 2005 | Sébastien Loeb/ Daniel Elena | Citroën Xsara WRC |
| 2006 | Marcus Grönholm/Timo Rautiainen | Ford Focus RS WRC06 |

*Non-championship event

### Stage Positions
| Position | Stage Numbers | 1 | 2 | 3 | 4 | 5 | 6 | 7 | 8 | 9 | 10 | 11 | 12 | 13 | 14 | 15 | 16 | 17 | 18 |
|---|---|---|---|---|---|---|---|---|---|---|---|---|---|---|---|---|---|---|---|
| | Grönholm | 1 | 1 | 1 | 1 | 1 | 1 | 1 | 1 | 1 | 1 | 2 | 1 | 2 | 2 | 2 | 2 | 1 | 1 |
| | Loeb | 2 | 2 | 2 | 2 | 2 | 2 | 2 | 2 | 2 | 2 | 1 | 2 | 1 | 1 | 1 | 1 | 2 | 2 |
| | Hirvonen | 3 | 3 | 3 | 3 | 3 | 3 | 3 | 3 | 3 | 3 | 3 | 3 | 3 | 3 | 3 | 3 | 3 | 3 |
| | Atkinson | 4 | 4 | 4 | 4 | 4 | 5 | 5 | 5 | 5 | 5 | 5 | 5 | 5 | 5 | 5 | 5 | 4 | 4 |
| | Latvala | 5 | 5 | 5 | 5 | 5 | 4 | 4 | 4 | 4 | 4 | 4 | 4 | 4 | 4 | 4 | 4 | 5 | 5 |
| | Sordo | 6 | 6 | 6 | 6 | 6 | 6 | 6 | 6 | 6 | 6 | 6 | 6 | 6 | 6 | 6 | 6 | 6 | 6 |
| | P.Solberg | 7 | 8 | 7 | 7 | 7 | 7 | 7 | 7 | 7 | 7 | 7 | 7 | 7 | 7 | 7 | 7 | 7 | 7 |
| | Aava | 11 | 11 | 10 | 9 | 9 | 9 | 9 | 8 | 8 | 8 | 8 | 8 | 8 | 8 | 8 | 8 | 8 | 8 |
| | H.Solberg | 10 | 9 | 8 | 8 | 8 | 8 | 8 | 10 | 10 | 10 | 10 | 10 | 9 | 9 | 9 | 9 | 9 | 9 |
| | Wilson | 12 | 12 | 11 | 10 | 10 | 10 | 9 | 9 | 9 | 9 | 9 | 9 | 10 | 10 | 10 | 10 | 10 | 10 |
| | Villagra | 15 | 17 | 14 | 11 | 11 | 11 | 11 | 11 | 11 | 11 | 11 | 11 | 11 | 11 | 11 | 11 | 11 | 11 |
| | Stohl | 9 | 10 | 9 | 13 | 34 | 32 | 31 | 22 | 22 | 20 | 16 | 15 | 13 | 13 | 13 | 13 | 12 | 12 |
| | P-Companc | 65 | 51 | 40 | 28 | 26 | 23 | 22 | 16 | 15 | 14 | 13 | 12 | 12 | 12 | 12 | 12 | 23 | 23 |
| | Pons | 8 | 7 | 28 | 37 | 46 | 43 | 41 | R | | | | | | | | | | |

### FIA CLASS WINNERS
| Class | Winner | Car |
|---|---|---|
| A8 Over 2000 cc | Grönholm/Rautiainen | Ford Focus RS WRC 07 |
| A6 1400-1600cc | Sasaki/Masuda | Honda Civic Si |
| N4 Over 2000 cc | Arai/Sircombe | Subaru Impreza WRX Sti |
| N3 1600-2000cc | Tapper/Cress | Ford Fiesta ST |

### RALLY LEADERS
Overall: SS1-10 Grönholm; SS11 Loeb; SS12 Grönholm; SS13-16 Loeb; SS17-18 Grönholm

PC: SS1 Arai; SS2-3 Hänninen; SS4-6 Araújo; SS7-16 McShea; SS17-18 Arai

### SPECIAL STAGE ANALYSIS
| | 1st | 2nd | 3rd | 4th | 5th | 6th |
|---|---|---|---|---|---|---|
| Loeb (Citroën) | 9 | 8 | - | 1 | - | - |
| Grönholm (Ford) | 8 | 9 | - | 1 | - | - |
| Atkinson (Subaru) | 1 | 1 | 3 | 4 | 7 | - |
| Hirvonen (Ford) | - | 2 | 9 | 1 | 2 | 3 |
| P.Solberg (Subaru) | - | - | 3 | 3 | 3 | 1 |
| Latvala (Ford) | - | - | 2 | 5 | 5 | 3 |
| Sordo (Citroën) | - | - | - | 1 | 1 | 11 |
| Stohl (Citroën) | - | - | - | - | - | - |
| H.Solberg (Ford) | - | - | - | - | 1 | - |
| Wilson (Ford) | - | - | - | - | 1 | - |

### WORLD CHAMPIONSHIP POINTS
**Drivers**
1 Grönholm 90; 2 Loeb 80; 3 Hirvonen 69; 4= P.Solberg, Sordo 31; 6 H.Solberg 28; 7 Atkinson 25; 8 Latvala 17; 9 Gardemeister 10; 10= Carlsson, Stohl 9 etc

**Manufacturers**
1 BP-Ford WRT 159; 2 Citroën Total WRT 113; 3 Subaru WRT 60; 4 Stobart M-Sport Ford RT 55; 5 OMV-Kronos Citroën WRT 35; 6 Munchi's Ford RT 6

**Junior World Championship**
1 Aava 32; 2 Andersson 28; 3 Sandell 19; 4 Mölder 17; 5 Prokop 16; 6 Burkart 14; 7 Beres 13; 8 Rautenbach 11; 9

### SS13 Te Hutewai 1 (11.22km)
1 Loeb/Elena (Citroën) 7m54.3s; 2 Grönholm/Rautiainen (Ford) 7m54.9s; 3 Hirvonen/Lehtinen (Ford) 7m58.7s; 4 Atkinson/Prevot (Subaru) 7m59.0s; 5 Solberg/Mills (Subaru) 8m00.0s; 6 Latvala/Anttila (Ford) 8m01.0s; PC Hänninen/Markkula (Mitsubishi) 8m28.3s

### SS14 Whaanga Coast 1 (29.81km)
1 Loeb/Elena (Citroën) 21m00.8s; 2 Grönholm/Rautiainen (Ford) 21m03.2s; 3 Atkinson/Prevot (Subaru) 21m08.0s; 4 Solberg/Mills (Subaru) 21m11.6s; 5 Latvala/Anttila (Ford) 21m12.9s; 6 Hirvonen/Lehtinen (Ford) 21m13.2s; PC Hänninen/Markkula (Mitsubishi) 22m26.0s

### SS15 Maungatawhiri 2 (5.34km)
1 Grönholm/Rautiainen (Ford) 2m39.7s; 2= Loeb/Elena (Citroën), Hirvonen/Lehtinen (Ford), Atkinson/Prevot (Subaru) 2m40.3s; 5= Solberg/Mills (Subaru), Latvala/Anttila (Ford) 2m40.8s; PC Hänninen/Markkula (Mitsubishi) 2m54.3s

### SS16 Te Hutewai 2 (11.22km)
1 Grönholm/Rautiainen (Ford) 7m43.0s; 2 Loeb/Elena (Citroën) 7m45.1s; 3 Hirvonen/Lehtinen (Ford) 7m45.5s; 4 Latvala/Anttila (Ford) 7m46.5s; 5 Atkinson/Prevot (Subaru) 7m46.7s; 6 Sordo/Martí (Citroën) 7m47.1s; PC Araújo/Ramalho (Mitsubishi) 8m19.0s

### SS17 Whaanga Coast 2 (29.81km)
1 Grönholm/Rautiainen (Ford) 20m32.1s; 2 Loeb/Elena (Citroën) 20m33.0s; 3 Atkinson/Prevot (Subaru) 20m34.2s; 4 M.Stohl/I.Minor (Citroën Xsara WRC) 20m37.8s; 5 Hirvonen/Lehtinen (Ford) 20m39.4s; 6 Sordo/Martí (Citroën) 20m39.5s; PC Hänninen/Markkula (Mitsubishi) 21m47.4s

### SS18 Mystery Creek 3 (3.14km)
1 Loeb/Elena (Citroën) 2m52.5s; 2 Grönholm/Rautiainen (Ford) 2m52.9s; 3 Solberg/Mills (Subaru) 2m53.0s; 4 Atkinson/Prevot (Subaru) 2m54.5s; 5 H.Solberg/C.Menkerud (Ford Focus RS WRC 06) 2m55.0s; 6= Hirvonen/Lehtinen (Ford), Sordo/Martí (Citroën) 2m55.3s; PC Arai/Sircombe (Subaru) 3m03.3s

### Cars which retired and subsequently re-started under SuperRally regs
| | | | | |
|---|---|---|---|---|
| 5 | Stohl/Minor | Citroën Xsara WRC | | |
| | Accident | | SS4 | Gr A |
| 14 | Pons/Amigo | Subaru Impreza WRC2007 | | |
| | Accident | | SS3 | Gr A |

### MAJOR RETIREMENTS
| | | | | |
|---|---|---|---|---|
| 14 | Pons/Amigo | Subaru Impreza WRC2007 | | |
| | Accident | | SS8 | Gr A |

Below: Loeb's superiority on asphalt, plus a smart call on tyres in the wet, helped him claw back four points to Grönholm in the title race

Right: Grönholm went back to school to try to improve his asphalt form, but by his own admission a single day's coaching was too little, too late

Far right: Sordo helped maximise the damage to Grönholm and Ford by finishing second to team-mate Loeb

Bottom right: The WRC mourned the loss of Colin McRae, who died in a helicopter crash in September. This was his former team Subaru's tribute

All photographs by McKlein

## The FIA World Rally Championship Round 12
# Rally Catalunya

SUCH was Marcus Grönholm's determination not to let his rival make a dent in his 10-point lead on the first pure asphalt outing of the season that he went back to school. By mid-morning on leg one of Rally Catalunya, and by the Finn's own admission, his having spent a solitary day with driver coach Rob Wilson was too little too late.

"I should have done it five years ago," grimaced Grönholm, while looking at a sheet of times that already had him down on not one Citroën, but both the C4 WRCs of Sébastien Loeb and Dani Sordo. From then on, Grönholm's rally was about damage limitation.

Loeb's advantage at the head of the field was near-enough doubled on one sodden run through Pratdip on Friday evening. In New Zealand, a month earlier, it had been Grönholm who had made the best of the wet conditions. This time, Loeb delivered a master class on how to get from A to B fastest within the tight confines of what's recognised as the World Rally Championship tyre selection. As the crews were readying themselves to leave the PortAventura theme park outside Salou for the final time on the opening day, the rain was coming; the gathering black clouds made that much obvious. The real question was how quickly it would find its way through the hills around Tarragona. Ford was confident the cars would be there and back before the worst of the rain fell. Wrong.

Citroën called the conditions as near perfect as anybody can with tyre choice these days. Its harder BFGoodrich rubber – with a small cut in – certainly slowed the cars down in the run from El Lloar to La Figuera which proceeded Pratdip, but where it counted, Loeb waltzed through the test taking half a minute out of the nearest none-C4; he *only* took half of that from team-mate Sordo.

"We got the weather wrong by 15 minutes," a member of the Ford team was heard to observe grimly. The numbers don't matter – fact is, the Focus RS WRCs were out there on the wrong boots.

At the end of the stage, Loeb was delighted. He talked of numerous moments in the test, of aquaplaning here and sliding there, but he'd done it. He knew he'd have to risk everything at some point in the three days. Now he could sit back and drive to the splits through the weekend. Grönholm, by comparison, was his usual blend of fury and frustration. Along with the half-minute Loeb had bagged in that stage, the Ford driver was well aware that he was set to claw back four championship points as well.

While it might have seemed like the weather was doing little to aid Grönholm on Friday evening, the sun which shone through legs two and three helped stave off what could have been a serious onslaught from Citroën 'privateer' François Duval. 'Employed' by the French firm, via the Kronos Team, the Belgian's job was to put his Xsara on the final step of the podium behind the C4s. In the end, the mainly dry conditions rendered his 2005-specification Citroën impotent against the more grunty current Fords. Had the weekend been wet, Duval's full compliment of active differentials would have given him a considerable edge in terms of traction over Grönholm and Mikko Hirvonen, who ended the event directly ahead of him.

# RALLY CATALUNYA

Below: Petter Solberg led home the Subarus in sixth place. He could manage no better with the car, despite recent asphalt testing

Right: Fifth-placed Duval was left cursing the dry weather – had it stayed wet the Citroën 'privateer' could have probably overhauled the Fords

Middle right: Changeable weather around the PortAventura rally base made tyre choice a tricky matter on the Friday evening

Far right: Hirvonen occupied something of a no-man's land in fourth – a minute ahead of Duval at the finish but almost the same distance behind Grönholm

Bottom right: Latvala found himself in another fight for position with Atkinson (Subaru), but this time the Ford man prevailed with a steady drive to seventh

All photographs by McKlein

Abu Dhabi
ultimate
Castrol

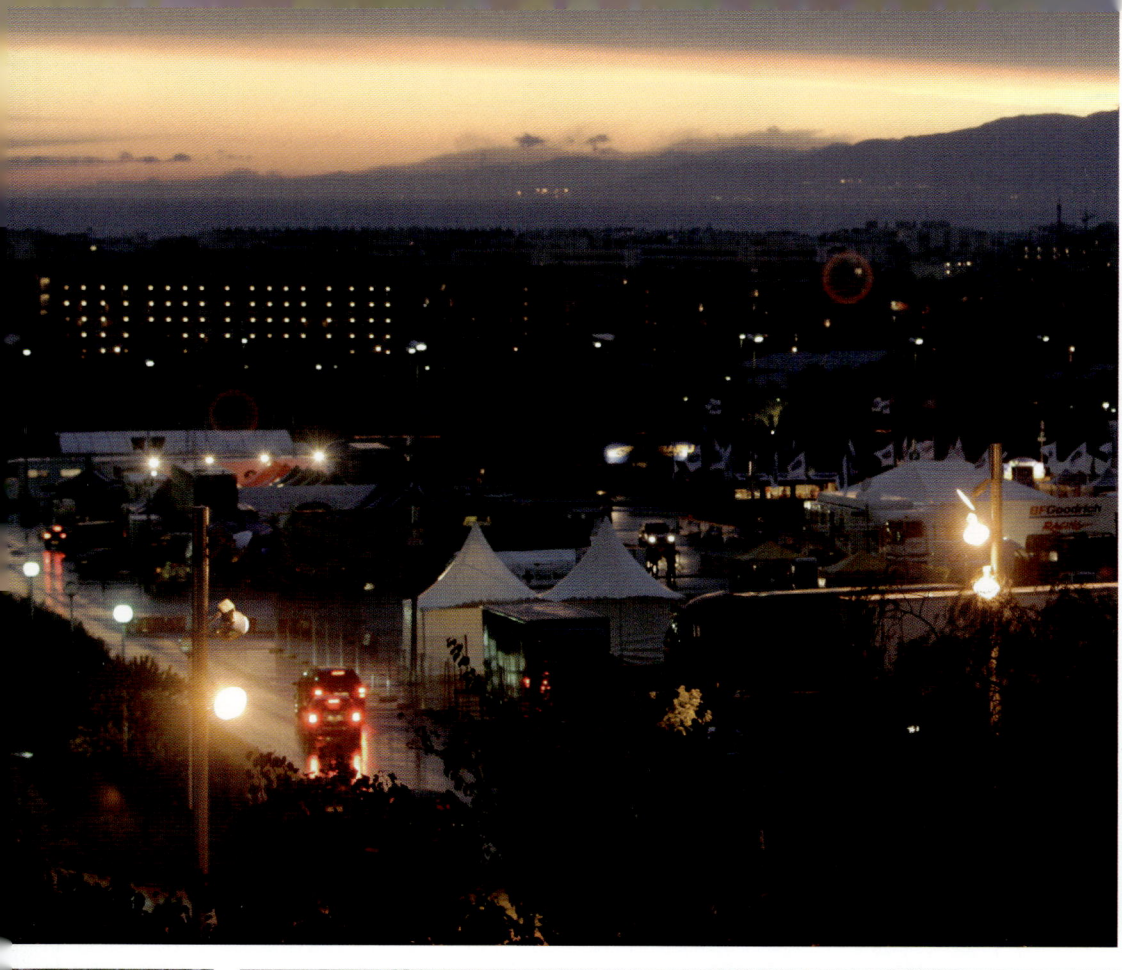

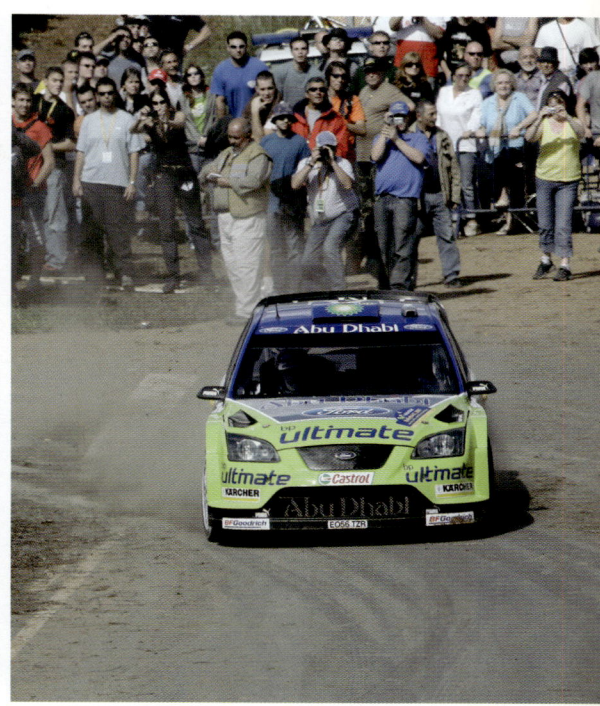

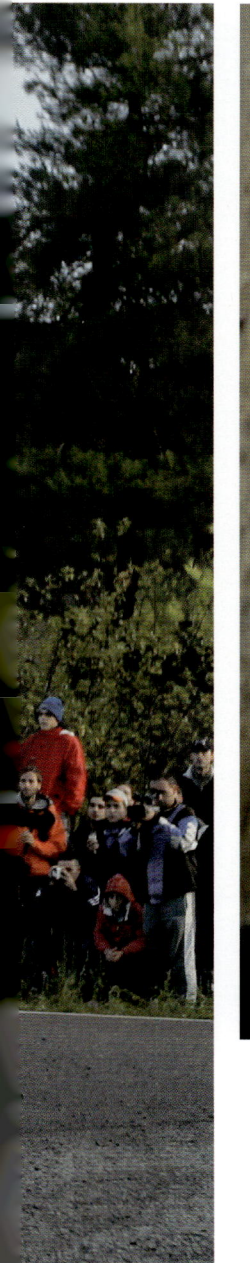

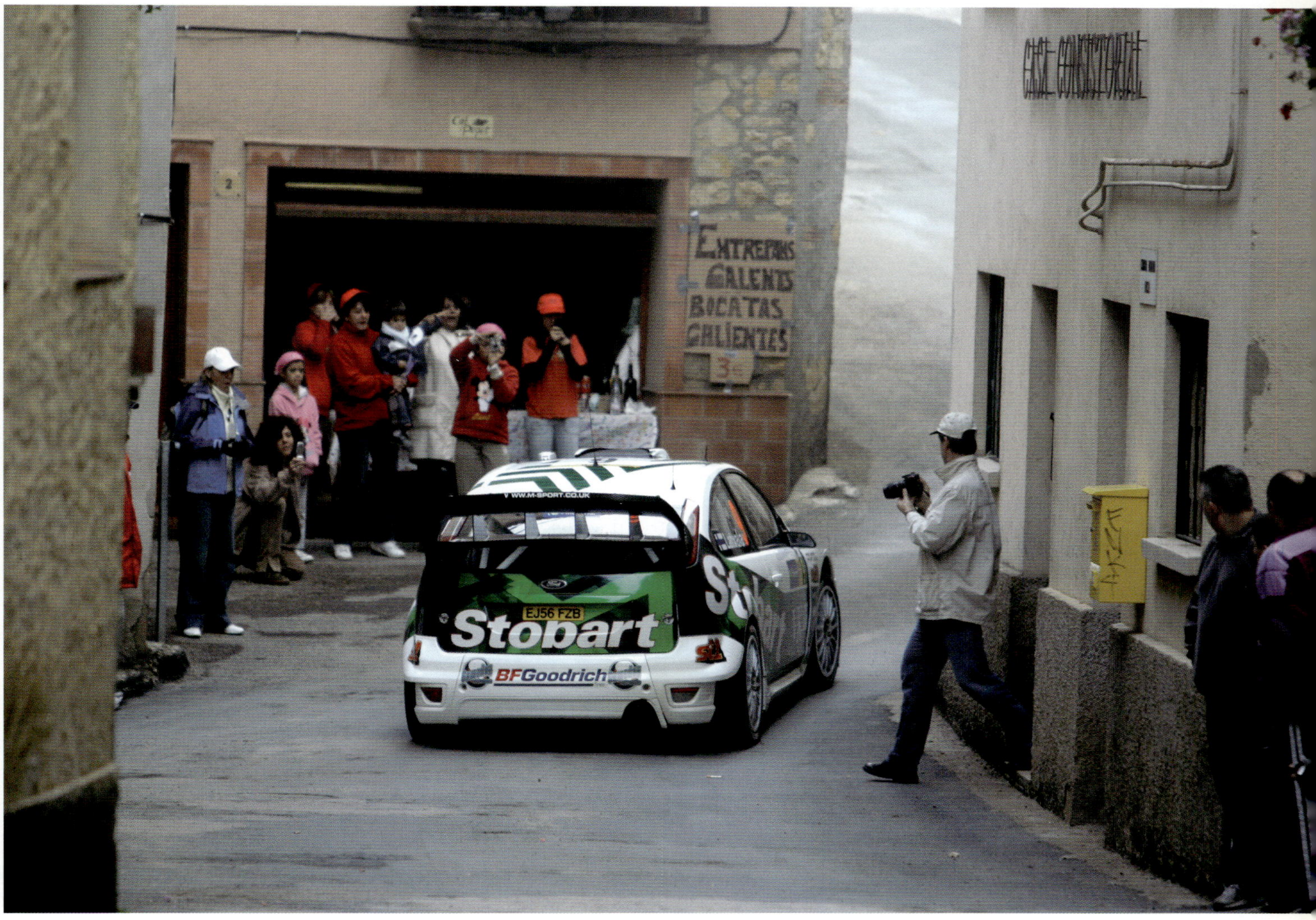
ENTREPANS
CALENTS
BOCATAS
CALIENTES
Stobart
BFGoodrich

Aigner was on impressive form to secure a dominant Group N win in his Mitsubishi
McKlein

## The FIA World Rally Championship Round 12
# Rally Catalunya Results
### October 5-7 2007

### FINISH LINES...

After what had been deemed a successful asphalt test, Subaru still failed to deliver, with Petter Solberg leading the trio of Impreza WRC2007s home in sixth place. There were no tears from the Norwegian this time, just the kind of cold, hard pragmatism which came with the acceptance that right now this was as good as it was going to get... After losing out to Solberg's team-mate Chris Atkinson on the last round, Stobart Ford man Jari-Matti Latvala edged the Aussie in Spain, taking seventh and leaving the Queenslander to content himself with eighth. Latvala's drive was as steady and self-assured as Atkinson's was lary and wild. On successive occasions – in stages eight and nine – Atko admitted he'd been close to binning the Subaru. The on-board footage was unbelievable. In the end, eighth and an unbruised Impreza was a result... Suzuki's Per-Gunnar Andersson played himself right back into the fight for this year's Junior title by taking four points out of his team-mate Urmo Aava. The Swede's job was made slightly easier by a puncture for the Estonian car. Martin Prokop placed his C2 Super 1600 between the two Suzukis to ensure the pair would go to the final round – a week later in Corsica – tied on points... Finally, Red Bull driver Andreas Aigner put in the kind of performance he had been threatening for some time to dominate Group N in his Mitsubishi Lancer.

### RUNNING ORDER

| | | |
|---|---|---|
| 3 | Marcus Grönholm/<br>Timo Rautiainen | Ford Focus RS WRC 07<br>Gr A |
| 1 | Sébastien Loeb/<br>Daniel Elena | Citroën C4 WRC<br>Gr A |
| 4 | Mikko Hirvonen/<br>Jarmo Lehtinen | Ford Focus RS WRC 07<br>Gr A |
| 7 | Petter Solberg/<br>Phil Mills | Subaru Impreza WRC2007<br>Gr A |
| 2 | Daniel Sordo/<br>Marc Martí | Citroën C4 WRC<br>Gr A |
| 10 | Henning Solberg/<br>Cato Menkerud | Ford Focus RS WRC 06<br>Gr A |
| 8 | Chris Atkinson/<br>Stéphane Prevot | Subaru Impreza WRC2007<br>Gr A |
| 9 | Jari-Matti Latvala/<br>Miikka Anttila | Ford Focus RS WRC 06<br>Gr A |
| 5 | Manfred Stohl/<br>Ilka Minor | Citroën Xsara WRC<br>Gr A |
| 6 | François Duval/<br>Patrick Pivato | Citroën Xsara WRC<br>Gr A |
| 17 | Jan Kopecky/<br>Filip Schovanek | Skoda Fabia WRC<br>Gr A |
| 14 | Xavier Pons/<br>Xavier Amigo | Subaru Impreza WRC2007<br>Gr A |
| 16 | Matthew Wilson/<br>Michael Orr | Ford Focus RS WRC 06<br>Gr A |
| 12 | Federico Villagra/<br>Jorge Pérez-Companc | Ford Focus RS WRC 06<br>Gr A |
| 11 | Luis Pérez-Companc/<br>Jose Maria Volta | Ford Focus RS WRC 06<br>Gr A |
| 15 | Khalid Al-Qassimi/<br>Nicky Beech | Ford Focus RS WRC 06<br>Gr A |
| 18 | Gareth Jones/<br>David Moynihan | Ford Focus RS WRC 04<br>Gr A |
| 19 | Andreas Mikkelsen/<br>Ola Floene | Ford Focus RS WRC 04<br>Gr A |
| 20 | Mark Van Eldik/<br>Michel Groenewoud | Subaru Impreza WRC2006<br>Gr A |
| 21 | Thomas Schie/<br>Goran Bergsten | Ford Focus RS WRC 04<br>Gr A |
| 22 | Peter Van Merksteijn/<br>Erwin Berkhof | Ford Focus RS WRC 06<br>Gr A |

### SPECIAL STAGE TIMES

**SS1 Querol 1 (25.43km)**
1 M.Grönholm/T.Rautiainen (Ford Focus RS WRC 07) 13m57.1s; 2 S.Loeb/D.Elena (Citroën C4 WRC) 13m59.7s; 3 D.Sordo/M.Martí (Citroën C4 WRC) 14m01.1s; 4 M.Hirvonen/J.Lehtinen (Ford Focus RS WRC 07) 14m12.8s 5 P.Solberg/P.Mills (Subaru Impreza WRC2007) 14m14.2s; 6 C.Atkinson/S.Prevot (Subaru Impreza WRC2007) 14m22.5s; JRC P-G.Andersson/J.Andersson (Suzuki Swift) 15m39.7s

**SS2 El Montmell 1 (24.13km)**
1 Loeb/Elena (Citroën) 12m56.4s; 2 Sordo/Martí (Citroën) 12m58.7s; 3 Grönholm/Rautiainen (Ford) 13m03.4s; 4 Hirvonen/Lehtinen (Ford) 13m10.4s; 5 F.Duval/P.Pivato (Citroën Xsara WRC) 13m11.8s; 6 Solberg/Mills (Subaru) 13m16.1s; JRC U.Aava/K.Sikk (Suzuki Swift) 14m34.2s

**SS3 Querol 2 (25.43km)**
1 Duval/Pivato (Citroën) 13m48.5s; 2 Loeb/Elena (Citroën) 13m49.0s; 3 Hirvonen/Lehtinen (Ford) 13m52.4s; 4 Sordo/Martí (Citroën) 13m52.6s; 5 Grönholm/Rautiainen (Ford) 13m57.8s; 6 Atkinson/Prevot (Subaru) 13m58.8s; JRC Aava/Sikk (Suzuki) 15m09.2s

**SS4 El Montmell 2 (24.13km)**
1 Sordo/Martí (Citroën) 12m31.4s; 2 Loeb/Elena (Citroën) 12m39.4s; 3 Duval/Pivato (Citroën) 12m42.0s; 4 Hirvonen/Lehtinen (Ford) 12m46.1s; 5 Solberg/Mills (Subaru) 12m48.6s; 6 Grönholm/Rautiainen (Ford) 12m50.5s; JRC Aava/Sikk (Suzuki) 13m58.3s

**SS5 El Lloar - La Figuera (22.43km)**
1 Hirvonen/Lehtinen (Ford) 12m27.7s; 2 Grönholm/Rautiainen (Ford) 12m27.8s; 3 Sordo/Martí (Citroën) 12m32.4s; 4 Loeb/Elena (Citroën) 12m35.3s; 5 Solberg/Mills (Subaru) 12m39.2s; 6 Duval/Pivato (Citroën) 12m40.0s; JRC Aava/Sikk (Suzuki) 13m47.2s

**SS6 Pratdip (26.47km)**
1 Loeb/Elena (Citroën) 16m16.7s; 2 Sordo/Martí (Citroën) 16m31.6s; 3 Hirvonen/Lehtinen (Ford) 16m40.3s; 4 Solberg/Mills (Subaru) 16m44.9s; 5 Duval/Pivato (Citroën) 16m49.1s; 6 Grönholm/Rautiainen (Ford) 16m50.5s; JRC Aava/Sikk (Suzuki) 17m50.2s

**SS7 Villaplana 1 (13.28km)**
1 Grönholm/Rautiainen (Ford) 7m54.4s; 2 Loeb/Elena (Citroën) 7m55.1s; 3= Sordo/Martí (Citroën), Duval/Pivato (Citroën) 7m55.5s; 5 Atkinson/Prevot (Subaru) 7m56.7s; 6 Hirvonen/Lehtinen (Ford) 7m56.9s; JRC Andersson/Andersson (Suzuki) 8m41.3s

**SS8 Coll del Grau 1 (26.32km)**
1 Loeb/Elena (Citroën) 13m59.5s; 2 Grönholm/Rautiainen (Ford) 14m00.5s; 3 Hirvonen/Lehtinen (Ford) 14m01.0s; 4 Duval/Pivato (Citroën) 14m01.4s; 5 Sordo/Martí (Citroën) 14m01.5s; 6 J-M.Latvala/M.Anttila (Ford Focus RS WRC 06) 14m13.9s; JRC J.Beres/P.Stary (Renault Clio) 15m29.2s

**SS9 Margalef - La Palma d'Ebre 1 (15.85km)**
1 Grönholm/Rautiainen (Ford) 9m45.8s; 2 Loeb/Elena (Citroën) 9m48.2s; 3 Sordo/Martí (Citroën) 9m49.9s; 4 Hirvonen/Lehtinen (Ford) 9m50.9s; 5 Latvala/Anttila (Ford) 9m51.6s; 6 Solberg/Mills (Subaru) 9m54.7s; JRC Aava/Sikk (Suzuki) 10m39.1s

**SS10 La Serra d'Almos 1 (4.11km)**
1 Sordo/Martí (Citroën) 2m38.3s; 2 Grönholm/Rautiainen (Ford) 2m38.4s; 3 Duval/Pivato (Citroën) 2m39.0s; 4 X.Pons/X.Amigo (Subaru Impreza WRC2007) 2m39.2s; 5 Loeb/Elena (Citroën) 2m39.3s; 6 Hirvonen/Lehtinen (Ford) 2m40.5s; JRC M.Prokop/J.Tomanek (Citroën C2) 2m54.7s

**SS11 Villaplana 2 (13.28km)**
1 Grönholm/Rautiainen (Ford) 7m44.1s; 2 Hirvonen/Lehtinen (Ford) 7m44.8s; 3 Sordo/Martí (Citroën) 7m44.9s; 4 Atkinson/Prevot (Subaru) 7m45.7s; 5 Solberg/Mills (Subaru) 7m46.1s; 6 Loeb/Elena (Citroën) 7m46.4s; JRC Aava/Sikk (Suzuki) 8m35.3s

**SS12 Coll del Grau 2 (26.32km)**
1 Sordo/Martí (Citroën) 13m59.0s; 2 Loeb/Elena (Citroën) 14m00.2s; 3 Grönholm/Rautiainen (Ford) 14m00.9s; 4 Hirvonen/Lehtinen (Ford) 14m04.7s; 5 Duval/Pivato

# RALLY CATALUNYA

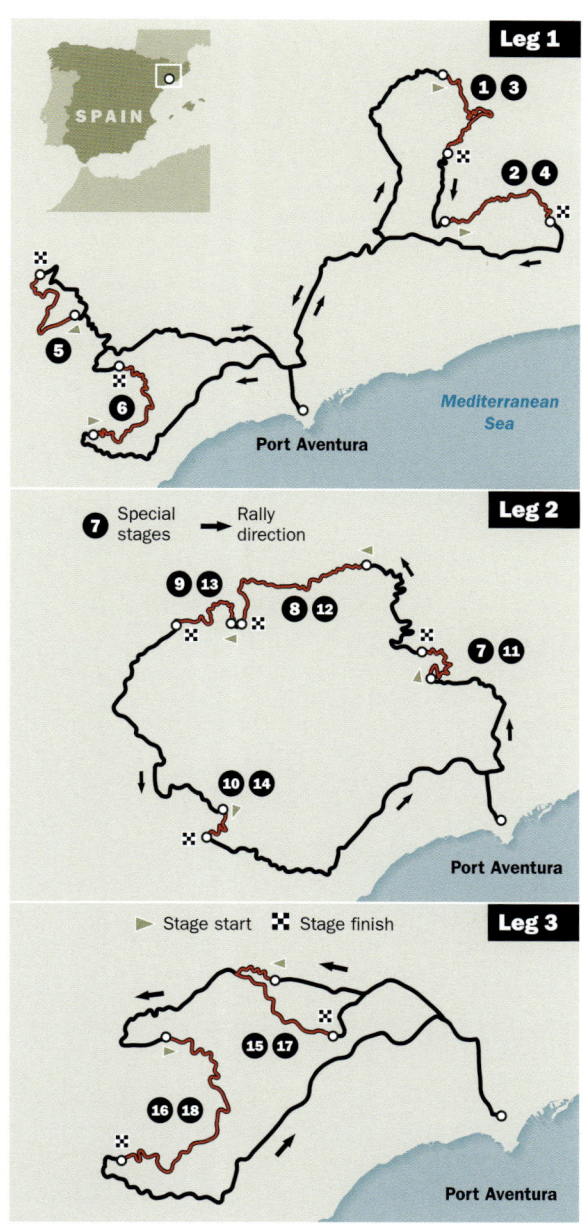

| Stage Numbers | 1 | 2 | 3 | 4 | 5 | 6 | 7 | 8 | 9 | 10 | 11 | 12 | 13 | 14 | 15 | 16 | 17 | 18 |
|---|---|---|---|---|---|---|---|---|---|---|---|---|---|---|---|---|---|---|
| Loeb | 2 | 1 | 1 | 2 | 2 | 1 | 1 | 1 | 1 | 1 | 1 | 1 | 1 | 1 | 1 | 1 | 1 | 1 |
| Sordo | 3 | 2 | 2 | 1 | 1 | 2 | 2 | 2 | 2 | 2 | 2 | 2 | 2 | 2 | 2 | 2 | 2 | 2 |
| Grönholm | 1 | 3 | 3 | 3 | 3 | 3 | 3 | 3 | 3 | 3 | 3 | 3 | 3 | 3 | 3 | 3 | 3 | 3 |
| Hirvonen | 4 | 4 | 4 | 4 | 4 | 4 | 4 | 4 | 4 | 4 | 4 | 4 | 4 | 4 | 4 | 4 | 4 | 4 |
| Duval | 11 | 6 | 5 | 5 | 5 | 5 | 5 | 5 | 5 | 5 | 5 | 5 | 5 | 5 | 5 | 5 | 5 | 5 |
| P.Solberg | 5 | 5 | 6 | 6 | 6 | 6 | 6 | 6 | 6 | 6 | 6 | 6 | 6 | 6 | 6 | 6 | 6 | 6 |
| Latvala | 10 | 10 | 7 | 8 | 7 | 7 | 7 | 7 | 7 | 7 | 7 | 7 | 7 | 7 | 7 | 7 | 7 | 7 |
| Atkinson | 6 | 11 | 8 | 7 | 8 | 8 | 8 | 8 | 8 | 8 | 8 | 8 | 8 | 8 | 8 | 8 | 8 | 8 |
| Pons | 8 | 7 | 9 | 9 | 9 | 9 | 9 | 9 | 9 | 9 | 9 | 9 | 9 | 9 | 9 | 9 | 9 | 9 |
| H.Solberg | 13 | 12 | 10 | 10 | 10 | 10 | 10 | 10 | 10 | 10 | 10 | 10 | 10 | 10 | 10 | 10 | 10 | 10 |
| Wilson | 17 | 16 | 12 | 12 | 11 | 11 | 11 | 11 | 11 | 11 | 11 | 11 | 11 | 11 | 11 | 11 | 11 | 11 |
| Villagra | 18 | 17 | 13 | 13 | 13 | 15 | 13 | 13 | 13 | 13 | 13 | 13 | 13 | 13 | 13 | 13 | 13 | 13 |
| Stohl | 7 | 8 | R | | | | | | | | | | | | | | | |
| Kopecky | 9 | 9 | R | | | | | | | | | | | | | | | |
| P-Companc | 15 | R | | | | | | | | | | | | | | | | |

(Citroën) 14m08.3s; 6 Pons/Amigo (Subaru) 14m09.5s; JRC Aava/Sikk (Suzuki) 15m20.4s

### SS13 Margalef - La Palma d'Ebre 2 (15.85km)
1 Loeb/Elena (Citroën) 9m38.8s; 2 Grönholm/Rautiainen (Ford) 9m40.2s; 3 Sordo/Martí (Citroën) 9m41.0s; 4 Latvala/Anttila (Ford) 9m45.7s; 5 Pons/Amigo (Subaru) 9m45.8s; 6 Duval/Pivato (Citroën) 9m46.1s; JRC Prokop/Tomanek (Citroën) 10m27.1s

### SS14 La Serra d'Almos 2 (4.11km)
1 Grönholm/Rautiainen (Ford) 2m37.7s; 2 Pons/Amigo (Subaru) 2m38.4s; 3 Atkinson/Prevot (Subaru) 2m39.1s; 4 Sordo/Martí (Citroën) 2m40.5s; 5 Latvala/Anttila (Ford) 2m41.2s; 6 Loeb/Elena (Citroën) 2m41.5s; JRC Aava/Sikk (Suzuki) 2m54.5s

### SS15 Riudecanyes 1 (16.31km)
1= Grönholm/Rautiainen, Loeb/Elena (Citroën) 10m19.2s; 3 Sordo/Martí (Citroën) 10m21.5s; 4 Hirvonen/Lehtinen (Ford) 10m22.6s; 5 Duval/Pivato (Citroën) 10m22.8s; 6 Atkinson/Prevot (Subaru) 10m26.3s; JRC A.Burkart/M.Koelbach (Citroën C2) 11m21.6s

### SS16 Colldejou 1 (26.51km)
1 Sordo/Martí (Citroën) 15m38.7s; 2 Loeb/Elena (Citroën) 15m39.5s; 3 Grönholm/Rautiainen (Ford) 15m47.0s; 4 Hirvonen/Lehtinen (Ford) 15m47.3s; 5 Solberg/Mills (Subaru) 15m50.5s; 6 Duval/Pivato (Citroën) 15m54.5s; JRC Burkart/Koelbach (Citroën) 17m17.8s

### SS17 Riudecanyes 2 (16.31km)
1 Grönholm/Rautiainen (Ford) 10m15.1s; 2 Duval/Pivato (Citroën) 10m19.3s; 3 Hirvonen/Lehtinen (Ford) 10m19.8s; 4 Latvala/Anttila (Ford) 10m20.5s; 5 Sordo/Martí (Citroën) 10m21.4s; 6 Atkinson/Prevot (Subaru) 10m21.5s; JRC Aava/Sikk (Suzuki) 11m17.6s

### SS18 Colldejou 2 (26.51km)
1 Grönholm/Rautiainen (Ford) 15m39.9s; 2= Loeb/Elena (Citroën), Sordo/Martí (Citroën) 15m44.3s; 4 Solberg/Mills (Subaru) 15m46.6s; 5 Hirvonen/Lehtinen (Ford) 15m48.6s; 6 Pons/Amigo (Subaru) 15m51.3s; JRC Aava/Sikk (Suzuki) 17m06.7s

### MAJOR RETIREMENTS
| | | | | |
|---|---|---|---|---|
| 5 | Stohl/Minor | Citroën Xsara WRC | | |
| | Accident | SS3 | Gr A | |
| 17 | Kopecky/Schovanek | Skoda Fabia WRC | | |
| | Accident | SS3 | Gr A | |
| 11 | P-Companc/Volta | Ford Focus RS WRC 06 | | |
| | Accident | SS2 | Gr A | |
| 18 | Jones/Moynihan | Ford Focus RS WRC 04 | | |
| | Mechanical | SS8 | | |
| 20 | Van Eldik/Gr'woud | Subaru Impreza WRC2006 | | |
| | Mechanical | SS18 | | |

### FIA CLASS WINNERS
| | | |
|---|---|---|
| A8 | Over 2000 cc | Loeb/Elena |
| | | Citroën C4 WRC |
| A7 | 1500-2000ss | Solá/Del Barrio |
| | | Honda Civic Type-R |
| A6 | 1400-1600 cc | Andersson/Andersson |
| | | Suzuki Swift |
| N4 | Over 2000 cc | Aigner/Wicha |
| | | Mitsubishi Lancer Evo 9 |
| N3 | 1600-2000cc | Godoy/Diaz |
| | | Ford Fiesta ST |

### RALLY LEADERS
Overall: SS1 Grönholm; SS2-3 Loeb; SS4-5 Sordo; SS6-18 Loeb
JRC: SS1-2 Andersson; SS3-7 Aava; SS8-18 Andersson

### SPECIAL STAGE ANALYSIS
| | 1st | 2nd | 3rd | 4th | 5th | 6th |
|---|---|---|---|---|---|---|
| Grönholm (Ford) | 8 | 4 | 3 | - | 1 | 2 |
| Loeb (Citroën) | 5 | 8 | - | 1 | 1 | 2 |
| Sordo (Citroën) | 4 | 3 | 7 | 2 | 2 | - |
| Hirvonen (Ford) | 1 | 1 | 4 | 7 | 1 | 2 |
| Duval (Citroën) | 1 | 1 | 3 | 1 | 4 | 3 |
| Pons (Subaru) | - | 1 | - | 1 | 1 | 2 |
| Atkinson (Subaru) | - | - | 1 | 1 | 1 | 4 |
| P.Solberg (Subaru) | - | - | - | 2 | 5 | 2 |
| Latvala (Ford) | - | - | - | 2 | 2 | 1 |

### WORLD CHAMPIONSHIP POINTS
**Drivers**
1 Grönholm 96; 2 Loeb 90; 3 Hirvonen 74; 4 Sordo 39; 5 P.Solberg 34; 6 H.Solberg 28; 7 Atkinson 26; 8 Latvala 19; 9 Duval 12; 10 Gardemeister 10 etc

**Manufacturers**
1 BP-Ford WRT 170; 2 Citroën Total WRT 131; 3 Subaru WRT 64; 4 Stobart M-Sport Ford RT 57; 5 OMV-Kronos Citroën WRT 39; 6 Munchi's Ford RT 6

**Junior Rally Championship**
1= Andersson, Aava 38; 3 Prokop 24; 4 Mölder 20; 5 Sandell 19; 6 Beres 18; 7 Burkart 16; 8 Rautenbach 15; 9 Pinomäki 8; 10= Cortinovis, Kosciuszko 6 etc

**Production Cup**
1 Arai 39; 2 Higgins 15; 3= Sohlberg, Pozzo 12; 5= M.Baldacci, McShea 11; 7= Svedlund, Villagra, Aigner, Nutahara 10 etc

### ROUTE DETAILS
Total route of 1359.96km of which 346.43km were competitive on 18 stages
**Leg 1** Friday 5 October, 6 Special Stages totalling 148.05km
**Leg 2** Saturday 6 October, 8 Special Stages totalling 119.16km
**Leg 3** Sunday 7 October, 4 Special Stages totalling 85.66km

### RESULTS
| | | | |
|---|---|---|---|
| 1 | Sébastien Loeb/ | Citroën C4 WRC | |
| | Daniel Elena | 3h22m50.5s | Gr A |
| 2 | Daniel Sordo/ | Citroën C4 WRC | |
| | Marc Martí | 3h23m04.3s | Gr A |
| 3 | Marcus Grönholm/ | Ford Focus RS WRC 07 | |
| | Timo Rautiainen | 3h23m30.3s | Gr A |
| 4 | Mikko Hirvonen/ | Ford Focus RS WRC 07 | |
| | Jarmo Lehtinen | 3h24m16.3s | Gr A |
| 5 | François Duval/ | Citroën Xsara WRC | |
| | Patrick Pivato | 3h25m19.2s | Gr A |
| 6 | Petter Solberg/ | Subaru Impreza WRC2007 | |
| | Phil Mills | 3h25m44.6s | Gr A |
| 7 | Jari-Matti Latvala/ | Ford Focus RS WRC 06 | |
| | Miikka Anttila | 3h26m28.7s | Gr A |
| 8 | Chris Atkinson/ | Subaru Impreza WRC2007 | |
| | Stéphane Prevot | 3h27m12.9s | Gr A |
| 9 | Xavier Pons/ | Subaru Impreza WRC2007 | |
| | Xavier Amigo | 3h27m54.6s | Gr A |
| 10 | Henning Solberg/ | Ford Focus RS WRC 06 | |
| | Cato Menkerud | 3h33m22.7s | Gr A |

81 starters, 66 finishers

### RECENT WINNERS
| | | |
|---|---|---|
| 1980* | Antonio Zanini/Jordi Sabater | Porsche 911SC |
| 1981* | Eugenio Ortiz/Guillermo Barreras | Renault 5 Turbo |
| 1982* | Antonio Zanini/Victor Sabater | Talbot Sunbeam Lotus |
| 1983* | Adartico Vudafieri/Tiziano Siviero | Lancia 037 Rally |
| 1984* | Salvador Servia/Jordi Sabater | Opel Manta 400 |
| 1985* | Fabrizio Tabaton/Luciano Tedeschini | Lancia 037 Rally |
| 1986* | Fabrizio Tabaton/Luciano Tedeschini | Lancia Delta S4 |
| 1987* | Dario Cerrato/Giuseppe Cerri | Lancia Delta HF 4x4 |
| 1988* | Bruno Saby/Jean-François Fauchille | Lancia Delta HF 4x4 |
| 1989* | Yves Loubet/Jean-Marc Andrié | Lancia Delta Integrale |
| 1990* | Dario Cerrato/Giuseppe Cerri | Lancia Delta Integrale 16v |
| 1991 | Armin Schwarz/Arne Hertz | Toyota Celica GT4 |
| 1992 | Carlos Sainz/Luis Moya | Toyota Celica Turbo 4wd |
| 1993 | François Delecour/Daniel Grataloup | Ford Escort RS Cosworth |
| 1994 | Enrico Bertone/Massimo Chiapponi | Toyota Celica Turbo 4wd |
| 1995 | Carlos Sainz/Luis Moya | Subaru Impreza 555 |
| 1996 | Colin McRae/Derek Ringer | Subaru Impreza 555 |
| 1997 | Tommi Mäkinen/Seppo Harjanne | Mitsubishi Lancer E4 |
| 1998 | Didier Auriol/Denis Giraudet | Toyota Corolla WRC |
| 1999 | Philippe Bugalski/Jean-Paul Chiaroni | Citroën Xsara Kit |
| 2000 | Colin McRae/Nicky Grist | Ford Focus WRC |
| 2001 | Didier Auriol/Denis Giraudet | Peugeot 206 WRC |
| 2002 | Gilles Panizzi/Hervé Panizzi | Peugeot 206 WRC |
| 2003 | Gilles Panizzi/Hervé Panizzi | Peugeot 206 WRC |
| 2004 | Markko Märtin/Michael Park | Ford Focus RS WRC04 |
| 2005 | Sébastien Loeb/Daniel Elena | Citroën Xsara WRC |
| 2006 | Sébastien Loeb/Daniel Elena | Citroën Xsara WRC |

*Non-championship event

The FIA World Rally Championship Round 13

# Tour de Corse

STANDING just north of Propriano at the start of the fourth stage of this year's Tour de Corse, there was no surprise in the body language of the two title protagonists. One was growing in confidence, fastest on every stage and building a lead; the other looking edgy, chewing nails and not loving his Friday morning. It will come as something of a surprise to learn that it was Sébastien Loeb, the man gunning for his third straight victory on the Tour de Corse, who would be needing the attention of a manicurist.

Marcus Grönholm's blistering pace out of the blocks had his rival worried. Sitting firmly in the back yard of Citroën and Loeb, Grönholm had clearly forgotten to read the script. His co-driver Timo Rautiainen had noticed Loeb's worry too.

"He looks a little concerned, hey?" muttered Rautiainen.

Unfortunately for the Finns, that was as good as it would get for them. After the cancelled first stage, a brace of scratch times and a 3.1-second lead over Loeb would be the pinnacle of their Corsican performance. From the next stage onwards, the reigning world champion – by his own admission not the fastest of fast starters – was bang on it. He stopped the rot in SS4 and hit the front straight after lunch with a corker of a time in Belvedere-Bocca Albitrina.

At the end of the rally, Grönholm said his drive had been one of his best on asphalt. Onlookers would be left pondering quite when he has bettered himself. This was an awesome effort from 'Bosse'. He knew he had to do something special, so he tightened his belts and launched the Focus down the rally of 10,000 corners. The mighty, mighty moment he had five miles into the first stage was testament to how hard he was trying.

That effort might not have been enough to conquer Loeb, but it was enough to lift him clear of Dani Sordo's second Citroën. Only time would tell how important those extra two points would be to Grönholm's end of season tally.

Loeb's performance was, once again, inch-perfect as he collected his second WRC win in as many weeks, narrowing the gap to Grönholm to just four points as the series turned its back on Mediterranean asphalt in favour of oriental gravel.

Sordo's chances of repeating the clean-sweep Citroën so desired were hobbled by his failure to find a comfortable set-up in the C4 on the Corsican lanes. Eventually, a gearbox change on the second day solved the problem. After that, he was on the pace of the two ahead, but unwilling to risk all in an effort to make a big dent in the half-minute gap to Grönholm.

As had been expected, Citroën did make major inroads into Ford's lead in the manufacturers' race. Mikko Hirvonen crashed the second Focus RS WRC on the first morning, ripping the left-rear wheel off the car and almost losing it to fire after brake fluid poured onto the red-hot exhaust. In the end, he saved the car, but could do nothing about the points his mistake had cost Ford.

Citroën team principal Guy Fréquelin laughed off suggestions that he might celebrate a fourth makes' title in five years. Despite Citroën taking 14 points out of Ford in the last two rallies, Fréquelin was wary of the 32 points that still split the two.

"Sure, I can think about [the title]", he said. "But it's just a dream…"

**Main:** Loeb was inch-perfect on the rally of 10,000 corners to further narrow the gap to Grönholm in the title chase

**Inset top:** 'Bosse' was on maximum attack in a damage-limitation exercise. Second place was his reward

**Inset bottom:** Such was Grönholm's pace at the start he had Loeb rattled, but the Citroën ace soon fought back

All photographs by McKlein

**Above:** The Suzuki SX4 made its first WRC appearance in the hands of Nicholas Bernardi. He posted one top-10 time before mechanical gremlins relegated the car to 31st overall

**Opposite top:** Sordo struggled with set-up issues but found more pace after a gearbox change. By then the best he could do was third

**Opposite middle:** A rare off for Hirvonen this year came at the worst possible time, allowing Citroën to make further inroads into Ford's manufacturers' lead

**Opposite bottom:** Another rare sight in '07 has been a smiling Petter Solberg, but Subaru scored well in Corsica with the Norwegian on top in fifth

**Right:** Things must have been going well at Citroën if some of the crew found time for fishing...

All photographs by McKlein unless specified

Suzuki team-mates Urmo Aava (left) and P-G Andersson waged war over the Junior Rally Championship in Corsica. Andersson took the title for a second time after Aava crashed out
McKlein

# The FIA World Rally Championship Round 13
# Tour de Corse Results
### October 12-14 2007

## FINISH LINES...

This event was a memorable one for Suzuki for two reasons. The first was the launch of the Sx4 WRC. Driven by Nicolas Bernardi, the car collected one top 10-time on its way to 31st overall. That position was not helped by the fact that the car had been forced to run under SupeRally rules on two of the three legs. An overheating problem had struck on Friday, while a blocked injector spoilt Saturday's run... The second highlight for Suzuki was Sweden's Per-Gunnar Andersson becoming the first champion of the season when he collected a second Junior Rally Championship. Suzuki drivers Andersson and Urmo Aava had arrived in Ajaccio level on points in a classic winner-takes-all situation. After setting a solid pace to lead through the first day, Aava slid off the road and out of the event on Saturday's second stage. Andersson also went off a kilometre up the road, but escaped with a puncture before going on to clinch the title... There was more cheer from the other Japanese manufacturer in the series beginning with S, as Subaru placed three factory Imprezas in points-paying positions for the first time this season, with Petter Solberg fifth, Chris Atkinson sixth and Xevi Pons eighth. Unfortunately for Subaru, Solberg just missed out on fourth after a fascinating fight with Stobart Ford driver Jari-Matti Latvala. Latvala, like the Ford-driving Finn two places up on him, turned in a wicked drive to eclipse his nightmare crash here in 2006.

## RUNNING ORDER

| | | |
|---|---|---|
| 3 | Marcus Grönholm/ | Ford Focus RS WRC 07 |
| | Timo Rautiainen | Gr A |
| 1 | Sébastien Loeb/ | Citroën C4 WRC |
| | Daniel Elena | Gr A |
| 4 | Mikko Hirvonen/ | Ford Focus RS WRC 07 |
| | Jarmo Lehtinen | Gr A |
| 2 | Daniel Sordo/ | Citroën C4 WRC |
| | Marc Martí | Gr A |
| 7 | Petter Solberg/ | Subaru Impreza WRC2007 |
| | Phil Mills | Gr A |
| 10 | Henning Solberg/ | Ford Focus RS WRC 06 |
| | Cato Menkerud | Gr A |
| 8 | Chris Atkinson/ | Subaru Impreza WRC2007 |
| | Stéphane Prevot | Gr A |
| 9 | Jari-Matti Latvala/ | Ford Focus RS WRC 06 |
| | Miikka Anttila | Gr A |
| 6 | François Duval/ | Citroën Xsara WRC |
| | Patrick Pivato | Gr A |
| 5 | Manfred Stohl/ | Citroën Xsara WRC |
| | Ilka Minor | Gr A |
| 15 | Jan Kopecky/ | Skoda Fabia WRC |
| | Filip Schovanek | Gr A |
| 17 | Xavier Pons/ | Subaru Impreza WRC2007 |
| | Xavier Amigo | Gr A |
| 14 | Matthew Wilson/ | Ford Focus RS WRC 06 |
| | Michael Orr | Gr A |
| 18 | Alessandro Bettega/ | Ford Focus RS WRC 06 |
| | Simone Scattolin | Gr A |
| 19 | Nicolas Bernardi/ | Suzuki SX4 WRC |
| | Jean-Marc Fortin | Gr A |
| 20 | Andreas Mikkelsen/ | Ford Focus RS WRC 04 |
| | Ola Floene | Gr A |
| 32 | Urmo Aava/ | Suzuki Swift |
| | Kuldar Sikk | Gr A |
| 35 | Martin Prokop/ | Citroën C2 |
| | Jan Tomanek | Gr A |
| 45 | P-G Andersson/ | Suzuki Swift |
| | Jonas Andersson | Gr A |

## SPECIAL STAGE TIMES

**SS1 Monti Rossu – Pila C 1 (18.10km)**
Cancelled due to spectator congestion

**SS2 Belvedere – Bocca Al 1 (16.62km)**
1 M.Grönholm/T.Rautiainen (Ford Focus RS WRC 07) 9m14.8s; 2 D.Sordo/M.Martí (Citroën C4 WRC) 9m17.6s; 3 S.Loeb/D.Elena (Citroën C4 WRC) 9m17.9s; 4 M.Hirvonen/J.Lehtinen (Ford Focus RS WRC 07) 9m18.7s; 5 F.Duval/P.Pivato (Citroën Xsara WRC) 9m23.1s; 6 C.Atkinson/S.Prevot (Subaru Impreza WRC2007) 9m23.8s; JRC M.Prokop/J.Tomanek (Citroën C2) 10m18.0s

**SS3 Arbellara - Aullene 1 (27.42km)**
1 Grönholm/Rautiainen (Ford) 15m34.6s; 2 Sordo/Martí (Citroën) 15m34.7s; 3 Loeb/Elena (Citroën) 15m35.6s; 4 P.Solberg/P.Mills (Subaru Impreza WRC2007) 15m49.8s; 5 Duval/Pivato (Citroën) 15m53.2s; 6 Atkinson/Prevot (Subaru) 15m55.1s; JRC U.Aava/K.Sikk (Suzuki Swift) 17m13.2s

**SS4 Monti Rossu – Pila C 2 (18.10km)**
1 Loeb/Elena (Citroën) 9m59.0s; 2 Grönholm/Rautiainen (Ford) 10m00.1s; 3 Sordo/Martí (Citroën) 10m03.5s; 4 J-M.Latvala/M.Anttila (Ford Focus RS WRC 06) 10m06.5s; 5 Solberg/Mills (Subaru) 10m07.4s; 6 Duval/Pivato (Citroën) 10m08.0s; JRC Prokop/Tomanek (Citroën) 11m05.9s

**SS5 Belvedere – Bocca Al 2 (16.62km)**
1 Loeb/Elena (Citroën) 9m12.1s; 2 Grönholm/Rautiainen (Ford) 9m15.2s; 3 Sordo/Martí (Citroën) 9m18.4s; 4 Latvala/Anttila (Ford) 9m22.0s; 5 Duval/Pivato (Citroën) 9m23.0s; 6 Atkinson/Prevot (Subaru) 9m23.2s; JRC Aava/Sikk (Suzuki) 10m17.4s

**SS6 Arbellara - Aullene 2 (27.42km)**
1 Loeb/Elena (Citroën) 15m25.1s; 2 Grönholm/Rautiainen (Ford) 15m29.8s; 3 Sordo/Martí (Citroën) 15m34.0s; 4 Duval/Pivato (Citroën) 15m40.2s; 5 Solberg/Mills (Subaru) 15m42.2s; 6 Latvala/Anttila (Ford) 15m44.8s; JRC Y.Bonato/B.Boulloud (Citroën C2) 17m02.6s

**SS7 Carbuccia - Scalella 1 (21.87km)**
1 Loeb/Elena (Citroën) 14m15.1s; 2 Grönholm/Rautiainen (Ford) 14m17.8s; 3 Duval/Pivato (Citroën) 14m19.5s; 4 Sordo/Martí (Citroën) 14m21.3s; 5 Solberg/Mills (Subaru) 14m31.4s; 6 X.Pons/X.Amigo (Subaru Impreza WRC2007) 14m32.2s; JRC Bonato/Boulloud (Citroën) 15m48.8s

**SS8 Calcatoggia - Plage du Liamone 1 (26.54km)**
1 Loeb/Elena (Citroën) 17m47.3s; 2 Grönholm/Rautiainen (Ford) 17m51.1s; 3 Sordo/Martí (Citroën) 18m00.6s; 4 Duval/Pivato (Citroën) 18m02.9s; 5 Latvala/Anttila (Ford) 18m03.4s; 6 Atkinson/Prevot (Subaru) 18m10.3s; JRC Bonato/Boulloud (Citroën) 19m31.7s

**SS9 Vico - Col St Roch 1 (13.30km)**
1 Loeb/Elena (Citroën) 8m39.6s; 2 Grönholm/Rautiainen (Ford) 8m40.9s; 3 Atkinson/Prevot (Subaru) 8m45.6s; 4 Duval/Pivato (Citroën) 8m48.9s; 5 Solberg/Mills (Subaru) 8m49.1s; 6 Sordo/Martí (Citroën) 8m49.6s; JRC Bonato/Boulloud (Citroën) 9m32.3s

**SS10 Carbuccia - Scalella 2 (21.87km)**
1 Sordo/Martí (Citroën) 14m19.7s; 2 Loeb/Elena (Citroën) 14m20.0s; 3 Grönholm/Rautiainen (Ford) 14m24.4s; 4 Duval/Pivato (Citroën) 14m25.3s; 5 Latvala/Anttila (Ford) 14m28.5s; 6 Atkinson/Prevot (Subaru) 14m32.2s; JRC Bonato/Boulloud (Citroën) 15m59.3s

**SS11 Calcatoggia - Plage du Liamone 2 (26.54km)**
1 Loeb/Elena (Citroën) 17m48.3s; 2 Grönholm/Rautiainen (Ford) 17m53.4s; 3 Sordo/Martí (Citroën) 17m55.0s; 4 Latvala/Anttila (Ford) 18m01.4s; 5 Solberg/Mills (Subaru) 18m03.1s; 6 Hirvonen/Lehtinen (Ford) 18m04.6s; JRC Bonato/Boulloud (Citroën) 19m33.2s

**SS12 Vico - Col St Roch 2 (13.30km)**
1 Loeb/Elena (Citroën) 8m38.6s; 2 Grönholm/Rautiainen (Ford) 8m44.0s; 3 Solberg/Mills (Subaru) 8m44.4s; 4 Atkinson/Prevot (Subaru) 8m44.6s; 5 Sordo/Martí (Citroën) 8m44.8s; 6 Latvala/Anttila (Ford) 8m46.9s; JRC Bonato/Boulloud (Citroën) 9m35.1s

**SS13 Penitencier - Pietra Rossa 1 (24.23km)**
1 Loeb/Elena (Citroën) 14m38.7s; 2 Grönholm/Rautiainen (Ford) 14m39.1s; 3 Hirvonen/Lehtinen (Ford) 14m43.2s; 4

# TOUR DE CORSE

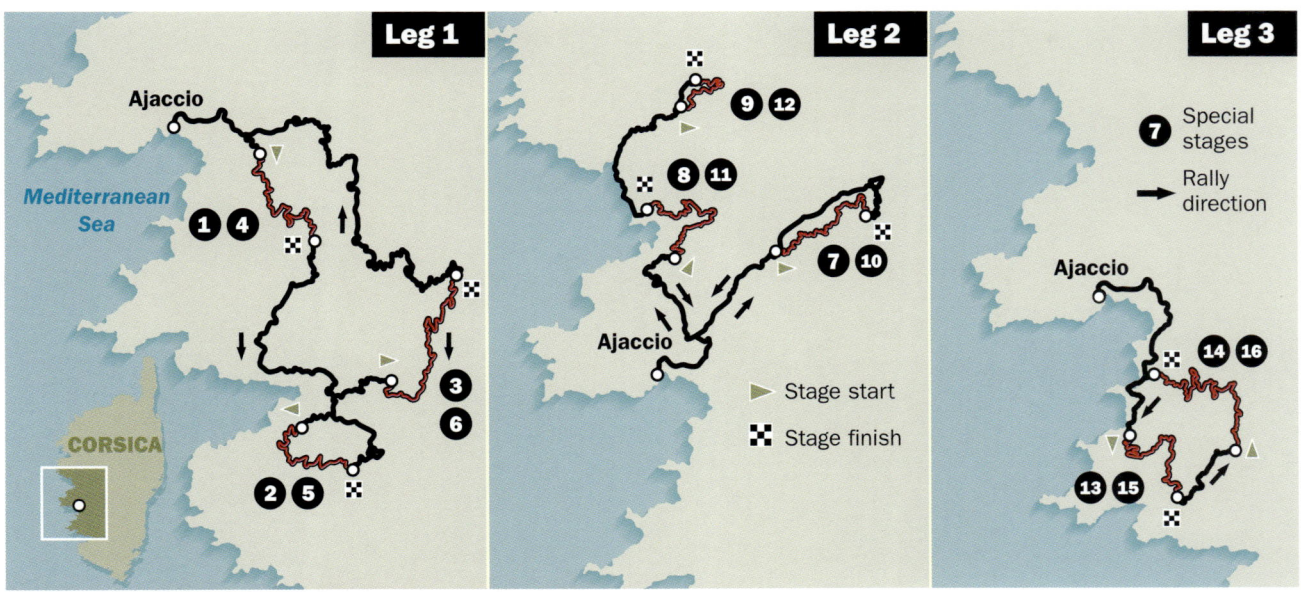

| Position | Stage Numbers | 2 | 3 | 4 | 5 | 6 | 7 | 8 | 9 | 10 | 11 | 12 | 13 | 14 | 15 | 16 |
|---|---|---|---|---|---|---|---|---|---|---|---|---|---|---|---|---|
| | Loeb | 3 | 2 | 2 | 1 | 1 | 1 | 1 | 1 | 1 | 1 | 1 | 1 | 1 | 1 | 1 |
| | Grönholm | 1 | 1 | 1 | 2 | 2 | 2 | 2 | 2 | 2 | 2 | 2 | 2 | 2 | 2 | 2 |
| | Sordo | 2 | 3 | 3 | 3 | 3 | 3 | 3 | 3 | 3 | 3 | 3 | 3 | 3 | 3 | 3 |
| | Latvala | 7 | 7 | 6 | 6 | 6 | 6 | 5 | 5 | 5 | 5 | 5 | 5 | 4 | 4 | 4 |
| | P.Solberg | 8 | 5 | 5 | 5 | 5 | 5 | 6 | 6 | 6 | 6 | 6 | 6 | 5 | 5 | 5 |
| | Atkinson | 6 | 6 | 7 | 7 | 7 | 7 | 7 | 7 | 7 | 7 | 7 | 7 | 6 | 6 | 6 |
| | Kopecky | 11 | 8 | 10 | 9 | 9 | 9 | 9 | 9 | 9 | 9 | 9 | 9 | 7 | 7 | 7 |
| | Pons | 9 | 8 | 8 | 8 | 8 | 8 | 8 | 8 | 8 | 8 | 8 | 8 | 8 | 8 | 8 |
| | H.Solberg | 12 | 13 | 12 | 10 | 10 | 11 | 10 | 10 | 10 | 10 | 9 | 9 | 9 | 9 | 9 |
| | Solá | 18 | 16 | 15 | 14 | 14 | 14 | 14 | 14 | 13 | 13 | 11 | 11 | 10 | 10 | 10 |
| | Bettega | 10 | 10 | 9 | 32 | 49 | 40 | 30 | 29 | 23 | 18 | 16 | 13 | 13 | 11 | 11 |
| | Hirvonen | 4 | 52 | 65 | 57 | 64 | 62 | 52 | 48 | 43 | 36 | 32 | 23 | 21 | 17 | 13 |
| | Stohl | 16 | 14 | 13 | 12 | 12 | 10 | 11 | 11 | 11 | 27 | 25 | 20 | 18 | 15 | 14 |
| | Bernardi | 15 | 12 | 31 | 56 | 61 | 49 | 46 | 42 | 36 | 43 | 46 | 40 | 37 | 33 | 31 |
| | Wilson | 14 | 15 | 14 | 13 | 13 | 13 | 13 | 13 | 13 | 12 | 12 | 10 | 10 | R | |
| | Duval | 5 | 4 | 4 | 4 | 4 | 4 | 4 | 4 | 4 | R | | | | | |

Solberg/Mills (Subaru) 14m44.9s; 5= Sordo/Martí (Citroën), Latvala/Anttila (Ford) 14m45.5s; JRC Bonato/Boulloud (Citroën) 16m21.8s

**SS14 Pont de Calzola 1 (31.80km)**
1 Sordo/Martí (Citroën) 18m54.6s; 2 Grönholm/Rautiainen (Ford) 18m57.0s; 3 Loeb/Elena (Citroën) 18m57.9s; 4 Latvala/Anttila (Ford) 19m04.0s; 5 Solberg/Mills (Subaru) 19m04.4s; 6 Hirvonen/Lehtinen (Ford) 19m08.4s; JRC Bonato/Boulloud (Citroën) 20m46.4s

**SS15 Penitencier - Pietra Rossa 2 (24.23km)**
1 Sordo/Martí (Citroën) 14m40.5s; 2 Hirvonen/Lehtinen (Ford) 14m42.1s; 3 Solberg/Mills (Subaru) 14m47.6s; 4 Loeb/Elena (Citroën) 14m49.1s; 5 Grönholm/Rautiainen (Ford) 14m49.4s; 6 Latvala/Anttila (Ford) 14m50.5s; JRC P-G.Andersson/J.Andersson (Suzuki Swift) 16m27.0s

**SS16 Pont de Calzola 2 (31.80km)**
1 Sordo/Martí (Citroën) 18m56.0s; 2 Hirvonen/Lehtinen (Ford) 18m58.3s; 3 Latvala/Anttila (Ford) 18m59.5s; 4 Grönholm/Rautiainen (Ford) 19m03.6s; 5= Loeb/Elena (Citroën), Solberg/Mills (Subaru) 19m07.2s; JRC A.Burkart/M.Koelbach (Citroën C2) 20m56.2s

Cars who retired and subsequently re-started and were classified under SuperRally regs:
| 4 | Hirvonen/Lehtinen | Ford Focus RS WRC 07 | | |
| | Accident | SS3 | Gr A |
| 18 | Bettega/Scattolin | Ford Focus RS WRC 06 | | |
| | Accident | SS5 | Gr A |
| 19 | Bernardi/Fortin | Suzuki SX4 WRC | | |
| | Hydraulics | SS5 | | |
| 19 | Bernardi/Fortin | Suzuki SX4 WRC | | |
| | Engine | SS11 | Gr A |

**MAJOR RETIREMENTS**
| 6 | Duval/Pivato | Citroën Xsara WRC | |
| | Alternator | SS12 | Gr A |
| 16 | Wilson/Orr | Ford Focus RS WRC 06 | |
| | Transmission | SS15 | Gr A |
| 20 | Mikkelsen/Floene | Ford Focus RS WRC 04 | |
| | Excluded | SS12 | Gr A |
| 32 | Aava/Sikk | Suzuki Swift | |
| | Accident | SS8 | Gr A |

**FIA CLASS WINNERS**
| A8 | Over 2000 cc | Loeb/Elena |
| | | Citroën C4 WRC |
| A7 | 1600-2000cc | Augoyard/Panseri |
| | | Renault Clio R3 |
| A6 | 1600-2000cc | Amourette/Marie |
| | | Citroën C2 |
| N4 | Over 2000cc | Solá/Del Barrio |
| | | Peugeot 207 S2000 |
| N3 | 1600-2000cc | Muselli/Follaci |
| | | Renault Clio RS |
| N1 | Upto 1400cc | Fabiani/Valli |
| | | Skoda Fabia 1.4L |

**RALLY LEADERS**
Overall: SS2-4 Grönholm; SS5-16 Loeb
(SS1 Cancelled)
JRC: SS2-4 Prokop; SS5-7 Aava; SS8-16 Prokop

## SPECIAL STAGE ANALYSIS

| | 1st | 2nd | 3rd | 4th | 5th | 6th |
|---|---|---|---|---|---|---|
| Loeb (Citroën) | 9 | 1 | 3 | 1 | 1 | - |
| Sordo (Citroën) | 4 | 2 | 5 | 1 | 2 | 1 |
| Grönholm (Ford) | 2 | 10 | 1 | 1 | 1 | - |
| Hirvonen (Ford) | - | 2 | 1 | 1 | - | 2 |
| P.Solberg (Subaru) | - | - | 2 | 2 | 7 | - |
| Latvala (Ford) | - | - | 1 | 4 | 3 | 3 |
| Duval (Citroën) | - | - | 1 | 4 | 3 | 1 |
| Atkinson (Subaru) | - | - | 1 | - | 1 | 5 |
| Pons (Subaru) | - | - | - | - | - | 1 |

## WORLD CHAMPIONSHIP POINTS

**Drivers**
1 Grönholm 104; 2 Loeb 100; 3 Hirvonen 74; 4 Sordo 45; 5 P.Solberg 38; 6 Atkinson 29; 7 H.Solberg 28; 8 Latvala 24; 9 Duval 12; 10= Gardemeister, Kopecky 10 etc

**Manufacturers**
1 BP-Ford WRT 179; 2 Citroën Total WRT 147; 3 Subaru WRT 71; 4 Stobart M-Sport Ford RT 64; 5 OMV-Kronos Citroën WRT 39; 6 Munchi's Ford RT 6

**Junior Rally Championship**
1 Andersson 43; 2 Aava 38; 3 Prokop 34; 4 Beres 26; 5 Mölder 20; 6 Sandell 19; 7 Burkart 18; 8 Rautenbach 16; 9 Bonato 12; 10 Cortinovis 9 etc

**Production Cup**
1 Arai 39; 2 Higgins 15; 3= Sohlberg, Pozzo 12; 5= M.Baldacci, McShea 11; 7= Svedlund, Villagra, Aigner, Nutahara 10 etc

## ROUTE DETAILS
Total route of 1045.68km of which 359.32km were competitive on 16 stages
**Leg 1** Friday 12 October, 6 Special Stages totalling 124.28km
**Leg 2** Saturday 13 October, 6 Special Stages totalling 122.94km
**Leg 3** Sunday 14 October, 4 Special Stages totalling 112.10km

## RESULTS

| 1 | Sébastien Loeb/ | Citroën C4 WRC | |
| | Daniel Elena | 3h28m31.5s | Gr A |
| 2 | Marcus Grönholm/ | Ford Focus RS WRC 07 | |
| | Timo Rautiainen | 3h28m55.2s | Gr A |
| 3 | Daniel Sordo/ | Citroën C4 WRC | |
| | Marc Martí | 3h29m15.8s | Gr A |
| 4 | Jari-Matti Latvala/ | Ford Focus RS WRC 06 | |
| | Miikka Anttila | 3h31m02.0s | Gr A |
| 5 | Petter Solberg/ | Subaru Impreza WRC2007 | |
| | Phil Mills | 3h31m13.6s | Gr A |
| 6 | Chris Atkinson/ | Subaru Impreza WRC2007 | |
| | Stéphane Prevot | 3h32m25.3s | Gr A |
| 7 | Jan Kopecky/ | Skoda Fabia WRC | |
| | Filip Schovanek | 3h36m34.4s | Gr A |
| 8 | Xavier Pons/ | Subaru Impreza WRC2007 | |
| | Xavier Amigo | 3h38m05.7s | Gr A |
| 9 | Henning Solberg/ | Ford Focus RS WRC 06 | |
| | Cato Menkerud | 3h38m43.7s | Gr A |
| 10 | Dani Solá/ | Peugeot 207 S2000 | |
| | Carlos Del Barrio | 3h46m29.1s | Gr A |

74 starters, 60 finishers

## RECENT WINNERS

| 1970 | Bernard Darniche/Guy Demange | Alpine Renault A110 |
| 1972 | Jean-Claude Andruet/'Biche' | Alpine Renault A110 |
| 1973 | Jean-Pierre Nicolas/Michel Vial | Alpine Renault A110 |
| 1974 | Jean-Claude Andruet/'Biche' | Lancia Stratos |
| 1975 | Bernard Darniche/Alain Mahé | Lancia Stratos |
| 1976 | Sandro Munari/Silvio Maiga | Lancia Stratos |
| 1977 | Bernard Darniche/Alain Mahé | Fiat Abarth 131 |
| 1978 | Bernard Darniche/Alain Mahé | Fiat Abarth 131 |
| 1979 | Bernard Darniche/Alain Mahé | Lancia Stratos |
| 1980 | Jean-Luc Thérier/Michel Vial | Porsche 911SC |
| 1981 | Bernard Darniche/Alain Mahé | Lancia Stratos |
| 1982 | Jean Ragnotti/Jean-Marc Andrié | Renault 5 Turbo |
| 1983 | Markku Alén/Ilkka Kivimäki | Lancia 037 Rally |
| 1984 | Markku Alén/Ilkka Kivimäki | Lancia 037 Rally |
| 1985 | Jean Ragnotti/Jean-Marc Andrié | Renault 5 Maxi Turbo |
| 1986 | Bruno Saby/Jean-François Fauchille | Peugeot 205 Turbo 16 E2 |
| 1987 | Bernard Béguin/Jean-Jacques Lenne | BMW M3 |
| 1988 | Didier Auriol/Bernard Occelli | Ford Sierra RS Cosworth |
| 1989 | Didier Auriol/Bernard Occelli | Lancia Delta Integrale |
| 1990 | Didier Auriol/Bernard Occelli | Lancia Delta Integrale 16v |
| 1991 | Carlos Sainz/Luis Moya | Toyota Celica GT4 |
| 1992 | Didier Auriol/Bernard Occelli | Lancia Delta HF Integrale |
| 1993 | François Delecour/Daniel Grataloup | Ford Escort RS Cosworth |
| 1994 | Didier Auriol/Bernard Occelli | Toyota Celica Turbo 4wd |
| 1995 | Didier Auriol/Denis Giraudet | Toyota Celica GT-Four |
| 1996 | Philippe Bugalski/Jean-Paul Chiaroni | Renault Maxi Mégane |
| 1997 | Colin McRae/Nicky Grist | Subaru Impreza WRC97 |
| 1998 | Colin McRae/Nicky Grist | Subaru Impreza WRC98 |
| 1999 | Philippe Bugalski/Jean-Paul Chiaroni | Citroën Xsara Kit |
| 2000 | Gilles Panizzi/Hervé Panizzi | Peugeot 206 WRC |
| 2001 | Jesús Puras/Marc Martí | Citroën Xsara WRC |
| 2002 | Gilles Panizzi/Hervé Panizzi | Peugeot 206 WRC |
| 2003 | Petter Solberg/Phil Mills | Subaru Impreza WRC2003 |
| 2004 | Markko Märtin/Michael Park | Ford Focus RS WRC04 |
| 2005 | Sébastien Loeb/Daniel Elena | Citroën Xsara WRC |
| 2006 | Sébastien Loeb/Daniel Elena | Citroën Xsara WRC |

The FIA World Rally Championship Round 14
# Rally Japan

*Opposite:* An on-form Hirvonen put his Corsican retirement behind him, to score his third WRC victory in Japan

*Above:* After Grönholm crashed out Hirvonen was fired up and ready to take on Loeb – until he retired too. From then on the Finn focused on finishing

*Top right:* Loeb was dismayed when an incorrect pace note from co-driver Daniel Elena ended his rally. He'd been poised to take over the championship lead

*Bottom right:* Stobart VK driver Henning Solberg made the final step of the podium on his first visit to Rally Japan

All photographs by McKlein unless specified

FRIDAY lunchtime at Kita Aikoku and Sébastien Loeb is smiling. He's trying not to, but he can't really help it. Given that the first part of the conversation was dedicated to Loeb explaining how ill at ease he felt with his C4 WRC, his cheerful demeanour might have appeared strange. That was until you discovered the man who stood between him and four straight world titles was going no further on Rally Japan. Marcus Grönholm had dropped his Ford Focus RS WRC07 on a spectator stage in Rikubetsu.

Fast-forward 24 hours and Loeb's face couldn't have been more different. He looked stricken, aghast even. He'd just watched his C4 get towed out of a ditch he'd parked it in after attempting a fourth-gear right-hander a ratio higher. Rather unsurprisingly, this rallying equivalent of circle into square didn't go. And a near-certain eight, possibly 10 points and a championship lead had gone begging. It was quite possible that Loeb's co-driver Daniel Elena was doing just those sums when he should have been saying the words "minus, minus" at the end of his call. Inexplicably, they came out "plus, plus".

"I gave him the wrong note," said the inconsolable Elena on Saturday night. "First time in 10 years…" There was no more to say on the issue. Not that Elena was overly keen on dissecting the incident further.

After a heavy night on the sake, Grönholm had been taking a late breakfast when his co-driver Timo Rautiainen called with the news. Having arrived in Japan four points to the good, the Finn had almost come to terms with the fact that he would possibly be heading home six down. But the good news was just that. Being a world champion, with world champion levels of competitiveness, it wasn't quite good enough. Grönholm was now kicking himself again.

"Okay," he said. "It's good. But if I hadn't gone off, it could have been very, very good."

He was right. A 14-point lead with only 20 on offer from the final two rounds of the season would have been something to get really excited about.

The good news for Ford was that Grönholm's team-mate Mikko Hirvonen did the perfect job, once again. Fired up and absolutely ready to take Loeb head on, Hirvonen almost seemed disappointed when the Frenchman failed to turn up to the scrap. Equally, Hirvonen realised Loeb's misfortune was good news for the title he so badly desired for his mentor. Not having to go flat-out also avoided a weekend of tricky meetings with team principal Malcolm Wilson, who never stopped pointing out that he wanted to see Hirvonen at the finish for manufacturer points.

This year's Rally Japan was one for the number twos, as Loeb's wingman Dani Sordo placed the sister C4 to Loeb's in second. With the gap approaching the minute mark, Citroën realised there was little point in sending the Spaniard out to chase his first win, instead preferring to test suspension parts for Rally GB. Japan's shift two months back in the calendar meant cooler conditions and heavy rain on Friday night, and the likes of the Puray and Penke stages were doing a passable impression of Rheola or Trawscoed.

日本
SUBARU
We WRC
We WRC
NAVY

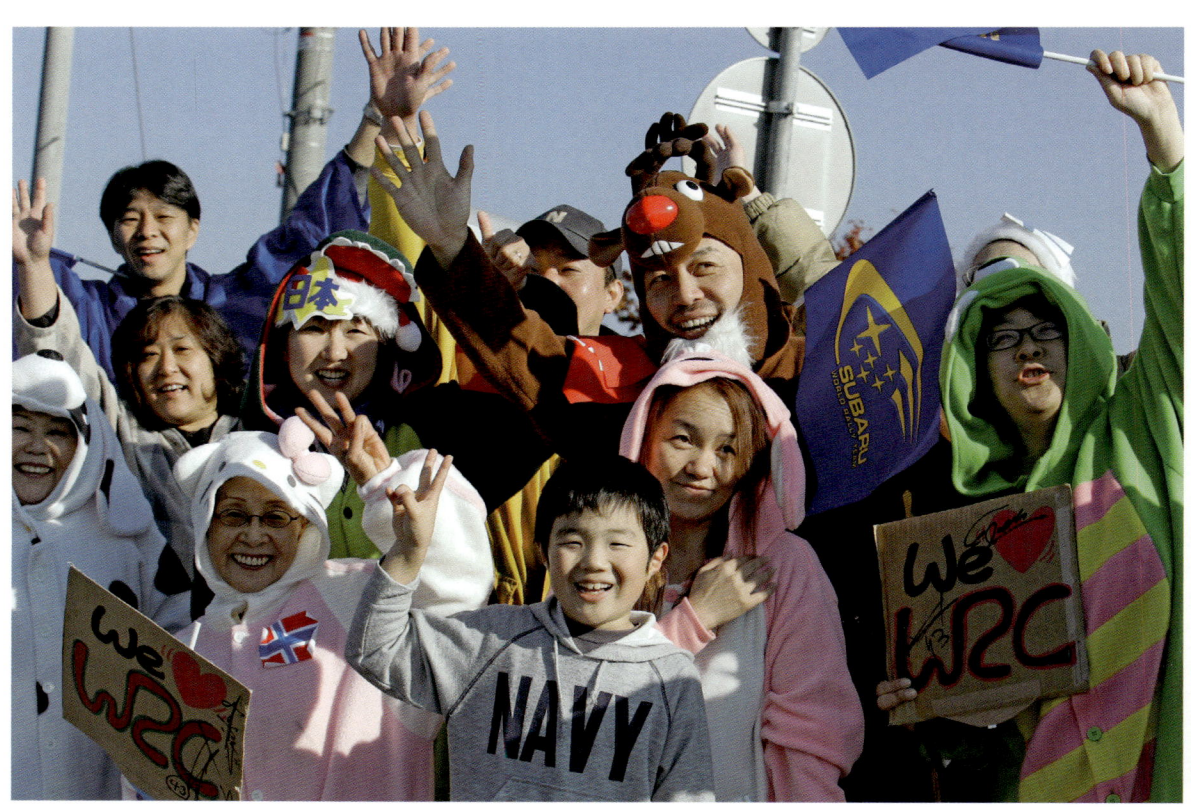

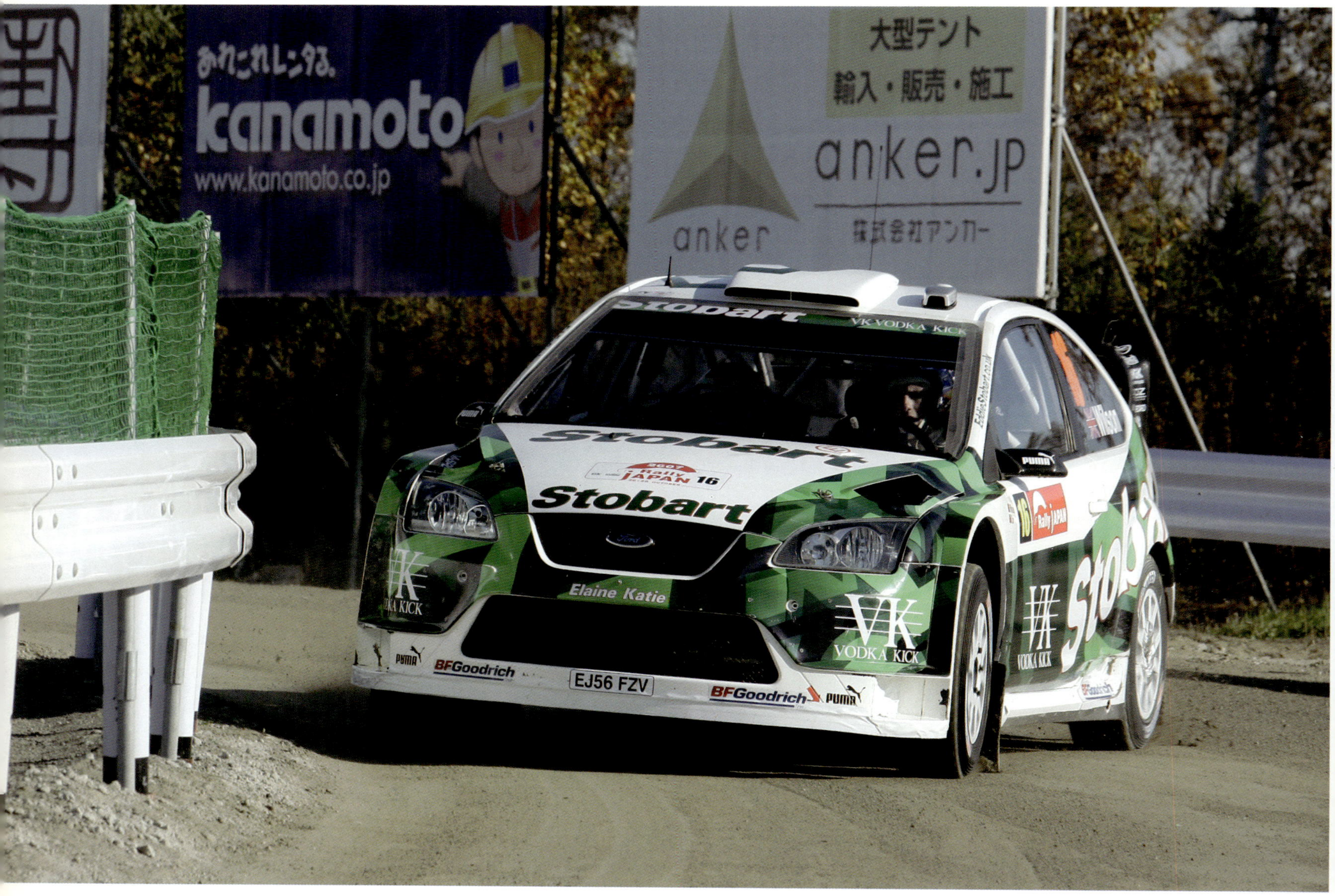
kanamoto
www.kanamoto.co.jp
大型テント
輸入・販売・施工
anker.jp
anker
株式会社アンカー
Stobart
VK VODKA KICK
Stobart
Stobart
Elaine Katie
VK VODKA KICK
BFGoodrich
EJ56 FZV
BFGoodrich
PUMA

Left: Grönholm had been looking down the barrel of a six-point deficit to Loeb after binning his Ford on a spectator stage on day one

Below: Like Hirvonen, Sordo took up the fight after his team leader retired. He and co-driver Marc Marti (left) celebrated with second

Opposite bottom: Young Brit Matthew Wilson turned in a composed drive in his Stobart VK Ford to score his best WRC finish to date in fourth

Opposite top: The Japanese fans are crazy for Subaru and Petter Solberg, but the Norwegian's rally was ruined by gearbox problems

All photographs by McKlein unless specified

Gabriele Pozzo kept himself in the fight for Production honours with a class win, as did fifth-placed Brit Mark Higgins
McKlein

## The FIA World Rally Championship Round 14
# Rally Japan Results
### October 26-28 2007

### FINISH LINES...

The Stobart VK Ford team had much to celebrate in Japan. Not only did Henning Solberg clinch the final podium position on his first trip to the Orient, but Matthew Wilson also turned in the drive of his 20-year-old life to edge Munchi's Ford man Luis Pérez Companc out of fourth. Wilson demonstrated composure and pace in equal measure to hunt down his rival through the final day, eventually clinching the place by 2.5 seconds... As the only Japanese manufacturer contesting the full World Rally Championship, Subaru was desperately hoping for a strong showing in front of its home crowd. It didn't come. In fact, it's hard to imagine a worse showing for the team. Chris Atkinson was third on the first stage, but then crashed his Impreza heavily in SS6. The fans' favourite Petter Solberg was halted by a gearbox fault that left him with only top gear. That the Norwegian returned under SuperRally to set a bunch of fastest times through the weekend meant little; the top two were out and everybody else was driving for a finish. In short, it was too little too late. To compile Subaru's agony, Xevi Pons put the third Impreza WRC2007 off the road as well... Mitsubishi men Gabriel Pozzo and Mark Higgins made the most of a Toshi Arai (Subaru) mistake to keep themselves in the fight for this year's Production Car title... Local Mitsubishi driver Katsu Taguchi, taking his first class win at WRC level, won the overall Group N category. The fact that he was eighth overall to score the final WRC point was even more reason for celebration.

### RUNNING ORDER

| | | |
|---|---|---|
| 3 | Marcus Grönholm/ Timo Rautiainen | Ford Focus RS WRC 07 Gr A |
| 1 | Sébastien Loeb/ Daniel Elena | Citroën C4 WRC Gr A |
| 4 | Mikko Hirvonen/ Jarmo Lehtinen | Ford Focus RS WRC 07 Gr A |
| 2 | Daniel Sordo/ Marc Martí | Citroën C4 WRC Gr A |
| 7 | Petter Solberg/ Phil Mills | Subaru Impreza WRC2007 Gr A |
| 8 | Chris Atkinson/ Stéphane Prevot | Subaru Impreza WRC2007 Gr A |
| 10 | Henning Solberg/ Cato Menkerud | Ford Focus RS WRC 06 Gr A |
| 9 | Jari-Matti Latvala/ Miikka Anttila | Ford Focus RS WRC 06 Gr A |
| 5 | Manfred Stohl/ Ilka Minor | Citroën Xsara WRC Gr A |
| 17 | Xavier Pons/ Xavier Amigo | Subaru Impreza WRC2007 Gr A |
| 16 | Matthew Wilson/ Michael Orr | Ford Focus RS WRC 06 Gr A |
| 11 | Luis Pérez-Companc/ Jose Maria Volta | Ford Focus RS WRC 06 Gr A |
| 12 | Federico Villagra/ Jose Luis Díaz | Ford Focus RS WRC 06 Gr A |
| 31 | Toshihiro Arai/ Tony Sircombe | Subaru Impreza WRX Sti Gr N |
| 34 | Mark Higgins/ Scott Martin | Mitsubishi Lancer Evo 9 Gr N |
| 54 | Gabriel Pozzo/ Daniel Stillo | Mitsubishi Lancer Evo 9 Gr N |
| 35 | Fumio Nutahara/ Daniel Barritt | Mitsubishi Lancer Evo 9 Gr N |
| 36 | Juha Hänninen/ Mikko Markkula | Mitsubishi Lancer Evo 9 Gr N |
| 46 | Armindo Arturo/ Miguel Ramalho | Mitsubishi Lancer Evo 9 Gr N |
| 50 | Patrik Flodin/ Maria Andersson | Subaru Impreza WRX Sti Gr N |
| 52 | Takuma Kamada/ Naoki Kase | Subaru Impreza WRX Sti Gr N |

### SPECIAL STAGE TIMES

**SS1 Pawse Kamuy Reverse 1 (9.20km)**
1 J-M.Latvala/M.Anttila (Ford Focus RS WRC 06) 4m48.9s; 2 S.Loeb/D.Elena (Citroën C4 WRC) 4m49.3s; 3 C.Atkinson/S.Prevot (Subaru Impreza WRC2007) 4m49.5s; 4 M.Hirvonen/J.Lehtinen (Ford Focus RS WRC 07) 4m50.2s; 5 M.Grönholm/T.Rautiainen (Ford Focus RS WRC 07) 4m50.8s; 6 P.Solberg/P.Mills (Subaru Impreza WRC2007) 4m51.7s; PC P.Flodin/M.Andersson (Subaru Impreza WRX Sti) 5m10.8s

**SS2 Cup Kamuy 1 (13.94km)**
1 Grönholm/Rautiainen (Ford) 8m29.7s; 2 Latvala/Anttila (Ford) 8m30.0s; 3 Hirvonen/Lehtinen (Ford) 8m33.7s; 4 H.Solberg/C.Menkerud (Ford Focus RS WRC 06) 8m38.8s; 5 D.Sordo/M.Martí (Citroën C4 WRC) 8m39.7s; 6 M.Stohl/I.Minor (Citroën Xsara WRC) 8m40.9s; PC Flodin/Andersson (Subaru) 9m09.5s

**SS3 Kimun Kamuy 1 (26.30km)**
1 Loeb/Elena (Citroën) 13m56.0s; 2 Grönholm/Rautiainen (Ford) 14m00.4s; 3 Latvala/Anttila (Ford) 14m03.0s; 4 Hirvonen/Lehtinen (Ford) 14m03.4s; 5 Solberg/Menkerud (Ford) 14m08.9s; 6 Sordo/Martí (Citroën) 14m14.4s; PC Flodin/Andersson (Subaru) 15m02.1s

**SS4 Rikubetsu 1 (2.73km)**
1 Sordo/Martí (Citroën) 2m05.4s; 2 Hirvonen/Lehtinen (Ford) 2m05.8s; 3 Solberg/Mills (Subaru) 2m05.9s; 4 Solberg/Menkerud (Ford) 2m06.1s; 5 Latvala/Anttila (Ford) 2m06.2s; 6 Loeb/Elena (Ford) 2m06.6s; PC T.Arai/T.Sircombe (Subaru Impreza WRX Sti) 2m11.2s

**SS5 Pawse Kamuy Reverse 2 (9.20km)**
1 Latvala/Anttila (Ford) 4m39.1s; 2 Hirvonen/Lehtinen (Ford) 4m40.3s; 3 Loeb/Elena (Ford) 4m40.4s; 4 Atkinson/Prevot (Subaru) 4m41.5s; 5 Sordo/Martí (Citroën) 4m42.2s; 6 Stohl/Minor (Citroën) 4m42.7s; PC J.Hänninen/M.Markkula (Mitsubishi Lancer Evo 9) 5m00.0s

**SS6 Cup Kamuy 2 (13.94km)**
1 Hirvonen/Lehtinen (Ford) 8m09.0s; 2 Loeb/Elena (Citroën) 8m11.9s; 3 Latvala/Anttila (Ford) 8m16.6s; 4 Solberg/Menkerud (Ford) 8m17.1s; 5 Sordo/Martí (Citroën) 8m17.6s; 6 Stohl/Minor (Citroën) 8m26.0s; PC Hänninen/Markkula (Mitsubishi) 8m56.9s

**SS7 Kimun Kamuy 2 (26.30km)**
1 Hirvonen/Lehtinen (Ford) 13m26.7s; 2 Loeb/Elena (Citroën) 13m32.2s; 3 Latvala/Anttila (Ford) 13m34.0s; 4 Sordo/Martí (Citroën) 13m36.3s; 5 Solberg/Menkerud (Ford) 13m37.4s; 6 Stohl/Minor (Citroën) 13m52.3s; PC F.Nutahara/D.Barritt (Mitsubishi Lancer Evo 9) 14m53.0s

**SS8 Rikubetsu 2 (2.73km)**
1 Sordo/Martí (Citroën) 2m04.2s; 2 Hirvonen/Lehtinen (Ford) 2m04.5s; 3 Latvala/Anttila (Ford) 2m05.1s; 4 Loeb/Elena (Citroën) 2m05.8s; 5 Solberg/Menkerud (Ford) 2m06.1s; 6 Stohl/Minor (Citroën) 2m06.8s; PC Nutahara/Barritt (Mitsubishi) 2m13.4s

**SS9 Obihiro 1 (1.35km)**
1 A.Araújo/M.Ramalho (PC Mitsubishi Lancer Evo 9) 1m18.5s; 2 Sordo/Martí (Citroën) 1m18.9s; 3 Loeb/Elena (Citroën) 1m19.1s; 4 Hirvonen/Lehtinen (Ford) 1m19.2s; 5= F.Villagra/J.L.Díaz (Ford Focus RS WRC 06), L.Pérez-Companc/J-M.Volta (Ford Focus RS WRC 06) 1m19.3s

**SS10 Obihiro 2 (1.35km)**
1 X.Pons/X.Amigo (Subaru Impreza WRC2007) 1m16.8s; 2 Sordo/Martí (Citroën) 1m17.4s; 3= Loeb/Elena (Citroën), Villagra/Díaz (Ford) 1m17.5s; 5 Araújo/Ramalho (PC Mitsubishi) 1m17.8s; 6 Hirvonen/Lehtinen (Ford) 1m18.0s

**SS11 Rikubetsu 3 (2.73km)**
1 Loeb/Elena (Citroën) 2m06.8s; 2= Hirvonen/Lehtinen (Ford), Solberg/Mills (Subaru) 2m06.9s; 4 Latvala/Anttila (Ford) 2m07.1s; 5 Solberg/Menkerud (Ford) 2m07.7s; 6 Sordo/Martí (Citroën) 2m08.8s; PC Nutahara/Barritt (Mitsubishi) 2m16.0s

**SS12 Puray 1 (34.95km)**
1 Hirvonen/Lehtinen (Ford) 19m28.4s; 2 Loeb/Elena (Citroën) 19m28.7s; 3 Sordo/Martí (Citroën) 19m40.9s; 4 Latvala/Anttila (Ford) 19m42.3s; 5 Solberg/Menkerud (Ford) 19m52.2s; 6 Solberg/Mills (Subaru) 20m01.2s; PC Hänninen/Markkula (Mitsubishi) 21m40.8s

RALLY JAPAN

| Position | Stage Numbers | 1 | 2 | 3 | 4 | 5 | 6 | 7 | 8 | 9 | 10 | 11 | 12 | 13 | 14 | 15 | 16 | 17 | 18 | 19 | 20 | 21 | 22 | 23 | 24 | 25 | 26 | 27 |
|---|---|---|---|---|---|---|---|---|---|---|---|---|---|---|---|---|---|---|---|---|---|---|---|---|---|---|---|---|
| | Hirvonen | 4 | 3 | 3 | 2 | 2 | 1 | 1 | 1 | 1 | 1 | 1 | 1 | 1 | 1 | 1 | 1 | 1 | 1 | 1 | 1 | 1 | 1 | 1 | 1 | 1 | 1 | 1 |
| | Sordo | 7 | 6 | 6 | 5 | 4 | 4 | 4 | 4 | 4 | 4 | 4 | 4 | 2 | 2 | 2 | 2 | 2 | 2 | 2 | 2 | 2 | 2 | 2 | 2 | 2 | 2 | 2 |
| | H.Solberg | 10 | 7 | 5 | 4 | 5 | 5 | 5 | 5 | 5 | 5 | 5 | 5 | 3 | 3 | 3 | 3 | 3 | 3 | 3 | 3 | 3 | 3 | 3 | 3 | 3 | 3 | 3 |
| | Wilson | 11 | 10 | 12 | 12 | 11 | 9 | 9 | 9 | 9 | 9 | 9 | 8 | 6 | 5 | 5 | 5 | 5 | 5 | 5 | 5 | 5 | 5 | 5 | 5 | 5 | 4 | 4 |
| | P-Companc | 12 | 11 | 11 | 11 | 10 | 8 | 8 | 8 | 8 | 8 | 8 | 7 | 5 | 4 | 4 | 4 | 4 | 4 | 4 | 4 | 4 | 4 | 4 | 4 | 4 | 5 | 5 |
| | Stohl | 8 | 8 | 8 | 7 | 7 | 6 | 6 | 6 | 6 | 6 | 6 | 6 | 4 | 6 | 6 | 6 | 6 | 6 | 6 | 6 | 6 | 6 | 6 | 6 | 6 | 6 | 6 |
| | Villagra | 14 | 13 | 13 | 13 | 12 | 10 | 10 | 10 | 10 | 10 | 10 | 9 | 9 | 7 | 7 | 7 | 7 | 7 | 7 | 7 | 7 | 7 | 7 | 7 | 7 | 7 | 7 |
| | Taguchi | 13 | 14 | 14 | 14 | 13 | 11 | 11 | 11 | 11 | 11 | 11 | 10 | 10 | 8 | 8 | 8 | 8 | 8 | 8 | 8 | 8 | 8 | 8 | 8 | 8 | 8 | 8 |
| | Pozzo | 21 | 19 | 20 | 20 | 21 | 16 | 13 | 13 | 13 | 13 | 13 | 13 | 12 | 11 | 9 | 9 | 9 | 9 | 9 | 9 | 9 | 9 | 9 | 9 | 9 | 9 | 9 |
| | Ishida | 24 | 29 | 29 | 28 | 28 | 25 | 24 | 24 | 22 | 22 | 22 | 18 | 16 | 13 | 11 | 12 | 12 | 12 | 12 | 12 | 12 | 12 | 12 | 12 | 12 | 13 | 10 |
| | Araujo | 22 | 21 | 25 | 29 | 26 | 19 | 14 | 14 | 14 | 14 | 14 | 24 | 22 | 17 | 15 | 14 | 13 | 13 | 13 | 13 | 13 | 13 | 13 | 13 | 13 | 10 | Ex |
| | P.Solberg | 6 | 5 | 6 | 6 | 6 | 28 | 36 | 46 | 60 | 65 | 63 | 51 | 47 | 39 | 36 | 29 | 28 | 26 | 26 | 25 | 22 | 21 | 20 | 20 | 19 | 17 | 16 |
| | Latvala | 1 | 1 | 2 | 1 | 1 | 2 | 2 | 2 | 3 | 3 | 3 | 3 | 8 | 10 | 18 | 26 | 27 | 30 | 34 | 39 | 36 | 34 | 33 | 32 | 32 | 26 | 25 |
| | Arai | 17 | 17 | 16 | 16 | 15 | 12 | 34 | 44 | 57 | 63 | 61 | 60 | 55 | 50 | 49 | 44 | 39 | 37 | 36 | 34 | 32 | 31 | 31 | 31 | 30 | 31 | 29 |
| | Pons | 9 | 9 | 10 | 10 | 9 | 7 | 7 | 7 | 7 | 7 | 7 | 11 | 21 | 28 | 32 | 36 | 36 | 41 | 47 | 50 | 49 | 47 | 47 | 45 | 43 | 37 | 35 |
| | Loeb | 2 | 4 | 4 | 3 | 3 | 3 | 3 | 3 | 2 | 2 | 2 | 2 | 7 | 9 | 16 | 24 | 26 | 29 | 33 | 38 | 33 | 32 | 30 | 30 | 28 | R | |
| | Nutahara | 16 | 16 | 17 | 17 | 16 | 13 | 12 | 12 | 12 | 12 | 12 | 12 | 11 | R | | | | | | | | | | | | | |
| | Atkinson | 3 | 12 | 9 | 9 | 8 | R | | | | | | | | | | | | | | | | | | | | | |
| | Grönholm | 5 | 2 | 1 | R | | | | | | | | | | | | | | | | | | | | | | | |

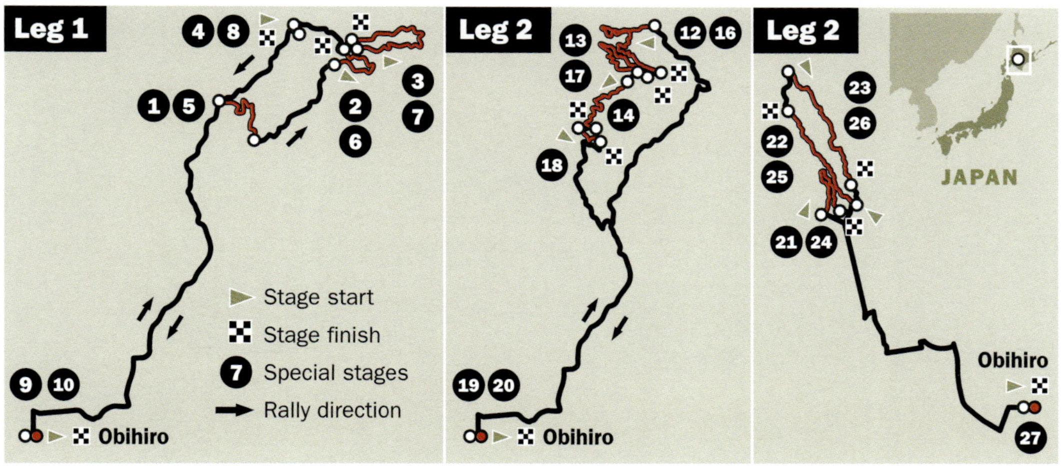


**SS13 Niueo 1 (20.75km)**
1 Sordo/Martí (Citroën) 12m31.3s; 2 Solberg/Menkerud (Ford) 12m35.2s; 3 Hirvonen/Lehtinen (Ford) 12m40.2s; 4 Solberg/Mills (Subaru) 12m42.4s; 5 Stohl/Minor (Citroën) 12m47.1s; 6 M.Wilson/M.Orr (Ford Focus RS WRC 06) 13m00.2s; PC Arai/Sircombe (Subaru) 13m31.6s

**SS14 Sipirkakim (22.43km)**
1 Solberg/Mills (Subaru) 12m13.1s; 2 Hirvonen/Lehtinen (Ford) 12m19.6s; 3 Sordo/Martí (Citroën) 12m24.0s; 4 Solberg/Menkerud (Ford) 12m29.1s; 5 Pérez-Companc/Volta (Ford) 12m38.4s; 6 Wilson/Orr (Ford) 12m48.5s; PC Arai/Sircombe (Subaru) 13m25.6s

**SS15 Rikubetsu 4 (2.73km)**
1 Solberg/Mills (Subaru) 2m05.6s; 2 Solberg/Menkerud (Ford) 2m07.0s; 3 Hirvonen/Lehtinen (Ford) 2m07.1s; 4 Sordo/Martí (Citroën) 2m07.6s; 5 Wilson/Orr (Ford) 2m09.9s; 6 Villagra/Díaz (Ford) 2m10.2s; PC Arai/Sircombe (Subaru) 2m15.0s

**SS16 Puray 2 (34.95km)**
1 Solberg/Mills (Subaru) 19m01.0s; 2 Sordo/Martí (Citroën) 19m13.2s 3 Hirvonen/Lehtinen (Ford) 19m17.4s; 4 Stohl/Minor (Citroën) 19m37.9s; 5 Solberg/Menkerud (Ford) 19m39.4; 6 Pérez-Companc/Volta (Ford) 19m49.2s; PC G.Pozzo/D.Stillo (Mitsubishi Lancer Evo 9) 21m09.8s

**SS17 Niueo 2 (20.75km)**
1 Sordo/Martí (Citroën) 12m17.5s; 2 Solberg/Mills (Subaru) 12m18.3s; 3 Hirvonen/Lehtinen (Ford) 12m29.2s; 4 Pérez-Companc/Volta (Ford) 12m38.9s; 5 Solberg/Menkerud (Ford) 12m40.3s; 6 Stohl/Minor (Citroën) 12m41.1s; PC Arai/Sircombe (Subaru) 13m23.8s

**SS18 Sipirkakim Short (4.67km)**
1 Solberg/Mills (Subaru) 2m42.4s; 2 Hirvonen/Lehtinen (Ford) 2m42.5s; 3 Solberg/Menkerud (Ford) 2m44.2s; 4 Sordo/Martí (Citroën) 2m47.1s; 5 Stohl/Minor (Citroën) 2m47.9s; 6 Pérez-Companc/Volta (Ford) 2m49.0s; PC Arai/Sircombe (Subaru) 3m01.4s

**SS19 Obihiro 3 (1.35km)**
1 Villagra/Díaz (Ford) 1m21.4s; 2 Sordo/Martí (Citroën) 1m22.3s; 3 Solberg/Mills (Subaru) 1m22.7s; 4 Wilson/Orr (Ford) 1m23.1s; 5 Solberg/Menkerud (Ford) 1m23.3s; 6 Hirvonen/Lehtinen (Ford) 1m23.6s; PC Hänninen/Markkula (Mitsubishi) 1m26.8s

**SS20 Obihiro 4 (1.35km)**
1 Villagra/Díaz (Ford) 1m22.0s; 2= Sordo/Martí (Citroën), Solberg/Menkerud (Ford) 1m23.0s; 4 Hirvonen/Lehtinen (Ford) 1m23.2s; 5 Wilson/Orr (Ford) 1m23.5s; 6 Stohl/Minor (Citroën) 1m23.9s; PC Hänninen/Markkula (Mitsubishi) 1m25.5s

**SS21 Rera Kamuy 1 (8.76km)**
1 Loeb/Elena (Citroën) 5m10.1s; 2 Hirvonen/Lehtinen (Ford) 5m11.0s; 3 Solberg/Mills (Subaru) 5m12.3s; 4 Sordo/Martí (Citroën) 5m13.9s; 5 Stohl/Minor (Citroën) 5m18.5s; 6 Pons/Amigo (Subaru) 5m18.6s; PC Arai/Sircombe (Subaru) 5m39.6s

**SS22 Panke Nikorpet 1 (17.40km)**
1 Sordo/Martí (Citroën) 9m35.0s; 2 Hirvonen/Lehtinen (Ford) 9m37.7s; 3 Loeb/Elena (Citroën) 9m38.3s; 4 Solberg/Mills (Subaru) 9m46.0s; 5 Latvala/Anttila (Ford) 9m47.3s; 6 Stohl/Minor (Citroën) 9m49.3s; PC Hänninen/Markkula (Mitsubishi) 10m19.0s

**SS23 Penke 1 (22.19km)**
1 Loeb/Elena (Citroën) 13m23.8s; 2 Hirvonen/Lehtinen (Ford) 13m28.0s; 3 Sordo/Martí (Citroën) 13m39.5s; 4 Latvala/Anttila (Ford) 13m43.6s; 5 Wilson/Orr (Ford) 13m51.3s; 6 Solberg/Mills (Subaru) 13m51.9s; PC Hänninen/Markkula (Mitsubishi) 14m22.0s

**SS24 Rera Kamuy 2 (8.76km)**
1 Loeb/Elena (Citroën) 5m02.5s; 2 Latvala/Anttila (Ford) 5m03.7s; 3 Solberg/Mills (Subaru) 5m07.6s; 4 Hirvonen/Lehtinen (Ford) 5m07.7s; 5 Sordo/Martí (Citroën) 5m08.0s; 6 Wilson/Orr (Ford) 5m11.2s; PC Arai/Sircombe (Subaru) 5m33.2s

**SS25 Panke Nikorpet 2 (17.40km)**
1 Loeb/Elena (Citroën) 9m17.9s; 2 Sordo/Martí (Citroën) 9m21.9s; 3 Hirvonen/Lehtinen (Ford) 9m25.3s; 4 Latvala/Anttila (Ford) 9m27.4s; 5 Solberg/Mills (Subaru) 9m34.5s; 6 Pérez-Companc/Volta (Ford) 9m35.3s; PC Hänninen/Markkula (Mitsubishi) 10m09.6s

**SS26 Penke 2 (22.19km)**
1 Sordo/Martí (Citroën) 13m05.4s; 2 Latvala/Anttila (Ford) 13m08.9s; 3 Hirvonen/Lehtinen (Ford) 13m12.3s; 4 Wilson/Orr (Ford) 13m14.8s; 5 Stohl/Minor (Citroën) 13m15.8s; 6 Pérez-Companc/Volta (Ford) 13m23.5s; PC Hänninen/Markkula (Mitsubishi) 13m59.5s

**SS27 Obihiro 5 (1.35km)**
1 Villagra/Díaz (Ford) 1m23.6s; 2 Solberg/Mills (Subaru) 1m23.8s; 3 Solberg/Menkerud (Ford) 1m24.1s; 4 Sordo/Martí (Citroën) 1m24.2s; 5 Pons/Amigo (Subaru) 1m24.7s; 6 Stohl/Minor (Citroën) 1m24.8s; PC Hänninen/Markkula (Mitsubishi) 1m26.1s

Cars who retired and subsequently re-started under SuperRally regs:

| | | | |
|---|---|---|---|
| 1 | Loeb/Elena | Citroën C4 WRC | |
| | Accident | SS13 | Gr A |
| 7 | Solberg/Mills | Subaru Impreza WRC2007 | |
| | Gearbox | SS6 | Gr A |
| 9 | Latvala/Anttila | Ford Focus RS WRC 06 | |
| | Accident | SS13 | Gr A |
| 17 | Pons/Amigo | Subaru Impreza WRC2007 | |
| | Accident | SS12 | Gr A |
| 31 | Arai/Sircombe | Subaru Impreza WRX Sti | |
| | Accident | SS7 | Gr N |
| 36 | Hänninen/Markkula | Mitsubishi Lancer Evo 9 | |
| | Accident | SS7 | Gr N |

## MAJOR RETIREMENTS

| | | | |
|---|---|---|---|
| 3 | Grönholm/Rautiainen | Ford Focus RS WRC 07 | |
| | Accident | SS4 | Gr A |
| 1 | Loeb/Elena | Citroën C4 WRC | |
| | Engine | SS26 | Gr A |
| 8 | Atkinson/Prevot | Subaru Impreza WRC2007 | |
| | Accident | SS6 | Gr A |
| 35 | Nutahara/Barritt | Mitsubishi Lancer Evo 9 | |
| | Mechanical | SS14 | Gr N |
| 46 | Araújo/Ramalho | Mitsubishi Lancer Evo 9 | |
| | Excluded | SS27 | Gr N |

## FIA CLASS WINNERS

| | | |
|---|---|---|
| A8 | Over 2000cc | Hirvonen/Lehtinen |
| | | Ford Focus RS WRC 07 |
| A7 | 1600-2000cc | Tokita/Jitkasem |
| | | Honda Integra Type-R |
| A6 | 1400-1600cc | Aava/Sikk |
| | | Suzuki Swift |
| A5 | Upto 1400cc | Onodera/Kuroda |
| | | Daihatsu Sirion |
| N4 | Over 2000cc | Taguchi/Stacey |
| | | Mitsubishi Lancer Evo 9 |
| N3 | 1600-2000cc | Oi/Toyama |
| | | Ford Fiesta ST |
| N2 | 1400-1600cc | Kato/Otani |
| | | Honda Civic Si |
| N1 | Upto 1400cc | Ito/Chigami |
| | | Daihatsu Sirion |

## RALLY LEADERS

Overall: SS1-2 Latvala; SS3 Grönholm; SS4-5 Latvala; SS6-27 Hirvonen

PC: SS1-5 Flodin; SS6 Arai; SS7-13 Nutahara; SS14-27 Pozzo

## SPECIAL STAGE ANALYSIS

| | 1st | 2nd | 3rd | 4th | 5th | 6th |
|---|---|---|---|---|---|---|
| Sordo (Citroën) | 6 | 6 | 3 | 5 | 4 | 2 |
| Loeb (Citroën) | 6 | 4 | 4 | 1 | - | 1 |
| P.Solberg (Subaru) | 4 | 3 | 4 | 2 | 1 | 3 |
| Hirvonen (Ford) | 3 | 9 | 7 | 5 | - | 2 |
| Villagra (Ford) | 3 | - | 1 | - | 1 | 1 |
| Latvala (Ford) | 2 | 3 | 4 | 4 | 2 | - |
| Grönholm (Ford) | 1 | 1 | - | - | 1 | - |
| Pons (Subaru) | 1 | - | - | - | 1 | 1 |
| Araújo (Mitsubishi) | 1 | - | - | - | 1 | - |
| H.Solberg (Ford) | - | 3 | 2 | 4 | 8 | - |
| Atkinson (Subaru) | - | - | 1 | 1 | - | - |
| Wilson(Ford) | - | - | - | 2 | 3 | 3 |
| Stohl (Citroën) | - | - | - | 1 | 4 | 9 |
| P-Companc (Ford) | - | - | - | 1 | 2 | 4 |

## WORLD CHAMPIONSHIP POINTS

**Drivers**
1 Grönholm 104; 2 Loeb 100; 3 Hirvonen 84; 4 Sordo 53; 5 P.Solberg 38; 6 H.Solberg 34; 7 Atkinson 29; 8 Latvala 24; 9= Duval, Stohl 12 etc

**Manufacturers**
1 BP-Ford WRT 189; 2 Citroën Total WRT 155; 3 Subaru WRT 73; 4 Stobart M-Sport Ford RT 71; 5 OMV-Kronos Citroën WRT 43; 6 Munchi's Ford RT 14

**Junior World Championship**
1 Andersson 43; 2 Aava 38; 3 Prokop 34; 4 Beres 26; 5 Mölder 20; 6 Sandell 19; 7 Burkart 18; 8 Rautenbach 16; 9 Bonato 10; 10 Cortinovis 9 etc

**Production Cup**
1 Arai 39; 2 Pozzo 22; 3 Higgins 19; 4 Sohlberg 12; 5= M.Baldacci, McShea 11; 7= Svedlund, Villagra, Aigner, Nutahara, Hänninen 10 etc

## ROUTE DETAILS

Total Route of 1575.79km of which 350.19km were competitive on 27 stages

**Leg 1** Friday 26 October, 10 special stages totalling 106.18km

**Leg 2** Saturday 27 October, 10 special stages totalling 146.68km

**Leg 3** Sunday 28 October, 7 special stages totalling 97.33km

## RESULTS

| | | | |
|---|---|---|---|
| 1 | Mikko Hirvonen/ | Ford Focus RS WRC 07 | |
| | Jarmo Lehtinen | 3h23m57.6s | Gr A |
| 2 | Dani Sordo/ | Citroën C4 WRC | |
| | Marc Martí | 3h24m35.0s | Gr A |
| 3 | Henning Solberg/ | Ford Focus RS WRC 06 | |
| | Cato Menkerud | 3h28m31.3s | Gr A |
| 4 | Matthew Wilson/ | Ford Focus RS WRC 06 | |
| | Michael Orr | 3h30m35.5s | Gr A |
| 5 | Luis Pérez-Companc/ | Ford Focus RS WRC 06 | |
| | Jose Maria Volta | 3h30m38.0s | Gr A |
| 6 | Manfred Stohl/ | Citroën Xsara WRC | |
| | Ilka Minor | 3h31m01.9s | Gr A |
| 7 | Federico Villagra/ | Ford Focus RS WRC 06 | |
| | Jose Luis Diaz | 3h35m12.9s | Gr A |
| 8 | Katsuhiko Taguchi/ | Mitsubishi Lancer Evo 9 | |
| | Mark Stacey | 3h44m37.7s | Gr N |
| 9 | Gabriel Pozzo/ | Mitsubishi Lancer Evo 9 | |
| | Daniel Stillo | 3h45m50.6s | Gr N |
| 10 | Masayuki Ishida/ | Mitsubishi Lancer Evo 9 | |
| | Keiji Seita | 3h48m30.0s | Gr N |

85 starters, 72 finishers

## PREVIOUS WINNERS

| | |
|---|---|
| 2001*Ishida/Ishida | Mitsubishi Lancer Evo |
| 2002*Possum Bourne/Mark Stacey | Subaru Impreza WRX |
| 2003*Toshihiro Arai/Tony Sircombe | Subaru Impreza WRX |
| 2004 Petter Solberg/Phil Mills | Subaru Impreza WRC2004 |
| 2005 Marcus Grönholm/ Timo Rautiainen | Peugeot 307 WRC |
| 2006 Sébastien Loeb/Daniel Elena | Citroën Xsara WRC |

*Non-championship event

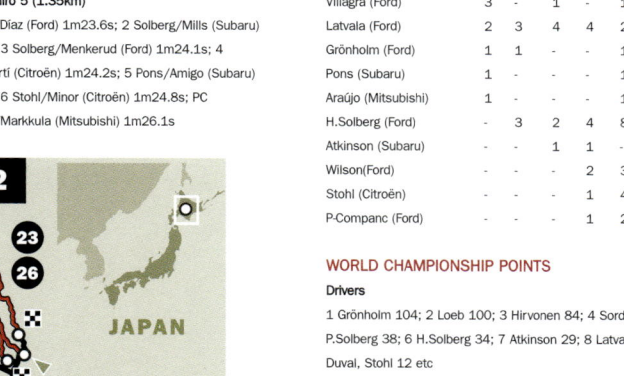

## The FIA World Rally Championship Round 15
# Rally Ireland

**Above:** Loeb overcame an early problem with the C4 to drive a perfect rally, gaining a crucial advantage over the unfortunate Grönholm in the championship race

**Right top:** For the second rally in a row Grönholm crashed out in the fourth stage. His title lead was turned into a six-point deficit to Loeb with only one round to go

**Right:** Subaru had another difficult event despite the return of David Richards and David Lapworth to the team. Petter Solberg was fifth, but Chris Atkinson and Xavier Pons crashed out

**Far right:** Dani Sordo was smiling, but in truth he'd have preferred to be let off the leash and challenge Loeb for the win instead of settling for second

All photographs by McKlein unless specified

TIGHTENING his belts before the first stage proper - run shortly after sunrise on Friday to the east of Sligo - Sébastien Loeb sighed and said to co-driver Daniel Elena: "I think we should go home now. This isn't going to be our rally."

The Citroën C4 WRC had developed a major problem with the left-rear damper on the way to SS2 Geevagh. A pipe carrying fluid from the reservoir to the strut had been damaged, and the upshot was an absence of shock absorbing on one of the car's four corners. In fact there were plenty of shocks to be absorbed over the next three stages. By the end of that loop, the rally - and indeed the championship - had taken a decisive turn. But that turn had come in Loeb's favour. Good job he hadn't gone home.

While the Frenchman was busy dealing with his problem, championship leader Marcus Grönholm had been pushing his Ford hard in an attempt to make the best of his title rival's troubled start. Unfortunately for the Finn, he pushed a little too hard in Lough Gill. Having emerged from the twisty section of the stage and onto the wider road, Grönholm stepped his pace up another notch in the Focus. He had been eight seconds up on Loeb at the previous split, and Grönholm really wanted to turn the screw and make this one count.

After a grippy section, one of a million or so surface changes on this event caught him out at an open 90-right that tightened. Having piled on one too many coals, he threw the car at the corner. With little resistance, the Focus skated across the road and slammed into a brick wall.

Grönholm was knocked out in the impact and - along with co-driver Timo Rautiainen - was taken to Sligo General Hospital for a check-up. He flew home the next morning. Having repeated his fourth stage exit from Rally Japan three weeks earlier, all he could hope was that Loeb would retire this time too.

The Frenchman failed to comply with Grönholm's wishes. After turning in a stunning drive through that opening loop, he was only a handful of seconds down on team-mate Dani Sordo. Unsurprisingly, he moved past the Spaniard on Friday afternoon and stayed ahead for the event's duration. There was no hiding his relief at turning a four-point deficit into a six-point championship lead with one round to go.

Sordo was frustrated at not being allowed off the leash, despite the exceptionally tricky conditions. These were made all the more difficult by heavy rain and the roads being covered in mud, which seems to be a given when rallying in these parts.

If Sordo's second place didn't mean that much to him, the man in third was as surprised as he was delighted. Stobart Ford driver Jari-Matti Latvala held off works Focus driver Mikko Hirvonen to clinch his first ever WRC podium. Hirvonen's mood reflected that of Sordo, but at least the Finn had helped clinch a second manufacturers' title in as many years for his employer to celebrate.

Ford was joined in its celebrations by the Rally Ireland organisers. After years of planning, the cross-border event ran to high acclaim from all concerned. From HRH The Princess Royal flagging the cars away, to a sell-out 16,000-strong crowd at Stormont - including political heavyweights Ian Paisley and Martin McGuinness - this was a major success. As winner Loeb pointed out, the only down side was the weather. Despite promoter Ronan Morgan's promise, the sunshine was the only area in which the event failed to deliver.

RALLY IRELAND

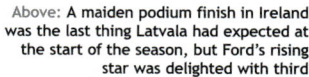

Above: A maiden podium finish in Ireland was the last thing Latvala had expected at the start of the season, but Ford's rising star was delighted with third

Opposite top: Ford wasted no time in celebrating its second manufacturers' title, although there was disappointment too at Grönholm's title blow

Opposite bottom: Driving a year-old Impreza, sixth-placed Guy Wilks turned in a mature performance to lead home fellow Brit Matthew Wilson (Stobart Ford)

Right: Ireland brought out the dancing girls to welcome the WRC. The country's debut in the world championship was considered a success and it'll be back in 2009

All photographs by McKlein

BP FORD
WORLD RALLY TEAM
2007 WORLD RALLY CHAMPIONS
KÄRCHER
Castrol

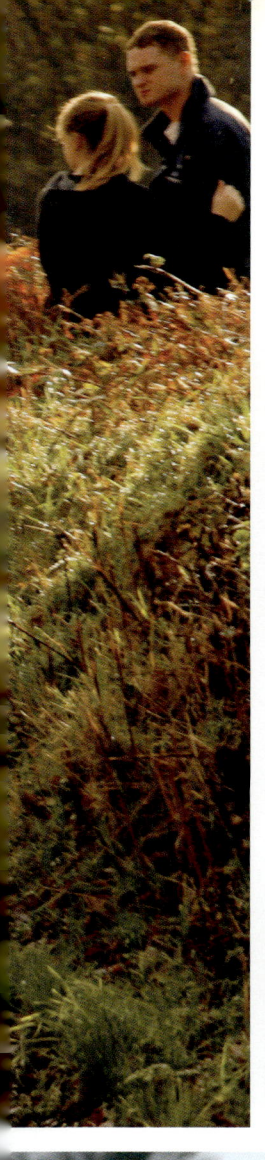

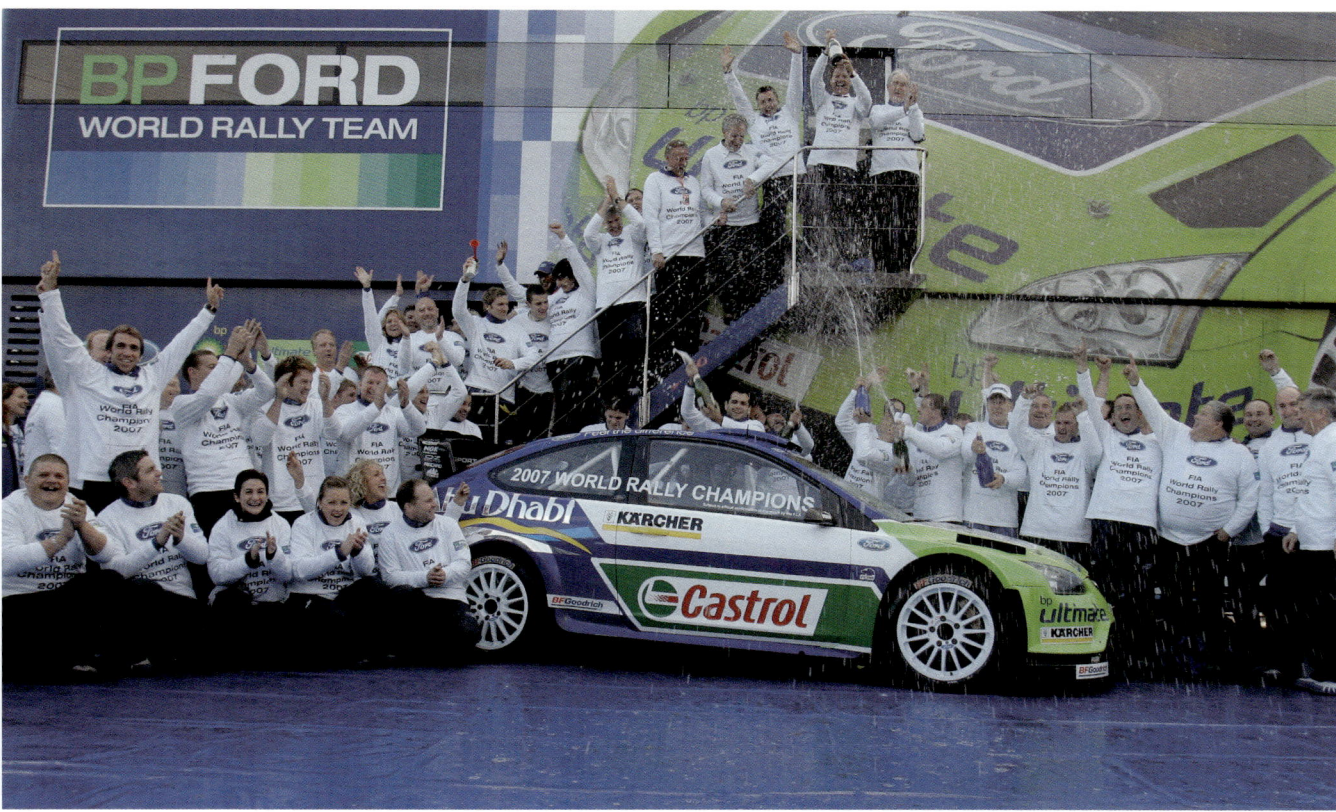

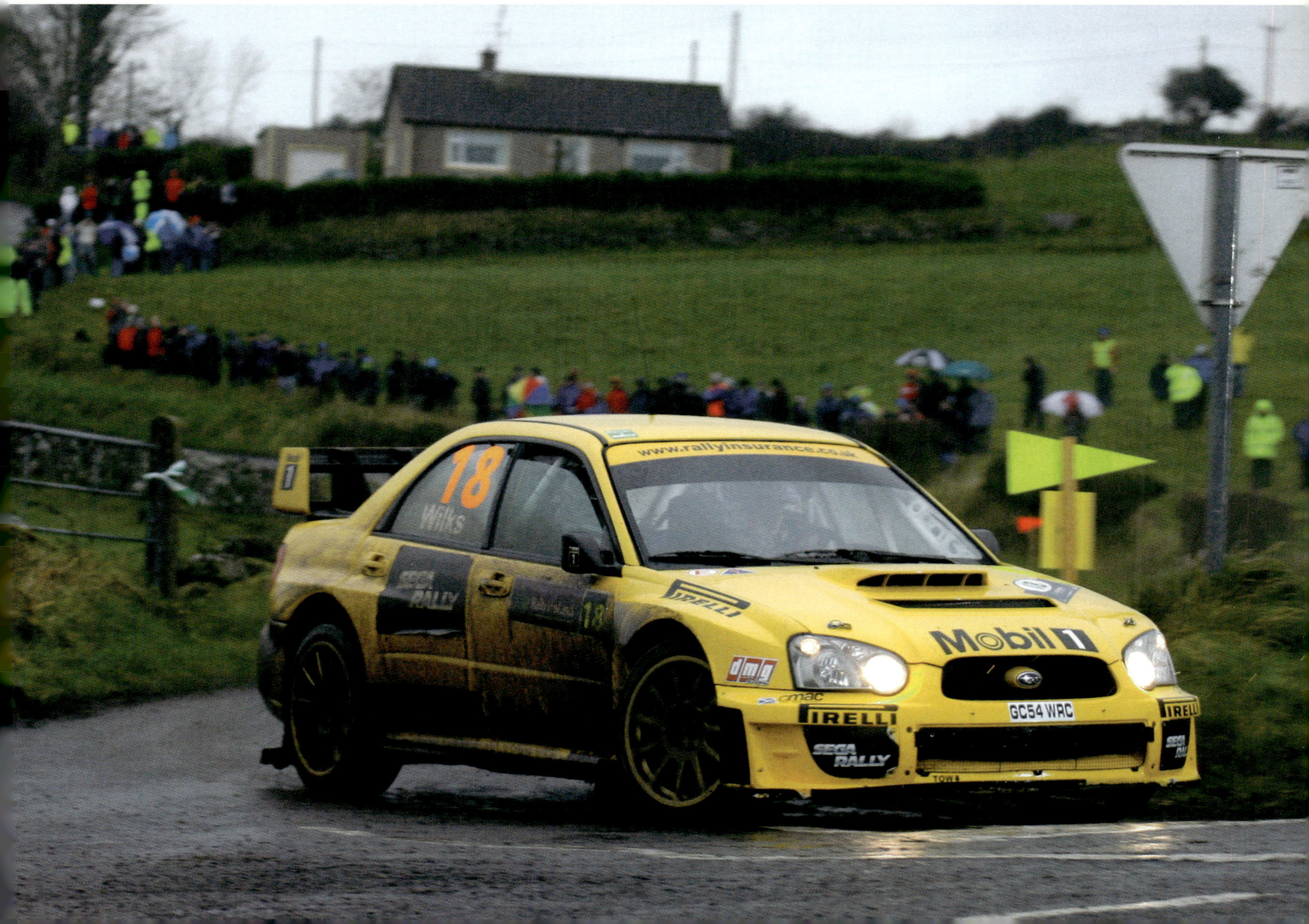
www.rallyinsurance.co.uk
18
Wilks
Mobil 1
PIRELLI
SEGA RALLY
GC54 WRC

*He may have been Production champion in 2004, but Niall McShea actually scored his first win the category on home soil in Ireland after scraping together the funds to compete*
McKlein

## The FIA World Rally Championship Round 15
# Rally Ireland Results
### November 16-18 2007

### FINISH LINES...

There was a deep sense of *deja vu* at the Subaru World Rally Team, as the two Davids - Richards and Lapworth - were back in blue. Following continued poor form from the Banbury-based team, Ireland was the first event since boss Richards' promise to "bang some heads together". Lapworth's presence was twofold: he was covering for chief engineer Graham Moore who had a prior engagement, and he wanted to cast his technical expertise over the Impreza WRC2007 on the battlefield. Unfortunately for Subaru the team's challenge never really got off the starting block, as both Chris Atkinson and Xevi Pons crashed on leg one, while Petter Solberg trundled around to fifth... If there wasn't much to smile about in the factory Imprezas, there was plenty of joy one place behind Solberg, as Guy Wilks guided his year-old Impreza to a career-best sixth overall. Wilks was the first to admit there had been an element of fortune in his position, following the demise of the likes of Kris Meeke - who had been the talking point of Thursday night when he posted an exceptional third quickest time before binning his Subaru on the final Friday stage... After his big haul in Japan, Matthew Wilson collected more points in Ireland by taking an untroubled seventh, while Gareth MacHale delighted local fans with eighth in his Focus... There was more joy for Irish fans when Niall McShea collected his first Production Car WRC win of the season. The former champion's victory followed an accident involving Mark Higgins that cost the Manxman his shot at this season's Production title. McShea admitted his success was even more outlandish given that a week prior to the start he had been on the verge of pulling his entry, as he had been unable to source the cash to carry on. How happy he was that he'd persevered in sourcing the necessary readies to tackle his nation's biggest ever motorsport event.

### RUNNING ORDER

| | | | |
|---|---|---|---|
| 3 | Marcus Grönholm/ Timo Rautiainen | Ford Focus RS WRC 07 | Gr A |
| 1 | Sébastien Loeb/ Daniel Elena | Citroën C4 WRC | Gr A |
| 4 | Mikko Hirvonen/ Jarmo Lehtinen | Ford Focus RS WRC 07 | Gr A |
| 2 | Daniel Sordo/ Marc Martí | Citroën C4 WRC | Gr A |
| 7 | Petter Solberg/ Phil Mills | Subaru Impreza WRC2007 | Gr A |
| 10 | Henning Solberg/ Göran Bergsten | Ford Focus RS WRC 06 | Gr A |
| 8 | Chris Atkinson/ Stéphane Prevot | Subaru Impreza WRC2007 | Gr A |
| 9 | Jari-Matti Latvala/ Miikka Anttila | Ford Focus RS WRC 06 | Gr A |
| 5 | Manfred Stohl/ Ilka Minor | Citroën Xsara WRC | Gr A |
| 16 | Matthew Wilson/ Michael Orr | Ford Focus RS WRC 06 | Gr A |
| 14 | Xavier Pons/ Xavier Amigo | Subaru Impreza WRC2007 | Gr A |
| 18 | Guy Wilks/ Phil Pugh | Subaru Impreza WRC2006 | Gr A |
| 21 | Andreas Mikkelsen/ Ola Floene | Ford Focus RS WRC 04 | Gr A |
| 17 | Khalid Al-Qassimi/ Nicky Beech | Ford Focus RS WRC 06 | Gr A |
| 19 | Kris Meeke/ Paul Nagle | Subaru Impreza WRC2006 | Gr A |
| 20 | Gareth MacHale/ Alan Harryman | Ford Focus RS WRC06 | Gr A |
| 22 | Eugene Donnelly/ Paul Kiely | Skoda Fabia WRC | Gr A |
| 23 | Eammon Boland/ Francis Regan | Subaru Impreza WRC2006 | Gr A |
| 24 | Andrew Nesbitt/ James O'Brien | Subaru Impreza WRC2006 | Gr A |
| 25 | Austin MacHale/ Brian Murphy | Ford Focus RS WRC 04 | Gr A |
| 26 | Aaron MacHale/ Killian Duffy | Ford Focus RS WRC 06 | Gr A |

### SPECIAL STAGE TIMES

**SS1 Stormont (1.82km)**
1 M.Grönholm/T.Rautiainen (Ford Focus RS WRC 07) 1m30.8s; 2 S.Loeb/D.Elena (Citroën C4 WRC) 1m31.7s; 3 K.Meeke/P.Nagle (Subaru Impreza WRC2006) 1m31.8s; 4 C.Atkinson/S.Prevot (Subaru Impreza WRC2007) 1m32.0s; 5 P.Solberg/P.Mills (Subaru Impreza WRC2007) 1m32.2s; 6= M.Hirvonen/J.Lehtinen (Ford Focus RS WRC 07), J-M.Latvala/M.Anttila (Ford Focus RS WRC 06) 1m32.5s; PC A.Aigner/K.Wicha (Mitsubishi Lancer Evo 9) 1m39.4s

**SS2 Geevagh 1 (11.47km)**
1 Loeb/Elena (Citroën) 6m05.7s; 2 Sordo/Martí (Citroën) 6m08.7s; 3 Grönholm/Rautiainen (Ford) 6m11.7s; 4 Hirvonen/Lehtinen (Ford) 6m14.7s; 5 Solberg/Mills (Subaru) 6m23.0s; 6 Atkinson/Prevot (Subaru) 6m24.6s; PC N.McShea/M.Clark (Subaru Impreza WRX Sti) 6m53.4s

**SS3 Arigna 1 (27.89km)**
1 Sordo/Martí (Citroën) 15m44.0s; 2 Grönholm/Rautiainen (Ford) 15m46.4s; 3 Loeb/Elena (Citroën) 15m47.5s; 4 Hirvonen/Lehtinen (Ford) 15m56.8s; 5 Latvala/Anttila (Ford) 16m00.8s; 6 Atkinson/Prevot (Subaru) 16m04.6s; PC M.Higgins/S.Martin (Mitsubishi Lancer Evo 9) 17m14.6s

**SS4 Lough Gill 1 (20.56km)**
1 Sordo/Martí (Citroën) 10m54.7s; 2 Loeb/Elena (Citroën) 10m57.4s; 3 Latvala/Anttila (Ford) 11m03.2; 4 Hirvonen/Lehtinen (Ford) 11m05.4s; 5 Solberg/Mills (Subaru) 11m09.5s; 6 H.Solberg/G.Bergsten (Ford Focus RS WRC 06) 11m16.3s; PC No Times, stage stopped

**SS5 Geevagh 2 (11.47km)**
1 Loeb/Elena (Citroën) 6m22.0s; 2 Sordo/Martí (Citroën) 6m28.6s; 3 Latvala/Anttila (Ford) 6m32.0s; 4 Hirvonen/Lehtinen (Ford) 6m33.9s; 5 Solberg/Bergsten (Ford) 6m35.5s; 6 A.Mikkelsen/O.Floene (Ford Focus RS WRC 04) 6m42.1s; PC Aigner/Wicha (Mitsubishi) 6m57.7s

**SS6 Arigna 2 (27.89km)**
1 Loeb/Elena (Citroën) 16m09.6s; 2 Sordo/Martí (Citroën) 16m13.5s; 3 Latvala/Anttila (Ford) 16m14.7s; 4 Solberg/Mills (Subaru) 16m27.9s; 5 Hirvonen/Lehtinen (Ford) 16m30.8s; 6 G.Wilks/P.Pugh (Subaru Impreza WRC2006) 16m32.0s; PC A.Araújo/M.Ramalho (Mitsubishi Lancer Evo 9) 17m20.3s

**SS7 Lough Gill 2 (20.56km)**
1 Sordo/Martí (Citroën) 10m55.5s; 2 Loeb/Elena (Citroën) 10m57.0s; 3 Hirvonen/Lehtinen (Ford) 11m08.6s; 4 Solberg/Mills (Subaru) 11m11.0s; 5 Latvala/Anttila (Ford) 11m12.9s; 6 Solberg/Bergsten (Ford) 11m16.7s; PC Higgins/Martin (Mitsubishi) 11m43.1s

**SS8 Glenboy (22.25km)**
1 Loeb/Elena (Citroën) 11m56.0s; 2 Latvala/Anttila (Ford) 11m58.0s; 3 Sordo/Martí (Citroën) 11m59.6s; 4 Solberg/Mills (Subaru) 12m01.8s; 5 Hirvonen/Lehtinen (Ford) 12m10.0s; 6 Wilks/Pugh (Subaru) 12m25.2s; PC Higgins/Martin (Mitsubishi) 13m01.8s

**SS9 Bencroy (15.43km)**
1 Sordo/Martí (Citroën) 8m21.3s; 2 Loeb/Elena (Citroën) 8m28.7s; 3 Latvala/Anttila (Ford) 8m36.3s; 4 Solberg/Mills (Subaru) 8m38.6s; 5 Hirvonen/Lehtinen (Ford) 8m40.7s; 6 Atkinson/Prevot (Subaru) 8m51.8s; PC Higgins/Martin (Mitsubishi) 9m26.5s

**SS10 Drumshanbo (8.65km)**
1 Loeb/Elena (Citroën) 5m00.3s; 2 Latvala/Anttila (Ford) 5m07.5s; 3 Sordo/Martí (Citroën) 5m08.5s; 4 Solberg/Mills (Subaru) 5m12.5s; 5 Hirvonen/Lehtinen (Ford) 5m15.7s; 6 Atkinson/Prevot (Subaru) 5m17.2s; PC Higgins/Martin (Mitsubishi) 5m40.8s

**SS11 Sloughan Glen 1 (20.95km)**
1 Loeb/Elena (Citroën) 11m37.7s; 2 Latvala/Anttila (Ford) 11m43.7s; 3 Sordo/Martí (Citroën) 11m44.0s; 4 Hirvonen/Lehtinen (Ford) 11m51.2s; 5 Atkinson/Prevot (Subaru) 11m51.6s; 6 Solberg/Mills (Subaru) 11m55.5s; PC P.Flodin/M.Andersson (Subaru Impreza WRX Sti) 12m32.3s

**SS12 Ballinamallard 1 (17.95km)**
1 Loeb/Elena (Citroën) 9m35.9s; 2 Latvala/Anttila (Ford) 9m39.6s; 3 Solberg/Mills (Subaru) 9m40.2s; 4 Atkinson/Prevot (Subaru) 9m44.8s; 5 Hirvonen/Lehtinen (Ford) 9m49.7s; 6 Wilks/Pugh (Subaru) 9m51.6s; PC Flodin/Andersson (Subaru) 10m14.6s

**SS13 Tempo 1 (13.46km)**
1 Loeb/Elena (Citroën) 7m31.6s; 2 Latvala/Anttila (Ford) 7m31.7s; 3 Sordo/Martí (Citroën) 7m31.9s; 4 Solberg/Mills

# RALLY IRELAND

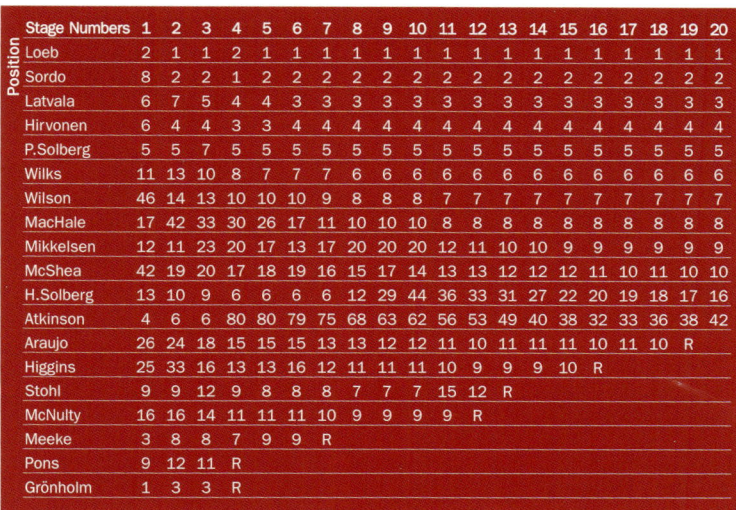

| Position | Stage Numbers | 1 | 2 | 3 | 4 | 5 | 6 | 7 | 8 | 9 | 10 | 11 | 12 | 13 | 14 | 15 | 16 | 17 | 18 | 19 | 20 |
|---|---|---|---|---|---|---|---|---|---|---|---|---|---|---|---|---|---|---|---|---|---|
| | Loeb | 2 | 1 | 1 | 2 | 1 | 1 | 1 | 1 | 1 | 1 | 1 | 1 | 1 | 1 | 1 | 1 | 1 | 1 | 1 | 1 |
| | Sordo | 8 | 2 | 2 | 1 | 2 | 2 | 2 | 2 | 2 | 2 | 2 | 2 | 2 | 2 | 2 | 2 | 2 | 2 | 2 | 2 |
| | Latvala | 6 | 7 | 5 | 4 | 3 | 3 | 3 | 3 | 3 | 3 | 3 | 3 | 3 | 3 | 3 | 3 | 3 | 3 | 3 | 3 |
| | Hirvonen | 6 | 4 | 4 | 3 | 4 | 4 | 4 | 4 | 4 | 4 | 4 | 4 | 4 | 4 | 4 | 4 | 4 | 4 | 4 | 4 |
| | P.Solberg | 5 | 5 | 7 | 5 | 5 | 5 | 5 | 5 | 5 | 5 | 5 | 5 | 5 | 5 | 5 | 5 | 5 | 5 | 5 | 5 |
| | Wilks | 11 | 13 | 10 | 8 | 7 | 7 | 7 | 6 | 6 | 6 | 6 | 6 | 6 | 6 | 6 | 6 | 6 | 6 | 6 | 6 |
| | Wilson | 46 | 14 | 13 | 10 | 10 | 10 | 9 | 8 | 8 | 9 | 7 | 7 | 7 | 7 | 7 | 7 | 7 | 7 | 7 | 7 |
| | MacHale | 17 | 42 | 33 | 30 | 26 | 17 | 11 | 10 | 10 | 8 | 8 | 8 | 8 | 8 | 8 | 8 | 8 | 8 | 8 | 8 |
| | Mikkelsen | 12 | 11 | 23 | 20 | 17 | 13 | 17 | 20 | 20 | 20 | 12 | 11 | 10 | 10 | 9 | 9 | 9 | 9 | 9 | 9 |
| | McShea | 42 | 19 | 20 | 17 | 18 | 19 | 16 | 15 | 17 | 14 | 13 | 12 | 12 | 12 | 11 | 10 | 11 | 10 | 10 | 10 |
| | H.Solberg | 13 | 10 | 9 | 6 | 6 | 6 | 6 | 12 | 29 | 44 | 36 | 33 | 31 | 27 | 22 | 20 | 19 | 18 | 17 | 16 |
| | Atkinson | 4 | 6 | 6 | 80 | 80 | 79 | 75 | 68 | 63 | 62 | 56 | 53 | 49 | 40 | 38 | 32 | 33 | 36 | 38 | 42 |
| | Araujo | 26 | 24 | 18 | 15 | 15 | 15 | 13 | 12 | 12 | 11 | 10 | 11 | 11 | 10 | 10 | 11 | 10 | R | | |
| | Higgins | 25 | 33 | 16 | 13 | 13 | 16 | 12 | 11 | 11 | 10 | 9 | 9 | 9 | 10 | R | | | | | |
| | Stohl | 9 | 9 | 12 | 9 | 8 | 8 | 8 | 7 | 7 | 15 | 12 | R | | | | | | | | |
| | McNulty | 16 | 16 | 14 | 11 | 11 | 11 | 10 | 9 | 9 | 9 | 9 | R | | | | | | | | |
| | Meeke | | 3 | 8 | 8 | 7 | 9 | 9 | R | | | | | | | | | | | | |
| | Pons | | 9 | 12 | 11 | R | | | | | | | | | | | | | | | |
| | Grönholm | 1 | 3 | 3 | R | | | | | | | | | | | | | | | | |

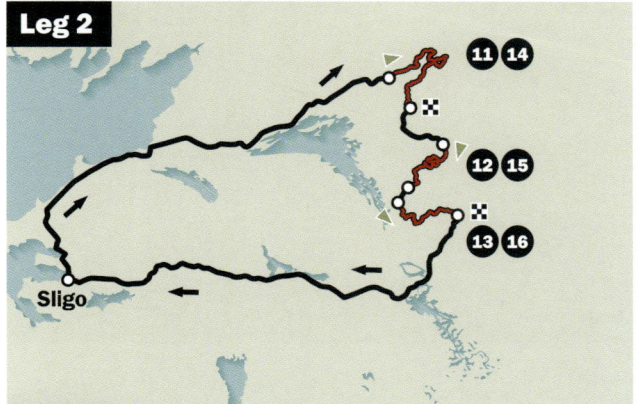

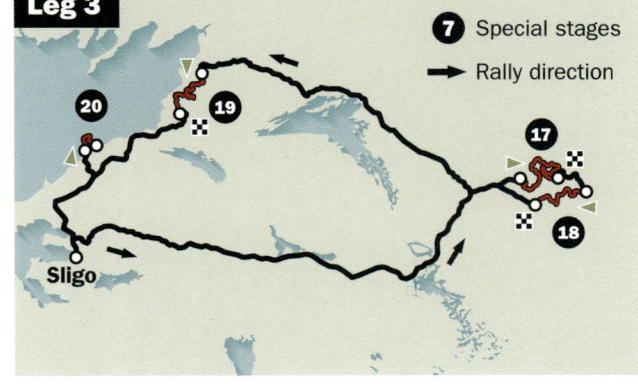

(Subaru) 7m32.0s; 5 Hirvonen/Lehtinen (Ford) 7m40.2s; 6 G.MacHale/A.Harryman (Ford Focus RS WRC 06) 7m42.9s; PC Flodin/Andersson (Subaru) 8m00.9s

**SS14 Sloughan Glen 2 (20.95km)**
1 Atkinson/Prevot (Subaru) 11m25.7s; 2 Sordo/Martí (Citroën) 11m27.1s; 3 Loeb/Elena (Citroën) 11m28.2s; 4 Hirvonen/Lehtinen (Ford) 11m33.0s; 5 Solberg/Mills (Subaru) 11m42.2s; 6 Wilks/Pugh (Subaru) 11m51.4s; PC P.Morrow/D.Senior (Mitsubishi Lancer Evo 9) 12m12.6s

**SS15 Ballinamallard 2 (17.95km)**
1 Loeb/Elena (Citroën) 9m30.7s; 2 Atkinson/Prevot (Subaru) 9m32.1s; 3 Solberg/Mills (Subaru) 9m32.3s; 4 Latvala/Antilla (Ford) 9m36.0s; 5 Hirvonen/Lehtinen (Ford) 9m37.4s; 6 Sordo/Martí (Citroën) 9m41.3s; PC McShea/Clark (Subaru) 10m14.9s

**SS16 Tempo 2 (13.46km)**
1 Latvala/Antilla (Ford) 7m28.9s; 2 Solberg/Mills (Subaru) 7m31.1s; 3 Hirvonen/Lehtinen (Ford) 7m32.2s; 4 Sordo/Martí (Citroën) 7m34.3s; 5 Loeb/Elena (Citroën) 7m35.2s; 6 Atkinson/Prevot (Subaru) 7m36.9s; PC McShea/Clark (Subaru) 8m10.9s

**SS17 Murley (24.70km)**
1 Hirvonen/Lehtinen (Ford) 13m19.9s; 2 Latvala/Antilla (Ford) 13m22.2s; 3 Sordo/Martí (Citroën) 13m23.4s; 4 Loeb/Elena (Citroën) 13m24.4s; 5 Mikkelsen/Floene (Ford) 13m31.2s; 6 Solberg/Mills (Subaru) 13m35.3s; PC McShea/Clark (Subaru) 14m03.7s

**SS18 Fardross (14.77km)**
1 Hirvonen/Lehtinen (Ford) 8m49.8s; 2 Loeb/Elena (Citroën) 8m54.4s; 3 Mikkelsen/Floene (Ford) 8m57.6s; 4 Latvala/Antilla (Ford) 9m00.2s; 5 Sordo/Martí (Citroën) 9m00.4s; 6 Wilks/Pugh (Subaru) 9m01.0s; PC G.Pozzo/D.Stillo (Mitsubishi Lancer Evo 9) 9m24.2s

**SS19 Donegal Bay (14.60km)**
1 Latvala/Antilla (Ford) 7m00.9s; 2 Wilks/Pugh (Subaru) 7m05.9s; 3 Hirvonen/Lehtinen (Ford) 7m13.1s; 4 Solberg/Mills (Subaru) 7m13.3s; 5 Loeb/Elena (Citroën) 7m15.8s; 6 Sordo/Martí (Citroën) 7m16.0s; PC McShea/Clark (Subaru) 7m39.4s

**SS20 Mullaghmore (2.38km)**
1 Solberg/Mills (Subaru) 1m16.9s; 2 Sordo/Martí (Citroën) 1m18.3s; 3= Loeb/Elena (Citroën), Solberg/Bergsten (Ford) 1m19.4s; 5 Wilks/Pugh (Subaru) 1m19.5s; 6 Latvala/Antilla (Ford) 1m19.8s; PC C.Murphy/G.Loughrey (Subaru Impreza WRX Sti) 1m25.2s

**Cars who retired and subsequently re-started under SuperRally regs**

| 10 | H.Solberg/Bergsten | Ford Focus RS WRC 06 |
| | Accident | SS8 | Gr A |
| 8 | Atkinson/Prevot | Subaru Impreza WRC2007 |
| | Engine | SS17 | Engine |
| 23 | Boland/Regan | Subaru Impreza WRC2006 |
| | Mechanical | SS7 | Gr A |
| 25 | MacHale/Murphy | Ford Focus RS WRC 04 |
| | Suspension | SS16 | Gr A |

**MAJOR RETIREMENTS**

| 3 | Grönholm/Rautiainen | Ford Focus RS WRC 07 |
| | Accident | SS4 | Gr A |
| 5 | Stohl/Minor | Citroën Xsara WRC |
| | Accident | SS13 | Gr A |
| 14 | Pons/Amigo | Subaru Impreza WRC2007 |
| | Accident | SS4 | Gr A |
| 19 | Meeke/Nagle | Subaru Impreza WRC2006 |
| | Accident | SS7 | Gr A |
| 22 | Donnelly/Kiely | Skoda Fabia WRC |
| | Mechanical | SS3 | Gr A |
| 24 | Nesbitt/O'Brien | Subaru Impreza WRC2006 |
| | Accident | SS11 | Gr A |

**FIA CLASS WINNERS**

| A8 | Over 2000cc | Loeb/Elena |
| | | Citroën C4 WRC |
| A6 | 1400-1600cc | McElhinney/McElhinney |
| | | Citroën C2 |
| N4 | Over 2000cc | McShea/Clark |
| | | Subaru Impreza WRX Sti |
| N3 | 1600-2000cc | Barry/Carroll |
| | | Honda Civic Type-R |
| N1 | Upto 1400cc | McHale/McCarthy |
| | | Toyota Yaris |

**RALLY LEADERS**
Overall: SS1 Grönholm; SS2-3 Loeb; SS4 Sordo; SS5-20 Loeb

PC: SS1-2 Aigner; SS3-5 Higgins; SS6 Aigner; SS7-15 Higgins; SS16 Araújo; SS17 McShea; SS18 Araújo; SS19-20 McShea

**SPECIAL STAGE ANALYSIS**

| | 1st | 2nd | 3rd | 4th | 5th | 6th |
|---|---|---|---|---|---|---|
| Loeb (Citroën) | 9 | 5 | 3 | 1 | 2 | - |
| Sordo (Citroën) | 4 | 5 | 5 | 1 | 2 | 2 |
| Latvala (Ford) | 2 | 6 | 4 | 2 | 2 | 2 |
| Hirvonen (Ford) | 2 | - | 3 | 6 | 7 | 1 |
| P.Solberg (Subaru) | 1 | 1 | 2 | 7 | 4 | 2 |
| Grönholm (Ford) | 1 | 1 | 1 | - | - | - |
| Atkinson (Subaru) | 1 | 1 | - | 2 | 1 | 6 |
| Wilks (Subaru) | - | 1 | - | - | 1 | 5 |
| H.Solberg (Ford) | - | - | 1 | - | 1 | 2 |
| Mikkelsen (Ford) | - | - | 1 | - | 1 | 1 |
| Meeke (Subaru) | - | - | - | 1 | - | - |
| G.MacHale (Ford) | - | - | - | - | - | 1 |

**WORLD CHAMPIONSHIP POINTS**
Drivers
1 Loeb 110; 2 Grönholm 104; 3 Hirvonen 89; 4 Sordo 61; 5 P.Solberg 42; 6 H.Solberg 34; 7 Latvala 30; 8 Atkinson 29; 9= Duval, Stohl 12 etc

Manufacturers
1 BP-Ford WRT 194; 2 Citroën Total WRT 173; 3 Stobart M-Sport Ford RT 80; 4 Subaru WRT 79; 5 OMV-Kronos Citroën WRT 43; 6 Munchi's Ford RT 14

Junior World Championship
1 Andersson 43; 2 Aava 38; 3 Prokop 34; 4 Beres 26; 5 Mölder 20; 6 Sandell 19; 7 Burkart 18; 8 Rautenbach 16; 9 Bonato 10; 10 Cortinovis 9 etc

Production Cup
1 Arai 39; 2 Pozzo 30; 3 McShea 24; 4 Higgins 19; 5 Nutahara 13; 6= Sohlberg, Al-Attiyah 12; 8 M.Baldacci 11; 9= Svedlund, Villagra, Aigner, Hänninen 10 etc

**ROUTE DETAILS**
Total route of 1389.70km of which 345.25km were competitive on 20 special stages

Leg 1 Thursday 15 – Friday 16 November, 10 special stages totalling 171.08km

Leg 2 Saturday 17 November, 6 special stages totalling 118.26km

Leg 3 Sunday 18 November, 4 special stages totalling 55.91km

**RESULTS**

| 1 | Sébastien Loeb/ | Citroën C4 WRC | | |
| | Daniel Elena | 3h01m39.2s | Gr A | |
| 2 | Daniel Sordo/ | Citroën C4 WRC | | |
| | Marc Martí | 3h02m32.6s | Gr A | |
| 3 | Jari-Matti Latvala/ | Ford Focus RS WRC 06 | | |
| | Miikka Anttila | 3h03m27.4s | Gr A | |
| 4 | Mikko Hirvonen/ | Ford Focus RS WRC 07 | | |
| | Jarmo Lehtinen | 3h03m56.9s | Gr A | |
| 5 | Petter Solberg/ | Subaru Impreza WRC2007 | | |
| | Phil Mills | 3h04m35.0s | Gr A | |
| 6 | Guy Wilks/ | Subaru Impreza WRC2006 | | |
| | Phil Pugh | 3h07m37.1s | Gr A | |
| 7 | Matthew Wilson/ | Ford Focus RS WRC 06 | | |
| | Michael Orr | 3h11m44.1s | Gr A | |
| 8 | Gareth MacHale/ | Ford Focus RS WRC 06 | | |
| | Alan Harryman | 3h12m47.5s | Gr A | |
| 9 | Andreas Mikkelsen/ | Ford Focus RS WRC 04 | | |
| | Ola Floene | 3h14m47.4s | Gr A | |
| 10 | Niall McShea/ | Subaru Impreza WRX Sti | | |
| | Marshall Clarke | 3h18m11.3s | Gr N | |

84 starters, 66 finishers

**PREVIOUS WINNERS**
2006*Eugene Donnelly/Paul Kiely    Toyota Corolla WRC
*Non-championship event

# The FIA World Rally Championship Round 16
# Rally GB

Right: Loeb drove Rally GB with the title in mind, finishing third to secure his fourth consecutive championship

Far right and above: Hirvonen took advantage of the championship situation to score his fourth WRC win. He led the rally from start to finish

Above right: Second-placed Grönholm was left to ponder what might have been as he headed into retirement

All photographs by McKlein unless specified

# RALLY GB

Allow me, Mr Elliot, to bastardise your words slightly:
This is the way the world *championship* ends;
Not with a bang, but a whimper.

THE final stanza of The Hollow Men was written about something far more serious than the World Rally Championship, but it did, rather neatly, sum up Rally GB.

After 15 rounds at a frenetic pace, this season was not meant to end with the top three drivers essentially tooling their way through the final leg. But while Sébastien Loeb sat in third place, there was no reason for second-placed man Marcus Grönholm to push. And while he wasn't pushing, Mikko Hirvonen was sitting pretty out in front.

That's a bit harsh on Hirvonen, who led from start to finish and, leg two aside (he didn't know those stages very well), looked to have the beating of Grönholm and Loeb. But wouldn't it have been fabulous to have seen the big two racing flat-chat to the line?

If Hirvonen's strongest opposition wasn't firing at 100 per cent all the time, then the weather was certainly doing its best to foul up the Finn's third win of the season. Friday was an unspeakably horrid day in the stages. The fog shrouded the tops of the mountains above Port Talbot, leaving the drivers to play a guessing game on braking points. And as if that wasn't bad enough, the second run through Rheola - in the dark - was a shocker. Torrential rain joined the fog to leave drivers talking of the toughest test of the season. Hirvonen emerged unscathed and even had the temerity to laugh in the face of what had been a devil of a stage.

"It was quite amazing, actually," he said. "Sometimes you couldn't really see if you were on the road or not. It was crazy!"

It didn't cause any problems for the podium sitters, but it did hit Jari-Matti Latvala hard. The Stobart driver had been fourth going into the stage, but a wiper linkage failure forced him to stop three times to clear the mud from his windscreen. He dropped 12 minutes, although the team eventually elected to SuperRally him at a cost of just 10 minutes.

Latvala was desperately disappointed at missing his chance of getting past Loeb in an effort to make it an all-Finnish and all-Ford podium, but he elected to just drive as quickly as he could to gain experience of the conditions and the stages. He drove superbly. Latvala was unbeaten on every other forest test in the event but missed out on setting fastest time on all the remaining stages when Grönholm went quickest around the Millennium Stadium superspecial.

Petter Solberg gave Subaru something to smile about by taking fourth. That allied to a heater matrix problem in the dark on Friday for Henning Solberg's Stobart Ford not only meant the 2003 champion beat his brother to fifth in the drivers' championship, it also meant Subaru edged Stobart for third in the makes' race.

Behind Solberg, Dani Sordo ended his season quietly in fifth, while Matthew Wilson turned in the drive of his year to beat Chris Atkinson to sixth.

Up at the front, Hirvonen and Loeb were celebrating: Hirvonen his fourth WRC win and Loeb his fourth WRC championship. That only left Grönholm to settle back and spend his retirement pondering what could have been a third championship win. If only…

Right: There was some unusual entertainment before the start of the Millennium Stadium Superspecial

Middle right: Andreas Mikkelsen made one of the more spectacular exits from the rally in his Ford Focus WRC

Far right: Latvala became a victim of the weather when the wipers on his Focus stopped working on leg one. He returned under SuperRally and was quickest on all the remaining forest stages

Bottom right: Wilson turned in another fine drive to finish sixth following a close battle with Atkinson's Subaru

Bottom: The longed-for final head-to-head between Grönholm and Loeb turned out to be something of a damp squib

Below: Petter Solberg had a bright end to what has been a difficult year, finishing fourth in the Welsh forests

All photographs by McKlein unless specified

# RALLY GB

Wilks and co-driver Phil Pugh had a rally to remember, winning in the Production Car class and claiming overall victory in the British Rally Championship
McKlein

## The FIA World Rally Championship Round 16
# Rally GB Results
### November 30 - December 02 2007

### FINISH LINES...

Manfred Stohl collected a point in eighth overall at Rally GB on the final outing for the OMV Kronos Team. After 15 years of backing Stohl, the Austrian oil firm has elected to move on from the WRC. Stohl has yet to decide what the future holds for him. Kronos, also leaving the series, will focus on running Peugeots in next year's Intercontinental Rally Challenge... They weren't the only ones leaving: BFGoodrich/Michelin also said its farewells in Cardiff after 34 years at the top and following its total domination of the sport since September 2005. Next year's world championship will be the domain of the Pirelli control tyre... Guy Wilks led Group N from Friday evening until Sunday afternoon to win the two rounds in this event that counted towards the British Rally Championship and clinch the title in a works-backed Mitsubishi Lancer. Wilks' only real threat for the crown was Mark Higgins, but punctures and transmission problems cost the Manxman any hope of clinching the silverware for a fourth time. Wilks also won the Production element of the WRC qualifier, comfortably beating PCWRC series regular Juho Hänninen in the process... Despite being half a world away, Toshi Arai was confirmed as this year's Production Car World Rally Champion. Argentinian Gabriel Pozzo was the only man able to stop Arai, and when he crashed off the road on leg one, the Japanese was free to celebrate his second award in three years...

### RUNNING ORDER

| | | | |
|---|---|---|---|
| 1 | Sébastien Loeb/ | Citroën C4 WRC | |
| | Daniel Elena | | |
| 3 | Marcus Grönholm/ | Ford Focus RS WRC 07 | |
| | Timo Rautiainen | Gr A | |
| 4 | Mikko Hirvonen/ | Ford Focus RS WRC 07 | |
| | Jarmo Lehtinen | Gr A | |
| 2 | Daniel Sordo/ | Citroën C4 WRC | |
| | Marc Martí | Gr A | |
| 7 | Petter Solberg/ | Subaru Impreza WRC2007 | |
| | Phil Mills | Gr A | |
| 10 | Henning Solberg/ | Ford Focus RS WRC 06 | |
| | Cato Menkerud | Gr A | |
| 9 | Jari-Matti Latvala/ | Ford Focus RS WRC 06 | |
| | Miikka Anttila | Gr A | |
| 8 | Chris Atkinson/ | Subaru Impreza WRC2007 | |
| | Stéphane Prevot | Gr A | |
| 5 | Manfred Stohl/ | Citroën Xsara WRC | |
| | Ilka Minor | Gr A | |
| 18 | Jan Kopecky/ | Skoda Fabia WRC | |
| | Filip Schovanek | Gr A | |
| 16 | Matthew Wilson/ | Ford Focus RS WRC 06 | |
| | Michael Orr | Gr A | |
| 11 | Luis Pérez-Companc/ | Ford Focus RS WRC 06 | |
| | Jose Maria Volta | Gr A | |
| 17 | Xavier Pons/ | Subaru Impreza WRC2007 | |
| | Xavier Amigo | Gr A | |
| 12 | Federico Villagra/ | Ford Focus RS WRC 06 | |
| | Jorge Pérez-Companc | Gr A | |
| 20 | Mads Østberg/ | Subaru Impreza WRC2006 | |
| | Ole Kristian Unnerud | Gr A | |
| 21 | Andreas Mikkelsen/ | Ford Focus RS WRC 06 | |
| | Ola Floene | Gr A | |
| 19 | Sebastian Lindholm/ | Suzuki SX4 WRC | |
| | Timo Tuominen | Gr A | |
| 22 | Gareth Jones/ | Ford Focus RS WRC 04 | |
| | David Moynihan | Gr A | |
| 23 | Mark Van Eldik/ | Subaru Impreza WRC2006 | |
| | Michel Groenewoud | Gr A | |
| 24 | Conrad Rautenbach/ | Citroën Xsara WRC | |
| | David Senior | Gr A | |
| 25 | Peter Van Merksteijn/ | Ford Focus RS WRC 06 | |
| | Hans Van Beek | Gr A | |

### SPECIAL STAGE TIMES

**SS1 Port Talbot 1 (17.40km)**

1 M.Hirvonen/J.Lehtinen (Ford Focus RS WRC 07) 9m15.2s; 2 S.Loeb/D.Elena (Citroën C4 WRC) 9m21.7s; 3 M.Grönholm/T.Rautiainen (Ford Focus RS WRC 07) 9m27.2s; 4 J-M.Latvala/M.Anttila (Ford Focus RS WRC 06) 9m29.9s; 5 C.Atkinson/S.Prevot (Subaru Impreza WRC2007) 9m34.2s; 6 P.Solberg/P.Mills (Subaru Impreza WRC2007) 9m34.5s; PC M.Higgins/S.Martin (Mitsubishi Lancer Evo 9) 10m30.2s

**SS2 Resolfen 1 (25.70km)**

1 Hirvonen/Lehtinen (Ford) 12m50.6s; 2 Grönholm/Rautiainen (Ford) 12m55.4s; 3 Loeb/Elena (Citroën) 12m59.5s; 4 Latvala/Anttila (Ford) 13m03.5s; 5 D.Sordo/M.Martí (Citroën C4 WRC) 13m06.8s; 6 Solberg/Mills (Subaru) 13m10.5s; PC Higgins/Martin (Mitsubishi) 14m18.6s

**SS3 Rheola 1 (27.90km)**

1 Hirvonen/Lehtinen (Ford) 15m55.7s; 2 Latvala/Anttila (Ford) 15m57.5s; 3 Grönholm/Rautiainen (Ford) 16m00.3s; 4 Loeb/Elena (Citroën) 16m02.7s; 5 Solberg/Mills (Subaru) 16m10.9s; 6 Sordo/Martí (Citroën) 16m13.1s; PC Higgins/Martin (Mitsubishi) 17m22.6s

**SS4 Port Talbot 2 (17.40km)**

1 Hirvonen/Lehtinen (Ford) 9m17.2; 2 Grönholm/Rautiainen (Ford) 9m21.4s; 3 Loeb/Elena (Citroën) 9m23.3s; 4 Solberg/Mills (Subaru) 9m26.0s; 5 Atkinson/Prevot (Subaru) 9m27.5s; 6 Latvala/Anttila (Ford) 9m30.1s; JWC G.Wilks/P.Pugh (Mitsubishi Lancer Evo 9) 10m37.0s

**SS5 Resolfen 2 (25.70km)**

1= Loeb/Elena (Citroën), Grönholm/Rautiainen (Ford) 13m20.9s; 3 Hirvonen/Lehtinen (Ford) 13m23.3s; 4 Latvala/Anttila (Ford) 13m27.3s; 5 Solberg/Mills (Subaru) 13m36.3s; 6 Sordo/Martí (Citroën) 13m45.5s; PC Wilks/Pugh (Mitsubishi) 15m07.1s

**SS6 Rheola 2 (27.90km)**

1 Hirvonen/Lehtinen (Ford) 16m39.3s; 2 Grönholm/Rautiainen (Ford) 16m55.7s; 3 Solberg/Mills (Subaru) 16m57.1s; 4 Loeb/Elena (Citroën) 17m11.1s; 5 Sordo/Martí (Citroën) 17m39.2s; 6 Atkinson/Prevot (Subaru) 18m26.5s; PC G.Evans/H.Lewis (Mitsubish Lancer Evo 9) 18m32.4s

**SS7 Crychan 1 (19.55km)**

1 Latvala/Anttila (Ford) 10m31.2s; 2 Grönholm/Rautiainen (Ford) 10m35.6s; 3 Loeb/Elena (Citroën) 10m41.7s; 4 Hirvonen/Lehtinen (Ford) 10m44.0s; 5 Sordo/Martí (Citroën) 10m46.8s; 6 X.Pons/X.Amigo (Subaru Impreza WRC2007) 10m47.0s; PC J.Hänninen/M.Markkula (Mitsubishi Lancer Evo 9) 11m38.2s

**SS8 Epynt 1 (13.76km)**

1 Latvala/Anttila (Ford) 7m33.2s; 2= Grönholm/Rautiainen (Ford), Hirvonen/Lehtinen (Ford) 7m36.2s; 4 Sordo/Martí (Citroën) 7m37.2s; 5 Loeb/Elena (Citroën) 7m41.5s; 6 Solberg/Mills (Subaru) 7m41.8s; PC Higgins/Martin (Mitsubishi) 8m18.9s

**SS9 Halfway 1 (18.37km)**

1 Latvala/Anttila (Ford) 10m28.3s; 2 Hirvonen/Lehtinen (Ford) 10m30.9s; 3 Grönholm/Rautiainen (Ford) 10m32.3s; 4 Sordo/Martí (Citroën) 10m34.4s; 5 Loeb/Elena (Citroën) 10m36.5s; 6 H.Solberg/C.Menkerud (Ford Focus RS WRC 06) 10m39.5s; PC Hänninen/Markkula (Mitsubishi) 11m18.7s

**SS10 Crychan 2 (19.55km)**

1 Latvala/Anttila (Ford) 10m39.8s; 2 Grönholm/Rautiainen (Ford) 10m41.1s; 3 Hirvonen/Lehtinen (Ford) 10m41.5s; 4 Loeb/Elena (Citroën) 10m43.4s; 5 Sordo/Martí (Citroën) 10m44.1s; 6 Solberg/Mills (Subaru) 10m46.3s; PC Wilks/Pugh (Mitsubishi) 11m44.0s

**SS11 Epynt 2 (13.76km)**

1 Latvala/Anttila (Ford) 7m40.1s; 2 Grönholm/Rautiainen (Ford) 7m41.0s; 3 Hirvonen/Lehtinen (Ford) 7m42.9s; 4 Solberg/Menkerud (Ford) 7m45.4s; 5 Sordo/Martí (Citroën) 7m46.0s; 6 Solberg/Mills (Subaru) 7m46.6s; PC Higgins/Martin (Mitsubishi) 8m27.1s

**SS12 Halfway 2 (18.37km)**

1 Latvala/Anttila (Ford) 10m39.6s; 2 Hirvonen/Lehtinen (Ford) 10m46.5s; 3 Loeb/Elena (Citroën) 10m46.6s; 4 Atkinson/Prevot (Subaru) 10m49.6s; 5 Solberg/Mills (Subaru) 10m50.8s; 6 Sordo/Martí (Citroën) 10m51.8s; PC Wilks/Pugh (Mitsubishi) 11m41.8s

**SS13 Cardiff Millenium Stadium (1.10km)**

1 Grönholm/Rautiainen (Ford) 1m03.8s; 2 Hirvonen/Lehtinen (Ford) 1m04.0s; 3 Solberg/Mills (Subaru) 1m04.2s; 4

# RALLY GB

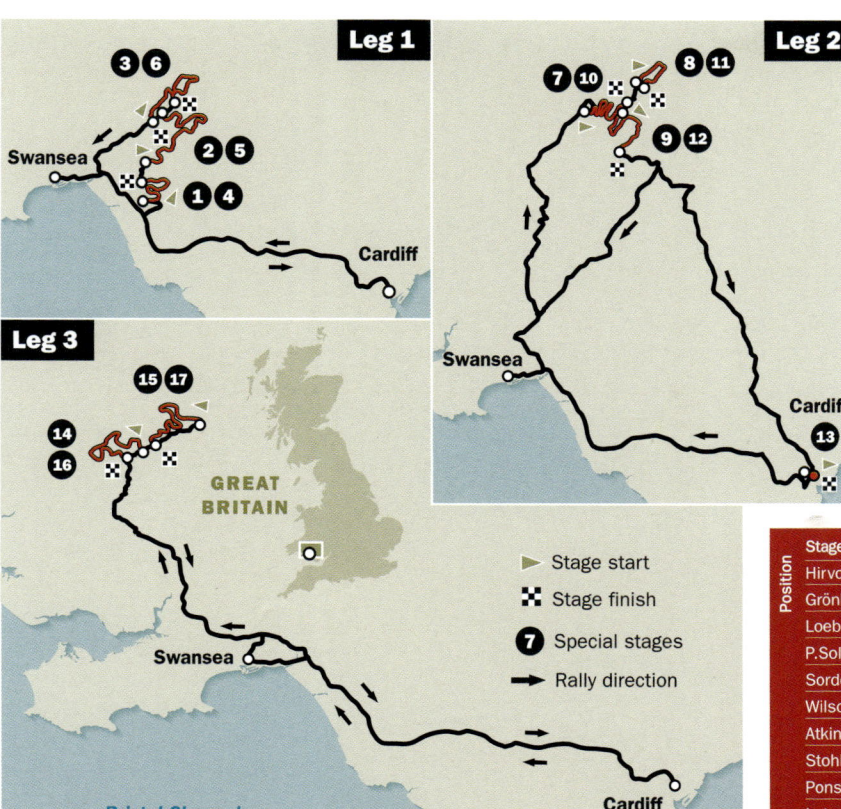

| | Stage Numbers | 1 | 2 | 3 | 4 | 5 | 6 | 7 | 8 | 9 | 10 | 11 | 12 | 13 | 14 | 15 | 16 | 17 |
|---|---|---|---|---|---|---|---|---|---|---|---|---|---|---|---|---|---|---|
| Position | Hirvonen | 1 | 1 | 1 | 1 | 1 | 1 | 1 | 1 | 1 | 1 | 1 | 1 | 1 | 1 | 1 | 1 | 1 |
| | Grönholm | 3 | 3 | 2 | 2 | 2 | 2 | 2 | 2 | 2 | 2 | 2 | 2 | 2 | 2 | 2 | 2 | 2 |
| | Loeb | 2 | 2 | 3 | 3 | 3 | 3 | 3 | 3 | 3 | 3 | 3 | 3 | 3 | 3 | 3 | 3 | 3 |
| | P.Solberg | 6 | 5 | 5 | 5 | 5 | 5 | 4 | 4 | 4 | 4 | 4 | 4 | 4 | 4 | 4 | 4 | 4 |
| | Sordo | 7 | 6 | 6 | 6 | 6 | 5 | 5 | 5 | 5 | 5 | 5 | 5 | 5 | 5 | 5 | 5 | 5 |
| | Wilson | 10 | 9 | 8 | 8 | 8 | 6 | 7 | 7 | 7 | 7 | 7 | 7 | 6 | 6 | 6 | 6 | 6 |
| | Atkinson | 5 | 7 | 7 | 7 | 9 | 7 | 6 | 6 | 6 | 6 | 6 | 6 | 7 | 7 | 7 | 7 | 7 |
| | Stohl | 11 | 8 | 9 | 9 | 7 | 8 | 8 | 8 | 8 | 8 | 8 | 8 | 8 | 8 | 8 | 8 | 8 |
| | Pons | 8 | 10 | 10 | 10 | 10 | 9 | 9 | 9 | 9 | 9 | 9 | 9 | 9 | 9 | 9 | 9 | 9 |
| | Latvala | 4 | 4 | 4 | 4 | 4 | 15 | 13 | 13 | 12 | 12 | 12 | 12 | 12 | 11 | 11 | 11 | 10 |
| | Østberg | 9 | 12 | 13 | 13 | 11 | 12 | 12 | 12 | 11 | 10 | 10 | 10 | 10 | 10 | 10 | 10 | 11 |
| | Kopecky | 13 | 14 | 14 | 14 | 13 | 11 | 11 | 11 | 10 | 11 | 11 | 11 | 11 | 12 | 12 | 12 | 12 |
| | H.Solberg | 15 | 13 | 11 | 11 | 24 | 38 | 35 | 33 | 30 | 27 | 23 | 18 | 18 | 18 | 16 | 16 | 15 |
| | Villagra | 21 | 16 | 16 | 16 | 16 | 32 | 32 | 30 | 26 | 25 | 24 | 22 | 22 | 22 | 19 | 18 | 18 |
| | Lindholm | 32 | 33 | 41 | 62 | 56 | 56 | 50 | 47 | 44 | 42 | 38 | 38 | 37 | 32 | 31 | 29 | 27 |
| | P.Companc | 14 | 15 | 15 | 15 | 14 | 18 | 16 | 16 | 13 | 13 | 13 | 13 | 13 | 13 | 13 | R | |
| | Mikkelsen | 12 | 11 | 12 | 12 | 12 | 10 | 10 | 10 | R | | | | | | | | |

Loeb/Elena (Citroën) 1m04.3s; 5 Atkinson/Prevot (Subaru) 1m04.6s; 6 Sordo/Martí (Citroën) 1m04.7s; PC A.Araújo/M.Ramalho (Mitsubishi Lancer Evo 9) 1m06.1s

**SS14 Brechfa 1 (28.88km)**
1= Hirvonen/Lehtinen (Ford), Latvala/Anttila (Ford) 16m14.2s; 3 Grönholm/Rautiainen (Ford) 16m16.2s; 4 Sordo/Martí (Citroën) 16m26.0s; 5 Loeb/Elena (Citroën) 16m29.1s; 6 Solberg/Mills (Subaru) 16m29.5s; PC Hänninen/Markkula (Mitsubishi) 17m29.5s

**SS15 Trawscoed 1 (28.23km)**
1 Latvala/Anttila (Ford) 16m39.7s; 2 Grönholm/Rautiainen (Ford) 16m41.9s; 3 Hirvonen/Lehtinen (Ford) 16m47.3s; 4 Loeb/Elena (Citroën) 16m50.9s; 5 Sordo/Martí (Citroën) 16m56.8s; 6 Solberg/Menkerud (Ford) 17m00.8s; PC Wilks/Pugh (Mitsubishi) 18m15.5s

**SS16 Brechfa 2 (28.88km)**
1 Latvala/Anttila (Ford) 16m11.6s; 2 Grönholm/Rautiainen (Ford) 16m13.0s; 3 Solberg/Mills (Subaru) 16m14.6s; 4 Hirvonen/Lehtinen (Ford) 16m15.3s; 5 Sordo/Martí (Citroën) 16m19.0s; 6 Loeb/Elena (Citroën) 16m19.6s; PC Hänninen/Markkula (Mitsubishi) 17m36.4s

**SS17 Trawscoed 2 (28.23km)**
1 Latvala/Anttila (Ford) 16m51.0s; 2 Grönholm/Rautiainen (Ford) 16m52.2s; 3 Sordo/Martí (Citroën) 16m59.2s; 4 Loeb/Elena (Citroën) 17m02.0s; 5 Solberg/Mills (Subaru) 17m03.9s; 6 Solberg/Menkerud (Ford) 17m06.0s; PC Hänninen/Markkula (Mitsubishi) 18m14.0s

**Cars who retired and subsequently re-started under SuperRally regs**

| 10 | Solberg/Menkerud | Ford Focus RS WRC 06 | | |
| | Misted Screen | SS6 | Gr A | |
| 9 | Latvala/Anttila | Ford Focus RS WRC 06 | | |
| | Wiper Failure | SS6 | Gr A | |
| 19 | Lindholm/Tuominen | Suzuki SX4 WRC | | |
| | Brakes | SS2 | Gr A | |

**MAJOR RETIREMENTS**

| 21 | Mikkelsen/Floene | Ford Focus RS WRC 06 | |
| | Accident | SS9 | Gr A |
| 11 | Pérez-Companc/Volta | Ford Focus RS WRC 06 | |
| | Accident | SS15 | Gr A |
| 24 | Rautenbach/Senior | Citroën Xsara WRC | |
| | Accident | SS8 | Gr A |

**FIA CLASS WINNERS**

| A8 | Over 2000cc | Hirvonen/Lehtinen |
| | | Ford Focus RS WRC 07 |
| A7 | 1600-2000cc | Solá/Sanchez |
| | | Honda Civic Type-R |
| A6 | 1400-1600cc | Gass/Shanks |
| | | Citroën C2 |
| N4 | Over 2000cc | Wilks/Pugh |
| | | Mitsubishi Lancer Evo 9 |
| N3 | 1600-2000cc | Evans/Edwards |
| | | Ford Fiesta ST |
| N2 | 1400-1600cc | Wozencroft/Ridge |
| | | Suzuki Swift |
| N1 | Up to 1400cc | Pinder/Taylor |
| | | MG ZR |

**RALLY LEADERS**
Overall: SS1-17 Hirvonen
PC: SS1-3 M.Higgins; SS4-17 Wilks

**SPECIAL STAGE ANALYSIS**

| | 1st | 2nd | 3rd | 4th | 5th | 6th |
|---|---|---|---|---|---|---|
| Latvala (Ford) | 10 | 1 | 1 | 3 | - | 1 |
| Hirvonen (Ford) | 6 | 4 | 4 | 2 | - | - |
| Grönholm (Ford) | 2 | 10 | 4 | - | - | - |
| Loeb (Citroën) | 1 | 1 | 3 | 6 | 3 | 1 |
| P.Solberg (Subaru) | - | - | 3 | 1 | 5 | 4 |
| Sordo (Citroën) | - | - | 1 | 3 | 7 | 4 |
| Atkinson (Subaru) | - | - | - | 1 | 3 | 1 |
| H.Solberg (Ford) | - | - | - | - | 1 | 3 |
| Pons (Subaru) | - | - | - | - | - | 1 |

**WORLD CHAMPIONSHIP POINTS**
Drivers
1 Loeb 116; 2 Grönholm 112; 3 Hirvonen 99; 4 Sordo 65; 5 P.Solberg 47; 6 H.Solberg 34; 7 Atkinson 31; 8 Latvala 30; 9 Stohl 13; 10 Duval 12 etc

Manufacturers
1 BP-Ford WRT 212; 2 Citroën Total WRT 183; 3 Subaru WRT 87; 4 Stobart M-Sport Ford RT 81; 5 OMV-Kronos Citroën WRT 45; 6 Munchi's Ford RT14

Junior World Championship
1 Andersson 43; 2 Aava 38; 3 Prokop 34; 4 Beres 26; 5 Mölder 20; 6 Sandell 19; 7 Burkart 18; 8 Rautenbach 16; 9 Bonato 10; 10 Cortinovis 9 etc

Production Cup
1 Arai 39; 2 Pozzo 30; 3 Higgins 25; 4 McShea 21; 5 Hänninen 18; 6 M.Baldacci 14; 7 Nutahara 13; 8= Sohlberg, Al-Attiyah 12; 10= Svedlund, Villagra, Wilks, Aigner, Araújo 10 etc

**ROUTE DETAILS**
Total route of 1259.74km of which 359.54km were competitive on 17 special stages

Leg 1 Friday 30 November, 6 special stages totalling 140.80km

Leg 2 Saturday 1 December, 7 special stages totalling 104.48km

Leg 3 Sunday 2 December, 4 special stages totalling 114.26km

**RESULTS**

| 1 | Mikko Hirvonen/ | Ford Focus RS WRC 07 | |
| | Jarmo Lehtinen | 3h22m50.9s | Gr A |
| 2 | Marcus Grönholm/ | Ford Focus RS WRC 07 | |
| | Timo Rautiainen | 3h23m06.1s | Gr A |
| 3 | Sébastien Loeb/ | Citroën C4 WRC | |
| | Daniel Elena | 3h24m23.9s | Gr A |
| 4 | Petter Solberg/ | Subaru Impreza WRC2007 | |
| | Phil Mills | 3h25m48.2s | Gr A |
| 5 | Daniel Sordo/ | Citroën C4 WRC | |
| | Marc Martí | 3h26m05.2s | Gr A |
| 6 | Matthew Wilson/ | Ford Focus RS WRC 06 | |
| | Michael Orr | 3h30m23.8s | Gr A |
| 7 | Chris Atkinson/ | Subaru Impreza WRC2007 | |
| | Stéphane Prevot | 3h31m20.4s | Gr A |
| 8 | Manfred Stohl/ | Citroën Xsara WRC | |
| | Ilka Minor | 3h21m45.5s | Gr A |
| 9 | Xavier Pons/ | Subaru Impreza WRC2007 | |
| | Xavier Amigo | 3h32m39.7s | Gr A |
| 10 | Jari-Matti Latvala/ | Ford Focus RS WRC 06 | |
| | Miika Anttila | 3h33m33.3s | Gr A |

108 starters, 86 finishers

**PREVIOUS WINNERS SINCE 1971**

| 1971 | Stig Blomqvist/Arne Hertz | Saab 96 V4 |
| 1972 | Roger Clark/Tony Mason | Ford Escort RS1600 |
| 1973 | Timo Mäkinen/Henry Liddon | Ford Escort RS1600 |
| 1974 | Timo Mäkinen/Henry Liddon | Ford Escort RS1600 |
| 1975 | Timo Mäkinen/Henry Liddon | Ford Escort RS1800 |
| 1976 | Roger Clark/Stuart Pegg | Ford Escort RS1800 |
| 1977 | Björn Waldegård/Hans Thorszelius | Ford Escort RS1800 |
| 1978 | Hannu Mikkola/Arne Hertz | Ford Escort RS1800 |
| 1979 | Hannu Mikkola/Arne Hertz | Ford Escort RS1800 |
| 1980 | Henri Toivonen/Paul White | Talbot Sunbeam Lotus |
| 1981 | Hannu Mikkola/Arne Hertz | Audi Quattro A1 |
| 1982 | Hannu Mikkola/Arne Hertz | Audi Quattro A1 |
| 1983 | Stig Blomqvist/Björn Cederberg | Audi Quattro A2 |
| 1984 | Ari Vatanen/Terry Harryman | Peugeot 205 Turbo 16 |
| 1985 | Henri Toivonen/Neil Wilson | Lancia Delta S4 |
| 1986 | Timo Salonen/Seppo Harjanne | Peugeot 205 Turbo 16 E2 |
| 1987 | Juha Kankkunen/Juha Piironen | Lancia Delta HF Turbo |
| 1988 | Markku Alén/Ilkka Kivimäki | Lancia Delta Integrale |
| 1989 | Pentti Airikkala/Ronan McNamee | Mitsubishi Galant VR-4 |
| 1990 | Carlos Sainz/Luis Moya | Toyota Celica GT4 |
| 1991 | Juha Kankkunen/Juha Piironen | Lancia Delta Integrale 16v |
| 1992 | Carlos Sainz/Luis Moya | Toyota Celica Turbo 4WD |
| 1993 | Juha Kankkunen/Juha Piironen | Toyota Celica Turbo 4WD |
| 1994 | Colin McRae/Derek Ringer | Subaru Impreza 555 |
| 1995 | Colin McRae/Derek Ringer | Subaru Impreza 555 |
| 1996 | Armin Schwarz/Denis Giraudet | Toyota Celica GT-Four |
| 1997 | Colin McRae/Nicky Grist | Subaru Impreza WRC97 |
| 1998 | Richard Burns/Robert Reid | Mitsubishi Carisma GT |
| 1999 | Richard Burns/Robert Reid | Subaru Impreza WRC99 |
| 2000 | Richard Burns/Robert Reid | Subaru Impreza WRC2000 |
| 2001 | Marcus Grönholm/Timo Rautiainen | Peugeot 206 WRC |
| 2002 | Petter Solberg/Phil Mills | Subaru Impreza WRC2002 |
| 2003 | Petter Solberg/Phil Mills | Subaru Impreza WRC2003 |
| 2004 | Petter Solberg/Phil Mills | Subaru Impreza WRC2004 |
| 2005 | Petter Solberg/Phil Mills | Subaru Impreza WRC2005 |
| 2006 | Marcus Grönholm/Timo Rautiainen | Ford Focus RS WRC 06 |

# Results 2007

## WORLD RALLY CHAMPIONSHIP FOR DRIVERS

| ROUND | | 1 | 2 | 3 | 4 | 5 | 6 | 7 | 8 | 9 | 10 | 11 | 12 | 13 | 14 | 15 | 16 | TOTAL |
|---|---|---|---|---|---|---|---|---|---|---|---|---|---|---|---|---|---|---|
| 1 | SÉBASTIEN LOEB | 10 | 8 | 0 | 10 | 10 | 10 | R | 8 | 6 | 10 | 8 | 10 | 10 | R | 10 | 6 | 116 |
| 2 | MARCUS GRÖNHOLM | 6 | 10 | 8 | 8 | 5 | 8 | 10 | 10 | 10 | 5 | 10 | 6 | 8 | R | R | 8 | 112 |
| 3 | MIKKO HIRVONEN | 4 | 6 | 10 | 6 | 4 | 6 | 8 | 5 | 8 | 6 | 6 | 5 | 0 | 10 | 5 | 10 | 99 |
| 4 | DANIEL SORDO | 8 | 0 | 0 | 5 | 6 | 3 | 6 | 0 | R | R | 3 | 8 | 6 | 8 | 8 | 4 | 65 |
| 5 | PETTER SOLBERG | 3 | R | 5 | R | 8 | R | 4 | 6 | R | 3 | 2 | 3 | 4 | 0 | 4 | 5 | 47 |
| 6 | HENNING SOLBERG | 0 | 5 | 6 | 0 | 0 | 4 | 5 | 4 | 4 | 0 | 0 | 0 | 0 | 6 | 0 | 0 | 34 |
| 7 | CHRIS ATKINSON | 5 | 1 | 0 | 4 | R | 2 | 0 | 3 | 5 | 0 | 5 | 1 | 3 | R | 0 | 2 | 31 |
| 8 | JARI-MATTI LATVALA | R | R | 4 | 2 | 1 | 5 | 0 | 0 | R | 1 | 4 | 2 | 5 | 0 | 6 | 0 | 30 |
| 9 | MANFRED STOHL | 0 | 2 | 0 | 3 | 0 | 1 | 2 | 1 | R | 0 | R | 0 | 3 | R | 1 | | 13 |
| 10 | FRANÇOIS DUVAL | - | - | - | - | - | - | - | R | - | 8 | - | 4 | R | - | - | - | 12 |
| 11 | MATTHEW WILSON | 0 | R | 0 | 1 | 0 | 0 | 0 | 0 | 0 | 0 | 0 | 0 | R | 5 | 2 | 3 | 11 |
| 12= | JAN KOPECKY | 1 | 0 | 1 | - | 0 | - | R | 2 | R | 4 | - | R | 2 | - | - | 0 | 10 |
| 12= | TONI GARDEMEISTER | 2 | 3 | R | - | EX | - | 3 | - | - | 2 | - | - | - | - | - | - | 10 |
| 14 | DANIEL CARLSSON | - | 4 | 2 | - | 3 | - | R | - | - | - | - | - | - | - | - | - | 9 |
| 15 | GIANLUIGI GALLI | - | 0 | 3 | - | 2 | - | - | - | - | - | - | - | - | - | - | - | 5 |
| 16= | LUIS PÉREZ-COMPANC | - | 0 | - | 0 | - | 0 | R | 0 | 0 | - | 0 | R | - | 4 | - | R | 4 |
| 16= | XAVIER PONS | 0 | R | 0 | - | - | - | - | - | 3 | 0 | R | 0 | 1 | 0 | R | 0 | 4 |
| 18= | GUY WILKS | - | - | R | - | R | - | - | 0 | 0 | 0 | - | - | - | - | 3 | 0 | 3 |
| 18= | URMO AAVA | - | - | 0 | - | 0 | - | - | 0 | 0 | 2 | 0 | 1 | 0 | R | 0 | - | 3 |
| 20 | FEDERICO VILLAGRA | - | - | - | - | - | 0 | 0 | 0 | 0 | - | 0 | 0 | - | 2 | - | 0 | 2 |
| 21= | MADS ØSTBERG | - | 0 | 0 | - | R | - | R | - | - | 1 | - | - | - | - | - | 0 | 1 |
| 21= | GARETH MACHALE | 0 | - | - | R | 0 | - | R | - | - | - | - | - | - | - | 1 | - | 1 |
| 21= | JUHA HÄNNINEN | - | EX | 0 | - | - | 0 | 1 | R | R | - | 0 | 0 | - | 0 | - | 0 | 1 |
| 21= | KATSUHIKO TAGUCHI | - | - | - | - | - | - | - | - | - | - | - | - | - | 1 | - | - | 1 |

## WORLD RALLY CHAMPIONSHIP FOR MANUFACTURERS

| ROUND | | 1 | 2 | 3 | 4 | 5 | 6 | 7 | 8 | 9 | 10 | 11 | 12 | 13 | 14 | 15 | 16 | TOTAL |
|---|---|---|---|---|---|---|---|---|---|---|---|---|---|---|---|---|---|---|
| 1 | BP-FORD WRT | 10 | 16 | 18 | 14 | 9 | 14 | 18 | 15 | 18 | 11 | 16 | 11 | 9 | 10 | 5 | 18 | 212 |
| 2 | CITROËN TOTAL WRT | 18 | 9 | 1 | 15 | 16 | 13 | 6 | 8 | 6 | 10 | 11 | 18 | 16 | 8 | 18 | 10 | 183 |
| 3 | SUBARU WRT | 8 | 2 | 5 | 4 | 8 | 2 | 5 | 9 | 5 | 5 | 7 | 4 | 7 | 2 | 6 | 8 | 87 |
| 4 | STOBART VK M-SPORT FORD | 1 | 5 | 10 | 3 | 2 | 9 | 7 | 4 | 4 | 5 | 5 | 2 | 7 | 7 | 9 | 1 | 81 |
| 5 | OMV KRONOS CITROËN WRT | 2 | 7 | 5 | 3 | 4 | 1 | 3 | 2 | 0 | 8 | 0 | 4 | 0 | 4 | 0 | 2 | 45 |
| 6 | MUNCHI'S FORD WRT | - | 0 | - | 0 | - | 0 | 0 | 1 | 5 | - | 0 | 0 | - | 8 | - | 0 | 14 |

KEY TO ROUNDS: 1-MONTE CARLO; 2-SWEDEN; 3-NORWAY; 4-MEXICO; 5-PORTUGAL; 6-ARGENTINA; 7-ITALY; 8-GREECE; 9-FINLAND; 10-GERMANY; 11-NEW ZEALAND; 12-SPAIN; 13-CORSICA; 14-JAPAN; 15-IRELAND; 16-GREAT BRITAIN

Race&motion

## JUNIOR RALLY CHAMPIONSHIP

| ROUND | | 1 | 2 | 3 | 4 | 5 | 6 | 7 | TOTAL |
|---|---|---|---|---|---|---|---|---|---|
| 1 | PER-GUNNAR ANDERSSON | 10 | 10 | 8 | - | - | 10 | 5 | 43 |
| 2 | URMO AAVA | 6 | 8 | 10 | - | 8 | 6 | R | 38 |
| 3 | MARTIN PROKOP | - | R | 6 | R | 10 | 8 | 10 | 34 |
| 4 | JOSEF BERES | - | 6 | 3 | R | 4 | 5 | 8 | 26 |
| 5 | JAAN MÖLDER | 5 | 5 | 4 | R | 3 | 3 | - | 20 |
| 6 | PATRICK SANDELL | 8 | 0 | 1 | 10 | EX | R | - | 19 |
| 7 | AARON NIKOLAI BURKART | 4 | - | 5 | 0 | 5 | 2 | 2 | 18 |
| 8 | CONRAD RAUTENBACH | - | 0 | R | 5 | 6 | 4 | 1 | 16 |
| 9 | YOAN BONATO | - | - | - | 1 | 2 | 1 | 6 | 10 |
| 10 | ANDREA CORTINOVIS | 2 | 4 | 0 | 0 | - | R | 3 | 9 |

KEY TO ROUNDS: 1-NORWAY; 2-PORTUGAL; 3-ITALY 4- FINLAND; 5-GERMANY; 6-SPAIN; 7-CORSICA

## PRODUCTION WORLD RALLY CHAMPIONSHIP

| ROUND | | 1 | 2 | 3 | 4 | 5 | 6 | 7 | 8 | TOTAL |
|---|---|---|---|---|---|---|---|---|---|---|
| 1 | TOSHIHIRO ARAI | 3 | 8 | 8 | 10 | 10 | R | - | - | 39 |
| 2 | GABRIEL POZZO | - | - | 5 | 2 | 5 | 10 | 8 | R | 30 |
| 3 | MARK HIGGINS | R | 10 | - | 5 | - | 4 | R | 6 | 25 |
| 4 | NIALL MCSHEA | - | - | 3 | - | 8 | - | 10 | - | 21 |
| 5 | JUHA HÄNNINEN | EX | - | 6 | R | 2 | 2 | - | 8 | 18 |
| 6 | MIRCO BALDACCI | 0 | 5 | R | 6 | 0 | - | - | 3 | 14 |
| 7 | FUMIO NUTAHARA | 4 | 2 | R | - | 4 | R | 3 | - | 13 |
| 8= | KRISTIAN SOHLBERG | 6 | 6 | R | R | - | - | - | - | 12 |
| 8= | NASSER AL-ATTIYAH | 2 | R | R | 4 | - | - | 6 | - | 12 |
| 10= | OSCAR SVEDLUND | 10 | - | - | - | - | - | - | - | 10 |
| 10= | FEDERICO VILLAGRA | - | - | 10 | - | - | - | - | - | 10 |
| 10= | GUY WILKS | - | - | - | - | - | - | - | 10 | 10 |
| 10= | ANDREAS AIGNER | 0 | 0 | 2 | 8 | - | - | R | 0 | 10 |
| 10= | ARMINDO ARAÚJO | 5 | - | - | R | 3 | EX | R | 2 | 10 |

KEY TO ROUNDS: 1-SWEDEN; 2-MEXICO; 3-ARGENTINA; 4-GREECE; 5-NEW ZEALAND; 6-JAPAN; 7-IRELAND 8-GREAT BRITAIN

# Technically speaking

Here's how the main runners in the 2007 World and Junior championships measured up to each other

## FORD FOCUS RS WRC07

**Team Principal:** Malcolm Wilson
**Chief Engineer:** Christian Loriaux
**Sponsors:** BP, Castrol, Abu Dhabi, BFGoodrich, OZ, Bremo, Sparco

### ENGINE
| | |
|---|---|
| Designation | Duratec WRC |
| Cylinders | Four in-line |
| Mounts | Transverse/front |
| Capacity | 1998cc |
| Bore & stroke | 85x88mm |
| Valves/camshaft | 16/DOHC |
| Fuel system | Ford/PI Research |
| Turbocharger | Garrett |
| Max power | 300bhp@6000rpm |
| Max torque | 550NM@4000rpm |
| Oil contract | Castrol |

### TRANSMISSION
| | |
|---|---|
| Gearbox | M-Sport/Ricardo 5-speed sequential |
| Drive type | 4WD |
| Clutch/differentials | M-Sport/Sachs multi-disc carbon clutch, M-Sport active centre diff. Pi electronic control units |

### DIMENSIONS
| | |
|---|---|
| Overall length | 4362mm |
| Overall width | 1800mm |
| Wheelbase | 2640mm |
| Weight | 1230kg |
| Front track | - |
| Rear track | - |
| Body | Three-door steel |

### CHASSIS
| | |
|---|---|
| Steering | Rack and pinion (power-assisted) |
| Front suspension | MacPherson struts, Reiger damping |
| Rear suspension | Trailing arm, Reiger damping |
| Wheel sizes | 7x15in (gravel) 8x18in (asphalt) |
| Tyres | BFGoodrich |
| Front brakes | 300/370mm Brembo discs, 4-8 piston caliper |
| Rear brakes | 300/370mm Brembo discs, 4-8 piston caliper |

## CITROËN C4 WRC

**Team Principal:** Guy Fréquelin
**Chief Engineer:** Xavier Mestelan-Pinon
**Sponsors:** Total, BFGoodrich, Meteo France, Eurodatacar

### ENGINE
| | |
|---|---|
| Designation | XU7JP4 |
| Cylinders | Four in-line |
| Mounts | Transverse/front |
| Capacity | 1998cc |
| Bore & stroke | - |
| Valves/camshaft | 16-valve/DOHC |
| Fuel system | Magneti Marelli MR3 |
| Turbocharger | Garrett |
| Max power | 315bhp@5500rpm |
| Max torque | 580Nm@2750rpm |
| Oil contract | Total |

### TRANSMISSION
| | |
|---|---|
| Gearbox | X-track 6-speed, sequential |
| Drive type | 4WD |
| Clutch/differentials | Triple-plate carbon, electronic control centre diff, mechanical front and rear |

### DIMENSIONS
| | |
|---|---|
| Overall length | 4274mm |
| Overall width | 1800mm |
| Wheelbase | 2608mm |
| Weight | 1230kg |
| Front track | 1598mm |
| Rear track | 1598mm |
| Body | Three-door steel |

### CHASSIS
| | |
|---|---|
| Steering | Rack and pinion (hydraulic power-assisted) |
| Front suspension | MacPherson strut with coil spring Citroën/Exe-TC damping |
| Rear suspension | MacPherson strut, with coil spring Citroën/Exe-TC damping |
| Wheel sizes | 7x15/8x15in |
| Tyres | BFGoodrich |
| Front brakes | 376x28mm Alcon discs, 6-/8 piston calipers |
| Rear brakes | 278x20mm Alcon discs, 6-8 piston calipers |

## CAR SPECIFICATIONS

## SUBARU IMPREZA WRC 2007

**Team Principal:** Richard Taylor
**Chief Engineer:** Christophe Chapelain
**Sponsors:** STi, BFGoodrich, BBS, Denso, Motul, PIAA, Snap-on, Sparco

### ENGINE
| | |
|---|---|
| Designation | EJ20 |
| Cylinders | Horizontally opposed four |
| Mounts Front | longitudinal |
| Capacity | 1997cc |
| Bore & stroke | 92x75mm |
| Valves/camshaft | 16/4 OHC |
| Fuel system | STi sequential injection |
| Turbocharger | IHI |
| Max power | 300bhp@5500rpm |
| Max torque | 600Nm@4000rpm |
| Oil contract | Motul |

### TRANSMISSION
| | |
|---|---|
| Gearbox | Prodrive 6-speed |
| Drive type | 4WD |
| Clutch/differentials | AP Carbon, electro-hydraulic active control centre diff, mechanical front and rear diffs |

### DIMENSIONS
| | |
|---|---|
| Overall length | 4465mm |
| Overall width | 1800mm |
| Wheelbase | 2540mm |
| Weight | 1230kg |
| Front track | 1510kg |
| Rear track | 1510kg |
| Body | Four-door steel |

### CHASSIS
| | |
|---|---|
| Steering | Rack and pinion (power-assisted) |
| Front suspension | MacPherson strut, Sachs damping |
| Rear suspension | MacPherson strut with longitudinal and transverse link, Sachs damping |
| Wheel sizes | BBS 7x15in (gravel) 8x18in (asphalt) |
| Tyres | BFGoodrich |
| Front brakes | AP 305-366x32mm discs 4-6 piston calipers |
| Rear brakes | AP 305x28mm discs 4-6 piston calipers |

## CITROËN XSARA WRC

**Team Principal:** Marc Van Dalen
**Chief engineer:** Jean-Pierre Debacker
**Sponsors:** OMV, BFGoodrich, OMP

### ENGINE
| | |
|---|---|
| Designation | XU7JP4 |
| Cylinders | Four in-line |
| Mounts | Transverse/front |
| Capacity | 1998cc |
| Bore & stroke | 86x86mm |
| Compression ratio | - |
| Valves/camshaft | 16-valve/DOHC |
| Fuel system | Magneti Marelli MR3 |
| Turbocharger | Garrett |
| Max power | 315bhp@5500rpm |
| Max torque | 570Nm@2750rpm |
| Oil contract | Total |

### TRANSMISSION
| | |
|---|---|
| Gearbox | X-track 6-speed, sequential |
| Drive type | 4WD |
| Clutch/differentials | Triple-plate carbon, electro-hydraulic active control |

### DIMENSIONS
| | |
|---|---|
| Overall length | 4167mm |
| Overall width | 1770mm |
| Wheelbase | 2555mm |
| Weight | 1230kg |
| Front track | 1568mm |
| Rear track | 1568mm |
| Body | Three-door steel |

### CHASSIS
| | |
|---|---|
| Steering | Rack and pinion (power-assisted) |
| Front suspension | MacPherson strut, Extreme Teck damping |
| Rear suspension | MacPherson strut, Extreme Teck damping |
| Wheel sizes | 7x15/8x15in |
| Tyres | BFGoodrich |
| Front brakes | 376x28mm Alcon discs, 6-8 piston calipers |
| Rear brakes | 278x20mm Alcon discs 6-8 piston calipers |

## CITROËN C2 S1600

### ENGINE
| | |
|---|---|
| Cylinders | Four in-line |
| Mounts Front | Transverse |
| Capacity | 1587cc |
| Bore & stroke | 78.5x82mm |
| Compression ratio | - |
| Valves/camshaft | 16/DOHC |
| Fuel system | Magneti Marelli MF-4M |
| Max power | 255bhp@8500rpm |
| Max torque | 205Nm@7000rpm |

### TRANSMISSION
| | |
|---|---|
| Gearbox | Sadev 6-speed sequential |
| Drive type | FWD |
| Clutch/differentials | 184mm dia.plate/passive mechanical |

### DIMENSIONS
| | |
|---|---|
| Overall length | 3660mm |
| Overall width | 1795mm |
| Wheelbase | 2326mm |
| Weight | 1000kg |
| Front track | 1600mm |
| Rear track | 1600mm |
| Body | Three-door steel |

### CHASSIS
| | |
|---|---|
| Steering | Rack and pinion (power-assisted) |
| Front suspension | MacPherson struts, Ohlins damping |
| Rear suspension | Trailing arms, Ohlins damping |
| Wheel sizes | 6x15in (gravel) 7x17in (asphalt) |
| Tyres | Pirelli |
| Front brakes | 300-355mm discs, 4 piston calipers |
| Rear brakes | 280mm discs, 2 piston calipers |

## SUZUKI SWIFT

### ENGINE
| | |
|---|---|
| Cylinders | Four in-line |
| Mounts Front | Transverse |
| Capacity | 1598cc |
| Bore & stroke | 81x77.5mm |
| Compression ratio | 12.9:1 |
| Valves/camshaft | 16/DOHC |
| Fuel system | Suzuki injection |
| Max power | 218bhp@8750bhp |
| Max torque | 186NM@7250rpm |

### TRANSMISSION
| | |
|---|---|
| Gearbox | Suzuki 5-speed sequential |
| Drive type | FWD |
| Clutch/differentials | Single-plate, 184mm dia./passive mechanical |

### DIMENSIONS
| | |
|---|---|
| Overall length | 3695mm |
| Overall width | 1805mm |
| Wheelbase | 2390mm |
| Weight | 1000kg |
| Front track | - |
| Rear track | - |
| Body | Three-door steel |

### CHASSIS
| | |
|---|---|
| Steering | Rack and pinion (power-assisted) |
| Front suspension | MacPherson struts, Kayaba/Reiger damping |
| Rear suspension | Trailing arms, coil springs, Reiger damping |
| Wheel sizes | 6x15in (gravel) 7x17in (asphalt) |
| Tyres | Pirelli |
| Front brakes | Brembo 300/355mm discs, 4 piston calipers |
| Rear brakes | Brembo 278mm discs, 2 piston calipers |

## MITSUBISHI LANCER EVO IX

### ENGINE
| | |
|---|---|
| Designation | 4G63 |
| Cylinders | Four in-line |
| Mounts | Front, Transverse |
| Capacity | 1997cc |
| Bore & stroke | 85x88mm |
| Valves/camshaft | 16/DOHC |
| Fuel system | ATL/Bosch |
| Turbocharger | Mitsubishi |
| Max power | 270bhp@4300rpm |
| Max torque | 550Nm@3200rpm |

### TRANSMISSION
| | |
|---|---|
| Gearbox | Ricardo 5-speed H-pattern dog gearbox |
| Drive type | 4WD |
| Clutch/differentials | Front and rear mechanical Ralliart; active centre GEMS |

### DIMENSIONS
| | |
|---|---|
| Overall length | 4490mm |
| Overall width | 1770mm |
| Wheelbase | 2625mm |
| Weight | 1330kg |
| Front track | - |
| Rear track | - |
| Body | Four-door steel |

### CHASSIS
| | |
|---|---|
| Steering | Rack and pinion (power-assisted) |
| Front suspension | Reiger adjustable/MacPherson struts |
| Rear suspension | Multi-link with Reiger adjustable |
| Wheel sizes | 8x17in (asphalt) 7x15in (gravel) |
| Front brakes | 300mm-355mm 4 piston calipers |
| Rear brakes | 295mm 4 piston calipers |

## SUBARU IMPREZA WRX

### ENGINE
| | |
|---|---|
| Designation | - |
| Cylinders | Horizontally opposed four |
| Mounts | Front, longitudinal |
| Capacity | 1994cc |
| Bore & stroke | 92mm/75mm |
| Valves/camshaft | 16/4 OHC |
| Fuel system | FT3-99 |
| Turbocharger | IHI |
| Max power | 270bhp@4500rpm |
| Max torque | 560Nm@3250rpm |

### TRANSMISSION
| | |
|---|---|
| Gearbox | Prodrive 5-speed H-pattern dog gearbox |
| Drive type | 4WD |
| Clutch/differentials | STi 6-paddle clutch, electro-mechanical locking centre diff, plated LSD front and rear diffs |

### DIMENSIONS
| | |
|---|---|
| Overall length | 4465mm |
| Overall width | 1800mm |
| Wheelbase | 2540mm |
| Weight | 1345kg |
| Front track | 1510mm |
| Rear track | 1515mm |
| Body | Four-door steel |

### CHASSIS
| | |
|---|---|
| Steering | Rack and pinion (power-assisted) |
| Front suspension | Prodrive-Ohlins MacPherson strut |
| Rear suspension | Prodrive-Ohlins MacPherson strut |
| Wheel sizes | 8x17in (asphalt) 7x15in (gravel) |
| Front brakes | 355mm-295mm 4 piston calipers |
| Rear brakes | 285mm 2 piston calipers |

Race&motion

## ABARTH GRANDE PUNTO

### ENGINE
| | |
|---|---|
| Designation | FTP |
| Cylinders | Four in-line |
| Mounts | Front, transverse |
| Capacity | 1997cc |
| Bore & stroke | 85mmx88mm |
| Valves/camshaft | 16/DOHC |
| Fuel system | Magneti Marelli MF-4M |
| Max power | 270bhp@8250bhp |
| Max torque | 225Nm@6500bhp |

### TRANSMISSION
| | |
|---|---|
| Gearbox | Sadev 6-speed sequential |
| Drive type | 4WD |
| Clutch/differentials | Sadev plated clutch, mechanical front, centre and rear differentials |

### DIMENSIONS
| | |
|---|---|
| Overall length | 4030mm |
| Overall width | 1800mm |
| Wheelbase | 2536mm |
| Weight | - |
| Body | Three-door steel |

### CHASSIS
| | |
|---|---|
| Steering | Rack and pinion (power-assisted) |
| Front suspension | Ohlins shock absorber MacPherson strut |
| Rear suspension | Ohlins shock absorber MacPherson strut |
| Wheel sizes | 8x18in (asphalt) 6.5x15in (gravel) |
| Front brakes | 300/355mm discs, 4 piston calipers |
| Rear brakes | 300 discs, 4 piston calipers |

Race&motion

## PEUGEOT 207 S2000

### ENGINE
| | |
|---|---|
| Designation | EW10J4s |
| Cylinders | Four in-line |
| Mounts | Front, transverse |
| Capacity | 1998cc |
| Bore & stroke | 86mmx86mm |
| Valves/camshaft | 16/DOHC |
| Fuel system | Magneti Marelli |
| Max power | 280bhp@8250rpm |
| Max torque | 250Nm@6500rpm |

### TRANSMISSION
| | |
|---|---|
| Gearbox | Sadev 6-speed sequential |
| Drive type | 4WD |
| Clutch/differentials | Twin disc Peugeot clutch, mechanical front, centre and rear differentials |

### DIMENSIONS
| | |
|---|---|
| Overall length | 4030mm |
| Overall width | 1800mm |
| Wheelbase | 2560mm |
| Weight | - |
| Body | Three-door steel |

### CHASSIS
| | |
|---|---|
| Steering | Rack and pinion (power-assisted) |
| Front suspension | Pseudo MacPherson/Peugeot damper |
| Rear suspension | Pseudo MacPherson/Peugeot damper |
| Wheel sizes | 8x18in (asphalt) 6.5x15in (gravel) |
| Front brakes | 300/355mm discs, 4 piston calipers |
| Rear brakes | 300mm discs, 4 piston calipers |

McKlein

# The challenge ahead

Rather than trying to rival the WRC, the IRC would be better off establishing itself as a GP2-style feeder series argues David Evans

**ROUND-BY-ROUND**

**1. SAFARI RALLY MARCH 9-11 (GRAVEL)**
Abarth drivers Andrea Navarra and Umberto Scandola were in the only Super 2000 cars. While Scandola was stopped by sand in the engine, Navarra won the IRC category followed by Japanese veteran Hideaki Miyoshi.

**2. RALLY OF TURKEY MAY 11-12 (GRAVEL)**
A full field attended the first 'proper' round of the IRC. Vouilloz took his first win on Peugeot's debut while Anton Alén finished fourth on his first rally with Abarth.

**3. YPRES WESTHOEK RALLY JUNE 22-23 (ASPHALT)**
Freddy Loix led in his Volkswagen before succumbing to transmission problems. Vouilloz rolled, while Bernd Casier in the Kronos Peugeot lost the chance to win with a small off.

**4. RALLY RUSSIA JULY 13-14 (GRAVEL)**
Anton Alén claimed his first overall rally victory. Dani Solà in the Honda was up to sixth overall before being forced into retirement after hitting a large hole in the road.

**5. MADEIRA RALLY AUGUST 2-4 (ASPHALT)**
Giandomenico Basso dominated, while Renato Travaglia's exclusion promoted Bruno Magalhaes to second. Had the Portuguese Peugeot driver not suffered an early misfire, he could have challenged for victory.

**6. BARUM RALLY ZLIN AUGUST 24-26 (ASPHALT)**
Alén made his asphalt debut and was up to fourth before hitting a wall. Loix led but went off following a puncture, while Navarra lost time after running over some chickens.

**7. SANREMO RALLY SEPTEMBER 28-30 (ASPHALT)**
Basso and Rossetti fought for the lead, while Paolo Andreucci's Mitsubishi was a contender until conditions dried up. Gilles Panizzi made his IRC debut but struggled with set-up and finished seventh.

**8. RALLYE DU VALAIS OCTOBER 25-27 (ASPHALT)**
By finishing first and second, Peugeot secured the manufacturers' title and the drivers' title for Ojeda. Honda claimed its best result with fifth for Luca Betti in the new R3.

**9. CHINA RALLY NOVEMBER 9-11 (GRAVEL)**
With the titles wrapped up, the IRC regulars stayed at home. David Higgins won the event in a Mitsubishi despite a day one misfire. Former British Rally Champion Martin Rowe was third.

THE IRC - or Intercontinental Rally Challenge - officially arrived at the end of last year promising a "new rally" and a "new generation."
In actual fact, the 2007 calendar contained an intriguing mix of old and new, with events such as the legendary Safari Rally but also Rally Russia: the first truly international motorsport event to be held behind the former Iron Curtain since the 1917 St Petersburg Grand Prix.

The series also provided a much-needed showcase for the new Super 2000 formula. Ironically, it could be that history will credit the IRC for forming the basis of tomorrow's World Rally Championship.

The biggest draw for competitors though was the prospect of unprecedented television exposure thanks to Eurosport - or to be precise, an average of more than eight hours per event (or 70 hours over the course of the year). Eurosport prides itself on being the biggest television channel in Europe so the attraction is easy enough to comprehend for teams and sponsors. Every highlights programme can also be watched online, opening up the potential audience to several millions of people.

This formula is not a new one: Eurosport successfully took over the World Touring Car Championship and turned it into a huge commercial success, with the presence of prestige manufacturers such as BMW, Alfa Romeo and SEAT, as well as some top drivers.

True, there were no big heroes in the IRC this year, and this was an area in which the championship probably suffered. Judging from the amount of media interest, the most popular event on the calendar was almost certainly Sanremo - and that was largely down to the presence of Gilles Panizzi, gunning for his fourth victory on the classic Italian event.

Enrique Garcìa Ojeda - the inaugural IRC champion - is an unassuming Spaniard who did not even win one rally this year, whereas his much better known team-mate, Nicolas Vouilloz, won three. This however is clearly the fault of the FIA scoring system (which the IRC has adopted) rather than the series itself: Niall McShea claimed the 2004 Production Car World Rally Championship in exactly the same way.

While Peugeot won five of the nine IRC rallies, Abarth driver Andrea Navarra hung onto the lead of the championship for half the season despite only winning one event - the Safari Rally - at the start of the year. Yet the Italian was one of the season's big disappointments: by his own admission he had lost his motivation, and he is unlikely to continue into 2008.

Abarth (née Fiat) did manage to uncover one real star: Anton Alén. Markku Alén's son - with whom he shares a striking physical resemblance as well as a number of typically Finnish mannerisms - marked himself out as forceful and marketable personality in a field of players that was sometimes lacking in charisma.

True, there were some household names in the IRC (in rallying circles at least) such as Simon Jean-Joseph, Freddy Loix, Brice Tirabassi and Dani Solà. But there were not enough of the really big personalities needed to sell a championship.

In fairness, as the series organisers are eager to point out, this is only the first year of the IRC and there is a long road ahead. Although this is not strictly true as the IRC has its roots in a four-round 2006 series called the International Rally Challenge, which was won by Fiat's Giandomenico Basso.

In 2007 though, things got serious. There was a full nine-round championship and some serious manufacturer involvement. In that context, the decision to start the championship with the Safari Rally in March seemed hard to comprehend - as few of the newly-signed manufacturers would be likely to show

## INTERCONTINENTAL RALLY CHALLENGE

themselves in such unusual (and expensive) conditions.

In the end only Abarth made the long trip down to Kenya, competing against some local Mitsubishi entries. By the time the championship got properly underway in Turkey, Peugeot, Citroën and Honda had joined those two manufacturers. Then for the Ypres Rally, Volkswagen made its first appearance as a registered manufacturer.

To see the championship entries in their proper context, however, it is important to understand how the whole concept of manufacturer registration works. The manufacturers pay a fee every year, in return for which their top two cars on every event are allowed to score manufacturer points. There are no nominated drivers, and in the case of Mitsubishi, for example, no fixed and permanent teams. If you turn up in a Mitsubishi Lancer for the Safari Rally next March and win it, then you score 10 manufacturer points for Mitsubishi. It's as simple as that. Also, local importers can register on behalf of a manufacturer. Volkswagen's entry is in reality Volkswagen South Africa, while Mitsubishi's entry is from Mitsubishi Ralliart Italy.

Most FIA-homologated cars are eligible, apart from four-wheel-drive Group A cars: part of the deliberate strategy to keep entry lists as wide open as possible and costs down. Super 2000 is counted as being within Group N, although strictly speaking these cars technically fall into Group A.

But there are complications. Those manufacturers not registered for the IRC, notably Subaru, do not appear in the IRC classification - which is fair enough. However this causes confusion when, as happened this year, Conrad Rautenbach wins the Safari Rally and Cody Crocker wins Rally China - both driving Imprezas. Effectively this results in two winners: an overall event winner and an IRC winner. Confused? Many people were.

Subaru is likely to sign up to the IRC in 2008, eliminating the problem once and for all. Nonetheless, conventional Group N machinery has not been in a strong position to compete with the Super 2000 cars this year. In fact, some Group N cars have fallen foul of the rules trying to keep up with their S2000 competition. On the two occasions that a Group N car has been on the podium in a European IRC rally, it has been subsequently excluded. Larry Cols (this year's Belgian Champion) decided that his Mitsubishi did not need the standard side impact bars incorporated within the doors of the road car in Ypres, while Renato Travaglia (no stranger to the concept of disqualification) had a creative arrangement with his turbo pipe in Madeira.

Along with Anton Alén's dominant performance on the WRC Rally Finland this year driving his Abarth Grande Punto (sadly curtailed by a broken engine), this proves that S2000 is indeed the way forward within the production car category. It provides better performance at pretty much the same cost, but most importantly allows many more manufacturers to become involved than just Mitsubishi and Subaru.

Peugeot and Abarth have been the pioneers in the category, but Skoda and Suzuki are currently working on a Super 2000 project while Citroën and Ford are likely to follow suit. Even more manufacturers will come on board if, as FIA president Max Mosley has indicated, S2000 forms the basis of tomorrow's WRC car from 2009 onwards. Would that spell the end of the road for the IRC? It's quite possible, but at least it would have the satisfaction of falling victim to its own success rather than failure. Or, as has been debated at length, the IRC could possibly merge or alternate with the WRC in some way - but these scenarios will all remain strictly hypothetical until the World Council has reached some sort of coherent decision about the future of the World Rally Championship.

**Opposite:** Nicolas Vouilloz won three rounds but finished as championship runner-up to his team-mate Ojeda

**Above left:** Former factory Ford WRC driver Solà revived his career with a season in a JAS Motorsport-run Honda Civic Type-R

**Above right:** Reigning champion Basso only competed on two IRC events as he focused on the Italian championship but won on his return in Madeira

**Top:** Panizzi was the centre of attention in Sanremo but his knowledge of the event failed to net a fourth win there following his WRC successes

All photographs by Photo4

## OJEDA'S SOFTLY-SOFTLY APPROACH

Enrique Garcia Ojeda proved that consistency pays - and he made no apology for it. After clinching the IRC crown by finishing second on the Rallye du Valais (a position he claimed four times from the seven rallies he contested), the Spaniard said: "Winning a championship is all about the results you obtain over the course of the year. This has been a very competitive season: you have to balance speed with the guarantee of finishing on every rally. I think we managed to find the best balance."

Ojeda came away with the spoils, but the star of the season was his team-mate Nicolas Vouilloz. The former mountain bike champion won three very different rallies (Turkey, Barum and Valais), making good use of the experience gained from his 10 world championship rallies in a World Rally Car.

What let the Frenchman down were two zero scores, in Ypres (where he crashed) and Madeira (where he finished ninth following some mechanical problems). The fact that he finished only five points behind his team-mate - who scored on every rally he contested - says a lot about Vouilloz's abilities.

Statistics can mean anything, but there was no doubt about who was the most successful driver. That man was the Italian Luca Rossetti, who chalked up a 100 per cent success rate by winning the only two events he contested: Ypres and Sanremo. The Peugeot Italy driver has been steadily improving all the time, and his victory in Sanremo was not such a surprise. But his win in Ypres was astonishing, particularly to the man himself. "I wasn't even sure if we should enter Ypres, because I thought we would be properly beaten and we ran a big risk of damaging the car," he said at the time.

Freddy Loix briefly led his home event, before succumbing to mechanical problems with his Volkswagen Polo S2000. Thereafter Loix switched to a privately-run Abarth following Pieter Tsjoen's retirement halfway through the season. The former WRC star was disappointing, only scoring points once, but he never felt as comfortable in the Italian car as he had in the VW.

Another disappointment was Abarth driver Andrea Navarra. The former European Champion was a shadow of his former self, switching co-drivers halfway through the year in an attempt to rediscover his mojo. His decline was matched by the rise of his young team-mate Umberto Scandola. After a shaky start, Scandola finished the season with fourth in Sanremo and third place in Switzerland - marking himself out as an asphalt specialist to be reckoned with in the future. A lot of the credit for that is down to Guido d'Amore - Gigi Galli's former co-driver in the WRC - who joined Scandola for those two events and re-worked his pace note system.

Abarth's benchmark on asphalt remains Giandomenico Basso, but the Italian champion only contested two IRC events this year (Madeira and Sanremo, finishing first and second). Had Abarth nominated him for the entire year, then the championship outcome could have been somewhat different…

# INTERCONTINENTAL RALLY CHALLENGE

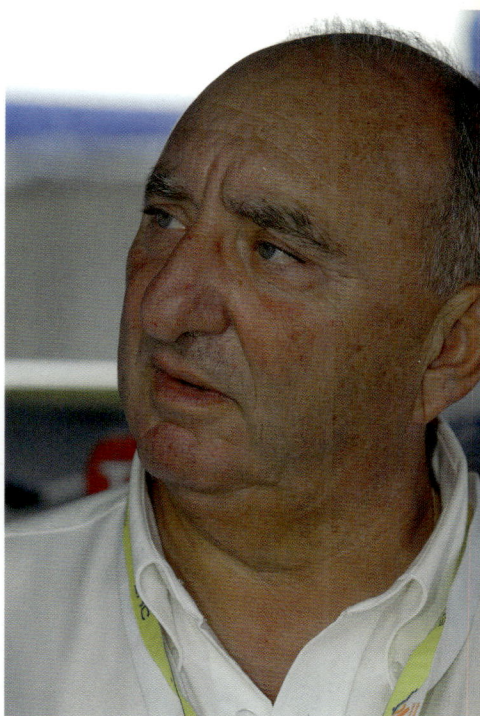

The openness and logic of the IRC came as a breath of fresh air in many ways: the entire regulations would fit comfortably onto just one sheet of A4 paper, compared to the rainforest-damaging levels of bureaucracy that threaten to engulf the world championship. There's no insistence on things like a single service park or SupeRally. For the record, not one single person was excluded for wearing the wrong type of underwear in the IRC all year and neither did the organisers top up their income with competitor fines (in contrast to the thousands gathered by the FIA).

But there is a price to pay for this policy of glasnost. By allowing competitors to dip in and out of the championship - not one single IRC driver contested every round - there is a risk of diluting the overall spectacle. There was a nucleus of factory drivers from Peugeot, Abarth and Honda competing on the majority of the rounds, but the three other registered manufacturers had no permanent factory teams.

It's a calculated risk. The IRC has deliberately chosen a different strategy to the WRC, to which it is (probably unfairly) frequently compared. The IRC aims to put the spotlight on local drivers at every round, by appealing to national distributors at the same time as multinational manufacturer teams. Peugeot won the IRC manufacturers' championship this year, but more specifically it was Peugeot Spain that claimed the title (as opposed to Peugeot Belgium or Peugeot Italy, which were also present in the series).

"This is one of the things that I think is really good about the IRC," says Peugeot Spain's champion Ojeda. "Ours is a really small national team, of about 20 people or so, which would never normally get the chance to compete at international level. But that's exactly what we've done this year, and we've ended up winning both championships. Essentially, the IRC has allowed us to punch above our weight - and the same opportunity exists for all the other teams. For me, the important thing is to keep it at this level and with these values: otherwise it becomes something too expensive, closer to the world championship."

The challenge for Eurosport will be to keep a clear vision in the years ahead, and not to get sucked into a rivalry with the WRC that many people seem keen to provoke. Thankfully, there is Jean-Pierre Nicolas - the former team principal of Peugeot who joined the IRC as motorsport development manager - to lend a firm guiding hand.

Experience pays: unusually for a new series priding itself on innovation, the IRC is actually looking to go back to some of rallying's traditional values - which have been missing in action at the top of the sport for quite some time.

As befits an unashamedly commercial series, the IRC has already constructed a strong brand identity for itself: now its exact sporting role. One of the championship's priorities is to develop young talent for the future (the much-vaunted "new generation"), which would place it in the role of GP2 to the WRC's Formula 1.

The problem is that it is hard to persuade ambitious people like those at Eurosport to limit their scope. The IRC has big plans for the future, essentially involving more rallies plus bigger and better coverage, all of which could inevitably lead to more expense and the inexorable boom and bust cycle that curses most forms of motorsport. The talk is of up to 12 rallies and 10 manufacturers by 2010: is this sustainable?

If the series is run along the same lines as the World Touring Car Championship, then such growth probably is. But while the WTCC's most successful driver - Andy Priaulx - may have achieved cult hero status, he is never going to be a global superstar like Mika Häkkinen or Jean Alesi - both of whom drove in the DTM, which is perceived by many to be the WTCC's rival.

The truth is that it's not - just as the IRC is no true rival to the WRC. Once this common misconception is cleared up, then the series will be in a strong position to move forwards. The ingredients are all there.

*Opposite: Ojeda won the championship despite not winning a round. He is expected to defend his title with Peugeot Spain in 2008*

*Above left: Alén Jr looks set to follow in his legendary father Markku's footsteps after a promising season with the Abarth team*

*Above right: Ex-Peugeot Sport boss Jean-Pierre Nicolas was brought in to manage the series and utilised his years of experience as a rally driver and team coordinator to keep things running smoothly*

*Below: The historic city of St Petersburg hosted the start of Russia's first international motorsport event since 1917 when the IRC came to town*

All photographs by Photo4

## DATES DESIGNED TO PLEASE

Having started off with a nine-round calendar, the IRC has expanded to 10 rounds for 2008. There are only minor changes: the Rally of Turkey is off the list (as it is back in the WRC) while the Portugal Rally and Principe de Asturias Rally in Spain join the calendar.

At first glance, the series seems quite unbalanced. There are only three events in the first half of the year followed by seven in the second half. Furthermore, there are also six asphalt rallies as opposed to just four gravel rallies, and two events held on Portuguese territory (Madeira and the former world championship Rally Portugal). However, the new calendar has been cleverly driven by commercial forces. The slow start to the season is designed to give teams and drivers the maximum amount of time to build up a budget. Most of the Super 2000 cars have been developed for asphalt, which generally entails cheaper running costs: hence the slight sealed-surface bias. Rally Portugal is a world-class event with a blue chip sponsorship package from Vodafone, so its inclusion makes perfect sense. And with a Spanish champion team and driver, an IRC round in Spain is equally logical. Originally, Mexico was to have formed part of the line-up as well - but at the last minute it returned to the world championship calendar.

Nonetheless, it's the more unconventional events that grab the attention. The IRC has been a successful pioneer of rallying in Russia and China: where even FIA president Max Mosley says that the WRC should eventually be heading.

Safari is more of a stand-alone showcase event, designed to provide a halo effect for the rest of the series through some spectacular images. It's hard to say how many manufacturers will make the trip down (only Abarth bothered in 2007) but in any case, rallies such as Africa and China allow conventional Group N cars to rack up some useful points: an important consideration when it comes to getting Subaru on board.

Other innovations for next year include some sort of two-wheel drive championship. This would allow manufacturers such as Citroën and Honda to gain more recognition for their efforts. Even without it, there have been some impressive acts of giant killing: Simon Jean-Joseph was regularly in the points for Citroën, while Luca Betti was a career-best fifth overall in Switzerland with his Honda Civic Type R R3.

PRODUCTION CAR WORLD RALLY CHAMPIONSHIP

# Arai left sitting pretty

The 2005 champion had an agonising wait to see if he would lift the Production crown again this year after opting out of the last two rounds. By Richard Rodgers

### ROUND-BY-ROUND

**ROUND 1 SWEDEN FEBRUARY 8-11**
Hänninen's joy following his debut win soon turns to despair when he's slung out of the results after his car is found to be running an additional fuel tank following post-event checks. Svedlund inherits the win as punctures delay Alén and Sohlberg, who lead for 12 out of 20 stages.

1. Oscar Svedlund (Subaru Impreza) 3h25m29.2s
2. Anton Alén (Subaru Impreza) +38.6s
3. Kristian Sohlberg (Subaru Impreza) +1m42.7s

**ROUND 2 MEXICO MARCH 9-11**
A brush with a bank is Higgins' only cause for concern as he breaks his victory duck after getting the better of a determined Baldacci. The San Marino driver drops out of contention late on with a puncture. Arai moves into second despite hitting a dog on the opening day.

1. Mark Higgins (Mitsubishi Lancer) 4h08m44.5s
2. Toshi Arai (Subaru Impreza) +1m20.9s
3. Kristian Sohlberg (Subaru Impreza) +2m30.7s

**ROUND 3 ARGENTINA MAY 3-6**
Although mechanical problems slow Arai in the closing stages he still takes second and the title lead. Villagra, a wildcard entrant, makes the most of his local knowledge to win and is rewarded with a programme of events in a World Rally Car. Erstwhile points leader Sohlberg crashes into retirement.

1. Federico Villagra (Mitsubishi Lancer) 3h08m53.7s
2. Toshi Arai (Subaru Impreza) +9.3s
3. Juho Hänninen (Mitsubishi Lancer) +28.2s

**ROUND 4 GREECE MAY 31-JUNE 1**
Arai takes advantage of Aigner's puncture for his first win in over 15 months months. Flodin crashes heavily for the second event on the bounce but he's uninjured. Punctures and bent steering delay Higgins, while his young countryman Stuart Jones retires on the opening stage when his Mitsubishi's gearbox breaks.

1. Toshi Arai (Subaru Impreza) 4h10m08.9s
2. Andreas Aigner (Mitsubishi Lancer) +2m58.4s
3. Mirco Baldacci (Subaru Impreza) +3m12.9s

**ROUND 5 NEW ZEALAND AUGUST 31-SEPTEMBER 2**
Arai beats McShea in a nail-biting final stage to claim win number two. McShea blames his road position and a sideways moment for his crucial time loss on the epic final morning. Local driver Mason impresses but a broken gearbox holds him back. A broken differential slows Araújo's charge.

1. Toshi Arai (Subaru Impreza) 4h13m35.8s
2. Niall McShea (Subaru Impreza) +2.6s
3. Richard Mason (Subaru Impreza) +1m10.2s

**ROUND 6 JAPAN OCTOBER 26-28**
Flodin leads but gets stuck in a ditch for 11 minutes. Arai inherits first but makes a mistake before a series of punctures leave him outside of the points and delay his title celebrations. When Nutahara crashes, Pozzo - who had recovered from a broken centre differential - is a comfortable winner.

1. Gabriel Pozzo (Mitsubishi Lancer) 3h45m50.6s
2. Leszek Kuzaj (Subaru Impreza) +2m40.1s
3. Takuma Kamada (Subaru Impreza) +2m48.4s

**ROUND 7 IRELAND NOVEMBER 15-18**
Araújo, still reeling after his exclusion from second in Japan, is edging to his first win when he's caught out on a slippery turn and suffers a huge crash. McShea, who had been in a close battle with the Portuguese, takes a home win. Higgins' retirement means only Pozzo can deny Arai the title.

1. Niall McShea (Subaru Impreza) 3h18m11.3s
2. Gabriel Pozzo (Mitsubishi Lancer) +44.1s
3. Nasser Al-Attiyah (Subaru Impreza) +4m31.1s

**ROUND 8 GREAT BRITAIN NOV 30-DEC 2**
With his production championship hopes over Higgins sets about defending his British title, run in tandem with the PWRC finale, but punctures leaves his rival Wilks, who is making a one-off guest appearance in main Group N class, with an unassailable lead. Hänninen ends his year on a high in second.

1. Guy Wilks (Mitsubishi Lancer) 3h44m23.7s
2. Juho Hänninen (Mitsubishi Lancer) +34.2s
3. Mark Higgins (Mitsubishi Lancer) +1m46.5s

| | | | | | | | | |
|---|---|---|---|---|---|---|---|---|
| Toshi Arai | 3 | 8 | 8 | 10 | 10 | 0 | - | 39 |
| Gabriel Pozzo | - | - | 5 | 2 | 5 | 10 | 8 | 0 | 30 |
| Mark Higgins | 0 | 10 | - | 5 | - | 4 | 0 | 6 | 25 |

Opposite page: Arai scored the first of two crucial wins in Greece. The champion's consistent approach paid dividends, especially when he opted to miss the final two rounds

A HOST of young drivers, several returning champions and a raft of national title-holders made for an action-packed season, which produced seven different winners, plenty of close finishes and a fair share of sizeable accidents.

It all came down to a final round showdown on Wales Rally GB in December where Toshi Arai and Gabriel Pozzo were bidding for their second showroom class crowns.

However, Arai was nowhere to be seen. Instead the 41-year-old was holed up in a hotel room in Tokyo waiting to give a live television interview for Japanese television in the event he claimed top honours.

Rules require production championship competitors to nominate six out of eight rounds on which to score points. Arai completed his half dozen on his home event, Rally Japan, in October meaning he sat out the final rounds in Ireland and Great Britain. Despite a brace of wins in Greece and New Zealand putting him within touching distance of a second title, Mark Higgins and Pozzo could still deprive him of the award after several punctures blighted Arai's charge on home soil, although the odds were firmly stacked against the pair.

Higgins arrived in Japan nursing a broken collarbone and left needing to take maximum points on the final two events to be champion. Pozzo, meanwhile, had a slightly less arduous task and required a win and a second place from the season-closing rallies if he was to emulate his championship success of 2001.

Higgins had driven the rally of his life on the tricky and narrow asphalt lanes in Ireland. Despite suffering great pain and relying on his co-driver Scott Martin to operate his Mitsubishi Lancer's handbrake, he held a commanding 35-second lead as he prepared to start the penultimate day's final stage. But then disaster: hamstrung by a slow puncture Higgins was struggling to keep control of his car. He was less than a mile from the finish when he slid into a ditch and retirement, his title dream over for another year.

Pozzo, who had only contested five asphalt rallies in his career, seized the initiative and, despite losing time on the second day with a spin, regained his composure and followed former champion Niall McShea home in the runner-up spot to keep his slender title hopes alive for two more weeks at least, after erstwhile leader Armindo Araújo crashed heavily.

In the event an off on the opening leg in Wales, where the 28-year-old Pozzo was making his first appearance, left his Lancer with smashed suspension and a missing wheel. Arai could now finally begin his celebrations, albeit from afar.

"After our punctures in Japan I had a really bad feeling about the championship," Arai recalls. "I was convinced 90 per cent I could still win but I couldn't do anything about it back home in Japan. I have never experienced waiting like that. When we won the title in 2005 it was our last rally. I didn't enjoy Higgins and Pozzo retiring. I was just relieved."

Although the title contest had gone down to the wire there was none of the drama and excitement that had been so prevalent when Nasser Al-Attiyah beat Fumio Nutahara to the class laurels on the season finale in New Zealand the previous year.

While organisers had cut the number of championship rounds from nine to eight for this season there was only one event, Greece, where the big guns actually went head to head. The format is the same for 2008 although a rule change to make all crews contest the final round is under discussion for future years.

Organisers blame the need to control costs for their reluctance to create an 'all rounds count' scenario, be that by increasing the number of points-scoring opportunities or through the imposition of mandatory event attendance. It's not an easy fix. In order to maintain its 'world' tag, the calendar must consist of events in at least three continents and the cheapest way to access these is by sea, rather than using the prohibitive airfreight alternative. While some drivers have access to two cars, organisers are keen for crews to complete their nominated programme of rallies in the same vehicle, hence the opt-out option.

Arai, for one, would certainly prefer a straight battle on all events. He says: "Rather than selecting six I would prefer to fight all the time because I think it's better for the championship and the fans."

Regardless of who he had to fight and when Arai put his title success this year down to strategy. When he won his first world title his tactic then was to go all out for wins rather than settle for points finishes. But he knew from sizing up the competition on the opening round in Sweden in February that a similar approach this year would be futile.

"The championship wasn't so important to me back in 2005 but on the first rally this year I realised there were so many fast drivers to beat. It was a lot harder this year because the competitors were of a high standard. Most years there are about five real challengers but this year there were at least ten.

"I had the confidence to win but my tactics were to fight over the long term rather than rally by rally because it was now important for me to win the championship."

While promising youngsters like Andreas Aigner, Patrik Flodin and Juho Hänninen enjoyed their respective moments in the limelight courtesy of some blistering stage times, their rise to hero status would tend to be short-lived due to their tendency for picking up punctures and making mistakes.

Arai, a veteran of 68 world rallies at the start of the season, not to mention countless appearances in the Asia Pacific championship, adopted a more controlled approach, particularly after a series of accidents had wrecked his challenge in 2006. He was cautious when the conditions required him to be - with the exception of a roll and a couple of off-road moments in Sweden - and when he was less confident with his Subaru's handling. But equally he was capable of turning on the speed with devastating effect, such as in New Zealand in September when he recovered to win despite dropping more than three and a half minutes changing a puncture.

Those closest to Arai's inner circle maintain that when he gets "in the zone" he is simply unbeatable and Arai describes his drive in New Zealand, when he started the final day more than one minute behind Briton Niall McShea, as his "best moment", adding: "I usually attacked about 80-90 per cent maximum as my aim was to be consistent throughout the year but in New Zealand it was more like 110 per cent."

The second round in Mexico was an "80-90 per cent" drive and his determination to avoid picking up any punctures meant

Above: Higgins scored his first long-awaited Production win in Mexico before injury and retirement in Ireland scuppered his championship hopes

Above middle: Pozzo kept his title bid alive with second in Ireland, despite it being only his sixth asphalt event. His campaign ended with an off in Wales on his Rally GB debut

Top: McShea was called up to replace Anton Alén at the TaCK team in Argentina, where he finished sixth. Budget problems then took hold, but he returned in Ireland to score his first Production win

All photographs by McKlein unless specified

**Above:** Aigner showed flashes of form and finished second in Greece, but there were too many incidents for him to really be a contender

**Opposite top:** Baldacci had an up-and-down year. He fought for victory in Mexico and was third in Greece, but suffered a variety of setbacks in Argentina, New Zealand and GB

**Opposite middle:** Sohlberg made a bright start, leading the series after round two, but poor results in Argentina and Greece prompted left the former WRC driver trailing and he quit

**Opposite bottom:** Defending champion Al-Attiyah had a torrid time in a season blighted by heavy accidents. Needless to say, like others before him he didn't retain his crown...

All photographs by McKlein

he was 1m20s behind event winner Higgins at the finish.

"I realised Higgins was a very fast driver in Mexico," Arai admits. "He made no mistakes and although he wasn't always consistent I had to watch him very closely after that."

Although he briefly moved to the front in Argentina, his eventual second place behind guest driver Federico Villagra was testament to his experience. A bolt in a hub bearing worked loose on day two, while two bolts in the subframe broke on the final day and caused a lack of stability under braking. With victory still up for grabs, a younger driver might have pressed on and paid the ultimate price, but Arai veered on the side of caution and made it to the finish in second, a result which put him seven points clear in the standings.

Arai's first of two victories came in Greece in June. After early leader Flodin had rolled out in spectacular fashion, Arai became engaged in a close battle with Aigner, until a puncture dropped the Austrian from first to seventh. Although he hurt his back in a heavy landing on the superspecial stage, based at a race course on the outskirts of Athens, Arai was able to control his lead to the finish and extend his title advantage to 14 points in the process ahead of the trip to New Zealand, where his win effectively sealed a second title.

"I was so pleased with that result because it was very good for the championship," he says. "I had a lot of time to make up so I attacked and drove as fast as I could."

Arai's choice of events also played into his hands. With little recent asphalt experience, Ireland was the first event to be crossed off the list at the start of the season. Entering Rally GB as a standalone event from his base in Japan made little sense logistically. "I don't like the rain you have in these rallies," he says. "It's slippery, muddy and foggy and I don't like any of these conditions. I would do them if they were in spring or summer as I have some experience of that weather from when I lived in the UK but I really don't like the winter conditions."

In contrast Higgins, 36, was expected to revel on the season-closing events. What points he lost on some of the earlier rounds he was confident he could make up on familiar territory. But the Isle of Man-born driver hadn't banked on Arai's consistency - the Japanese was on the podium on four occasions, while Higgins appeared there just twice - nor his injury, which he sustained exercising at home in his adoptive Wales in the build-up to Rally Japan.

That he attempted to start in the Far East let alone made the finish was a miraculous achievement although it very nearly ended in failure. He needed four points to maintain his title challenge but his injury, coupled with a road penalty caused when his car developed an electrical glitch, restricted him to sixth place. He and co-driver Scott Martin were on a train heading to Sapporo airport for the flight home when Martin received a call telling him Araújo's car had failed post-event scrutineering and Higgins had been promoted to that all important fifth place as a result. Before Araújo's penalty, Higgins was left to rue his decision not to finish in Sweden under SupeRally regulations when he rolled out on the final day following a troubled return to the series he had last contested in 2005.

Pozzo's 2006 season ended in shame when he and his fellow Tango Rally Team drivers were thrown out of the series after their cars were found to be running illegal turbochargers. The Argentine returned to head a scaled-down Tango effort. With the exception of Rally GB, he scored on all other five outings including an impressive victory in Japan.

McShea had all but given up on his dream of returning to the world championship when a call out of the blue heralded an unlikely comeback in the production series he won in 2004. Despite that success, the Northern Irishman's career

## PRODUCTION CAR WORLD RALLY CHAMPIONSHIP

lost momentum and he had been largely forgotten when he was called up to replace Anton Alén in the Russian-backed TaCK operation. Alén, the young son of rally legend Markku, finished second in Sweden but had found the lure of a ride with the factory Abarth team in the Intercontinental Rally Challenge too good to turn down. Although he wanted to combine the roles, TaCK refused permission and McShea was drafted in for Rally Argentina in May.

It was a difficult start - McShea was one of several drivers left stranded overnight in a Buenos Aires airport following the trip to the Argentine capital for the event opening superspecial - but he finished in sixth place nevertheless. Delays readying his entry for Greece prompted him to replace that event with a trip to Japan instead, although that ultimately never materialised after various funding issues took hold. His participation in New Zealand came after an 11th-hour rescue deal and his appearance on Rally Ireland was a similarly late affair.

Despite the setbacks the 34-year-old was just grateful for the opportunity and his victory on the penultimate round proved a popular triumph. Sadly for McShea his future appears just as uncertain as it did before his call to fly to Argentina, although he was actively pursuing options in the fledgling IRC at the time of writing.

After a couple of years dabbling in World Rally Cars, Kristian Sohlberg stepped back to the production championship in a Subaru Impreza prepared by the Belgium-based SYMS team. Although a broken driveshaft in Sweden robbed him of a shot at victory, the third place finishes he bagged there and in Mexico propelled him to the top of the drivers' standings after two rounds. He led briefly during the next event in Argentina but a crash on day two left his car with broken suspension and he was forced to retire. When his fortunes continued to wane in Greece in June - he lost 14 minutes changing a broken steering arm on one stage - he quit the series having slumped 17 points behind Arai with only two events remaining.

Like Sohlberg, Mirco Baldacci also started the year with high hopes but his season soon turned to disappointment. Although he challenged Higgins for the win in Mexico, a puncture dropped him to fourth, while an engine-induced retirement in Argentina left him hopelessly adrift in the championship race. He hit back with third in Greece but a broken turbo and failed brakes ruined his hopes in New Zealand. There was a further kick in the teeth on Rally GB when gearbox and engine maladies slowed his progress.

Fumio Nutahara came within five points of clinching the production title in 2006 but there was to be no repeat performance this season. Rally Japan provided a rare highlight when he led for seven stages only to inflict sizeable damage to his Lancer when he crashed. With the production championship switching to the control Pirelli rubber next season Nutahara, who receives major backing from Japanese tyre firm Advan, looks to have departed the world stage with a proverbial whimper rather than a bang.

Hänninen emerged as a star of the future with several impressive showings and more stage wins than any of his rivals, although his victory in Sweden was cancelled out due to a fuel tank irregularity and was handed to guest driver Oscar Svedlund. Hänninen was on the podium in Argentina and again on Rally GB, where Guy Wilks wrapped up his domestic title with first place in the production standings to boot.

Araújo showed promise and will star next year if he gets funding for another programme. Aigner also sparkled from time to time but hit trouble too often to be a contender. Flodin enjoyed more Group N success away from the pressure-cooker environment of the PWRC but has the talent to shine in the future after a retirement-strewn year.

### AL-ATTIYAH SUFFERS A WOBBLY DEFENCE

No driver has ever defended the production world title before and that trend continued in 2007 when Nasser Al-Attiyah failed to recapture the form that brought him his first crown in 2006.

The Qatari, 37, was combining the defence of his production and Middle East championship crowns with a programme of cross-country events for the German X-Raid team, including the Dakar Rally in January.

Although he was successful in his efforts to retain the Middle East title - albeit in a tense final round - and impressed in his desert raid outings, his performances in the PWRC failed to match up to the high standards he set the previous year.

His campaign was punctuated by heavy accidents - he even missed out on the trip to New Zealand when he sustained head injuries filming a television commercial - and it was only on his last event, Rally Ireland, that he showed any true form, surviving the atrocious conditions to net third place.

Seventh in Sweden was a decent result given it was only his second snow rally but his season quickly went downhill from there when he rolled five times after a slow puncture caused him to go off the road on the second stage in Mexico.

Another crash in Argentina, when he ripped a wheel off his car on leg two's final stage, did nothing to help his cause, although fifth in Greece gave him a much needed lift, despite a costly puncture and a broken fuel pump.

## JUNIOR RALLY CHAMPIONSHIP

# P-G beats his speed demons

Suzuki driver Andersson lost his driving licence before Rallye Deutschland but still claimed a second Junior championship.
By Anthony Peacock

### RALLIES

**ROUND 1 NORWAY FEBRUARY 16-18**
Andersson won the rally with a massive margin of more than seven minutes over Sandell. Aava had to settle for third after hitting a tree stump on the opening day.

1. P-G Andersson (Suzuki Swift) 3h49m37.9s
2. Patrik Sandell (Renault Clio) +7m33.7s
3. Urmo Aava (Suzuki Swift) +15m12.4s

**ROUND 2 PORTUGAL MARCH 29-APRIL 1**
A duel between Andersson and Aava was settled after the latter punctured on the penultimate stage. Prokop rolled five times, the biggest accident all year in the Juniors.

1. P-G Andersson (Suzuki Swift) 4h22m43.4s
2. Urmo Aava (Suzuki Swift) +3.7s
3. Jozef Béres (Renault Clio) +7m48.9s

**ROUND 3 SARDINIA MAY 18-20**
Aava beat his team-mate fair and square while Prokop bounced back well from his accident. Sandell stopped with an engine problem on the last day while Béres rolled.

1. Urmo Aava (Suzuki Swift) 4h15m03.9s
2. P-G Andersson (Suzuki Swift) +1m09.4s
3. Martin Prokop (Citroën C2) +6m22.8s

**ROUND 4 FINLAND AUGUST 2-5**
Suzuki chose to skip this event. Prokop led until he went off, leaving room for a Renault monopoly. Bettega took two fastest times and was set for third until a wheel came off.

1. Patrik Sandell (Renault Clio) 3h25m14.5s
2. Kalle Pinomäki (Renault Clio) +1m19.1s
3. Michal Kosciuszko (Renault Clio) +4m13.7s

**ROUND 5 GERMANY AUGUST 17-19**
Andersson, serving a driving ban, was replaced by James Wozencroft. Prokop claimed 10 stage wins and victory while Aava cruised to second ahead of an impressive Conrad Rautenbach.

1. Martin Prokop (Citroën C2) 3h52m26.9s
2. Urmo Aava (Suzuki Swift) +49.5s
3. Conrad Rautenbach (Citroën C2) +2m15.9s

**ROUND 6 SPAIN OCTOBER 5-7**
Aava led until he picked up a puncture on SS8. He fought back but just missed out on second place. Irishman Shaun Gallagher won the rookie championship in his C2-R2.

1. P-G Andersson (Suzuki Swift) 3h44m24.5s
2. Martin Prokop (Citroën C2) +33.9s
3. Urmo Aava (Suzuki Swift) +39.9s

**ROUND 7 FRANCE OCTOBER 12-14**
Andersson and Aava started equal on points, but the Estonian crashed out of the lead on SS8. Prokop took the lead and the win, while fourth for Andersson sealed the title.

1. Martin Prokop (Citroën C2) 3h52m31.0s
2. Jozef Béres (Renault Clio) +12.5s
3. Yoann Bonato (Citroën C2) +1m14.2s

### CHAMPIONSHIP

1. P-G Andersson (Suzuki Swift) 43pts
2. Urmo Aava (Suzuki Swift) 38pts
3. Martin Prokop (Citroën C2) 34 pts

THE champagne makers of northern France have been known to spend days locked in heated debate as to whether or not to declare the new harvest of a particular year a vintage.

It depends on many factors - principally soil and weather - but ultimately it boils down to just one man's opinion. If the cellar master believes it is a good year then the champagne is triumphantly labelled as a vintage - no matter what anybody else thinks.

"Well, from my point of view, it's been a really really good season!" says P-G Andersson, and who are we to disagree with the chief taster of this year's Junior Rally Championship action?

After all, it's simply a question of perspective. Elements of this year's Junior championship were quite strange though. Realistically, there were only ever going to be two people who stood a proper chance of winning it. But the man who won it was bereft of a driving licence for two months, while the man who finished second - his team-mate Urmo Aava - won fewer rallies than the person who finished third. Surprisingly, Aava's solitary win in Sardinia was only the second of his whole Junior championship career (Andersson has won 12 in a lot less time) - but the Estonian was hardly humiliated over the course of the season.

Aava traditionally has the luck of a black cat walking under a ladder on Friday 13th and his legendary misfortune was exemplified by Rally Portugal, where he had a puncture on the penultimate stage that cost him the win.

As it happened, the exploding tyre made little difference to the championship result, given that Aava ended up with 38 points to Andersson's 43. The Swede was forced to miss Rallye Deutschland, however, after his over-zealous home police force "borrowed" his driving licence following a bit of sportsmanship on public roads. At least that's how he vaguely described it.

This shouldn't have presented too serious a problem: if one driving licence is broken you simply replace it with a different one that works. Several of the sport's top stars have managed to ply their trade thanks to driving licences from places as diverse as China, Dubai, Kenya and Monaco in the past. Like Alabama though, where it is illegal to mow the lawn between midnight and daybreak, Sweden has this quirky little law. Specifically, it prevents its nationals from holding driving licences issued by any other country.

So it was adios to the plan of becoming a newly qualified driver in South America and guten morgen to the idea of spectating during Rallye Deutschland. In any other year, this calamity would have done for Andersson's chances.

But Aava could only manage second on the challenging Mosel stages - and then a win for Andersson on his return in Spain meant that they would both start the final round of the season equal on points. Corsica was consequently the most exciting Junior round in the championship's history - for a day and a half. The Suzuki drivers battled it out for the rally lead and the championship: a microcosm of the entire season in fact.

Then, with a 13-second lead, Aava dropped it on stage eight. Andersson claimed that he had not been pushing too hard himself: a statement that was greeted with frank derision from his team-mate. It stopped short of a public slanging match, but there was certainly enough needle between the two Suzuki drivers to make life interesting.

Of course the stakes were a lot higher for them, as they were battling for a career as well as a title. Suzuki team principal Nobuhiro 'Monster' Tajima has never hidden his desire to see one of Suzuki's Junior drivers at the wheel of the new SX4 World Rally Car - but only one, as the team needs to employ an experienced driver as well to push development forwards.

Neither of them would particularly want to be judged on their 2007 season though. Urmo was often a bit faster than P-G (he won 39 stages during the year as opposed to P-G's 33) but his raw talent still needs polishing. P-G had the debacle of his driving ban, and did not quite exhibit the same effortless superiority of his last championship win in 2004 (against stronger opposition).

Up until now, a rookie driver has won every Junior title. This year, none of the rookies even won a rally. There were several reasons behind his, chiefly the fact that there were fewer new drivers in Super 1600 cars this year - which still seem to have the upper hand over the latest R3 machinery. But even the lucky rookies in a S1600 car (such as Vilius Rozukas from Lithuania) were never going to challenge the established stars in the way that Dani Sordo had in 2005 for instance. Even young Vilius figured that one out, wisely stepping down to a Citroën C2-R2 at the end of the year.

The only newcomer who might have been able to spring a surprise - had he been given a proper chance - was Alessandro Bettega. As last year's winner of the Fiesta Sporting Trophy, he was given the dubious prize of a Fiesta S1600 for the year. Nicknamed the 'Fiasco Super 1600' by several people, it was about as desirable as a three-week holiday in Dagenham.

In desperation Bettega switched to a Suzuki Swift S1600 and a Renault Clio R3, before concluding his season with a Ford Focus WRC in Corsica. At the wheel of that, he managed to break into the top 10 overall before ending the rally 11th. With more time in a reliable Super 1600 car, the Italian would have probably had the speed to challenge for victories on asphalt rather than spending most of his time by the side of the road.

Instead, the driver who pushed the leading duo the hardest was Martin Prokop, in a Citroën C2 S1600. Prokop was the most improved driver of the year, and his finest hour was Rallye Deutschland when he beat Urmo Aava fair and square. Aava would later claim that he was taking no risks, but the Estonian was still pushing hard enough to go off briefly.

Two weeks earlier, Prokop won seven out of the first eight stages in Rally Finland before going off after mishearing a pace note. Prokop was expected to be good this season, in his third year of the championship with one of the best-sorted cars out there. On asphalt - his favoured surface - the Czech driver was a genuine contender, taking 18 points from the last two rallies and claiming 22 fastest stage times at the end of the year. Conrad Rautenbach, in another C2, was also much improved this year and had his moments of promise.

Nonetheless, Citroën was missing a consistent top-line driver to take the fight to Suzuki (even though the Juniors was never a manufacturers' championship). An ironic state of affairs as Citroën was the manufacturer that invested most heavily in the series, with the all-new C2 Junior Experience this year, and also the manufacturer that unearthed the real star of the season.

That man was Yoann Bonato, who contested three rallies in a C2-R2 before ending his year with a C2 S1600 drive in Corsica. Finland was not only his first Junior event, but also his first-ever gravel event. He won the C2-R2 class convincingly and even scored an overall Junior championship point. It was exactly the same story in Germany and Spain. The fairy tale seemed too good to last: he dropped around two minutes on the opening day of Corsica changing a puncture on his C2 S1600. But on the second and third days he won all the stages bar two, to end up on the podium.

It was a tantalising glimpse of what might have been for Citroën. Nonetheless, it proved the effectiveness of the C2 Junior Experience scheme - which has a generous enough prize fund to undoubtedly tempt several top people into the C2 next year.

If the winner of next year's Junior championship is driving a Citroën, he will get two rallies in a Citroën WRC car. If he's second he gets one drive and if he's third (like Prokop this year) he gets a test.

By coming out with such an exciting incentive scheme, Citroën tackled one of the biggest issues facing the Junior championship this year: the rising costs of Super 1600. As David Richards - during his time as the sport's commercial rights-holder -was fond of saying, it's all about adding value.

The cost of S1600 is what has forced several drivers and manufacturers down the road of the new R3 category: a cheaper, less hi-tech alternative, which is meant to have broadly similar levels of performance. The most active manufacturer in the class is currently Renault but Honda also made its debut with the R3 Civic Type R in Spain this year, which Dani Solà drove to what would have been fourth in the Juniors, had he been eligible.

It's hard to know which manufacturers are likely to follow suit by building an R3 car, but the experiment didn't really work out for reigning Junior champion Patrik Sandell in the all-new Clio R3. It wasn't by any means a disastrous year: it got off to a good start with second in Norway and then of course there was the Swede's win in Finland, which he described as "an ambition since my childhood". On fast roads the R3 cars are good, whereas on more twisty and technical sections the superior handling of a S1600 car makes a difference. In the end, what let Sandell down were a couple of engine problems and a somewhat harsh exclusion in Germany. But the Swede retains a stoical outlook that is typical of his countrymen. "In the end, we always knew it was going to be tricky to defend the title with a completely new car," he says. "It's been a positive year: we've done a lot of work and the potential is certainly there."

Nonetheless, Sandell would have been less impressed to note that Jozef Béres - a man from Slovakia who used to have the crazy frog stuck to the inside of his rally car - beat him in the overall championship by seven points driving his old Clio S1600.

It was that sort of year really. It may not have quite been a vintage season but it was certainly full of big flavours, with a complex bouquet and a long finish.

### GROUP R VERSUS SUPER 1600

World motorsport's governing body, the FIA, is introducing the new Group R regulations from the start of 2008. Essentially there are two 'R' categories: R2 for front-wheel drive cars with an engine size of up to 1600cc and R3 for front-wheel drive cars with an engine size of up to 2000cc.

The new R rules (which stand simply for 'rally') are designed to cut costs by demanding the use of several components that are directly derived from road cars. Citroën has led the way in the R2 class with its C2-R2, while Renault has pioneered the R3 category thanks to the Clio R3.

By using a two-litre engine, the R3 cars are intended to have roughly the same performance as a Super 1600 car, although there are obviously compromises in terms of suspension and handling. The Group R cars also look less dramatic than their Group A counterparts, as they do not have the wide bodywork and big wheels permitted under the S1600 rules.

The other important area covered by the Group R regulations is the engine. There are strict rules limiting specifications such as valve lift and compression ratio, in order to bring down the cost of engine development.

In practice, the R3 category has resulted in a cheap and quick car that isn't quite so capable at stopping and going around corners - hence a Clio R3 one-two in Finland this year. Nonetheless Patrik Sandell is very complimentary about his new machine. "It's very easy to drive," he points out. "You can have a lot of confidence with it straight away."

Opposite page: Eventual champion Andersson scored a vital win in Catalunya - and his first on asphalt - as team-mate and rival Aava crashed out

Top: Aava showed his promise by scoring points in WRC machinery in New Zealand (pictured) and Finland, driving a Mitsubishi Lancer, but missed out on the Junior crown

Above: Béres switched to a Renault Clio from a Suzuki Ignis for the season but despite running newer machinery couldn't secure a breakthrough wine

Left: Reigning champion Sandell broke the mould by switching to the new-generation R3 machinery, but the Clio's lack of development limited his ambitions, though he did win in Finland

All photographs by McKlein unless specified

# No simple task for Simon

Former European champion Simon Jean-Joseph overcame budget problems and a power disadvantage to land a second crown in 2007 - with some help from Citroën. By Richard Rodgers

Simon Jean-Joseph won the European title for a second time, despite getting by on a round-by-round deal

Above right: Five dominant wins handed Conrad Rautenbach the African championship although there were problems along the way

| EUROPEAN RALLY CHAMPIONSHIP |
|---|

**ROUND 1 RALLYE MILLE MIGLIA APRIL 20-22**
The local contingent of Super 2000 stars, led by reigning European champion Basso in a works Grande Punto, dominate the leaderboard. Jean-Joseph makes an encouraging start but he's delayed by a puncture before dropping out with an electrical fault, leaving Iliev to top the points.

1. Dimitar Iliev (Mitsubishi Lancer) 3h20m55.5s
2. Michal Solowow (Fiat Grande Punto) +5m22.4s
3. No other registered drivers finished

**ROUND 2 FIAT RALLY MAY 11-13**
The stakes are raised with the addition of several Intercontinental Rally Challenge regulars claiming their share of the European points. The all-new gravel event provides a tough test. Despite an early puncture Vouilloz moves into the lead on the final afternoon to record an impressive win on his debut run in the Peugeot.

1. Nicolas Vouilloz (Peugeot 207) 2h31m28.7s
2. Andrea Navarra (Abarth Grande Punto) +24.2s
3. Enrique García Ojeda (Peugeot 207) +1m13.0s

**ROUND 3 INA CROATIA DELTA RALLY MAY 24-26**
Croatia's first appearance in the European championship is marked by a home win for Sebalj, although he has to rely on Isik, who was 29s clear after day one, coming unstuck with an electrical problem, and Polish driver Solowow dropping from second to fourth.

1. Juraj Sebalj (Mitsubishi Lancer) 2h44m4.7s
2. Dimitar Iliev (Mitsubishi Lancer) +28.4s
3. Simon Jean-Joseph (Citroën C2) +1m19.8s

**ROUND 4 PLATINUM RALLY POLAND JUNE 8-10**
The high-speed gravel event in the heart of Poland's lake district provides a tough challenge. While a thrilling battle for the lead between the non-registered Holowczyc and Svedlund dominates the headlines, Travaglia overcomes a puncture to head home the European regulars.

1. Renato Travaglia (Mitsubishi Lancer) 2h39m21.1s
2. Michal Solowow (Fiat Grande Punto) +2m2.6s
3. Volkan Isik (Fiat Grande Punto) +5m49.4s

**ROUND 5 BELGIUM YPRES WESTHOEK RALLY JUNE 22-24**
With overall winner Rossetti not eligible for the championship it is left to Ojeda to score maximum points on the rain-hit event, after team-mate Vouilloz crashes out. Navarra recovers from a costly puncture on the opening leg to land second. Iliev avoids the numerous hazards to claim a solid third.

1. Enrique García Ojeda (Peugeot 207) 2h39m02.5s
2. Andrea Navarra (Abarth Grande Punto) +1m45.3s
3. Dimitar Iliev (Mitsubishi Lancer) +8m27.9s

**ROUND 6 RALLY BULGARIA JULY 6-8**
Iliev becomes only the second local driver to win the event and credits his victory to a storming opening charge, which enabled him to build a comfortable lead at the end of leg one. With third-placed Bulgarian Popov not scoring it is left to another home driver Donchev to clinch the final podium spot.

1. Dimitar Iliev (Mitsubishi Lancer) 2h42m50.2s
2. Simon Jean-Joseph (Citroën C2) +17.9s
3. Krum Donchev (Mitsubishi Lancer) +51.2s

**ROUND 7 RALLYE VINHO DA MADEIRA AUGUST 2-4**
There's post-event drama when Travaglia is excluded and hands the top European points to Ojeda. Navarra is out before the first stage with an electrical glitch, while a clutch problem ruins Vouilloz's challenge on day one. Basso wins outright but isn't a contender for championship points.

1. Enrique García Ojeda (Peugeot 207) 3h09m06.2s
2. Corrado Fontana (Fiat Grande Punto) +2m45.8s
3. Simon Jean-Joseph (Citroën C2) 3m10.7s

**ROUND 8 BARUM RALLY ZLIN AUGUST 24-26**
Vouilloz claims the honours as a driveshaft breakage on the final morning costs Ojeda the lead, which he inherits from the non-scoring Loix, who suffers a puncture and crashes out. A brake problem costs Jean-Joseph almost three minutes but he fights back to claim five vital points.

1. Nicolas Vouilloz (Peugeot 207) 2h28m10.8s
2. Enrique García Ojeda (Peugeot 207) +16.3s
3. Andrea Navarra (Abarth Grande Punto) +4m47.7s

**ROUND 9 ELPA RALLY OCTOBER 5-7**
Jean-Joseph is able to keep close to the flying Isik on the opening leg's asphalt stages but can't hold on when the rally moves onto gravel for leg two. He drops behind Travaglia and Donchev but is able to get back ahead of the Bulgarian when he picks up a puncture on the final stage and drops one minute.

1. Volkan Isik (Fiat Grande Punto) 3h04m42.2s
2. Simon Jean-Joseph (Citroën C2) +3m33.8s
3. Michal Solowow (Fiat Grande Punto) +3m51.2s

**ROUND 10 RALLYE D'ANTIBES OCTOBER 19-21**
While Travaglia, having switched to a Grande Punto, ends his season on a high note with a crushing win it's not enough to deny Jean-Joseph the title. He remains in second place throughout the three-day finale and despite erring on the side of caution he's still able to set a handful of fastest stage times on the challenging mountainous event.

1. Renato Travaglia (Fiat Grande Punto) 3h16m24.3s
2. Simon Jean-Joseph (Citroën C2) +2m13.0s
3. Volkan Isik (Fiat Grande Punto) +3m54.3s

| | | | | | | | | | | |
|---|---|---|---|---|---|---|---|---|---|---|
| Simon Jean-Joseph | 1 | 2 | 7 | 0 | 5 | 12 | 8 | 5 | 10 | 14 | 64 |
| Volkan Isik | 2 | 6 | 3 | 7 | 0 | 7 | 4 | 3 | 16 | 9 | 57 |
| Renato Travaglia | 3 | 5 | 0 | 16 | 5 | 0 | 0 | 6 | 0 | 19 | 54 |

SIMON Jean-Joseph wasn't expected to challenge for the European championship crown. Although his driving credentials were never in doubt - he had won the title in 2004 following a lengthy stint in the World Rally Championship - he only had a deal for three events and his Super 1600-specification Citroën C2 lacked the outright pace and traction necessary to beat the hoards of Super 2000 and Group N models that dominated the entry this year, especially on gravel or in wet conditions.

Save for a brief test in the build-up to the season, he also lacked knowledge of his new mount and treated the first leg of the opening round, the Rallye Mille Miglia in Italy in April, as an extended test session. His prospects diminished even further when an electrical fault struck on the first stage of day two and he headed home from northern Italy with a paltry single point, his bonus for being the third highest European runner at the end of day one, under the new scoring system introduced for 2007.

But consistency rather than ultimate speed mattered most over the next nine rounds. After securing his drive with the factory-blessed PH Sport squad for the remainder of the season he only once failed to score, which meant he was able to capitalise when arch-rival Renato Travaglia suffered the indignity of two exclusions due to technical infringements.

The Italian was set to claim second place - and top European points - in Madeira in August, only for post-event checks to reveal his Mitsubishi Lancer was running a dodgy turbo. He was second on the Elpa Rally in Greece in early October, but this time officials discovered an illegal rear differential mounting and promptly threw him out of the results. Although he lodged an official protest, the FIA's International Court of Appeal didn't find in his favour and Jean-Joseph was declared champion for a second time after triumphing in a classic David versus Goliath contest.

"It was difficult having to wait but once it was confirmed it was an excellent feeling," Jean-Joseph says of his eventual title triumph, which was confirmed in late November. "We did not expect to do many rallies and our start was not so good. But after the Ypres Rally in June we decided we would try to do each rally one by one to see how we went, although it was never easy.

"Although PH Sport knew the car very well and we always had good balance on asphalt and gravel, we only had two-wheel drive and had to fight with cars with four-wheel drive and bigger engines. We also faced new events and there were up to six drivers who could have won the championship.

"Travaglia was very experienced but also very fast and that made him the most dangerous for me and the championship. Volkan Isik made some big, big progress during the year and Dimitar Iliev also improved."

After his disappointment on the Mille Miglia, Jean-Joseph's run to eighth overall on round two in Turkey didn't point to a title tilt either. Run on new gravel stages on the outskirts of Istanbul rather than on the asphalt roads used in the past, he struggled for traction during the early exchanges. With several regulars from the Intercontinental Rally Challenge - which ran in tandem with the ERC on a total of four events including Turkey - also eligible for European points the Martinique-based driver found himself facing a mountain to climb.

His prospects improved slightly after the all-asphalt Delta Rally in Croatia in late May when Jean-Joseph finished third, despite being delayed by a puncture on day one and a spark plug failure on the second leg.

His result on the Zagreb-based event secured a drive on the

# REGIONAL CHAMPIONSHIPS

## CONRAD'S AFRICAN ROUT

ON paper you could have been forgiven for thinking that Conrad Rautenbach had it easy during his capture of his first African title after he stormed to the crown by 17 points courtesy of five dominant wins.

And while the 23-year-old from Zimbabwe was one of only a handful of career-minded drivers taking part in the seven-round series, he still had to endure some extremely tough terrain and several unexpected hazards, with errant motorists straying onto stages an occasional problem.

Rautenbach, who dovetailed his African campaign with a season in the FIA Junior Rally Championship and a programme of British events, didn't enjoy the best of starts to his year. Persistent damper problems and a series of punctures aboard his Subaru Impreza limited him to fifth place overall on February's opening round in Tanzania behind eventual winner Hideaki Miyoshi.

He made amends on the Safari Rally in Kenya in March with an impressive victory against the factory Abarth Grande Puntos of Andrea Navarra and Umberto Scandola, who were contesting the combined Intercontinental Rally Challenge event. However, Miyoshi's run to second place enabled the Japanese to preserve his championship lead.

"That was the highlight." Rautenbach admits. "It's a famous event and I also beat the factory Super 2000 cars. We had problems with the dampers again so we took it easy on the first leg. But we pushed a bit on day two and Navarra got a puncture."

The Ugandan round in April, which included a superspecial in the grounds of King Mutebi II's home, was hit by heavy rain. Although torrential showers left many of the stages decimated, Rautenbach was still able to claim another win to move one point clear of Miyoshi in the title race.

He won again in the mountains of Rwanda in May, while a spate of punctures hindered Miyoshi to the extent he pulled out of the championship following the event, convinced that his title hopes were over.

With regular co-driver Peter Marsh honouring a commitment to local driver Johnny Gemmell for Zulu Rally South Africa at the end of May - which also counted as a round of the domestic series - Rautenbach called up his junior championship partner David Senior from Britain for the Durban-based event. Despite coming up against a host of S2000 machines in their four-year-old Group N Impreza, Rautenbach landed top African points in an impressive second overall.

"It was impossible to keep up with the Volkswagen Polo Super 2000 [driven by local driver Hergen Fekken] in the forests on the second day because there was so much dust about but second was still a good result," Rautenbach recalls.

With the title in the bag following a third successive win on this home event in July and a clashing junior championship round in Germany, Rautenbach skipped the season-closing Zambia Rally. In his absence local driver Muna Singh took advantage to claim his first and only victory of the campaign, while his co-driver David Sihoka deprived Marsh of the navigators' crown.

### AFRICAN RALLY CHAMPIONSHIP

**ROUND 1 RALLY OF TANZANIA FEBRUARY 9-11**
1. Hideaki Miyoshi (Mitsubishi Lancer) 3h03m7s
2. Asad Anwar (Mitsubishi Lancer) +10m45s
3. Lola Verlaque (Subaru Impreza) +12m07s

**ROUND 2 KCB SAFARI RALLY KENYA MARCH 9-11**
1. Conrad Rautenbach (Subaru Impreza) 2h30m43s
2. Carl Tundo (Subaru Impreza) +2m01s
3. Hideaki Miyoshi (Mitsubishi Lancer) +9m20s

**ROUND 3 PEARL OF AFRICA UGANDA RALLY APRIL 13-15**
1. Conrad Rautenbach (Subaru Impreza) 2h52m52s
2. Hideaki Miyoshi (Mitsubishi Lancer) +3m28s
3. Muna Singh (Subaru Impreza) +3m33s

**ROUND 4 RWANDA MOUNTAIN GORILLA RALLY MAY 4-6**
1. Conrad Rautenbach (Subaru Impreza) 3h12m55s
2. Muna Singh (Subaru Impreza) +5m33s
3. Hideaki Miyoshi (Mitsubishi Lancer) +9m06s

**ROUND 5 ZULU RALLY SOUTH AFRICA MAY 24-27**
1. Conrad Rautenbach (Subaru Impreza) 2h59m59s
2. Muna Singh (Subaru Impreza) +4m47s
3. No other registered drivers finished

**ROUND 6 DUNLOP ZIMBABWE CHALLENGE RALLY JULY 13-15**
1. Conrad Rautenbach (Subaru Impreza) 3h08m22s
2. Muna Singh (Subaru Impreza) +7m12s
3. Lola Verlaque (Subaru Impreza) +10m48s

**ROUND 7 ZAMBIA INTERNATIONAL RALLY AUGUST 17-19**
1. Muna Singh (Subaru Impreza) 2m47m14s
2. Lola Verlaque (Subaru Impreza) +6m15s
3. No other registered drivers finished

| | | | | | | | | |
|---|---|---|---|---|---|---|---|---|
| Conrad Rautenbach | 6 | 16 | 15 | 16 | 16 | 16 | 0 | 85 |
| Muna Singh | 0 | 8 | 8 | 12 | 12 | 12 | 16 | 68 |
| Hideaki Miyoshi | 16 | 10 | 10 | 8 | 0 | 0 | 0 | 44 |

---

next round in Poland in June, although funds could only stretch to the lower-specification C2-R2. He was nevertheless the fourth best European runner after the first leg but failed to go the distance when an anti-torque clevis screw sheered on the final morning and forced him to retire.

He hit back in the Belgian rain on the Ypres Westhoek Rally later on in the month with fourth place, despite constantly searching for traction on the narrow and slippery country lanes. That result convinced the Citroën hierarchy to sanction Jean-Joseph's participation in the remaining five events. Although their decision was based solely on being able to exploit a new market for their hot hatch, it was vindicated when the 38-year-old - back behind the wheel of the C2 S1600 - bagged second overall behind local driver Dimitar Iliev on Rally Bulgaria in early July, which propelled Jean-Joseph into the thick of the title battle.

He left Madeira, where he finished seventh overall in August, eight points adrift of championship leader Iliev. A miraculous recovery from 23rd to 10th - as the fifth highest European contender - on the Barum Rally in the Czech Republic in August following brake problems, underlined Jean-Joseph's fighting qualities garnered from his lengthy driving career and provided a further boost to his championship ambitions.

After inheriting second on the mixed-surface Elpa Rally following Travaglia's exclusion he was one of five drivers separated by 14 points prior to the season-closing Antibes Rally in France, which uses several classic Monte Carlo Rally stages. Although a freak snowstorm led to the cancellation of the Col de Turini stage, the event was held in largely dry conditions and Jean-Joseph made the most of the ample grip to claim second place behind Travaglia.

While Jean-Joseph is quick to highlight the challenge he faced from the Super 2000 and Group N runners and was undoubtedly a worthy champion, the series again lacked real strength in depth with only Isik, Travaglia and veteran Pole Michal Solowow mounting extended campaigns.

The continued emergence of the Intercontinental Rally Challenge had again diminished the series' appeal, but with events taking place in several important markets and certainly not lacking in quality, the regional series still plays a key role on the rallying calendar.

With four events doubling as IRC rounds, registrations were up on previous years with the Peugeot Sport Espana squad one of the notable additions. Its drivers Enrique García Ojeda and Nicolas Vouilloz both claimed two maximum scores apiece but with championship regulations requiring a driver to contest a minimum of six events in order to figure in the final standings, their results were discounted from the final tally. That rule also undermined Croatian Juraj Sebalj's achievement of winning his home event in a Mitsubishi Lancer.

Of Jean-Joseph's rivals who did go the distance Turkey's Volkan Isik was a constant threat in his S2000 Fiat Grande Punto. He was unlucky not to have landed a podium finish on home soil in May when he was delayed by an alternator problem in the closing stages. Mechanical woes also cost him in Croatia, although he made up for those disappointments with victory in Greece. Travaglia scored top European points in Poland in the summer and on the final round in France. Bulgarian Iliev was a twice a maximum scorer in his Lancer, claiming the class laurels in Italy and outright victory on his home rally.

## RUSSIANS BEST IN BURGEONING BAJAS

Two Russians took centre stage in the consciousness of those who followed the FIA International Cup for Cross-Country Bajas closely, well particularly those living in Great Britain.

While Boris Gadasin became champion with a win and a second place at the wheel of a Nissan Navara, it was his countryman and Mitsubishi Pajero driver Miroslav Zapletal who sprung to prominence when he won Baja GB, which marked the UK's first appearance in the emerging off-road contest.

Bajas start and finish at the same location (it's a Mexican word meaning loop), and while the sport permits the same T1 and T2 vehicles that feature in desert raids to take part, the stages are shorter and are based around a central service. Although the sport is still in its infancy, the 2008 calendar will feature two new events in Hungary and Saudi Arabia, bringing the total number of rounds to six.

After Gadasin's victory on the Italian Baja in March, it was the might of the factory Mitsubishi Cross Country Rally World Cup team that took centre stage when the series resumed in Spain in July.

The Franco-Japanese outfit was taking part at the behest of its main sponsor Repsol, the Spanish petroleum giant. Despite the local patronage, it was the squad's French star Stéphane Peterhansel who won ahead of his Spanish team-mate Nani Roma. Britain's Colin McRae was also in action in an X-Raid BMW X3. Although he won the opening leg, a road penalty dropped him to third.

And so to Builth Wells in mid-Wales in August for Baja GB. After a successful candidate event in 2006 elevated the competition to FIA championship status much was expected of the British round. While a scant 18-car entry took the start after as many as 40 crews had been lined up to participate, the event was still considered a success, particularly as more than £100,000 had been spent upgrading several forest roads. The effort paid off when the event was confirmed on the 2008 Baja calendar.

The sport has already developed a strong following in Britain and that looks set to continue to grow, particularly in the build-up to Baja GB next September. Indeed privateer competitor Richard Hopkins entered the season-closing Baja Anta Da Serra in Portugal, won by local pilot Miguel Barbosa, after being inspired to do so when he tackled his home event in the summer, while several car constructors including the creators of the McRae Enduro are becoming established.

| | | | | | |
|---|---|---|---|---|---|
| Boris Gadasin | 15 | 0 | 11 | 0 | 26 |
| Hamad Bin Eid Al Thani | 5 | 0 | 11 | 3 | 19 |
| Miroslav Zapletal | 3 | 0 | 15 | 0 | 18 |

## NASSER'S LATE LIFT-OFF

THE stakes were high when the crews left the start ramp in Damascus, Syria's capital, for the fifth round of the Middle East championship in June.

Nasser Al-Attiyah, champion for the past two seasons, was eight points behind Khalid Al-Qassimi in the standings after crashes in Oman and Jordan had derailed his bid for a fourth regional title.

A puncture and an overheating engine had restricted Al-Qassimi to fourth on April's Troodos Rally in Cyprus, but prior to that a brace of wins and a second-place finish behind Al-Attiyah on the opening round in Qatar had given him a healthy lead in the championship he last won in 2004.

Put simply, if Al-Attiyah slipped up again in Syria and Al-Qassimi claimed a decent score, the Qatari could all but relinquish his title defence.

Despite claiming a much-needed maximum score in Syria, Al-Qassimi's capture of second meant Al-Attiyah and co-driver Chris Patterson would have to win the remaining three events, including the rescheduled Rally of Lebanon in November, to reclaim the top honours.

The significance of the Lebanese round was all to do with the scoring system adopted by the organisers. They decreed that as well as making drivers drop their worst scores, in the event of a tied result the winner of the longest round in the series would take the overall prize on countback.

At nearly 600 miles the Lebanon event was the longest on the calendar. Although Al-Attiyah trailed local driver Roger Feghali in the final results, because the Mitsubishi pilot wasn't eligible for Middle East points, Al-Attiyah landed a maximum score. It meant the 37-year-old started the final round in Dubai in late November in the knowledge that if the scores were tied then he'd be champion.

Al-Attiyah did win the finale but it proved to be a controversial end to the season. He was 36 seconds ahead of his rival when organisers took the decision to cancel the remaining three stages after several reports of quad bikes being ridden in the opposite direction on live tests and obstacles being laid in the path of competing cars. Because the event had gone over half distance full points were awarded and the title went to Al-Attiyah.

"I'm very disappointed it had to finish like that," he admitted.

There was controversy too on the second visit to Cyprus in October - where an extra round had been scheduled - when a protest by a rival motoring club disrupted the first two stages.

While Al-Attiyah's tally of six wins was never bettered, the Subaru driver's car-wrecking off in Oman, followed two rounds later by an opening stage crash in Jordan, somewhat took the shine of his campaign. But his sequence of four successive late-season victories under considerable pressure meant his championship success was richly deserved.

In fairness Al-Qassimi had bigger fish to fry. He had landed a four-event programme of world championship events in a factory Ford Focus thanks to a hefty injection of cash from the Abu Dhabi Tourism Authority, which would increase to 10 rounds in 2008. To say it affected Al-Qassimi's application would be wrong given his diligent approach, but he never seemed properly equipped to fend off Al-Attiyah's recovery.

Of the other regulars, Jordanian Amjad Farrah and Al-Qassimi's younger brother Abdullah bagged four podiums apiece, while Lebanese veteran Michel Saleh was rarely outside the points in his Impreza.

Youngster Misfar Al-Marri from Qatar impressed, particularly when he deputised for his countryman Al-Attiyah on the PCWRC round in New Zealand in September while Nasser was convalescing from head wounds sustained in a road accident. Fortunately the injuries weren't severe and occurred during the lengthy summer break.

### MIDDLE EAST RALLY CHAMPIONSHIP

**ROUND 1 QATAR INTERNATIONAL RALLY FEB 16-18**
1. Nasser Al-Attiyah (Subaru Impreza) 2h05m01.9s
2. Khalid Al-Qassimi (Subaru Impreza) +1m35.7s
3. Abdullah Al-Qassimi (Mitsubishi Lancer) +11m06.3s

**ROUND 2 RALLY OMAN MARCH 14-16**
1. Khalid Al-Qassimi (Subaru Impreza) 2h26m37s
2. Abdullah Al-Qassimi (Subaru Impreza) +5m53s
3. Amjad Farrah (Mitsubishi Lancer) +10m10s

**ROUND 3 TROODOS RALLY APRIL 20-22**
1. Nasser Al-Attiyah (Subaru Impreza) 4h04m54s
2. Amjad Farrah (Mitsubishi Lancer) +13m0s
3. Michel Saleh (Subaru Impreza) +13m26s

**ROUND 4 JORDAN RALLY MAY 10-12**
1. Khalid Al-Qassimi (Subaru Impreza) 3h17m44s
2. Amjad Farrah (Mitsubishi Lancer) +1m12s
3. Michel Saleh (Subaru Impreza) +5m57s

**ROUND 5 SYRIAN INTERNATIONAL RALLY JUNE 7-9**
1. Nasser Al-Attiyah (Subaru Impreza) 2h20m35s
2. Khalid Al-Qassimi (Subaru Impreza) +36s
3. Abdullah Al-Qassimi (Subaru Impreza) +8m35s

**ROUND 6 CYPRUS RALLY OCTOBER 12-14**
1. Nasser Al-Attiyah (Subaru Impreza) 3h05m29s
2. Khalid Al-Qassimi (Subaru Impreza) +6m01s
3. Amjad Farrah (Mitsubishi Lancer) +6m30s

**ROUND 7 RALLY OF LEBANON NOVEMBER 9-11**
1. Nasser Al-Attiyah (Subaru Impreza) 3h07m10s
2. Khalid Al-Qassimi (Subaru Impreza) +7m54s
3. Nick Georgiou (Mitsubishi Lancer) +16m40s

**ROUND 8 DUBAI INTERNATIONAL RALLY NOV 29-DEC 1**
1. Nasser Al-Attiyah (Subaru Impreza) 1h44m13s
2. Khalid Al-Qassimi (Subaru Impreza) +36s
3. Abdullah Al-Qassimi (Subaru Impreza) +7m32s

## SAINZ LEADS RACE TO DAKAR

"They were ideal conditions for Dakar," confirmed one team boss. "It's perfect preparation for Dakar," agreed another. "I think we are now ready for Dakar," a leading driver would say.

Even though the legendary desert raid from Lisbon to the Senegalese capital Dakar wasn't a round of the five-event FIA Cross Country Rally World Cup, it dominated the season. And while the destination of the title wasn't confirmed until the UAE Desert Challenge finale, it was never really a true contest as teams drifted in and out of the series, depending on their testing schedules aligned to their Dakar preparations.

That meant the big three (Mitsubishi, Volkswagen and the BMW-blessed X-Raid team) only went head to head on the Dubai-based Desert Challenge in late October, where Carlos Sainz and Volkswagen prevailed as drivers' and manufacturers' champions respectively.

The lack of serious competition was underlined by the fact that Brazilian privateer Paulo Nobre was a title contender heading into the final round. Not wishing to talk down his achievements but Nobre, whose BMW X3 was prepared by the German X-Raid outfit, only really shone with third-place finishes on the African Heritage Cross Country in South Africa and the nine-day Por las Pampas, which crossed into Chile from Argentina. Nobre could have scored higher in South Africa but for a road penalty and a late crash, which damaged his BMW's steering and necessitated major repairs in order to reach the finish. His delay and the lack of serious competition helped Norwegian Ivar Tollefsen to claim victory in a Nissan Navara, the only occasion when he threatened the leaderboard. The lack of opposition was also demonstrated by the fact Riccardo Garosci, in a production-specification Mitsubishi Pajero, took second overall.

There was plenty of competition on the opening Rally Vodafone Transiberico in late May, however. Sainz found the narrow and twisty Portuguese stages to his liking as he took his first victory for his German employer, after second-placed works Mitsubishi driver Nani Roma's challenge was hamstrung by a time-consuming puncture on leg three.

Mitsubishi sent a single car to South America in late August for the Por las Pampas. Luc Alphand was handed the job of negotiating the 2557-mile route, which subjected crews to sub-zero temperatures on the mountainous passes and the increased heat of arid desert-like plains. Although there was a late engine scare, Alphand's victory, in the absence of Volkswagen, moved him ahead of Nobre to the top of the drivers' standings.

The VW team returned for Morocco's round in September where two punctures on the final day for Sainz robbed the Spaniard of victory and handed maximum points to his team-mate Giniel de Villiers. But Sainz recovered to take second and a five-point lead over Alphand heading into the last round in the Middle East after Mitsubishi elected to skip the event.

After Nobre dropped out of contention when he rolled on the first leg, Alphand needed Sainz to hit trouble in order to keep his title dream alive. But what distant hopes the ex-skiing champion had evaporated when he retired with broken suspension after hitting a pothole on the penultimate day.

But rather than celebrate their respective achievements - Volkswagen had two titles to savour, Mitsubishi's Stéphane Peterhansel won the rally, while Nasser Al-Attiyah starred for X-Raid - the Dakar was the main talking point for competitors as references to January's showcase went into overdrive.

Although the Desert Challenge had produced plenty of drama and lead changes, time and again it was Dakar on the minds of the team bosses and drivers rather than championship points. The series may include several established events, but without the Dakar it's hard to comprehend what real value it has.

| | | | | | |
|---|---|---|---|---|---|
| Carlos Sainz | 15 | 0 | 0 | 11 | 11 | 37 |
| Giniel de Villiers | 0 | 0 | 0 | 15 | 7 | 22 |
| Luc Alphand | 5 | 0 | 15 | 0 | 0 | 20 |

# REGIONAL CHAMPIONSHIPS

## CODY BREAKS THE OPPOSITION

CODY Crocker didn't panic when he got his Asia Pacific title defence underway on the second round in New Zealand even though Jussi Välimäki, the champion in 2005 and the man expected to provide him with his sternest test, had established a 15-point lead at the top of the table.

Championship rules require teams to miss one of the seven scheduled rounds and Crocker's Singapore-based Motor Image team elected to skip the season opener in New Caledonia, where Välimäki made the most of the Australian's absence to claim maximum points.

Crocker's reason for remaining calm was simple. He knew Välimäki's RaceTorque Engineering squad wouldn't be making the trip to the second round in Whangarei where Crocker was confident he could clean up.

His self-belief was justified when he followed up his maximum points haul in New Zealand with three further wins, including his tenth consecutive Asia Pacific success in the searing heat of Malaysia in August. He secured the championship on the next round in Indonesia before underlining his impressive campaign with a fifth win on the China Rally in November.

Although Crocker endured a troubled run in Indonesia - a puncture on day one wiped out his bid for an 11th straight win - his problems were small fry compared to those experienced by Välimäki.

Even his winning run in New Caledonia wasn't without its share of woes. A driving error on the fourth stage resulted in a "big moment" for the Finn, while a troublesome gearbox caused consternation throughout the first leg. But there were no such problems on day two when Välimäki clawed back his team-mate Katsuhiko Taguchi's 24-second lead on the mountainous stages to win by almost 20 seconds thanks to an inspired tyre choice. He opted for mud tyres to cope with a section of the route where it had rained heavily prior to the start. Taguchi, who won on the island in 2006, chose a dry cut alternative and struggled for grip as a result.

When Välimäki resumed his bid on the Rally of Canberra in Australia in early June, Crocker had edged into a one-point lead thanks to a greater total of bonus scores in New Zealand. Välimäki's hopes took a further battering when a puncture on leg one caused considerable delay, although he admitted he was no match for Crocker and Taguchi on day two. The stages were based in an area badly affected by a forest fire a few years earlier and the lack of natural landmarks affected Välimäki's driving as he struggled to find suitable braking points.

There was a minor scare for Crocker in Australia when he was forced to complete the final stage of leg one nursing a bent steering arm, which enabled Taguchi to cut his lead to 12 seconds. But a turbo boost problem dogged the Japanese on day two and Crocker was able to take a comfortable victory after winning 10 of the 16 stages.

It was discovered after the event that the engine in Välimäki's Mitsubishi Lancer was down on power, a problem that intensified when it broke in the build-up to Rally Hokkaido in Japan. Although the broken motor prevented Välimäki's MRF Tyres-backed team from fine-tuning his car's set-up before the start, a serious bout of food poisoning was of greater concern to the 33-year-old. He was also slowed by a puncture on day one and had to settle for a distant third place at the finish as Crocker took advantage of Taguchi's down on power engine to win again.

Välimäki started the fifth round in Malaysia knowing he had to win to stand any chance of claiming the title after falling 31 points behind Crocker. In ambient temperatures of 45 degrees centigrade Välimäki led after two stages, but he lost almost a minute on stage three after a mistake on the recce when he and co-driver Jarkko Kalliolepo missed out more than a mile of the stage when they made a wrong turn at a junction. It meant they had to drive the section blind in the rally proper and were unable to attack as a result.

Worse was to come for Välimäki on day two when he was forced to retire on the 10th stage with rear differential failure. Team-mate Taguchi was hit by the same fault and would also go no further. "I noticed something was wrong with the transmission at the end of leg one," Välimäki remembers. "I reported it to the team but there was no time in the 10-minute service for anyone to check it."

There were no such problems for Crocker. Despite being beaten to the overall win by Toshi Arai, who was making a one-off appearance for the Motor Image team, the Melbourne driver's maximum score meant he now required four points on the next event in Indonesia to be champion for a second time. Although Crocker's puncture on day one meant he was powerless to prevent Välimäki claiming a morale-boosting win, his run to fifth was enough to make him and co-driver Ben Atkinson champions again with one round remaining.

"I was a bit apprehensive at the start of the season because I was with a new team and I knew Taguchi and Välimäki would be tough to beat," Crocker admits. "They had their problems so perhaps the pressure wasn't on us like it could have been. But I always felt comfortable in my car and with my team so I was confident I could have taken the fight to them."

Crocker, 36, will defend his title in 2008 under a two-year deal with the Motor Image squad. And he hopes he will face a tougher test as he bids for a third title. "As a driver you're always looking for more competition although I don't think people realise now physically demanding these events are," he says. "It really is a unique challenge dealing with the heat and you're always covering big distances."

With Välimäki set to continue in the series - he returned to the Asia Pacific ranks for 2007 because he felt it provided his best chance of a regular drive after he failed to secure a ride in the world championship - Crocker certainly won't have things all his own way. David Higgins, who helped the WY Rally Team to the prestigious entrants' title in the Chinese championship, could be rewarded with a season of Asia Pacific action, while Crocker is tipping his young team-mate Rifat Sungkar from Indonesia to make considerable progress under his tutelage. MRF-supported Indian Guaurav Gill will also benefit from a full programme after missing three events in 2007 when he destroyed his car on the opening round in New Caledonia.

Organisers have made a raft of changes to encourage more entries for 2008. They have created the Asia and Pacific cups to allow competitors who can only afford to travel to a handful of events to chase an award over three rounds instead of the current mandatory six. The launch of Subaru's new generation Impreza will create added interest, while the Australian-built Super 2000 Ford Fiesta is set to be homologated for use in the series, which could trigger and influx of S2000 machinery and, ultimately, more competition.

### ASIA PACIFIC RALLY CHAMPIONSHIP

**ROUND 1 RALLYE DE NOUVELLE CALÉDONIE APRIL 13-15**
1. Jussi Välimäki (Mitsubishi Lancer) 2h54m15s
2. Katsuhiko Taguchi (Mitsubishi Lancer) +19s
3. Patrick Yanai (Mitsubishi Lancer) +4m48s

**ROUND 2 RALLY OF WHANGAREI MAY 11-13**
1. Cody Crocker (Subaru Impreza) 2h52m33s
2. Hiroshi Yanagisawa (Subaru Impreza) +2m43s
3. Rifat Sungkar (Subaru Impreza) +9m35s

**ROUND 3 RALLY OF CANBERRA JUNE 1-3**
1. Cody Crocker (Subaru Impreza) 2h30m51s
2. Katsuhiko Taguchi (Mitsubishi Lancer) +1m03s
3. Jussi Välimäki (Mitsubishi Lancer) +2m16s

**ROUND 4 RALLY HOKKAIDO JULY 6-8**
1. Cody Crocker (Subaru Impreza) 2h32m13s
2. Katsuhiko Taguchi (Mitsubishi Lancer) +1m23s
3. Jussi Välimäki (Mitsubishi Lancer) +1m59s

**ROUND 5 MALAYSIAN RALLY AUGUST 10-12**
1. Cody Crocker (Subaru Impreza) 2h49m46s
2. Naren Kumar (Mitsubishi Lancer) +5m57s
3. Brian Green (Mitsubishi Lancer) +16m10s

**ROUND 6 INTERNATIONAL RALLY OF INDONESIA SEPT 7-9**
1. Jussi Välimäki (Mitsubishi Lancer) 3h06m36s
2. Katsuhiko Taguchi (Mitsubishi Lancer) +1m41s
3. Hiroshi Yanagisawa (Subaru Impreza) +2m45s

**ROUND 7 CHINA RALLY NOVEMBER 9-11**
1. Cody Crocker (Subaru Impreza) 3h28m03s
2. Brian Green (Mitsubishi Lancer) +16m36s
3. No other registered drivers finished

| | | | | | | | |
|---|---|---|---|---|---|---|---|
| Cody Crocker | 0 | 16 | 16 | 16 | 16 | 6 | 16 | 86 |
| Jussi Välimäki | 15 | 0 | 9 | 8 | 1 | 16 | 0 | 49 |
| Katsuhiko Taguchi | 13 | 0 | 11 | 10 | 2 | 11 | 0 | 47 |

Brian Young - LINEAR Photography

**Top:** Nasser Al-Attiyah reclaimed the Middle East honours in a controversial final showdown in Dubai

**Above left:** Carlos Sainz added the Cross Country award to his brace of World Rally Championship titles

**Above Right:** Australian Cody Crocker took little time to adapt to a new team by defending his Asia Pacific crown

All words by Richard Rodgers

# Mitsubishi's number one Guy

Guy Wilks ended Mitsubishi's long struggle for British Rally Championship success by stealing Mark Higgins' crown.

### By Gillian Bell

Above: Wilks won five from seven BRC rounds to score maximum points, including a dominant class victory in Higgins' backyard on the Isle of Man

Top left: Super 2000 machinery came to Britain in the form of the Toyota S2000R. David Higgins and the RED team struggled for results, however, before parting company

Top right: Defending champion Mark Higgins won twice, but his Subaru Impreza didn't have the pace of the works-backed Lancers

Bottom left: Suzuki Swift driver Smith showed great consistency to secure the ladies' titles in both Britain and Ireland, as well as the Irish Group N crown

Bottom right: Gwyndaf Evans, in possibly his last British campaign, joined forces with Wilks to claim the teams' title for a jubilant Mitsubishi

All photographs by Gavin Lodge

IT'S probably fair to say that there were a lot of chewed fingernails at Mitsubishi Motors UK by the end of Wales Rally GB. Here the team was, on the verge of winning both the driver and team titles in this year's British Rally Championship, providing the man it had pinned all its hopes on could deliver. That man was Guy Wilks, and deliver he did.

Wilks and co-driver Phil Pugh's success in this year's BRC not only gave the works-blessed team the success it has so desperately chased for the past few seasons, it also signalled the end of Mark Higgins' series domination. Well, for now anyway. Wilks and Higgins' rivalry was the big story of this year, and what a rivalry it was. It gave the British series a much-needed injection of excitement, as former Junior WRC driver Wilks announced himself ready to take on and beat the three-time champion.

Before the BRC outlawed the use of World Rally Car machinery, there hadn't really been anyone to hold a candle to Higgins. He utterly dominated the series in 2005 and still made winning look fairly easy last year as Group N machinery came to the fore. So when Wilks won the season-opening Pirelli Rally in April, having replaced the unfortunate Ryan Champion at Mitsubishi, you sensed that Higgins wouldn't be having it all his own way this year.

Of course being the driver he is Higgins fought back on the next round, the Jim Clark, and won again in Ulster. His TEGSport-run Subaru Impreza didn't have the legs of the works Lancers, but it was the more reliable car, and Higgins used it well to take advantage of the Mitsubishis' continued transmission maladies. After a mistake on the Jim Clark and a gearbox-related retirement in Ulster, Wilks was left fearing for his title hopes, but he shouldn't have. In between those setbacks he took a dominant class win in Higgins' backyard on the Isle of Man, where the locals did not appreciate his bating of the Manxman. He went to Yorkshire needing a victory to stay in the fight and led from start to finish.

Then came Rally GB, which counted as the final two points-scoring rounds of the championship (leading to horrible confusion in the timesheets). Wilks started the rally with mechanical dramas when the wrong diff settings were loaded onto the Lancer. But with the problem sorted at the day's first service, he turned speed demon to pass erstwhile leader Higgins, who collected punctures on three of the day's six stages. Mark's renowned bad luck had struck, and he had the look of a beaten man. Through days two and three, which counted as the final round, he struggled with transmission and suspension problems on the Impreza, and with continued pain from the broken collarbone injury he'd sustained in October. Against such strong competition, it was just too much. In the end Wilks took maximum points (100) from the series once two dropped scores were taken into account, while Higgins finished on 94.

Had Higgins taken on too much this year? He'd chased three titles - the British, the Production Car World Rally Championship and the Irish Tarmac Championship - and came away with none. But he had absolutely no regrets. In all three series he'd marked himself out as the man to beat. Armed with an Impreza WRC he'd had Eugene Donnelly psychologically beaten in the Irish series, but had been forced to switch back to his Group N Impreza for the three rallies that counted as rounds of both the British and Irish championships, damaging his title chances. Production winner Toshi Arai has said he hopes Higgins is back to challenge him in 2008, and Wilks spoke of how much he'd relished the competition with Mark in the British series. At the time of writing Higgins was unsure of his plans for '08, but wherever he ends up he'll be a contender.

As for Wilks, Mitsubishi has already made overtures to the 26-year-old Darlington driver. His first overall championship win was something that Guy cherished, but having achieved what he set out to do in this year's BRC, will he really be up for a repeat? Wilks has made no secret of the fact that he wants to be in the WRC, and so he should be. He ran a limited WRC campaign with the Ramsport team this year, and though there were a couple of slip-ups, he did finish sixth in Ireland. WRC seats aren't exactly flying off the shelves, but if Wilks got the sniff of a chance he'd surely take it.

Should neither Wilks nor Higgins return, the BRC would undoubtedly be losing its two biggest names. Add to those that of Gwyndaf Evans, the former champion who undertook possibly his last British campaign this year as team-mate to Wilks and finished third in the points. Given that he was in the same machinery as Guy, Gwyndaf could have reasonably expected to join the title fight. But he suffered the majority of the Mitsubishi's transmission woes, retiring with gearbox-related problems on the first two rounds and in Yorkshire. A heavy

# BRITISH RALLY CHAMPIONSHIP

landing over a jump in Rally GB meant Evans retired from the final round, but not before he'd enjoyed possibly his finest moment of the season in the wild and wet final forest stage on the Friday evening, where he'd set a seventh quickest time overall, even against WRC machinery, to end the day as runner-up to Wilks. Also competing in that event was Evans' son Elfyn, who has a promising driving career ahead of him. Not surprisingly Evans, now 48, is considering stepping back to oversee his progress.

So who will be back in 2008? Well, there is of course another former champion in the shape of David Higgins. This was a year Higgins would probably like to forget in parts. With backing from TQ, he had teamed up with renowned rally preparation firm RED to give the Toyota S2000R its British debut. It was a marriage that was soon heading for the divorce courts. Much had been made of the Super 2000 car's arrival in Britain, given that the formula is working well in the Intercontinental Rally Challenge and has even been hailed as the future of the WRC. But when Higgins' Toyota finally made it from South Africa to Cumbria for the Pirelli, the RED team discovered fuel pump problems and Higgins failed to take the start. He returned the next day to set some impressive times, and then overcame further mechanical dramas to finish second in class on the car's asphalt debut at the Jim Clark. That was the high point. When the car overheated on the Isle of Man, Higgins' frustration was clear, and when the Toyota succumbed to a wiring fault in Ulster, the cracks in the Higgins/RED relationship were also clear. It therefore came as little surprise when the two parties parted company, leaving David to contest the final three rounds in an Autotek-run Impreza, in which he scored some useful points but still only finished sixth in the points.

The younger Higgins is now working on plans with TQ to run his own team in the 2008 BRC - fingers crossed it will come to fruition. One team that won't be present, well, in its current form anyway, is Suzuki. Team Dealer Suzuki ran two new Swifts in the class R2 category for lower-spec production cars this season, but following a directive from Japan, it is launching the new Swift Sport Cup next year in place of the R2 class effort. The one-make series is attracting the right sort of attention - the Swift is a good car and the top prize is a paid-for drive in Super 1600 machinery on next year's Rally GB. Plus Suzuki is a well-organised firm - look at its Junior success on the world stage. Quite what impact all this will have on the Citroën C2R2 Cup remains to be seen. Another one-make series, again for class R2 cars, the Cup had a shaky debut this year, with parts supply problems and fewer drivers running the cars than expected. Overall entry levels in the BRC were respectable, with 22 drivers competing in the final round, but the competition was, shall we say, rather strung out at times.

Still there are some drivers worth keeping an eye on in 2008, and chief among those is Phillip Morrow, the 24-year-old Northern Irishman who dominated this year's Mitsubishi Evo Challenge to earn himself a seat in the works team. Whether he takes that up will depend on the result of the Pirelli Star Driver Award, a scheme that will give one of six selected drivers the chance to win a drive in next year's BRC. Competing with him for that drive is this year's Junior champion Darren Gass who, at just 19, is worth keeping an eye on. Class R2 rivals Matt Beebe and James Wozencroft have also shown potential (see sidebar). Then there's this year's surprise championship leader at the halfway point, Wyn Humphreys. Team-mate to Higgins at TEGSport, Humphreys showed good consistency on his BRC debut, but he was no match for Mark on pace and ended up fourth in the points. Having said that, this was the first in a two-year learning programme.

There's reason to stay tuned to the BRC but, as always, everyone's plans seem to rest on money, or the worrying lack of it in the sport. The series can take comfort in the fact that it has strong backing from tyre supplier Pirelli; its organisers just have to hope that the boys and girls behind the wheel can find cash enough to come out and play.

## BEEBE IS BEST OF THE REST

Behind the top guys, the category for lower-spec production cars was the most hotly-contested in this year's BRC, with Matt Beebe beating James Wozencroft to the Class R2 title by a single point.

Beebe started the year in one of the Citroën C2R2s, but switched back to his old faithful MG ZR for round two and promptly scored a class win. Thereafter the fight for honours fell to a three-way tussle between the 26-year-old and Suzuki pairing Wozencroft and Lorna Smith, who also contested the Irish Tarmac Championship in Group N2. The consistent Smith won that title, and picked up the Ladies' awards in both series. Wozencroft, last year's British Super 1600 champion, ultimately came away empty-handed, although he will fight for a prize drive in next year's BRC via the Pirelli Star Driver Award scheme and is trying to raise the budget for a S1600 drive in the meantime, with the continued support of Suzuki.

The highlight for the 23-year-old this year was undoubtedly his WRC debut in P-G Andersson's Swift when the WRC Junior champion was forced to miss Rally Deutschland after earning a driving ban. Wozencroft impressed with his sensible yet pacey approach, but retired with gearbox failure.

Vesa Mikkola should have been a title contender in this class, but he had a torrid time in an Autosport Technology-run Honda Civic, falling prey to a mixture of accidents and mechanical drams. For example, he'd look set for a class win in Yorkshire when the car's bonnet flew open on stage, leading to the inevitable accident.

In the Citroën C2R2 Cup, Jason Pritchard and George Thomas showed the most potential, but both lacked the consistency to reap the rewards. That left Martin Laverty, at 57 the oldest competitor in the field, to take the title. His prize is to join a test session at Citroën Sport. Doubtless he won't be what Citroën was expecting...

And classes R3 and R1? Well they were, er, sadly lacking in numbers but for the record were won by Darren Gass and Steve Graham. Those BRC entry levels could still do with a bit of work...

# Weathering the storm

National rallying has had its problems - including a fair amount of freak weather this year - but there were still plenty of winners to celebrate. By Andrew Haill

**Above:** John Price's bid for a 13th Asphalt Rally Championship proved unlucky when he crashed out of contention on the final round

**Top right:** Jimmy McRae's Historic campaign was understandably cut short, but he still managed third in the points

**Bottom right:** Steve Simpson did battle with Price for Asphalt honours - victory on the final round gave the Hyundai Accent driver the title

All photographs by Mark Griffin

WHETHER it be a result of the greenhouse effect or global warming, already-stressed rally organisers have had to add an extra item to the list of 'things we have no control over but still have to contend with' during 2007 - the weather. Despite vast leaps forward in the technology used for forecasting, the predictions have been woefully adrift on several occasions this season.

While one could be forgiven for being caught out by the M5 motorway's closure as a result of flooding in mid-July, heavy snow at the start of February is hardly unique. Nevertheless, a question mark hung over the Wyedean Rally's very existence as competitors and officials battled their way to the start in Chepstow. The organisers were fully on the case, but the main worry was that public roads through the Forest of Dean would be impassable to 'normal' traffic, preventing marshals, medical and radio teams accessing their allotted posts. In the event, a thaw set in late on the Friday and normal service was resumed.

The monsoon season came early to Southwell Racecourse the day before the Dukeries Rally in June, leading to a swift change of start/finish venue as the facilities rapidly disappeared under several inches of water. Once again, the organisers were on top of the situation and were able to keep the show on the road, albeit in a slightly altered form.

Although the opening round of the MSA Asphalt Rally Championship, the Tour of Epynt in March, could easily have floated away under the vast amounts of water being deposited on the Brecon Beacons at the time, it was actually fuel that derailed the smooth course of events.

For reasons best known to themselves, the MSA are at variance with the FIA over the level of permitted fuels in any UK championship. The FIA allows 102 octane to be used, while the MSA's Blue Book of rules has long stated that 100 is the legal limit over here. From mid-2006, the MSA had been warning that fuel testing would be carried out during the season and so it came to pass that certain competitors on the Tour of Epynt were singled out for scrutiny. The whole episode was a fiasco during which no fuel actually changed hands, let alone was tested, but it set the tone for the rest of the season and gave competitors in a number of other disciplines food for thought.

Those caught up in the fracas on Epynt took no further part in the Asphalt Championship, which developed into a fascinating tussle between 12-times winner John Price in his familiar MG Metro 6R4 and the Hyundai Accent WRC of Steve Simpson, who led the series through much of the season and was chasing his first national title. After a steady start, Price was the best of the mainland contingent on the series' visit to the Sligo Stages, but then really stamped his authority on proceedings by winning the Ulster National Rally outright in the face of some serious local opposition. Price and Simpson headed for the final round, the Cheviot National Rally, tying on points. An uncharacteristic off on Otterburn put Price out of the running and Simpson went on to win the event and the championship.

In the MSA Gravel Championship it was business as usual, with Marcus Dodd piloting his Hyundai Accent WRC to a third title, securing victory with a maximum score on the penultimate round in Killarney. The Poole driver's season began in the best possible fashion with a win - his fifth - on Rallye Sunseeker, while main rival Steve Perez brought his Focus home in second. Dodd went on to take four wins in all, putting the outcome beyond doubt prior to the Bulldog Rally. Although he and co-driver Andrew Bargery went to Oswestry for the final round free of title constraints and intent on putting the Hyundai through its paces, an unscheduled roll scuppered their plans on the second stage.

Rallye Sunseeker, which brings the sport to the masses on the south coast, traditionally opens with two stages along Bournemouth seafront on the Friday evening. For the past four

## BRITISH NATIONAL REVIEW

### BRITISH HISTORIC RALLY CHAMPIONSHIP

It is pleasing to record that historic rallying in the UK is still a growth industry, with organisers of the 2007 MSA British Historic Rally Championship receiving in excess of 100 driver registrations. After several near-misses (he lost out by one point in 2005), David Stokes and co-driver Guy Weaver finally got their hands on the trophy this year, but the result hung in the balance until the final whistle.

Not only is the number of competitors in this branch of the sport on the increase, the standard of car preparation is also constantly moving forward. The machinery on display prior to the first round, the Robin Hood Forest Stages, gave the lie to the season ahead and so it was that 'Stoker' had to work very hard for the victory.

The Yorkshire forests played host to the final round of the series, where a win for Dessie Nutt and Geraldine McBride in their Porsche 911 would have seen Stokes' Escort RS1600 relegated to the rank of bridesmaid once more. In the end Stokes' winning margin was just two points!

Jimmy McRae made his mark on the championship at the wheel of a Stobart-sponsored MkII Escort and, while understandably missing from the last round, he and Andy Richardson secured third overall in the points table. After a tremendous run in Yorkshire, a class win confirmed Neil Calvert and Arlene Cookson's Lotus Cortina in fourth place.

Escort RS1600, Porsche 911, Escort MkII and Lotus Cortina - just some examples of the wide variety of machinery that has found a new lease of life with the upsurge in interest in this form of motorsport. Oh, and by the way, it's fun!

### FIESTA SPORTING TROPHY

Having fielded impressive numbers in its debut year, the Fiesta Sporting Trophy set sail once again on the Malcolm Wilson Rally (the series is run out of M-Sport), when 22 of the two-litre Group N machines lined up in the main street in Cockermouth for the start of an eight-round series.

Irishman Jonathan Greer, 19, the son of former driver and now top preparation expert David, claimed the 2007 title with co-driver Jonny Hart on the penultimate round, the McRae Stages. They then journeyed to the Bulldog Rally and, free of championship constraints, were able to show off their prowess there as well.

Second in the final reckoning was Alastair Fisher, nephew of the late Bertie, while third place went to Elfyn Evans, whose progress was closely monitored by his dad Gwyndaf.

There was also an Irish Fiesta Sporting Trophy and the roles were reversed there, with Fisher claiming victory from Greer.

years, Paul Bird has shown everyone else a clean pair of heels, going to bed as overnight leader. Despite an unquestionable turn of speed, however, the popular Cumbrian Superbike team owner and former National Gravel Rally Champion has yet to translate that into an outright win. It can only be a matter of time…

Contenders for both the MSA Asphalt and MSA Gravel championships meet on the RBS International Manx Rally (don't ask!) and since it first ran back in 1980, the list of winners has made impressive reading. Phil Collins was the first person to win it three times - that was in 1990, and he was joined by the late Bertie Fisher in '92. In recent years, however, Ulsterman Kenny McKinstry has made the rally his own. He and Noel Orr scored 'triple top' in 2004, then put themselves into the record books by going one better two years later and followed it up in 2007 with a fifth victory. Against top-notch opposition, their speed over the closed public roads on the Isle of Man has become legendary, and one gets the feeling that their domination is not over just yet.

After a year chasing British Rally Championship glory, the Mitsubishi Evolution Challenge returned to the ANCRO-run MSA Gravel Championship and no-one can dispute that the presence of large numbers of Group N Lancers did wonders for the entry levels on several events - there were 25 on the first round! Indeed, on occasions the lure of a fully funded works drive in the 2008 BRC saw them posting top-five results on a number of qualifying rounds. After a frustrating 2006 Phillip Morrow returned to dominate the series, claiming the title with an event to spare, while Sebastian Ling took the runner-up spot.

Although not immune from the falling registration levels that are prevalent across the sport, the BTRDA Rally Series is still the most popular 'national' championship as it continues to provide a source of affordable motorsport to large numbers of competitors. Retaining its 'three-in-one' format, the series promotes competition at all levels with its Gold Star (all-comers), Silver Star (two-wheel drive) and 1400cc championships. With 10 events from which to choose, the scoring system takes into account a competitor's best six results from their first nine starts.

Once again this year a number of drivers staked their claim to the Gold Star title, only for their challenges to fade as the winning post came into sight. For a while Tristan Pye and David Howells, both in Group N Imprezas, were virtually inseparable as they knocked in one good score after another. Although his Hyundai Accent retired from three of the first five events, Damian Cole then found reliability to the point that, with just the Cambrian Rally to go, he had moved ahead of the duelling Subarus. But - and it was a big but - he had contested all nine rounds to date and had to sit out the traditional end-of-season thrash through the North Wales forests.

Will Nicholls, on the other hand, did not make an appearance until the North Humberside rally at the end of March and, although trailing prior to the Cambrian, he was in a position to count every point his Impreza WRC could earn. It paid off and the trophy will now spend the next 12 months on the Isle of Wight. Having finished third in 2006 and runner-up this time, Cole has vowed to try and maintain his improvement.

Such is the level of competition, however, that nothing can be taken for granted.

Despite the plethora of four-wheel drive turbo-charged machinery now available at reasonable cost, there is still a place for two-wheel drive machines, to the point that a number of popular regional series allow nothing else. In this way the BTRDA Silver Star Championship has long been the preserve of well-driven - and very quick - Ford Escorts, with a similarly configured Opel Manta nudging its way through on occasion. Not only has 2007 seen them knocked off their pedestal, but a front-wheel drive car was the perpetrator of the deed.

Graham Middleton took the Gold Star Championship by storm in 2005 at the wheel of a Hyundai Accent WRC and this year the plan was to add the Silver Star to his portfolio. His chosen mode of transport was a Hyundai Coupe, but he too left it late - a retirement in the Forest of Dean and absences from the Malcolm Wilson and North Humberside rallies meant his bid didn't get off the ground until April's Somerset Stages. In a situation akin to that of Will Nicholls, he wasn't certain of the title until he returned to Llandudno at the completion of the Cambrian, but success was his.

Rumours abound that Middleton is now planning to complete the set by entering the 1400 Championship at some point, but 2007 was Clive Wheeler's year at this level. Although it has been copied in recent times, the original format was the brainchild of the BTRDA. This time, the imposition of a control tyre for the new season caused a great deal of controversy and the formation of a breakaway 1400 Club. The BTRDA stood firm and, although registrations were undoubtedly affected, yet another ultra-competitive championship was under way.

There were raised eyebrows when - as cars emerged from the snow-covered Forest of Dean on a day when power was obviously an embarrassment - the Enduro-spec Nova of Dale Glover topped the time sheets. Wheeler's Citroën C2 moved into the series lead on the Malcolm Wilson and stayed there for the rest of the year. To be fair, that doesn't tell the whole story - the fact that a retirement and a non-start mid-season brought the chasing pack perilously close to the leader, and that there were six different drivers scoring top points in the first eight events, gives some idea of the nature of the beast.

The culmination of the Scottish Championship came with the Colin McRae Forest Stages in October, but proceedings were overshadowed by the tragic events near Lanark a fortnight earlier. Gary Adam had already secured the title after the Speyside Stages in August, while third place on the McRae gave veteran Jimmy Girvan the runner-up spot.

Not a classic year, but each of the aforementioned series was very competitive on its own. Cost is still the main stumbling block to further development of the sport, but there are many other factors to add to the equation. The ongoing changes to K37 (concerning vehicle eligibility) in the Blue Book have prompted a degree of uncertainty, the problems over fuel have kept some away and familiarity is starting to breed contempt. Put simply, a degree of boredom with the same old events and stages being wheeled out year on year is having a negative effect on entries, but that is a whole new can of worms.

*Above:* In the Gravel Championship it was business as usual, with Marcus Dodd scoring four wins on his way to a third title

*Middle:* Steve Perez was Dodd's main opposition on Rallye Sunseeker, where he finished second to the eventual champ

*Top:* As his rivals' challenges faded, Will Nicholls kept racking up the points in the BTRDA Gold Star championship to take the top prize

All photographs by Mark Griffin